JOHN DERIAN STICKER BOOK

ARTISAN / NEW YORK

For Mary

Discover the full line of John Derian puzzles and stationery at artisanbooks.com/johnderianpapergoods

---

ISBN 978-1-64829-101-2

Author photo by Julia Cumes

Published by Artisan,
an imprint of Workman Publishing,
a division of Hachette Book Group, Inc.
1290 Avenue of the Americas
New York, NY 10104
artisanbooks.com

Printed in China on responsibly sourced paper

3 5 7 9 10 8 6 4

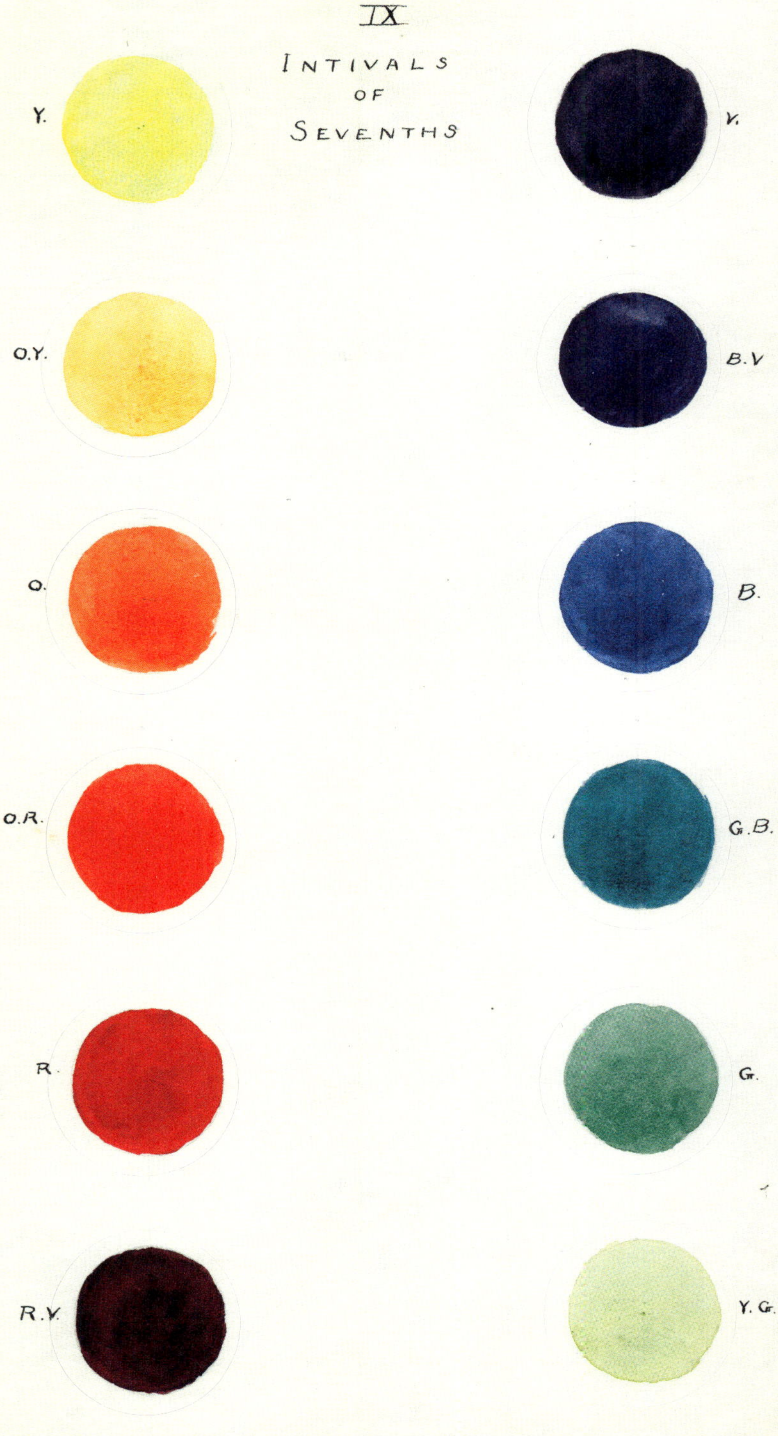
IX
INTIVALS OF SEVENTHS
Y.
O.Y.
O.
O.R.
R.
R.V.
V.
B.V
B.
G.B.
G.
Y.G.

ABOUT THIS BOOK

The images in this sticker book are from my ever-growing personal archive. I would say that roughly 80 percent of them were found without any identifying details about the artist or source, but almost all the images here are prints that came from various eighteenth- and nineteenth-century natural history books. In 2016, I published a collection of these images in my first book, *John Derian Picture Book*. This book is a revised version of the original, but now hundreds of the images have been turned into stickers, which you will find on every other spread.

I hope you have fun with all the stickers I've created—and all the colorful pages to sticker on in between.

Enjoy,
John Derian

Freshman I

Shogher Baghdoyan.

Nov. 6, 1935

C+

Complements determined by means of the After Image.

Lettering too large

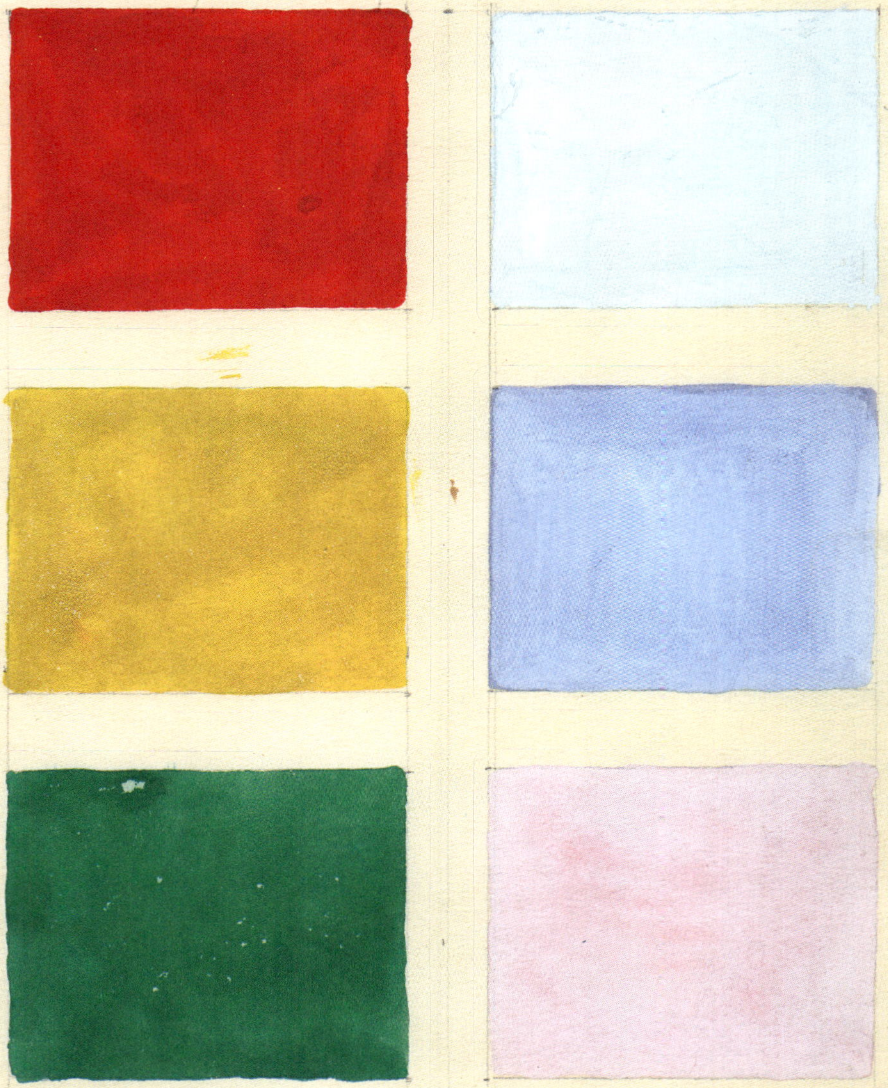

Needs little more gr

Cloudy Day

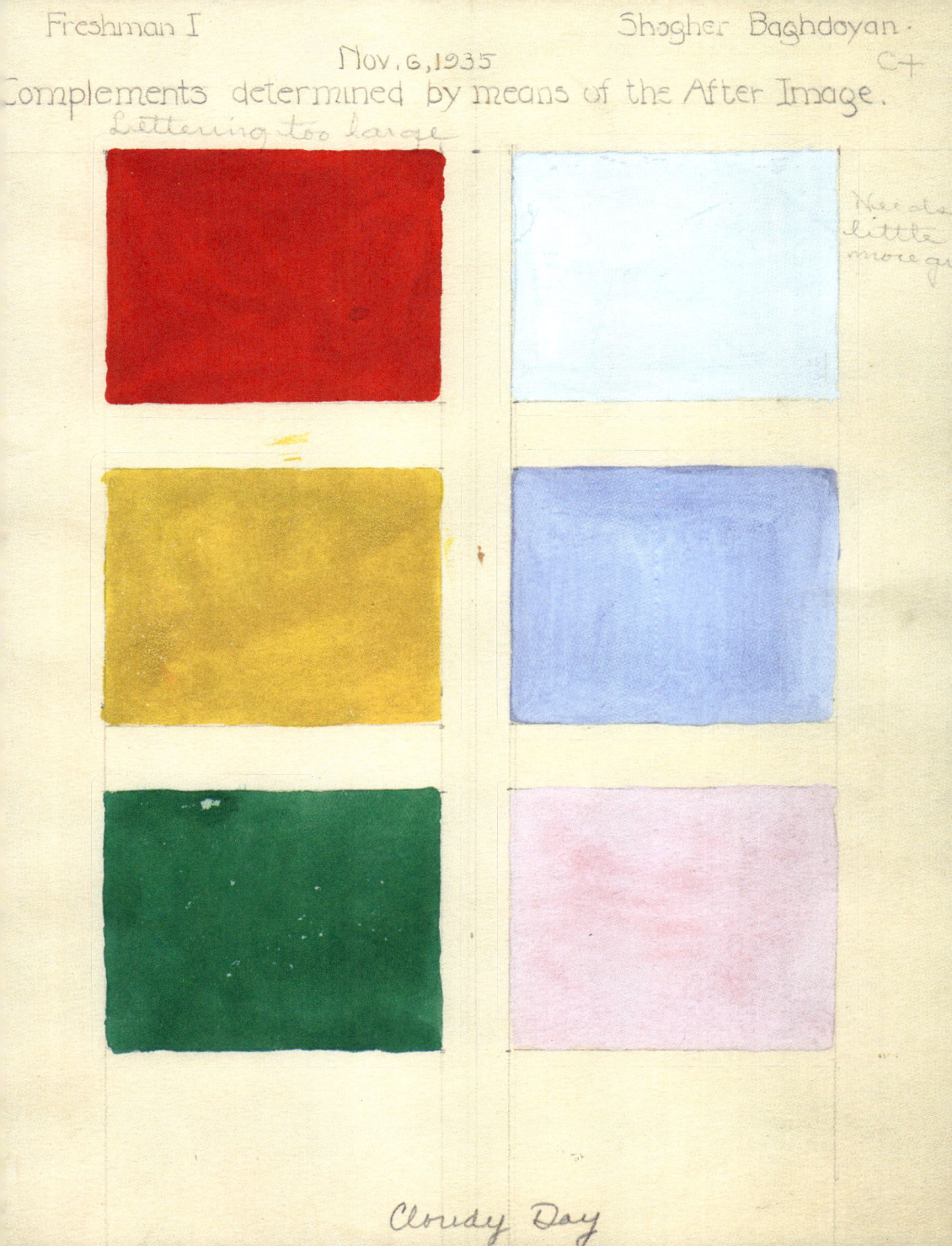

Sorry to appear insistant , but I must have my trinkets. This is the last chance.

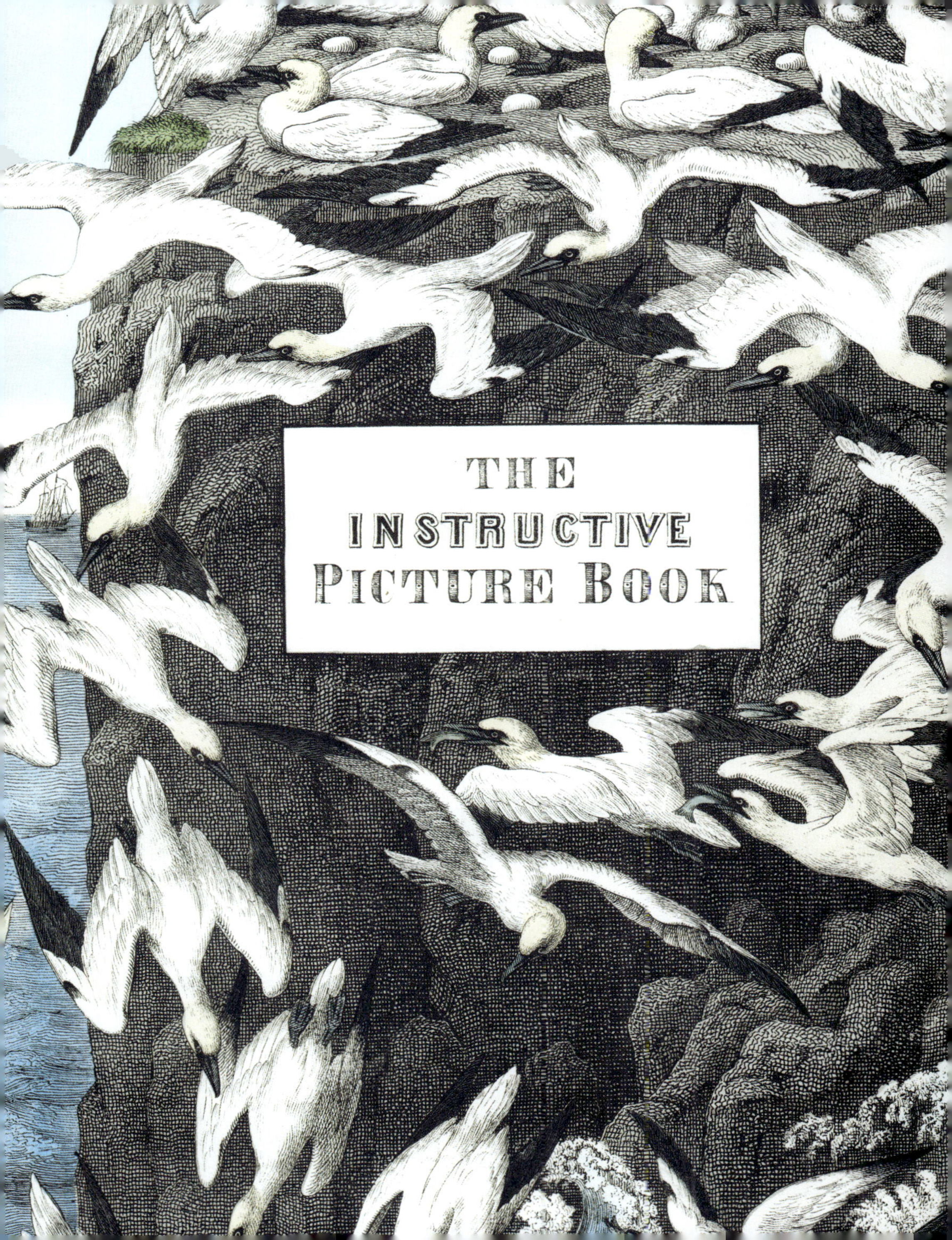
THE
INSTRUCTIVE
PICTURE BOOK

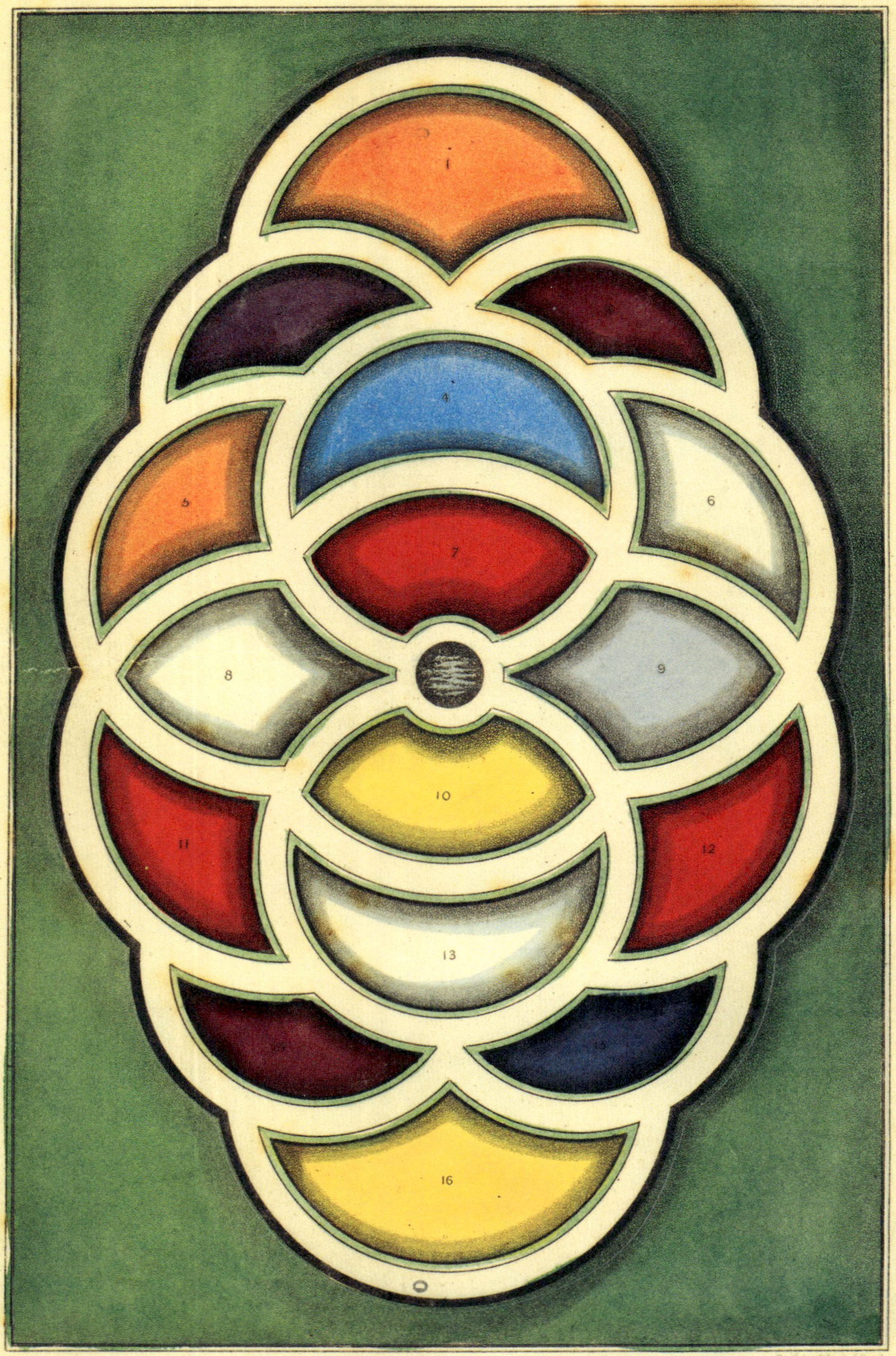

Engd. by Alfred Adlard

THINGS I LIKE

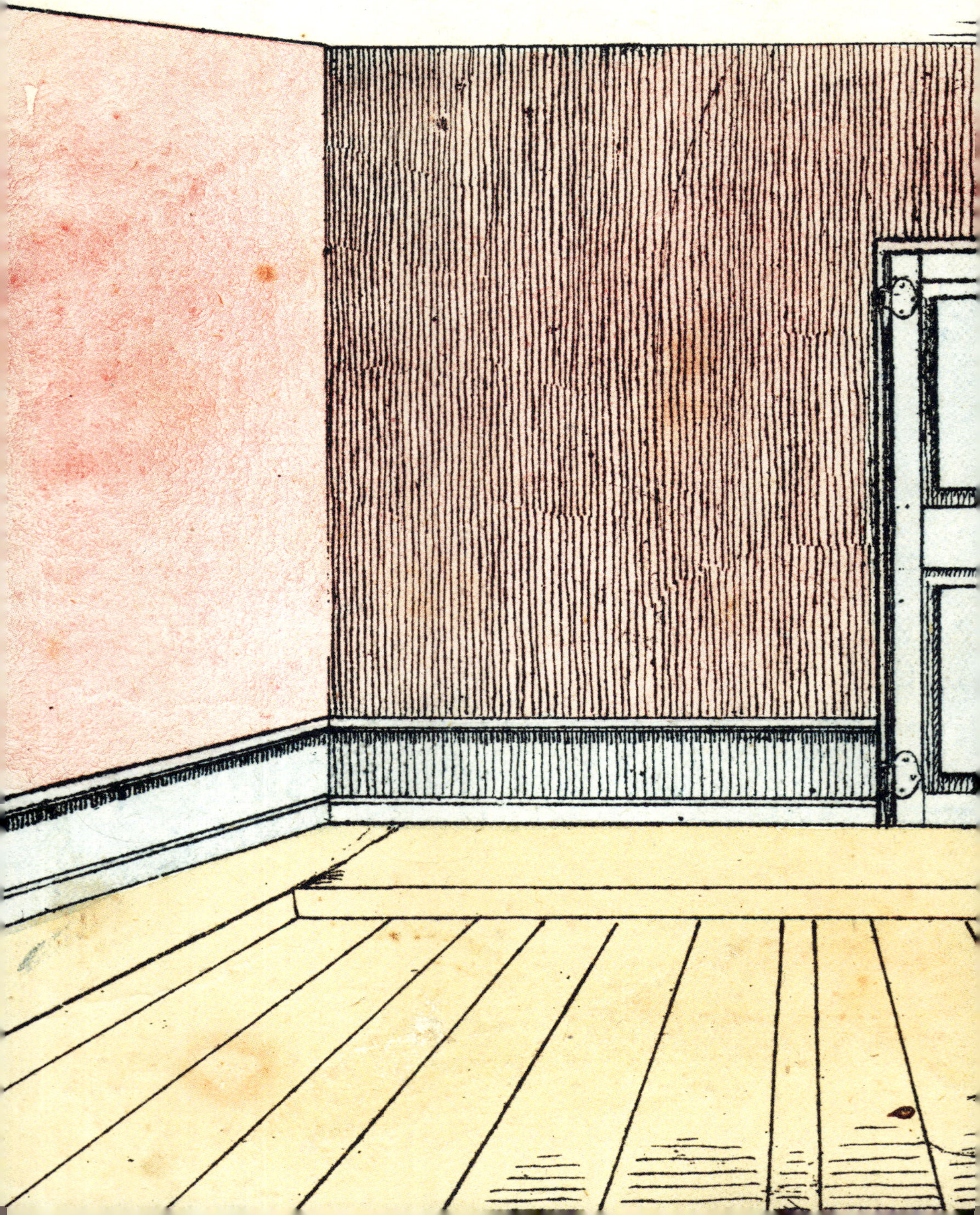

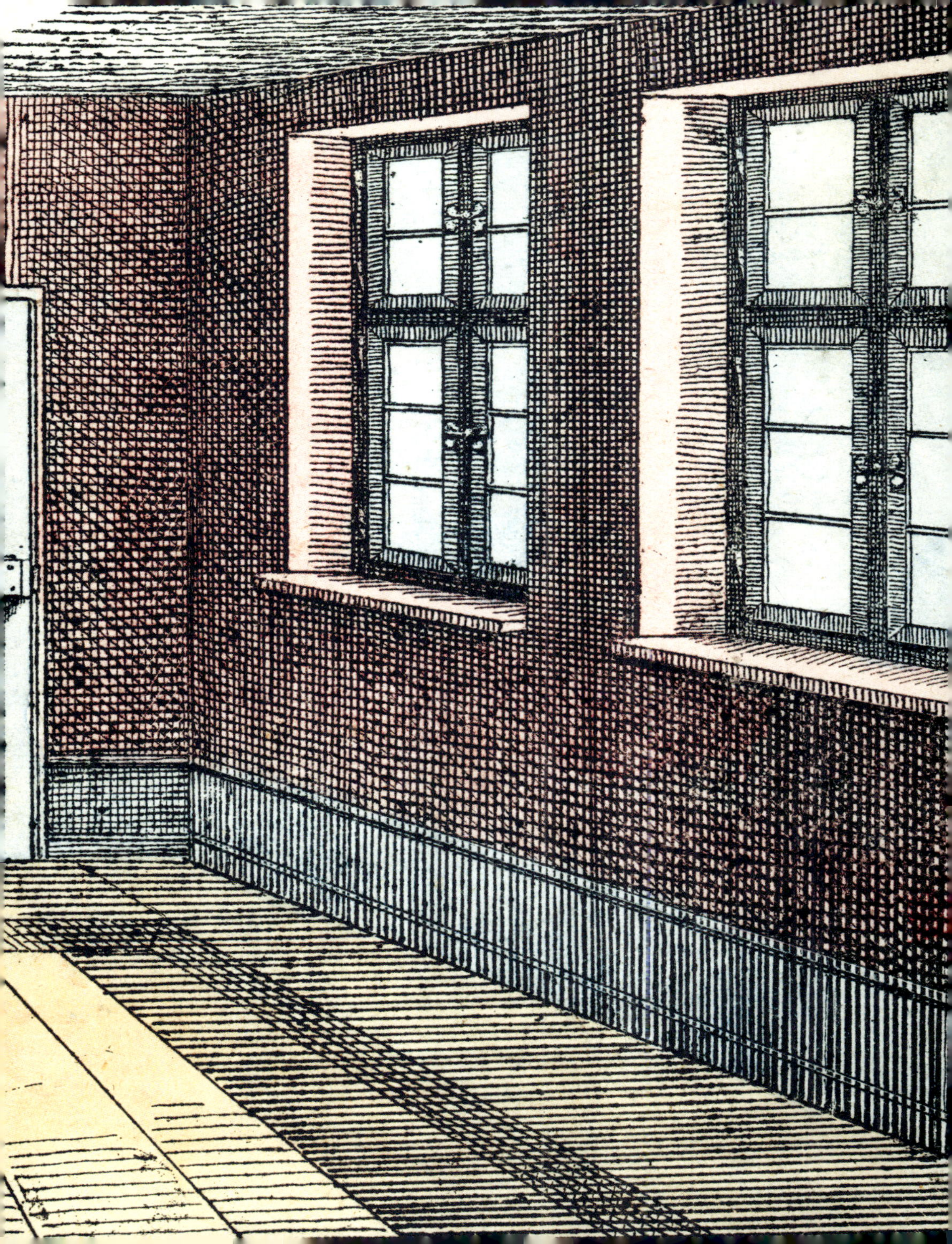

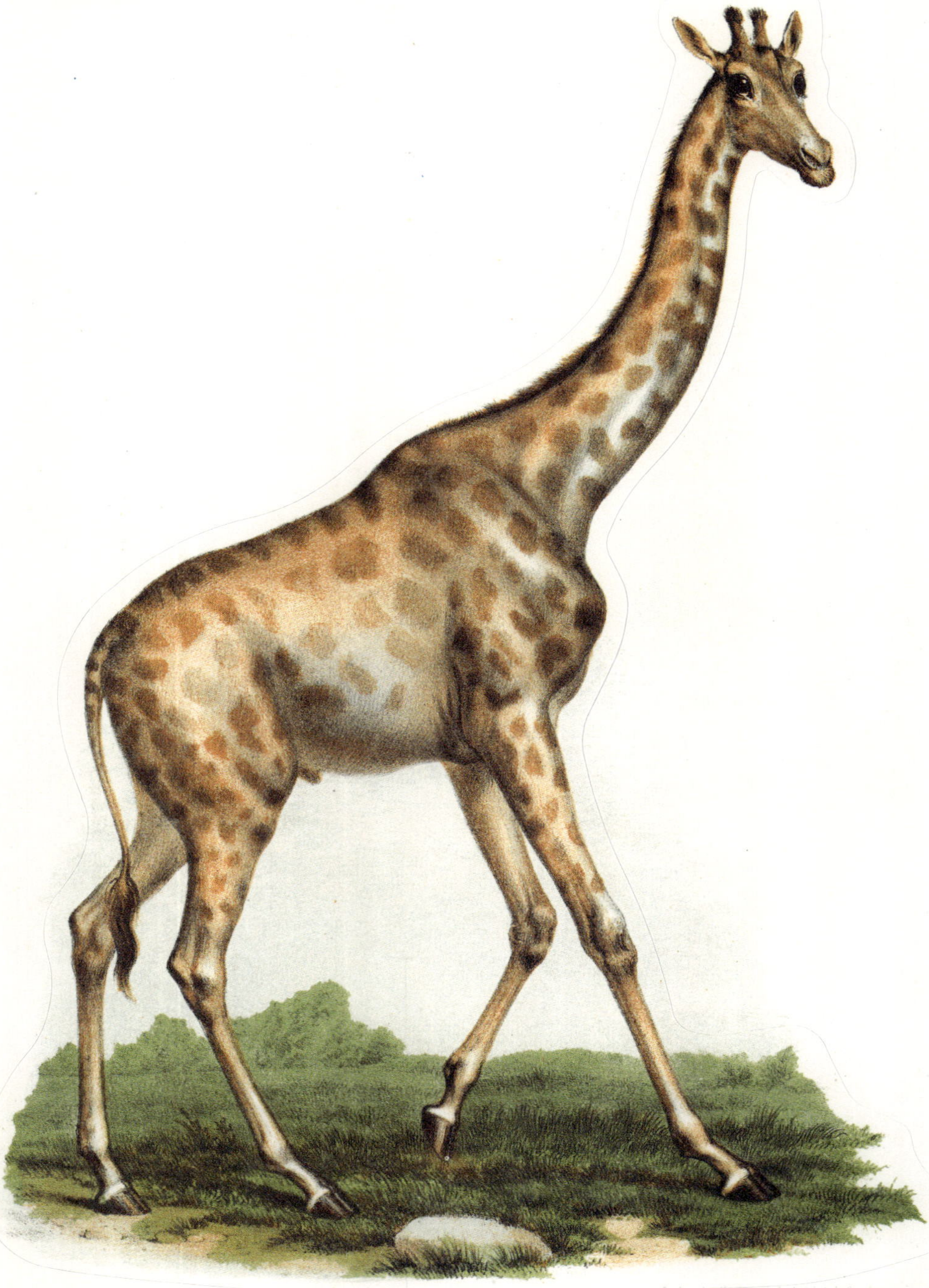

Fig. 194. Die gemeine Giraffe. *Camelopardalis Giraffa.*

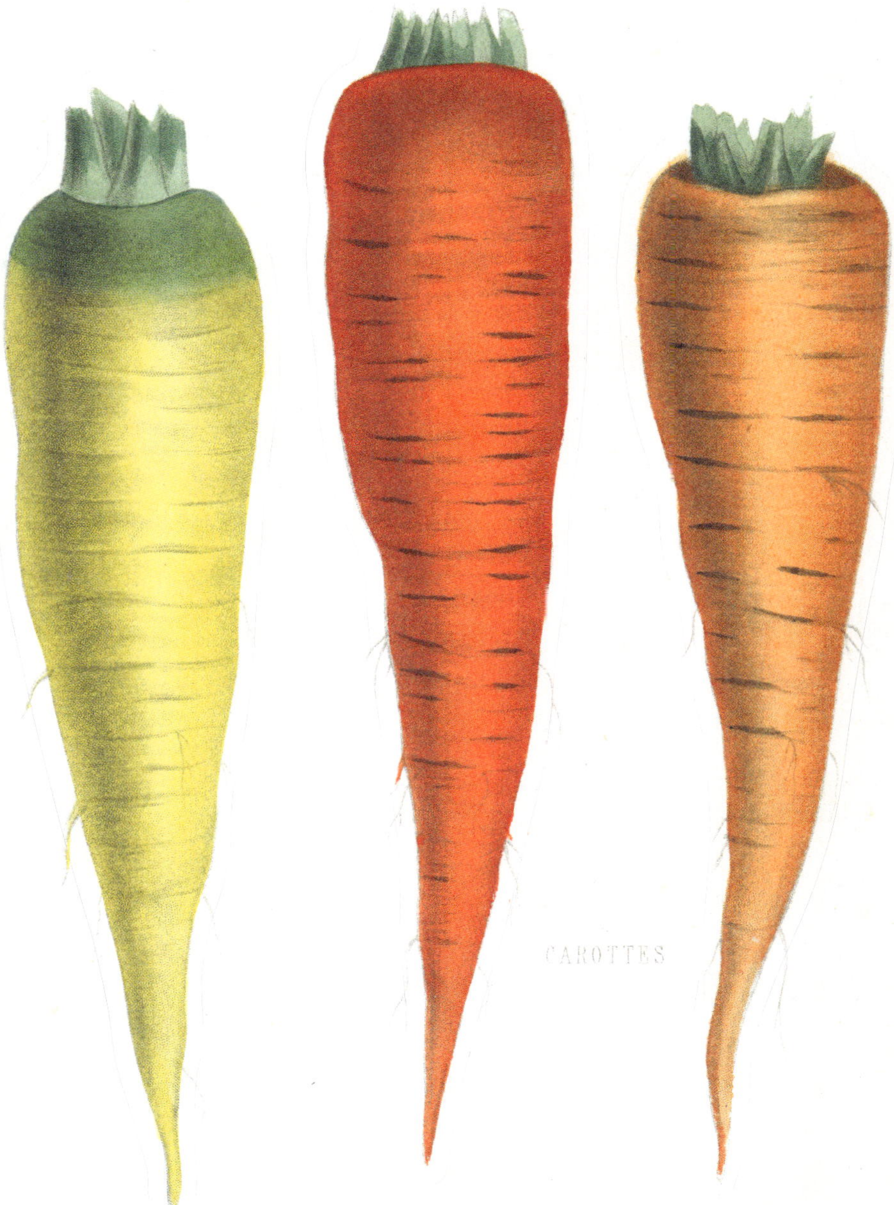

CAROTTES

C. jaune d'Achicourt — C. rouge longue. — C. rouge pâle de Flandres.

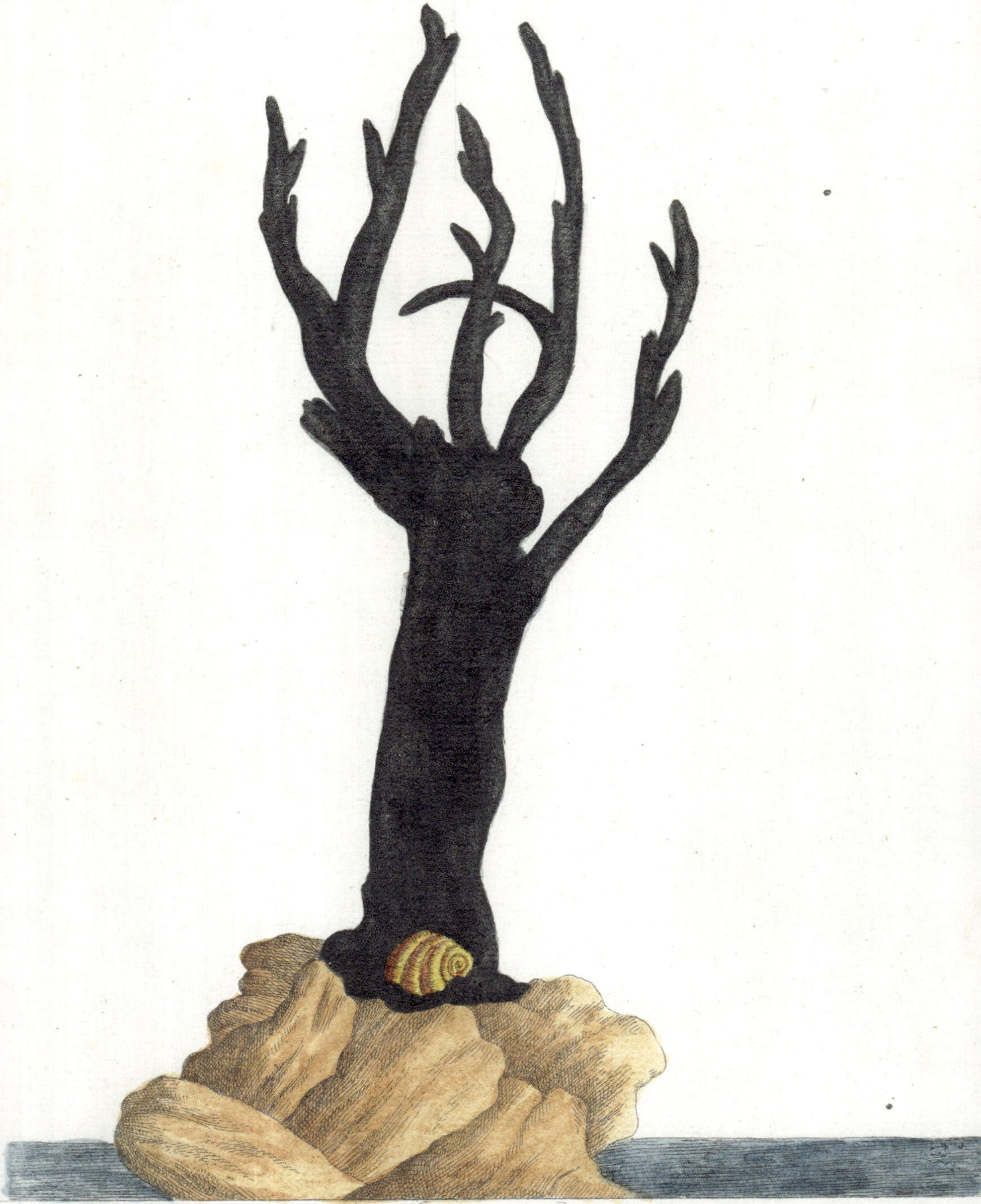

Corallium nigrum. Schwartze Corallen

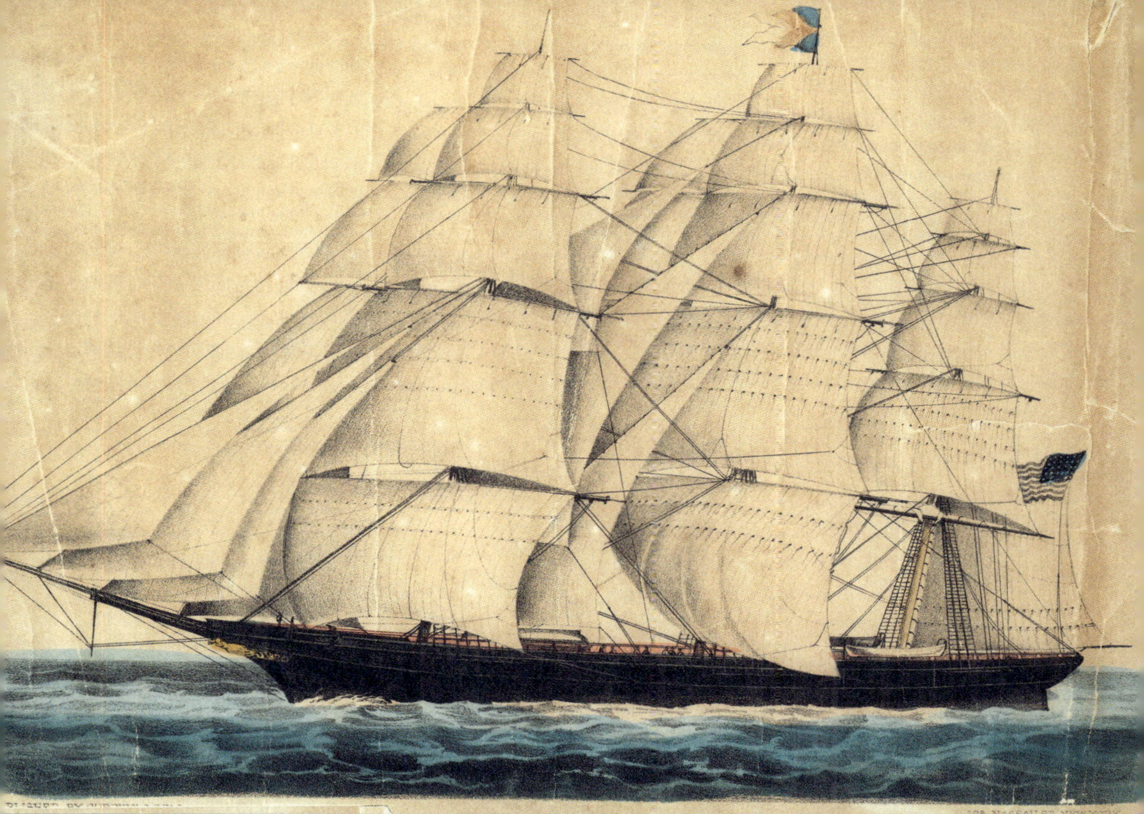

1835

Mr Moses Morse

Bradford N.H.

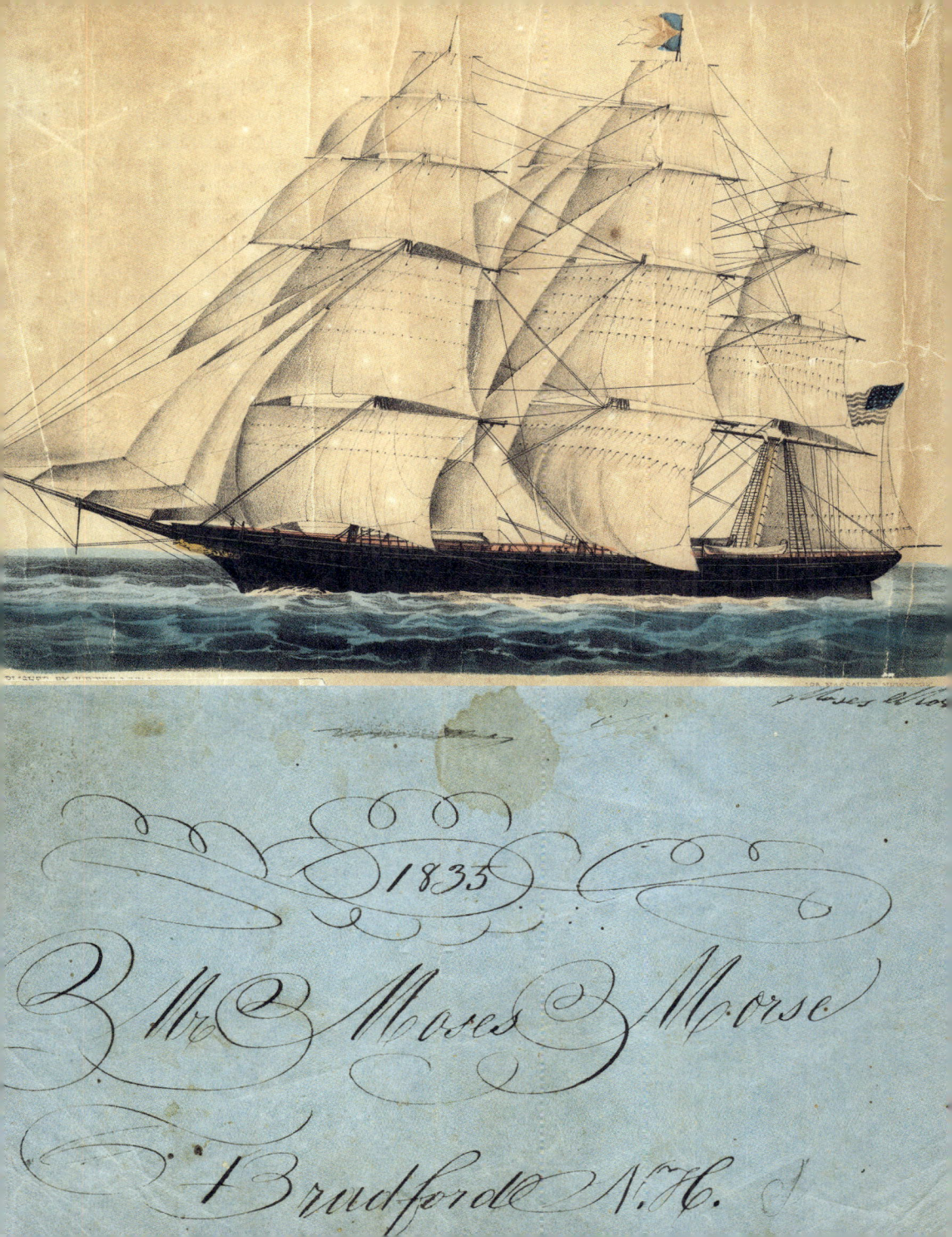

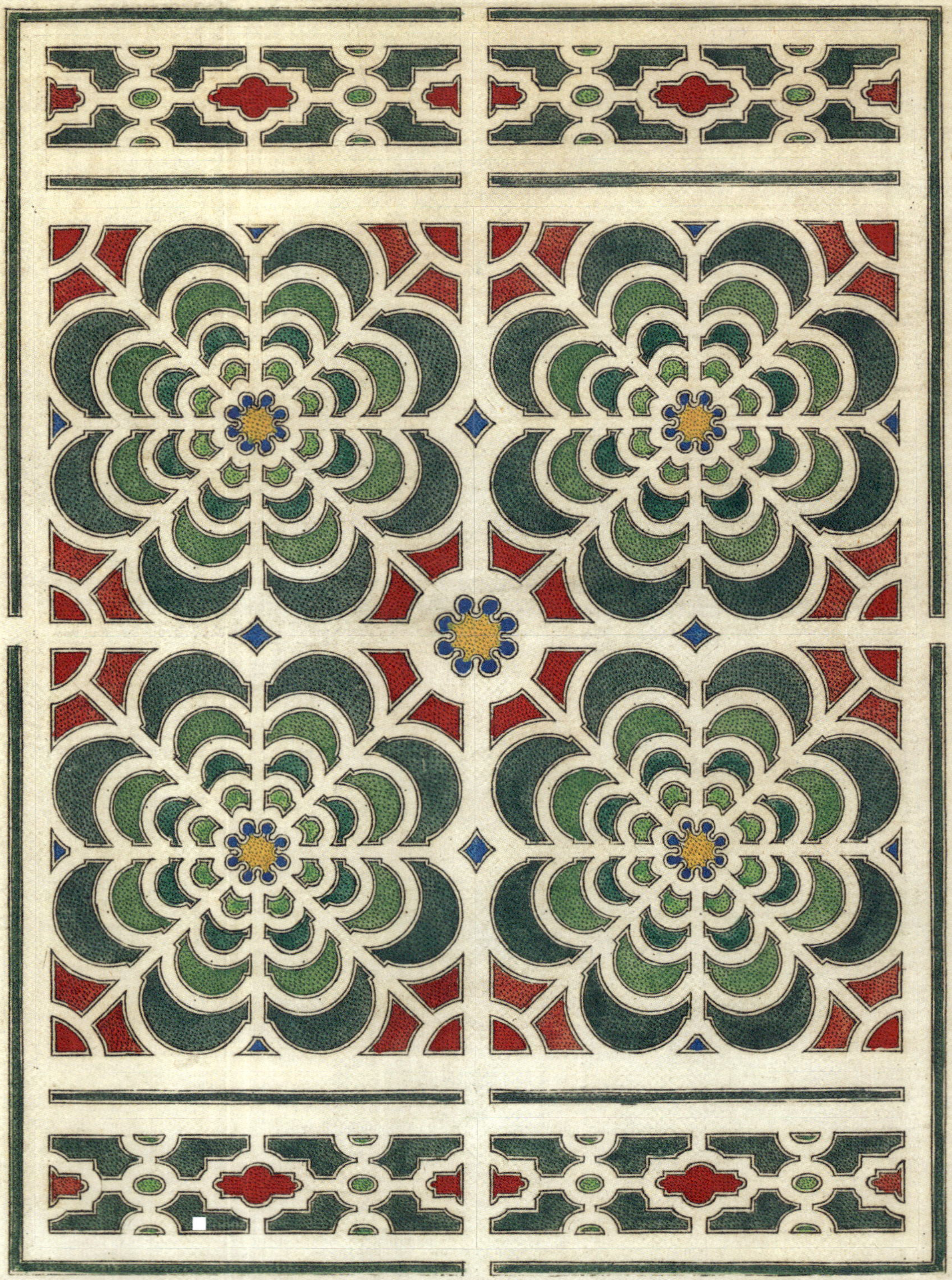

Si uelis deniq; floreæ curæ quàm facilem aditum, tam difficilem exitum hortensi repræsentare simulacro: tuos hortos in labyrinthum implica, cuius hic imago aliqua exhibetur. Possunt autem labyrinthi areolæ uel cæterarum instar humiles subsidere, ut oculi tantùm implicatis flexibus irretiantur: uel ad quatuor circiter palmos lateritia structura excitari, ut pedes quoq; inter flores errabundi iucundissimè impediantur.

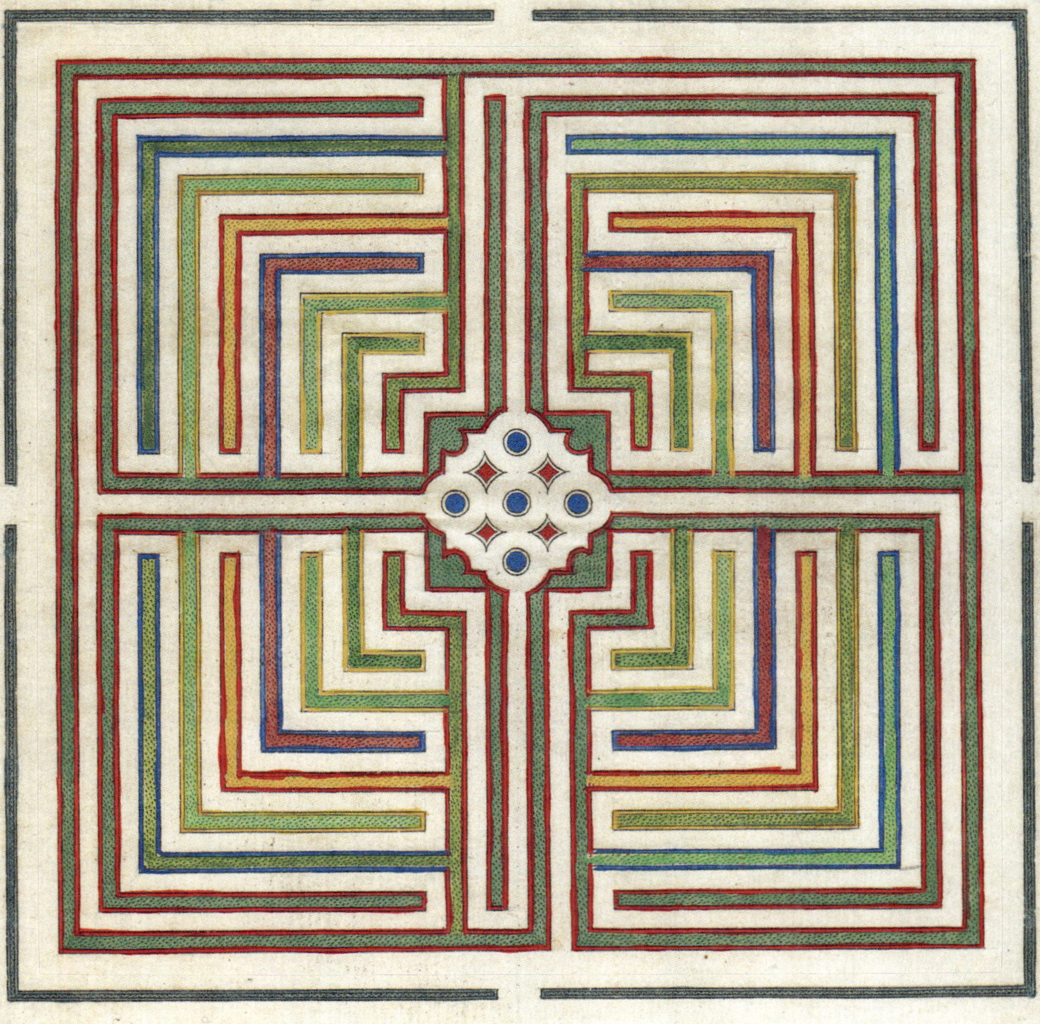

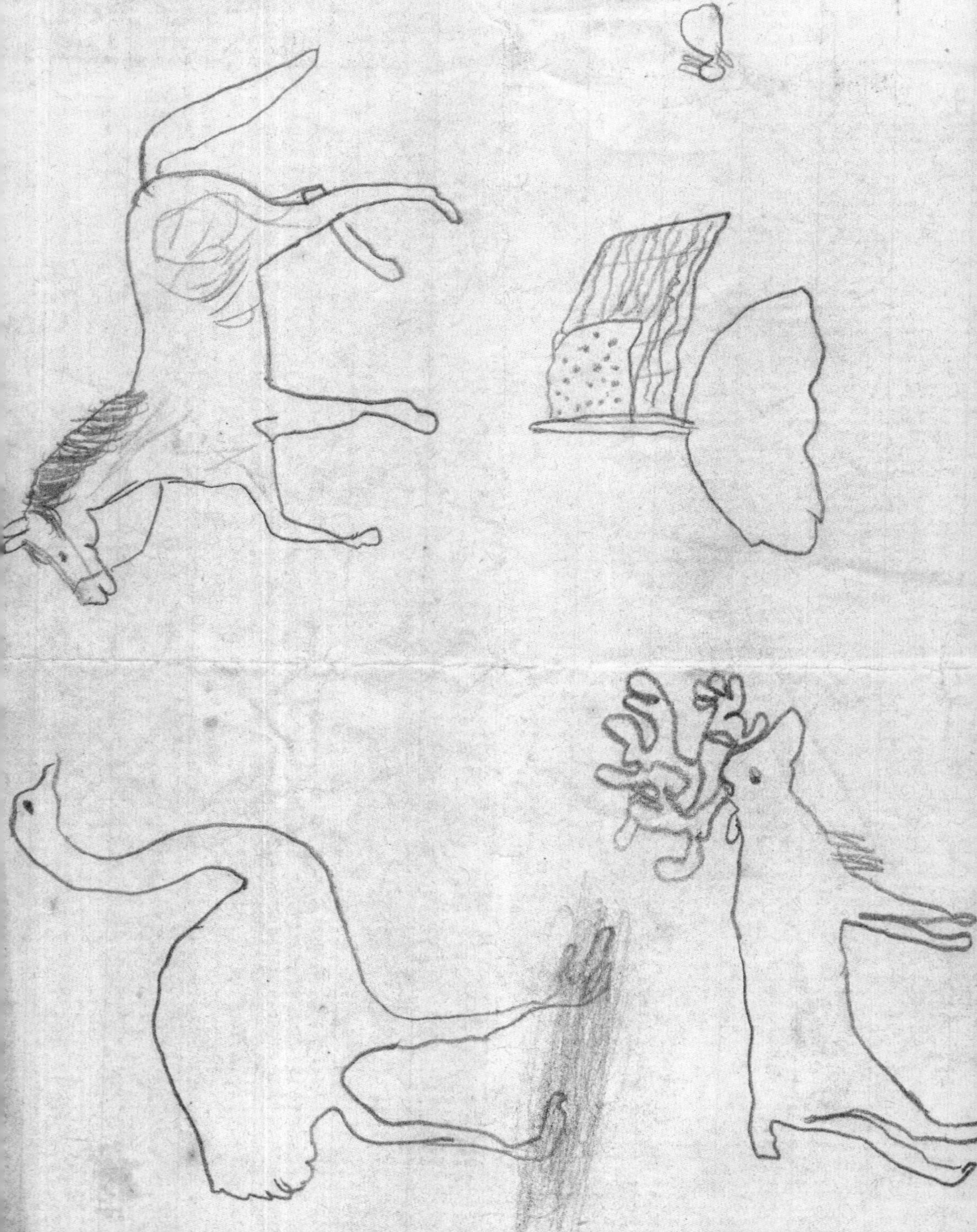

T. LXV.

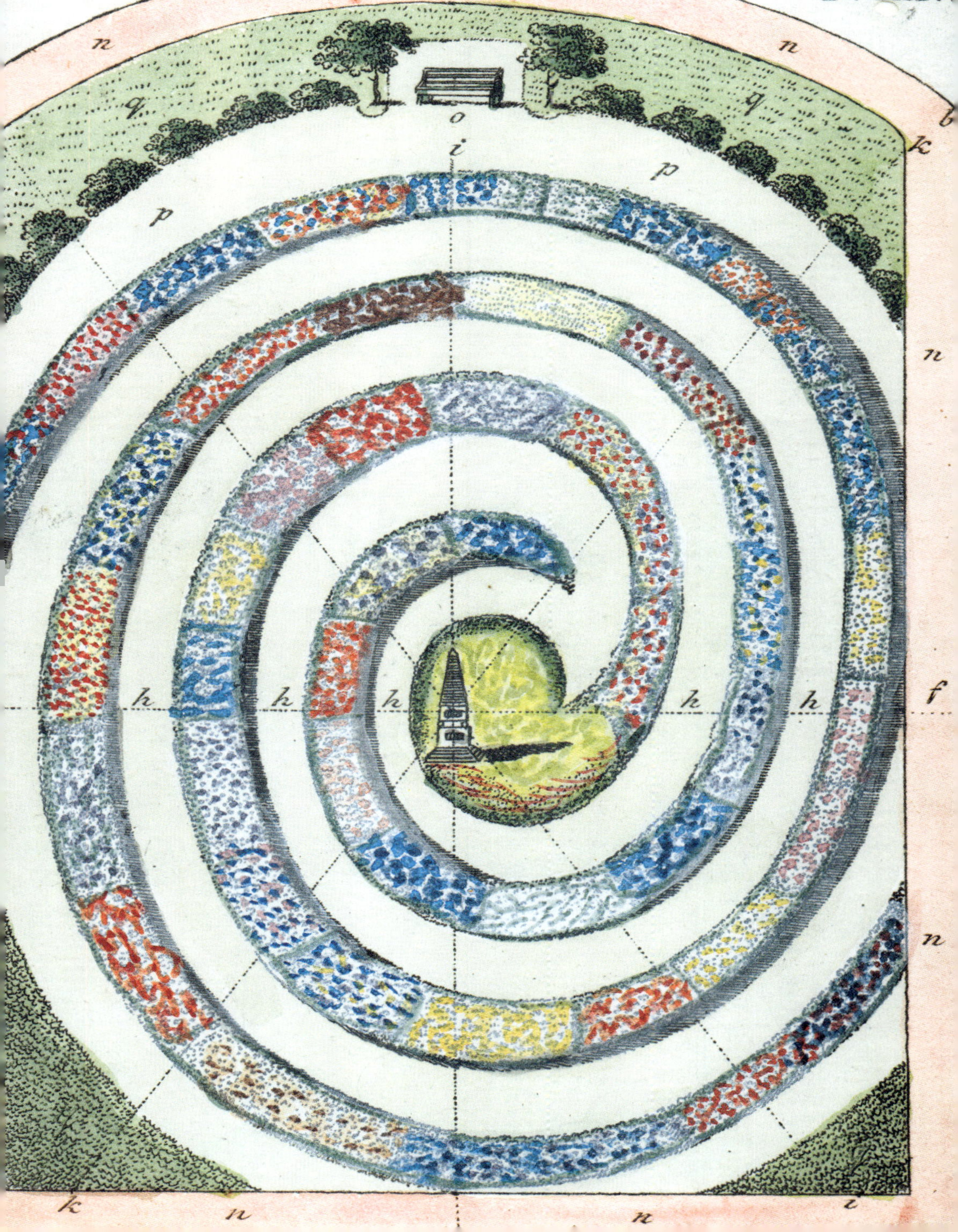

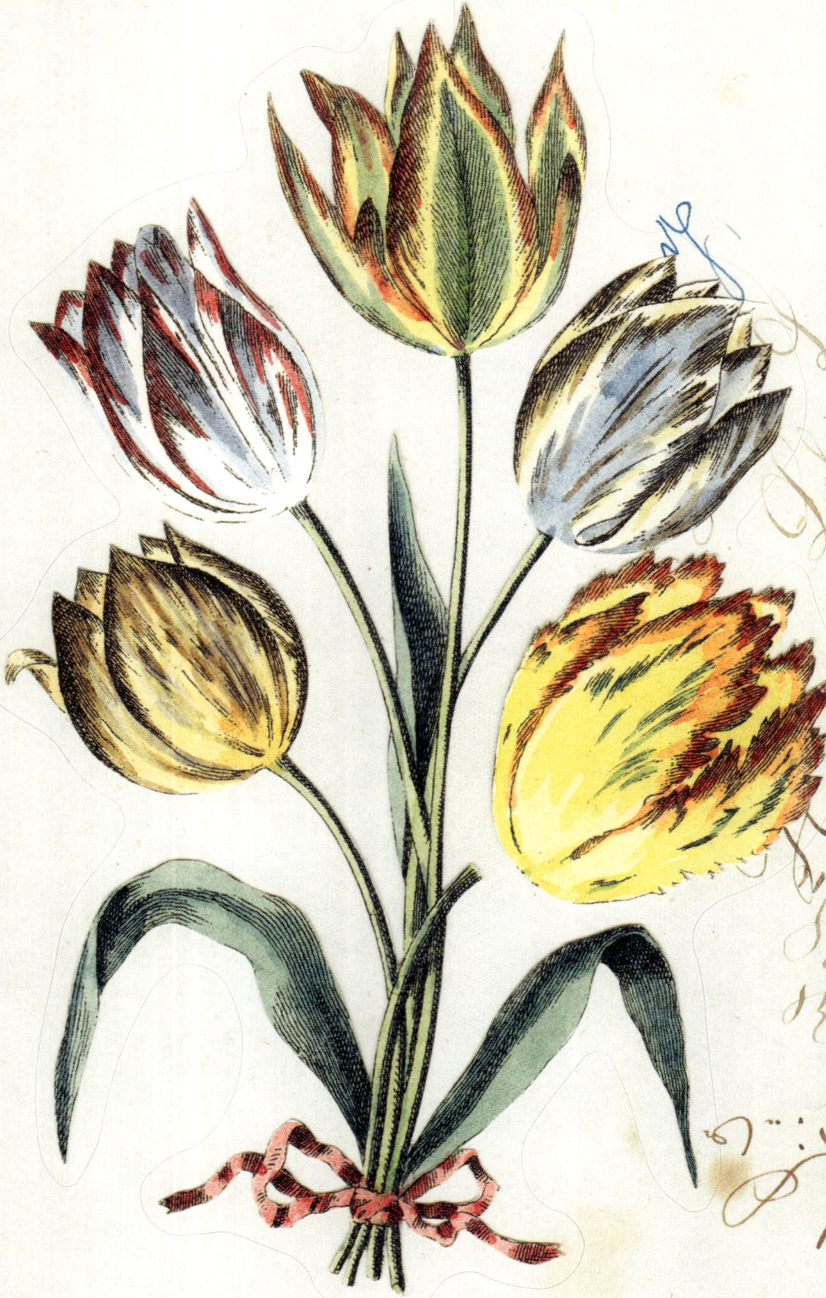

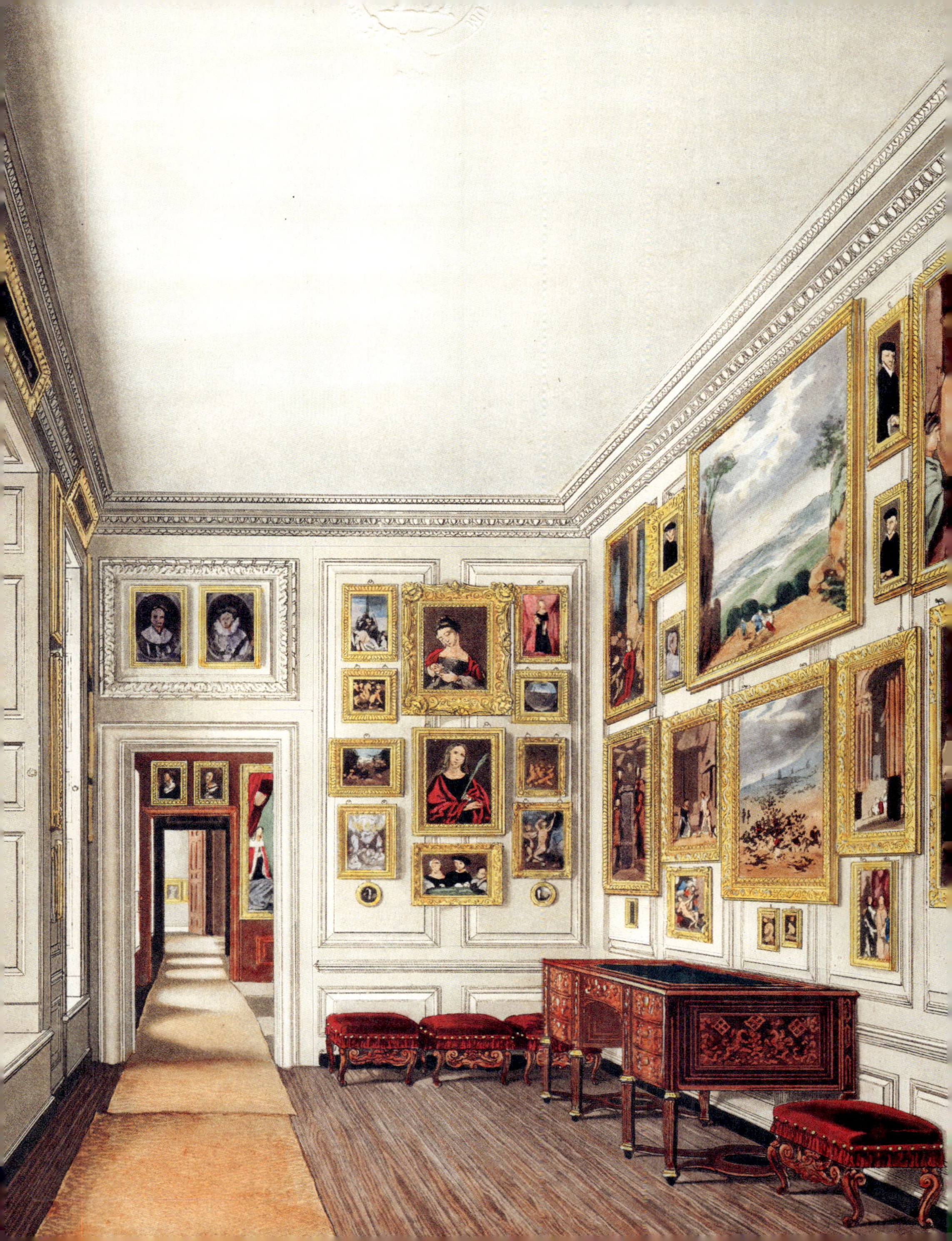

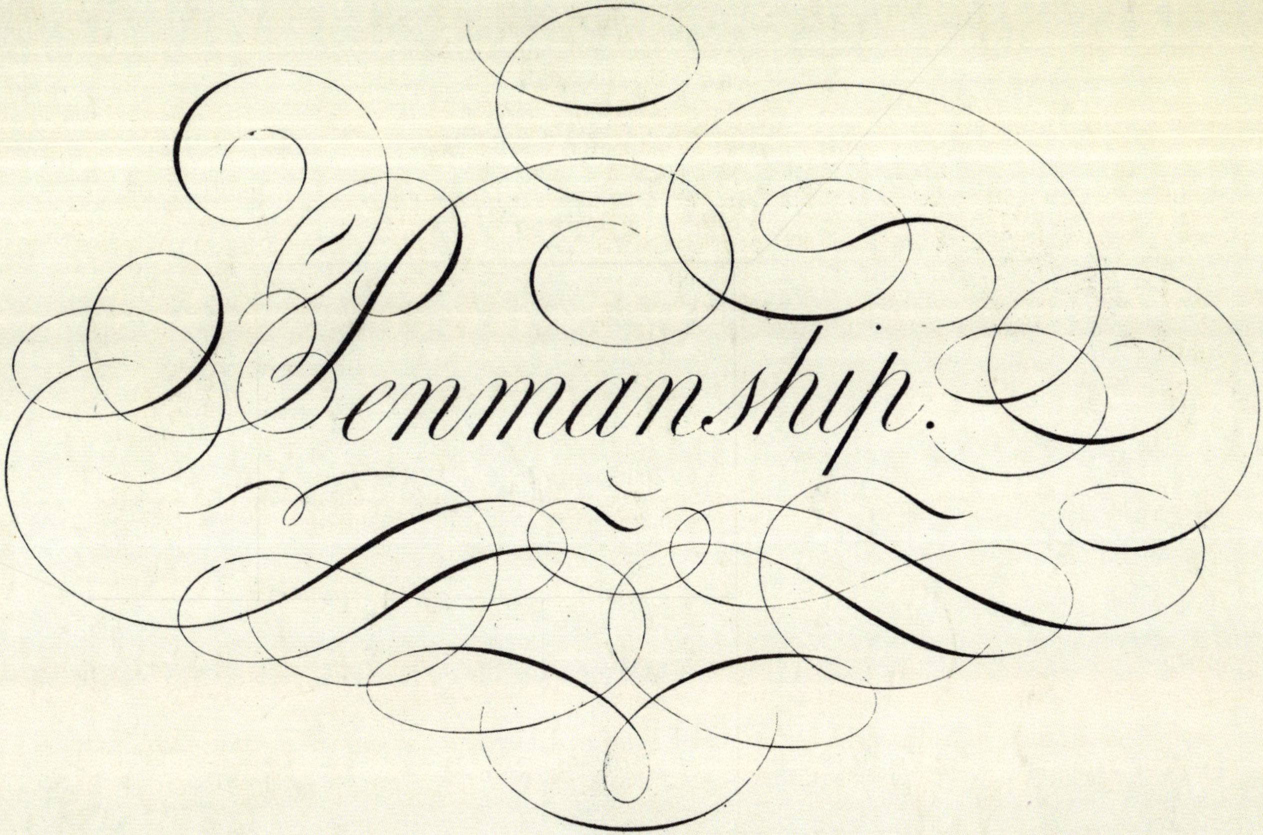
Penmanship.

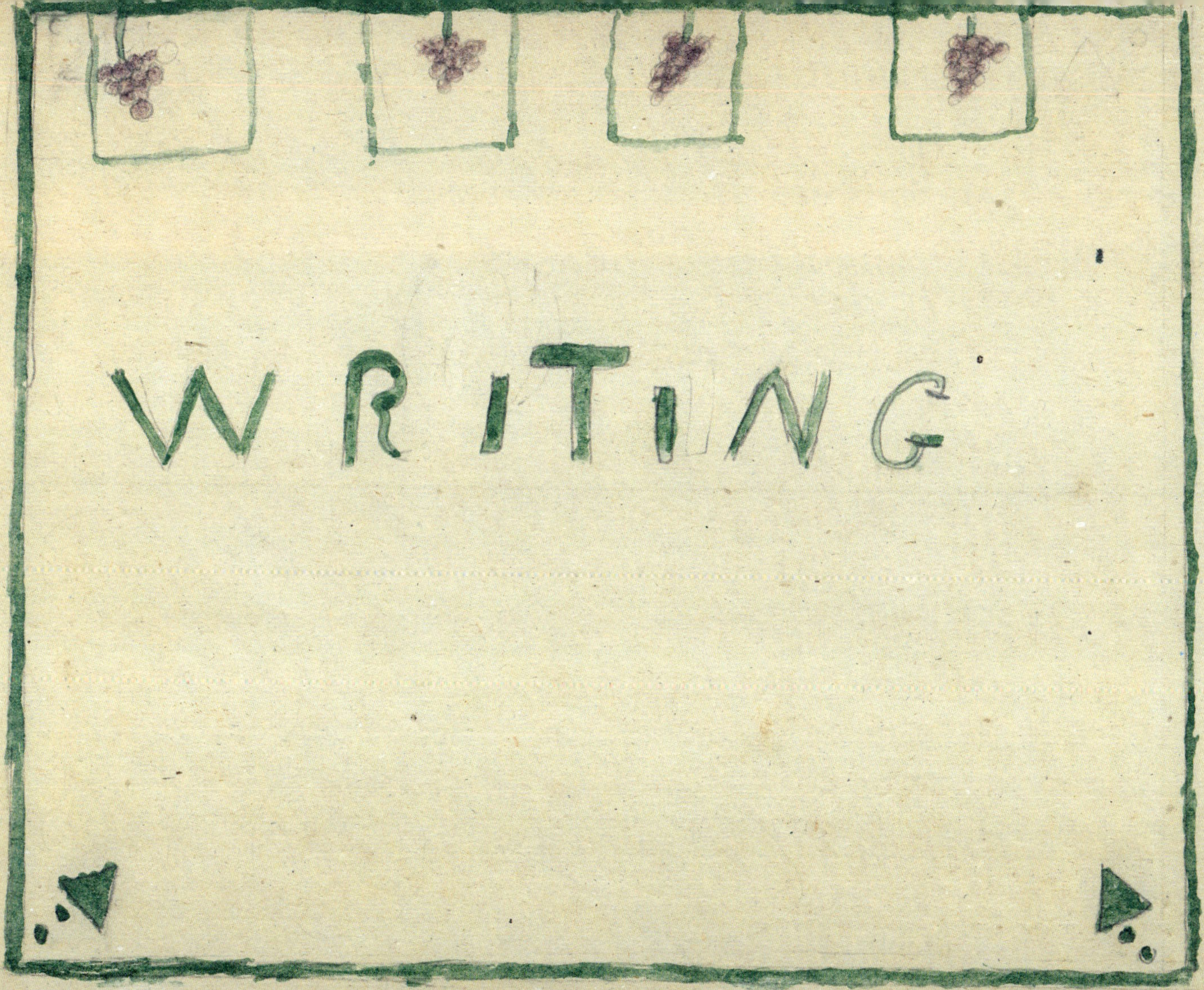
WRITING

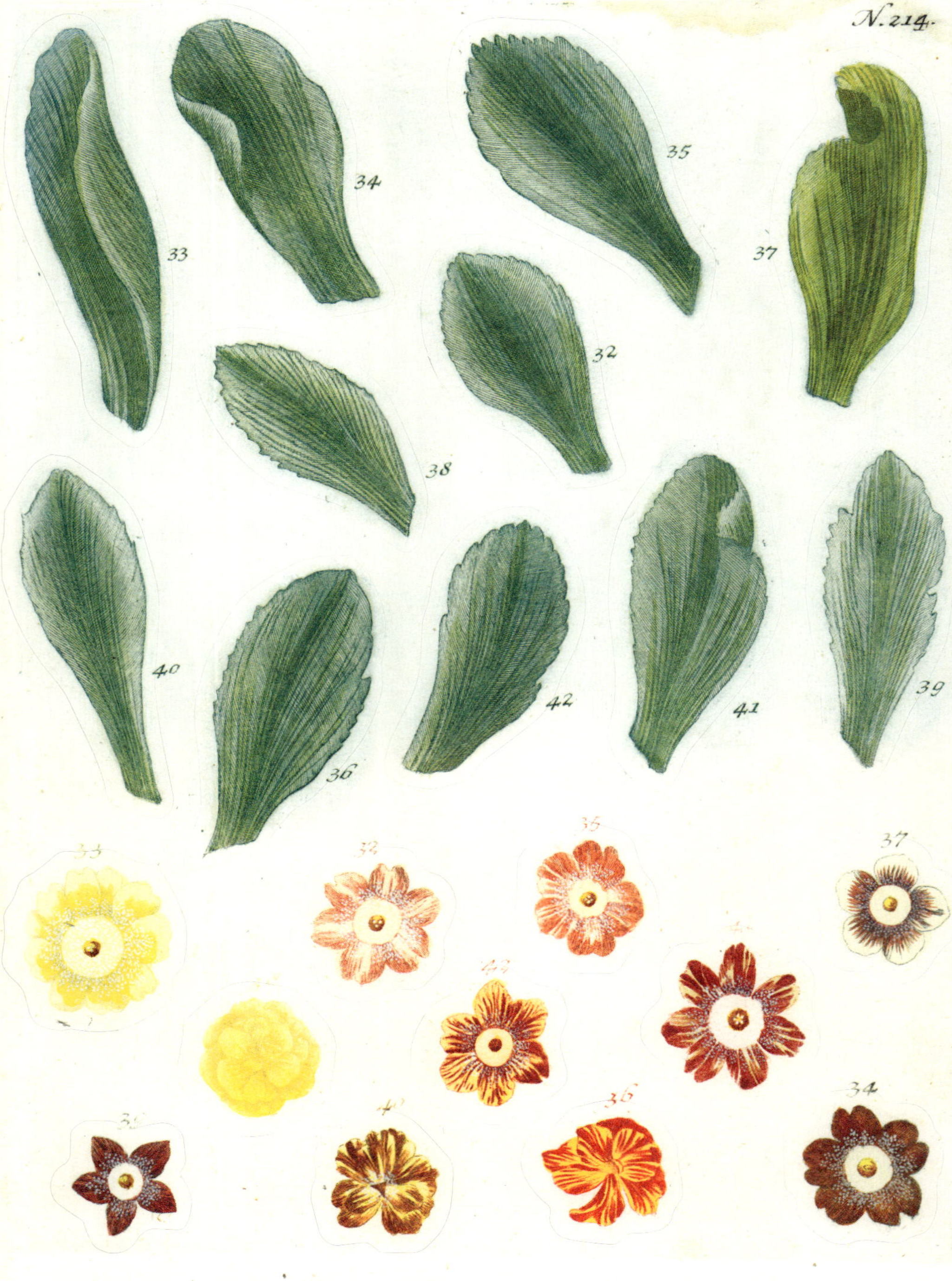

Auricularum ursi variorum Colorum Species.

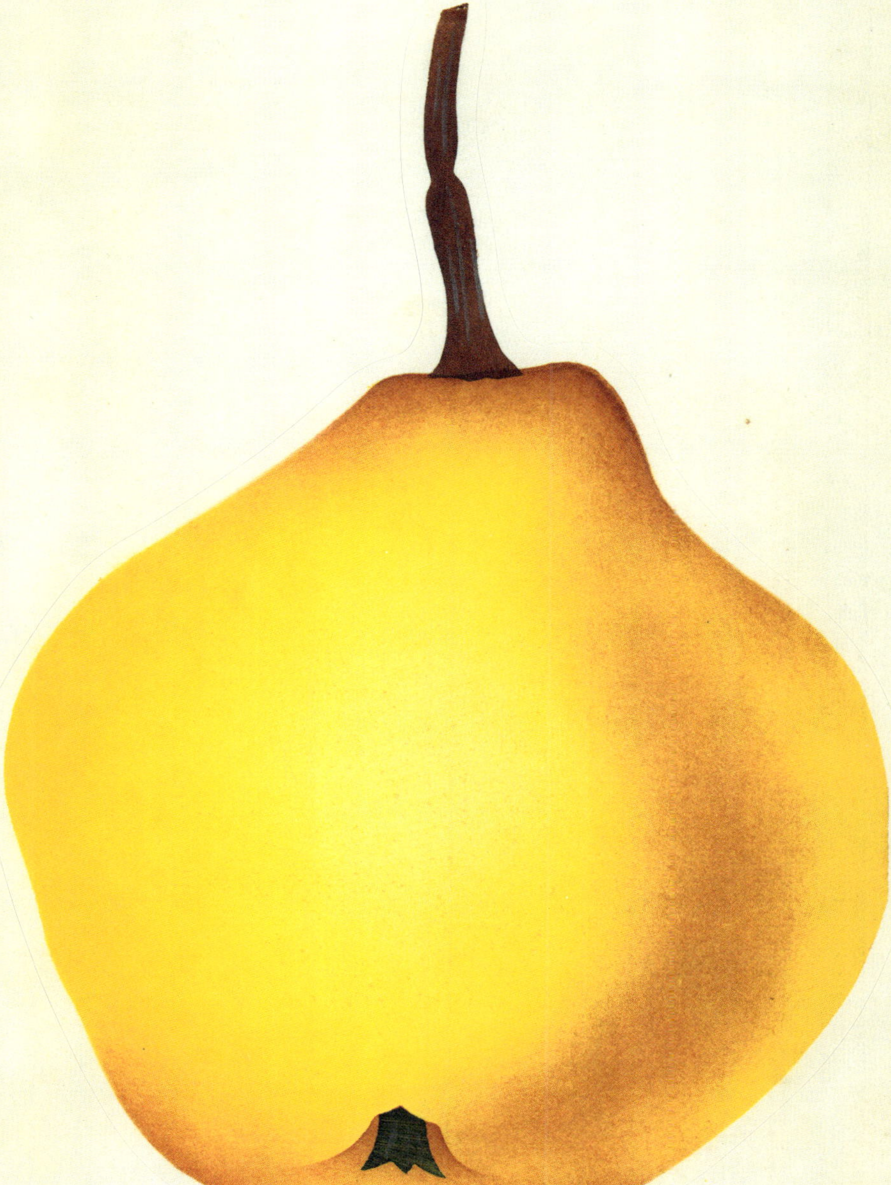

CHAMPION QUINCE.

Of recent introduction, and by far the largest Quince grown. Skin fair and smooth ; flesh of fair quality and late keeper.

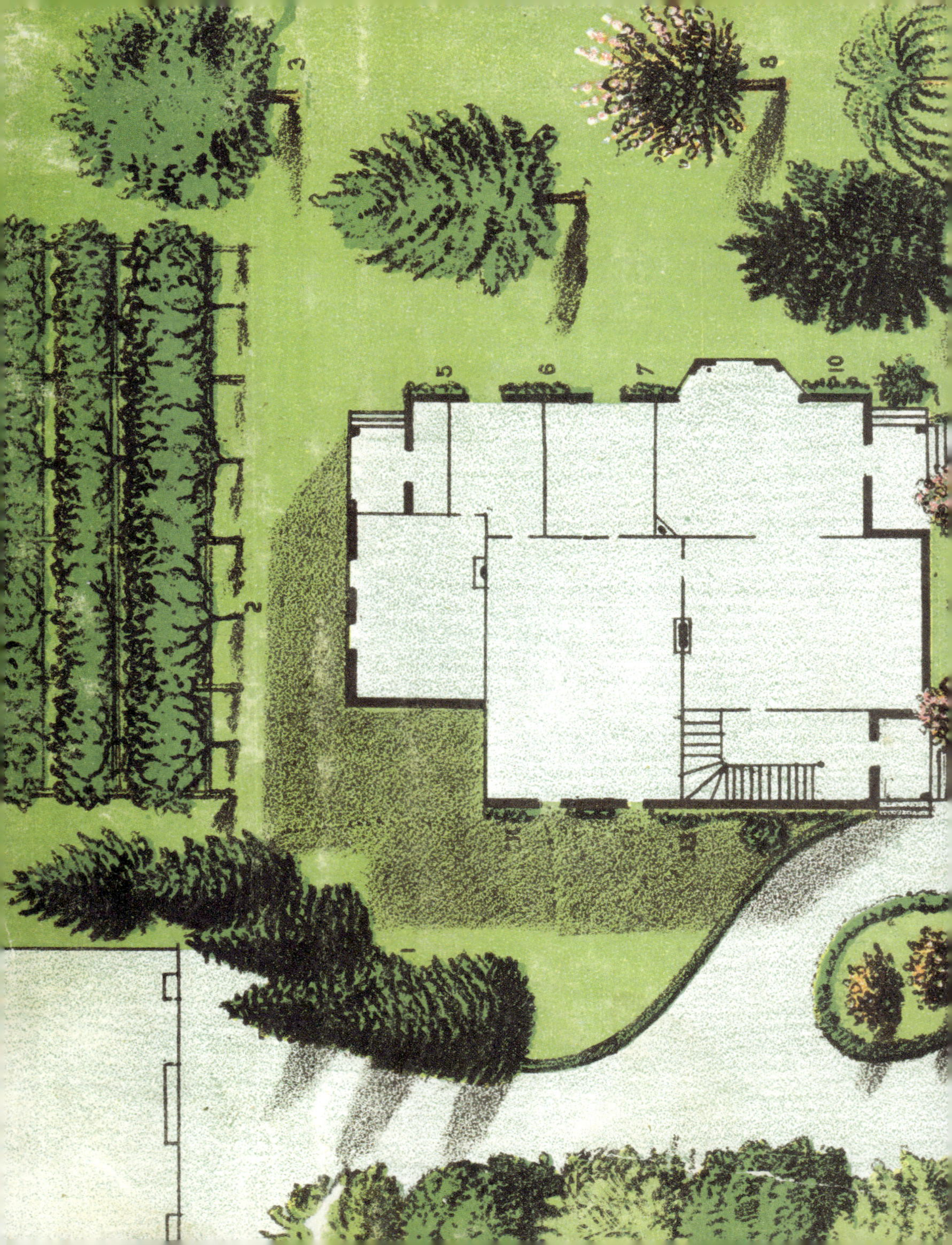
3
8
5
6
7
10
2
1

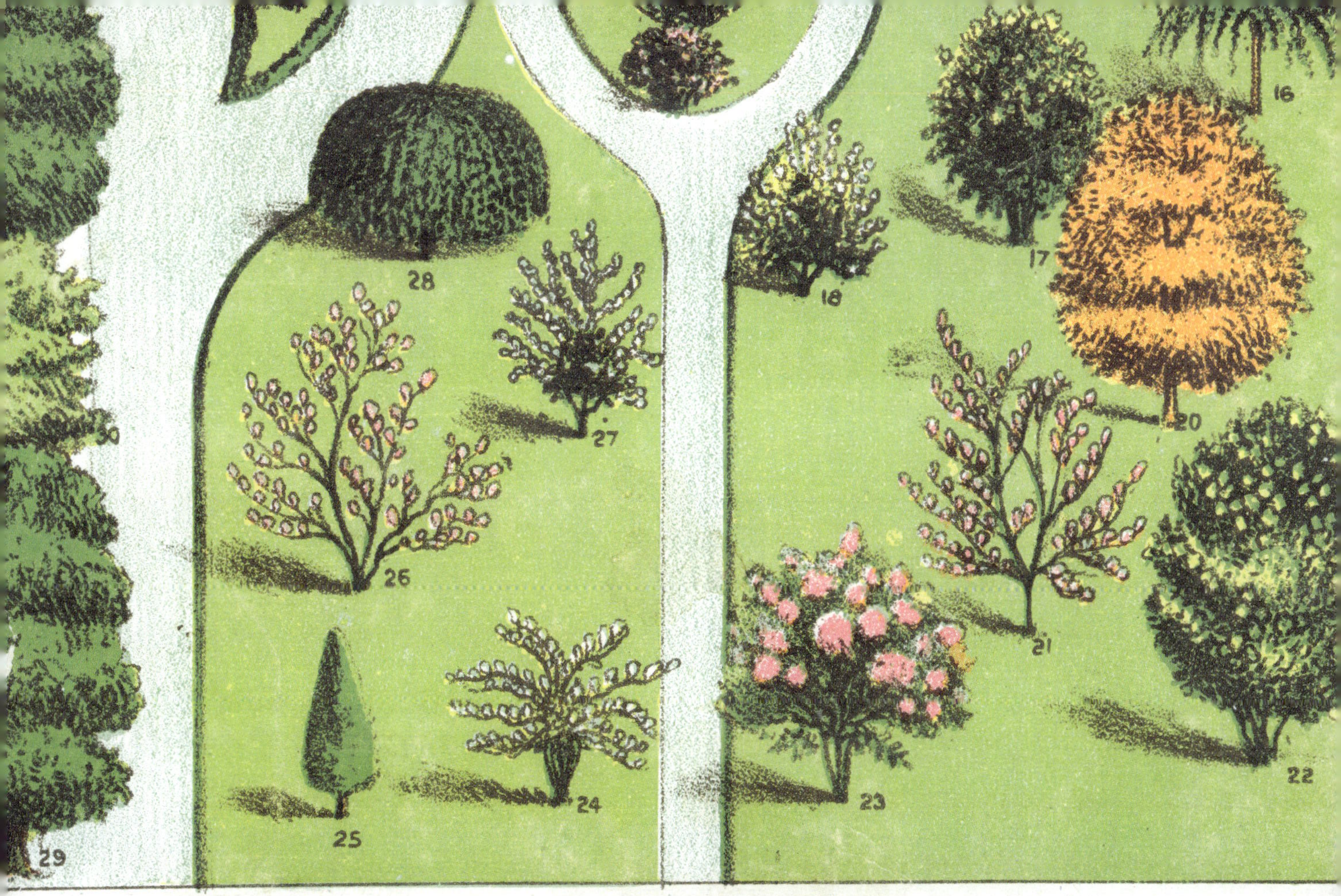

New Ornamental Front Lawn.

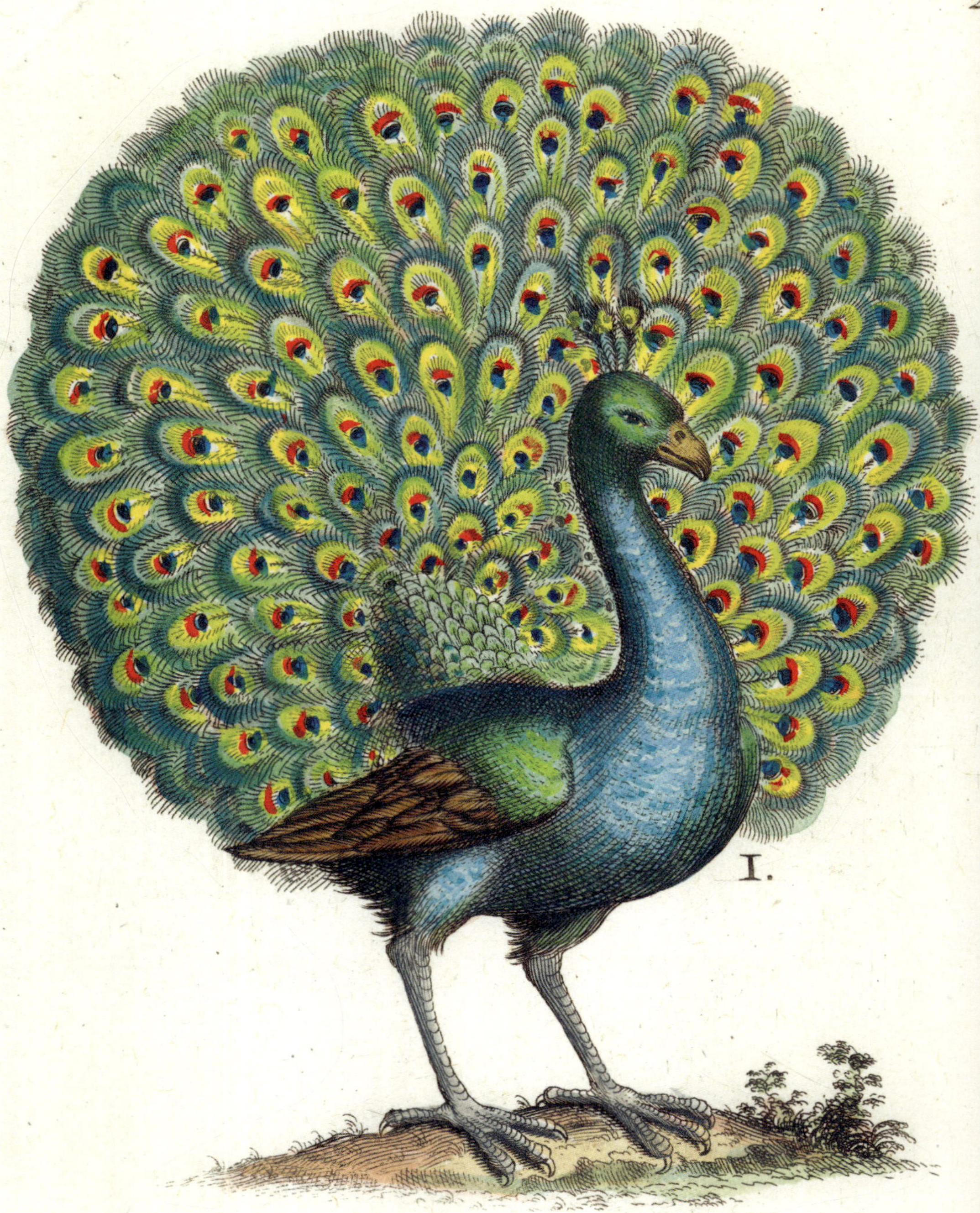

I.

T. XXIV.

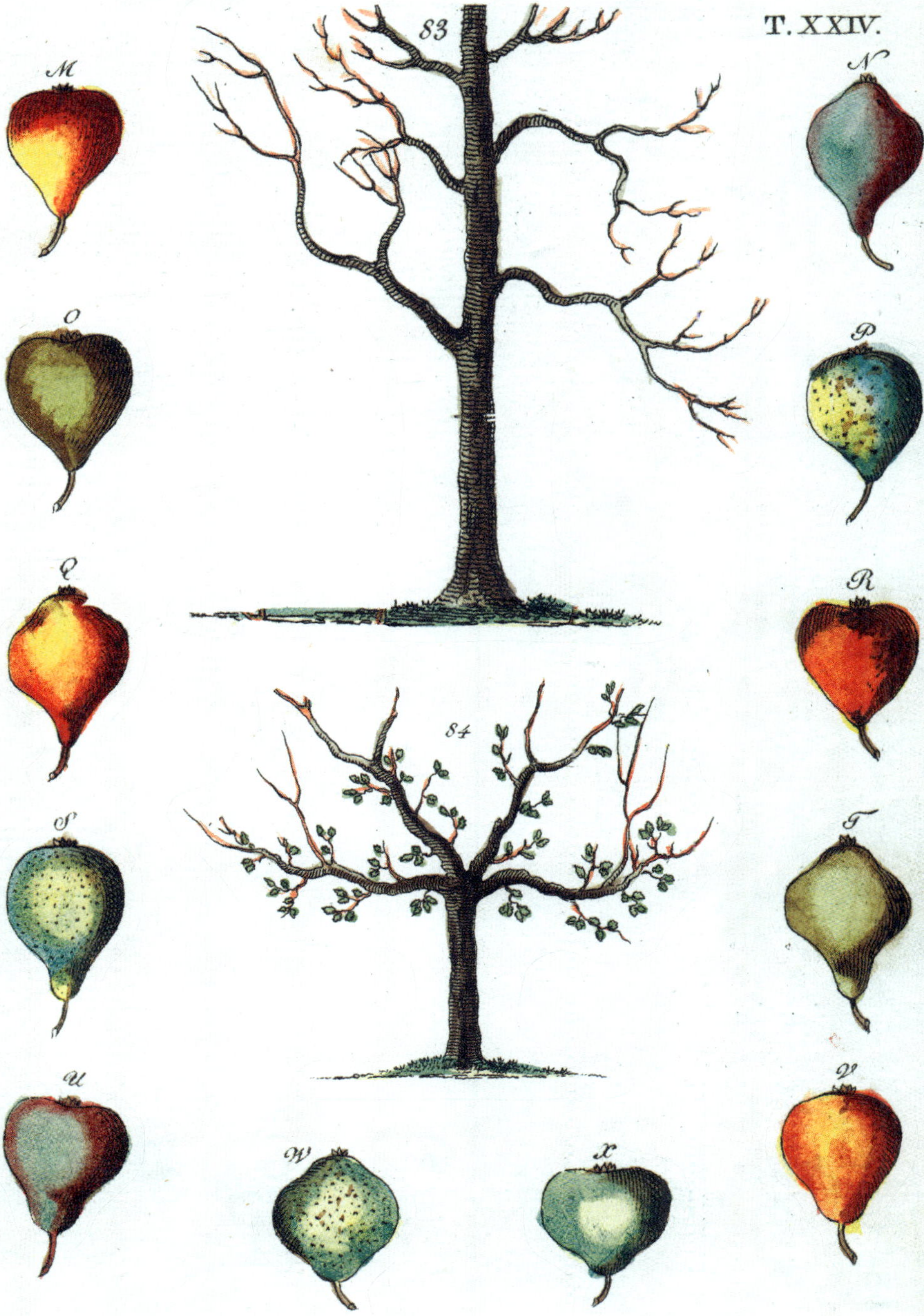

76.

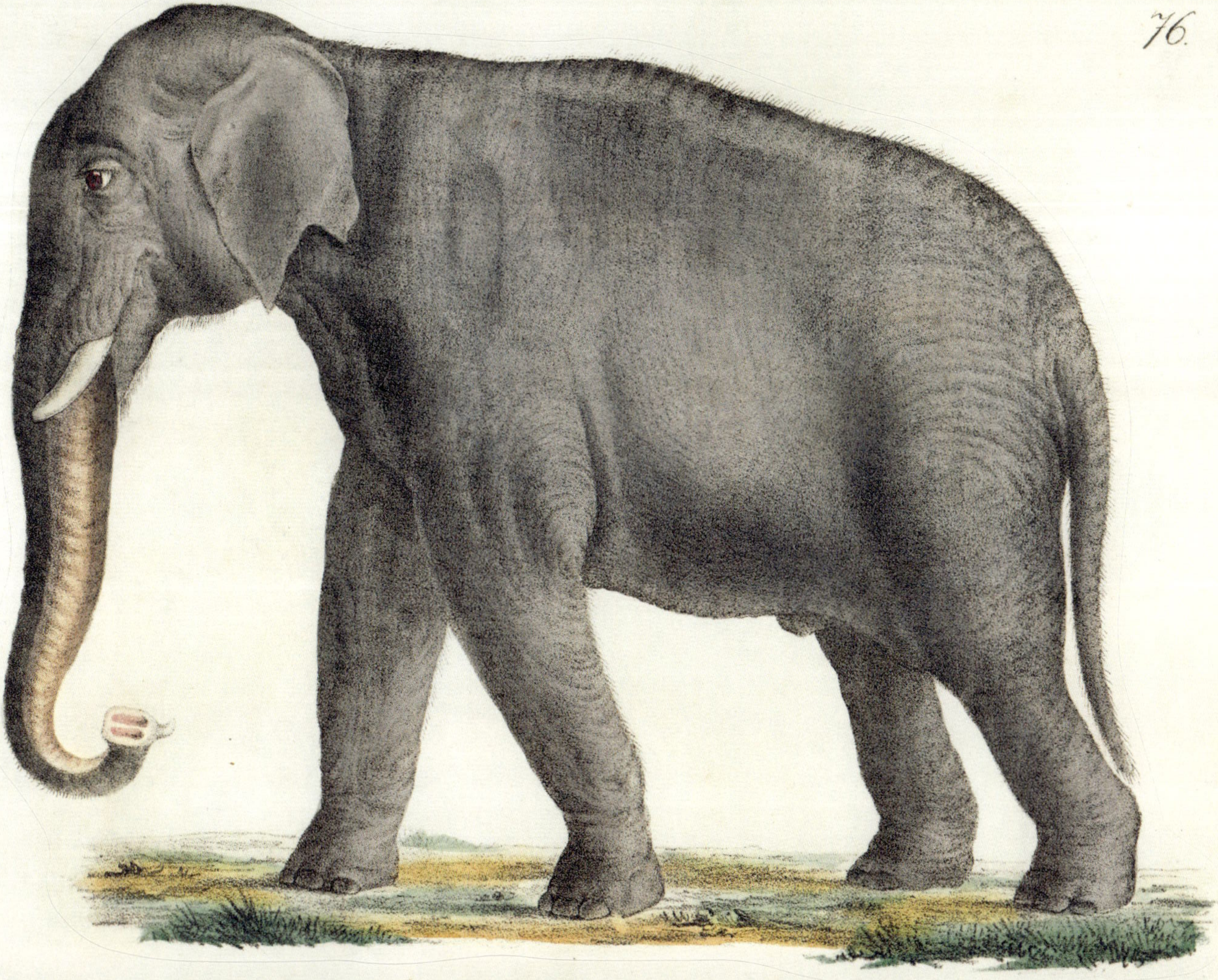

B

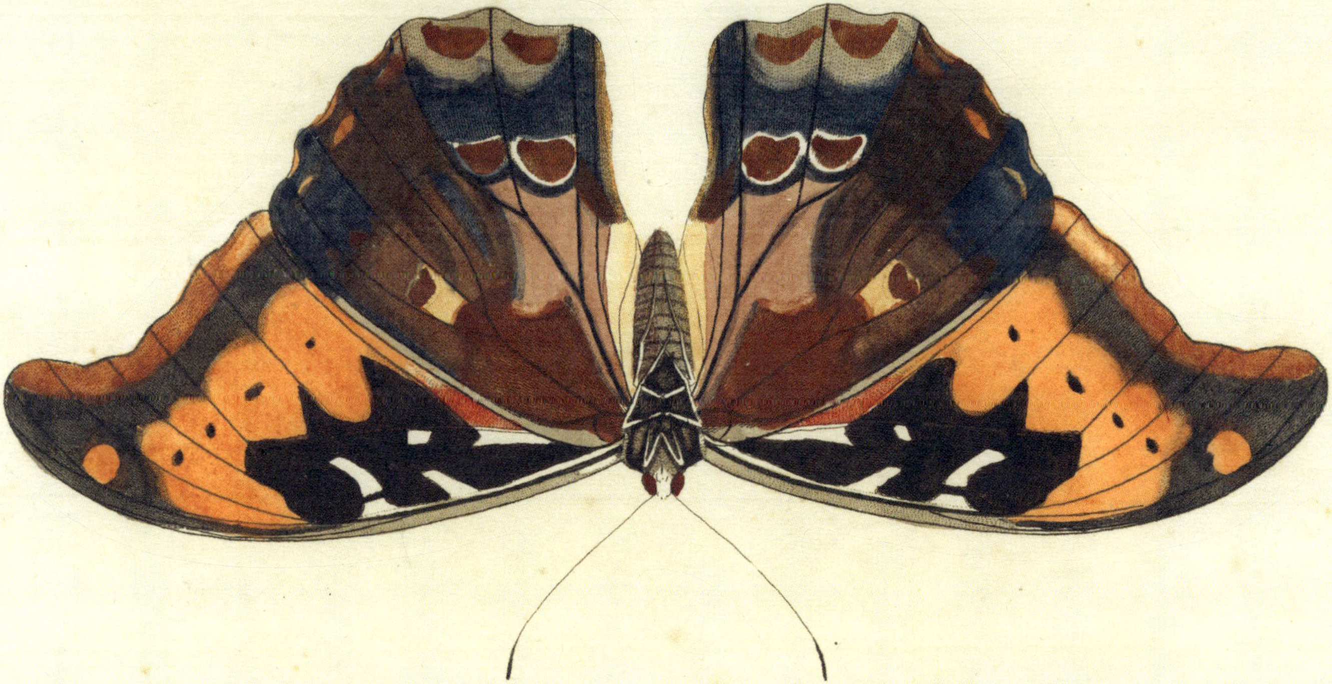

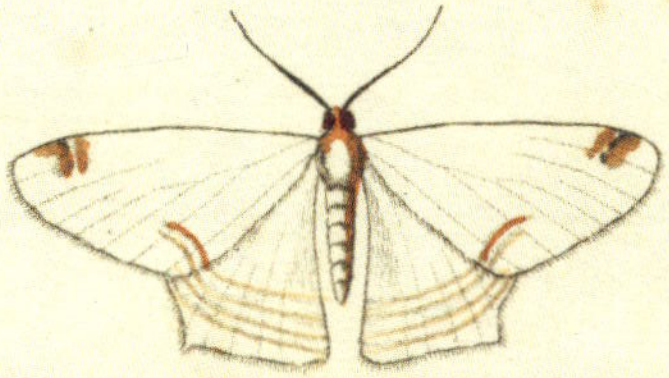

D

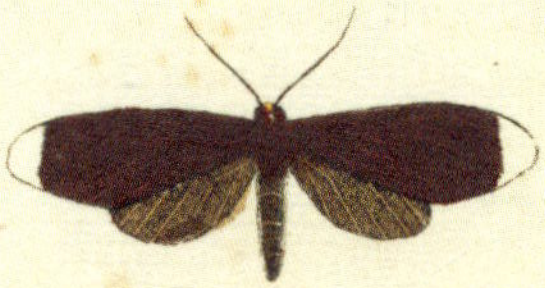

E

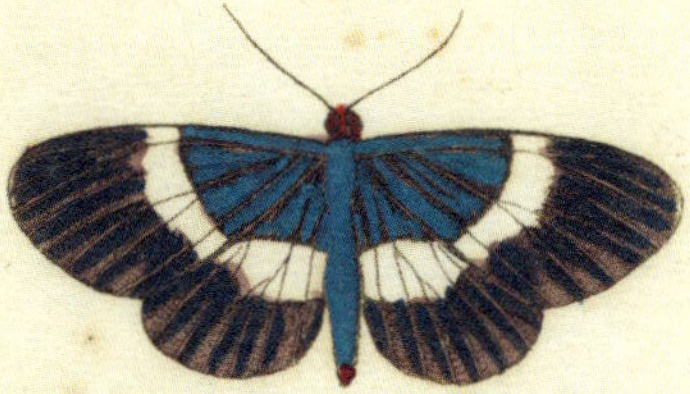

C

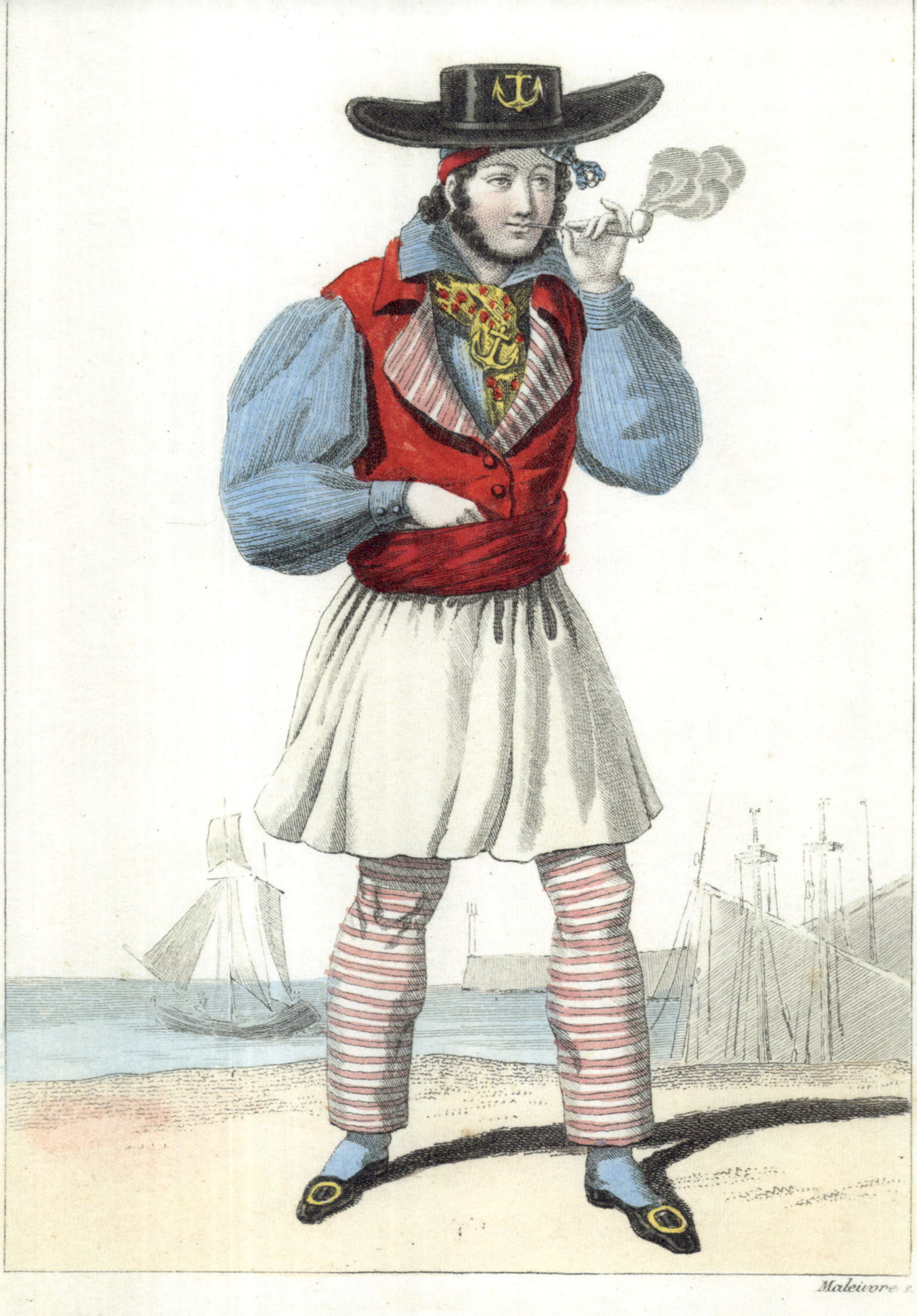

Maleuvre s.

Chez Hautecœur Martinet, Libraire et M.^d d'Estampes, rue du Coq, N.º 13 et 15, Paris.

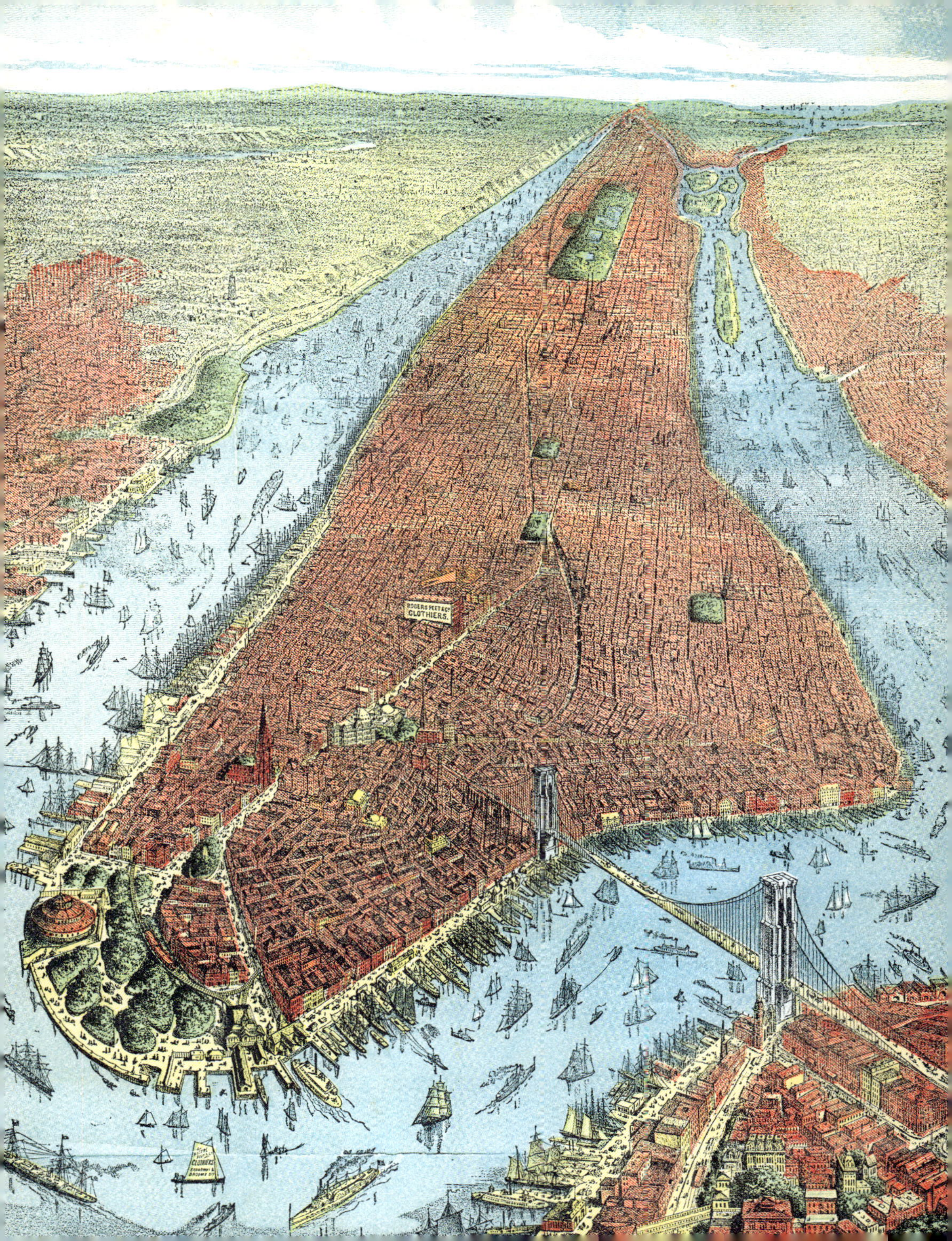
ROGERS PEET & Co
CLOTHIERS.

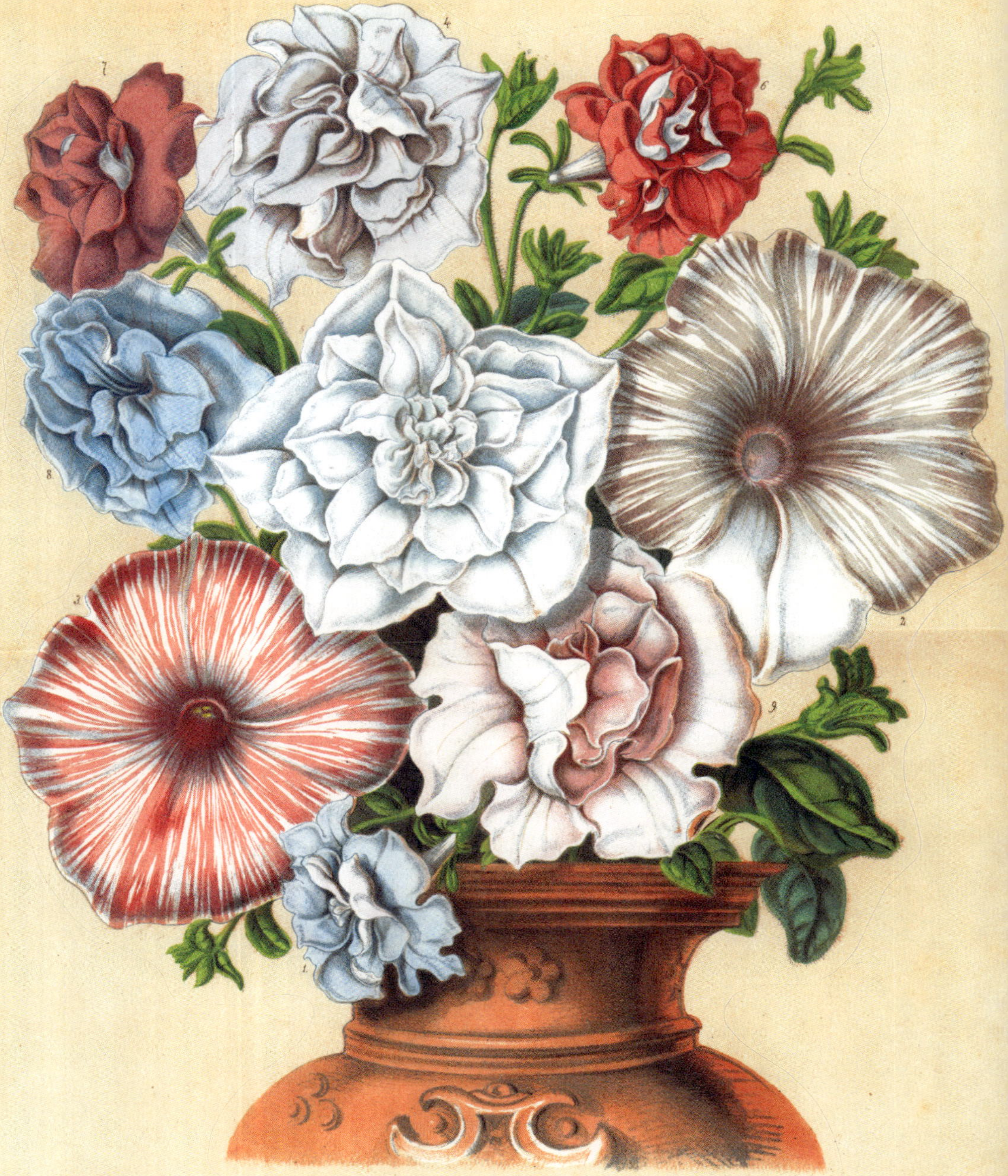

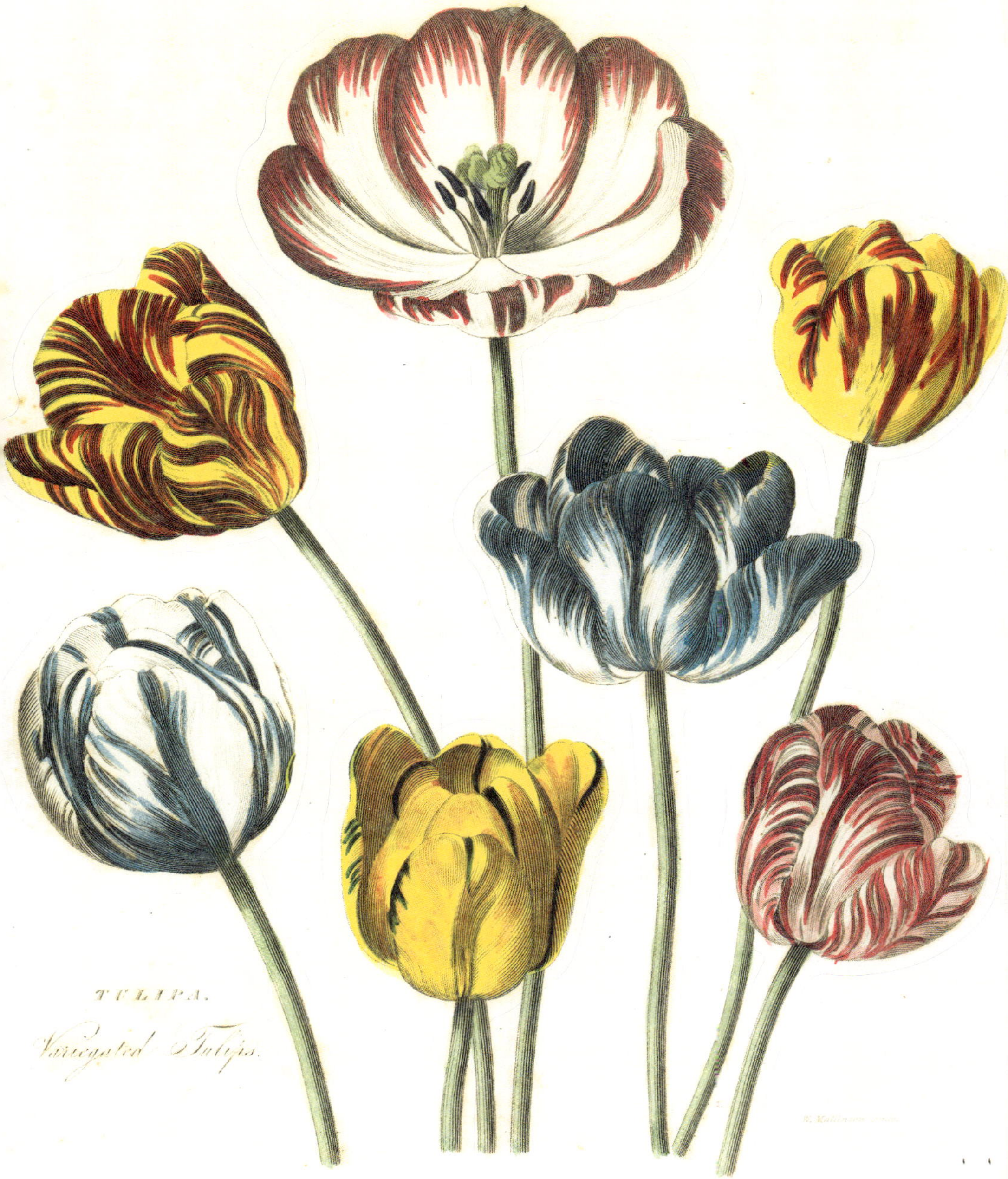

TULIPA.

Variegated Tulips.

Published by Henry Fisher, Caxton, Liverpool. Aug. 1819.

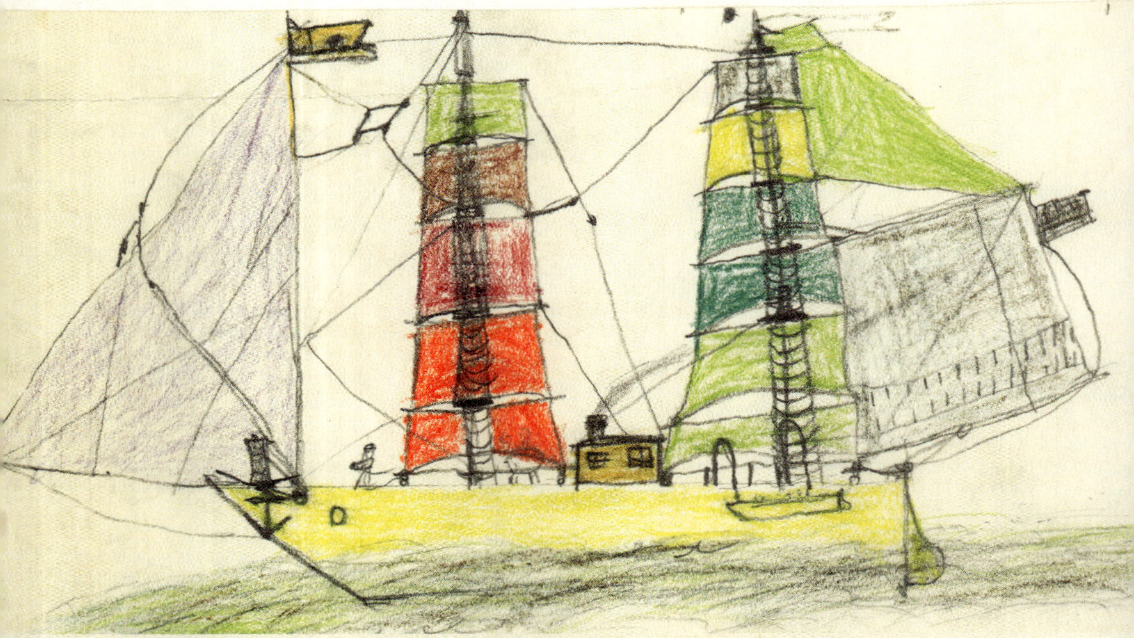

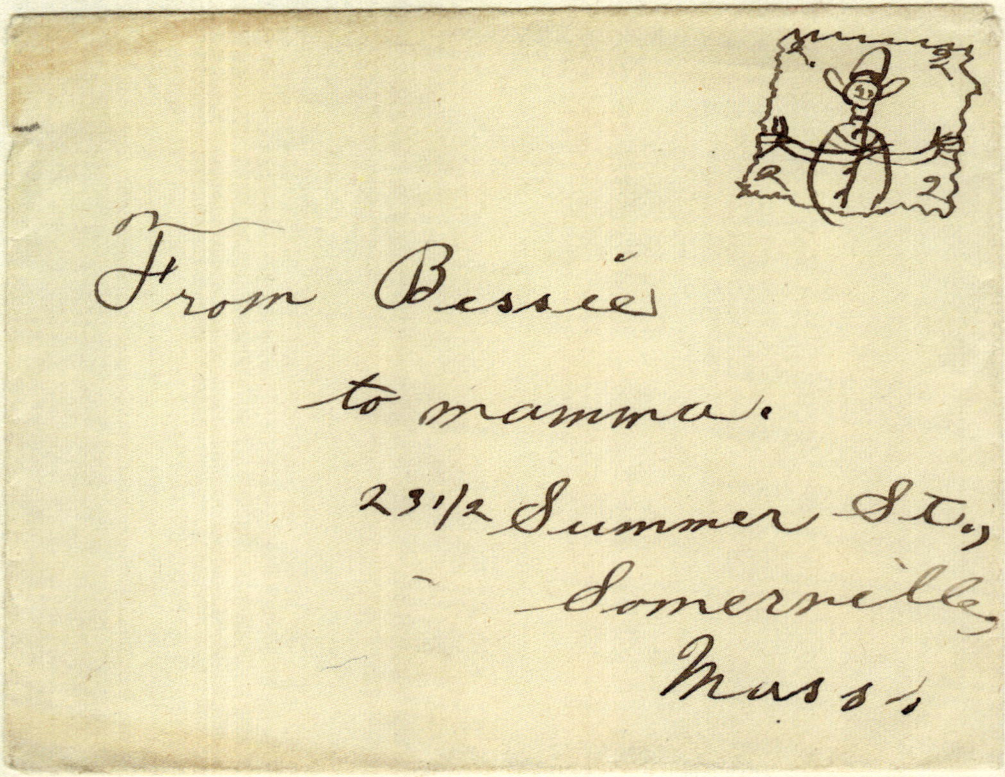

From Bessie
to mamma.
23 1/2 Summer St.,
Somerville
Mass.

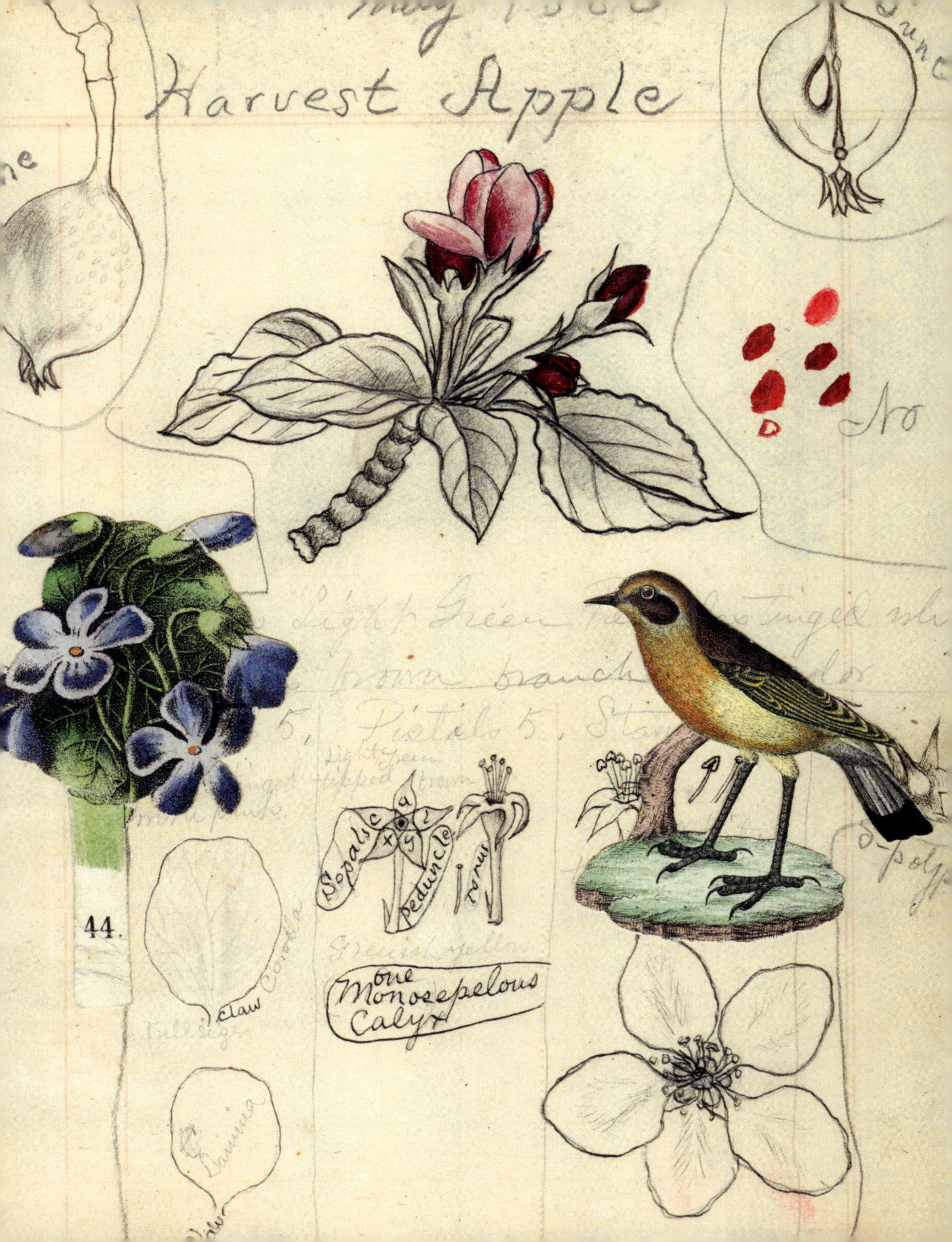

Harvest Apple
No
Light Green
Pistals 5,
Light green tipped brown
Sepals
peduncle
Torus
Greenish yellow
one Monosepelous Calyx
44.
claw
Corolla
Full size

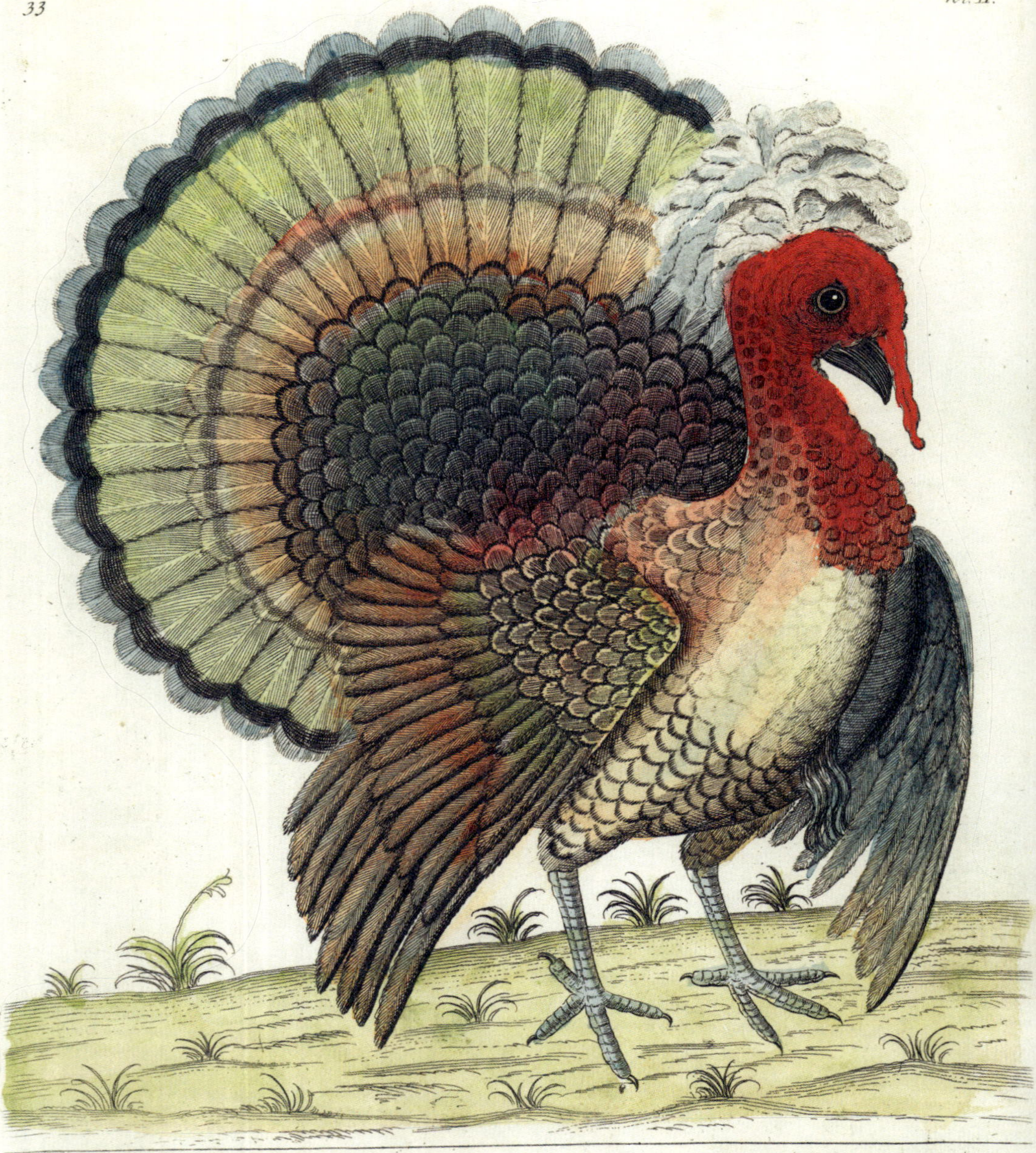

Gallopavo Cristatus. *The Crested Turkey Cock.*

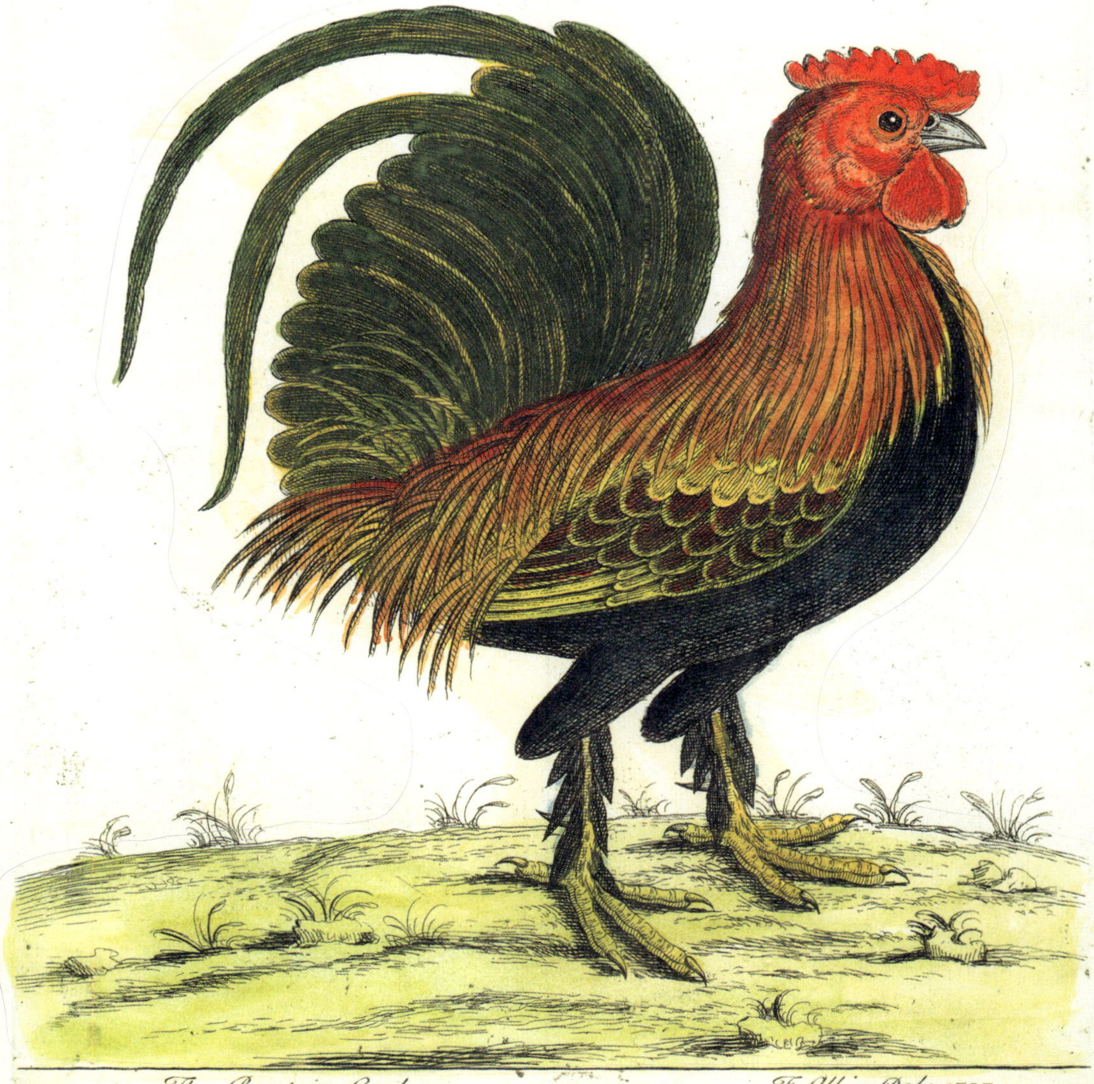

The Bantam Cock. *F. Albin Del: 1737.*

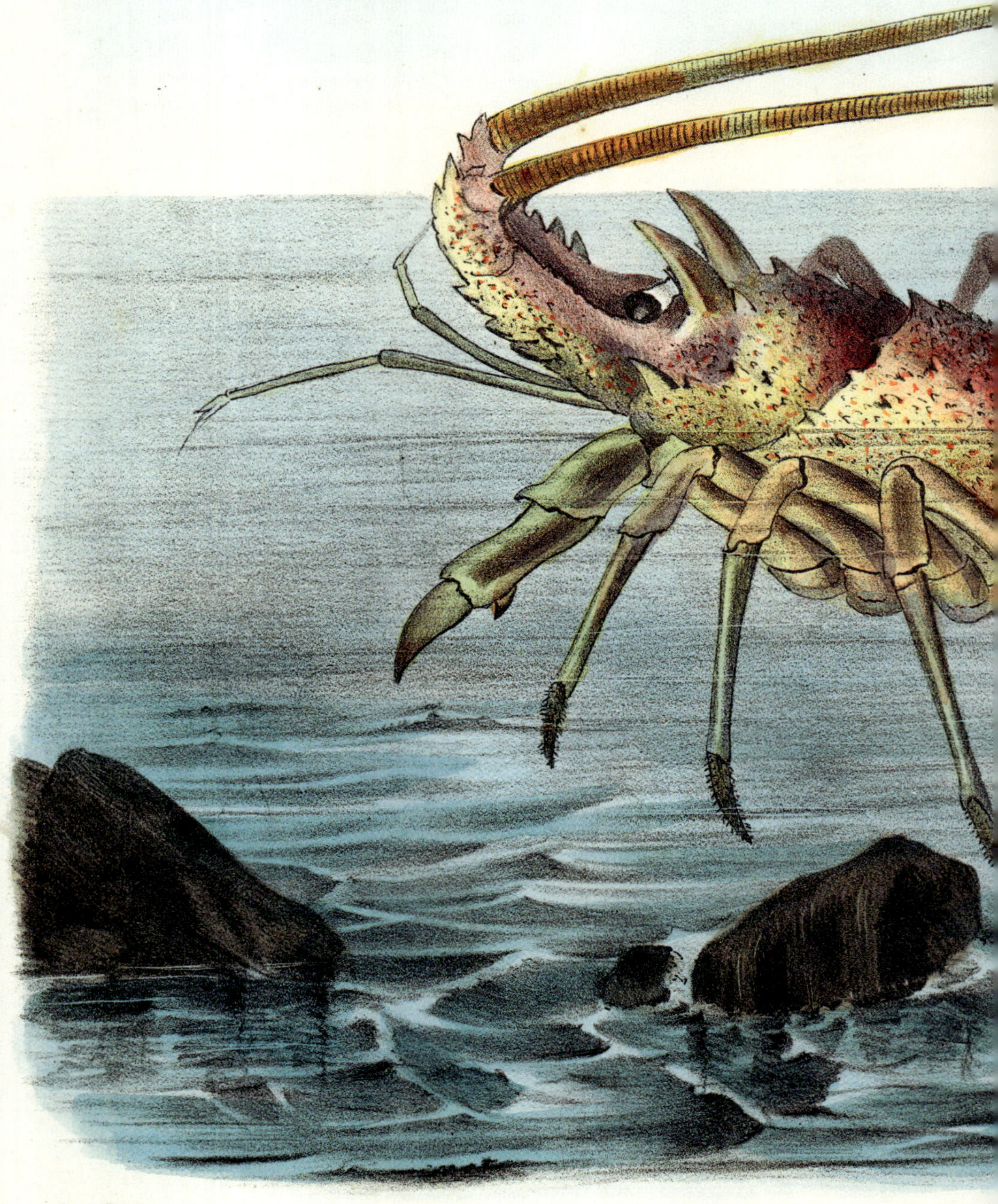

Lit. Petraroja

ALIUSTA COMUNE

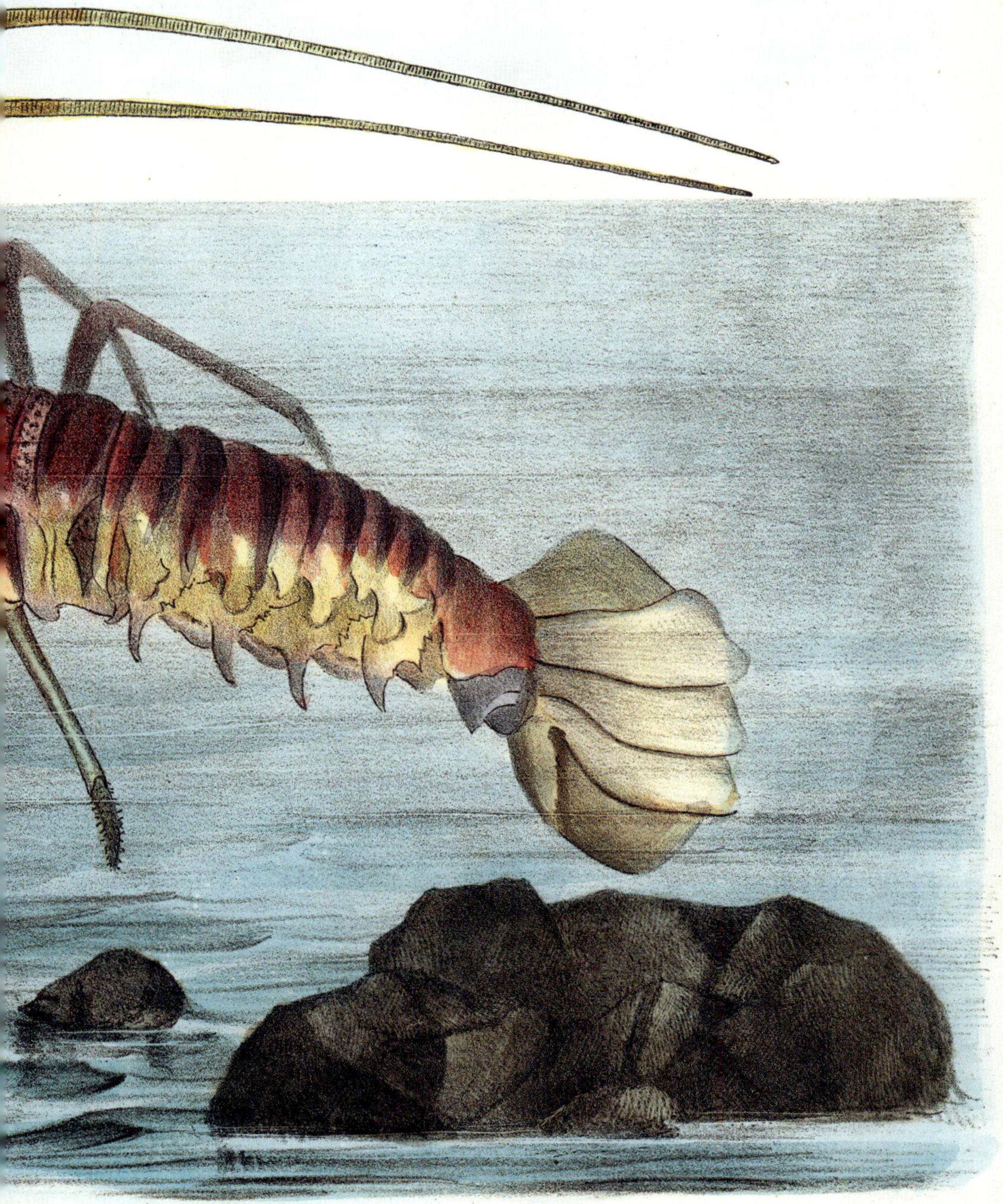

G. Irolli dis.

Palinurus vulgaris (Latr.)

Der Beutelkrebs von Oben

Fig. 1.

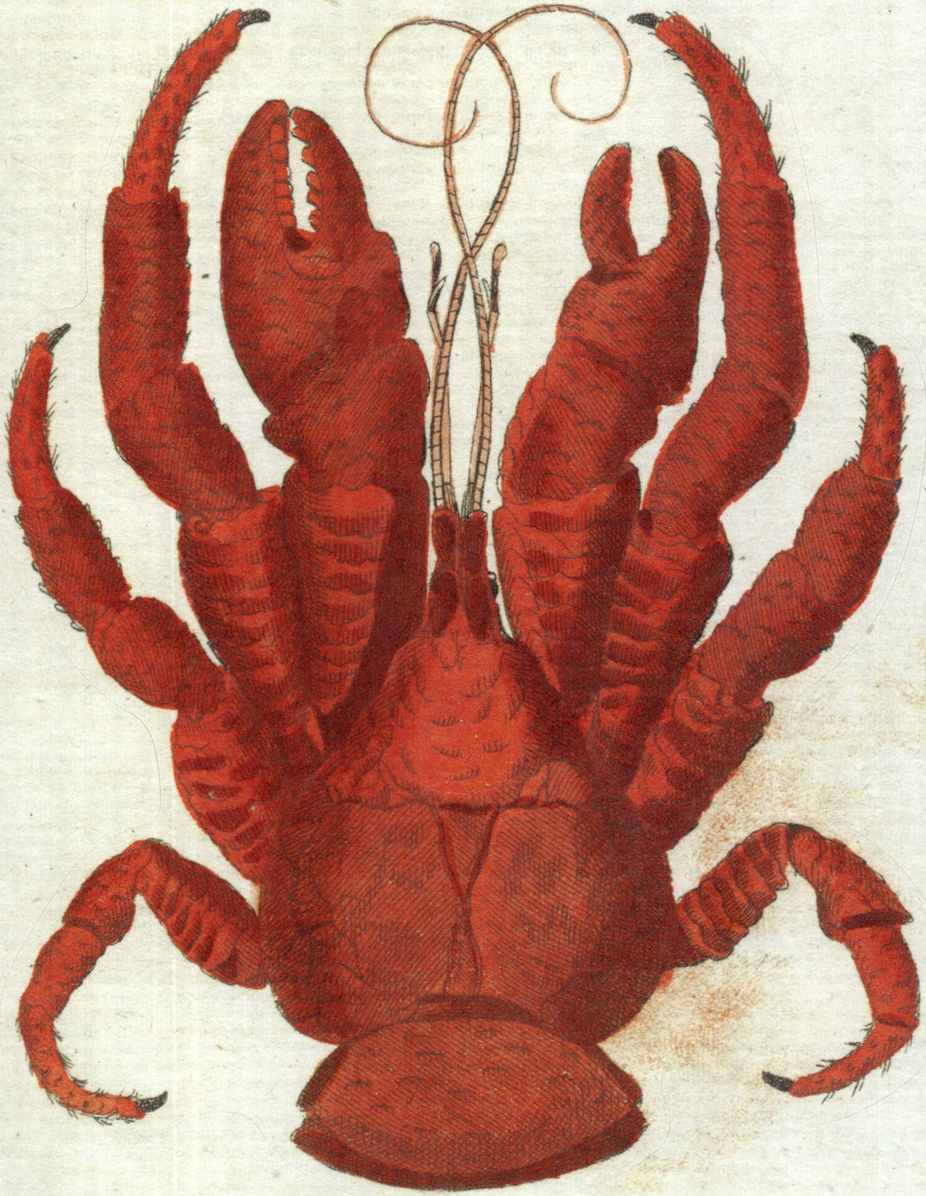

Fig. 2.

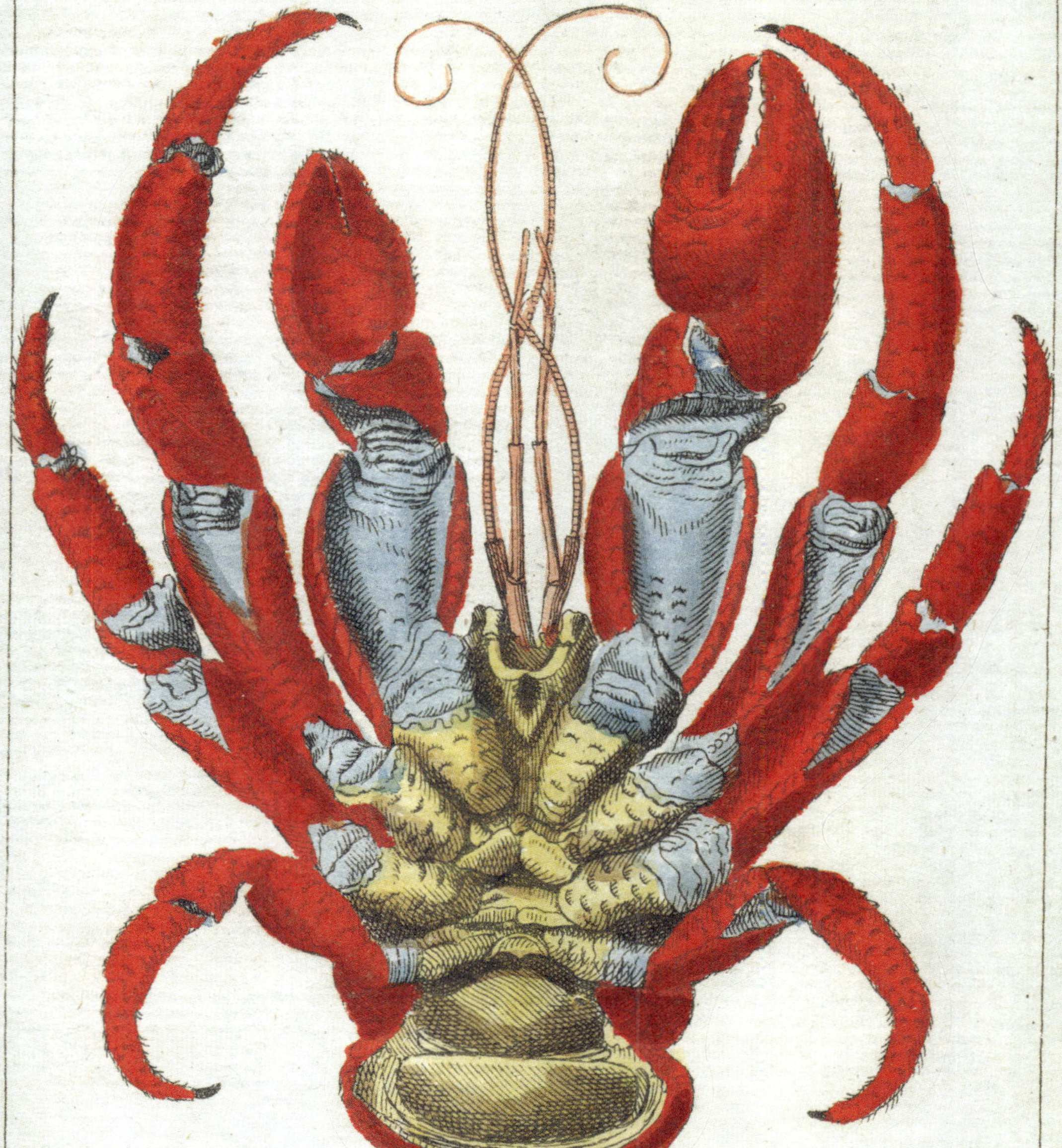

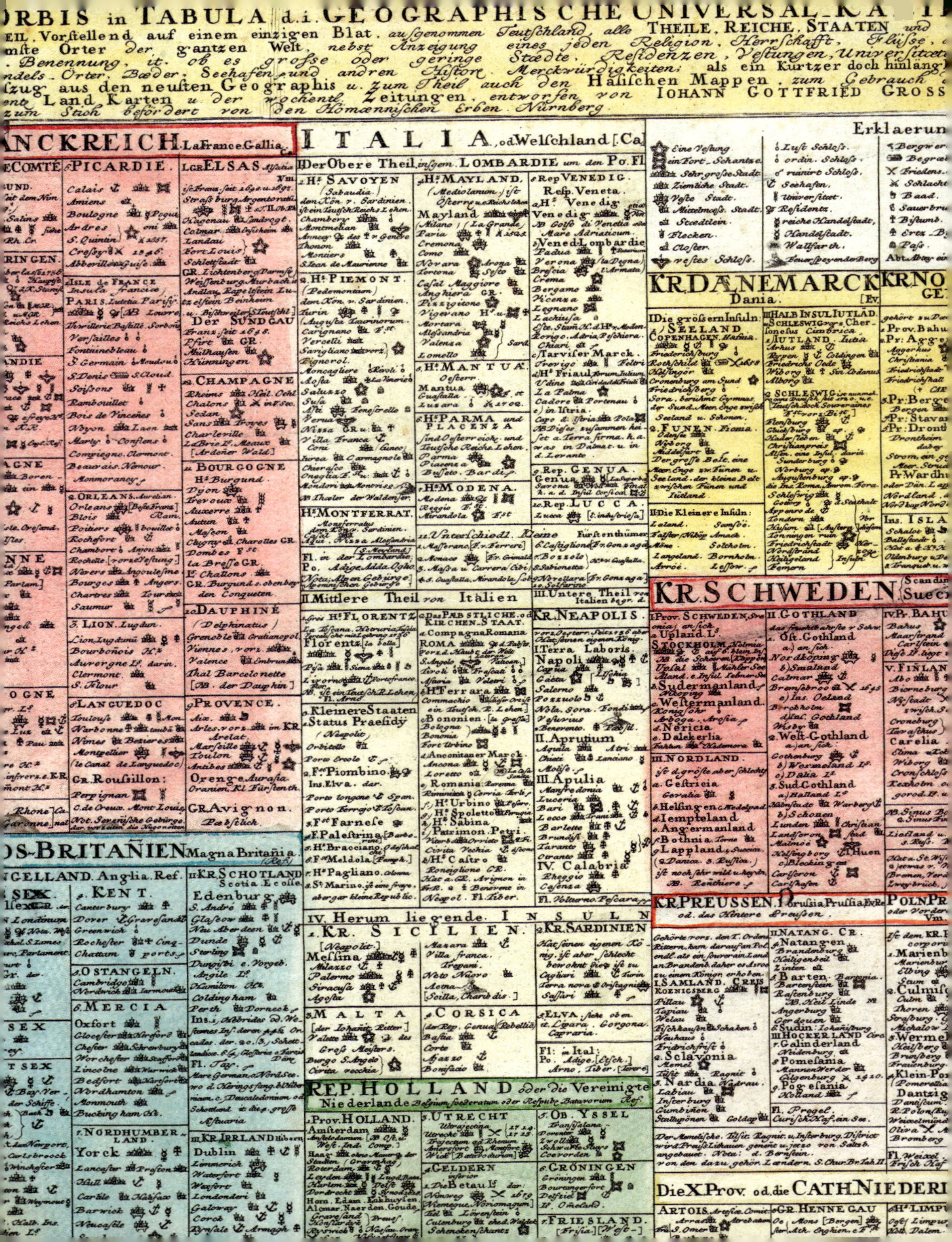
ORBIS in TABULA d.i. GEOGRAPHISCHE UNIVERSAL-KA
Vorstellend auf einem einzigen Blat, ausgenommen Teutschland, alle THEILE, REICHE, STAATEN und
Land Karten u. der wochentl. Zeitungen, entworfen von IOHANN GOTTFRIED GROSS
zum Stich befördert von den Homænnischen Erben Nürnberg
NCKREICH. La France, Gallia
ITALIA, od. Welschland
Erklaerung
KR. DÆNEMARCK
Dania
KR. SCHWEDEN
OS-BRITANNIEN Magna Britania
REP. HOLLAND oder die Vereinigte Niederlande
KR. PREUSSEN. Borussia, Prussia
Die X Prov. od. die CATH. NIEDERL
PICARDIE
ELSAS
CHAMPAGNE
BOURGOGNE
DAUPHINÉ
PROVENCE
LANGUEDOC
LOMBARDIE
SAVOYEN
PIEMONT
MAYLAND
Rep. VENEDIG
MANTUA
PARMA und PLACENZA
MODENA
LUCCA
MONTFERRAT
GENUA
Mittlere Theil von Italien
FLORENTZ
KR. NEAPOLIS
KR. SICILIEN
KR. SARDINIEN
MALTA
CORSICA
SEELAND
IUTLAND
SCHLESWIG
FUNEN
KENT
KR. SCHOTLAND
KR. IRRLAND
MERCIA
UTRECHT
OB. YSSEL
GELDERN
GRÖNINGEN
FRIESLAND

in qua totius Orbis Imperia, Status atque Provinciæ cum suis ditionibus, urbibus nobi-
s. Sedibus Principum, munimentis, academiis, emporiis, portubus, castellis, arcibus, fontibus
ribus, fluviis insignioribus, nec non cujusque religione, dominio directo reliquisque memo-
bus historicis ex probatissimis nostræ ætatis scriptis et tabulis Geogr. præser
Hasianis per signa et scripturæ compendia accurate delineantur, et ad usum
rum, ut vocant, Geographicarum et relationum publicarum accomodantur, per IOH.
TOFR. GROSSIUM. pars I. omnia reliqua. præter Germaniam continens. Sumtibus Homanianis.

eichen.

Kr. Königreich.	begr. begreifft.	
Ls. Landschafft.	d. (der. die. das.	
MGR. Marggrafschafft.	d. (dar) darinnen	
Mah. Mahomedisch.	e. ein. eg. zum Exempel	
Pr. Provinz.	geh. gehört, gehörig	
Rep. Republic	h. a. hat auch (nemlich	
Ref. Reformirt.	auswärtige Länder	
Vm. Vermischter Relig.	o (od) oder	
Vorg. Vorgebürg.	s. u. siehe unten	
a. auch.	vorz. vorzeiten.	

A S I A.

GELOBTE LAND. PALÆSTINA o. Terra Sancta.

I. L. IUDÆA
1. Stam Iuda
Bethlehem Hebron Gaza Asdod Ls. Gosen
2. Stam Benjamin
Ierusalem & Iericho
3. Stam Dan
4. Stam Simeon
Bersabe. Ascalon

II. L. SAMARIA
1. St. Ephraim
Samaria & Sichem
½ St. Manasse
Basan Chorazin
III. L. GALILÆA
1. St. Asser
Berg Saron Grentz Syrien
2. St. Naphtali
Capernaum X. Staedte
3. St. Sebulon
Nazareth Cana Tiberias

4. St. Iaschar
Israel Berg Carmel
IV. L. PERÆA
a. Trachonitis b. Idumæa
c. Batanea
1. St. Ruben
Bethabara
2. St. Gad
Ls. Gilead
3. Der andere ½ St. Manasse.

See Genezareth Todte Meer Flus Iordan

Die Große TATAREY Mag. Tataria.
Relig. Mahomet. u. Heydn.

IRUSS. TATAREY
Gen Westen:
I. Königr. CASAN.
a. Eigentl. Casan
Casan
b. Bulgar Ls.
II. Königr. ASTRACAN
Astracan
Grebinskischen Cosacke
Steppe. eine Wüste.
III. CIRCASSIA
Donskisch. Cosacken.
Eigentl. Circassien
Terki
Gen Nord u. Osten:
I. Prov. TOBOLSKY. das eigentl. SIBERIEN.
Tobolsky
Ostiaken Volk.
Surgut [Samoyeden]
II. Prov. IENISESKOY
Tungusen. Volck
Ieniseskoy
Fret. Weygats. [Samoyedi]
III. Prov. IRKUTSKOY.
Irkutskoy
Dauria Ls.
Iakutskoy
IV. Prov. OCHOTSKOY.
Prov. Kamtschatka
Udskoy Ochotskoy

Fl. Wolga. Oby. Ienisey. Amur. Casp. Meer.

SOUVERAINE TATAREY.
Gen Osten:
I. Kön. d. CANTAISCHA od. Gr. Cans
KALMAKKIA.
Marcus. Urga &
BUKARIA Ls.
Casgar Coten
Turquestan
(Nord-Wärts)
II. TIBET. TANYU.
Boutan Königr.
Regenten:
1. Dalai Lama. ein Oberster Priester.
2. Can Taischa ein Welt. Fürst.
Berg Poutala. Lama Toncker
Gen Westen:
I. TURQUESTAN
Taschkunt
Karakalpakki. Volck.
USBECK. Chiwa. Königr.
Turcomannen. Volck.
Mawaralnahra L.
Bactriana L.
II. Kleine Tatarey. siehe oben.
Cubanische Tatarn
Circassier. Dagestaner.
Lesgi

Fl.
Oby. Irtis. Sir. Hoang Yangtsé. Schun. Gilun

SINESISCHE TATAREY
I. MANTSCHEUX. Mogolistan der Ost Mungalen
1. Gouvern. CHINIANG.
Leaotong.
Chiniano
2. Gouvernem. KIRIN
Ninguta [Diese Tatar. Mantschen besitzen Sina]
3. Gouvernem. TCITCICAR
Dauria Ls.
Unbekandte Laender:
Ls. YESSO. Matsumay
Ins. Staatenland.
II. Die West MUNGALEN
Eigentl. Mogolistana.
1. Naymanni. Volck.
Farin Karakotö
2. Kalkas Ls.
Paras
Urga & eines falschen Lama
III. Ein Theil der eigentl. Tatarey.
Hami Tourfan.
Koko Nor. ein See.
Koko norische Tatarn

Fl. Leao. Amur. Tumeen. Gelbe fl. od. Hoang ho. Kerlon Selenga.

ASIATISCH TURCKEY. Turcia Asiatica. Mahomet.

I. NATOLIA Levante. vorz. ASIA MINOR.
Treibt grosse Handlung.
Smirna
Bergamo
Bursia vorz. &
Abydo e Dardanelle
Sesto, gegen über.
Isnyren vorz. Nicæa
[Concilium 325 787]
Scutari. vorz. Chrysopolis
Amasan. Tocat
Taurus. ein Gebürg.
vorz. auch Troja
Ephesus. Halicarnasso.
Sardis. Philadelphia
Thyatira. Laodicea
Colossen. Nazianzum.
Tarso. Trapezunt
Chalcedon. [Concil. 451
It. Landschaften:
Phrygia. Ionia. Doris.
Lydia. Caria. Bithynia
Pontg. Paphlagonia.
Galatia. Cappadocia.
Cilicia.
Pamphilia.
II. SORIA. vorz. Syria
1. Ls. Aleppo
Aleppo
Scanderona
Antiochia. wo e. Patriarch der Cath. Christen. am B. Libano. die Maroniten heisse
Libanus, ein Gebürg.
[vorz. Ls. Laodicea. Seleucia]
2. Tripoli. vorz. Phoenicia
Tripoli Syriæ
3. Damasco vorz. Canaan. Palæstina.
Damas vorz. Damasc
Sayd vorz. Sidon.
Sur vorz. Tyrus.
Iaffa vorz. Ioppe
[vorz. auch Samaria
Gaza
Ierusalem]

ARABIA. Mah.
Hat seine eigene Fürsten
1. Das Steinigt Arab [Petræa]
Herat
Horeb u. Sinai Gebürg
Paran. Z in. Cades. sind grosse Wüsteneyen.
vorz. Amalekiter. Moabiter Amoniter. Ismaeliter]
2. Wüste Arabien. [Arabia Deserta.]
Anna
Balsora
3. Glücks Arabien. [Arabia felix.]
Mocca Mahom. Grab
Medina Mascate
Fartach. Fürstenth.
Königr. YEMEN
hat s. eigen Koenig.
Mocca & Aden. Moab.
III. GEORGIEN.
hat [Cathol. Christen]
Caucasus. Gebürg.
[vorz. Colchis. Iberia.]
IV. TURCOMANIA
[vorz. Gr. Armenien]
Erzerum
Ararat Geb.
V. DIARBECK
Bagdad
Mosul vor. Ninive
Ophra. Haran.
Ls. Babylonia od. Chaldæa dar Babel
Ls. Assyria Mesopotamia]
VI. Hiezu gehör. INSUL
1. u. Kr. CYPERN. Cypr.
Nicosia
Famagosta
2. Ins. RHODIS vorz. der Malt. Ritter.
Rhodis
3. Ins. Scio, Metellino. Lesbus.

Königr. SINA. Heydn.
Grose u. Volckreich von Klugen Einwohnern. wird beherrscht vom Tatar Can
Gen Nord:
I. Pr. v. PETCHELI
Peking
II. Pr. CHANSI
Tsientcheou
III. Pr. CHENSI
Xinyan
[Haben die Grosse Mauer zur Grentze.]
IV. Pr. HONAN
Hanyang
Gen Ost:
V. CHANTONG
Tsinan.
VI. KIANGNAN
Nanking
VII. TCHEKIANG
Tchutcheou
VIII. FOKIEN
Linghoa
Ins. Formosa.
Gen Mittag:
IX. HOUQUANG.
X. KOEITCHEOU.
XI. YUNNAN.
Yunnan
XII. QUANGSI
XIII. QUANGTONG
Quangtcheou
[Porcellain]
Macao Ins. [Portug.]
Ins. Hainan
Gen West:
XIV. SETCHUEN
Mahou
Tchingtou
am Sines. Meer ist:
COREA. eine Halb-Ins. u. Königr.
Kingki

Fl. Hoangho. oder Gelbe flus.
Kiuchakiang. oder Blaue flus.

KÖNIGR. PERSIEN. Regnum Persiæ Mahom.

I. Pr. IRACAZEMI
Hispahan
Casbin
II. Pr. SUSISTAN
Suster
III. Pr. SCIRUAN
Derbent. Russ.

VI. Pr. SABLUSTAN
VII. Pr. SESISTAN
VIII. Pr. ADHERBEITZAN
Tabris. Tauris
IX. Pr. CANDAHAR
Candahar

XII. Pr. KERMAN
Gamron
Ins. Ormus
[Sin. Persicus]
XIII. Pr. FARISTAN
Schiras
vorz. Staedte Persepolis.

A F R I C A

I. Am NIL-Strom:
1. ÆGYPTEN. Aegyptus [Türckisch] Mah.
a. Das Niedere Bahri
Alexandria
Damiate. Rosete. in Delta.
b. Mittlere. Vostani.
Cahiro
[vorz. Memphis. Labyrinth u. Mumien. Pyramiden]
c. Obere. Said.
Gerge. Assuana. Ibrim.
[vorz. Thebe. Coptus.]
d. Gen Ost. am Roth. Meer:
Suez & Cosser
e. Gen West:
Bouhera Pr.
II. ÆTHIOPIEN unter Egypten
1. KR. NUBIEN. Mah.
a. KR. Sennar
Doncola. Meroë Ins.
Kr. Dequin
b. am Meer: Abex.
Suaquem
2. KR. ABESSINIEN.
Christl.
a. Eigentl. Abessinien [Konig Neguz]
Königreiche. Amara.
Bagemder. Dambea.
Samen. Bugna. Goyam.
Gongo. Midrabahr. &c.
b. Gallanische Prov.
c. Gen West: Schankala
Falassan. Völcker.
d. am Meer gen Ost:
Crocco. Dancale Kr.

III. BARBAREY Mahomet.
A. BARBAREY ansich
1. KR. FEZ u. MAROCCO
a. Disseits d. B. Atlas
Kr. Fez. Fez
Mequinet. Salée
Tanger. Tetuan.
Ceuta, Hisp.
Kr. Marocco. Marocco
Mazagan. Port.
Kr. Sus. Vera Cruz.
b. Ienseit. B. Atlas:
Kr. Darha Kr. Tafilet.
Kr. Segelmesse
Kr. Fighig
II. Unter TURKISCH. Sch.
1. Kr. u. Rep. ALGIER
Alger
Constantine. Bugie.
Tremesen. Oran. Sp.
Kr. Labes
2. Kr. u. Rep. TUNIS
Tunis Goulette.
Prov. Biledulgerid.
3. Kr. Rep. TRIPOLIS
Tripoli
Ezzab. Prov.
Kr. Barca
III. Souver. Laender:
Tikorte Kr. Gadames Kr.
Huerguela Prov.
B. SARA. Wusten.
a.) Zanzaga Wüste.
Cap blanc.
Ins. Argorin [Franz.]
Tasset. Tagaza.
b.) Zwenziga. Wüste.
c.) Targa d.) Lemta
e.) Berdoa [vorz. Lybia]

III. Vorder ÆTHIOPIEN. Mahom.
I. NIGRITEN LAND. od. Land d. Schwartzē
Gegē d. Atlant. Meer zu:
Gualata Kr. Senega Pr.
Ialoffi pop.
Cajor. Kr. Fort. Louis [Fr.]
Cap. Ver de. I. Goree [Fr.]
S. Iames. Ins. [Angl.]
Cacheo, [Port.]
Bisseaux [Fr.]
Foulles. pop. Calam Kr.
Bambouc pr. Cassou Kr.
Iaga Kr. Melly Kr.
Mandinga Kr.
2. Im Land einwaert
Guber Kr. Tombut Kr.
Agades Kr. Gago Kr
Cano Kr. Zanfara Kr.
Bournou Kr.
Gaoga Kr.
Fl. Senega. Senegal. Gambia. Riogrande.
II. OBERE GUINEA Heydn.
1. am Æthiop. Meer
a. Malagetta
Ufer Serra Liona
Kr. Mitombo
Malaguetta. Grey Küst
Petit Dieppe [Fr.]
Kr. Sanguin
Grand Sestre
Petit Sestre
Sestre Crou
(Französ.)
Bassa
b. GUINEA [eigentl.]
1. Elfenbein Küst, litus dentium
Quaqua Küst.
2. Goud Kust
Asiante Kr.
Abim Pr.
Aquambou Kr.
Issini [Fr.]
Fridricsburg Holl.
Mina Holl.
Conradsburg Holl.
Cabo Corso Engl.
Fredricsburg Dæn.
Mouree
Cormantin
Crevecoeur
(Holl.)
Castell. Angl. im Kr. Accara.
Christiansburg Den.
3. Gen Ost:
Dahome Kr.
Ardra Kr. Iuda Kr.
Gregoi [Engl.] [Fr.]
Pawpaw Kr.
Benin Kr.
Biaffara Kr.
Malays. Volck.
Calbongos. Volck.
Flu. Camaronum
Cap. Lobo Gonsalez
II. Einwär. im Land
Ist alles unbekant.

Vorgebürge: Capo Verga
Cap de Palmas
Cap de 3 Puntas

IV. Hinter ÆTHIOPIEN
vorz. Ober Æthio
A.) NIEDRE G
a.) am Æthiopi Meer:
Loango Kr.
Cacongo Kr.
Malemba
Angoy Kr.
Congo Kr.
Gr. Sonho H.
Pemba. Mor.
Batta H. Pongo
Sundi H.
Angola. o. D.
[Portug.] Rel.
Loanda S. Pau
Oarij Kr.
Moseche. Quisa
Iumbi
Benguela Kr.
b.] Einwärt
Matamba Kr
Fl. Zaire. Berbe
(B.) Nieder ÆTHIOPIEN.
Bororos Kr. u.
Mumbos. Z
Giaghas. Dong
Menschen Fr
Nimeamaje
Macoco. Kr.
Galli. Volck.
(C.) Küste ZAN u. AYAN
a.] In Zangh
Moruca Kr.
Mozambique
Quiloa Kr. Qu
Monbaza Kr
Melinde Kr.
Melinde
Brava Resp.
b.] In Ayan:
Adea Kr.
Adel Kr. [od.
V. [D.] CAFRE
Heydn
1. Gen West
Com. bebe. Vol
Cafferische Nat
dar. Hotentot
Cap de bonna Sp
od. Vorgeb. d. gu
[Holl.]
2. Gen Ost
Monomotapa
Sene. Tete. S. Iag
Massapa
Sofala Kr.
Inhaqua [P
VI. INSULN AFRICA
Gen West: I
a.] Canariæ.
Canaria. Tenerif
Palma. Ferro.
b. Ins. Madera
c. Ins. Porto Santo
II. Classe Ins. C
S. Iago. Boa
Del Fuogo
III. Classe in Æth
Ins. S. Helena
Anobon. [Por
Gen Ost:
1. Zocotora 2. In
tis 3. Ins. Com
4. I. Madagasc
5. I. Bourbon
6. I. S. Mauritz

AMERICA. India Occidentalis

od. West Indien. Las Indas Occidentales. America genañt v.
Vesputio, welcher d. veste Land A. 1497 erfunden. Vor ihm ab
ste Erfinder gewesen Christoph. Columbus A. 1492. Die Wahr
Gold, Silber, Edelgesteine, Cacao, Indigo, Zucker, Cochen. Biber,

I. NORD-AMERICA
1. ARCTISCHE LÆNDER
S. Iacobs Insuln
Neu Gröenland Ls.
[Meer Enge Hudson Davis]
2. TERRA LABRADOR od. Neu Britania. od. der Esquimeaux.
3. CANADA od. Neu-FRANCIA [Franz.]
Saguenay Ls.
Canada Ls.
Quebec
Montreal
Fl. S. Laurentii
LOVISIANA [Franz.]
Neu Orleans
Iroquois Heydn.

6. NEU-MEXICO. Ca.
[Span.]
S. Fé de Granada
Neu Granada Ls.
Quivira. Ls.
Fl. Assomtion
7. MEXICO od. NEU SPANIEN. Ca.
[Span.]
a. Audienza Mexico
Mexico
Vera Cruz
Iucatan Ls.
Campeche
Aquapulco
Tlascala
b. Aud. Guadalaxara.
c. Guatimala.

2. PERU KR
[Span.] am S
a. Aud. di Quito
b. Aud. de lo
Lima
Cusco Tru
Ylo
Oropesa
c. Aud. de los
Potosi
[Silber Berg
Arica
3. CHILI. Ca.
[Span.] am
a. Chili Ls.
S. Iago

ISCHE REICH Imper. Russicum. Griech. Relig.
sche Kayserthum.

USSLAND Nord:
eral
AND
cholm.
SSLAND.
Laponia. Russica
naiqua.
Kargapol
Plescow
OD WELIKI
rod
A.
RDENSER
ER. rotus
IA Europæ
Asiatische]
rov.
Prov.
Prov.
Prov.
Prov.
propria
Prov.

A.
1.) Gen Sude:
BIELO OZERO. H.
Bielo Ozero
2. IAROSLAW H.
Iaroslaw
3. TWEER H.
Tweer
4. ROSTHOW H.
Rosthow.
5. SUSDAL H.
Susdal
6. WOLODIMER H.
Wolodimer
7. MOSCOW H.
Moscow
8. WOROTIN H.
Worotin
9. REZAN H.
Pereslaw. Tula.
10. NISINOVOGOROD
Nisinovogorod
Pop. Czeremissi
Eigentlichs RUSSLAND.
11. RZEWA H.
Rschow
12. BIELA H. Biela
13. SMOLENSKO H.
Smolensko

Klein RUSSLAND.
14. CZERNICHOW H.
Czernichow
15. SEVERIA H.
Novogorod Severski
16. RUSS. UKRAINE.
1. Pop. Zaporogische Cosacke
Kiow
Betzura
Trechimerow
Bachurin
Pereslaw. Pultawa
2. Bielgorod. Cosacke
Woronez
Bielgorod
[Nota. Ukrain. Linie]
3. Donische Cosacken
Panschine. Babey.
Czerkaskoy.
[Asiatische Cosaken s. in Asia]

Fl. Wolga: darein Occa. Kama fallen
Don [Tanais] darein Donnecz.
Dwina. Dniper.

Nota:
Den Asiatischen Theil Russlands siehe in d. Grossen Tatarey.

RISCHE LÆNDER
Oster. theils Türck.

RN. Vm. Oester
Ungarn
Ca. Er.
Freystadt.
Berg. St.
Parkan
Ins. S. Andr.
Freystadt
ok. Wein
adein
Ref.
edin
1691
Ungarn
Wein Wachs
Ca. Er.
burg
S. Gothard
rg
fkirchen
2. 6. Ludor II
Türck.
NIEN. Oester
[Brücke]
dein
mit. Sirmien
mit.
opranitz
1699
ürck
des Bassa
Arnaut.
Bassa
Raub Nest

4. SIEBENBÜRGEN.
Transylvania. Oest. Vm.
Hermanstadt Er.
Cibinium
Cronstadt Er.
Weissenburg [Carlsburg] Ca.
Nösen [Beiterze]
Medwisch [Medwais]
Schesburg. Claussenburg
Millenbach, Neumarkt
Bierthelmen Er.
Türzburg
Rothe Thurn
Das eiserne Thor
NB. Die Relig. ist Ca. Er. Ref. Socin. u. a. Griech.
Hat ☉ und. ☾ NB die Zeckler
5. CROATIEN.
meist Oest.
Carlstadt
Petrina Sissecz
Wihicz Türck.
6. SERVIEN
Oest. u. Türck.
Belgrad o. Griechisch Weissenburg
Passarowitz 1718.
Nissa. Widdin. Türck.
7. DALMATIEN.
a) Venet.
Morlachia Ls. dar.
Cliña Spalatro
Zara Hauptst.
Sebenigo Nona
Traw Clissa
Narenza Sing
Cattaro Salone Segla
b) Oester.
Zeng
[Uscocken bes. Völcker]
c.) Türck.
Arcegowina d. Bassa
Scardona. Clino.
RAGUSA Rep. S. Croix
Ins. Meleda. Die übrig. Ins. sind Venet.
Ungarn. hies vorz. Panonia.
Servien. Moesia.
Fl. Donau. Sau. Drau. Leitha u. Arabo.

EUROPÆISCHE TURCKEY
I. ROMANIEN Mah. Türck.
Liegt am Schw. Meer.
CONSTANTINOPEL.
Stambul. vorz. Byzanz
des Gros. Sult. Seraglio
Adrianopel
Philippopoli
Gallipoli
Dardanelli. Sesto u.
[Avido gegenüber in Asia
[Mare] Nigrum seu Pontus Eux. 2.) Mare Ægeum. [Archipelagus]
3.) Fret. Dardan. s. Hellesp.
4.) Fret. Constant. s. Bosphor. Thraciæ 5.) Propontis.]
Man duldet a. die Christen gegen e. gewissen Tribut.
II. BULGARIEN Türck.
Sophia oh. Mauer
Nicopolis oh. Mauer
Silistria Varna
in Russl. ist a. e. Bulgaria
III. Fr. MOLDAU unter Türck. Schutz.
Iassy d. Fürstens
Chozim
Schantz d. H. Dreyf.
Fl. Pruth.
IV. WALLACHEY. Griec. Unt. Türk. Schutz.
Buckerest d. Furst
Tergovist
Kempelung Messe.
Czerneteft Weinwachs.
Oesterr. hat auch was darinnen]

Fl. Donau. Pruth. Waag.] Carpathische Gebürg.] vorz. hies es Dacia, Mysia, oder Illyricum orientale.
NB Siehe ferner Grichenland u. d. Kleine Tatarey.

CHENLAND. Graecia Levante Griech. u. Mahom. Rel.
tens den Türcken.

6. LIVADIA o. Achaja.
Hellas. Attica
Livadia Lepanto
Athen (Setines
Pireo. port. Piræus
Marathon Ls.

7. Herum liegende INSULN.
1. Candia vorz. Creta.
Canea. Retimo

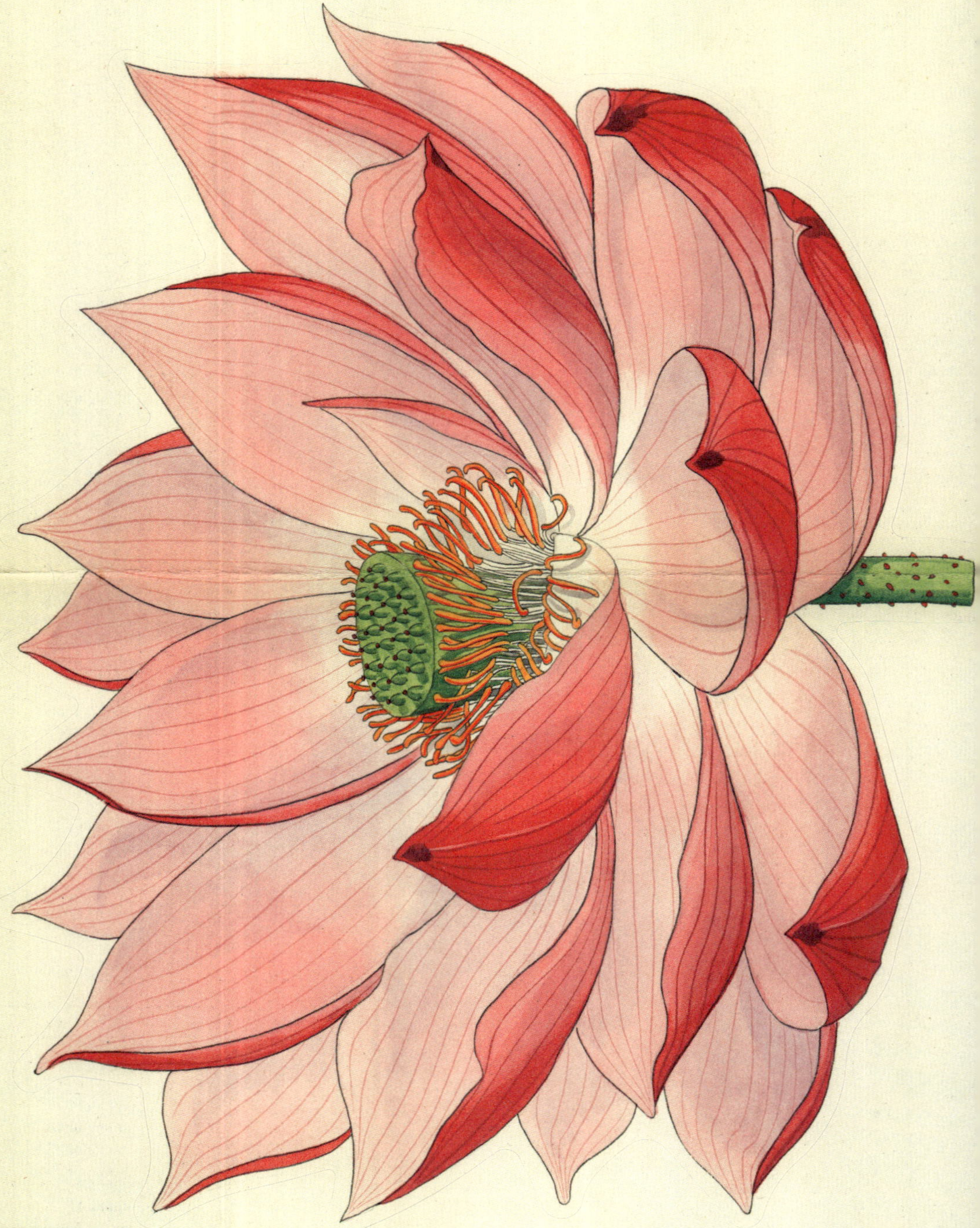

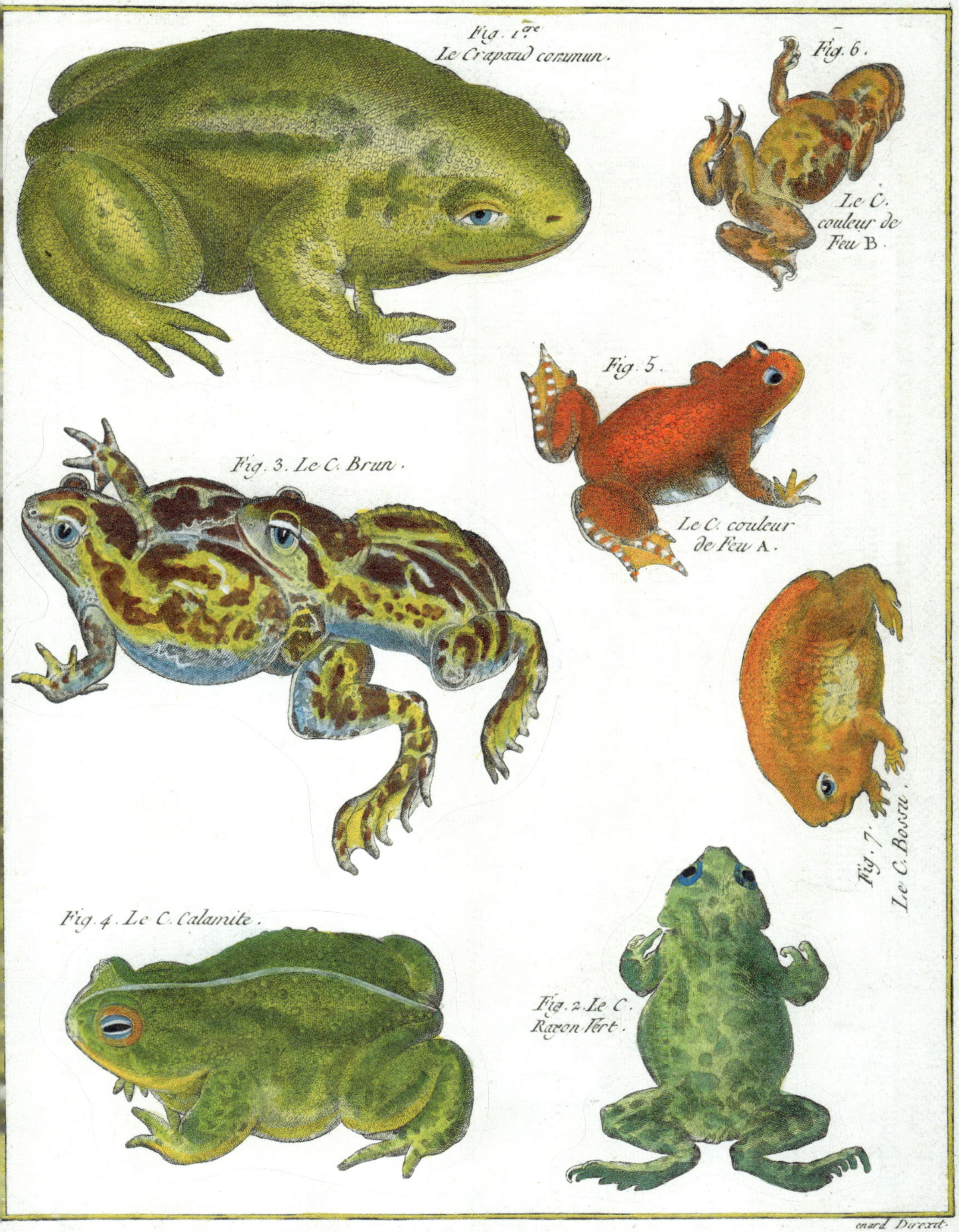

enard Direxit.

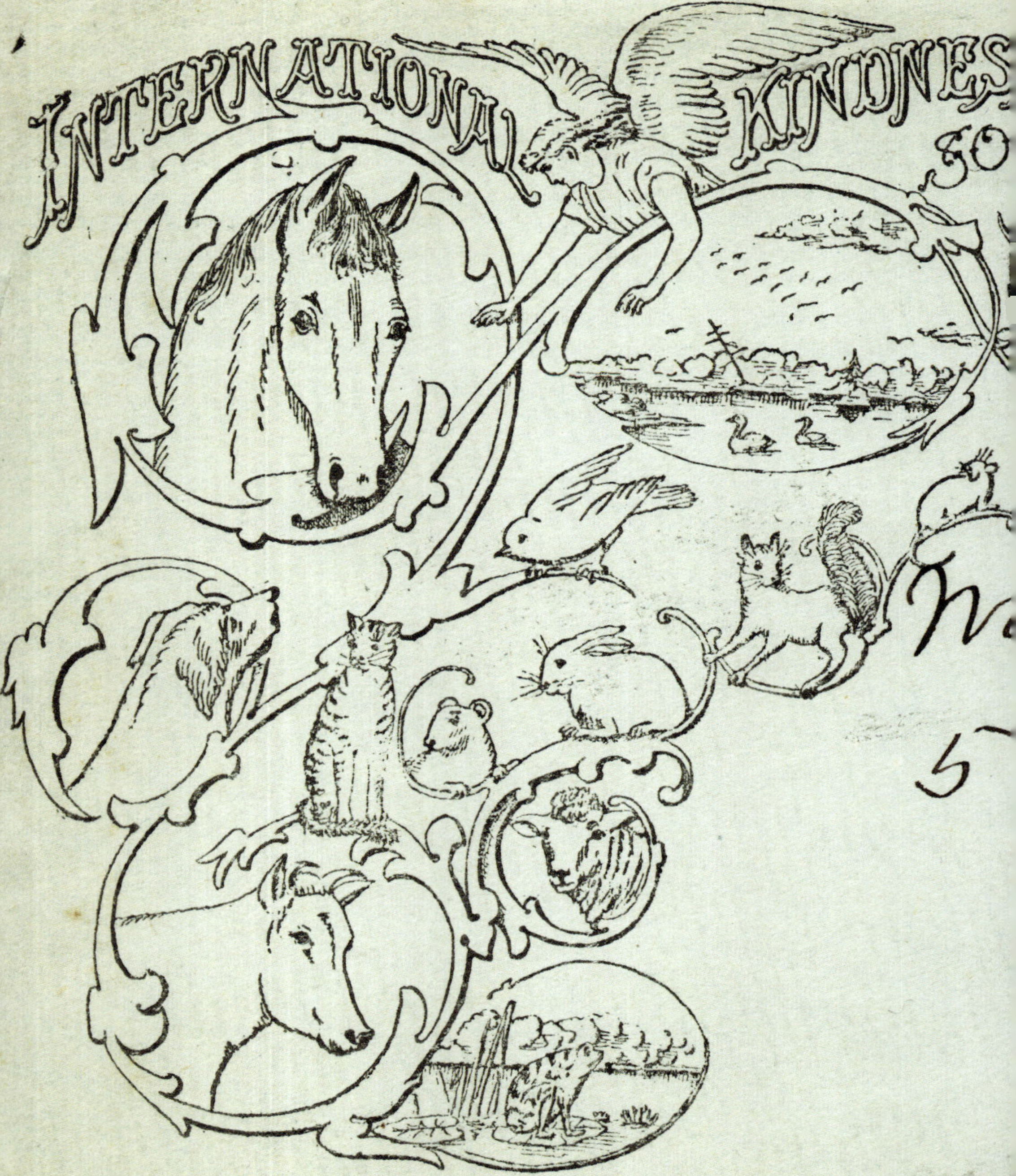

275 E. FORTY-SECOND STREET, CHICAGO, ILL.

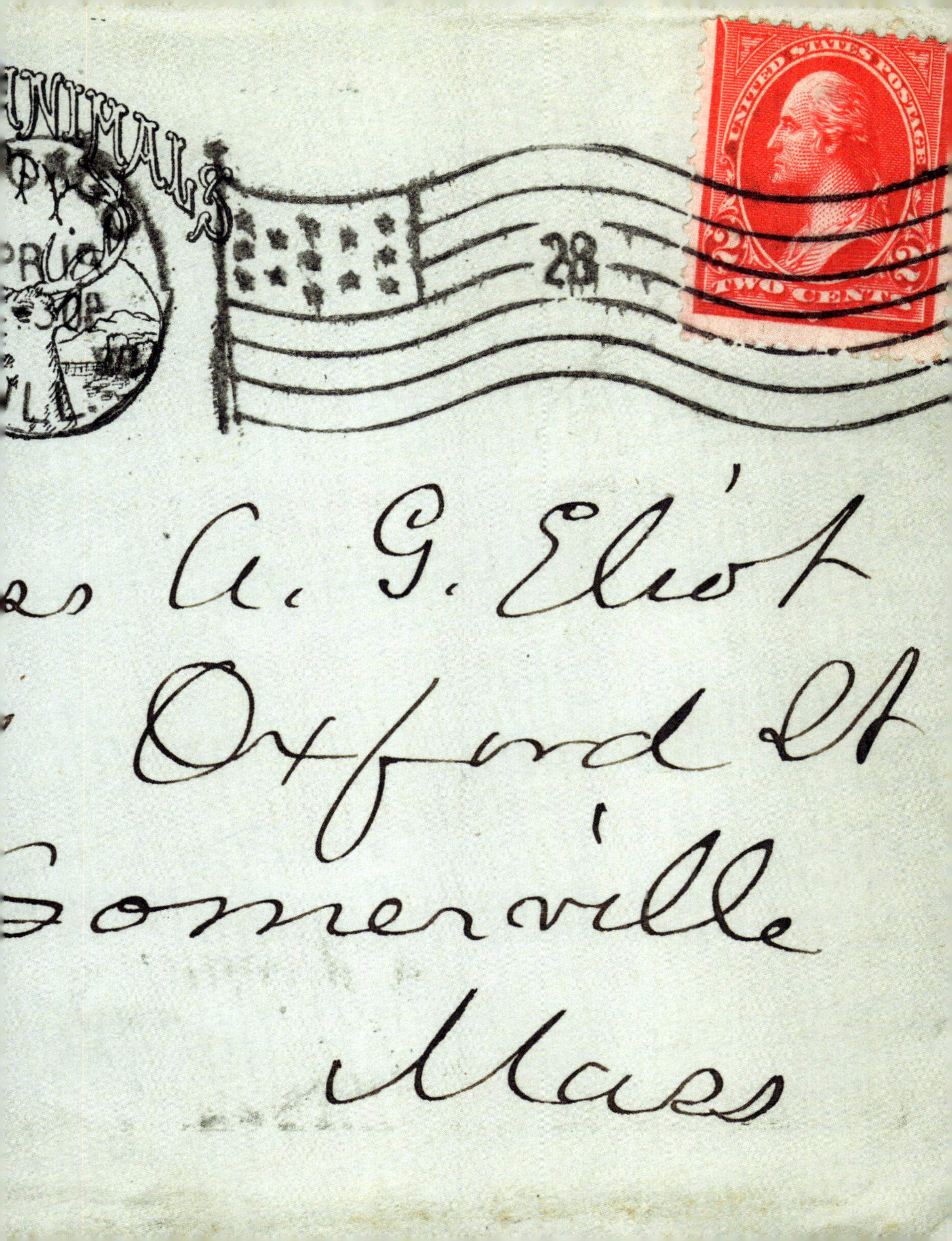
UNITED STATES POSTAGE
TWO CENTS
28
A. G. Eliot
Oxford St
Somerville
Mass

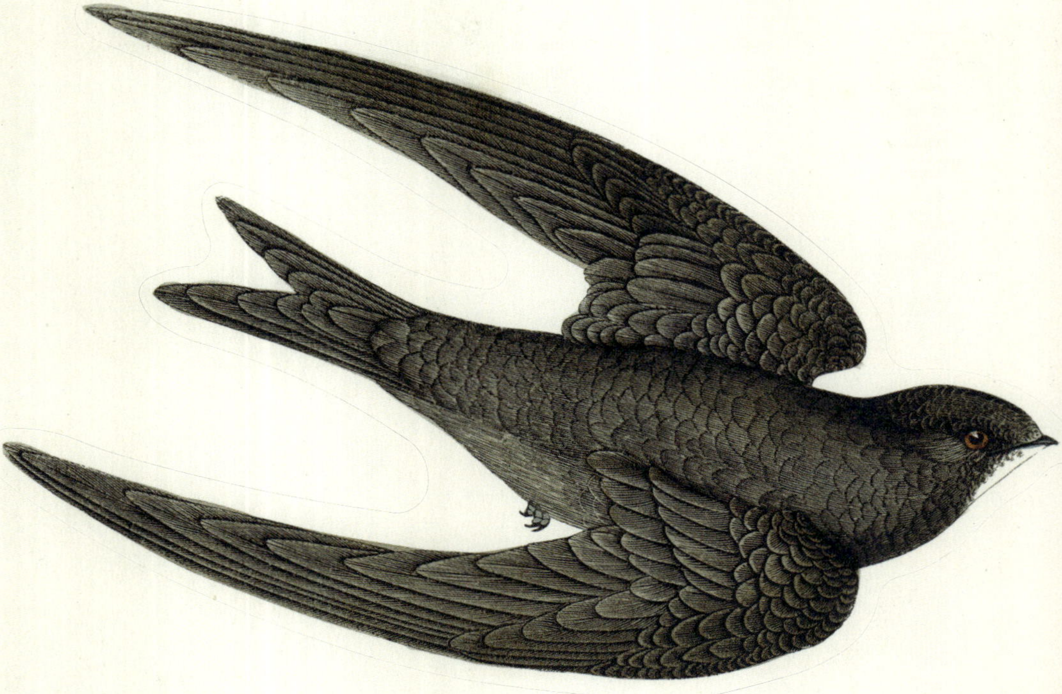

SWIFT.

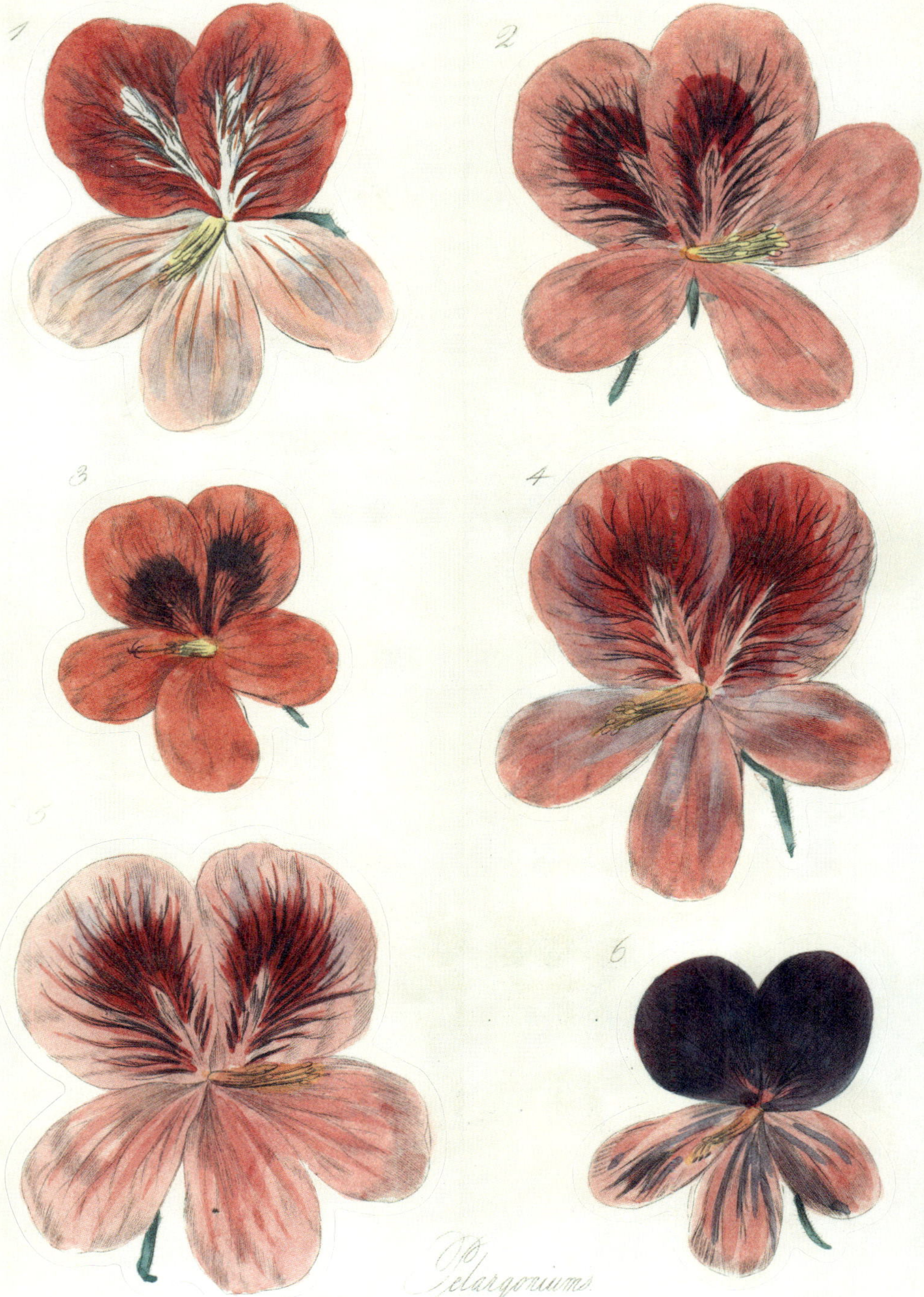

Pelargoniums.

J. & J. Parkin Sc

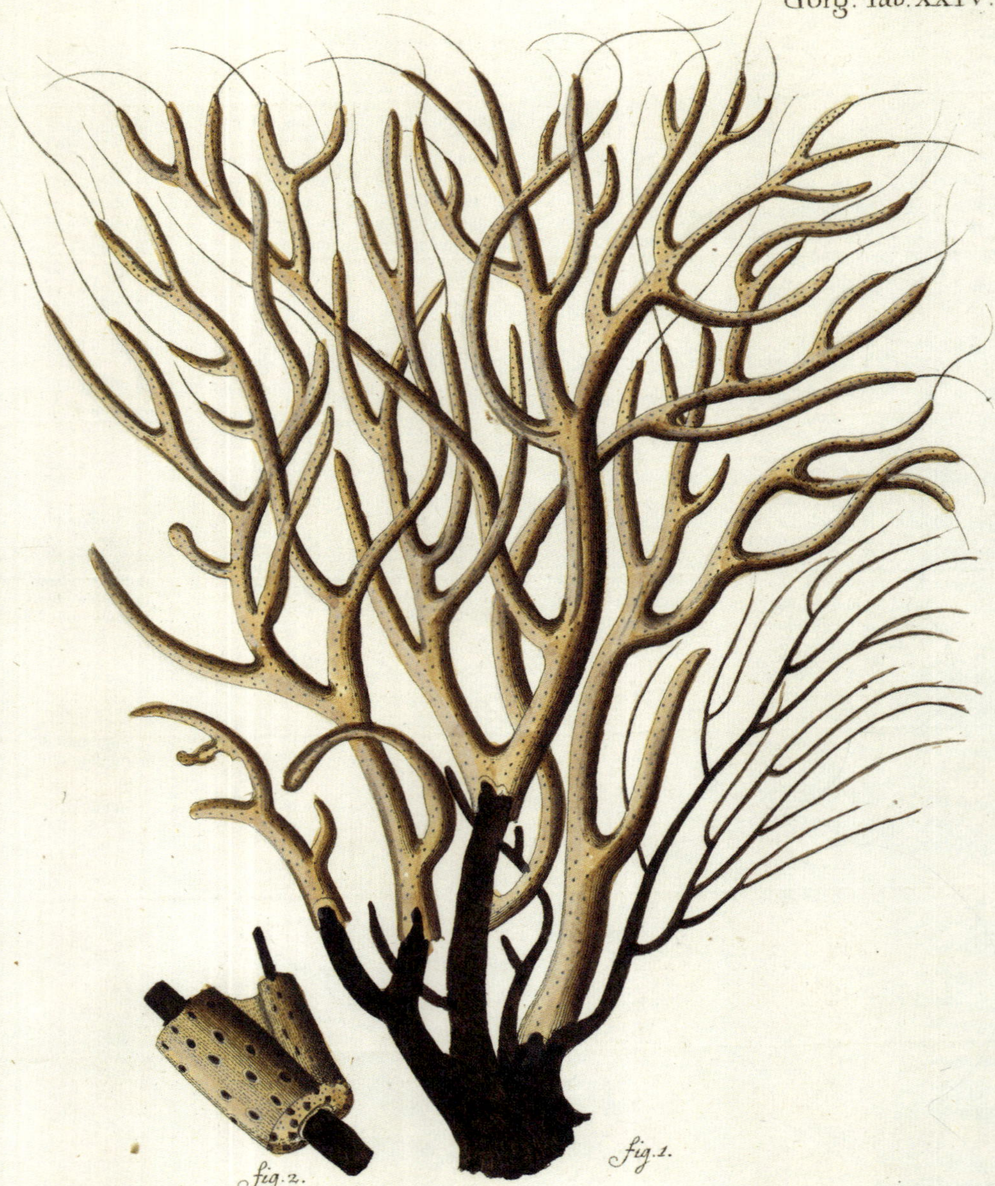

Gorgonia Antipathes.
Variet. β.

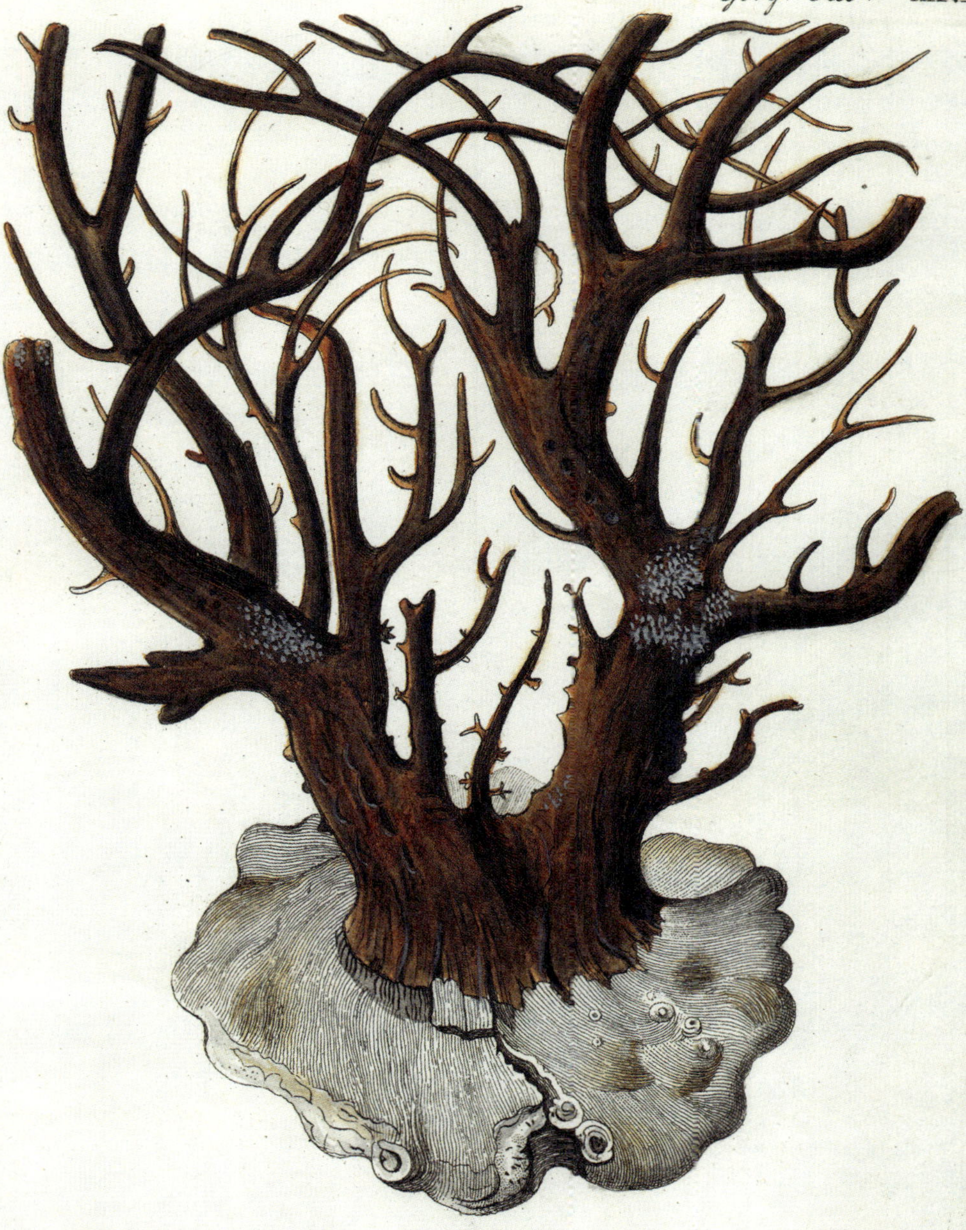

Gorgonia Antipathes.
decorticata. Var.

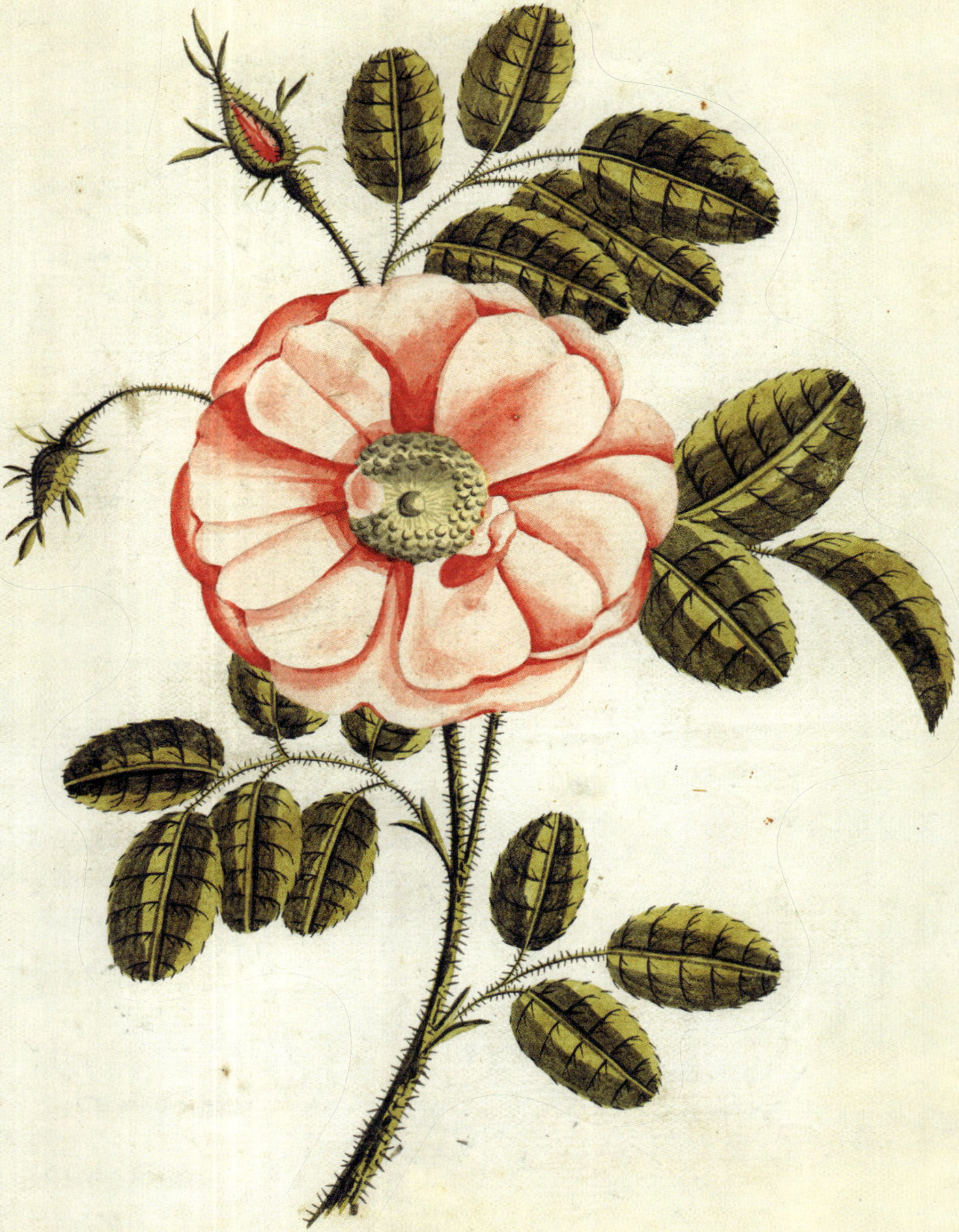

La Rosa Epanouie

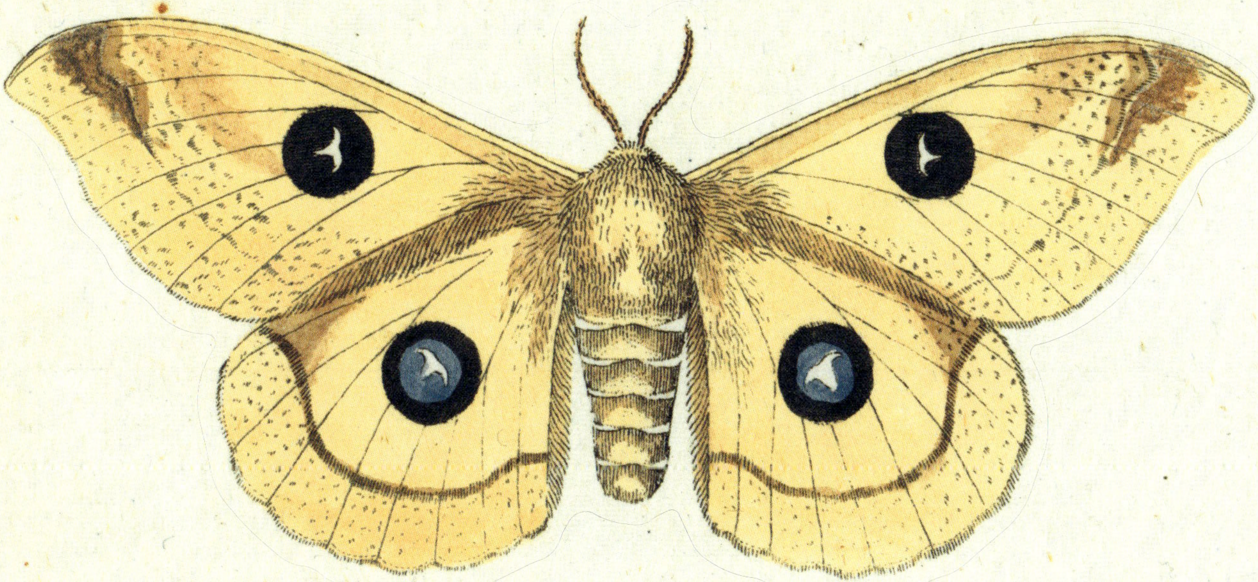

Bombyx Tau fem. Fabr.

Jac. Sturm fec.

36

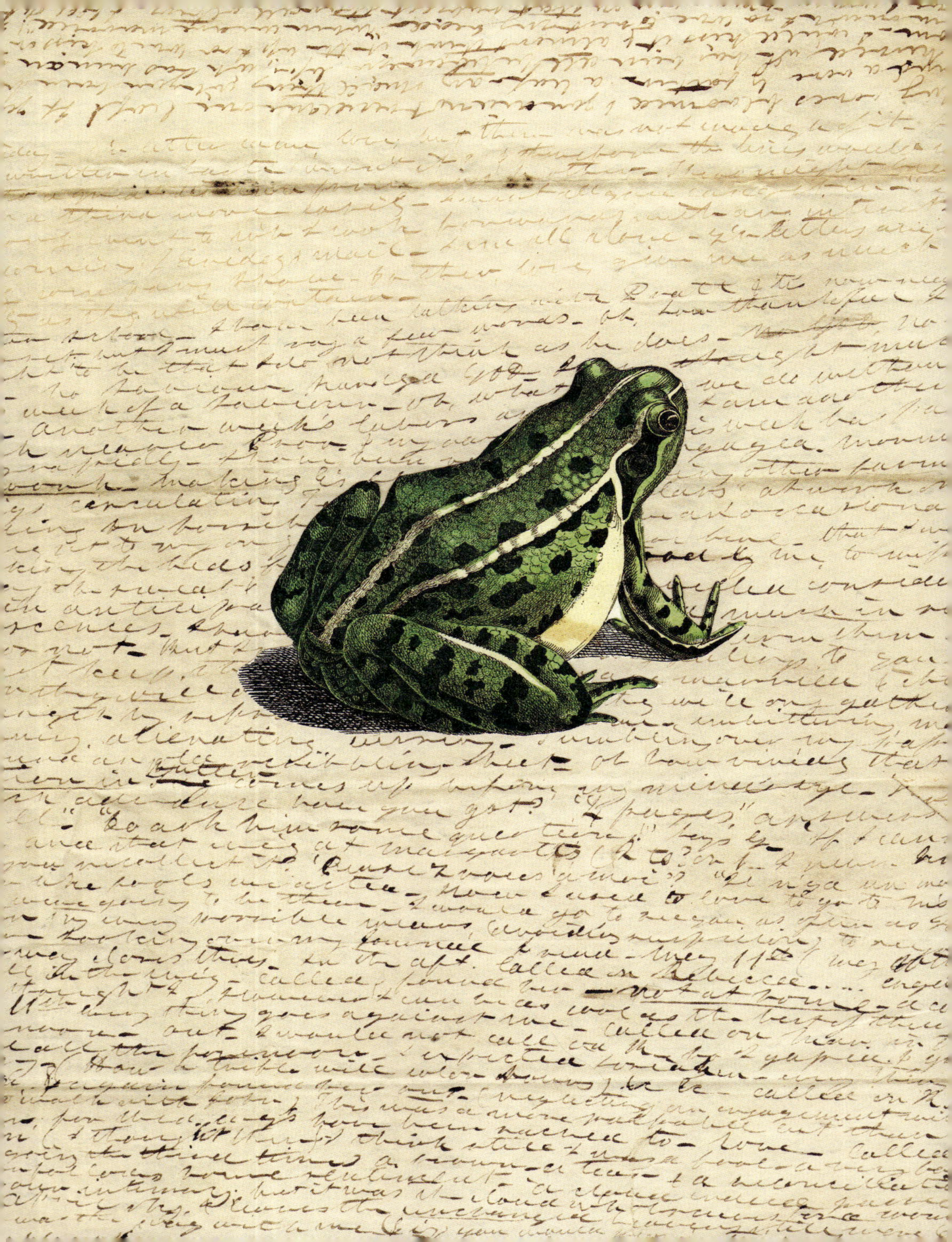

pqrſstllſtst vwxyz

pqrſstllſtst vwxyz & John

pqrſstllſtst vwxyyz & John Moorhou

pqrſstllſtst vwxyz & John Moorhouse

pqrſstllſt vwxyz & John

pqrſstllſt vwxyz & John

pqrſstllſtst vwxyz & John M

pqrſstllſtst vwxyz & John

pqrſstllſtst vwxyz & John M

pqrſstllſtst vwxyz & John Jo

pqrſstllſtst vwxyz & John Jo

John Moorhouse Booke 1732

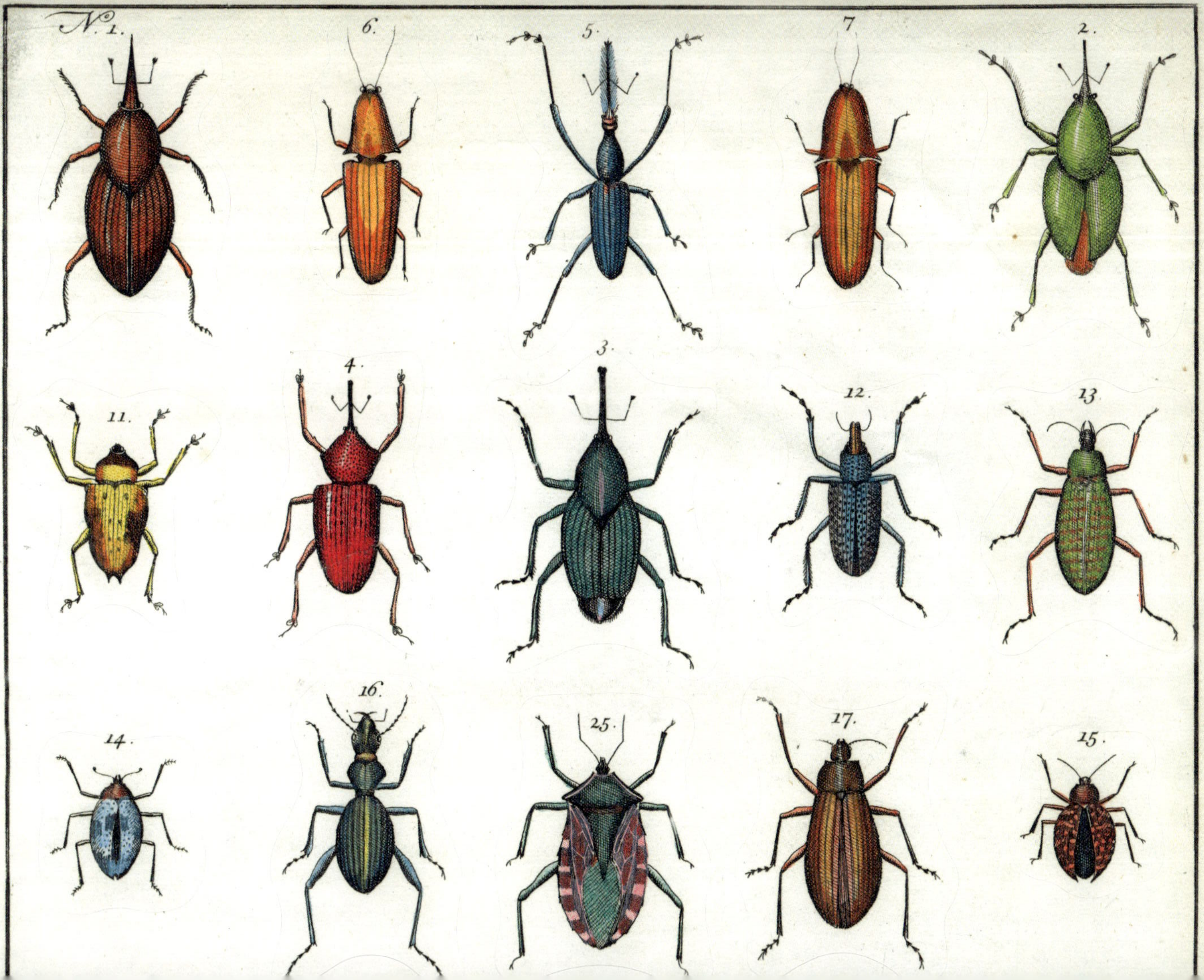

N°. 1.
6.
5.
7.
2.
3.
4.
11.
12.
13
16.
25.
17.
14.
15.

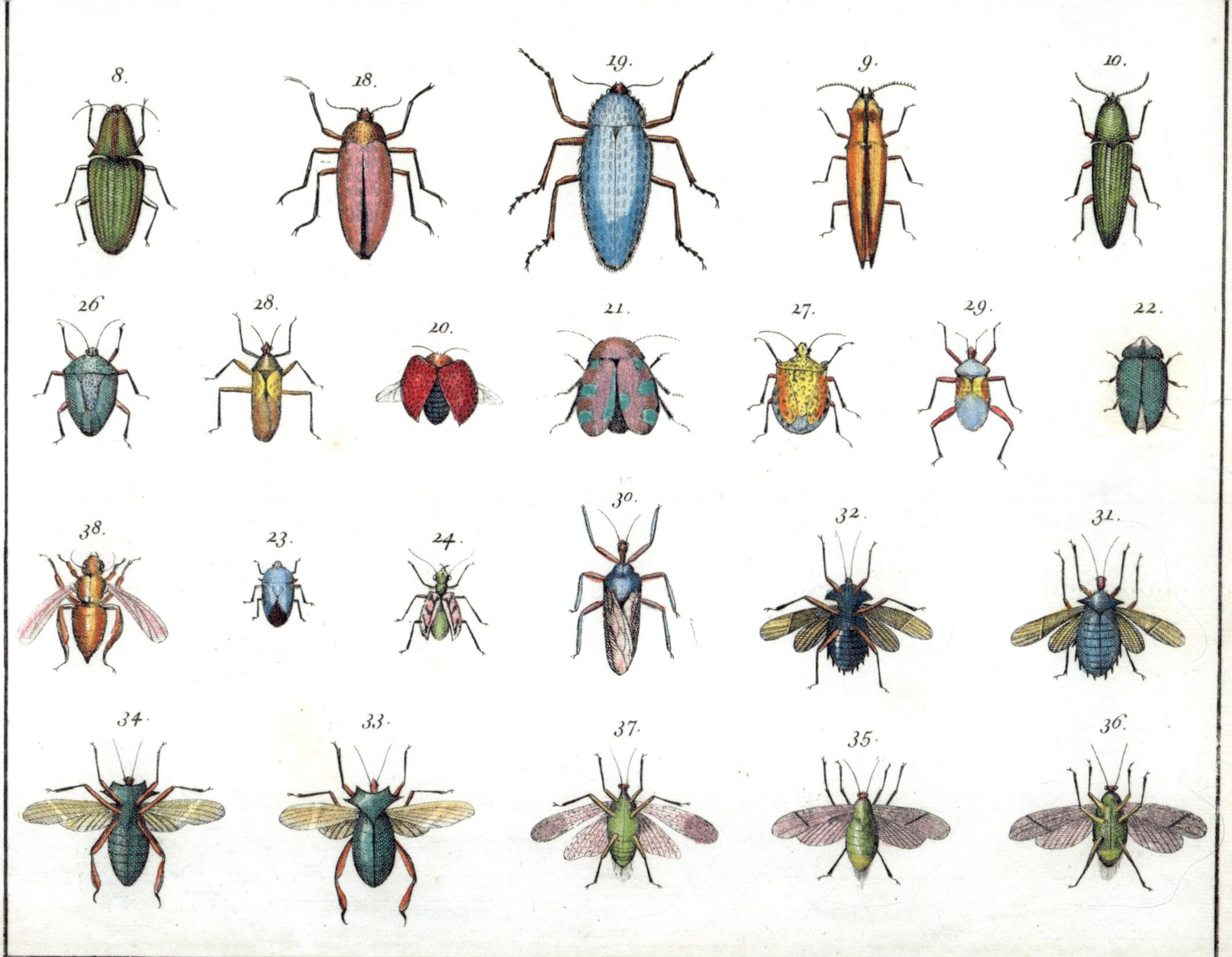
8.
18.
19.
9.
10.
26
28.
20.
21.
27.
29.
22.
38.
23.
24.
30.
32.
31.
34.
33.
37.
35.
36.

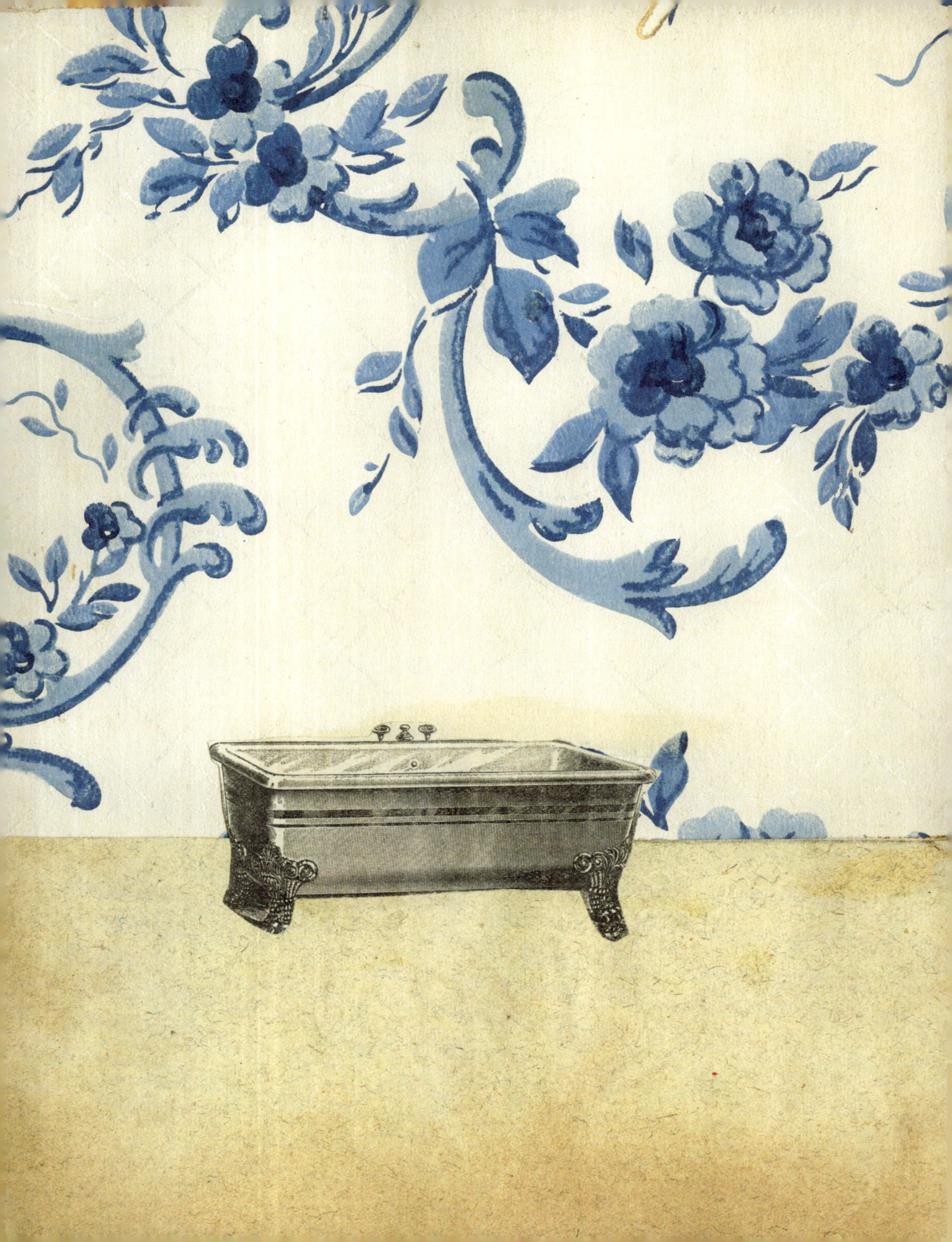

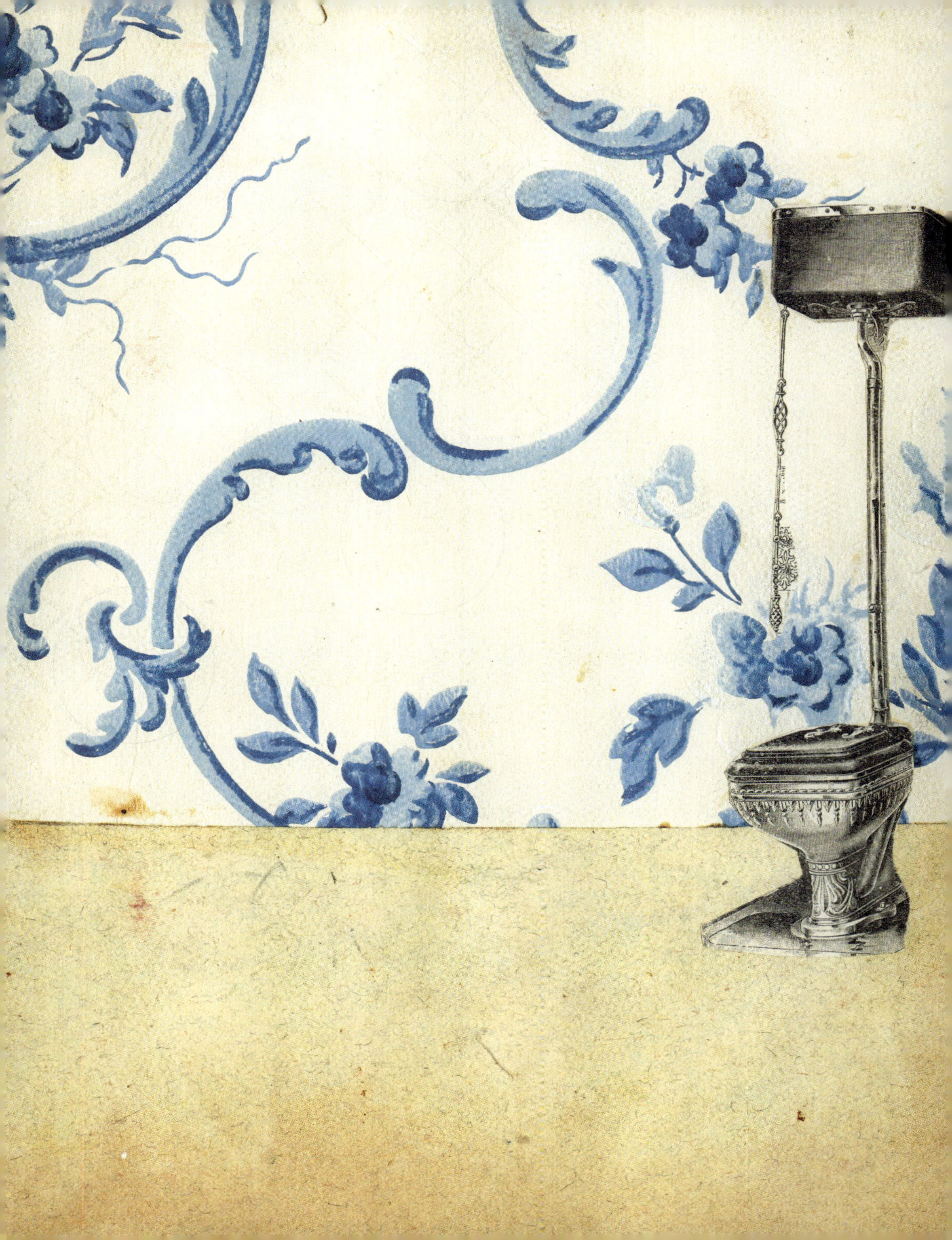

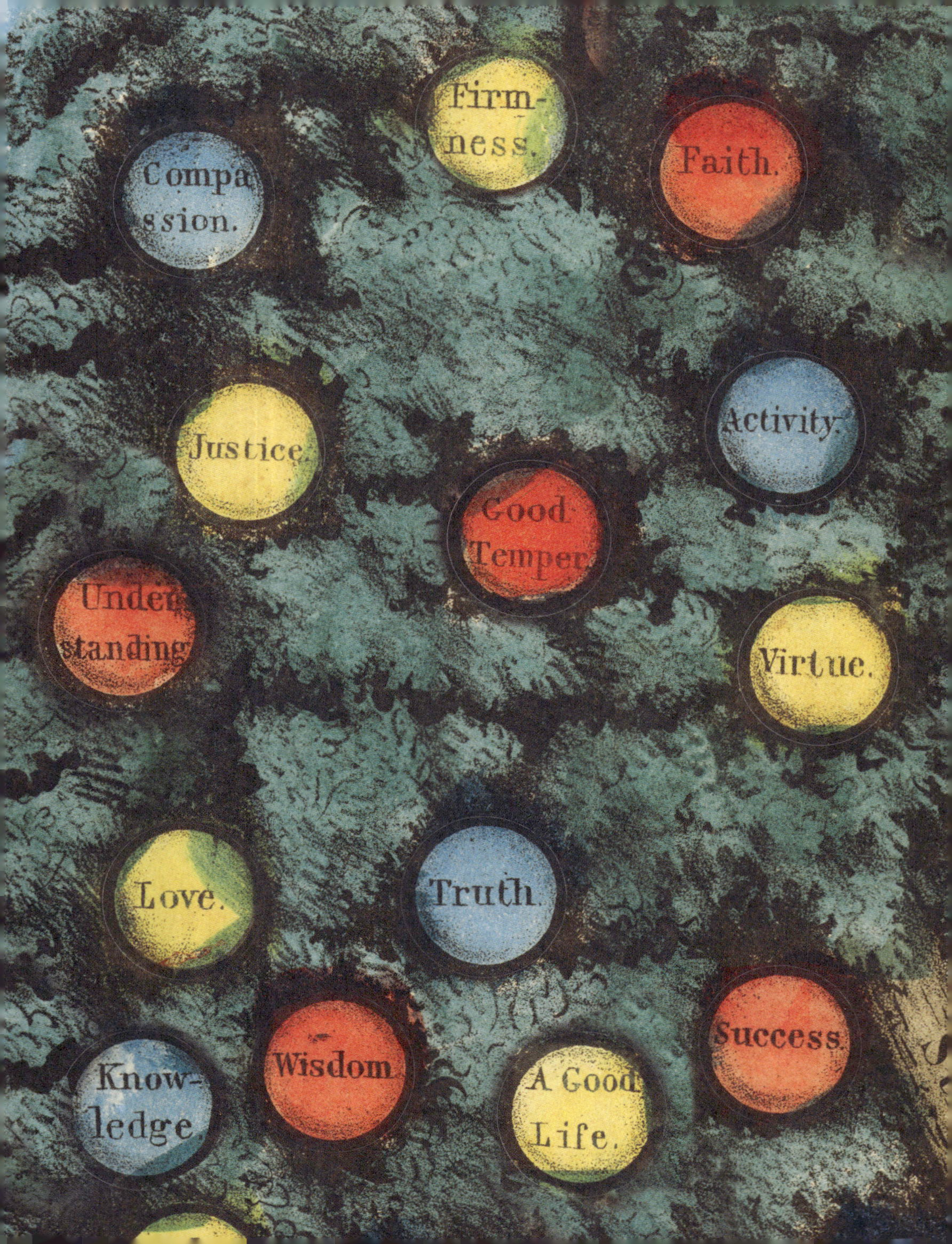
Firm-
ness.
Faith.
Compa
ssion.
Activity.
Justice.
Good
Temper.
Under
standing
Virtue.
Love.
Truth.
Success.
Wisdom.
Know-
ledge.
A Good
Life.

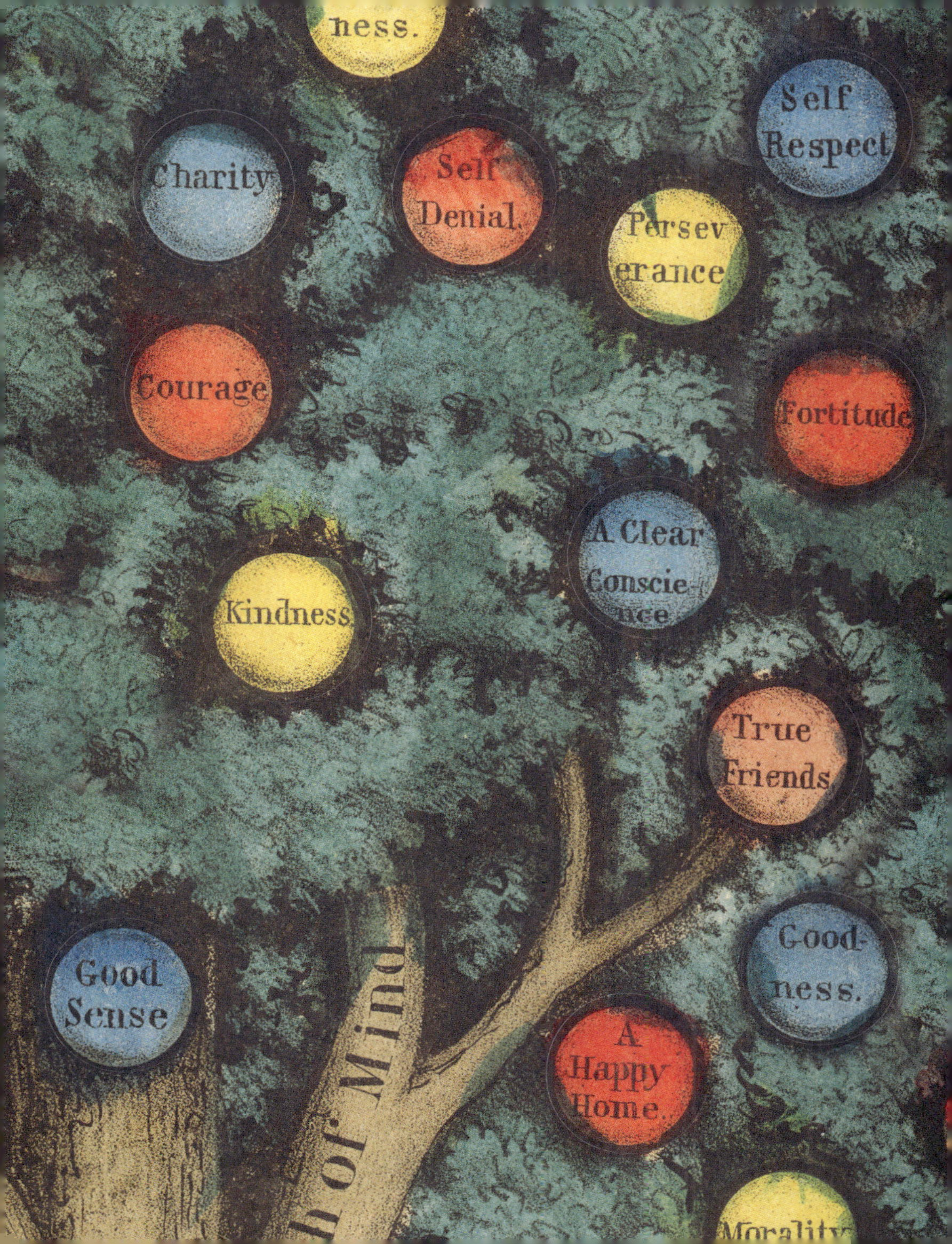
ness.
Charity
Self Denial.
Self Respect
Persev erance
Courage
Fortitude
A Clear Conscie- nce
Kindness
True Friends
Good Sense
h of Mind
Good- ness.
A Happy Home.
Morality

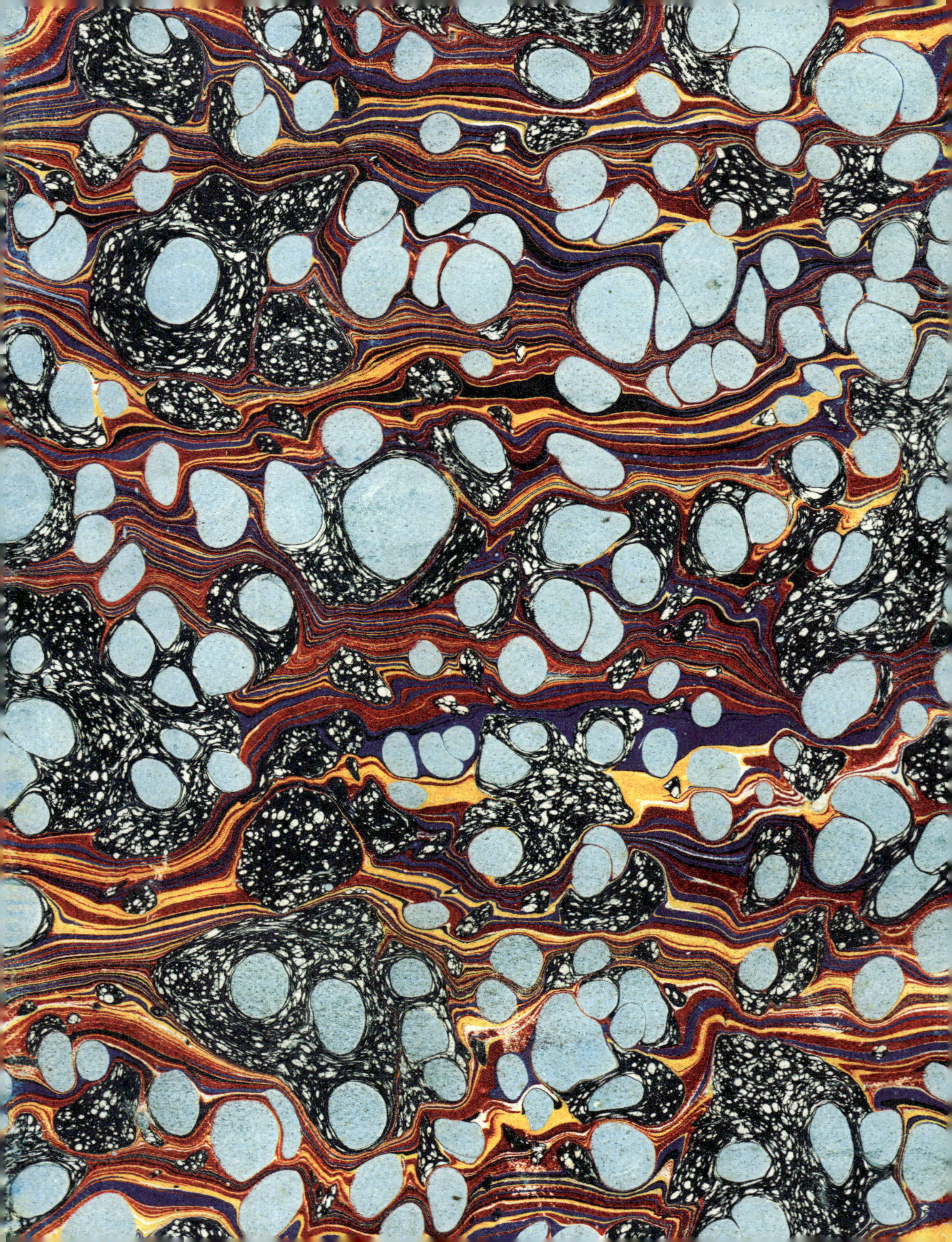

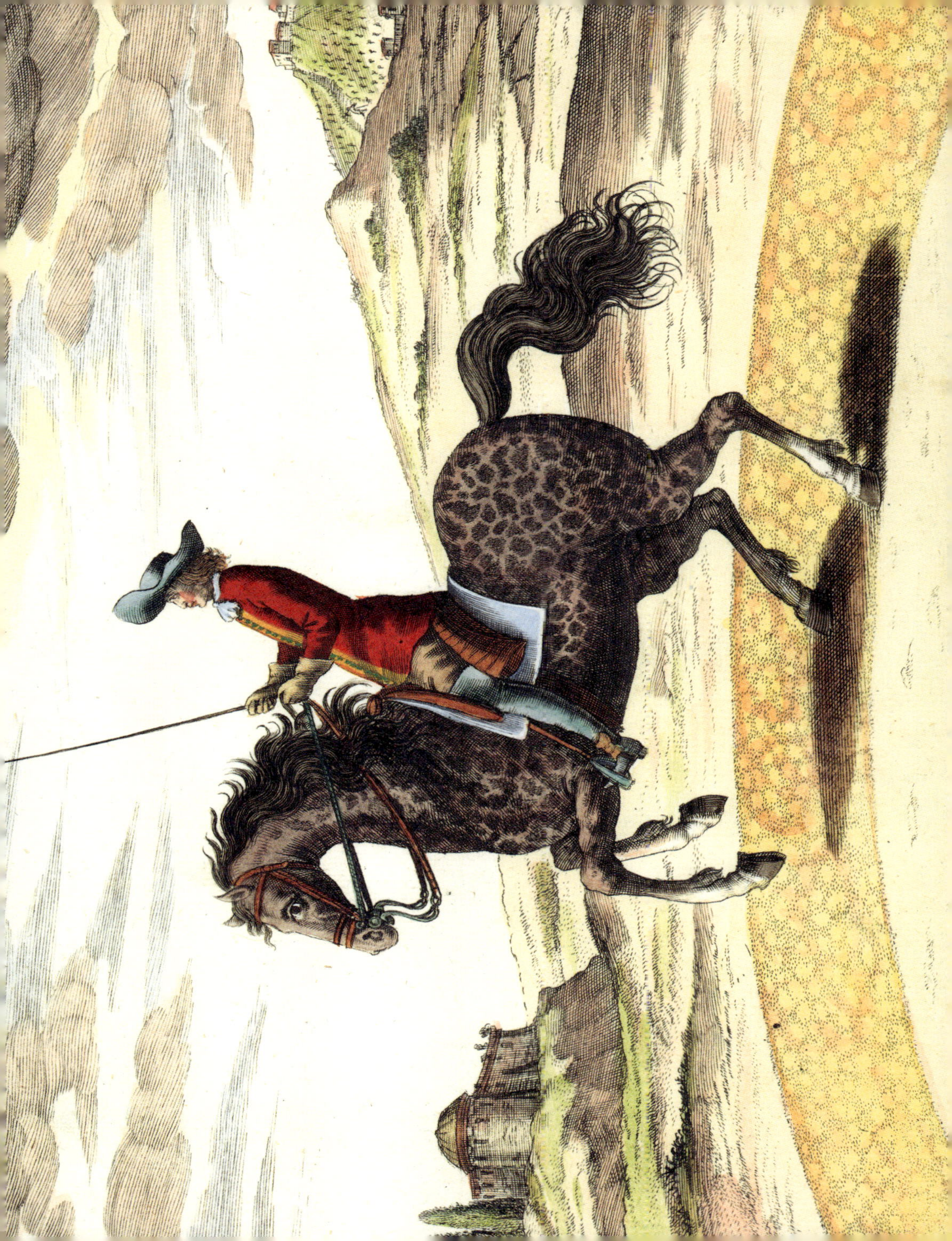

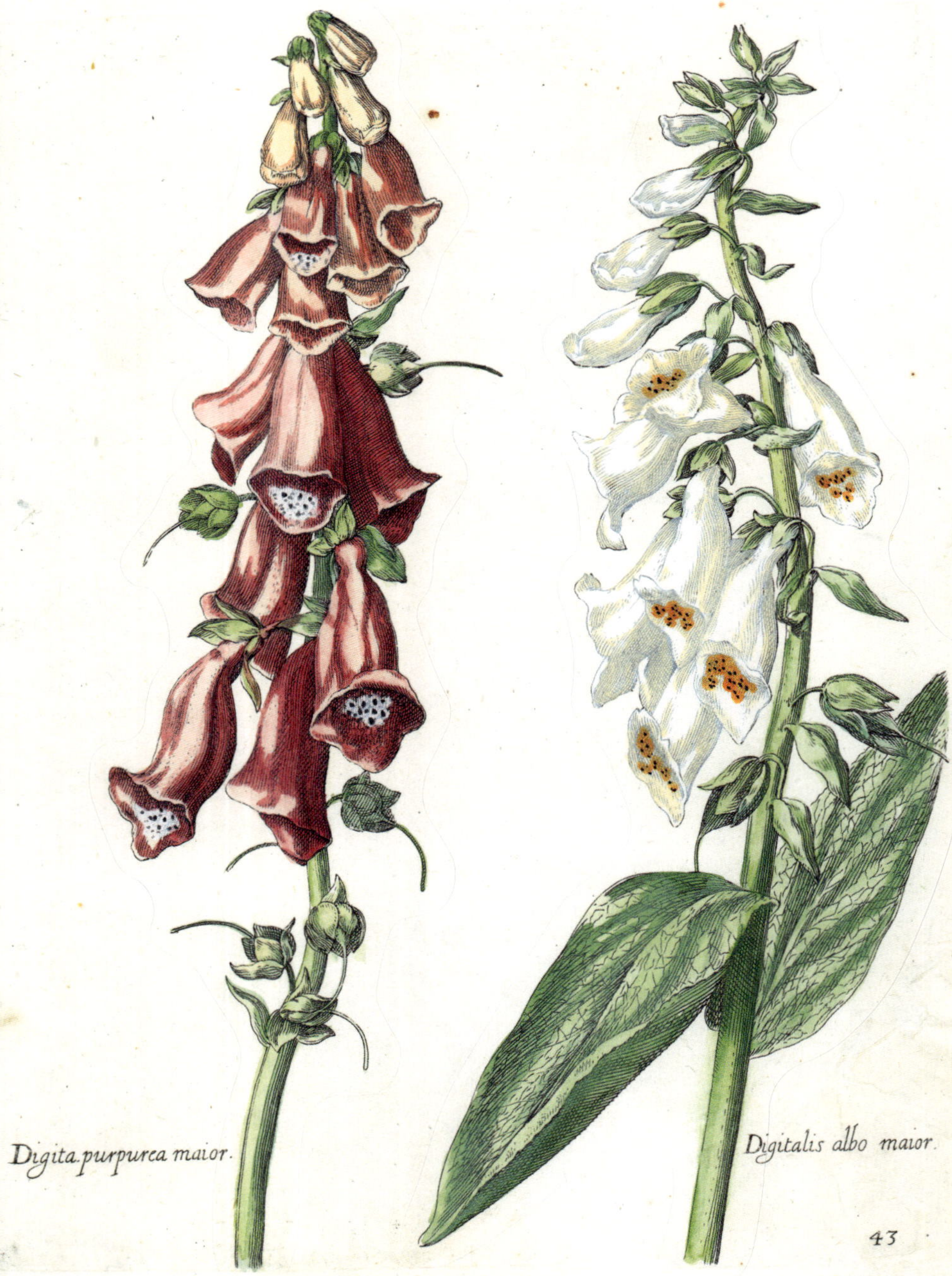
Digita.purpurea maior.
Digitalis albo maior.

CANIS. Plate I.

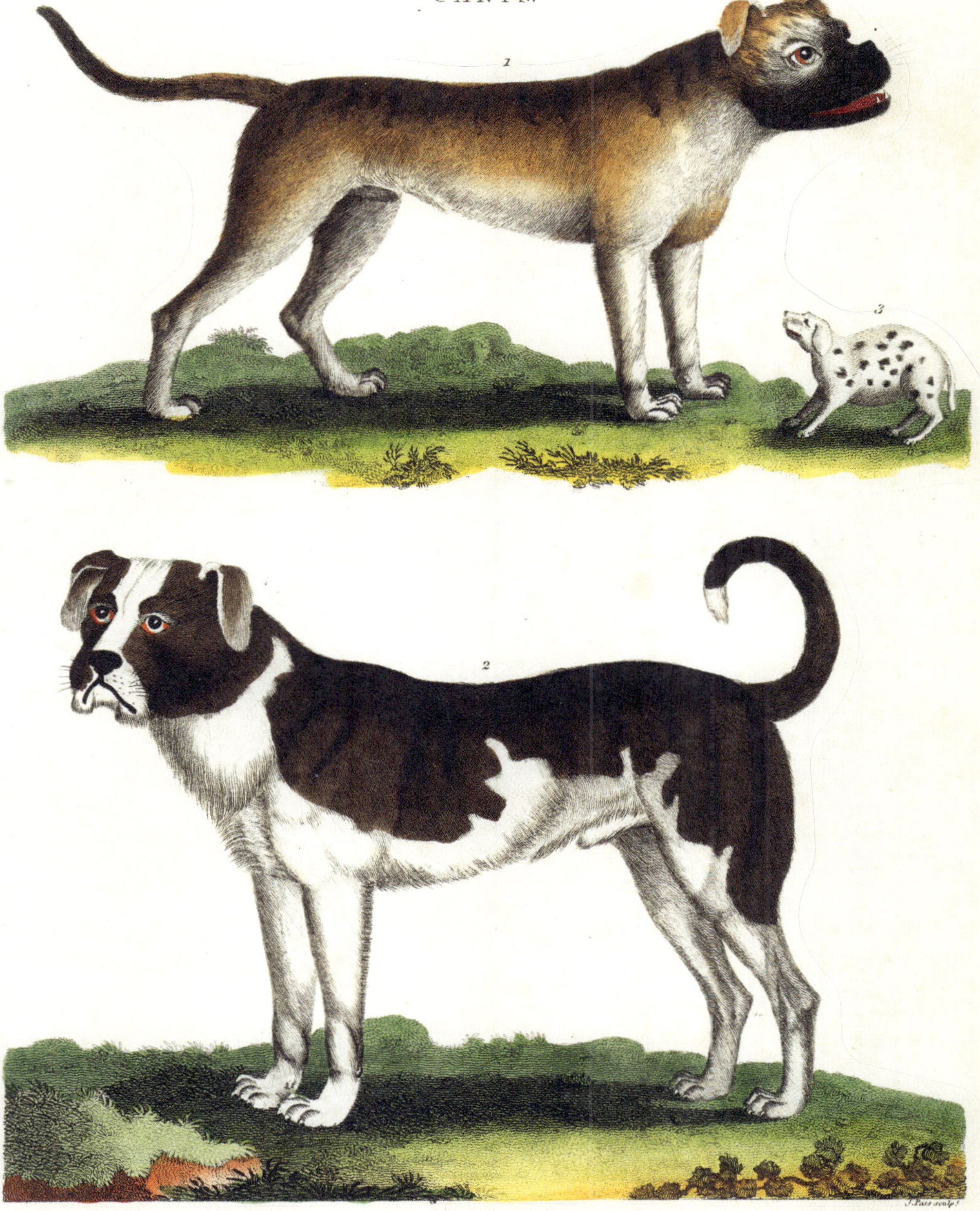

1 – The British Bull-dog. – 2. The Old English Mastiff. – 3. The Alco, or American Dog.

London. Published as the Act directs. April 8. 1800 by J. Wilkes.

Alecia Read

Anne Parsners

Boardingschool 1817

Alecia — Reed's

Book Pleasant Vally

February 2. 1817

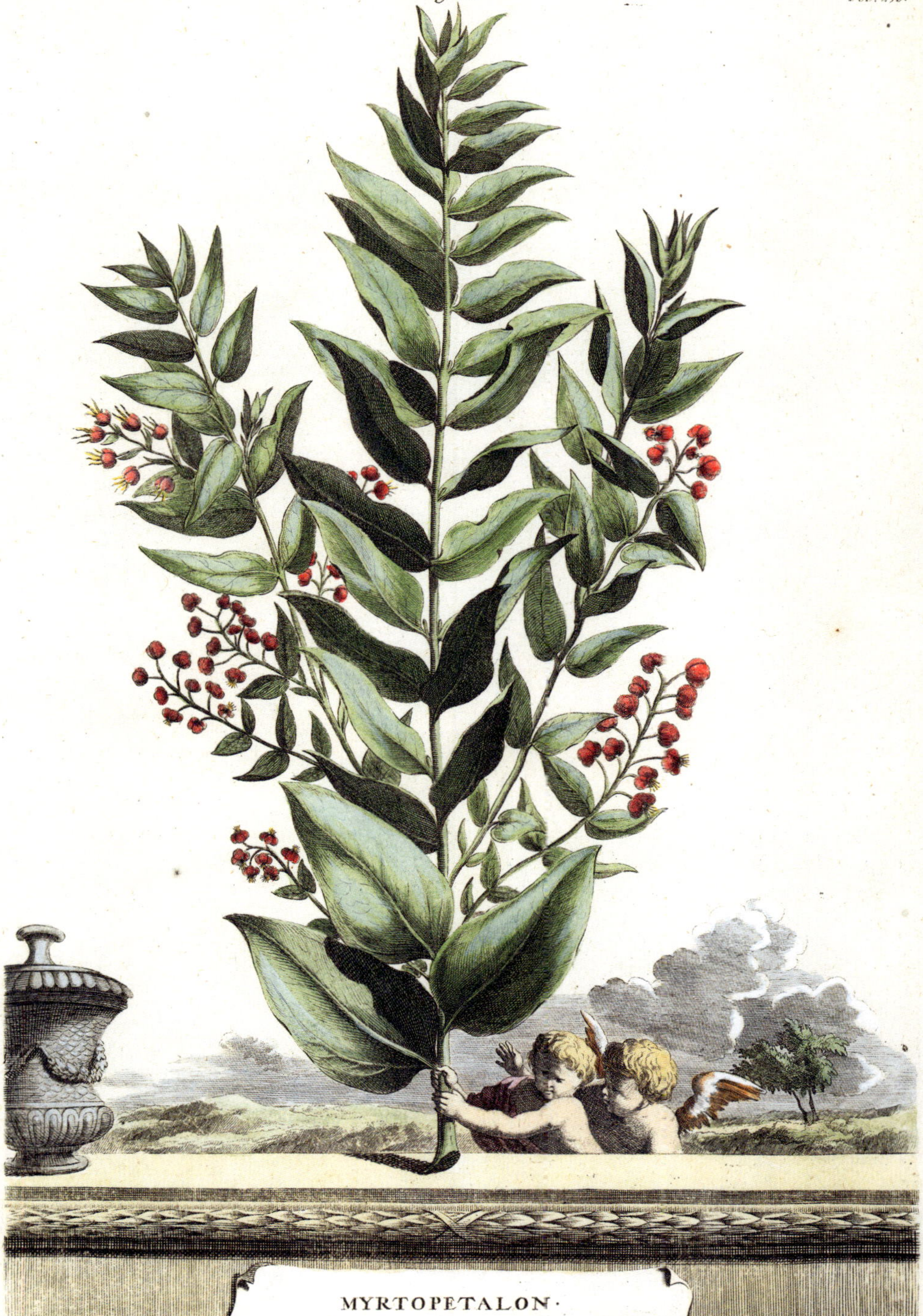
MYRTOPETALON·

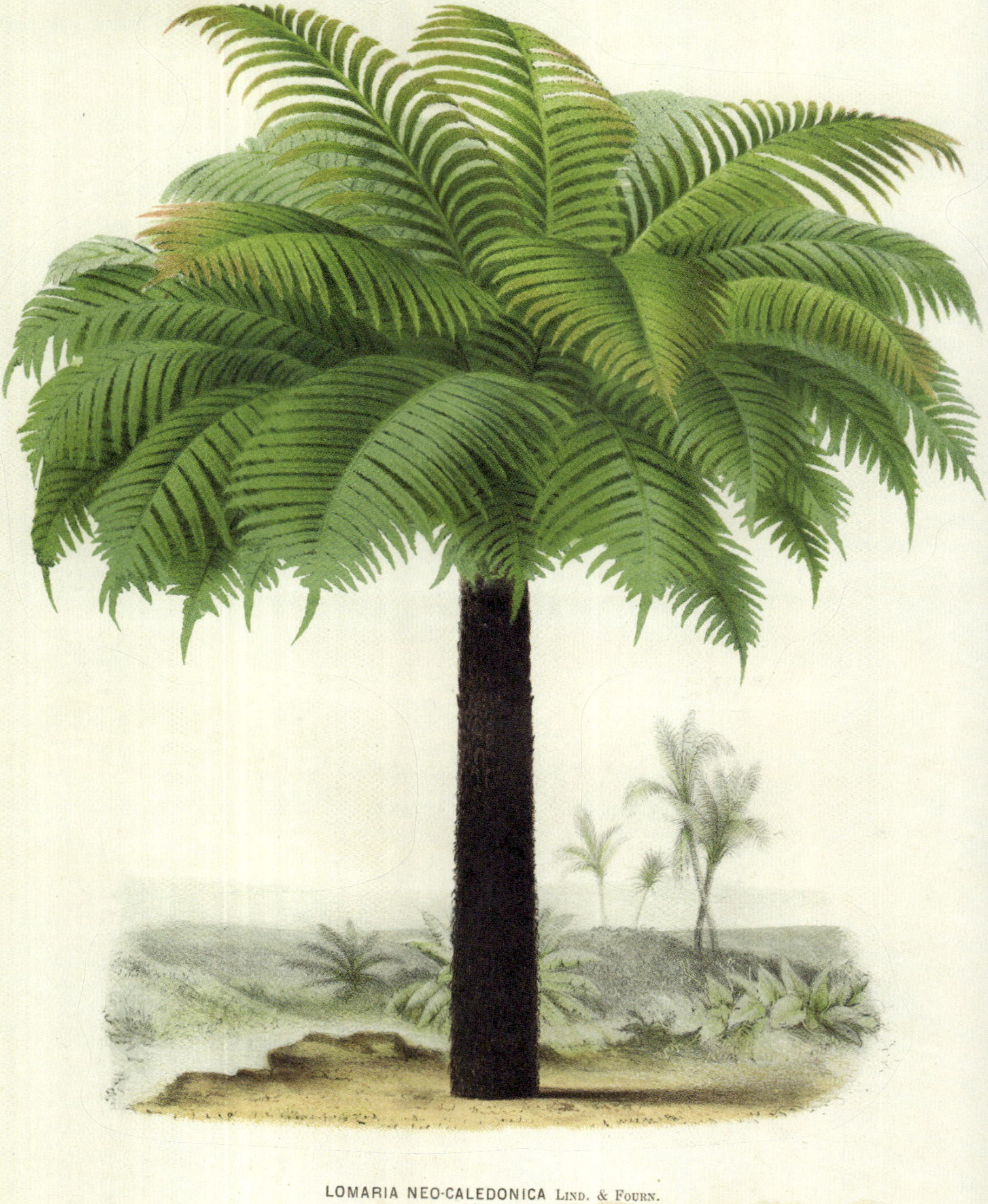

LOMARIA NEO-CALEDONICA Lind. & Fourn.

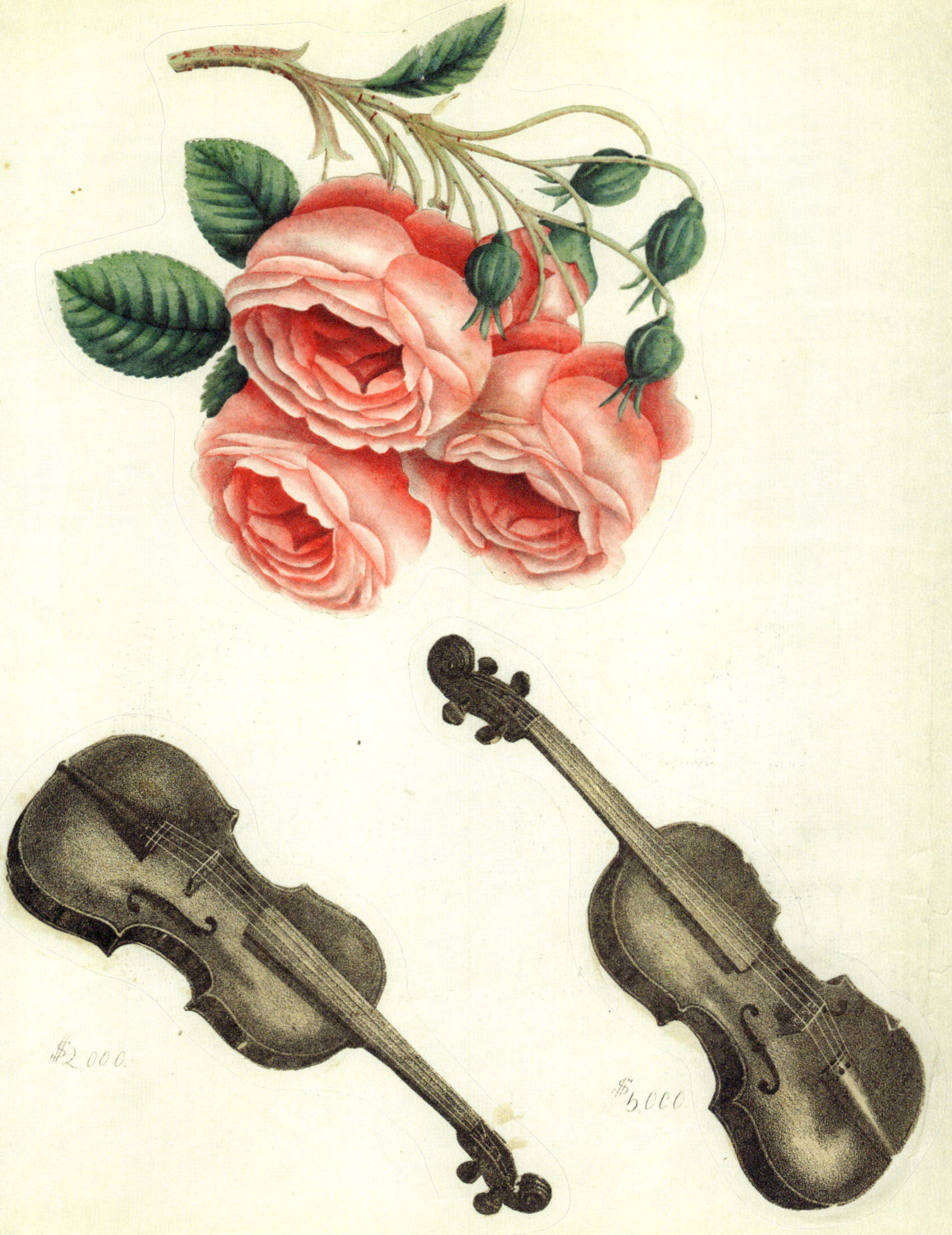
$2,000.
$5,000.

THE
SUMMER HOUSE,
AND
Other Stories.

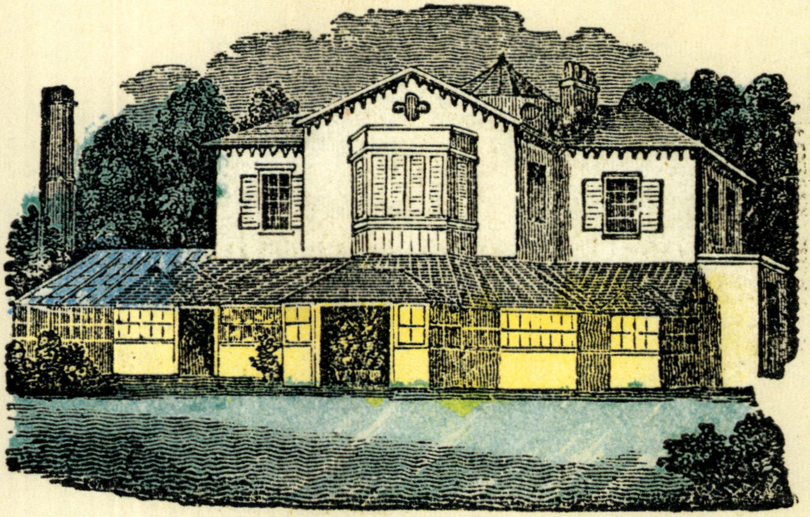

NEW YORK:
LEAVITT & ALLEN.

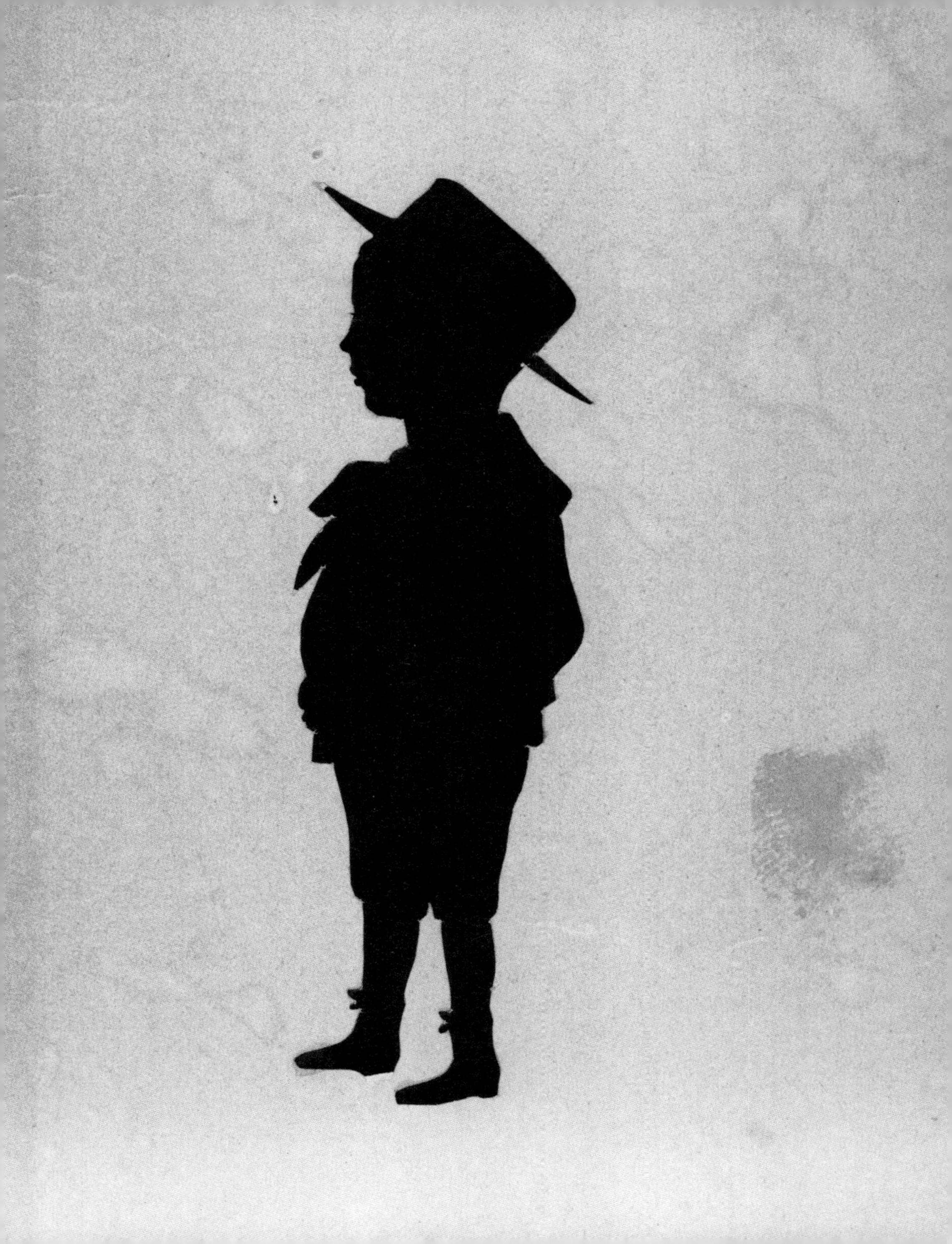

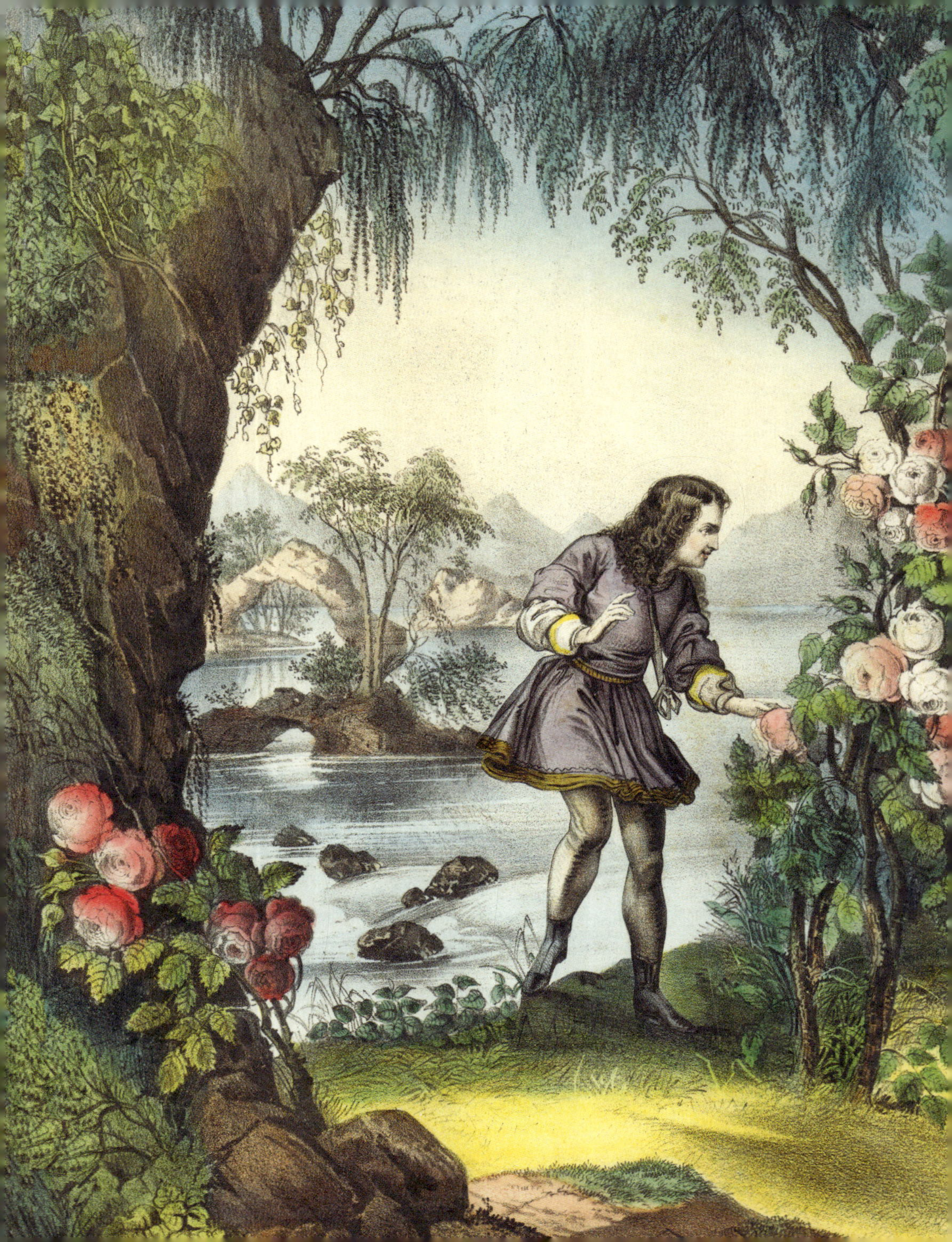

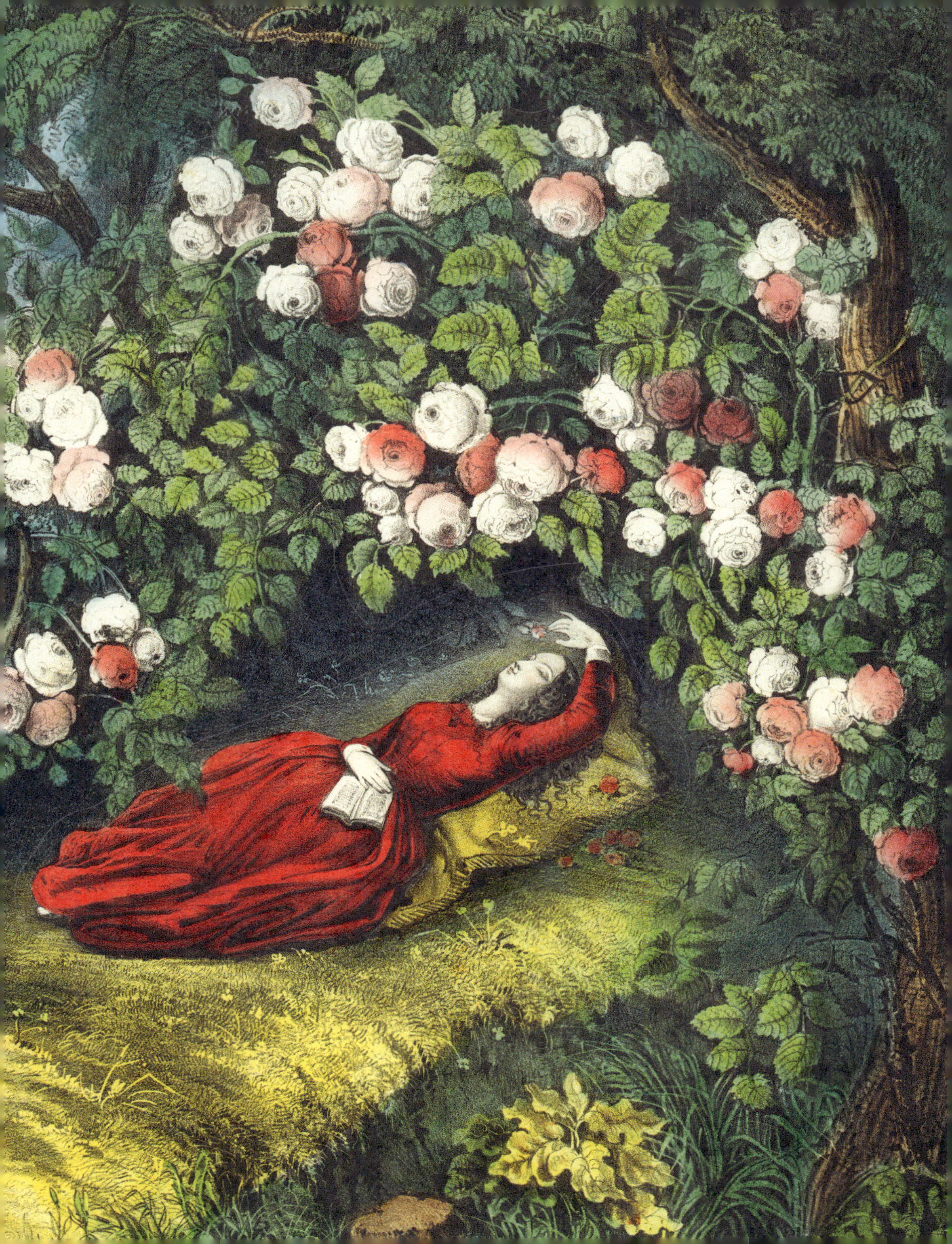

The Central Park

The Central park is a large tract of land in the Central part of the island of manhatten which has been laid out in to roads paths grass plots ponds drives rides and also contains the Croton Reservoirs. on the right side of the enterance on fifth avenue there is a path leading to a building that formerly used to be the arsenal and is now used as a menagerie and is full of animals there are Grisly bears Black bears leopards Panthers wild cats ocelots opposums munkeys wolfs boffaloes Prarie dogs eagles owls Parrots Rabbits Guinepigs hawks and Mocking Birds there are stuffed animals and a great many other kinds of animals. there are a great many swans and fish in the ponds. a great many people go there to ride and walk every called Mount St vincent or house of refreshment where people can stop and get refreshments when ever they want to. there is a Deer Park with several differant kinds of Deer in it. there are a great many Sheep let out every Summer to graze. and also a great many Rabbits. there are numerous Statutes in bronze there is the statute of Humbolt of Commerce of the tigress. there is a boys play house. there is a building behind mount st vincent that is used for keeping statuary and Paintings in. every saturday they on the lawn there is a very pretty drinking fountain for horses. but now as I cannot think of anything else to say I will end my Compisition

Arthur P Wadsworth

284 words

October 1st 1869

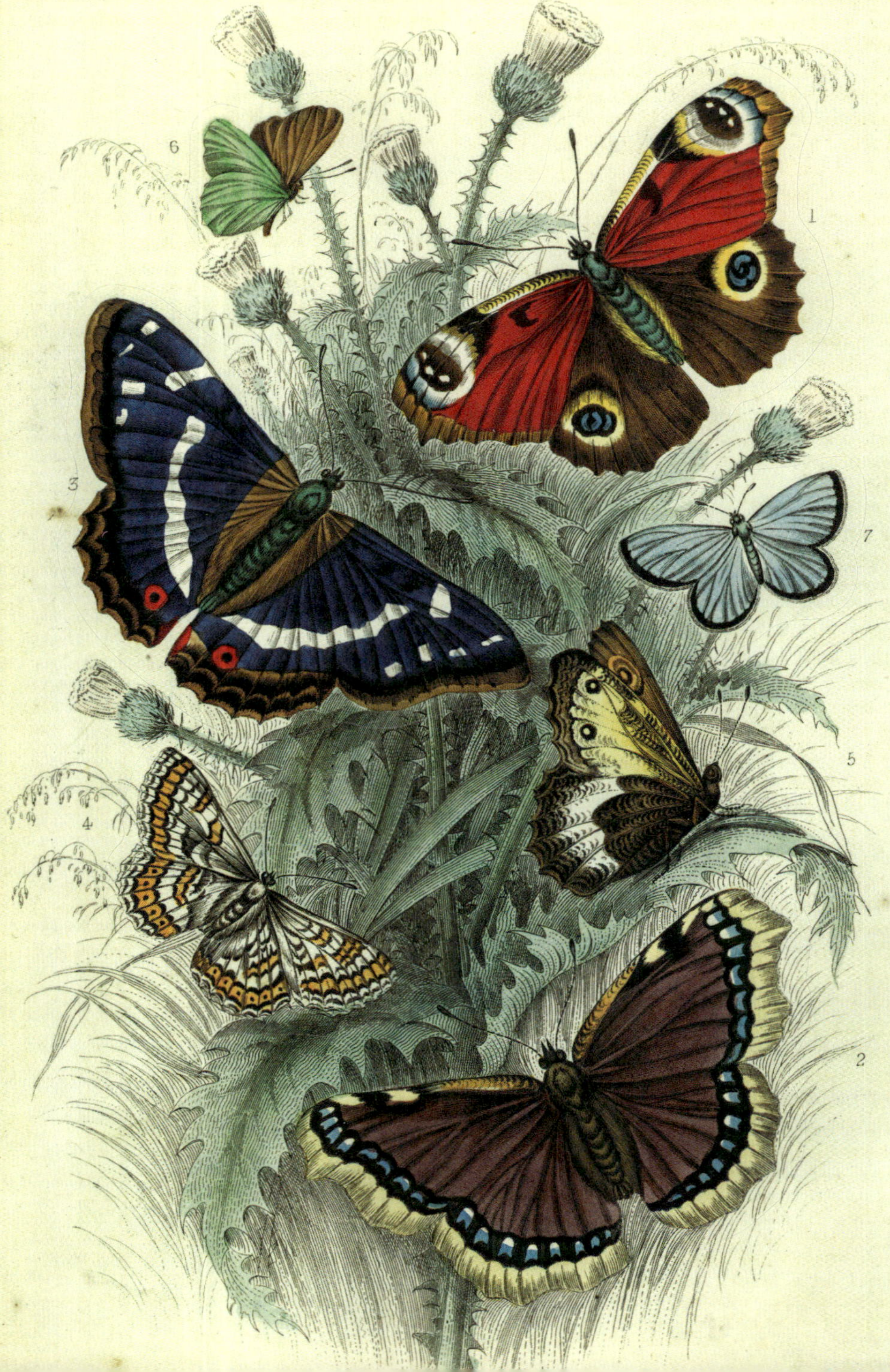
6
1
3
7
5
4
2

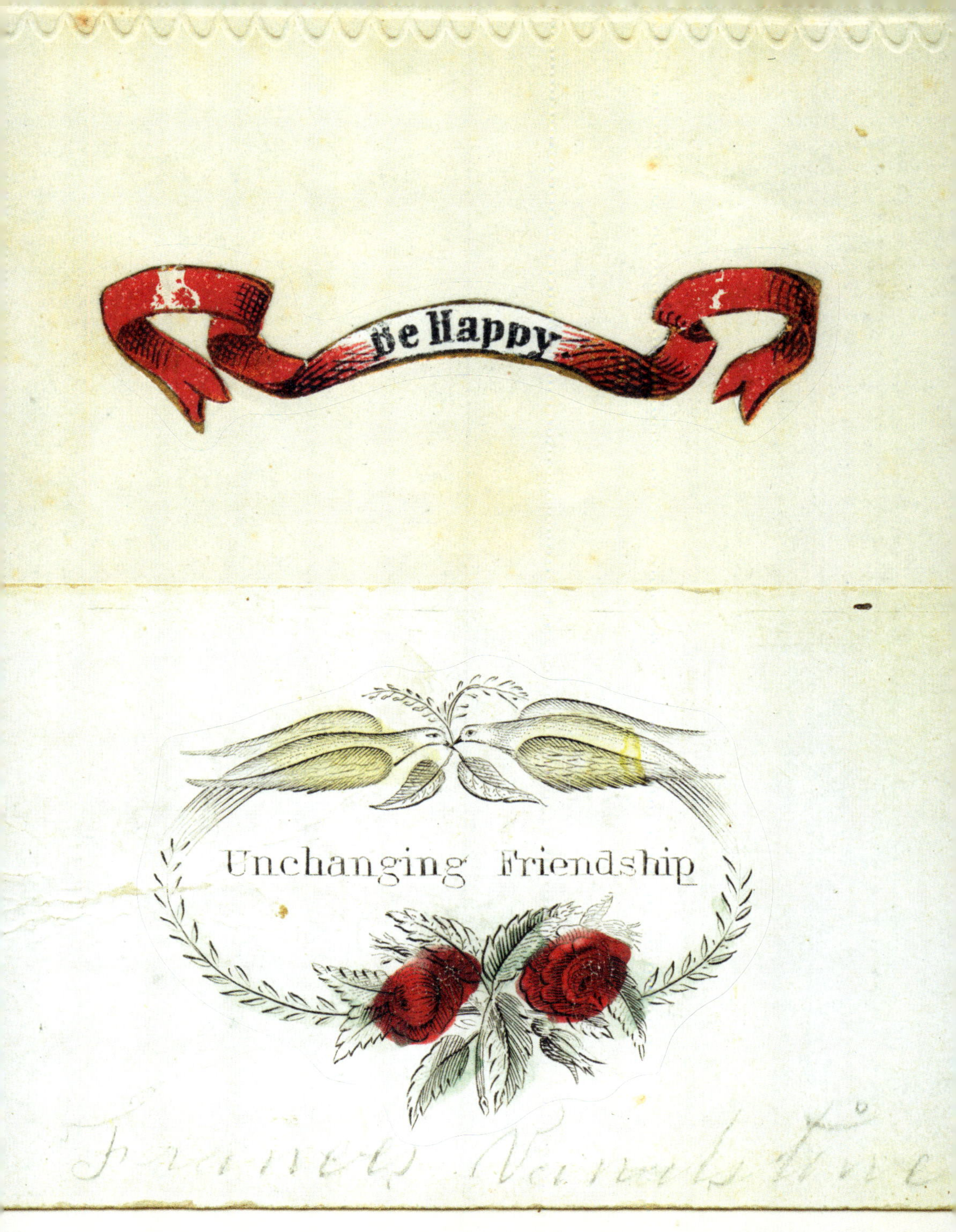
Be Happy
Unchanging Friendship

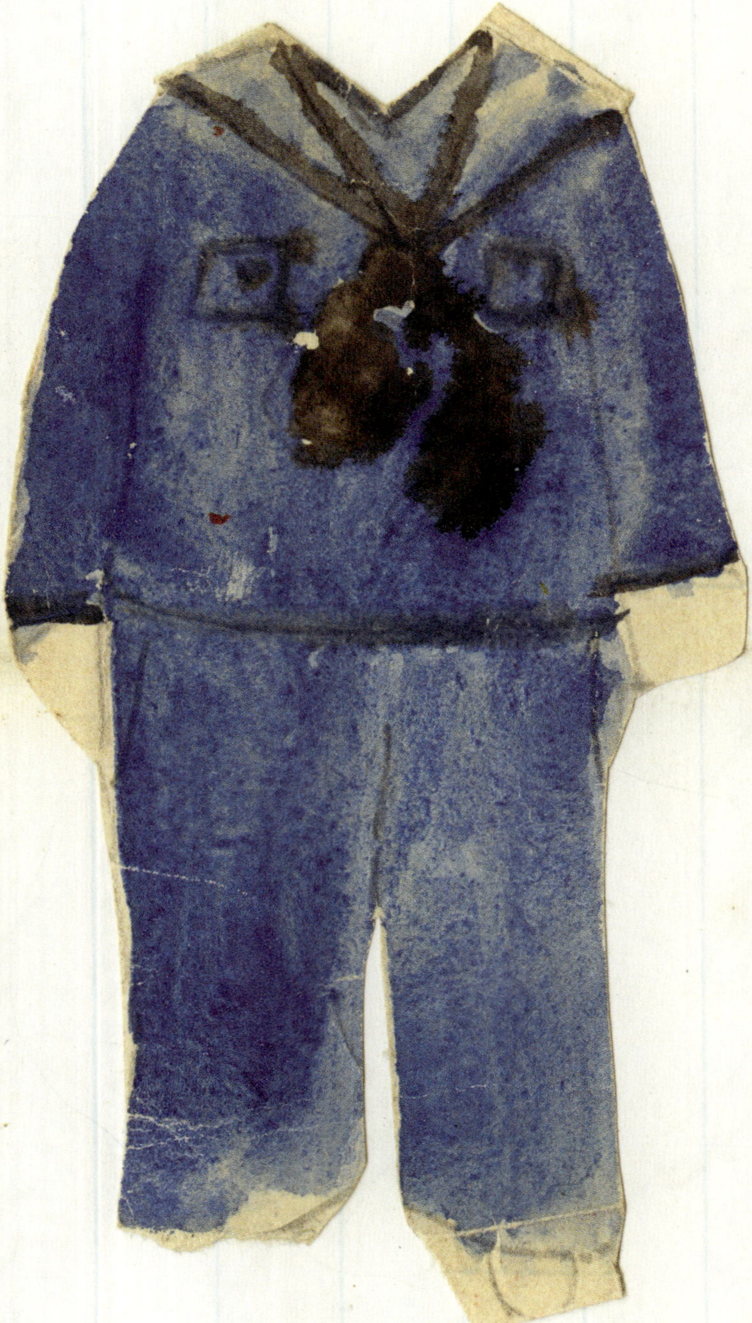

a No. 74

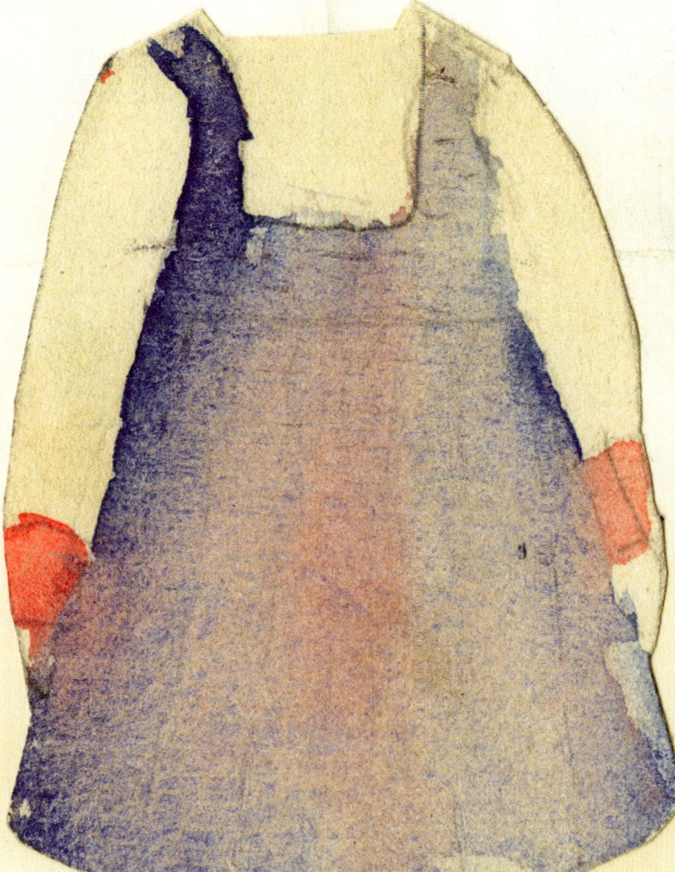

Fig. 1.

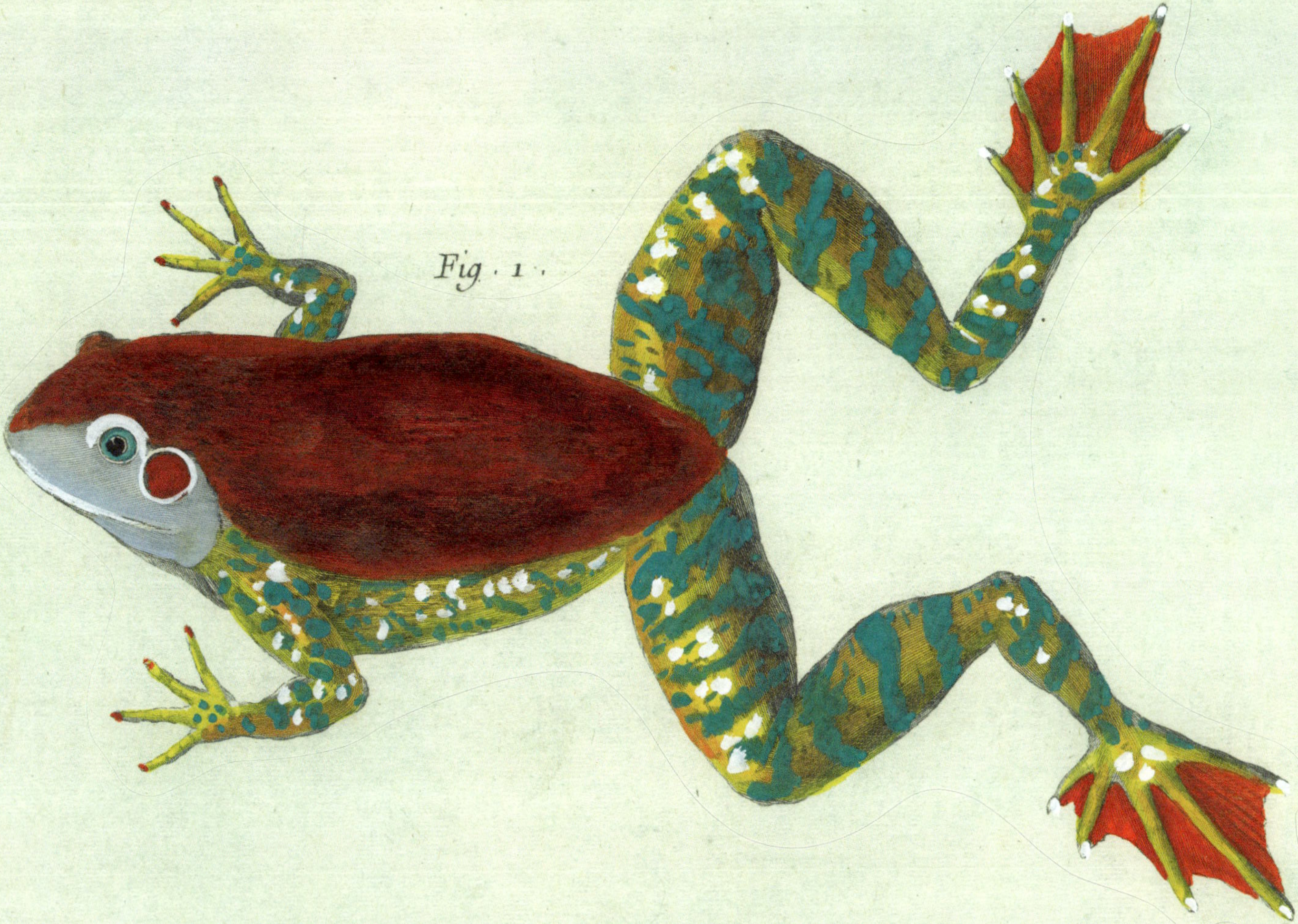

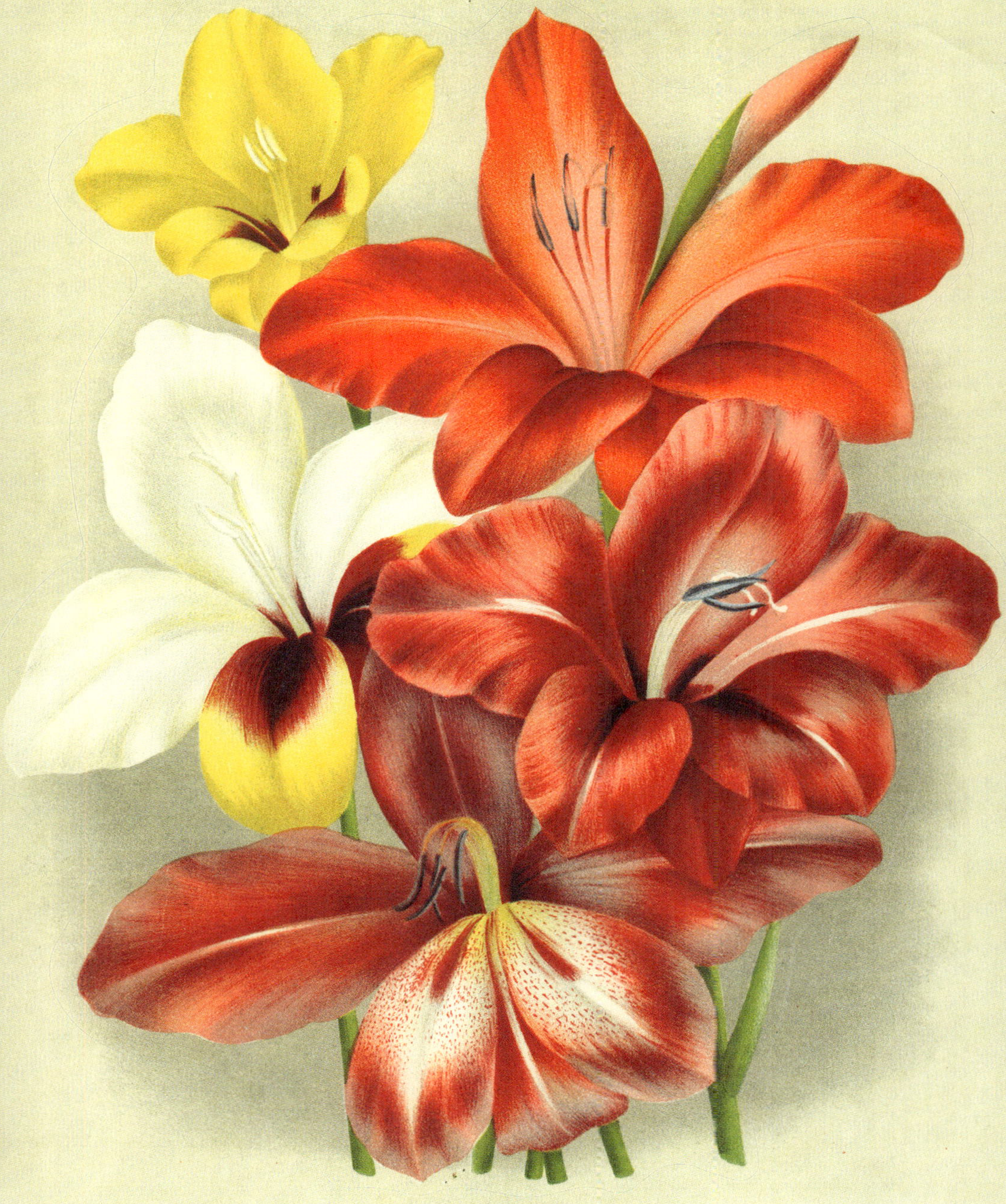

GLADIOLUS HYBRIDUS HORT.
NOUVEAUX HYBRIDES DE GLAIEULS

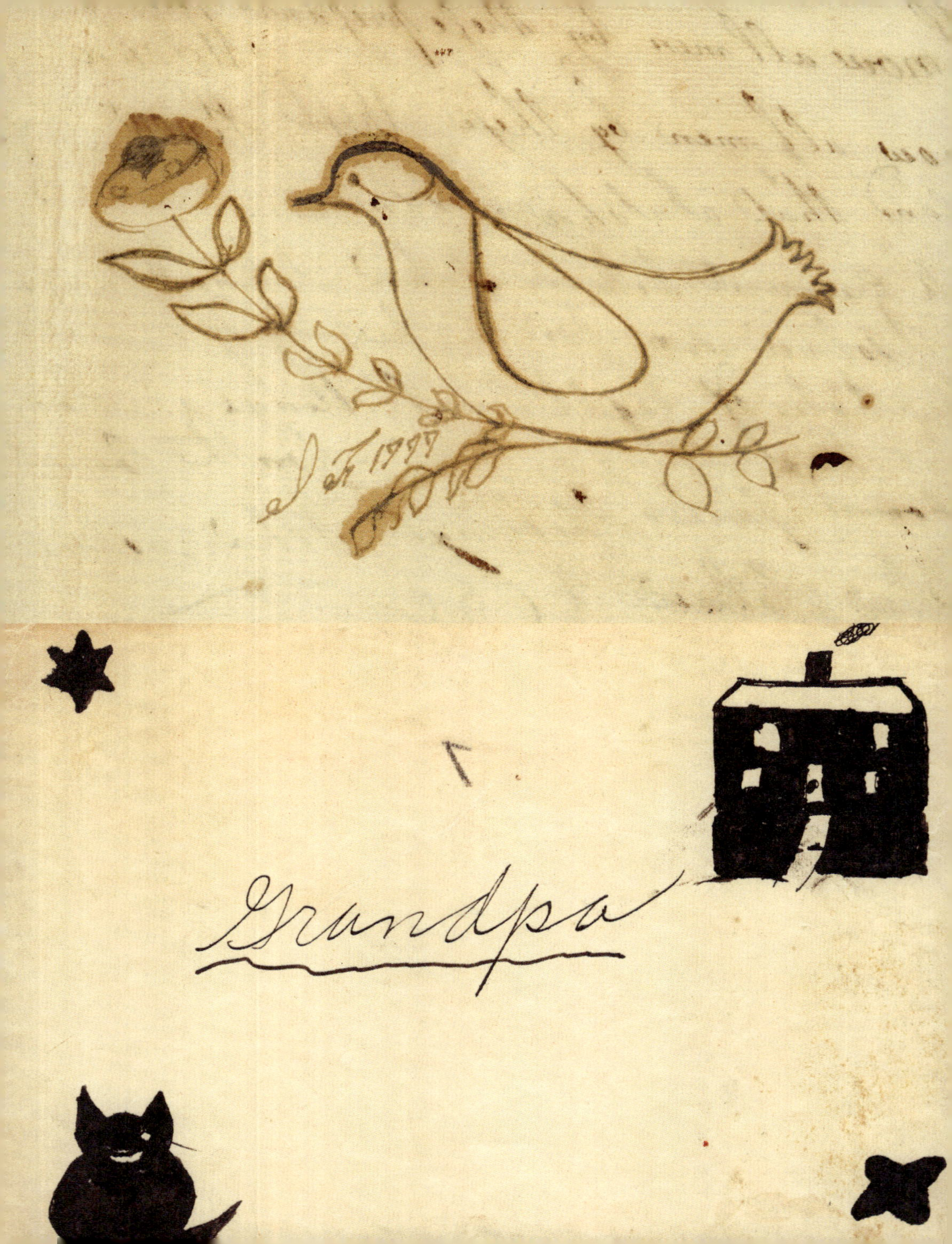
Grandpa

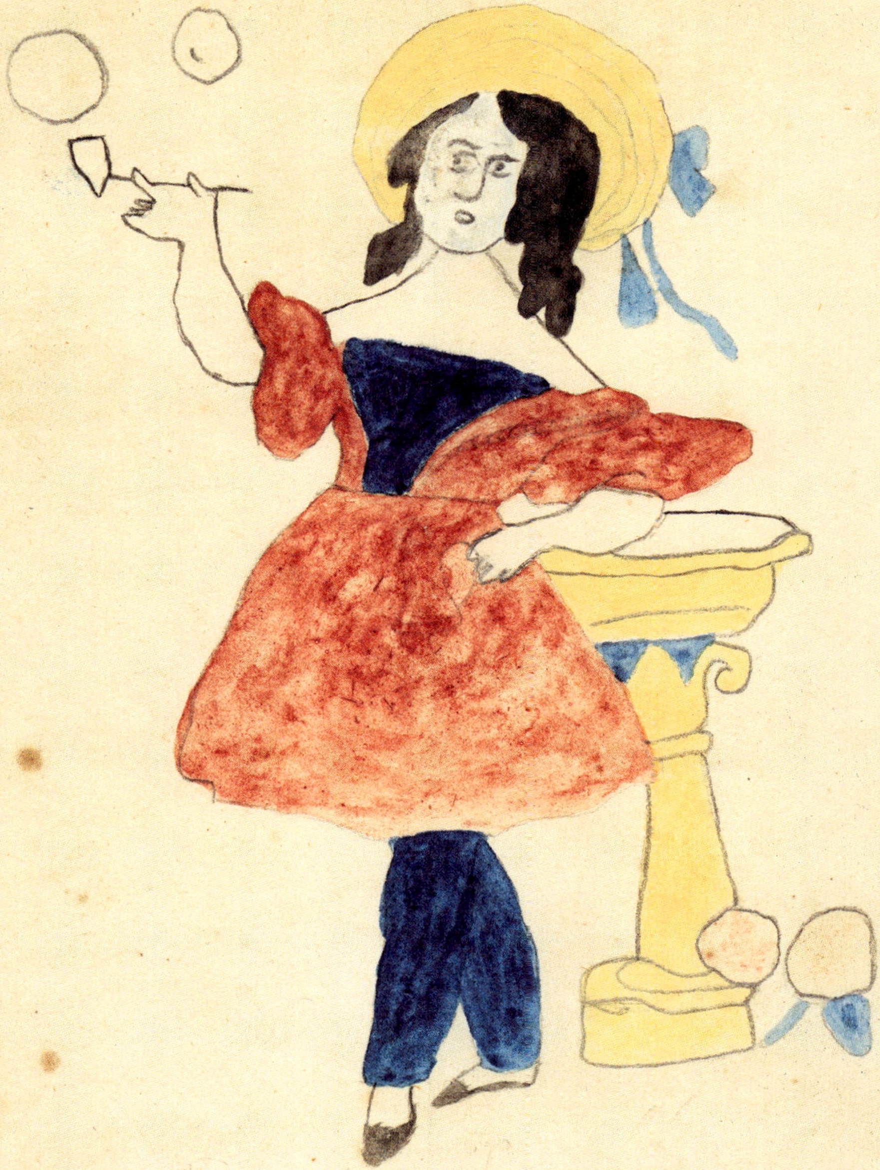

Blowing Bubbles.

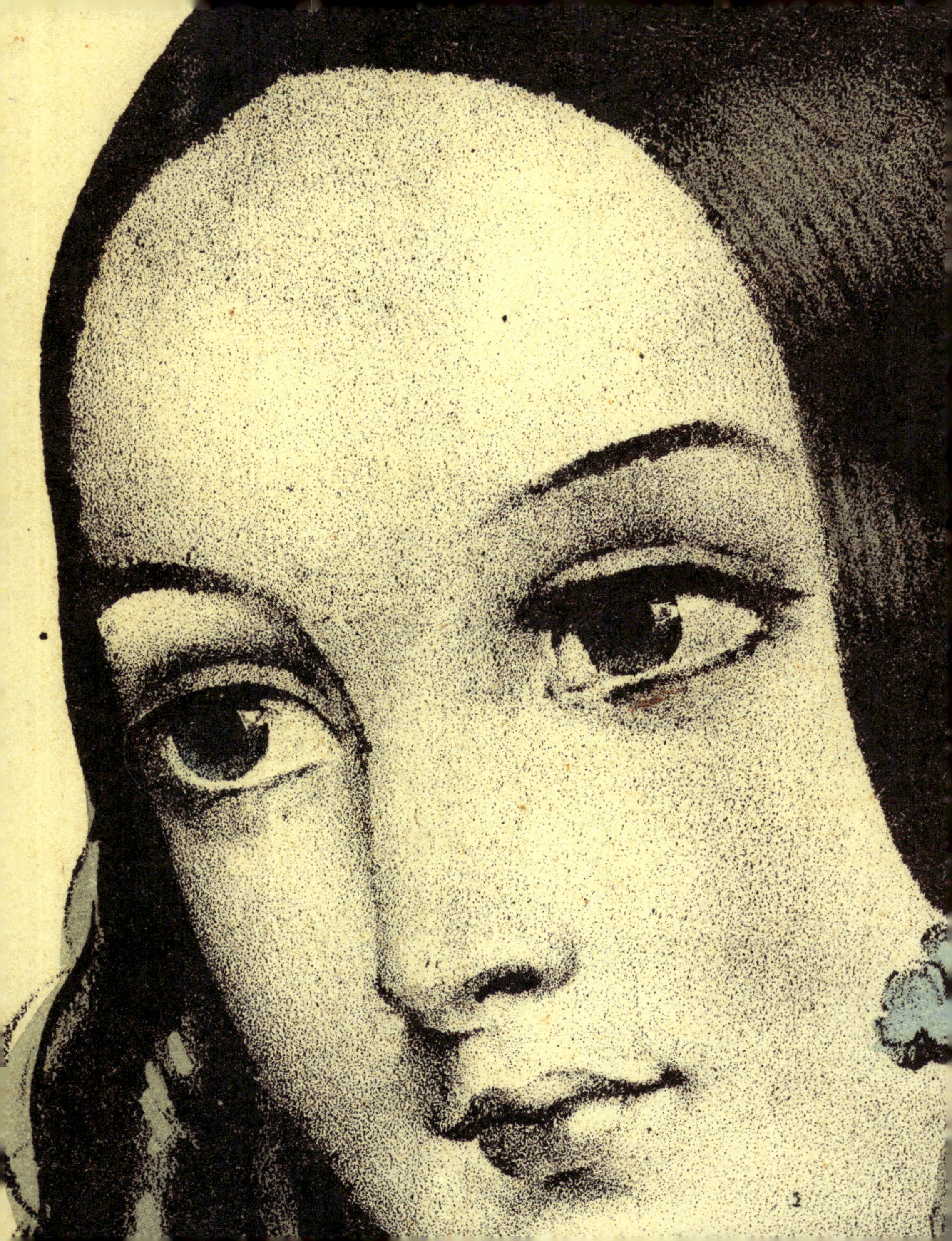

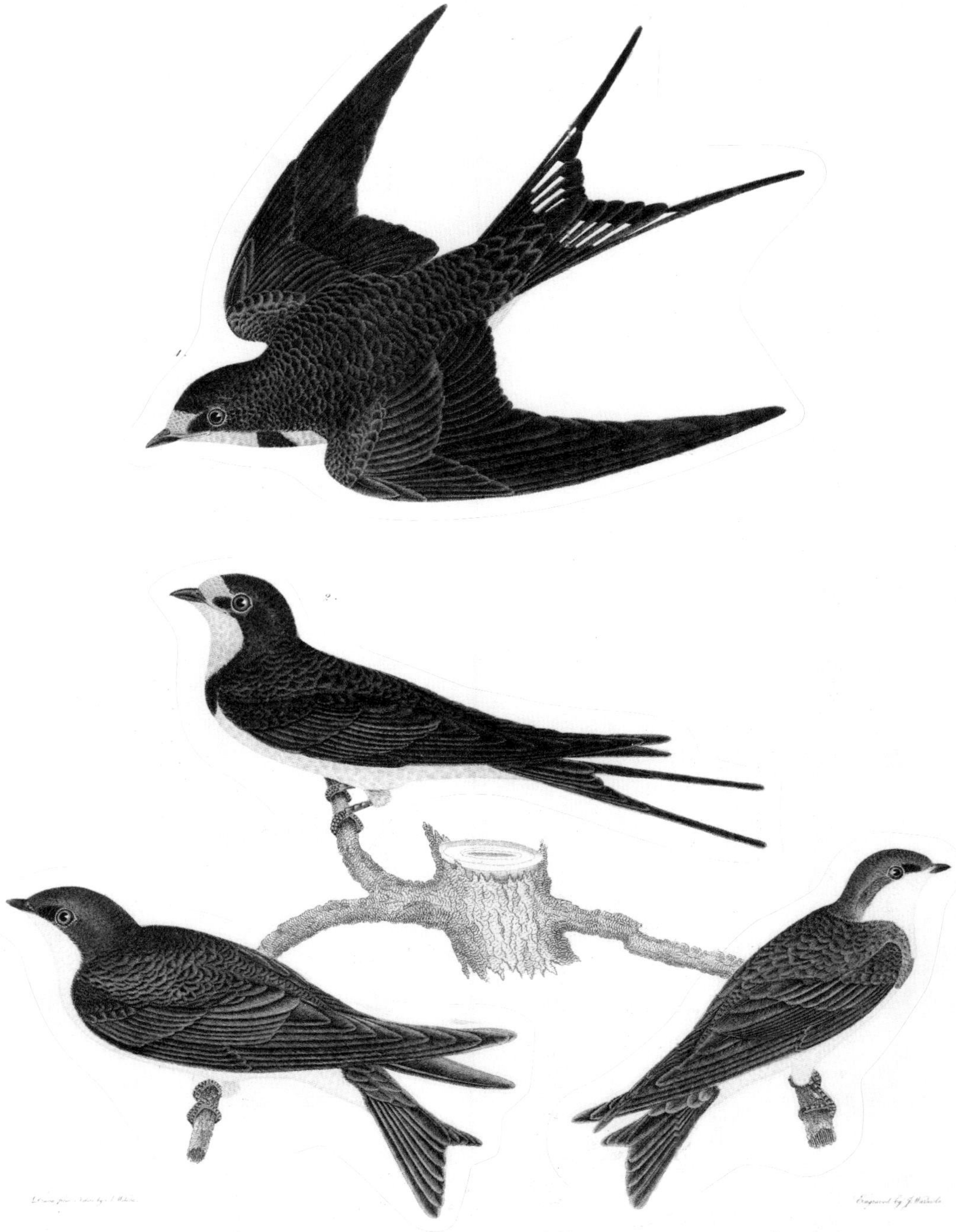

Drawn from Nature by A. Wilson.

Engraved by J. Warnicke

1. Barn Swallow. 2. Female. 3. White bellied S. 4. Bank S.

38

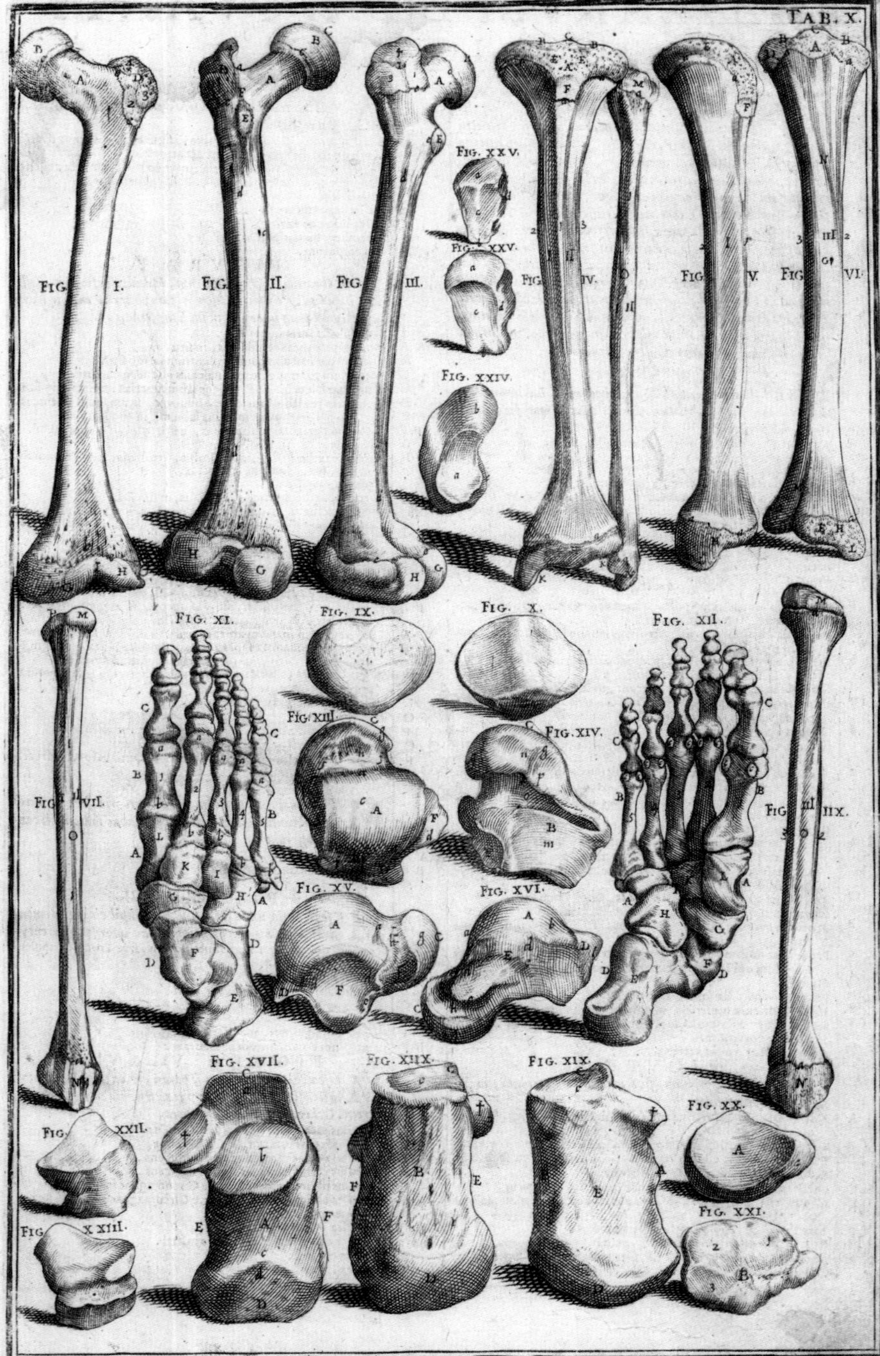
TAB. X.
FIG. I.
FIG. II.
FIG. III.
FIG. IV.
FIG. V.
FIG. VI.
FIG. XXV.
FIG. XXV.
FIG. XXIV.
FIG. IX.
FIG. X.
FIG. XI.
FIG. XII.
FIG. VII.
FIG. XIII.
FIG. XIV.
FIG. IIX.
FIG. XV.
FIG. XVI.
FIG. XVII.
FIG. XIIX.
FIG. XIX.
FIG. XX.
FIG. XXI.
FIG. XXII.
FIG. XXIII.

19

June N

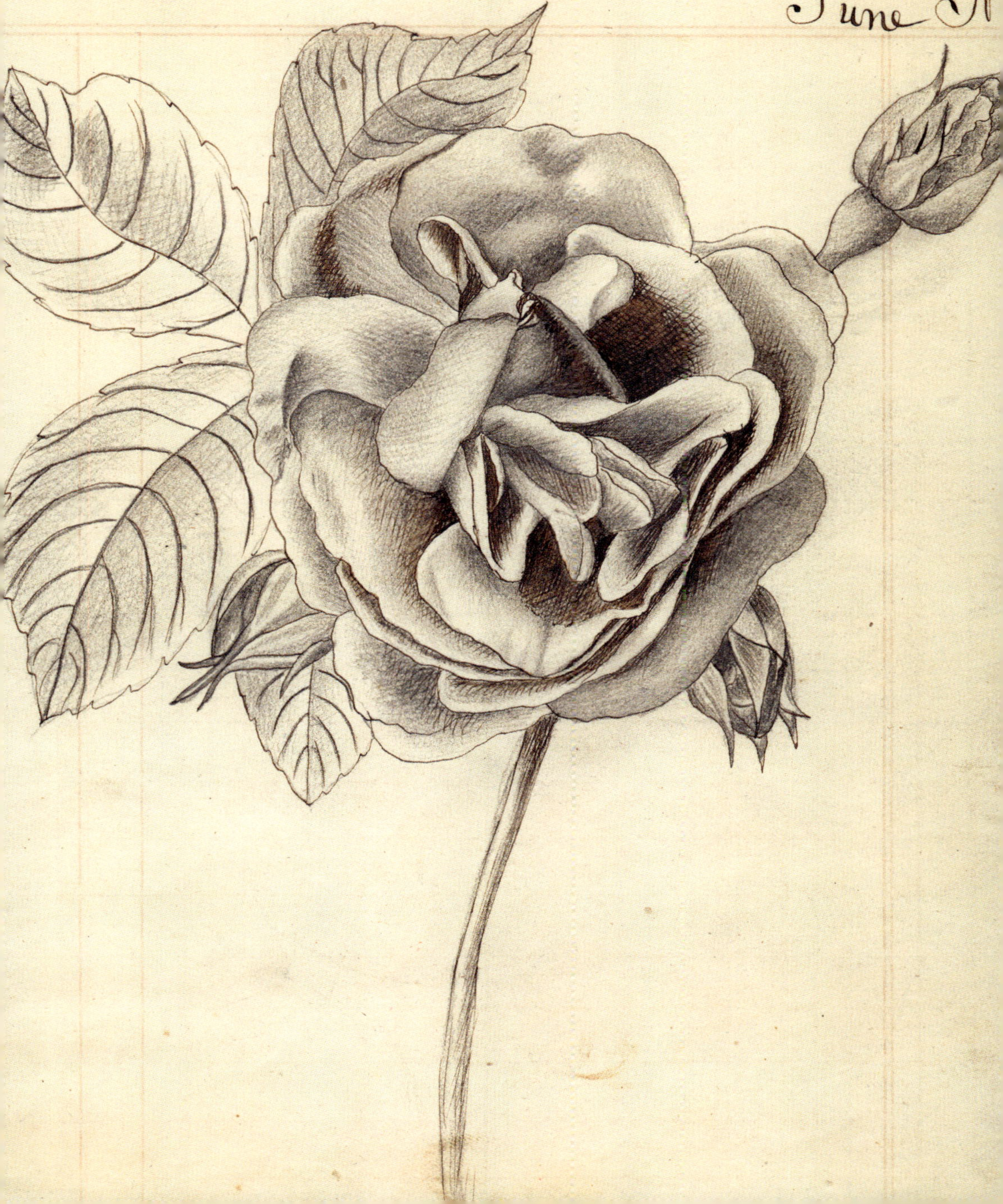

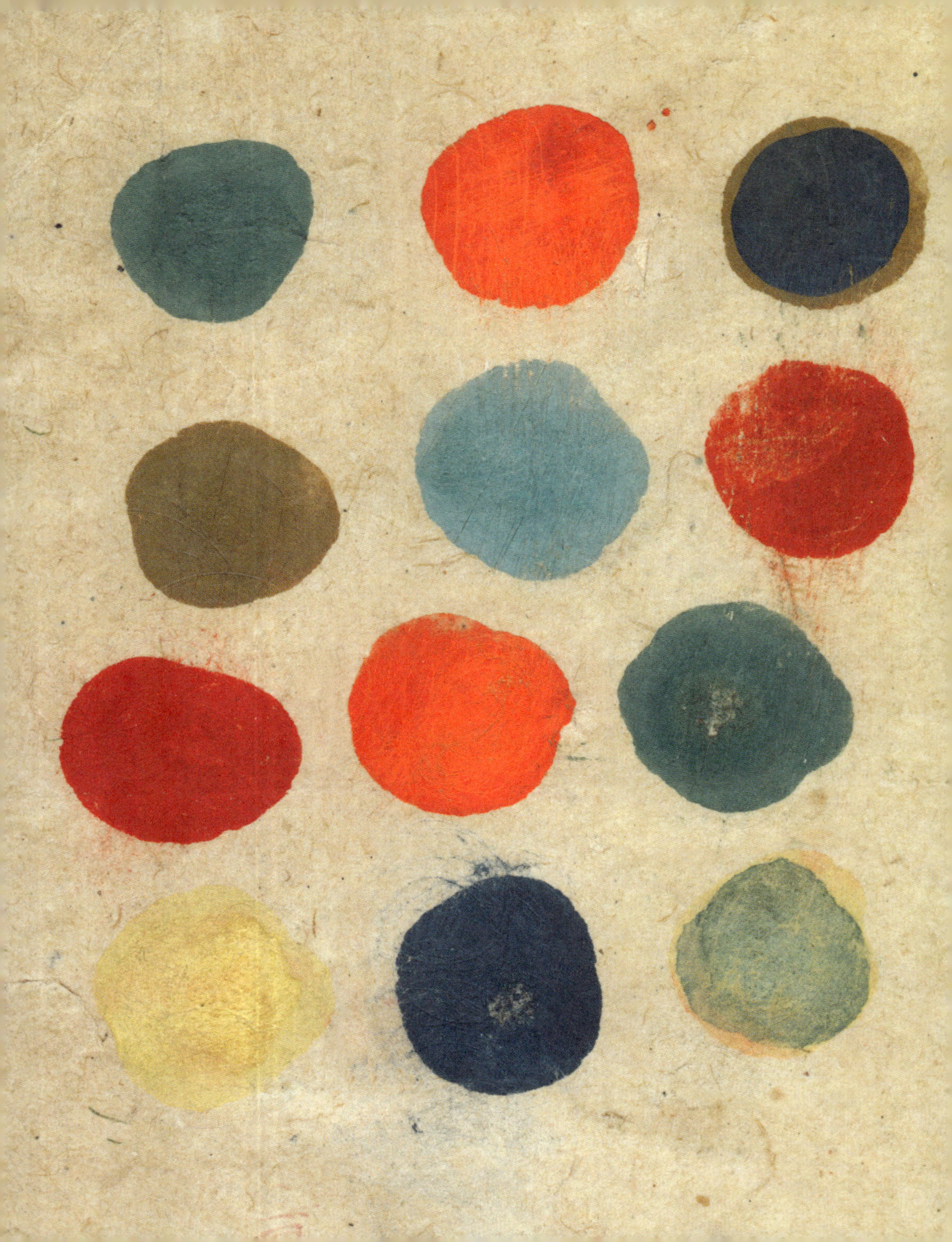

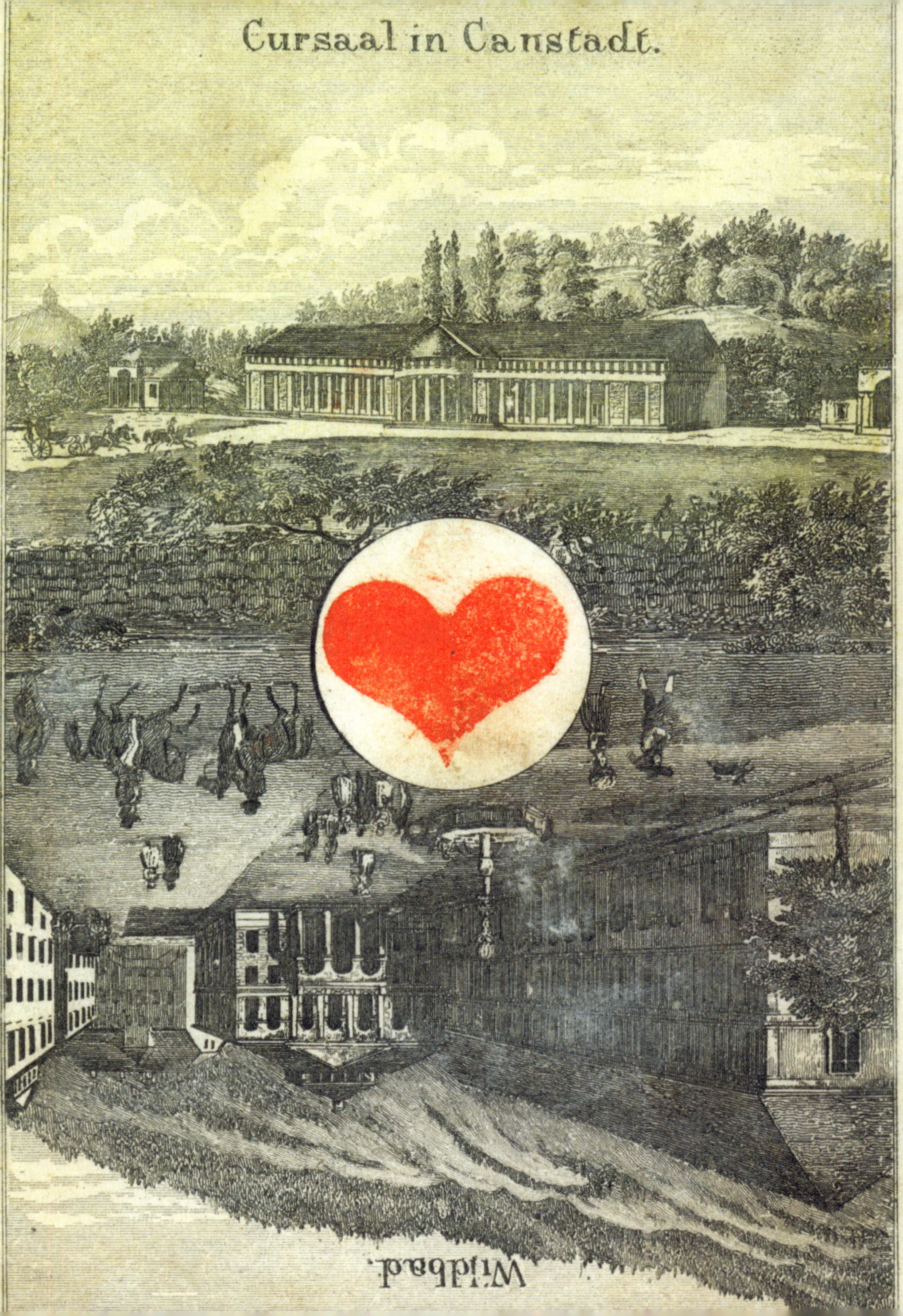
Cursaal in Canstadt.
Wildbad.

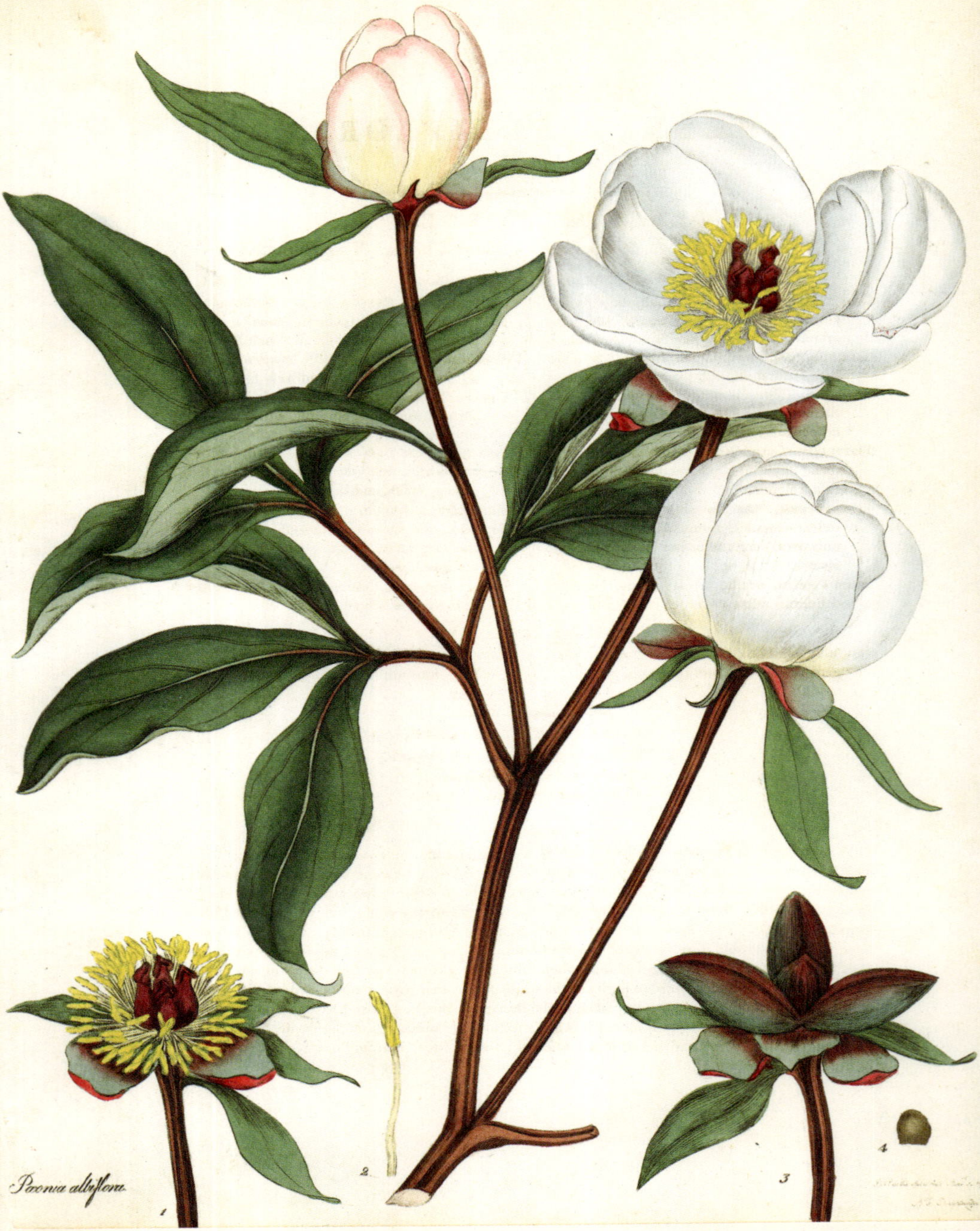

Pæonia albiflora

L. L.

1.

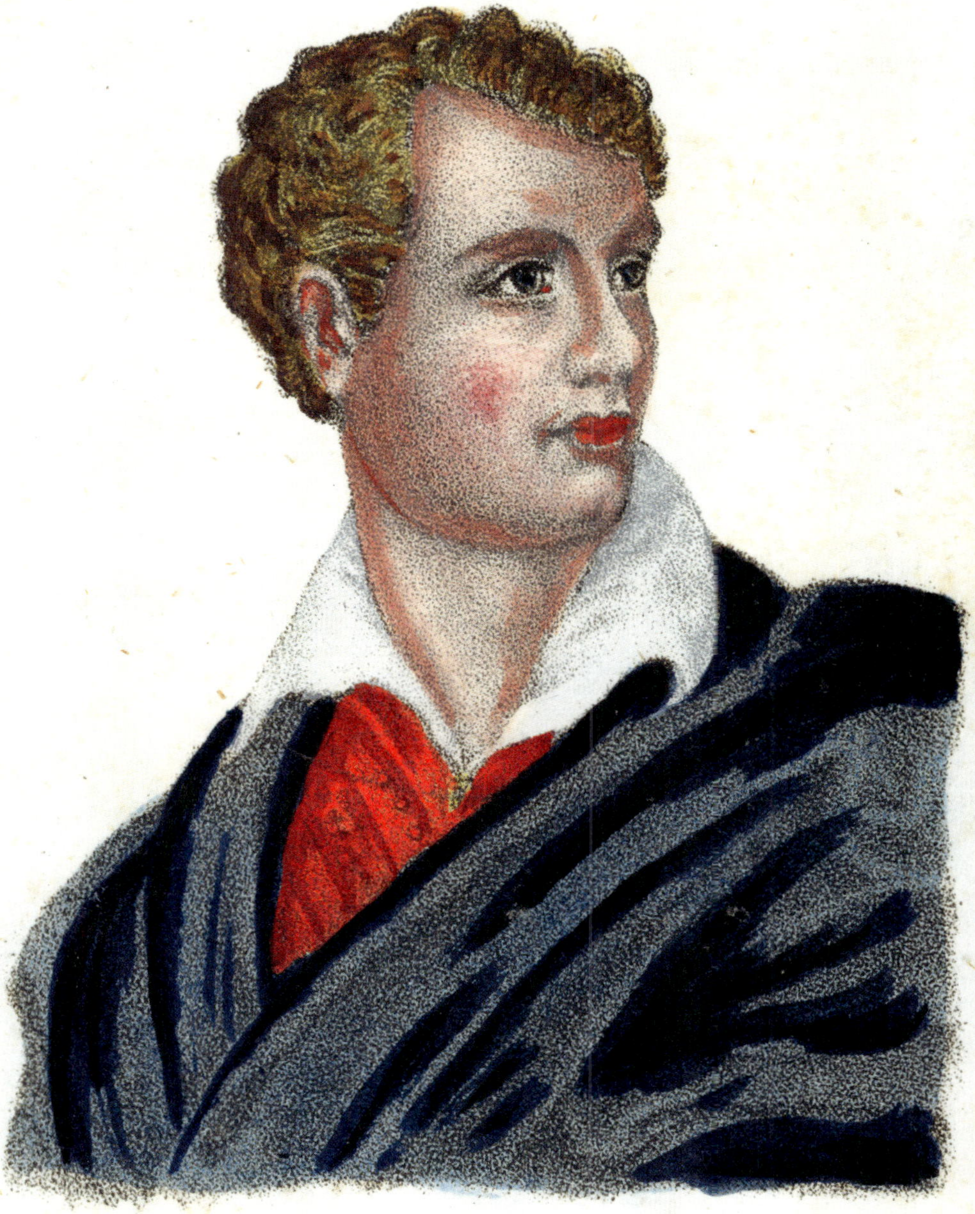

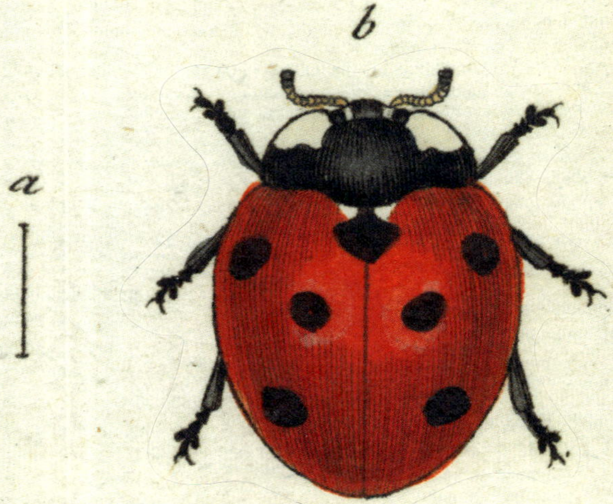

Coccinella septempunctata Fabr.

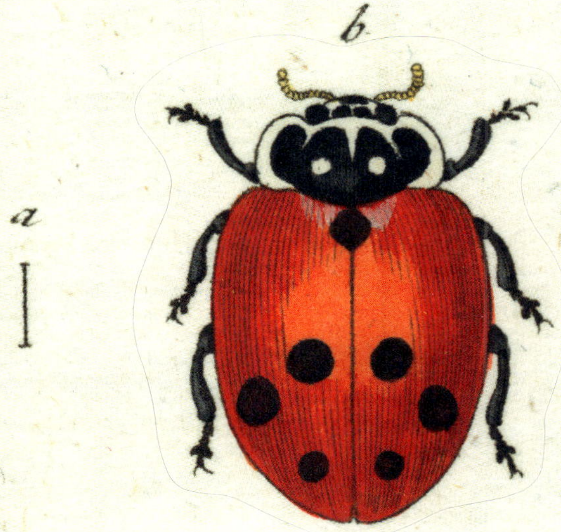

Coccinella ſeptemnotata Fabr.

J. S

NOTES

ARTIST'S BR

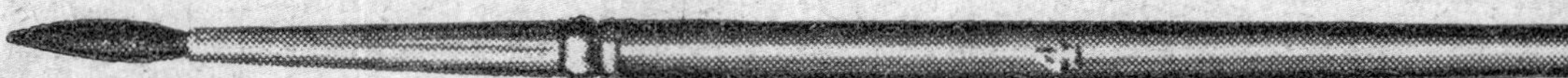

Series 20 No. 3

MY LOVE A

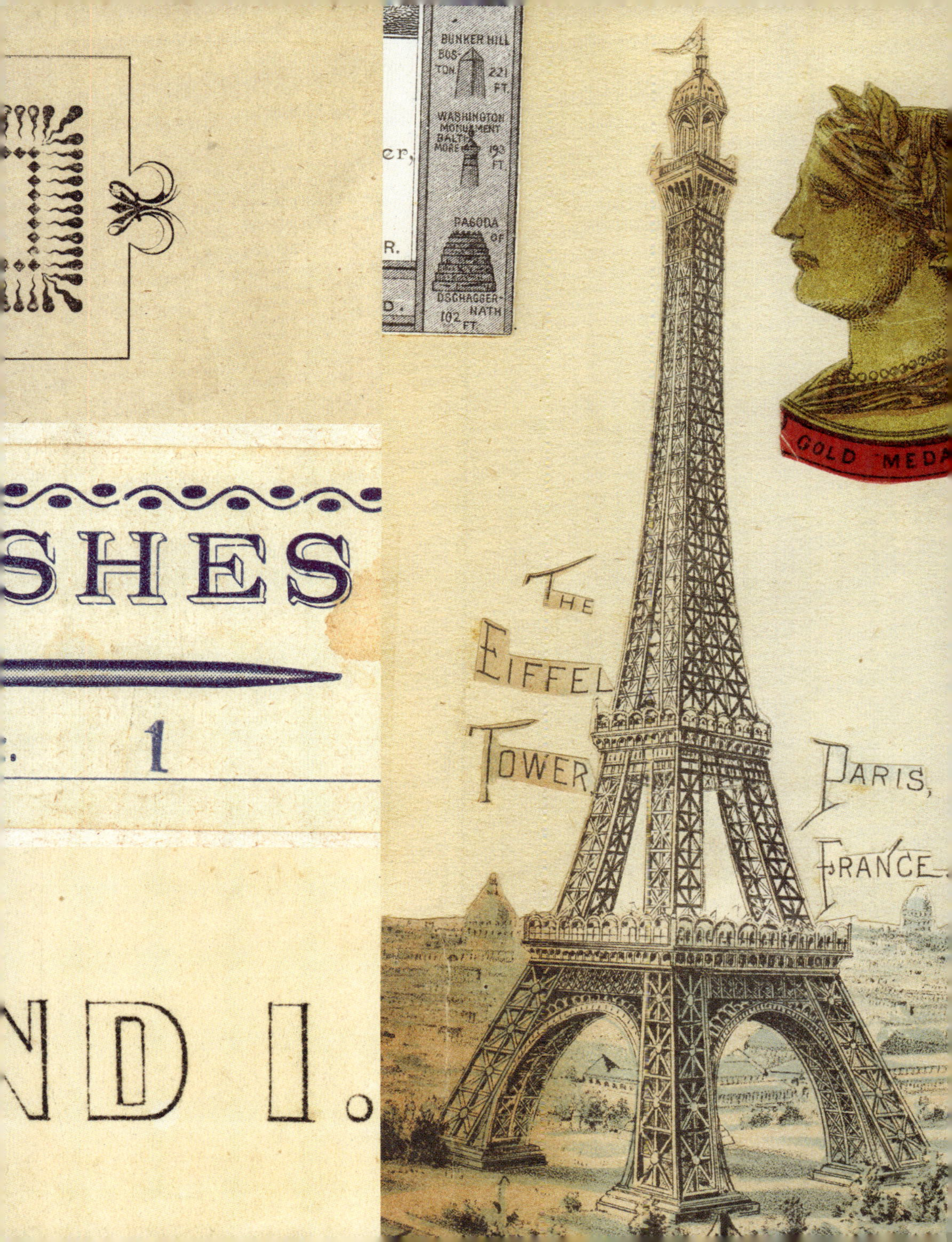
BUNKER HILL
BOSTON 221 FT.
WASHINGTON MONUMENT
BALTIMORE 193 FT.
PAGODA OF DSCHAGGERNATH
102 FT
SHES
1
GOLD MEDA
THE
EIFFEL
TOWER
PARIS,
FRANCE.
ND I.

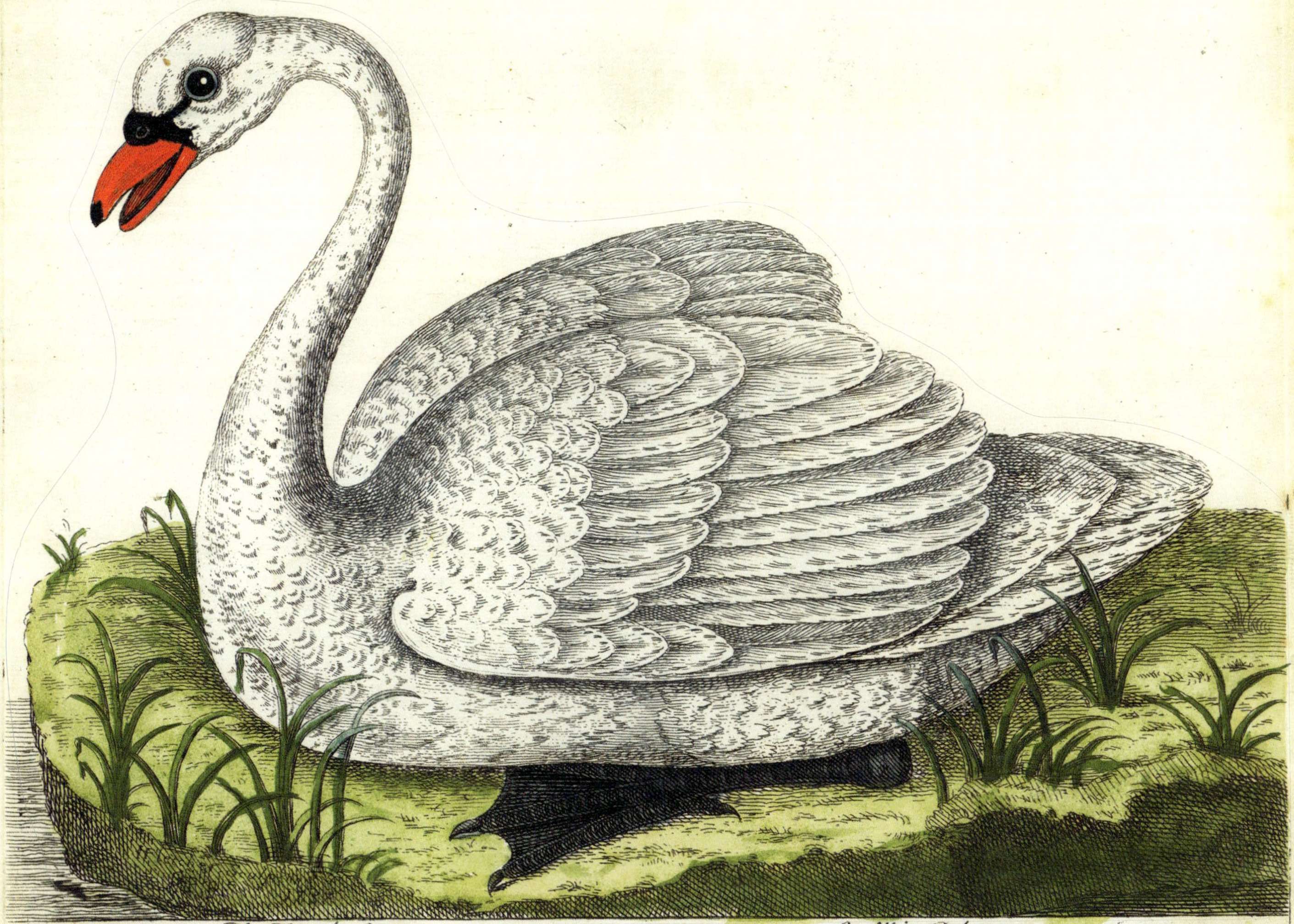

The Female Swan.

E. Albin Del: 1737.

T. LXVI.

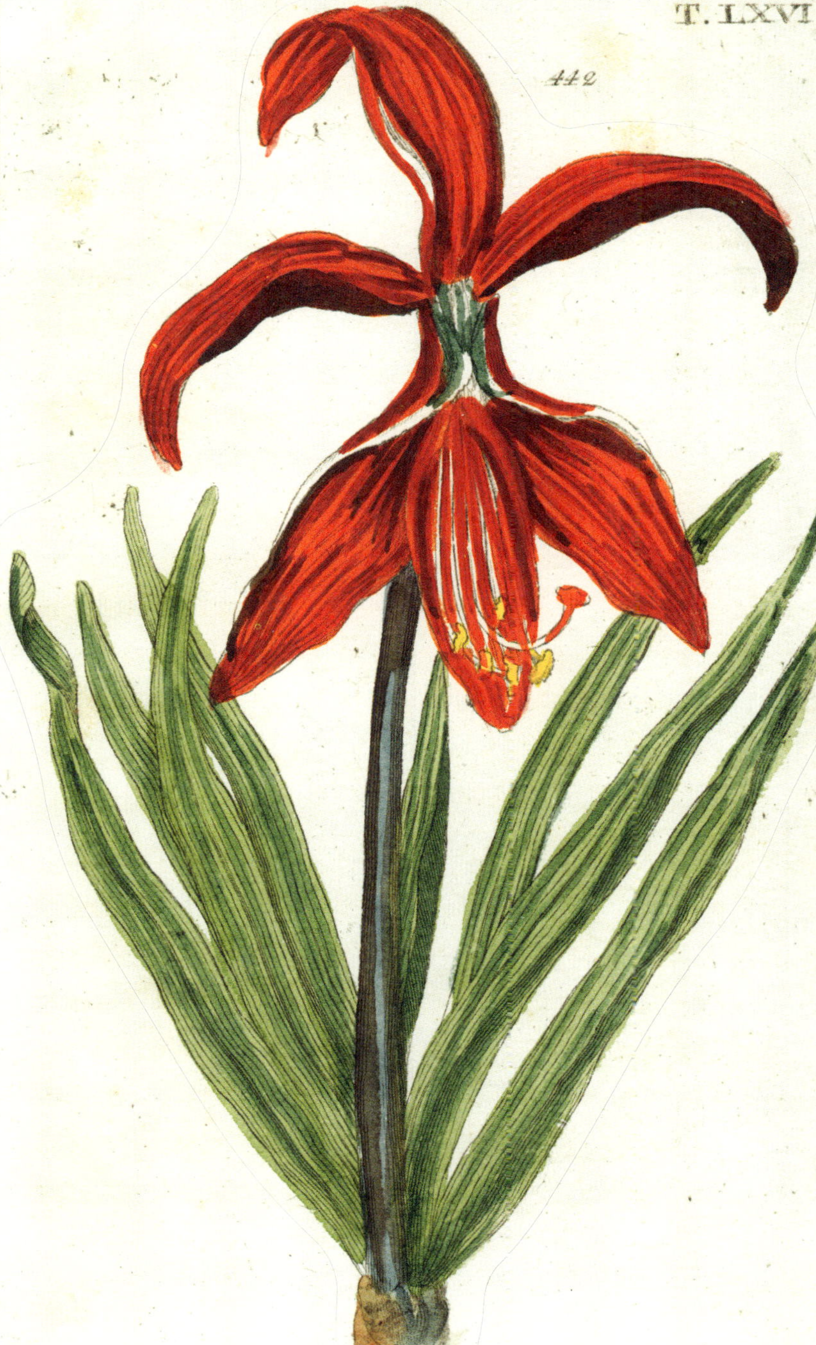

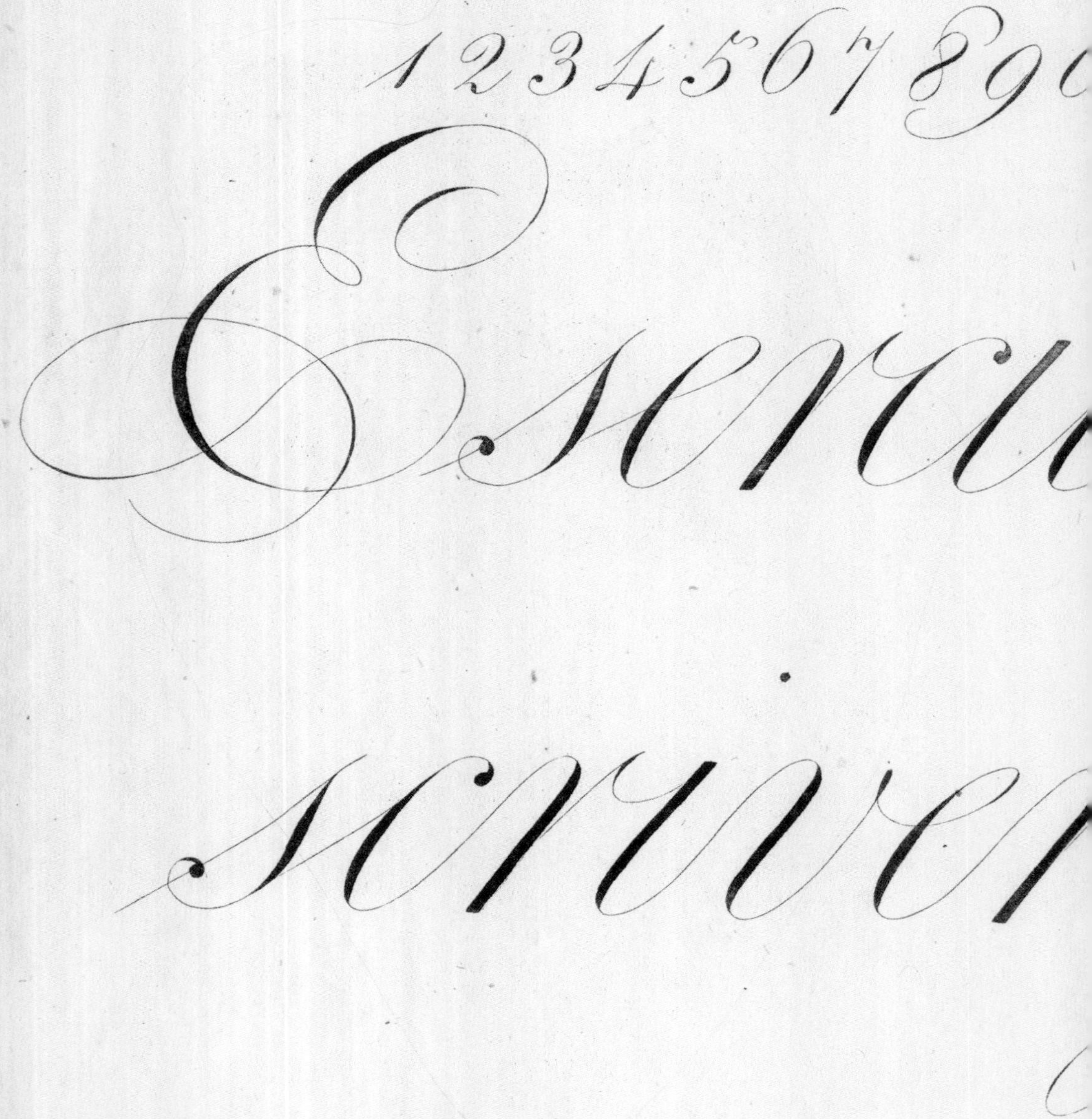
1 2 3 4 5 6 7 8 9

1234567890

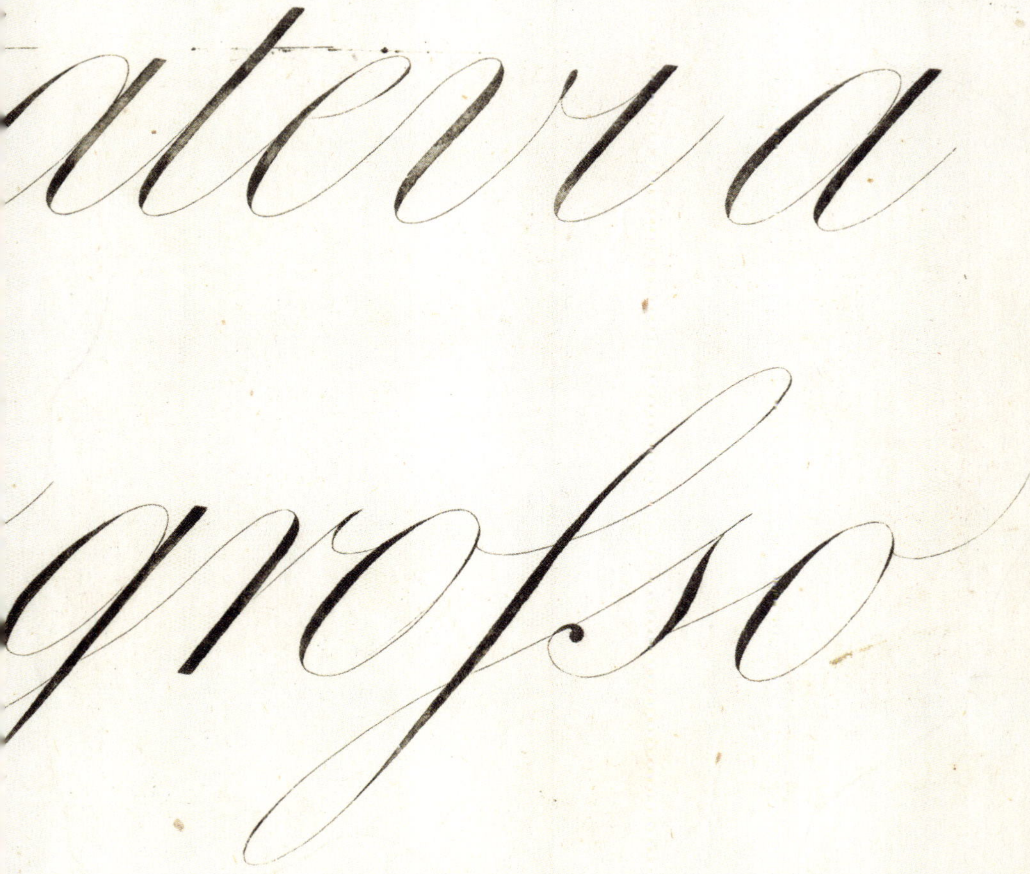

LA TRIBUNE HORTICOLE.
(Supplément)
2 Janvier 1909 Pl. 125.

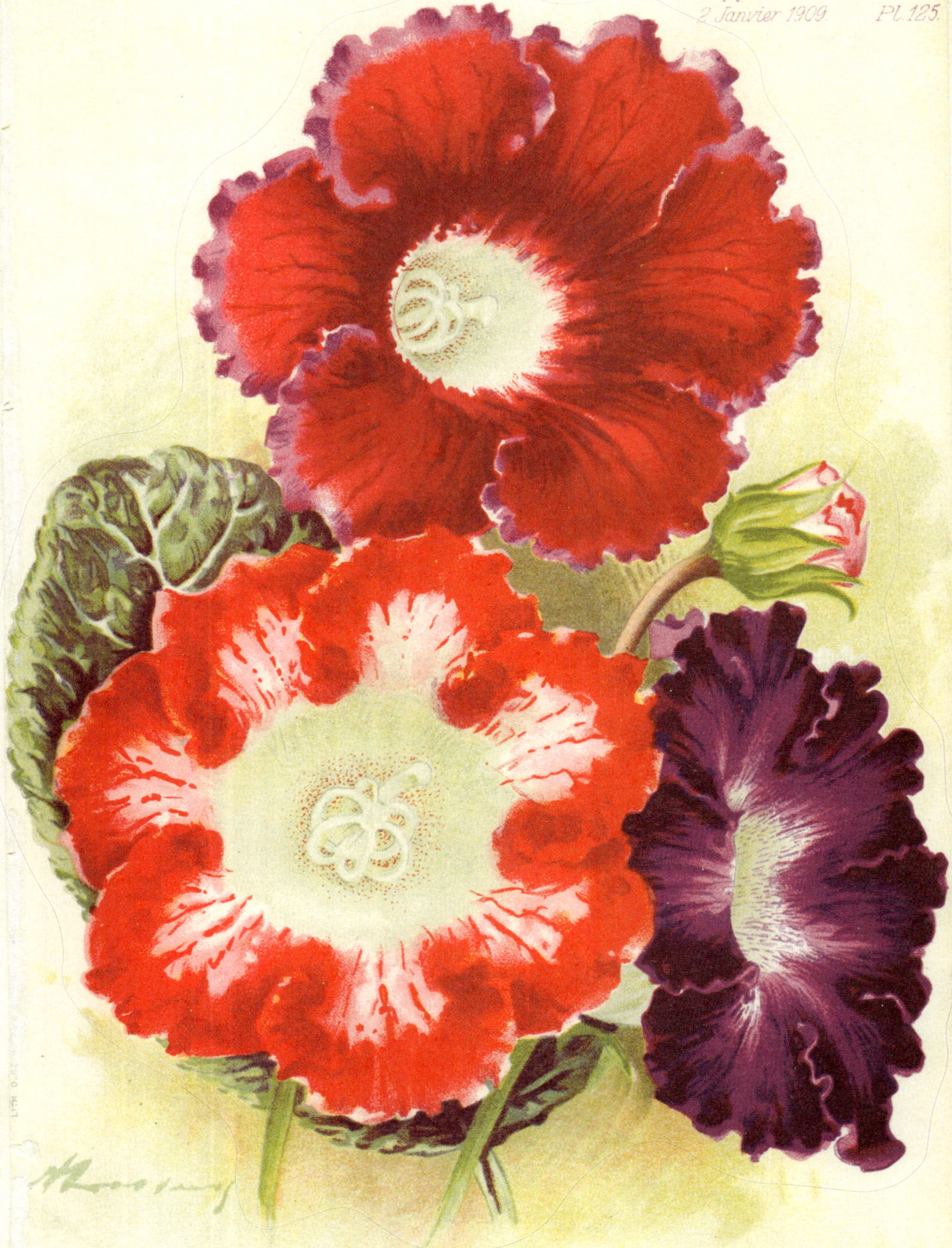

TROIS BEAUX TYPES DE FLEURS DES GLOXINIAS
DE LA RACE KEGELJAN DE NAMUR

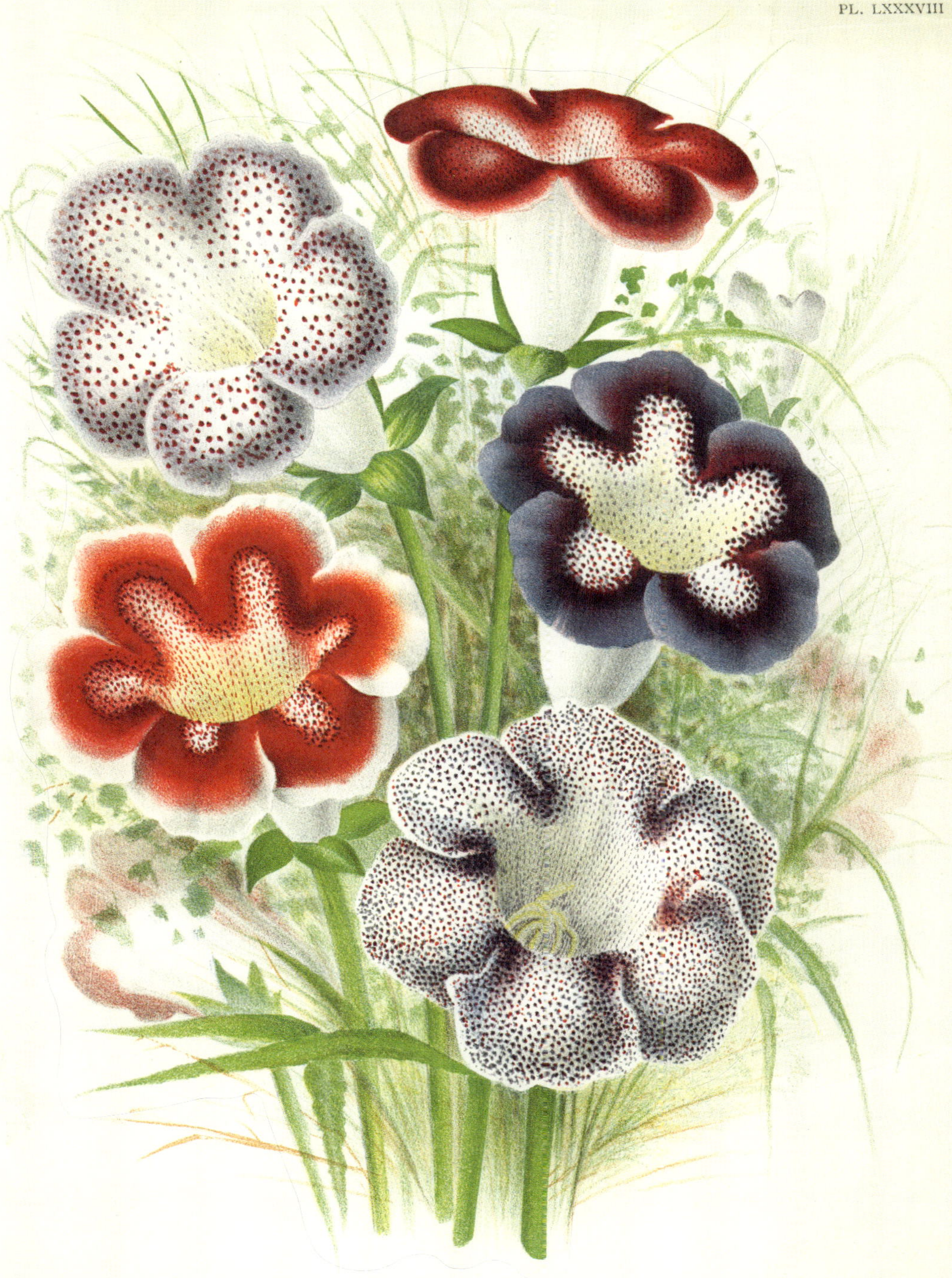

VARIÉTÉS DE GLOXINIA

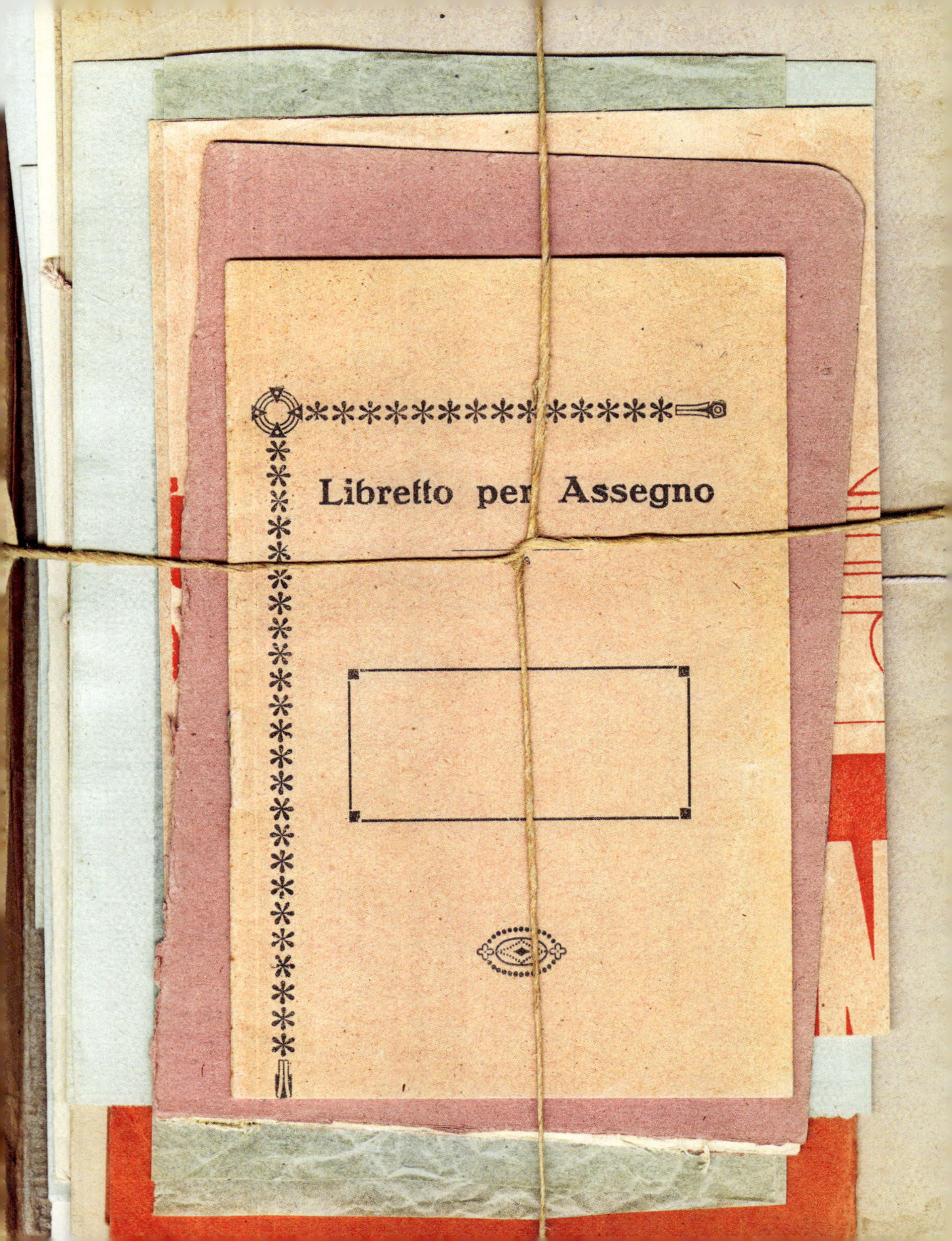
Libretto per Assegno

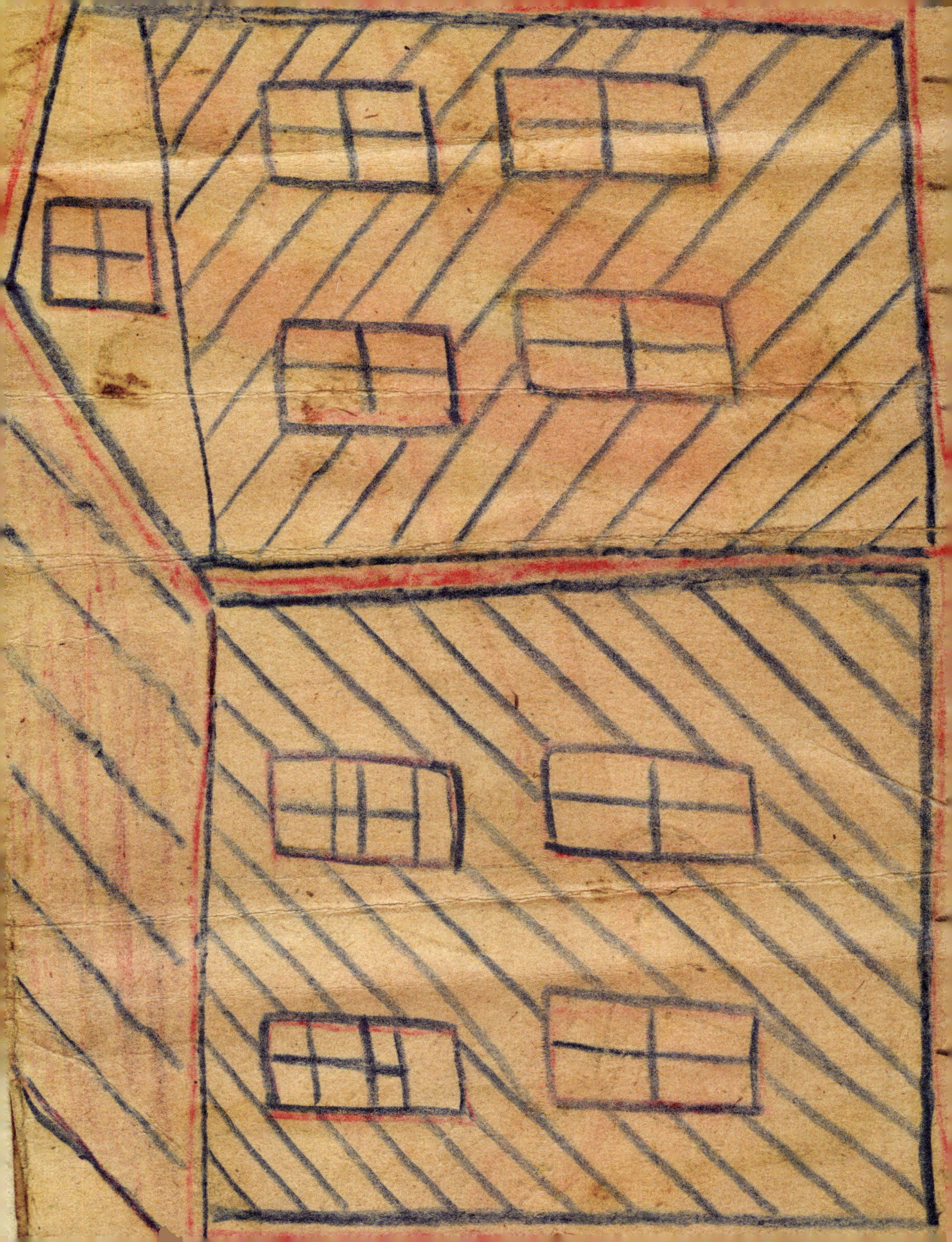

N.695.

a. *Malva rosea semiplena*. b. *Malva rosea flore rubro pleno, Rose de Tramee,* Bautren Rosen. c. *Malva rosea flore nigricante*. d. *Malva rosea flore sulphureo pleno*. e. *Malva rosea flore luteo pleno*.

x.

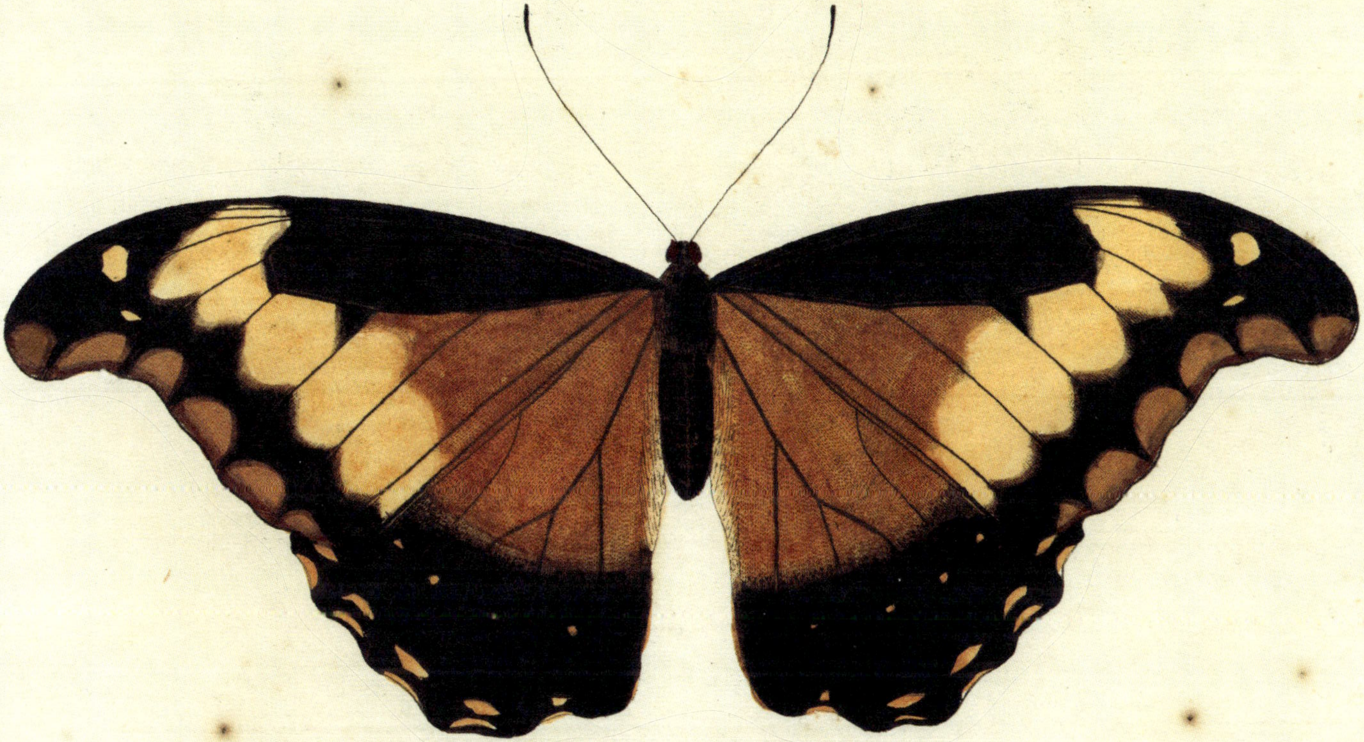

A

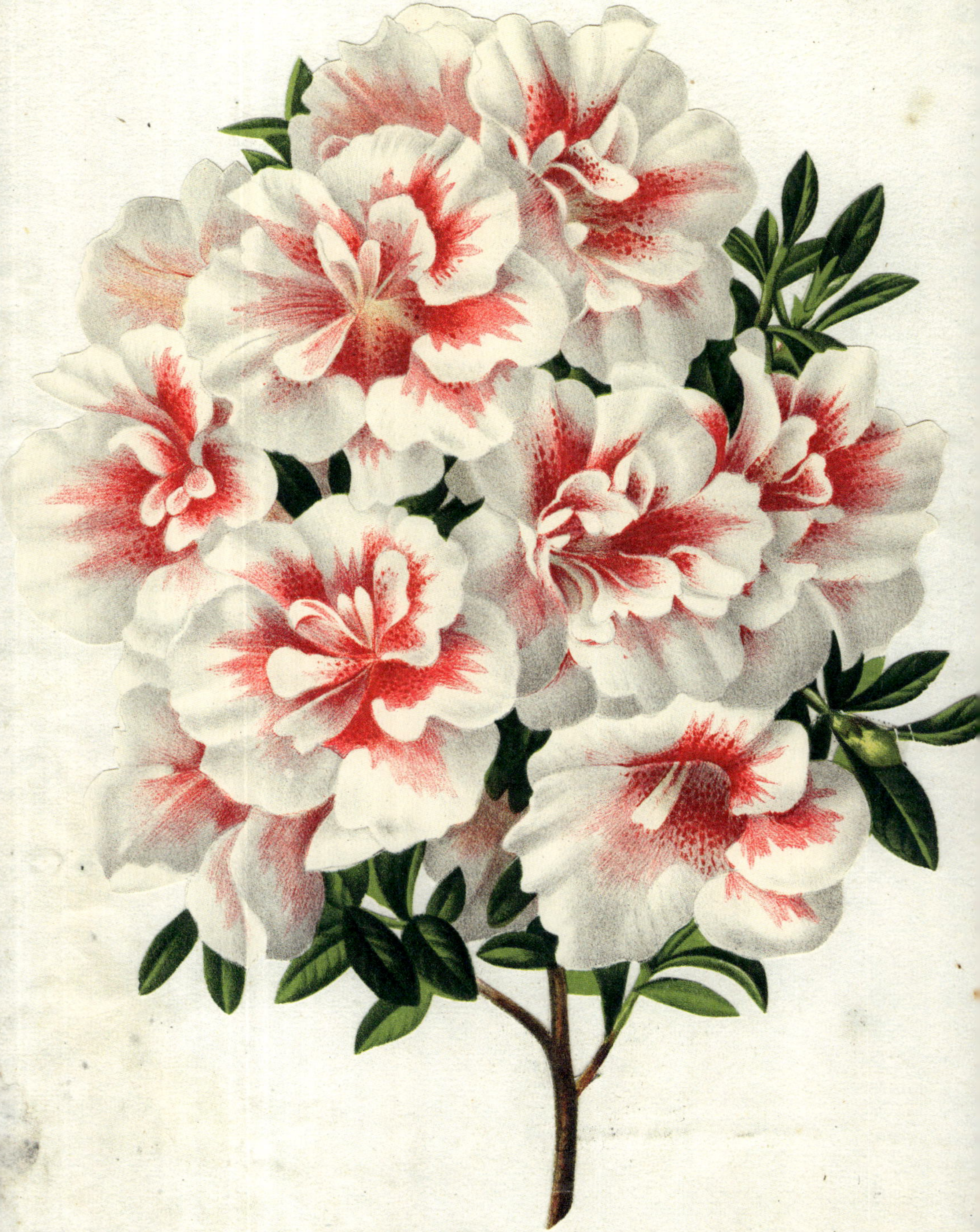

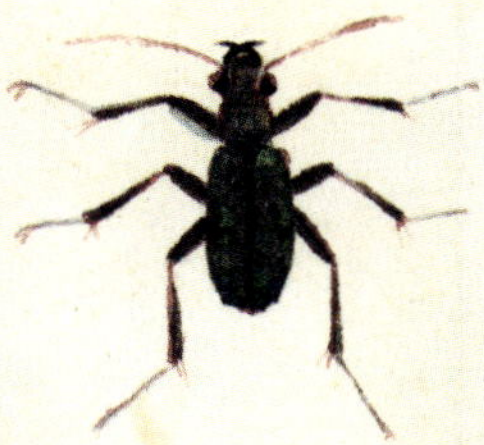

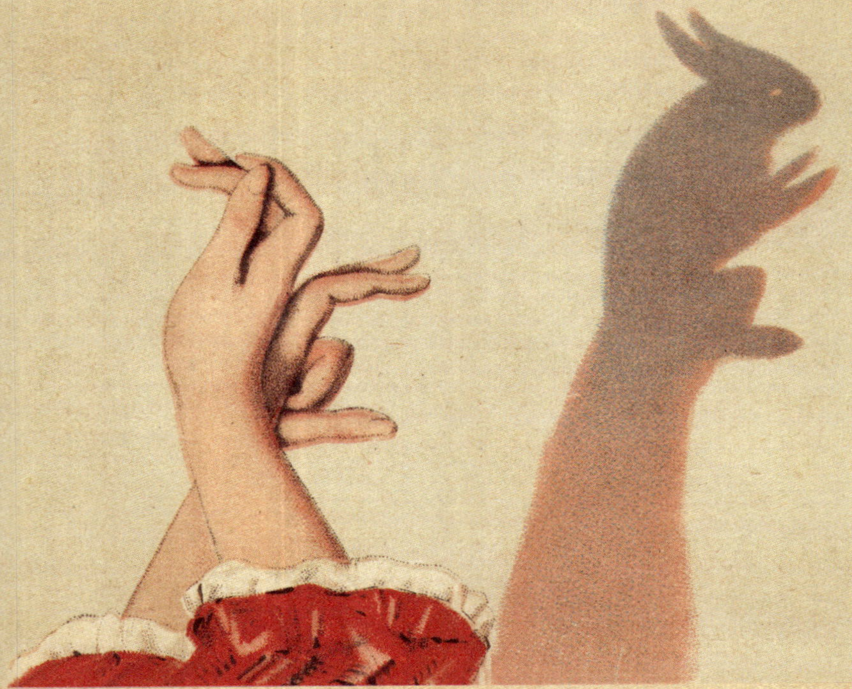

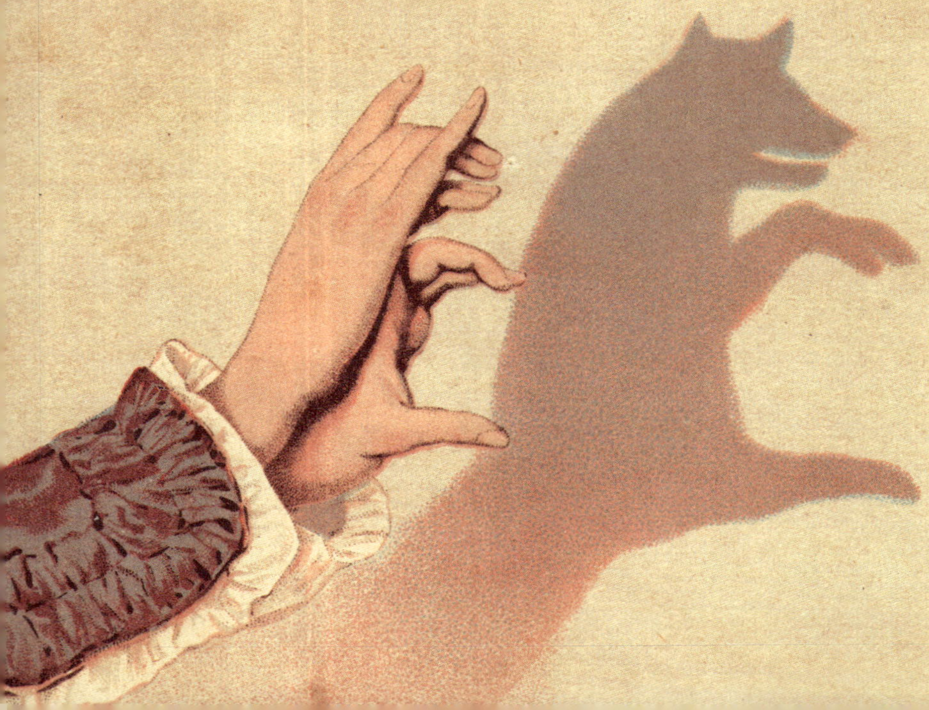

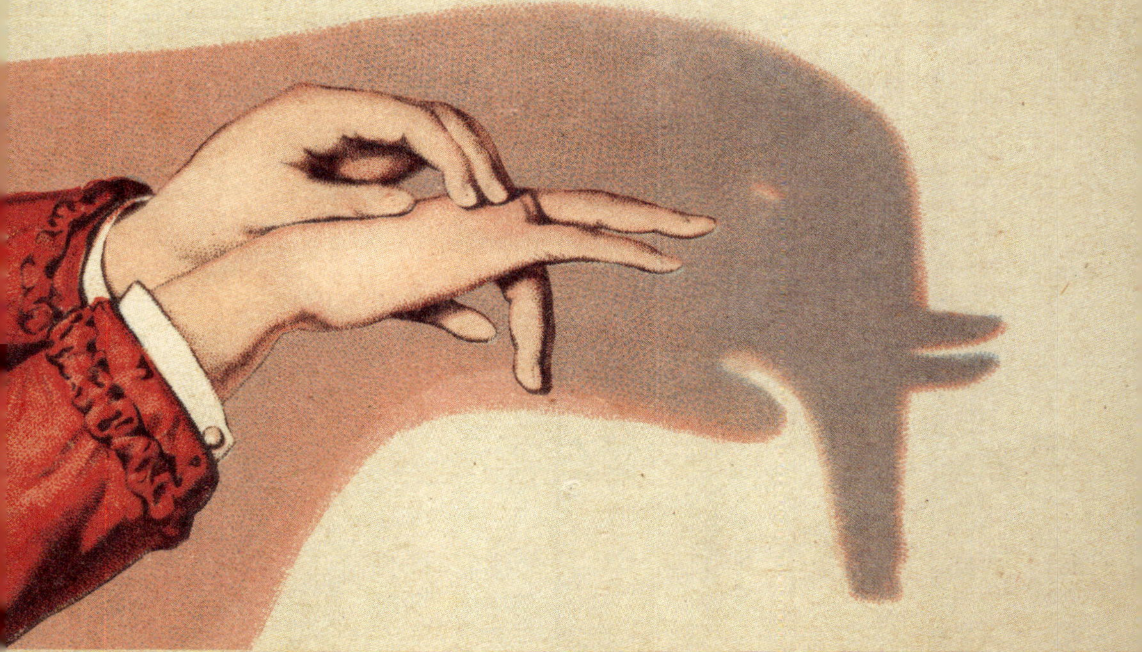

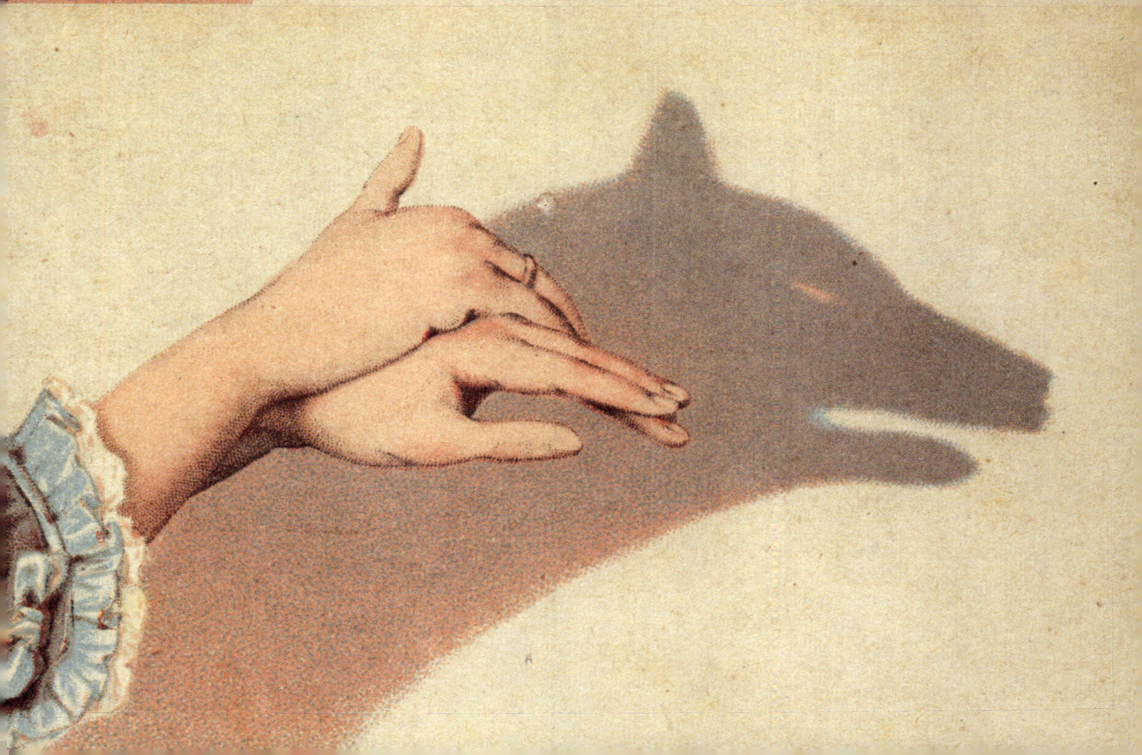

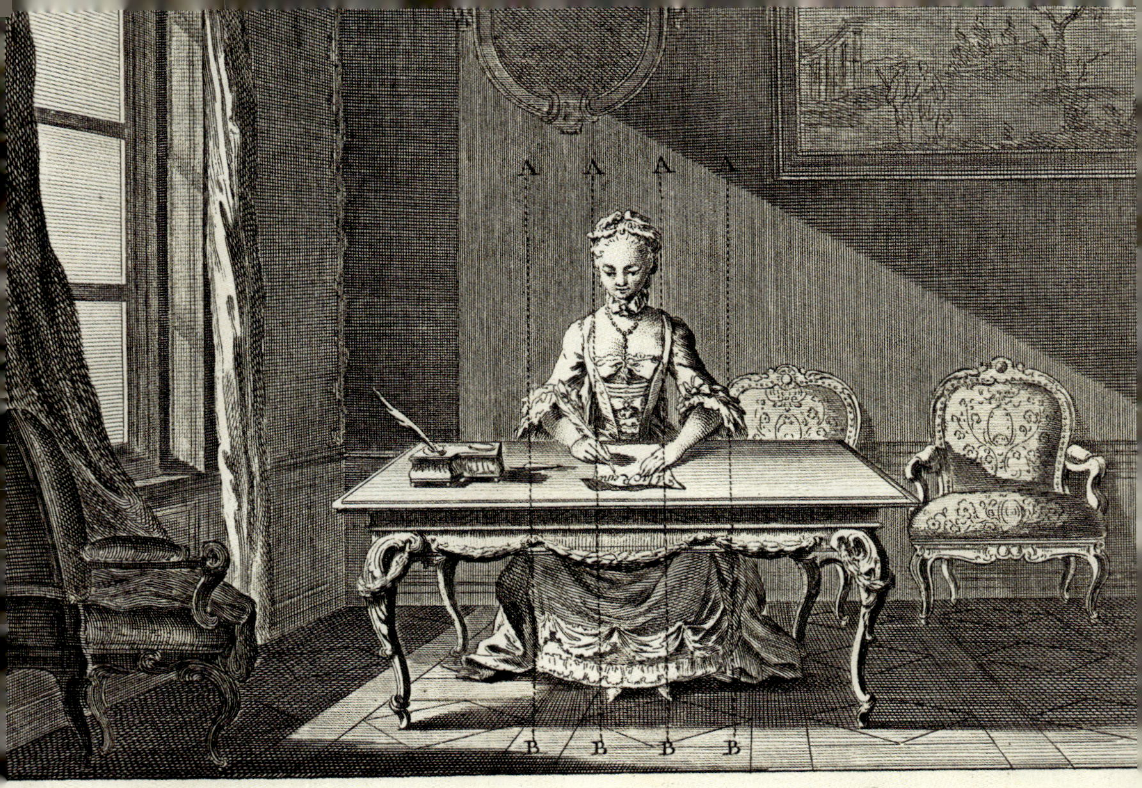
A A A A
B B B B

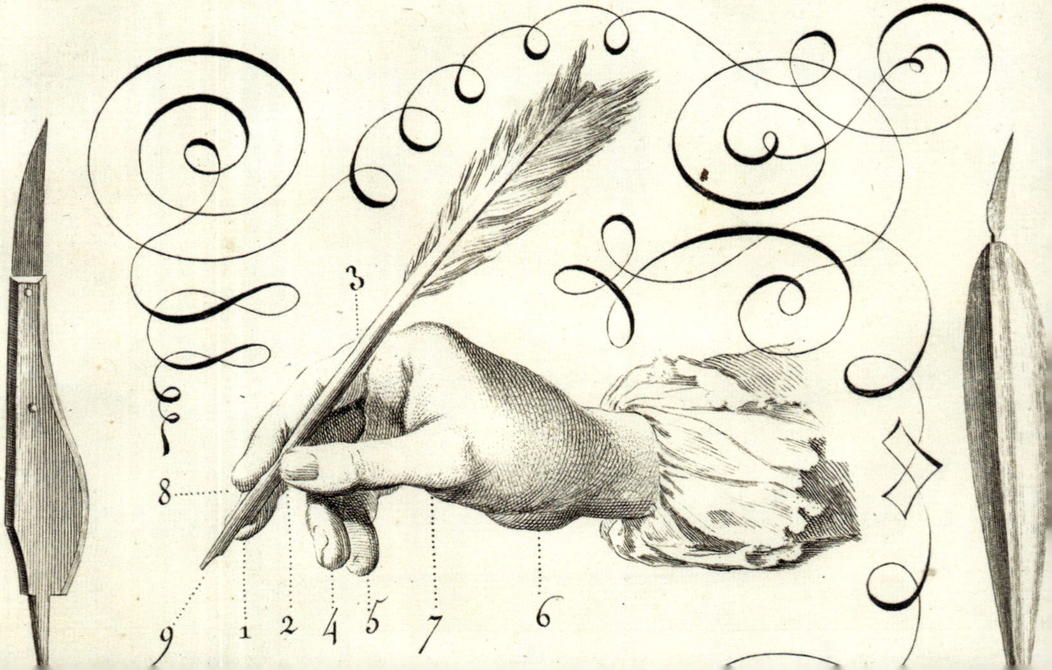
3
8
9 1 2 4 5 7 6

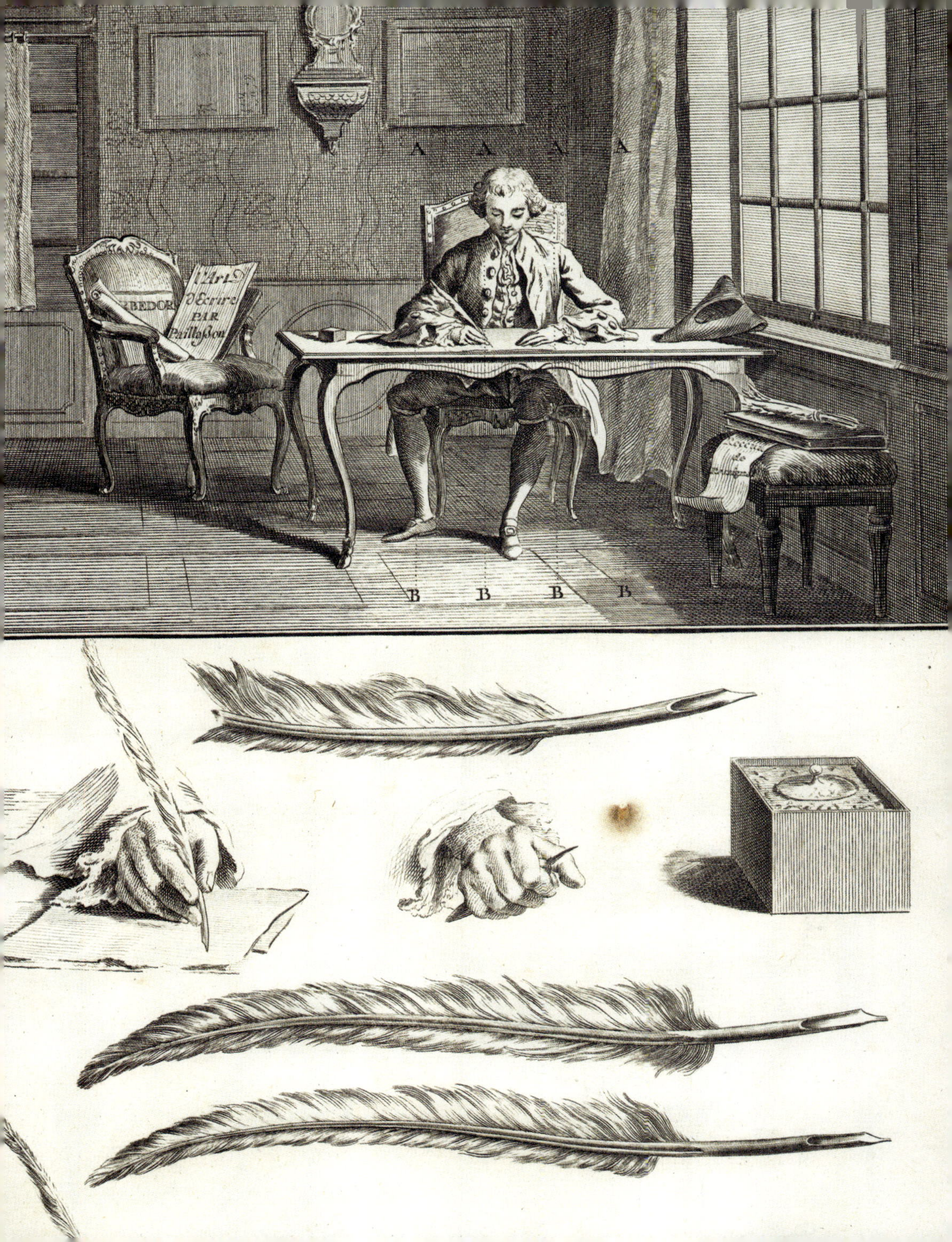
A A A A
l'Art d'Ecrire PAR Paillaßon
B B B B

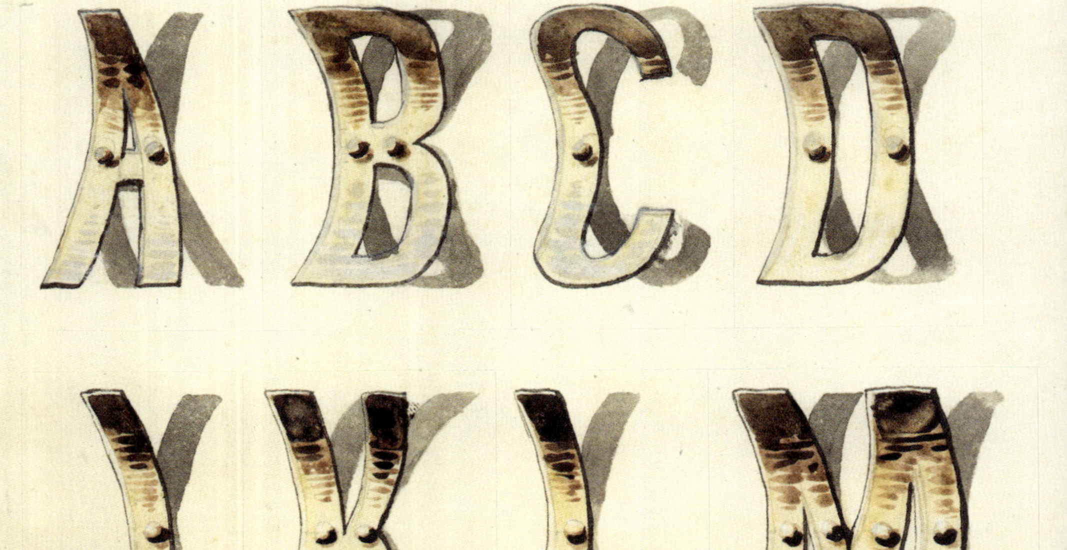
A B C D
J K L M
R S T U V

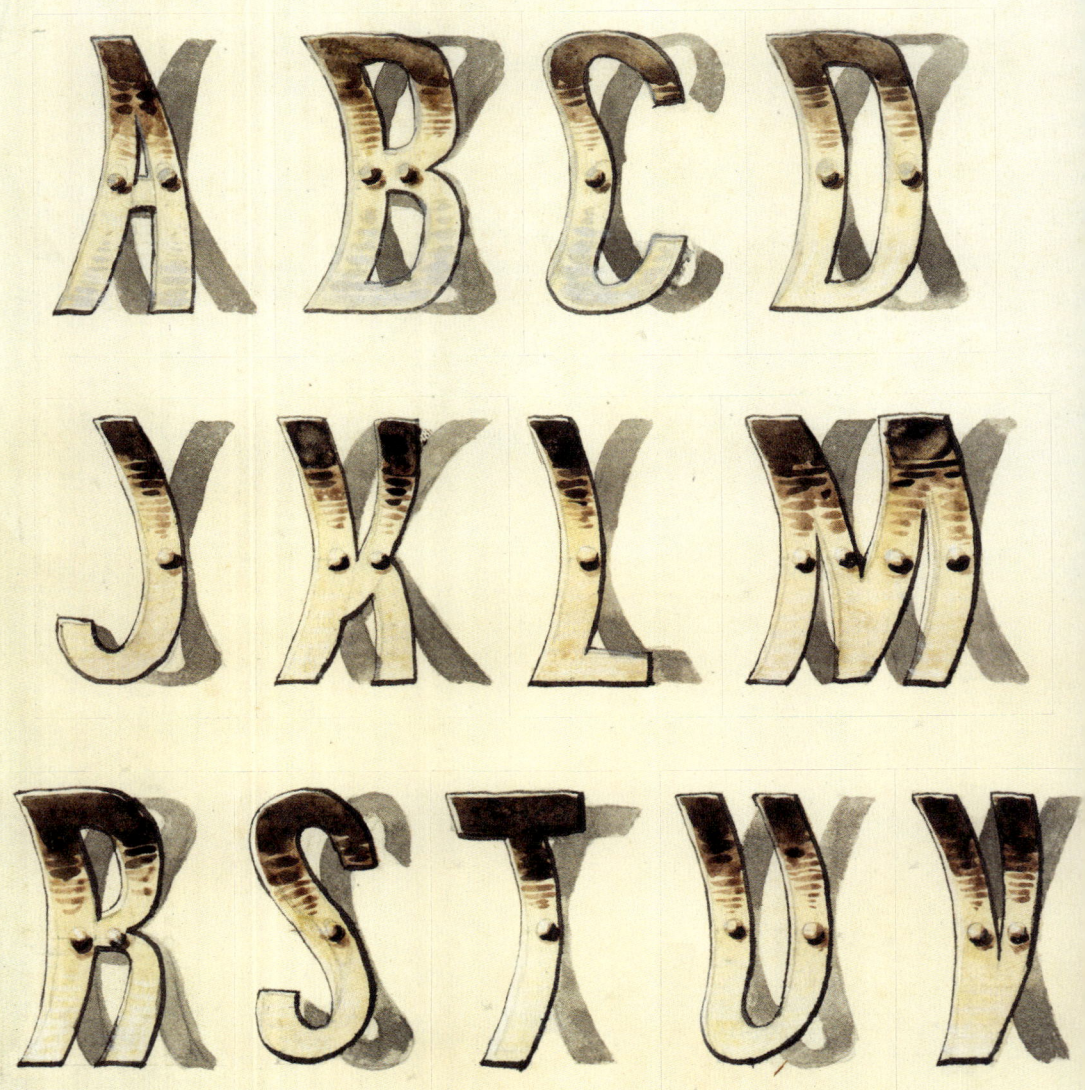

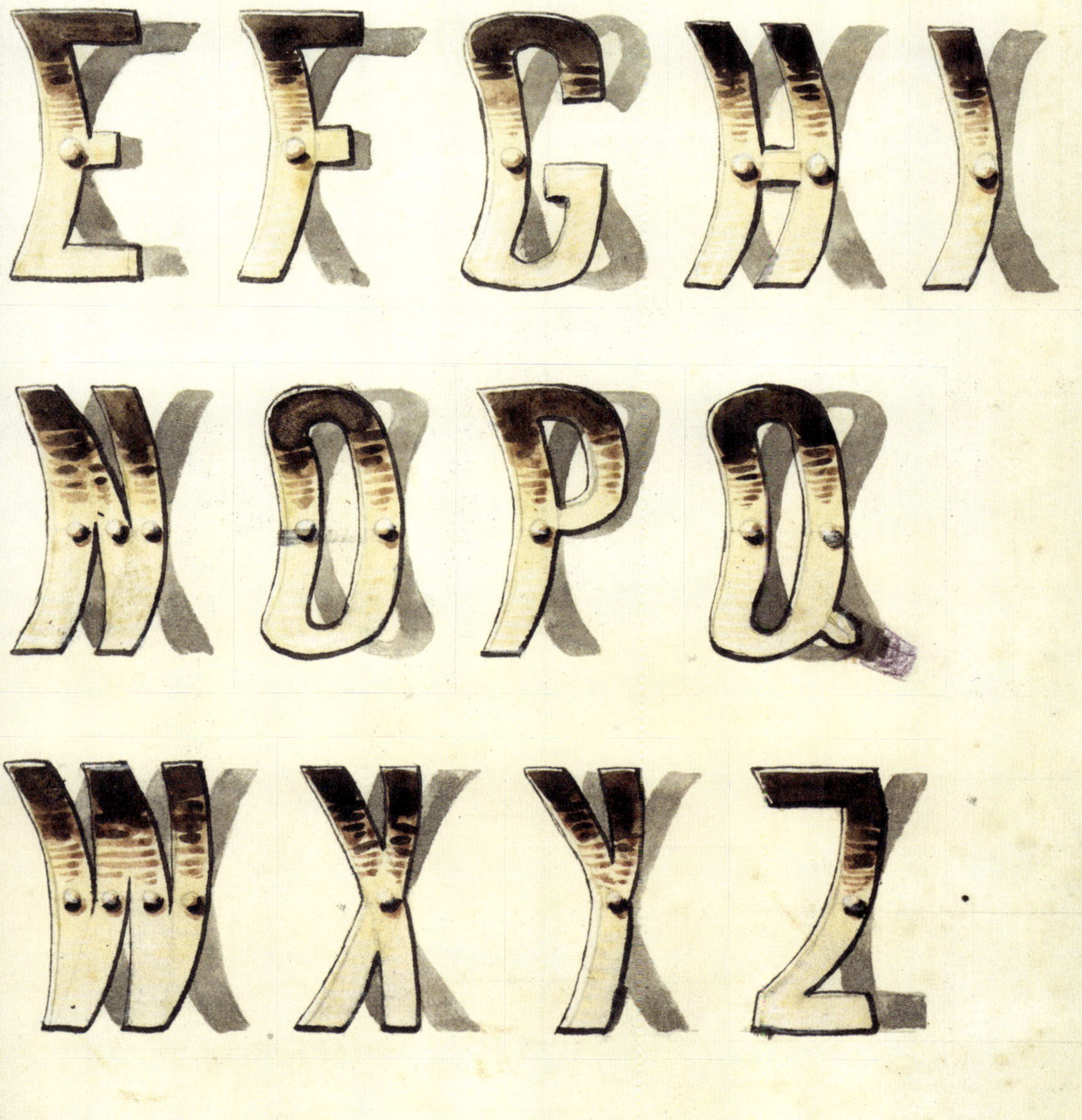
E F G H I
N O P Q
W X Y Z

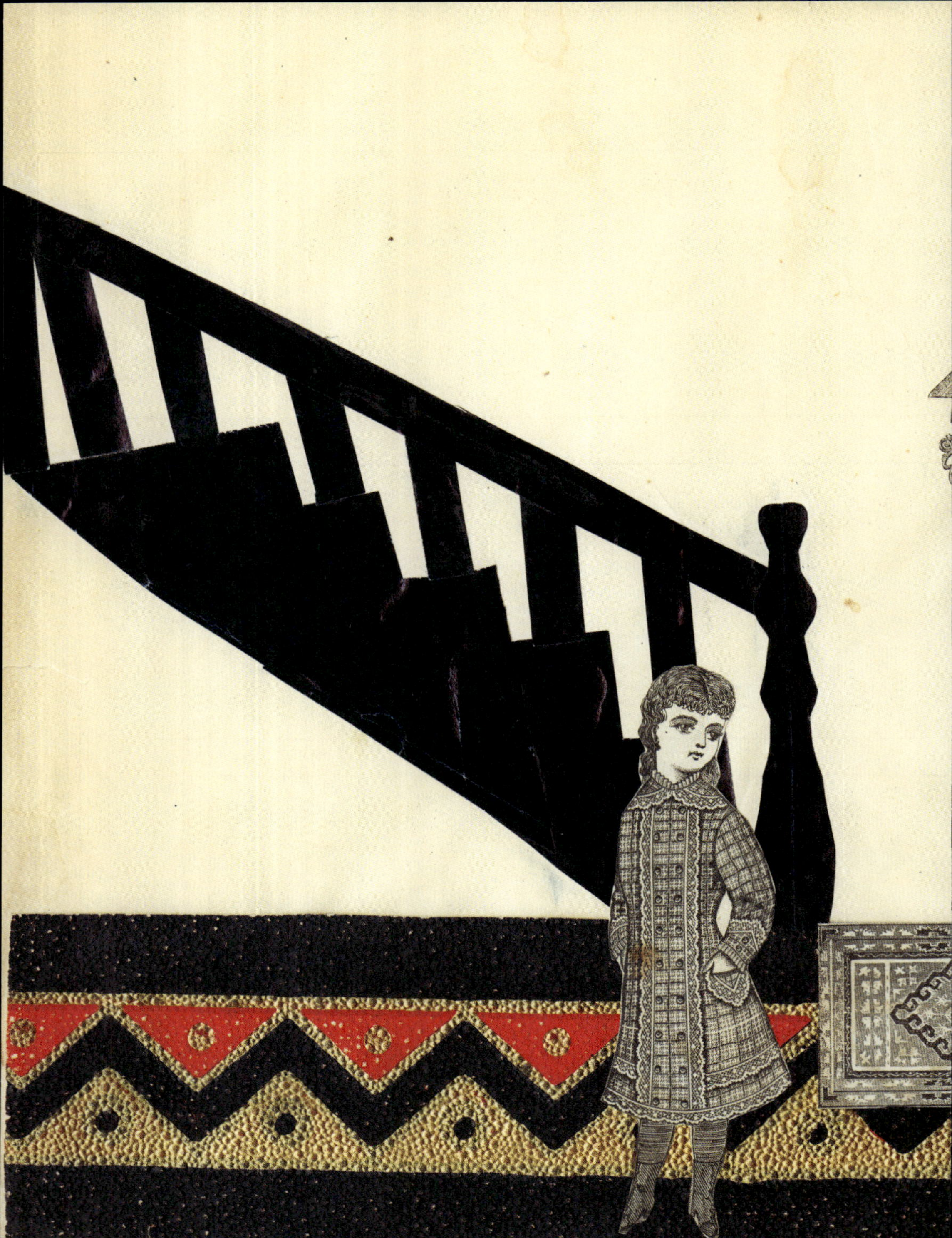

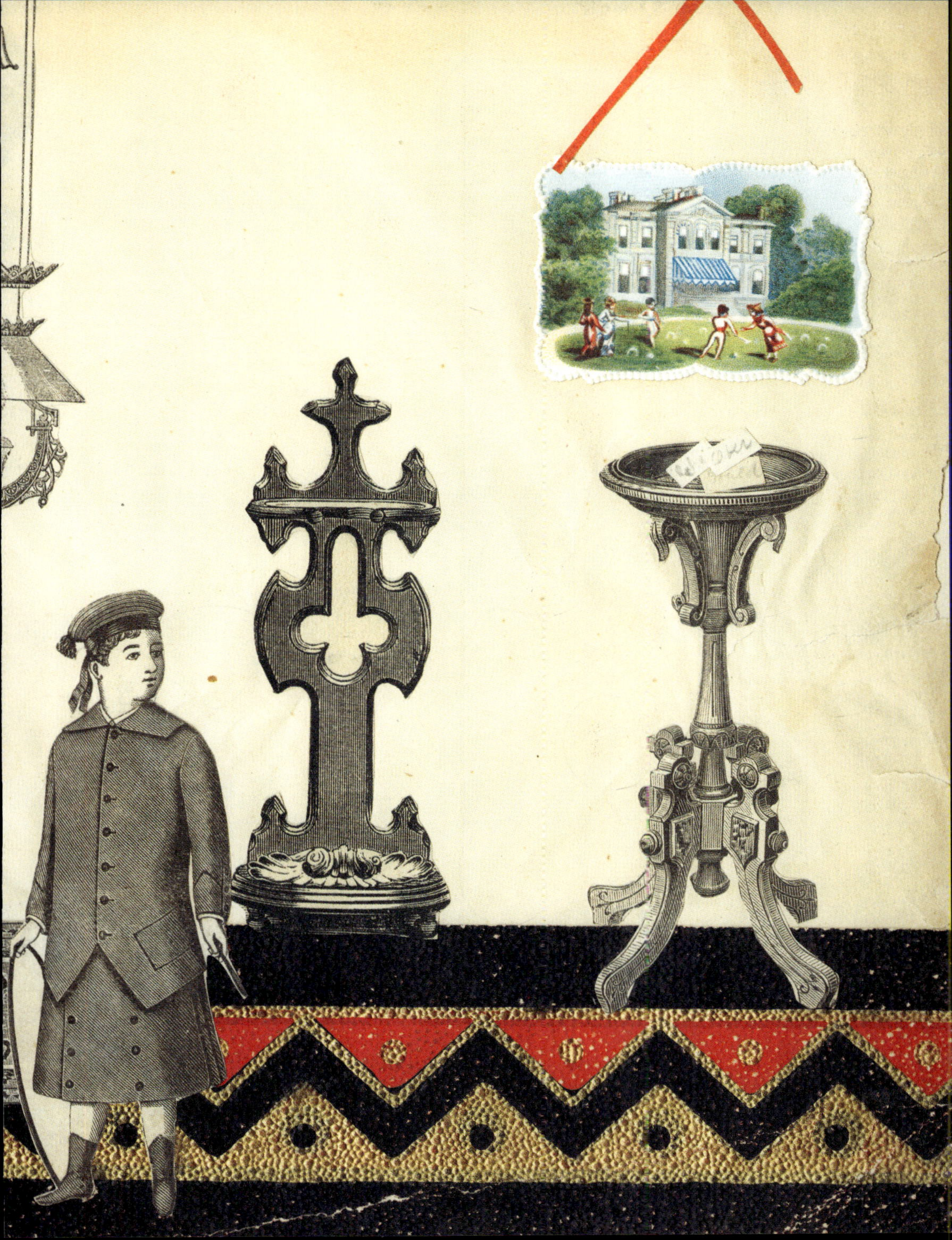

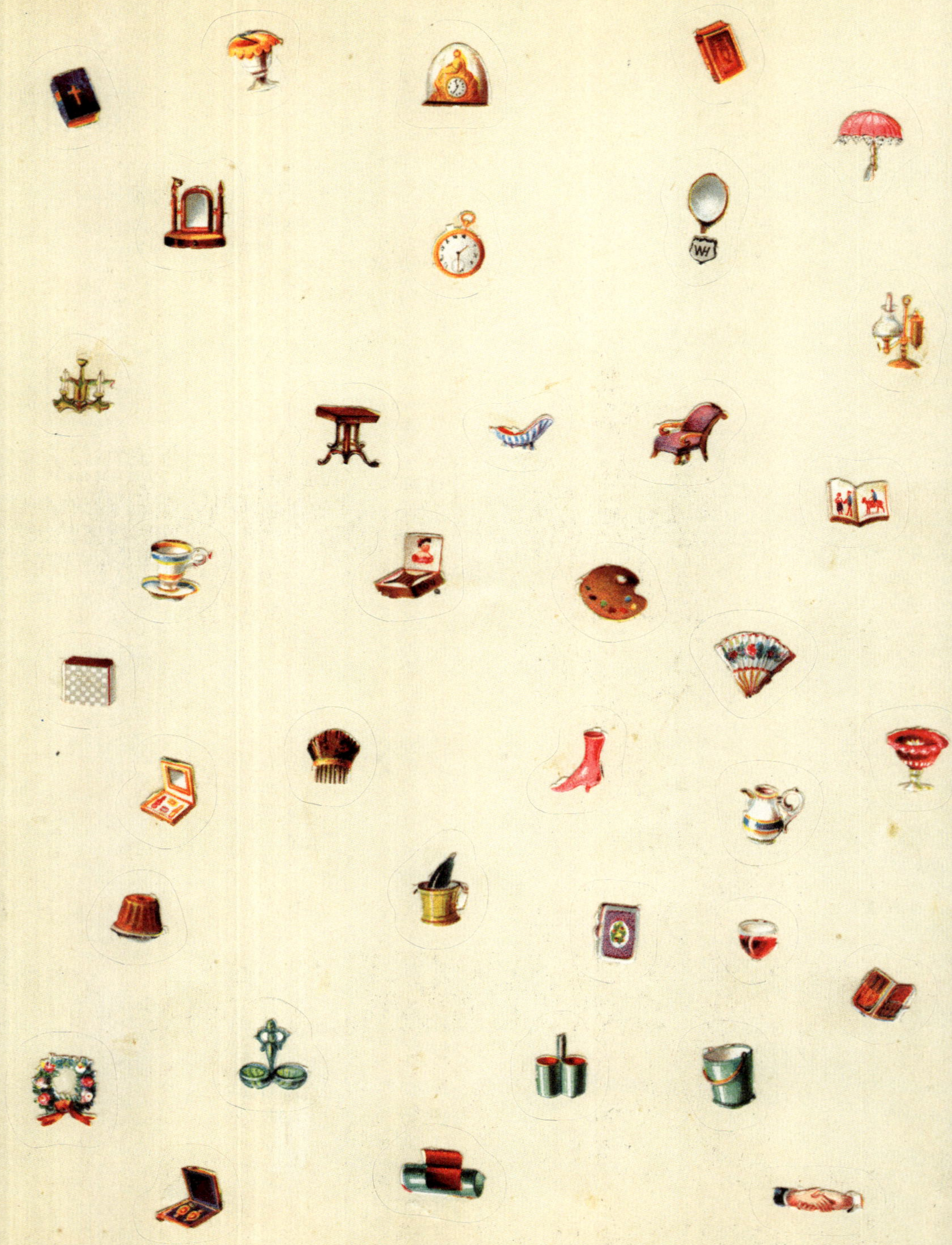

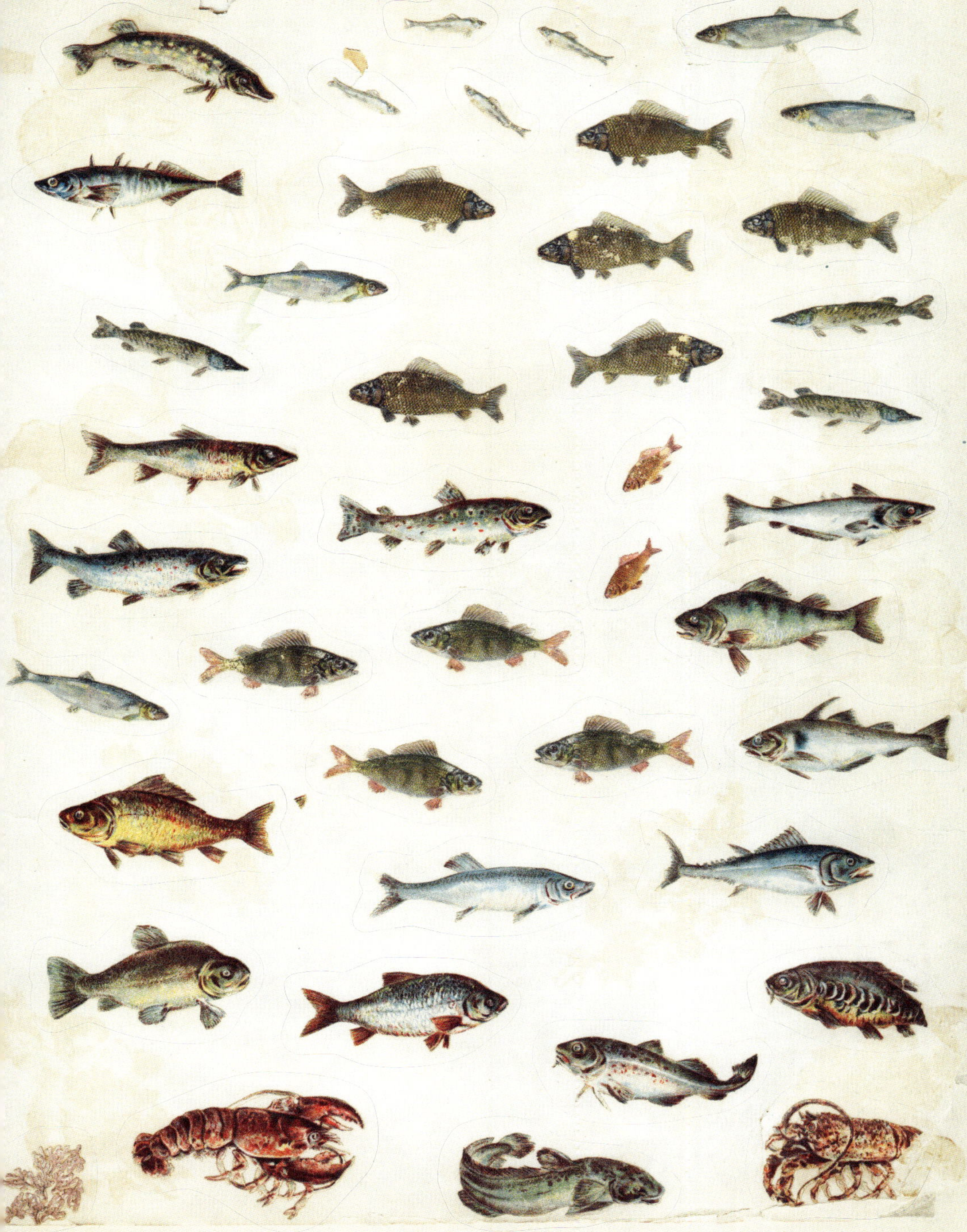

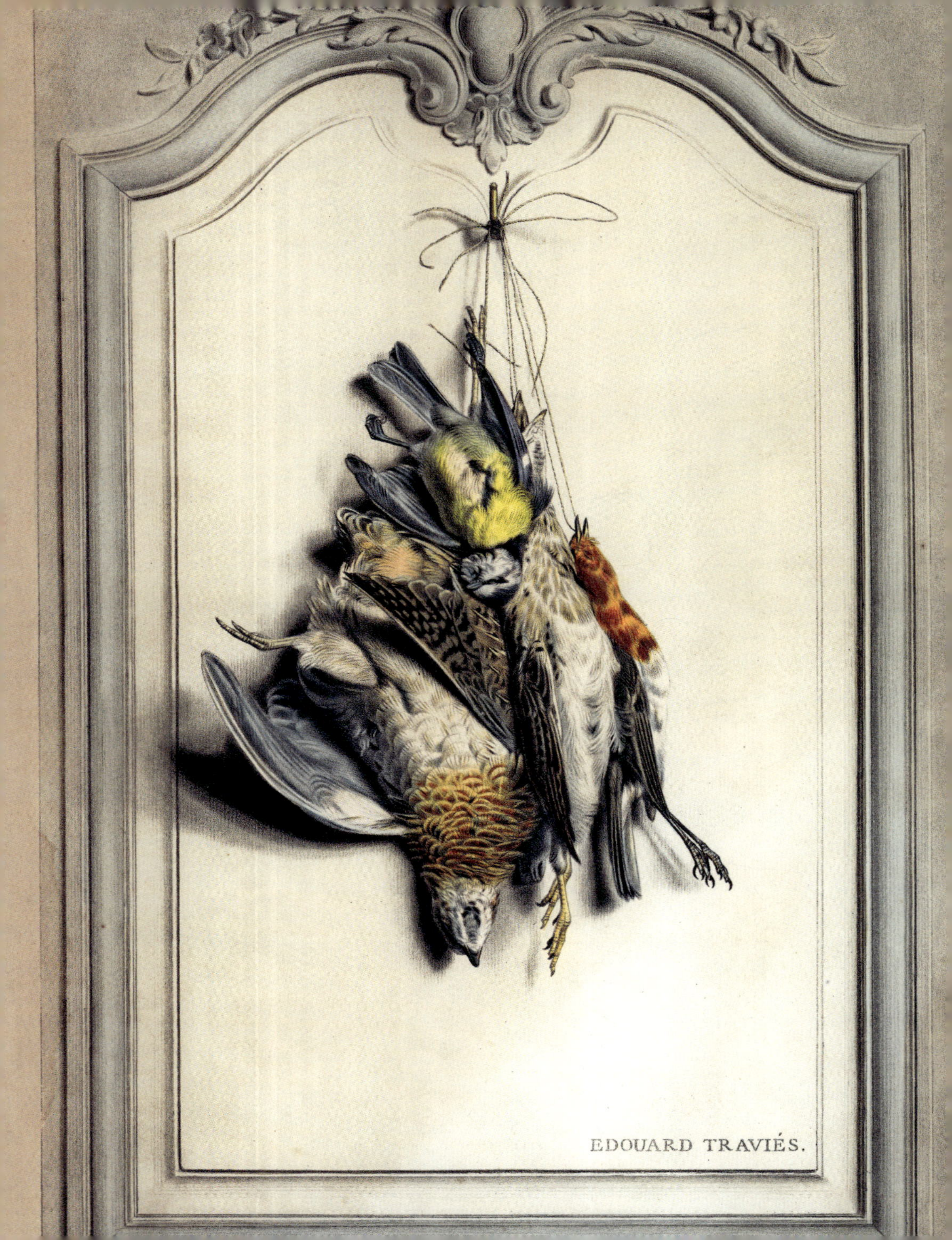
EDOUARD TRAVIÉS.

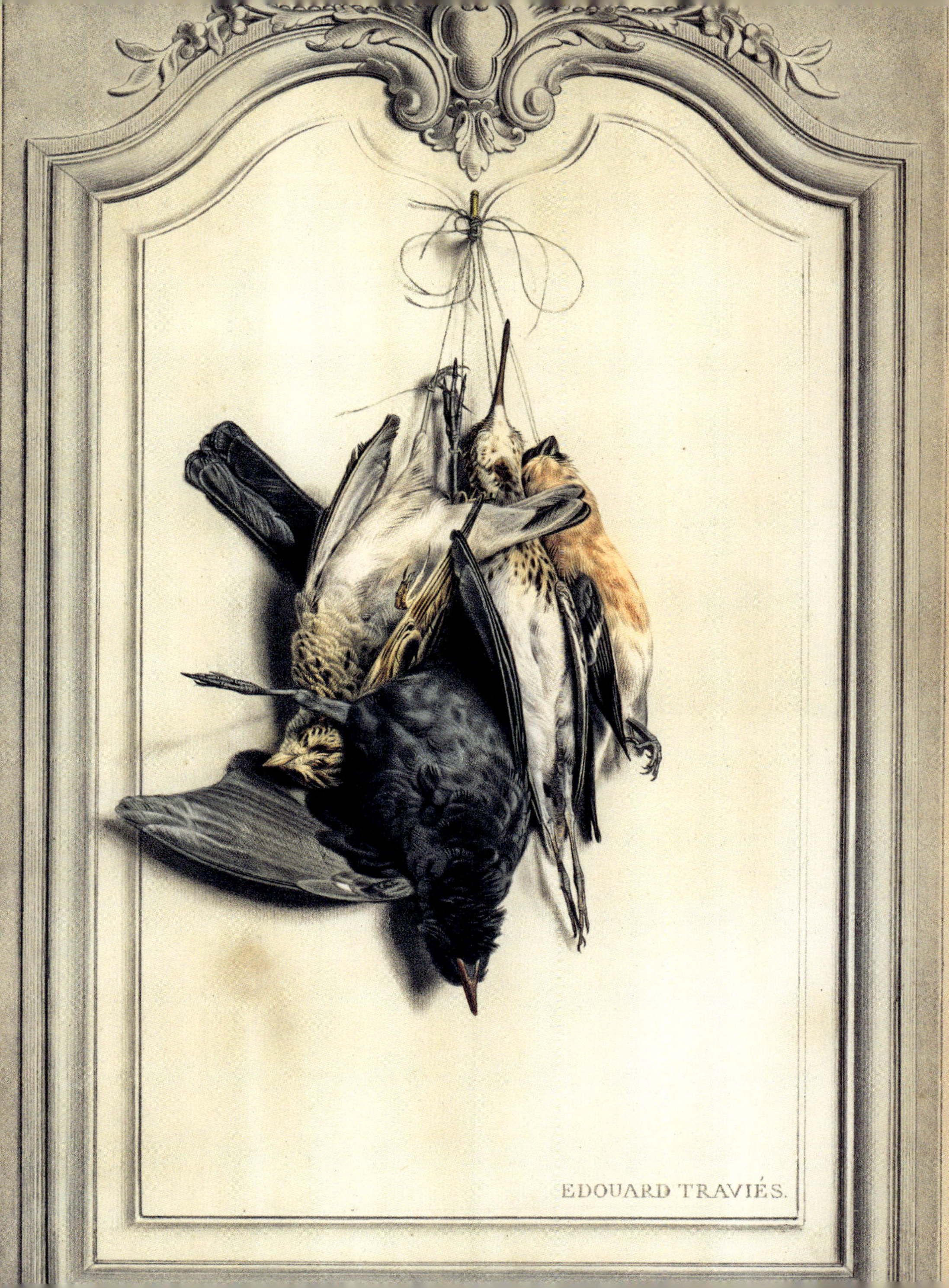
EDOUARD TRAVIÉS.

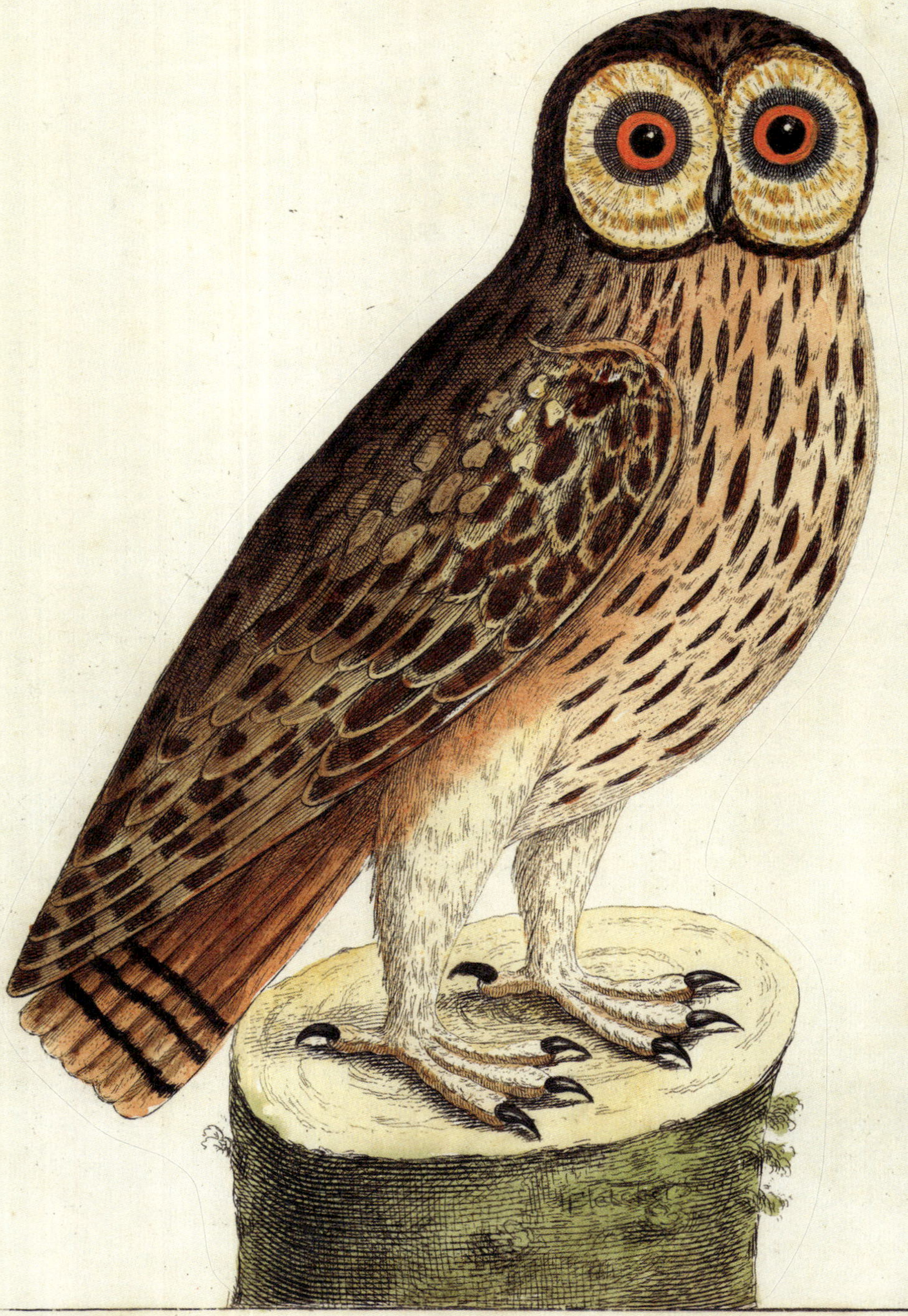

The great Brown Owl: *E. Albin Del. 173*

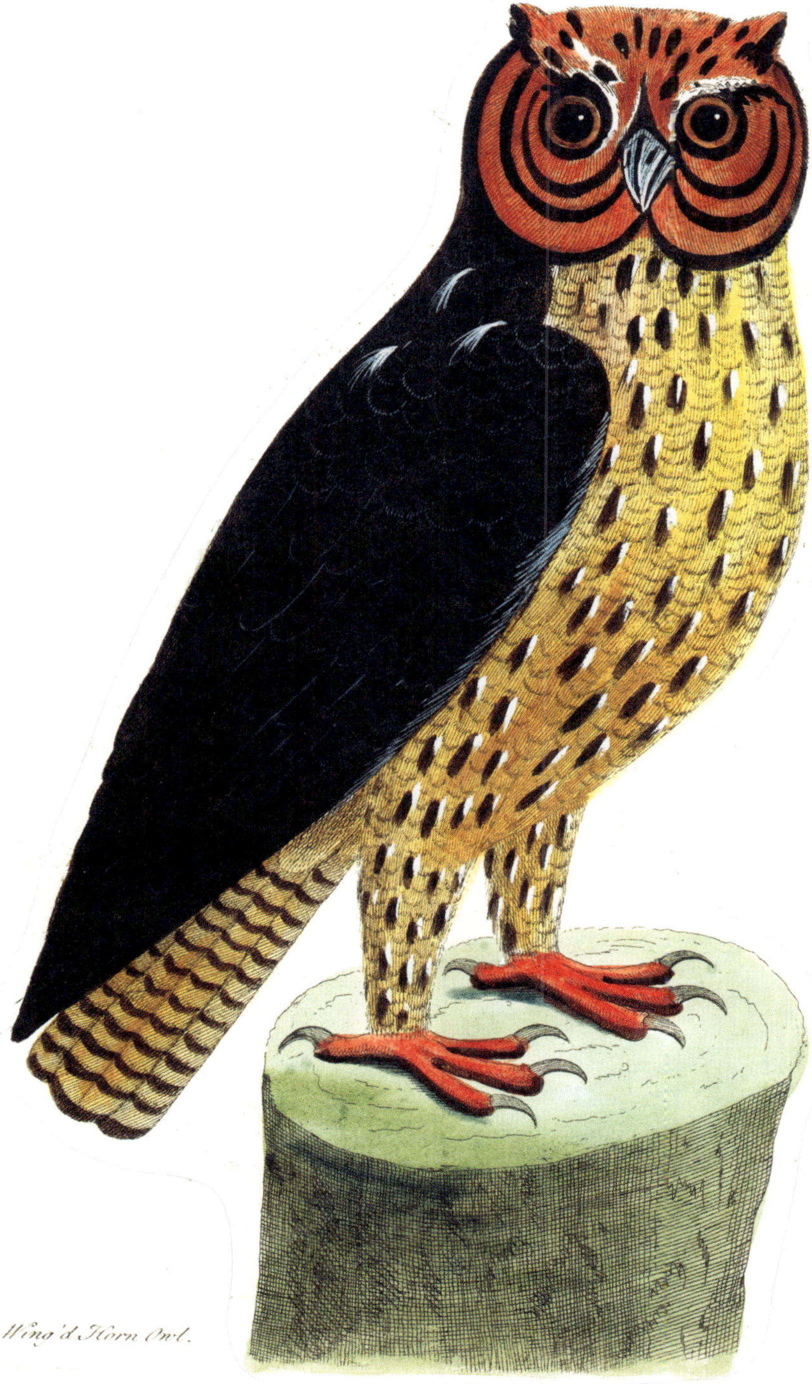

The Black Wing'd Horn Owl.

E. Albin Del: 1737.

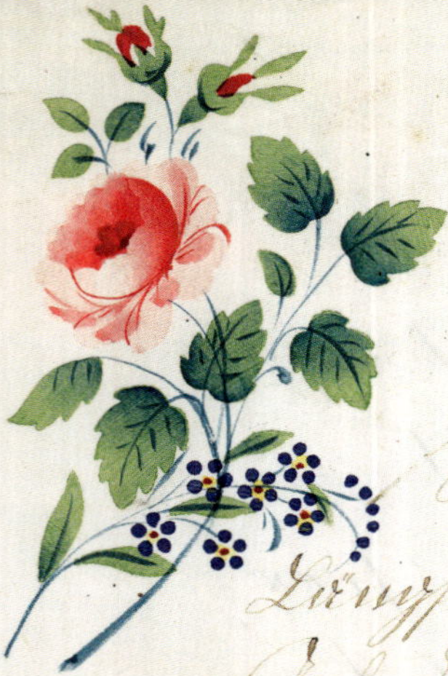

Weihnachtslied.

Willkommen schönes Weihnachtsfest
Längst freuten wir uns sehr
Auf dich, du bringst uns Wonn' und läßt
An Gaben uns nicht leer.

Da steht der schöne Tannenbaum
Mit hellem Lichterschein;
Da liegen auf des Tisches Raum
Geschenke groß und klein.

Die guten Eltern sind erfreut
An ihrer Kinderlust,
Und frei und froher schlaget heut
Ihr Herz in treuer Brust.

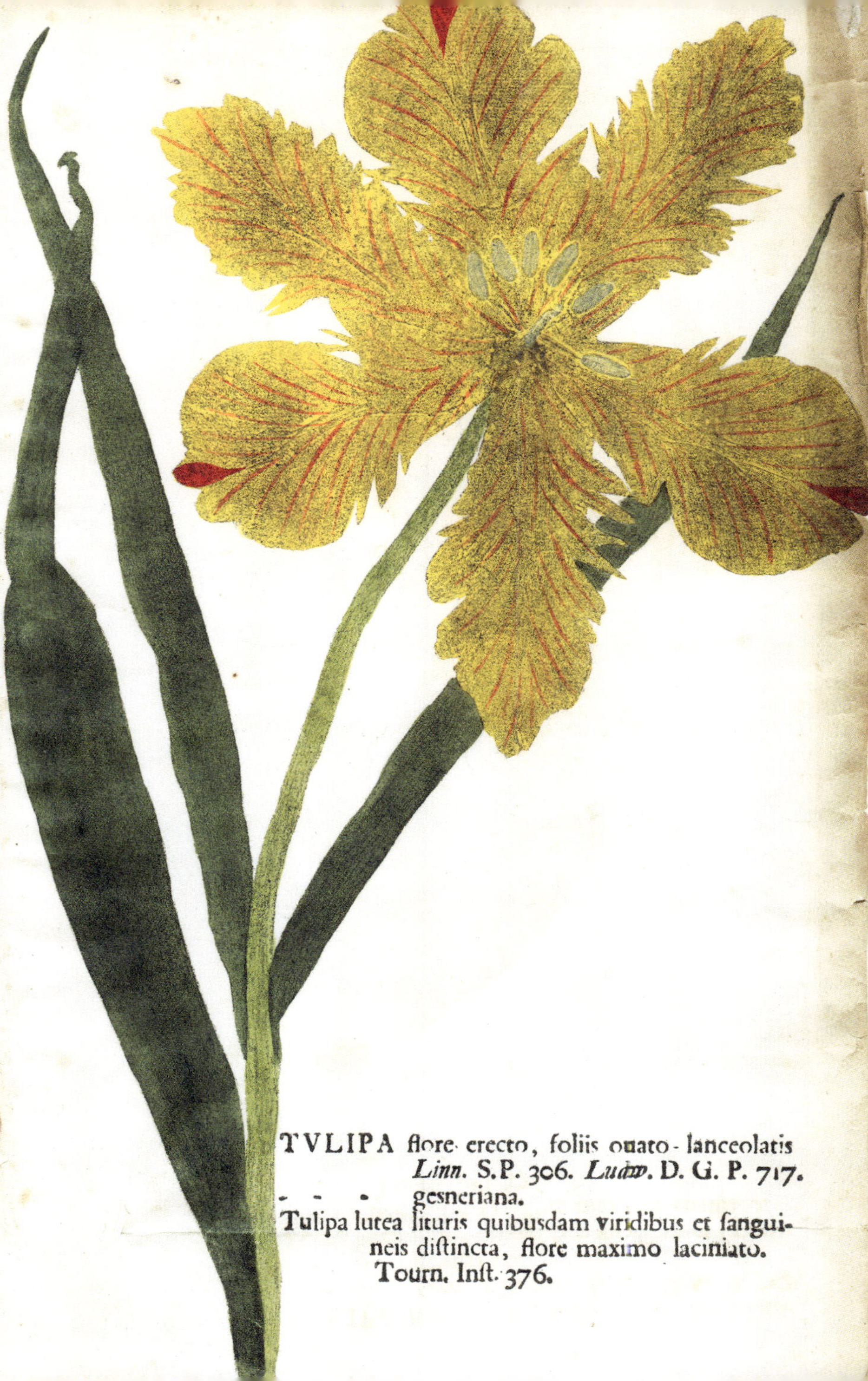

TVLIPA flore erecto, foliis ouato-lanceolatis
Linn. S.P. 306. *Ludw.* D. G. P. 717.
- - - gesneriana.

Tulipa lutea lituris quibusdam viridibus et ſanguineis diſtincta, flore maximo laciniato.
Tourn. Inſt. 376.

T 75.

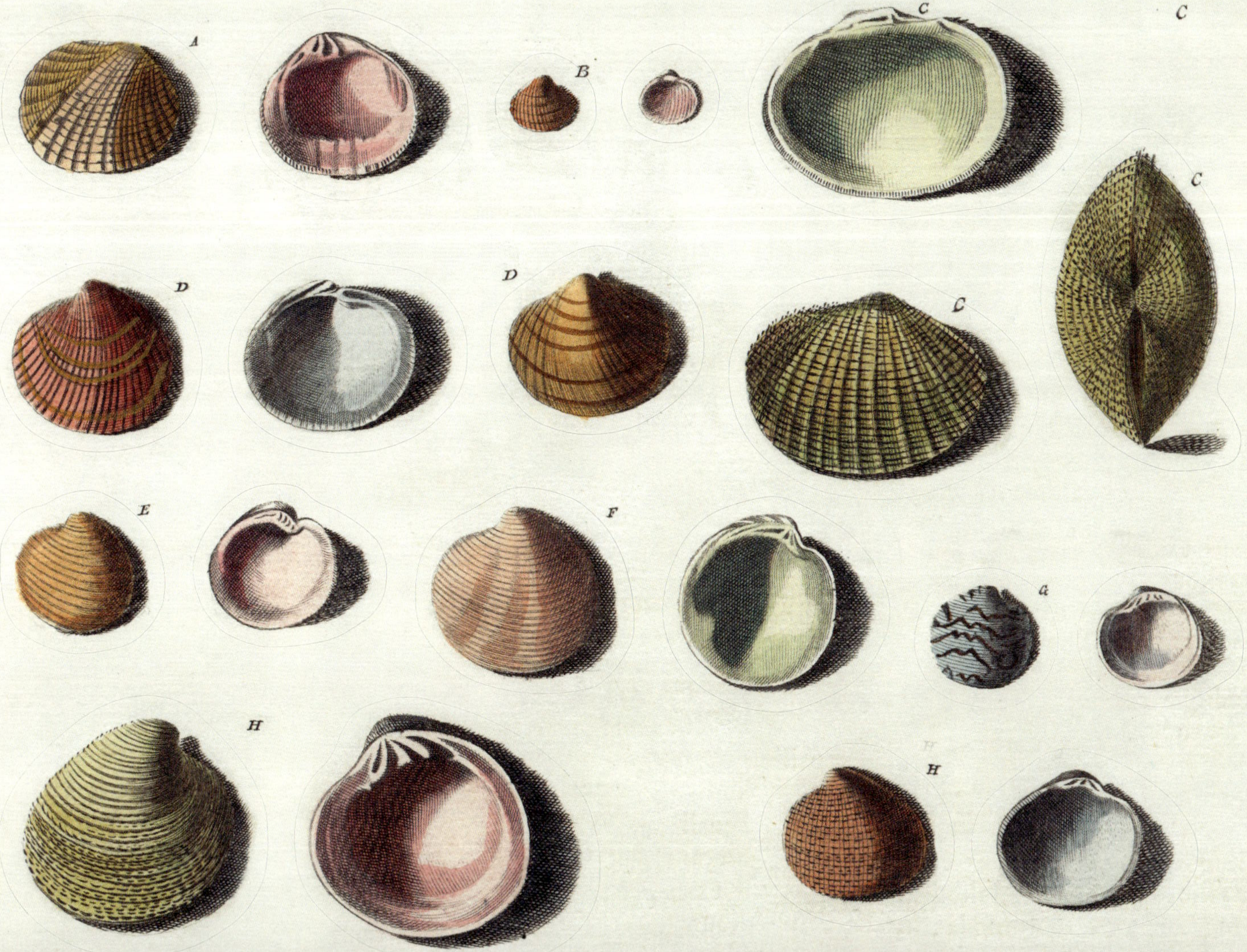

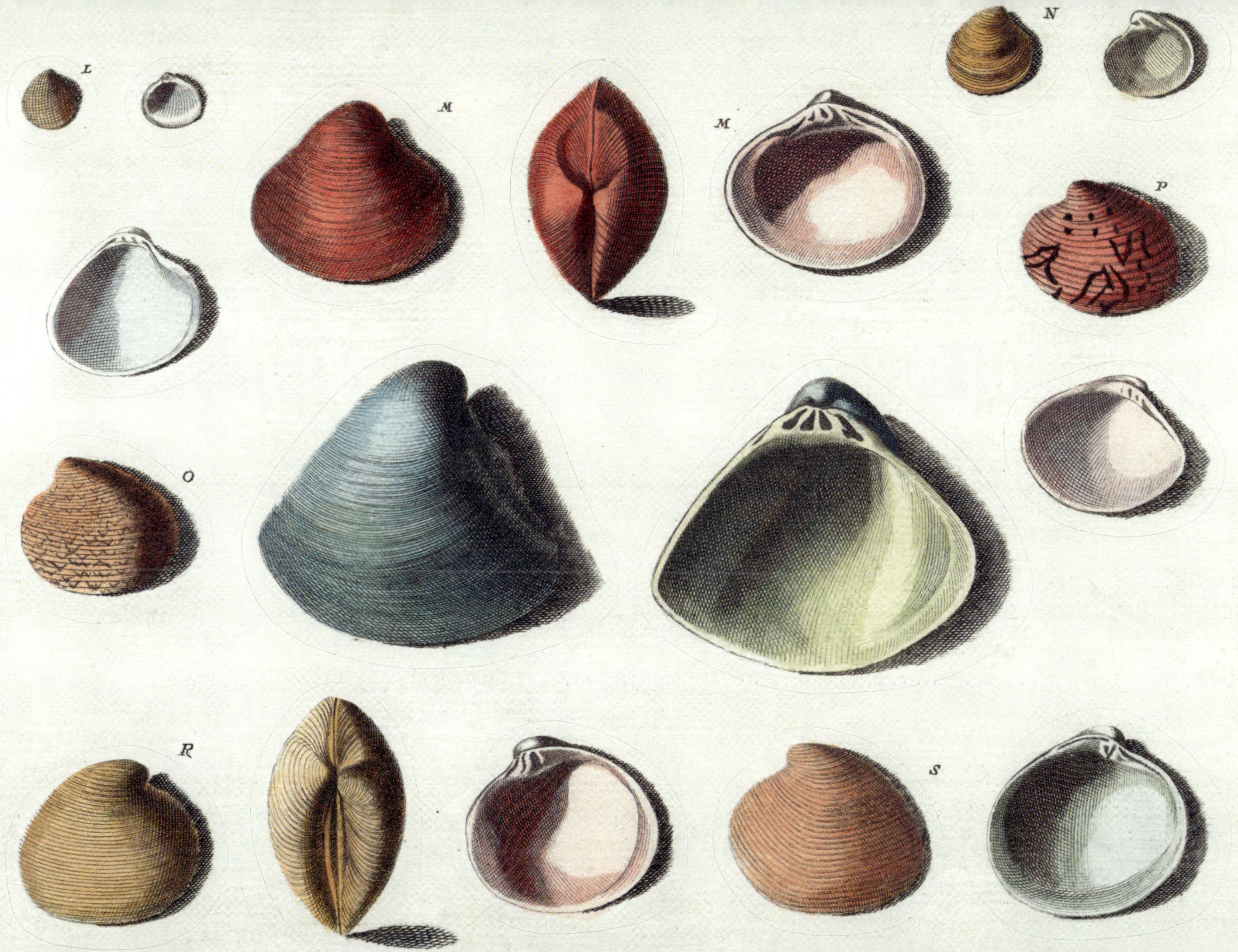

Ios. Menabuoni del   P. Ant. Pazzi sc.

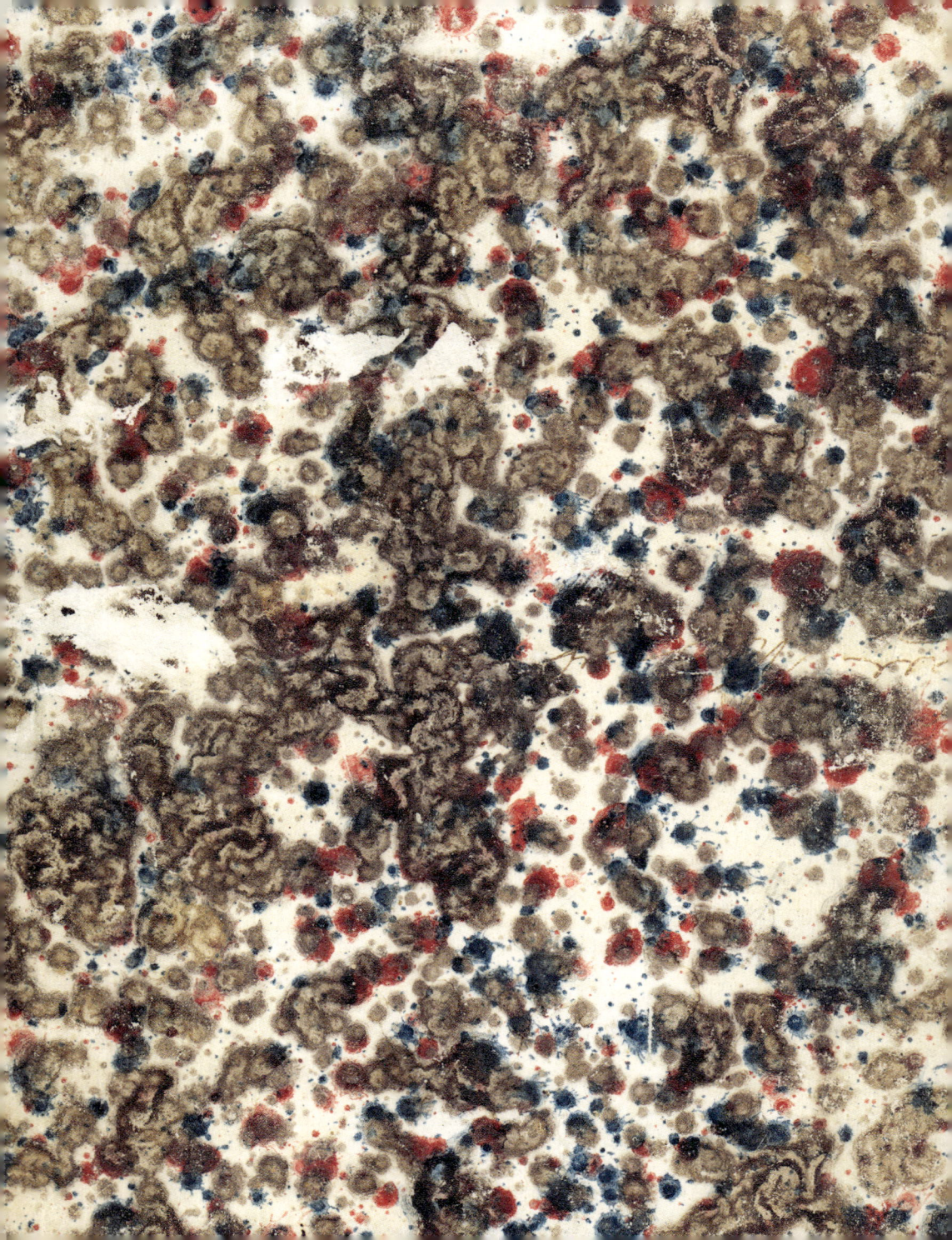

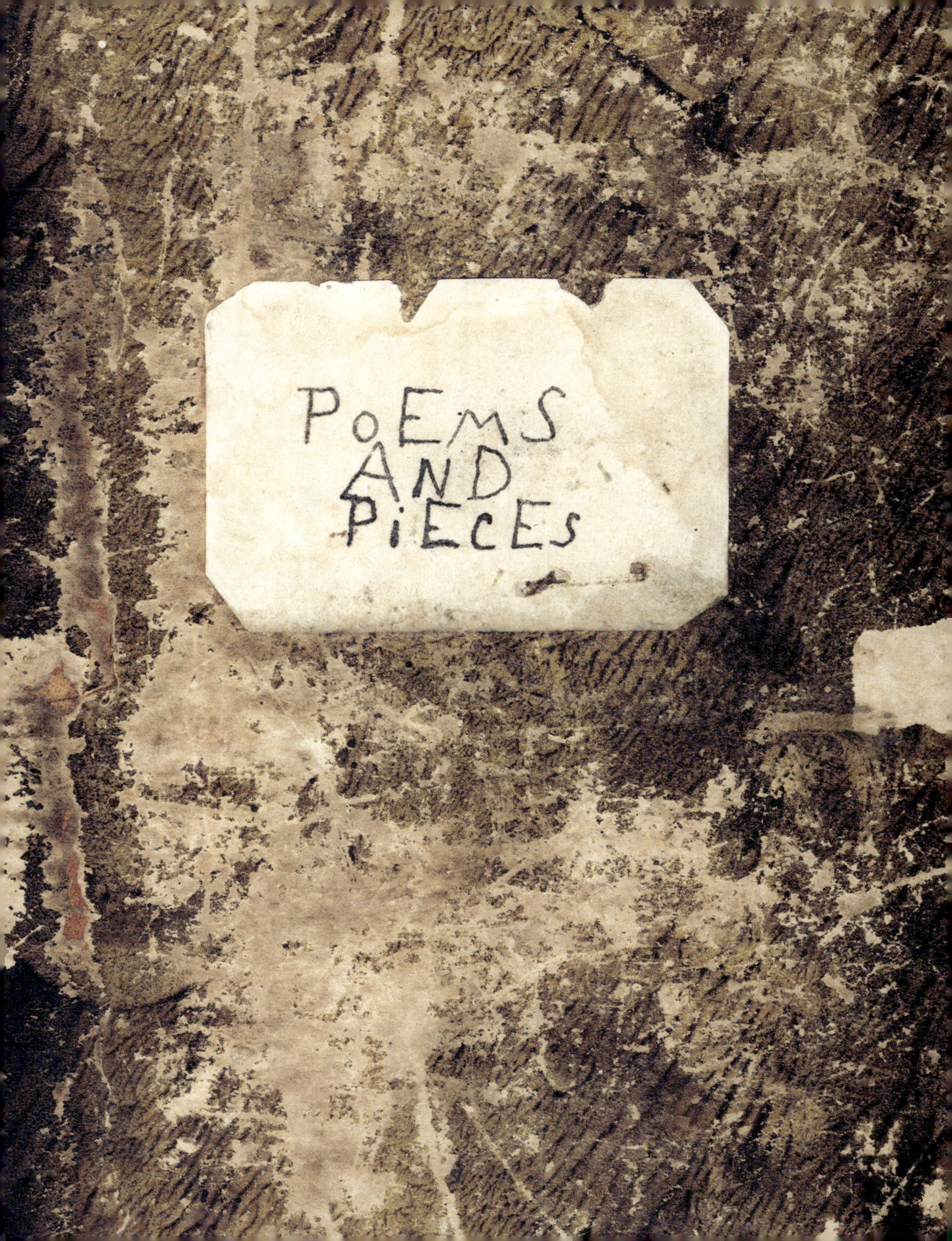
POEMS
AND
PIECES

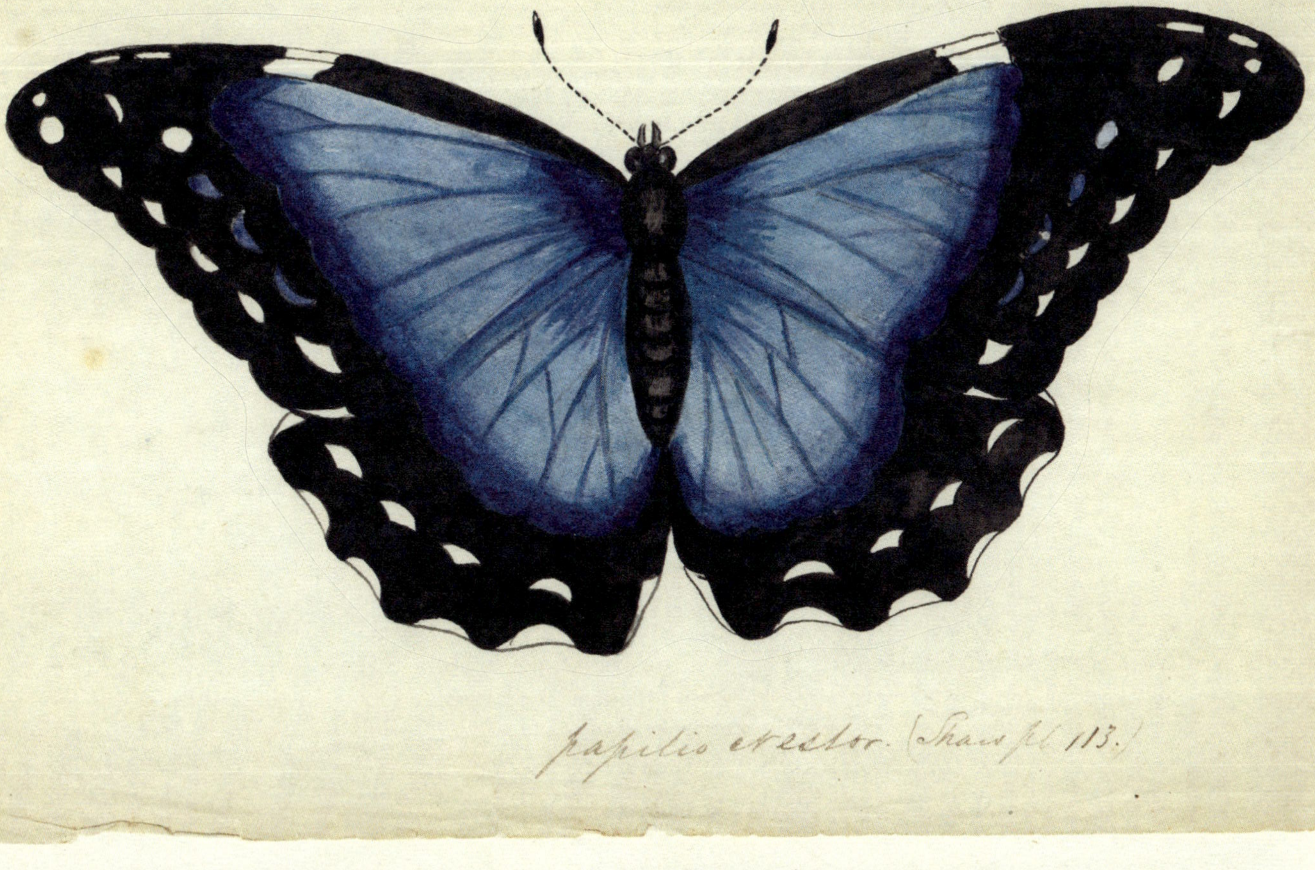

papilio erestor. (Shaw pl 113.)

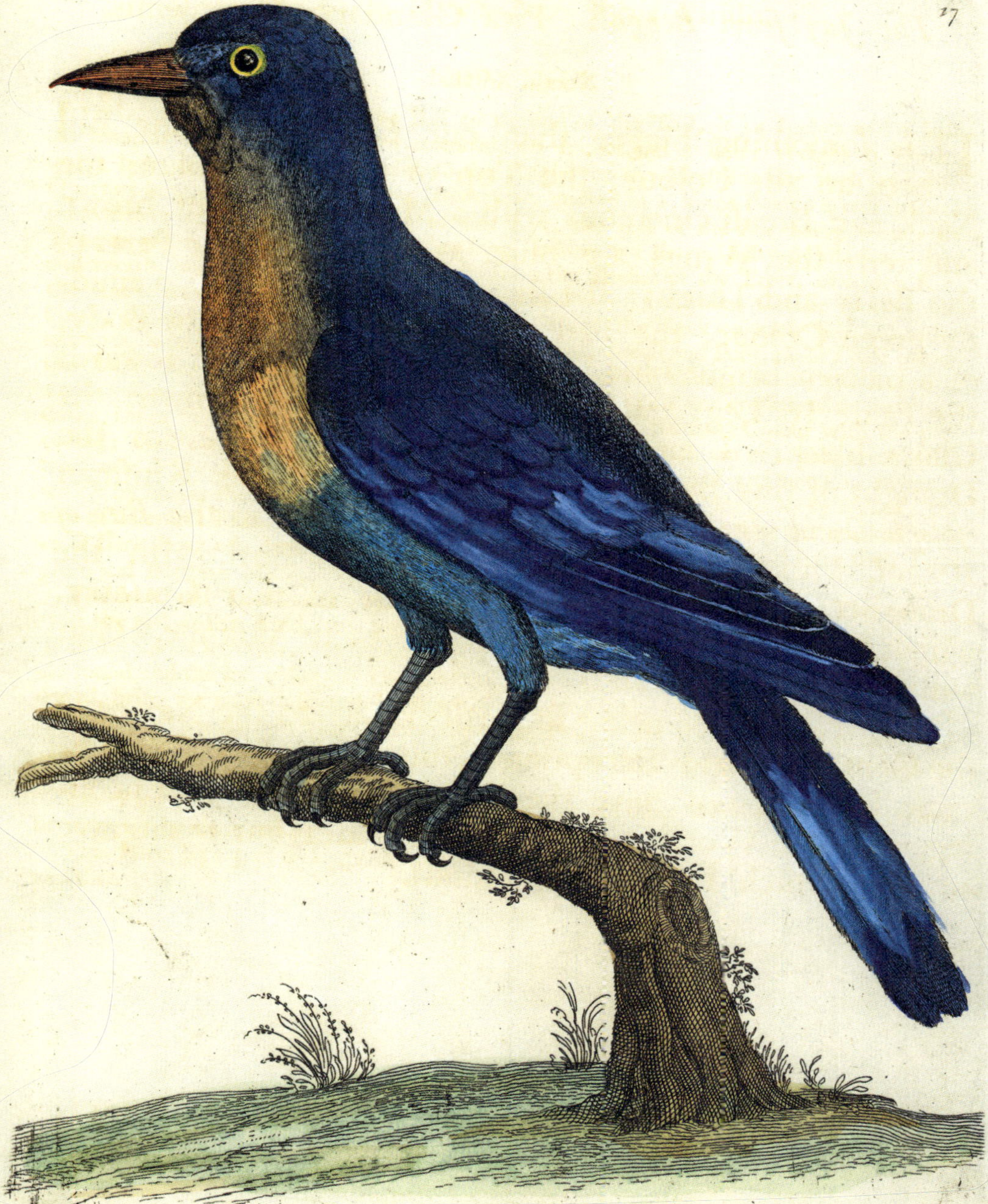

Eliz. Albin delin. Pica Glandaria Capensis. The Jay from the Cape of Good Hope.

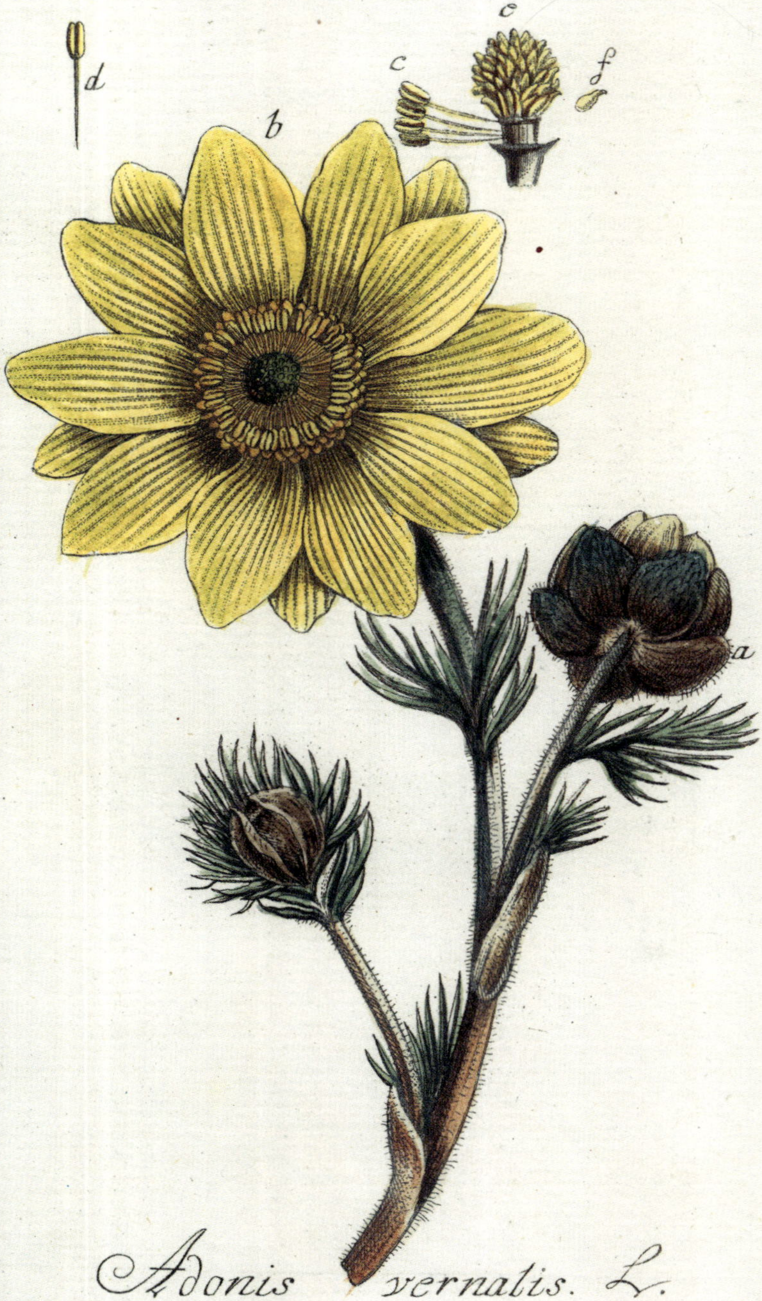

Adonis vernalis. L.

B. Thanner. del. J. C. Claußner. sc.

T.XIX.

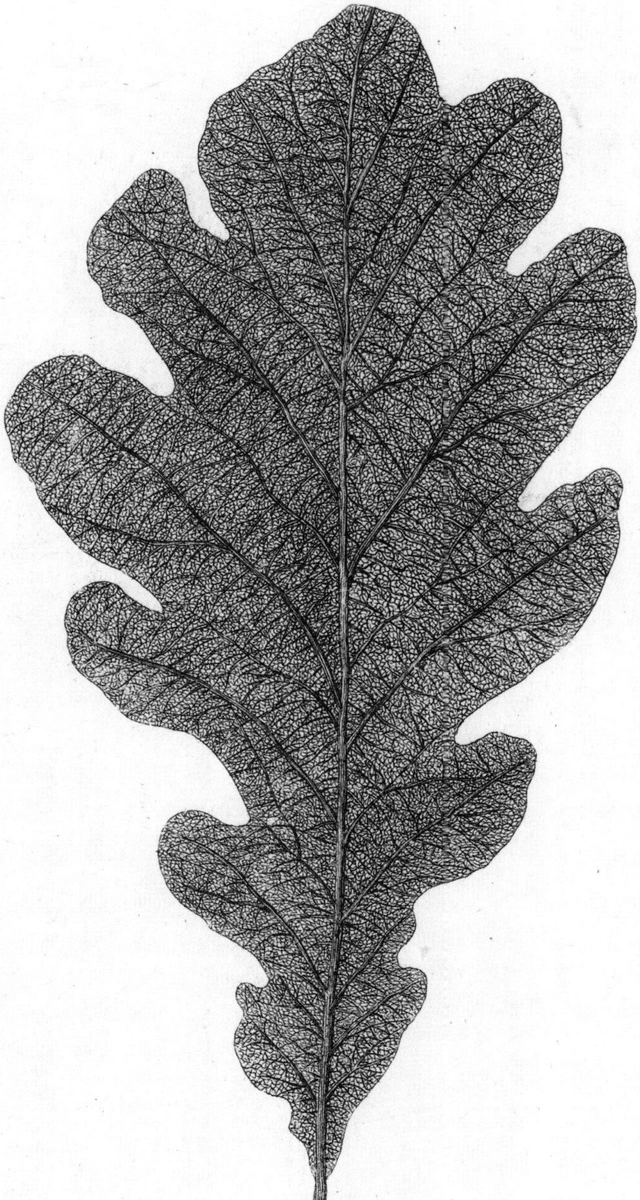

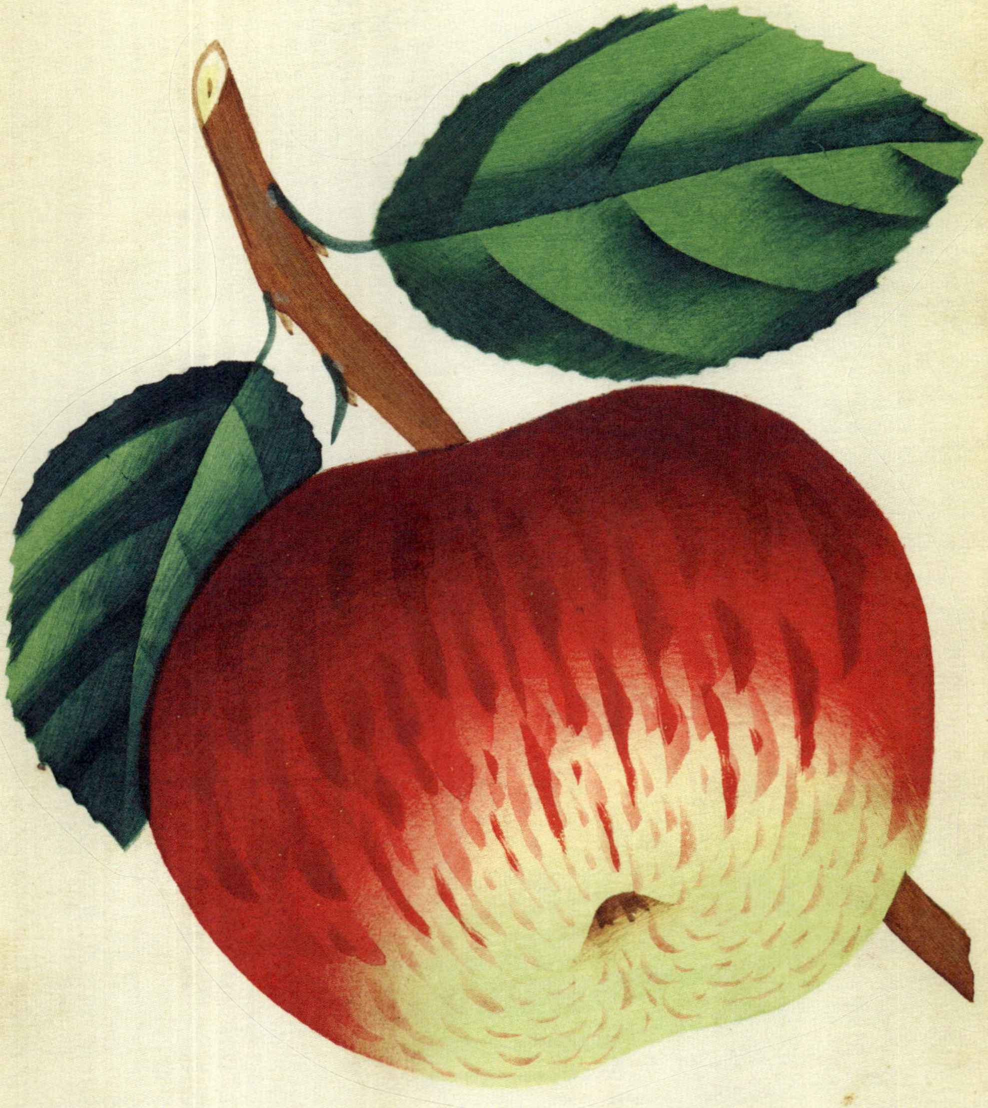

DUCHESS OF OLDENBURG—RUSSIAN

Large size flavor slightly sub,acid. A hardy Russian variety indispensable in the North. One of the most desirable sorts for market or for garden and domestic use September.

M. BRUNSWICK & CO. B ROCHESTER, N. Y.

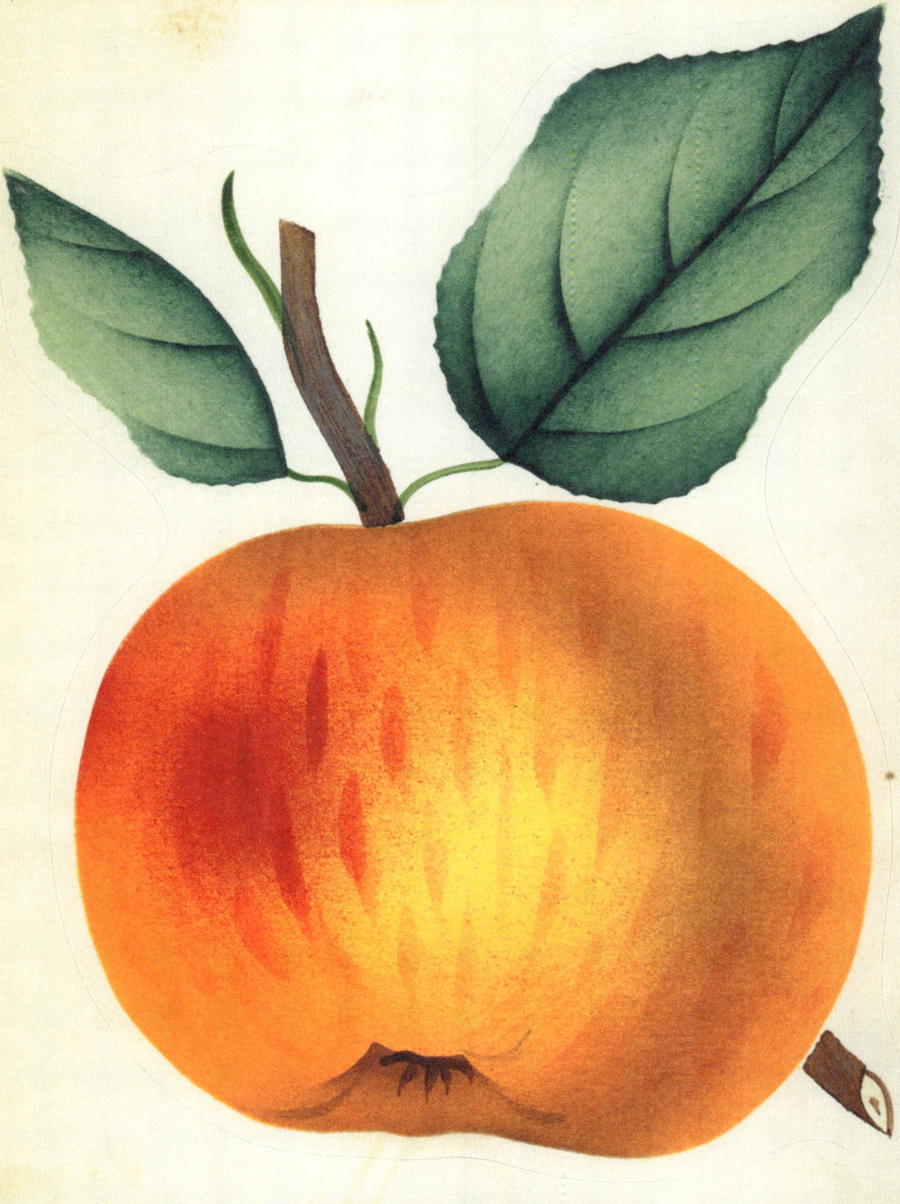

GRAVENSTEIN.

A superb looking German Apple, which originated in Gravenstein in Holstein, and is thought one of the finest apples of the North of Europe. Tree very vigorous, spreading, forming a large head. Very productive, an early bearer. Flesh tender and crisp, with a high-flavored, somewhat aromatic taste. Very good. September and October.

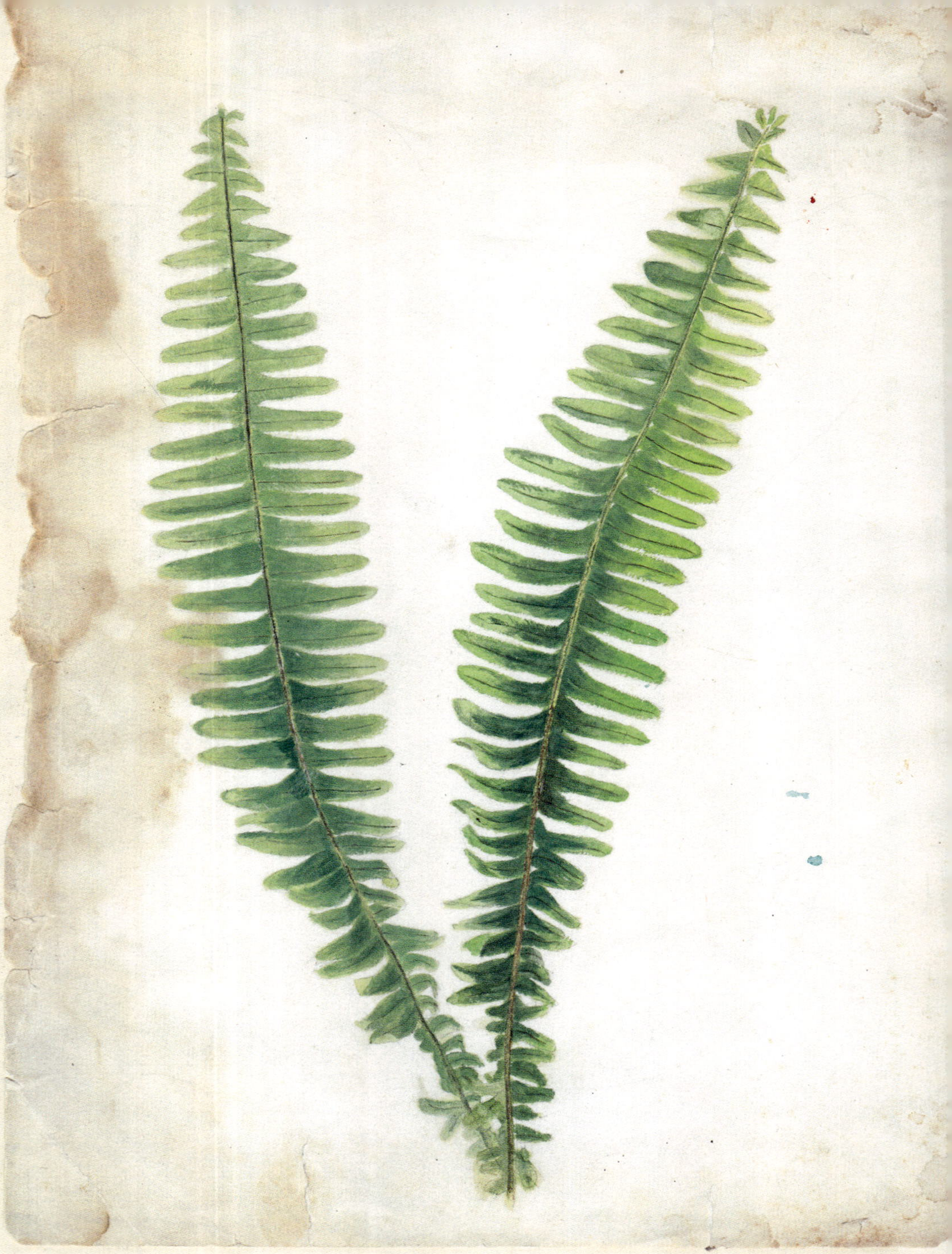

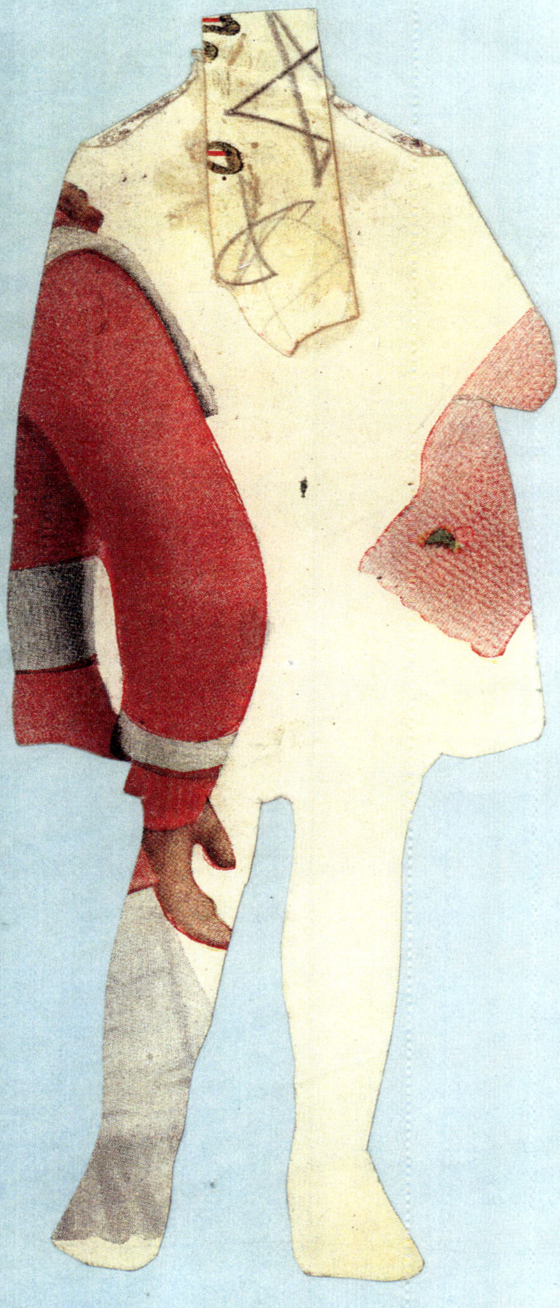

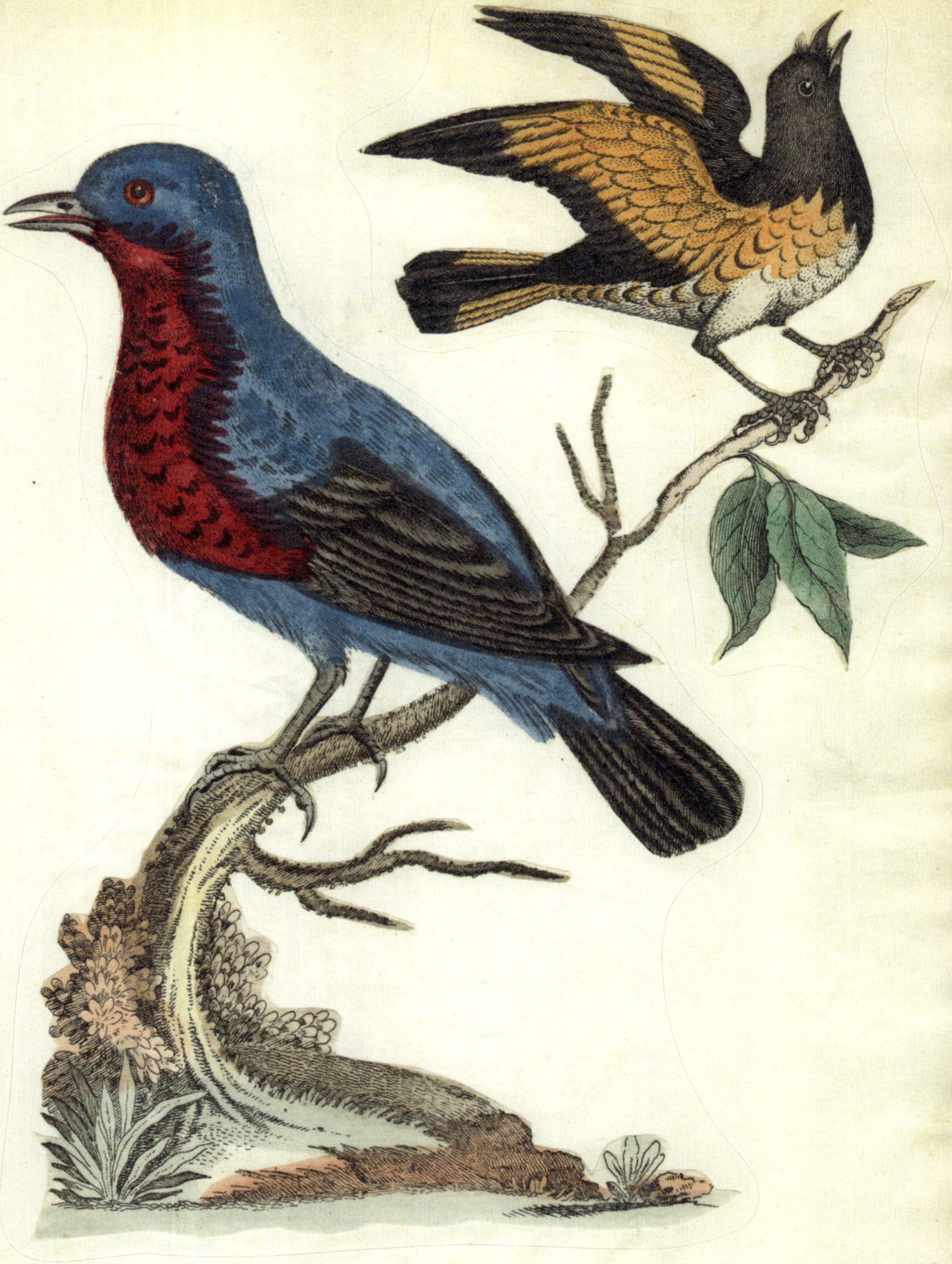

The Purple breasted blue Manakin.

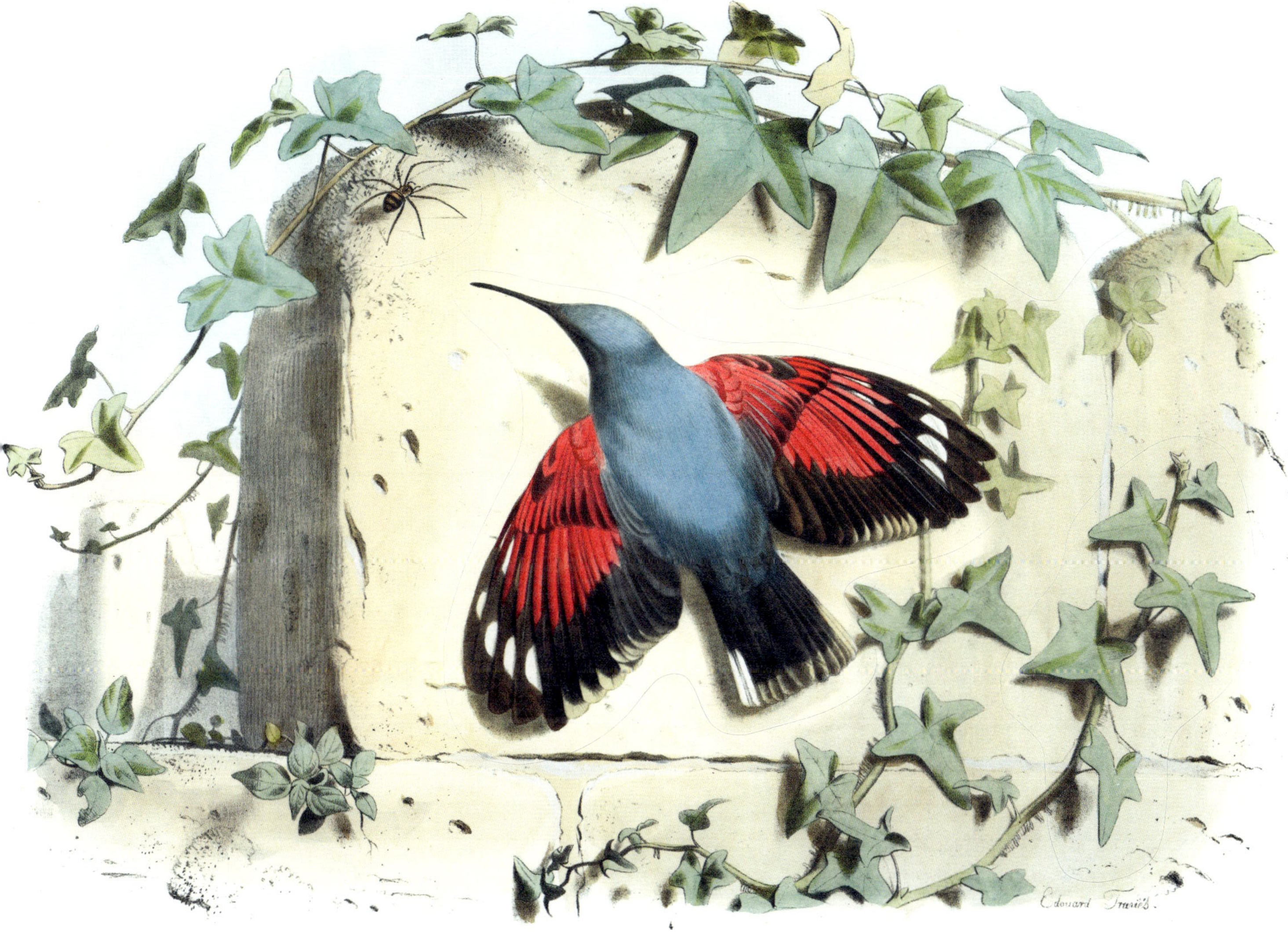

4

Le Grimpereau de muraille

Certhia muraria (Linnée) Grandeur naturelle

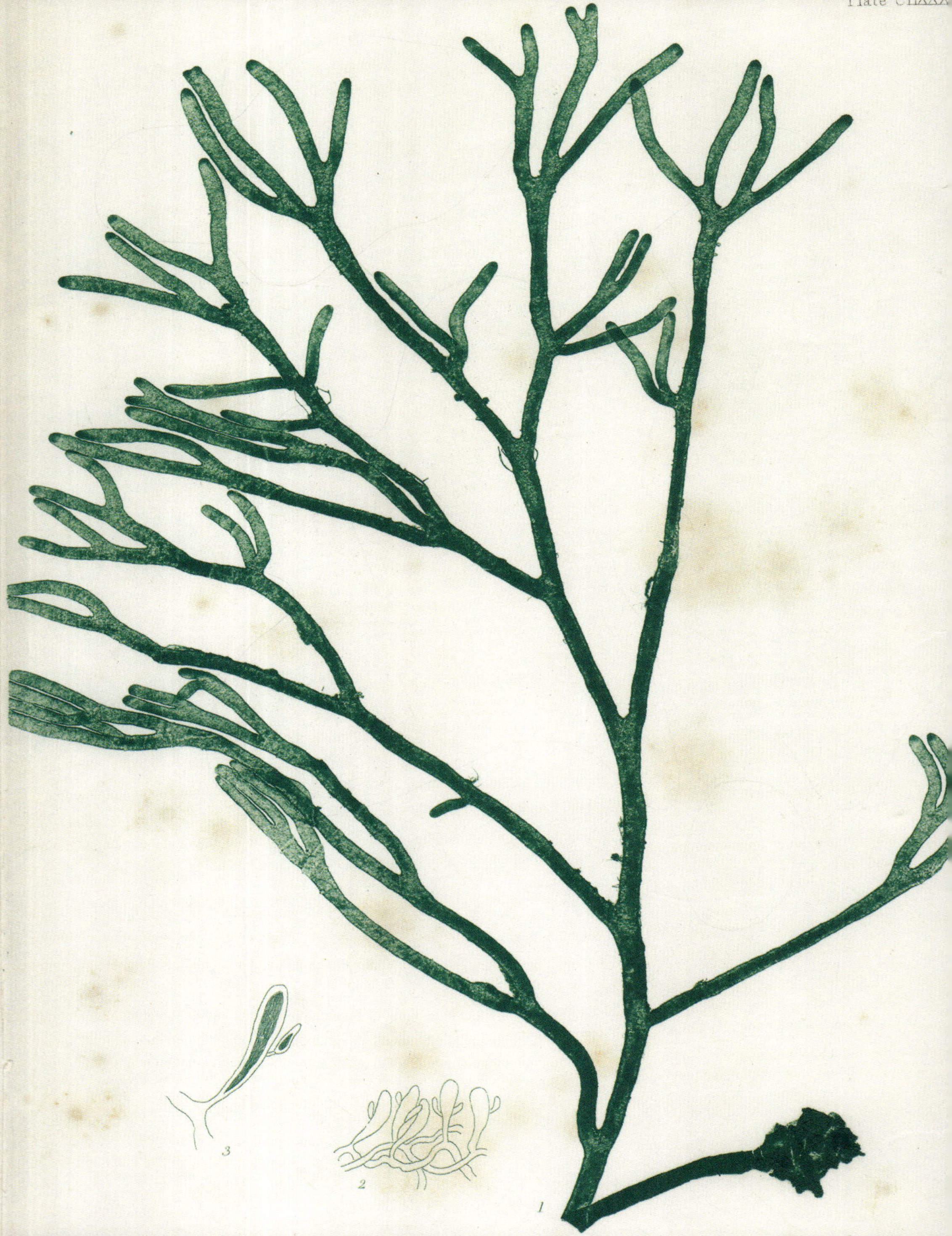
3
2
1

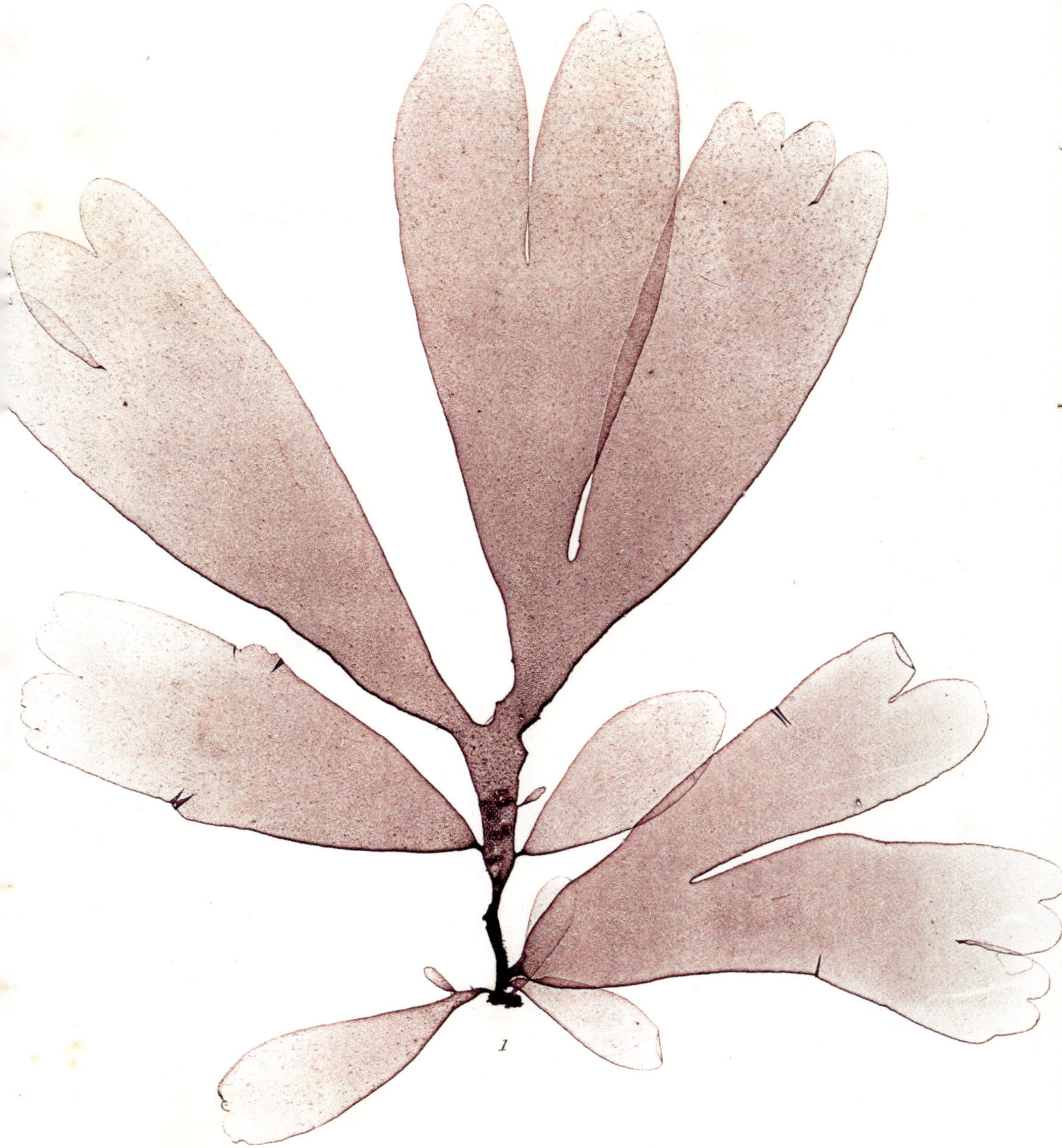

1

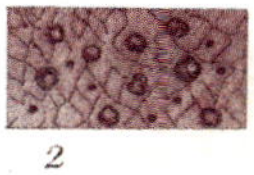

2

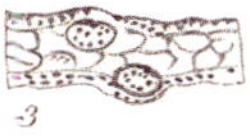

3

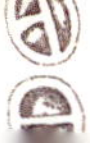

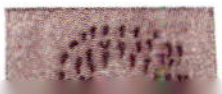

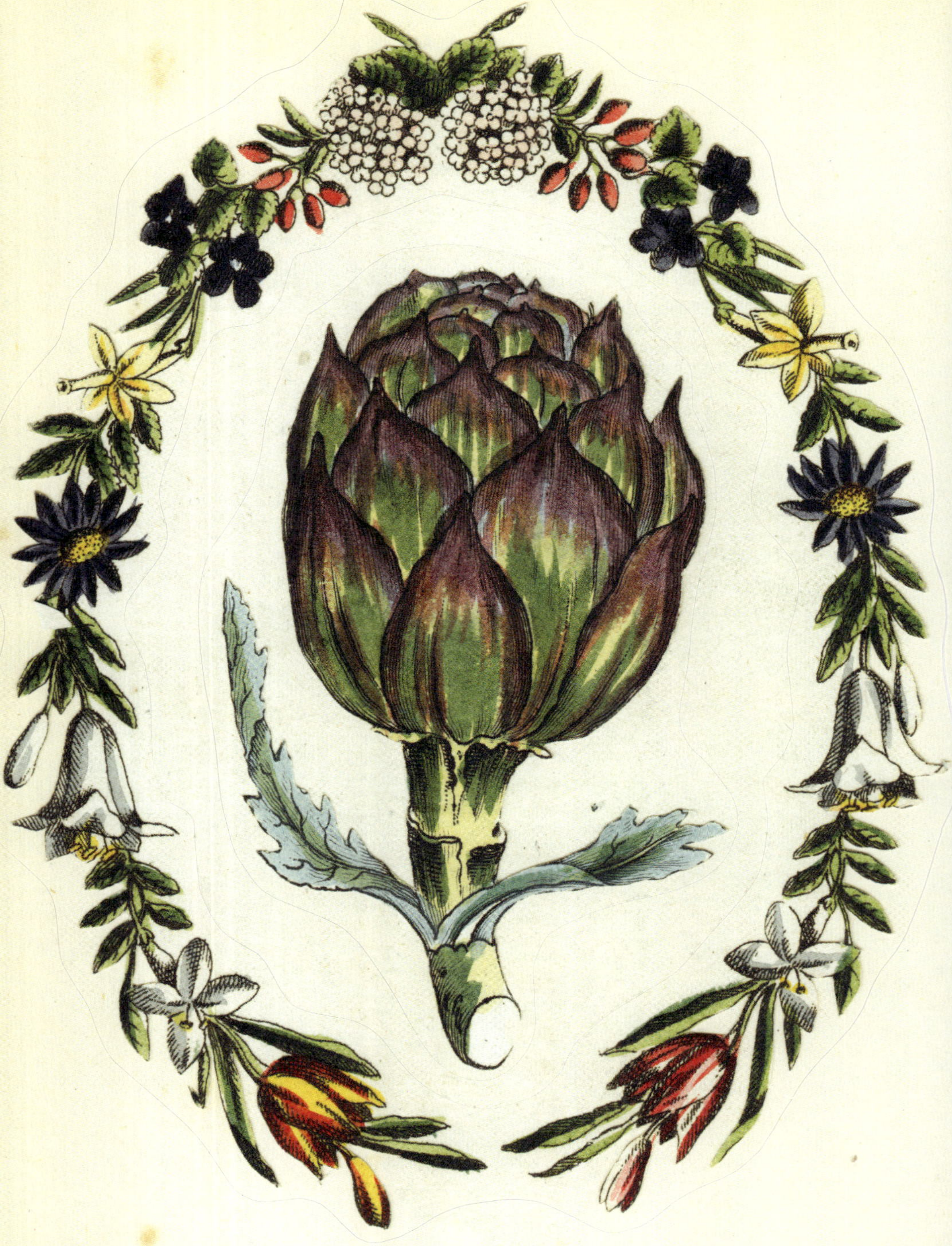

Fig. 1.

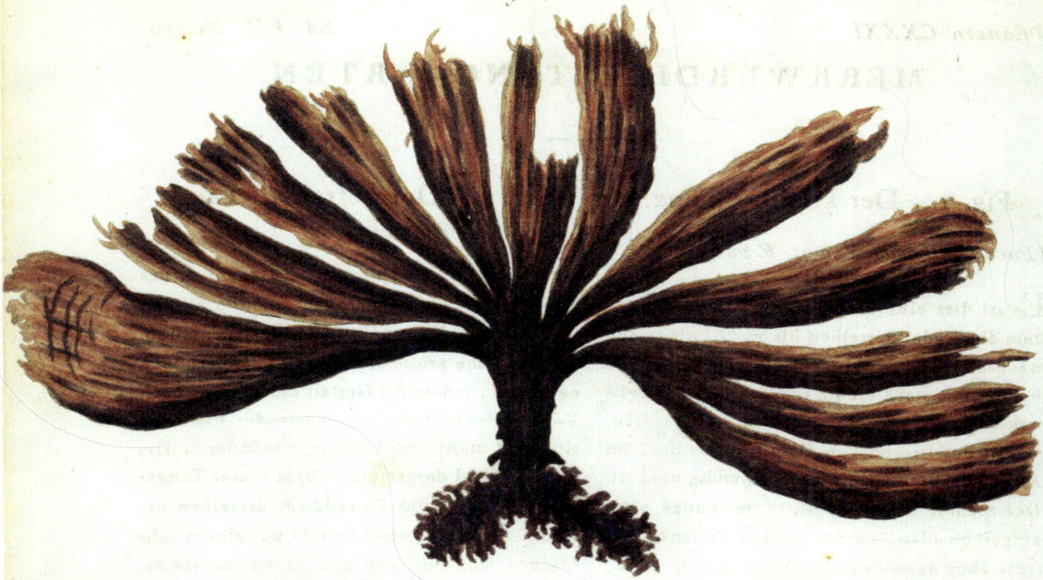

Fig. 2.

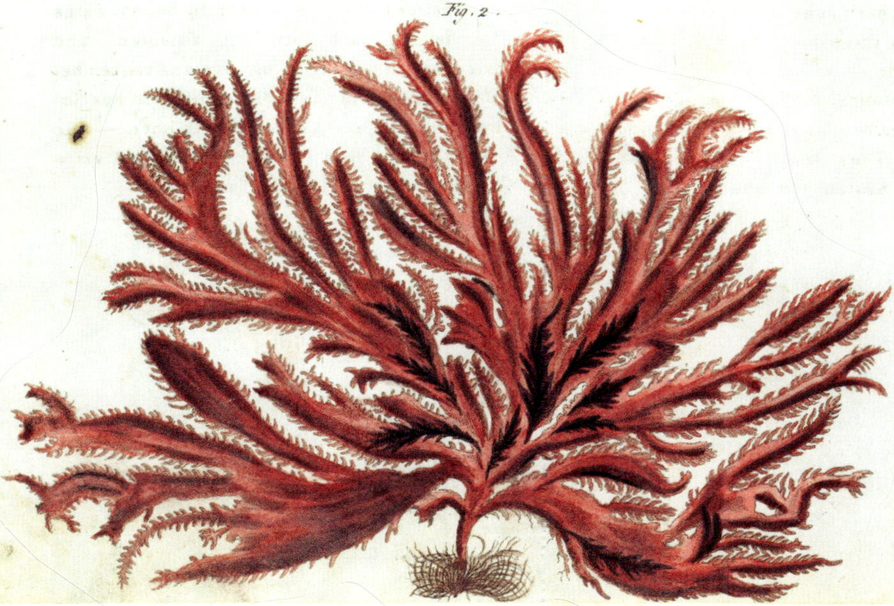

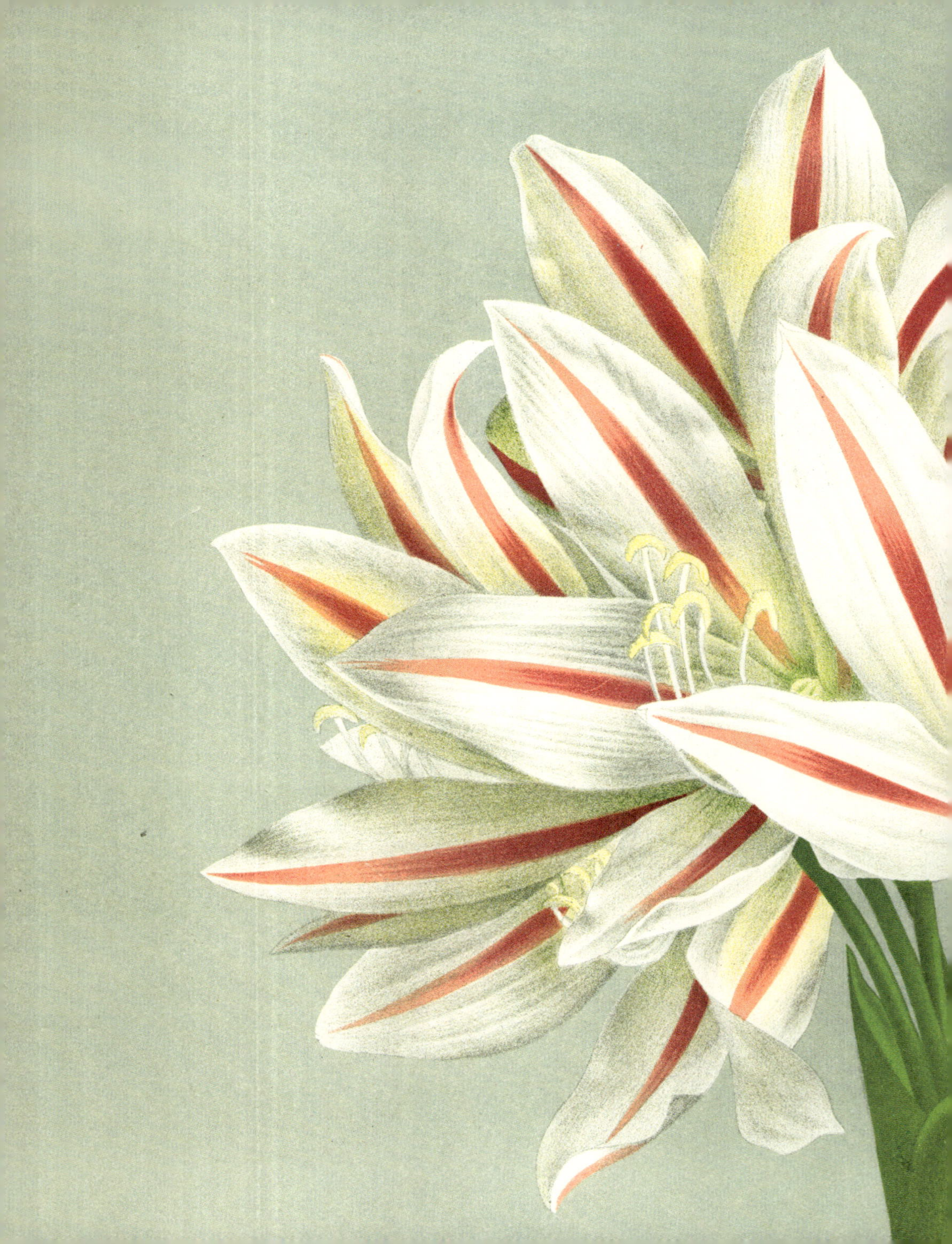

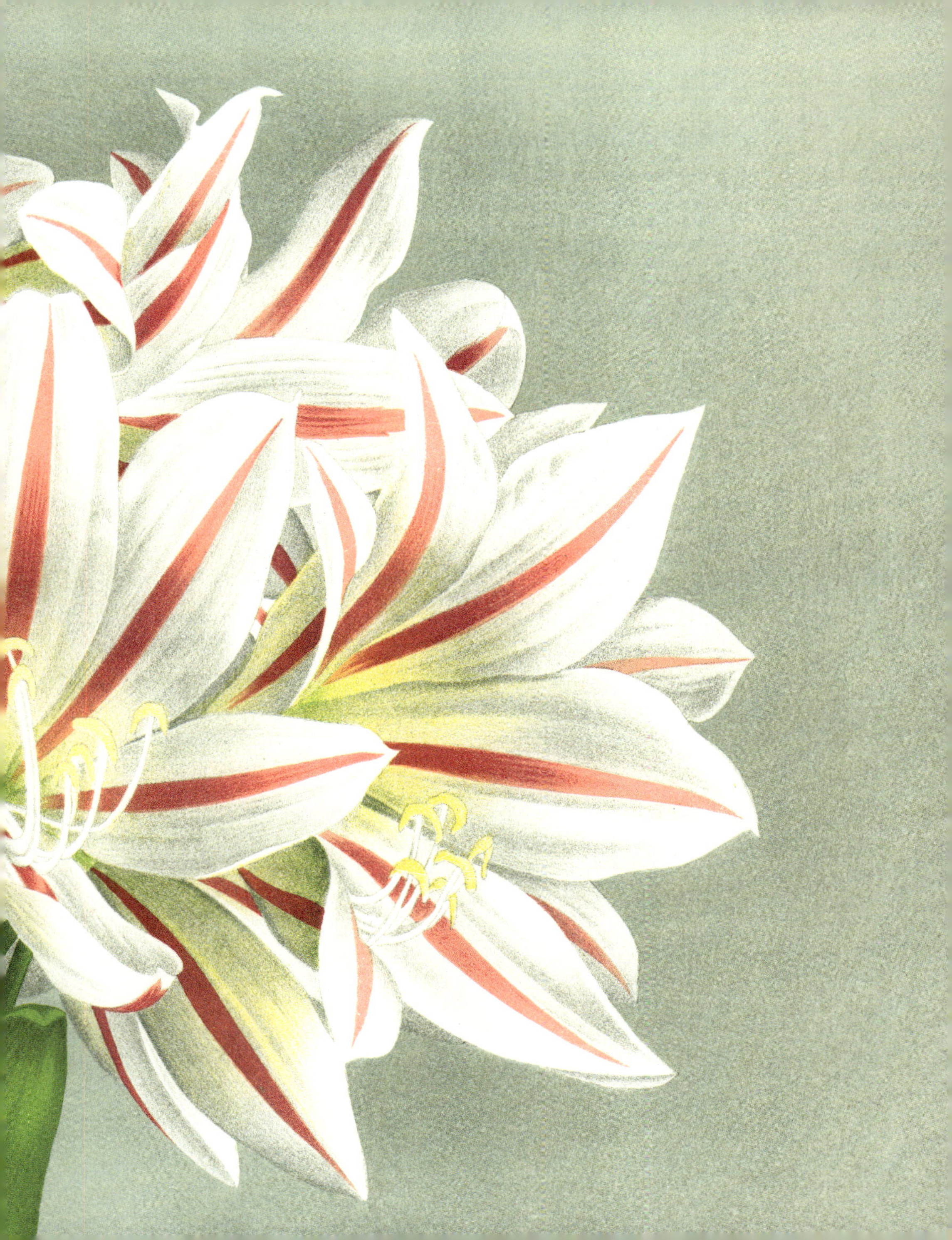

Pl. 396.

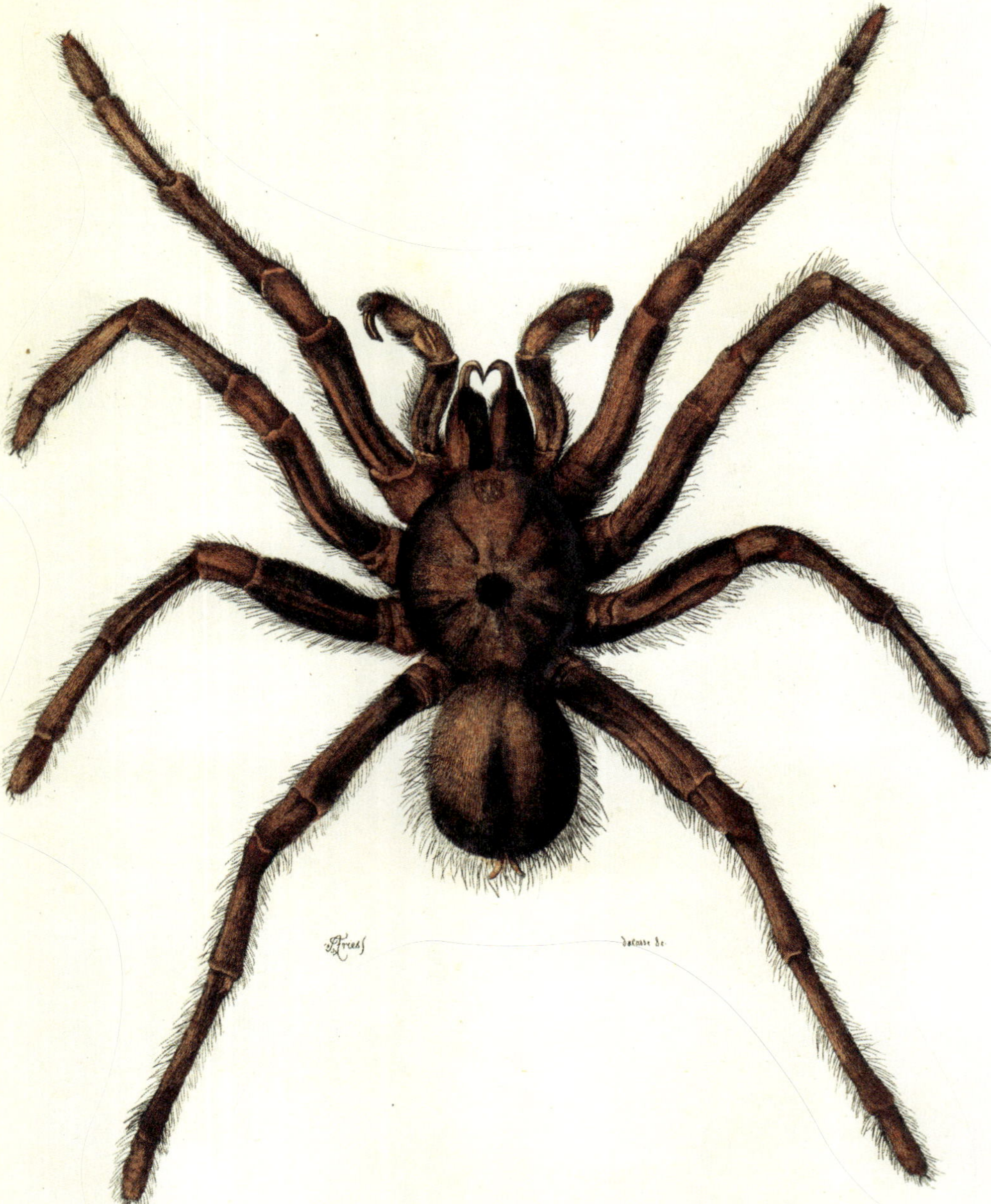

Mygale de Leblond (*grandeur naturelle*)

Pl 1.

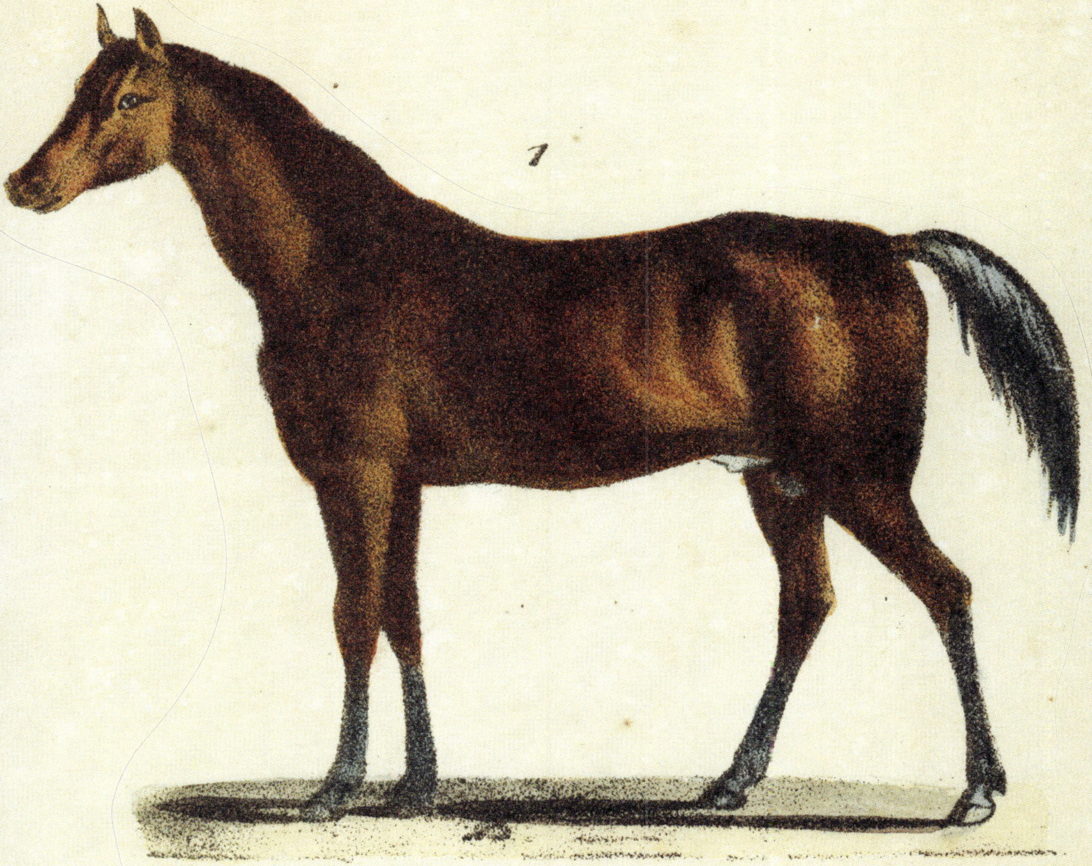

1

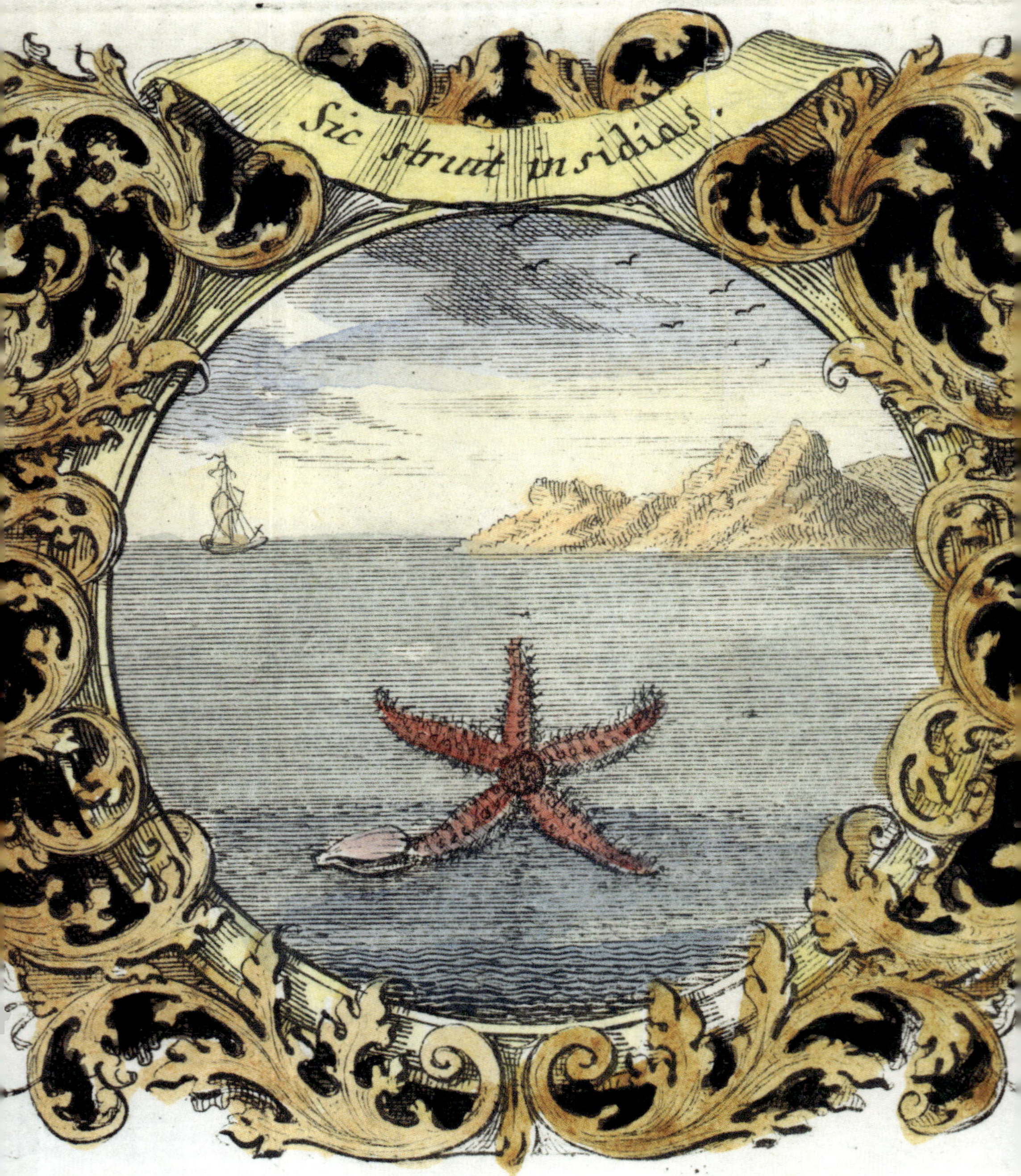
Sic struit insidias.

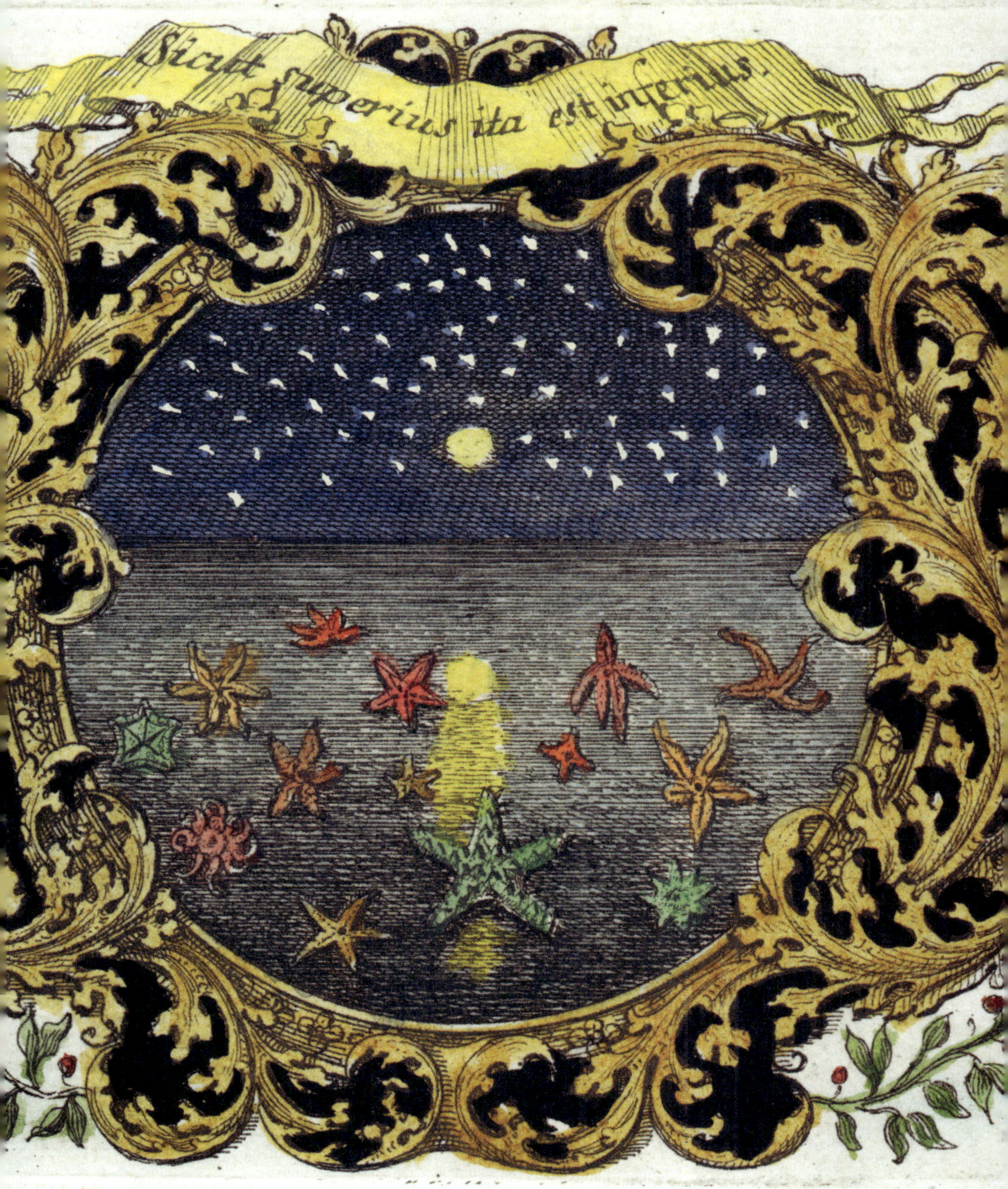
Sicut superius ita est inferius

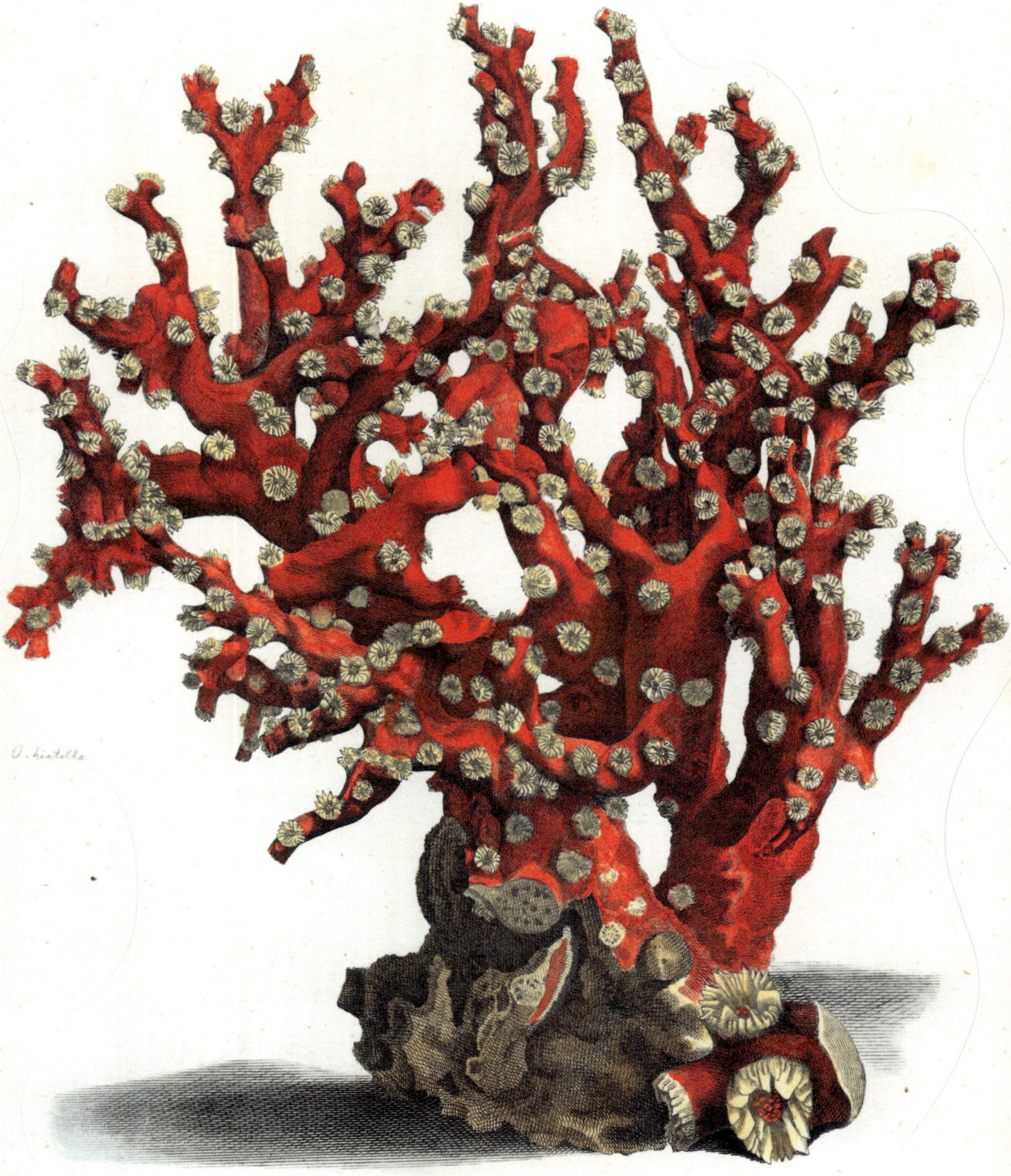

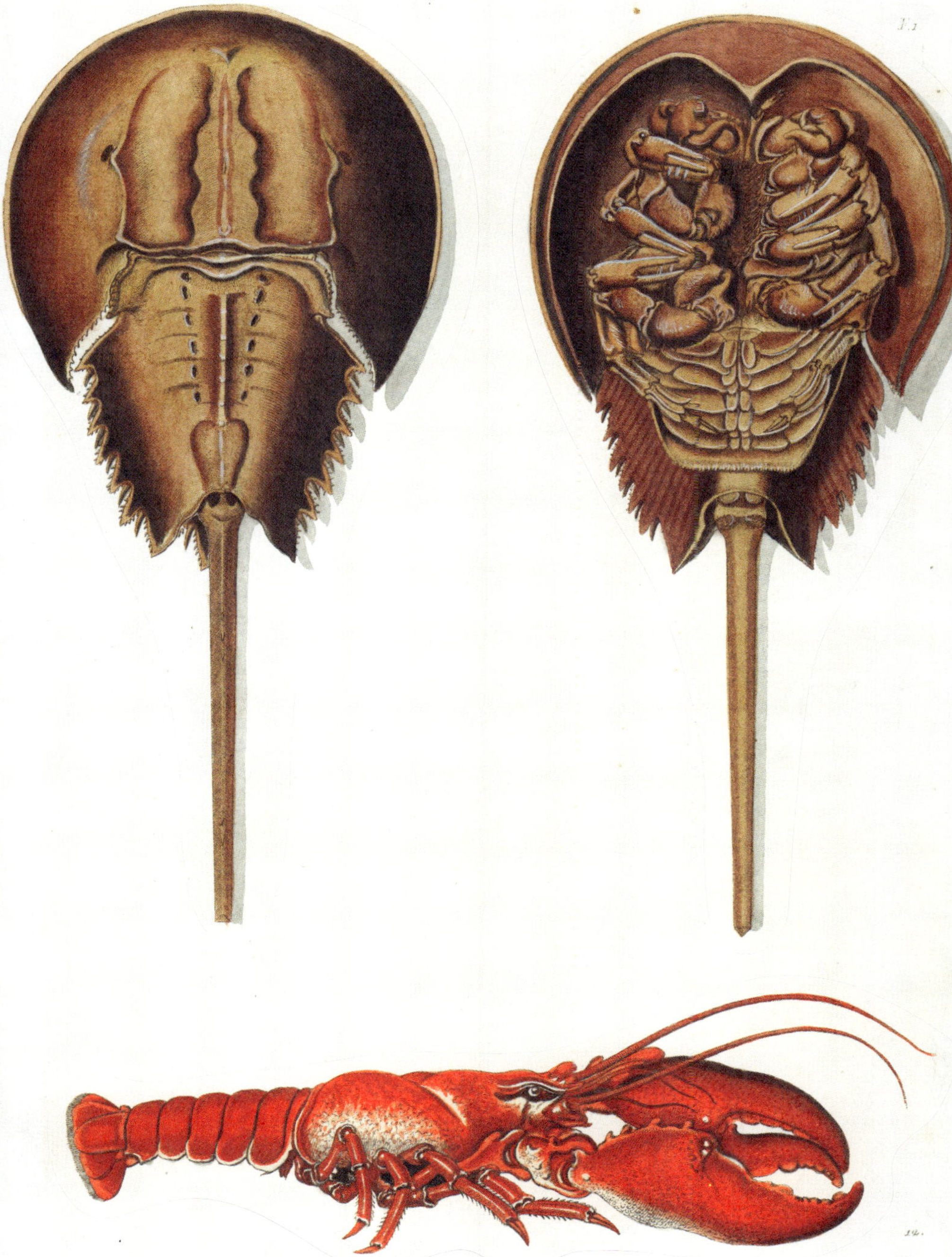

Ex Collect. G. W. Knorri.

N. 427.

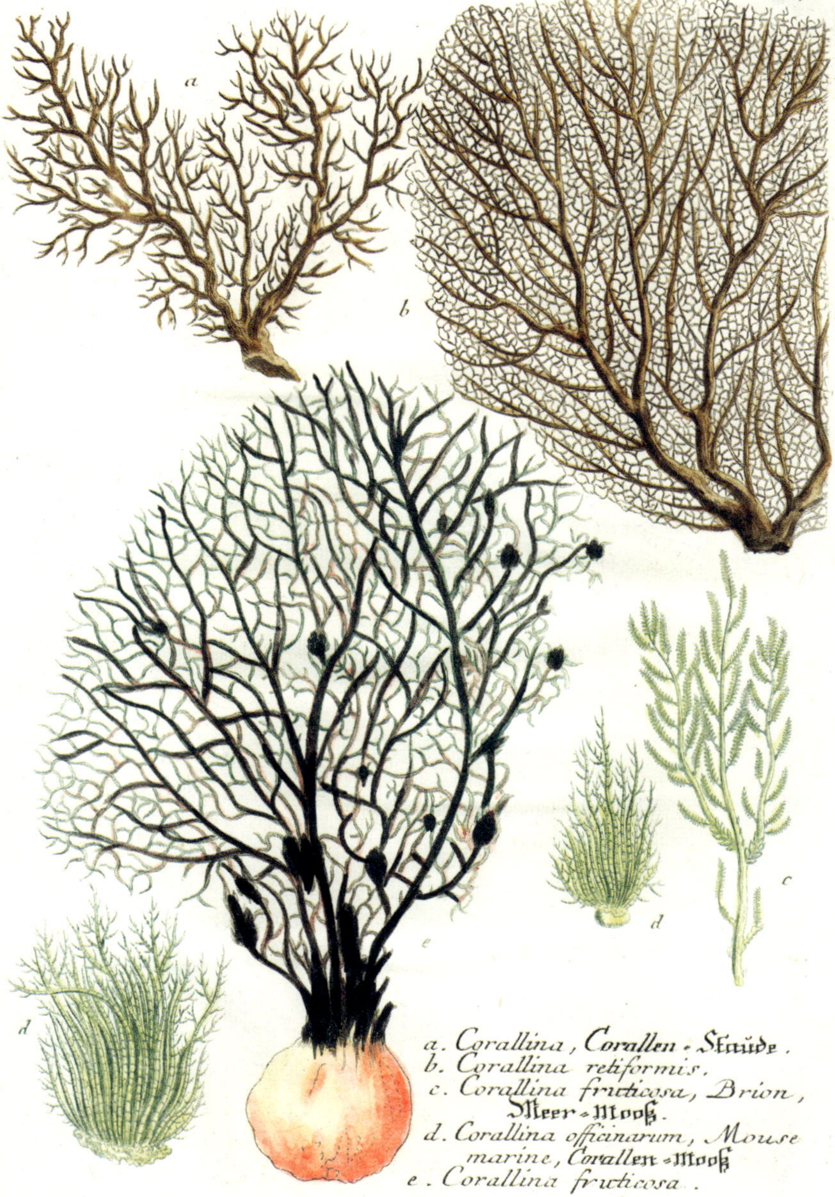

a. Corallina, Corallen-Staude.
b. Corallina retiformis.
c. Corallina fruticosa, Brion, Meer-Mooß.
d. Corallina officinarum, Mouse marine, Corallen-Mooß
e. Corallina fruticosa.

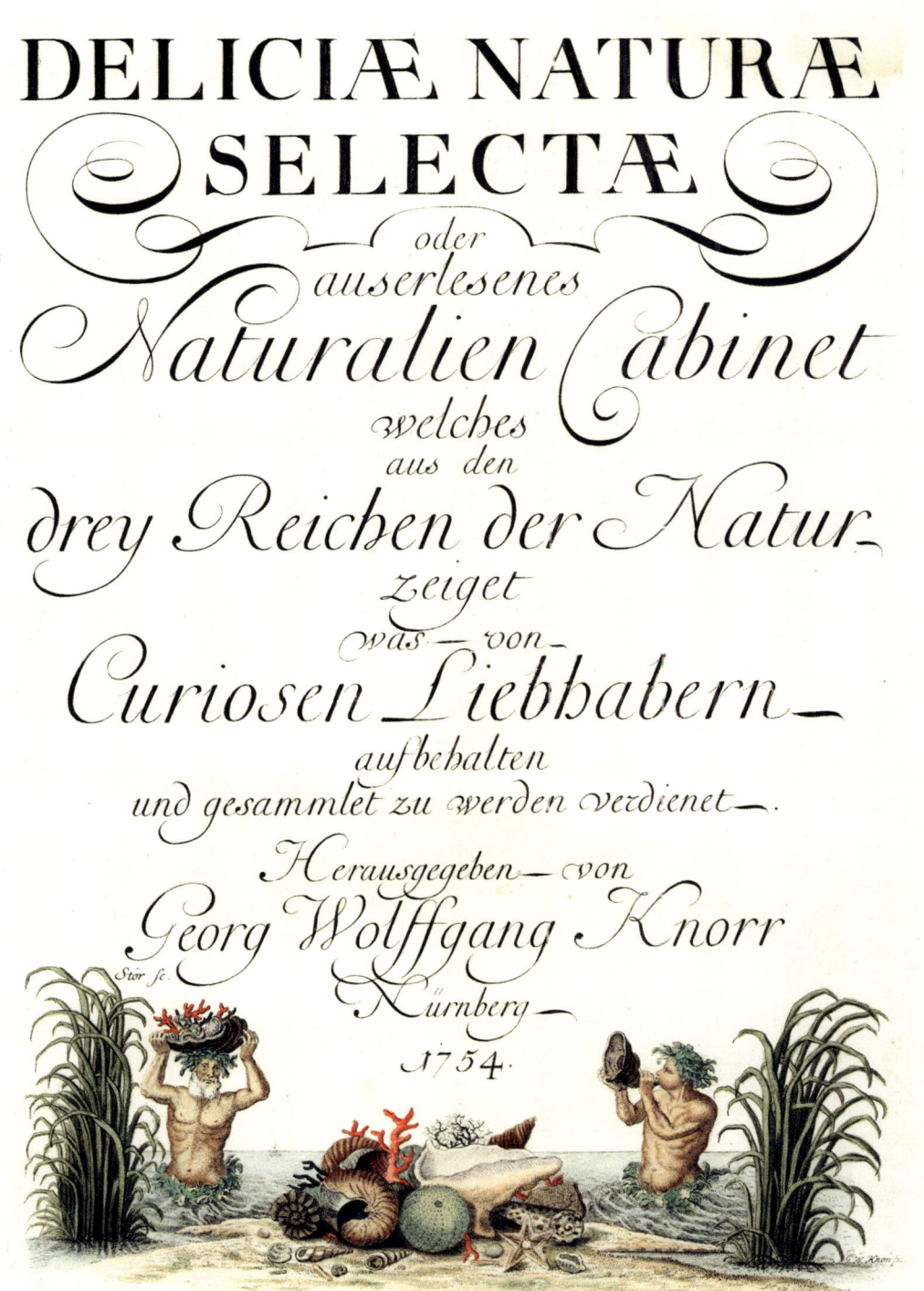

DELICIÆ NATURÆ SELECTÆ

oder

auserlesenes

Naturalien Cabinet

welches

aus den

drey Reichen der Natur

zeiget

was von

Curiosen Liebhabern

aufbehalten

und gesammlet zu werden verdienet.

Herausgegeben von

Georg Wolffgang Knorr

Stör sc.

Nürnberg

1754.

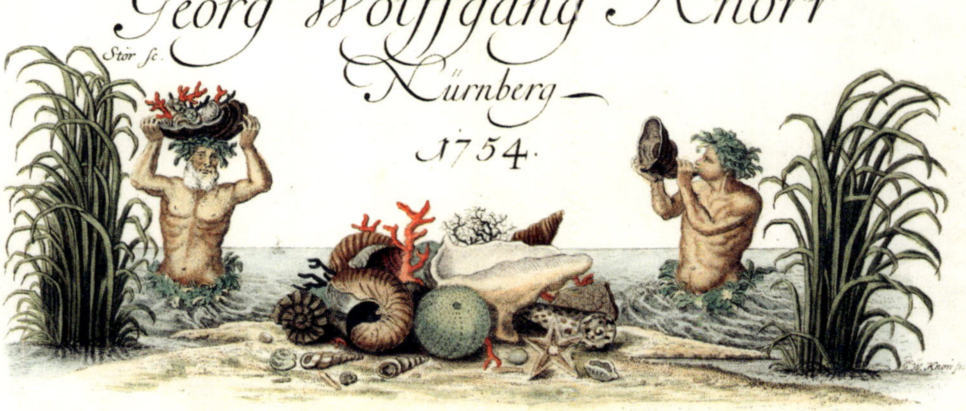

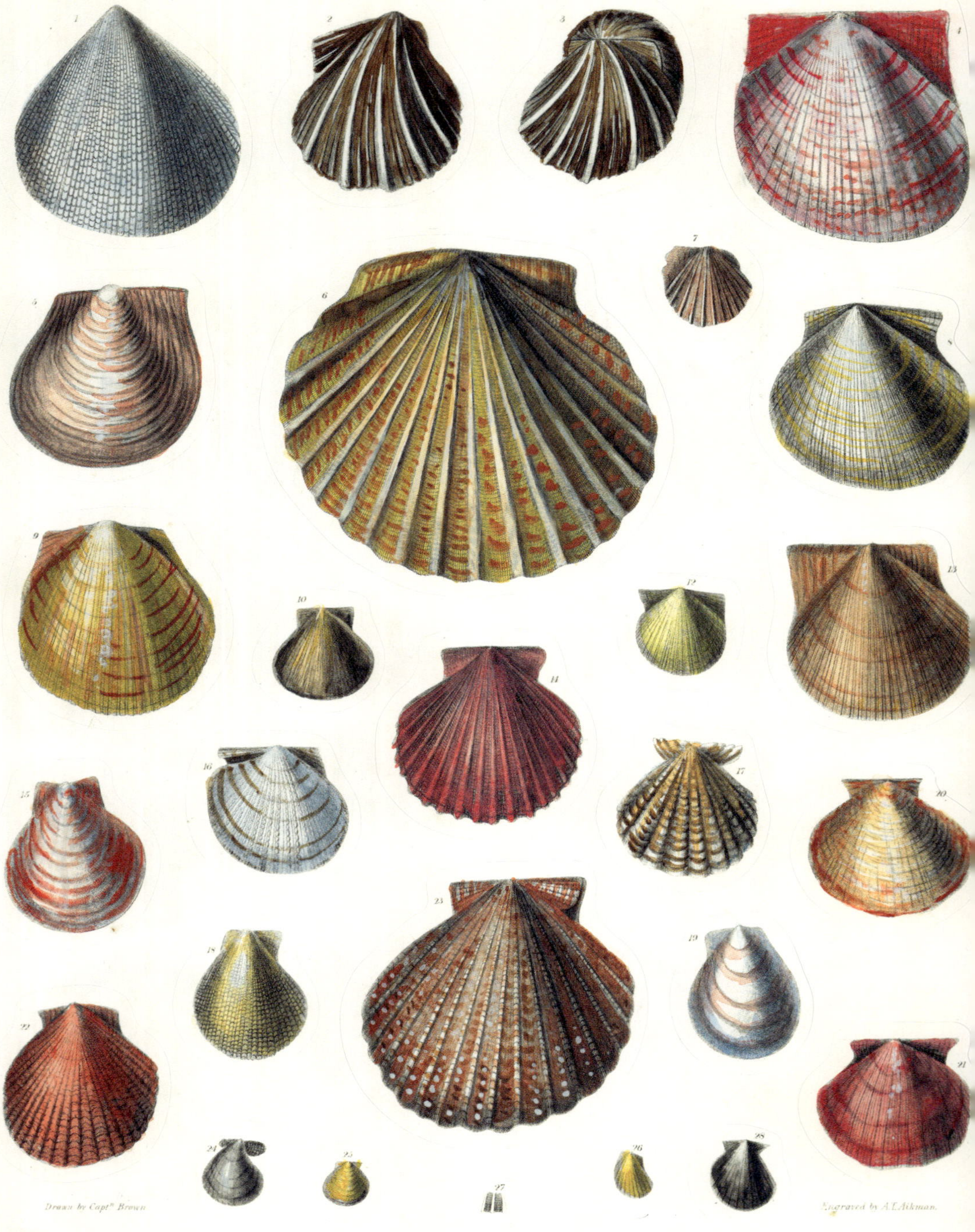

Drawn by Captⁿ Brown

Engraved by A.L. Aikman.

LXII.

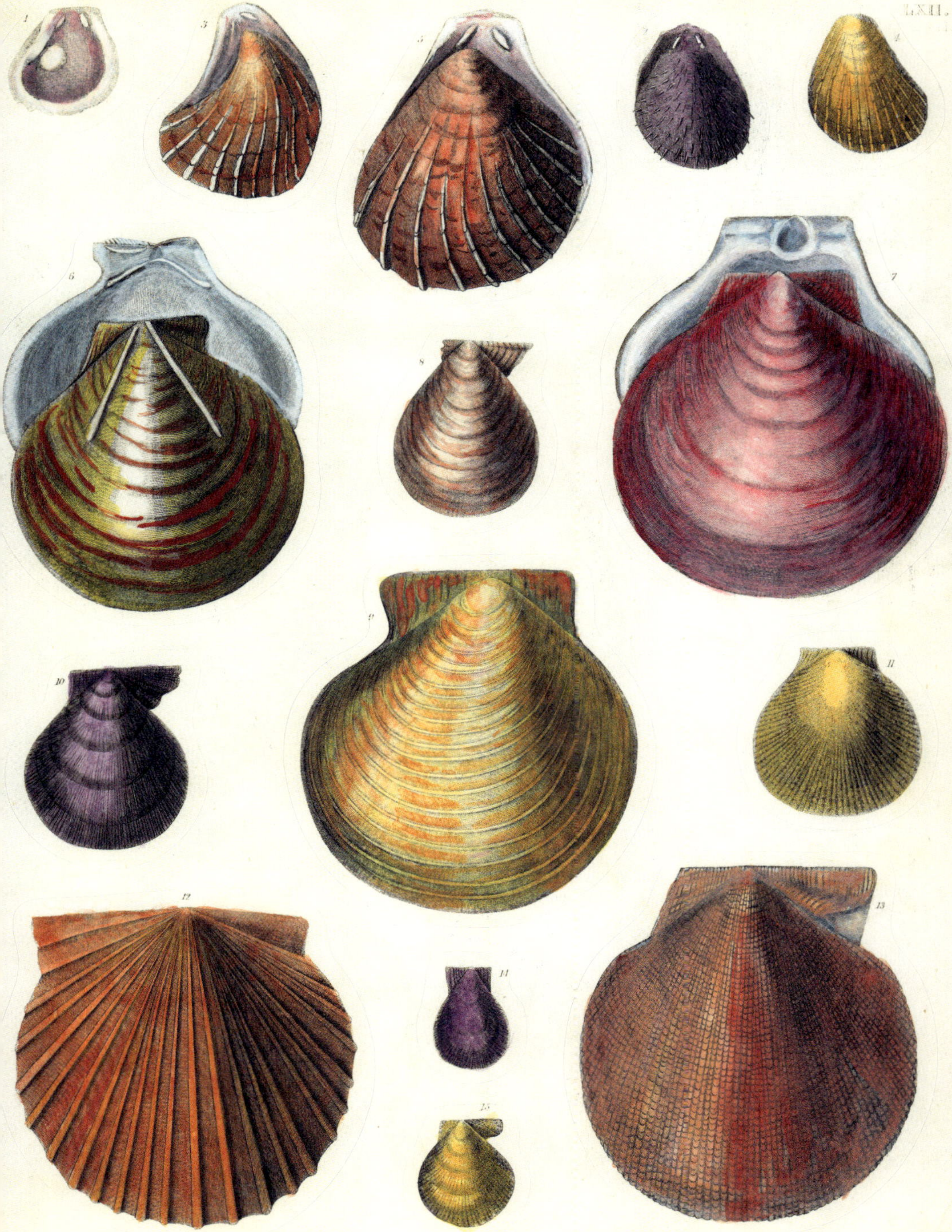

Drawn by Captn Brown

Engraved by A.T. Hkman

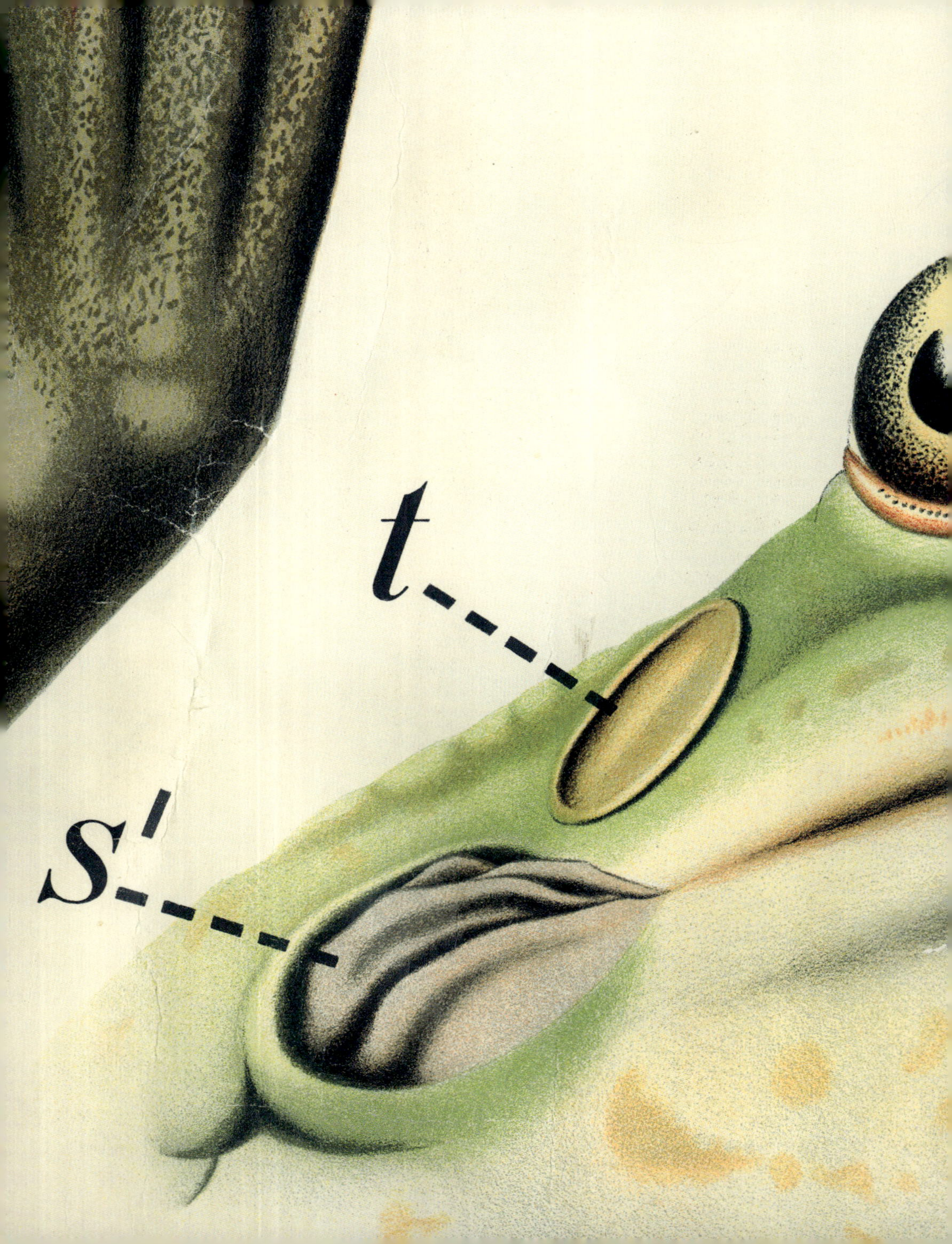
t
s

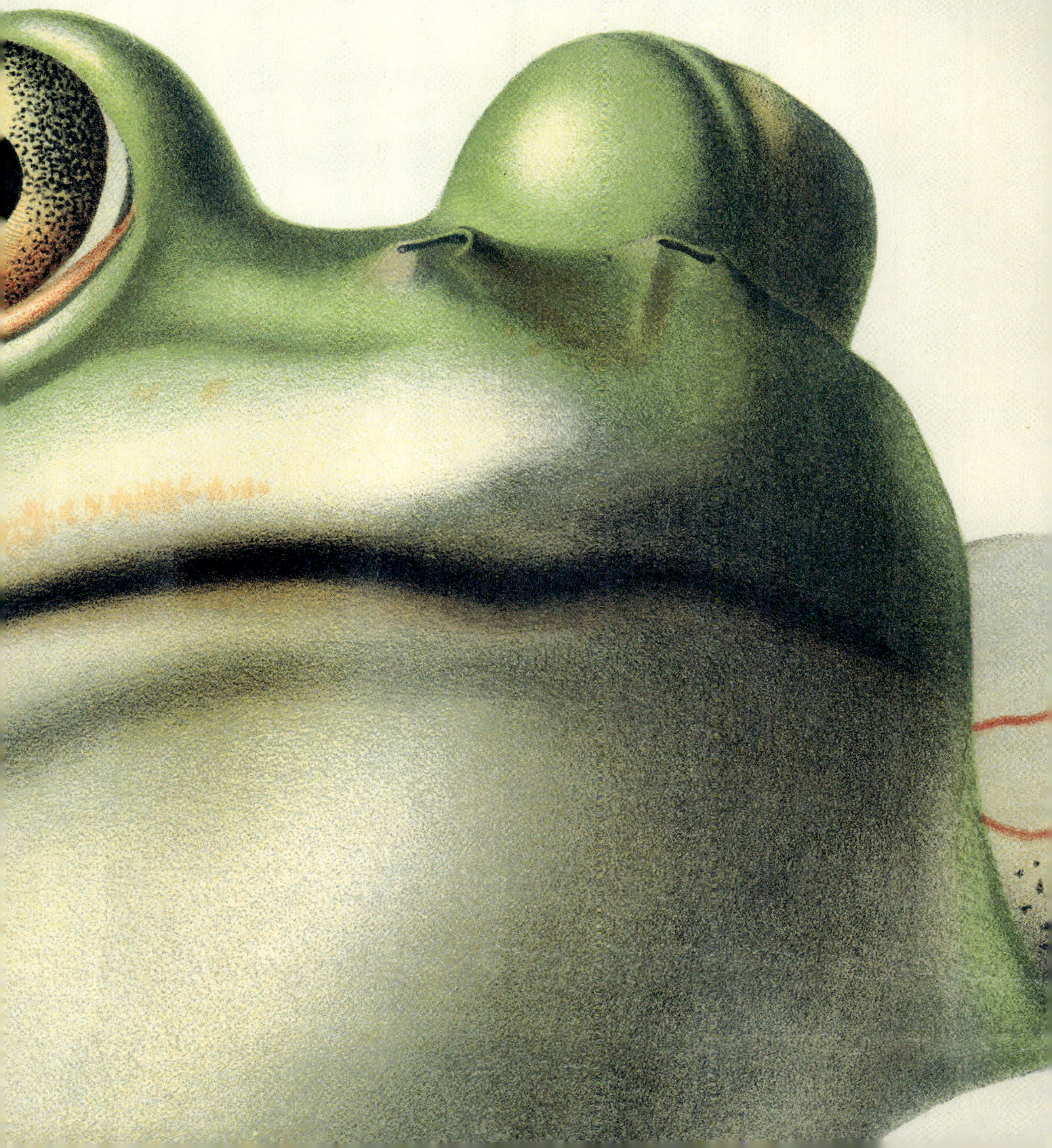

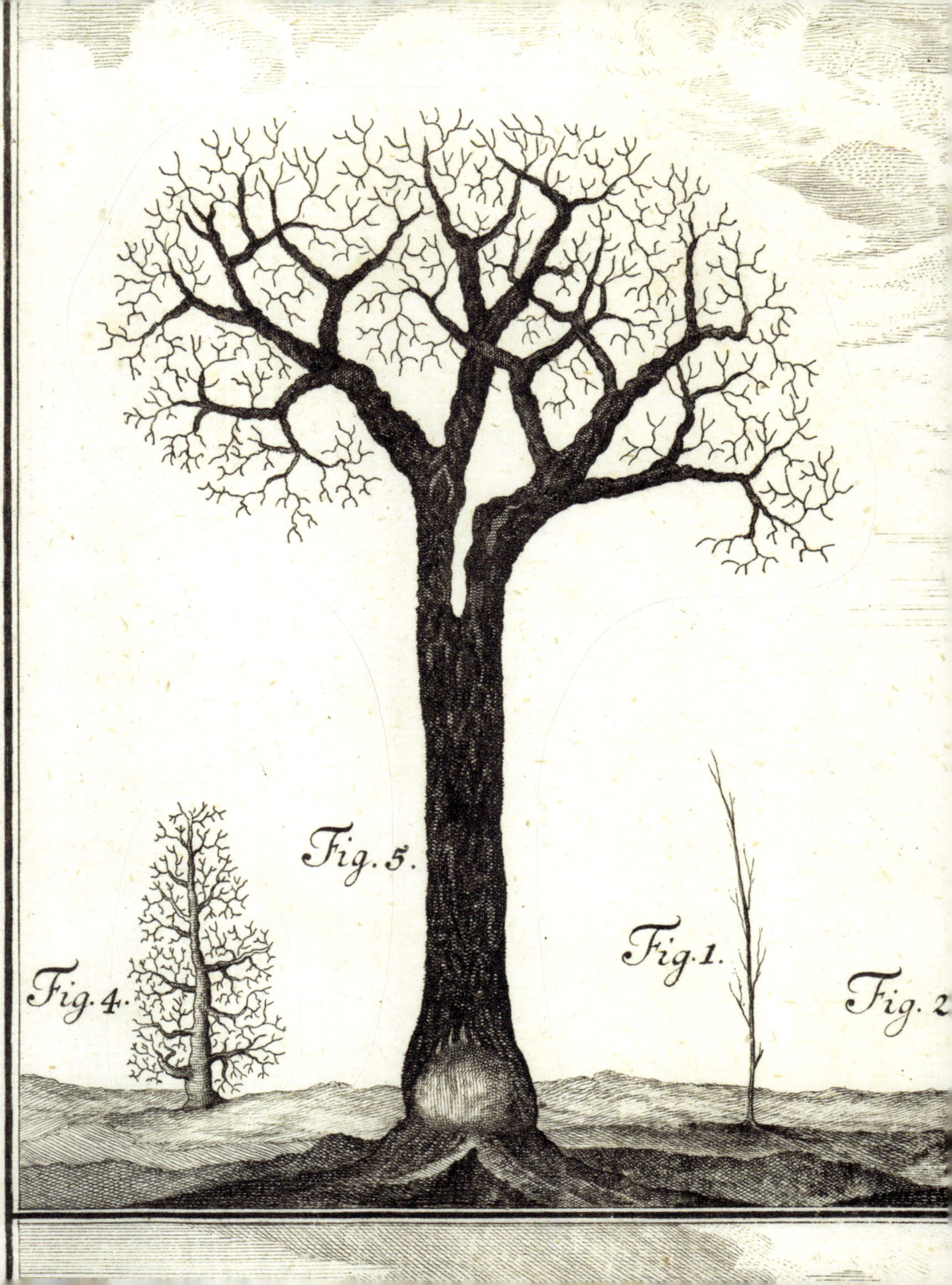
Fig. 5.
Fig. 4.
Fig. 1.
Fig. 2

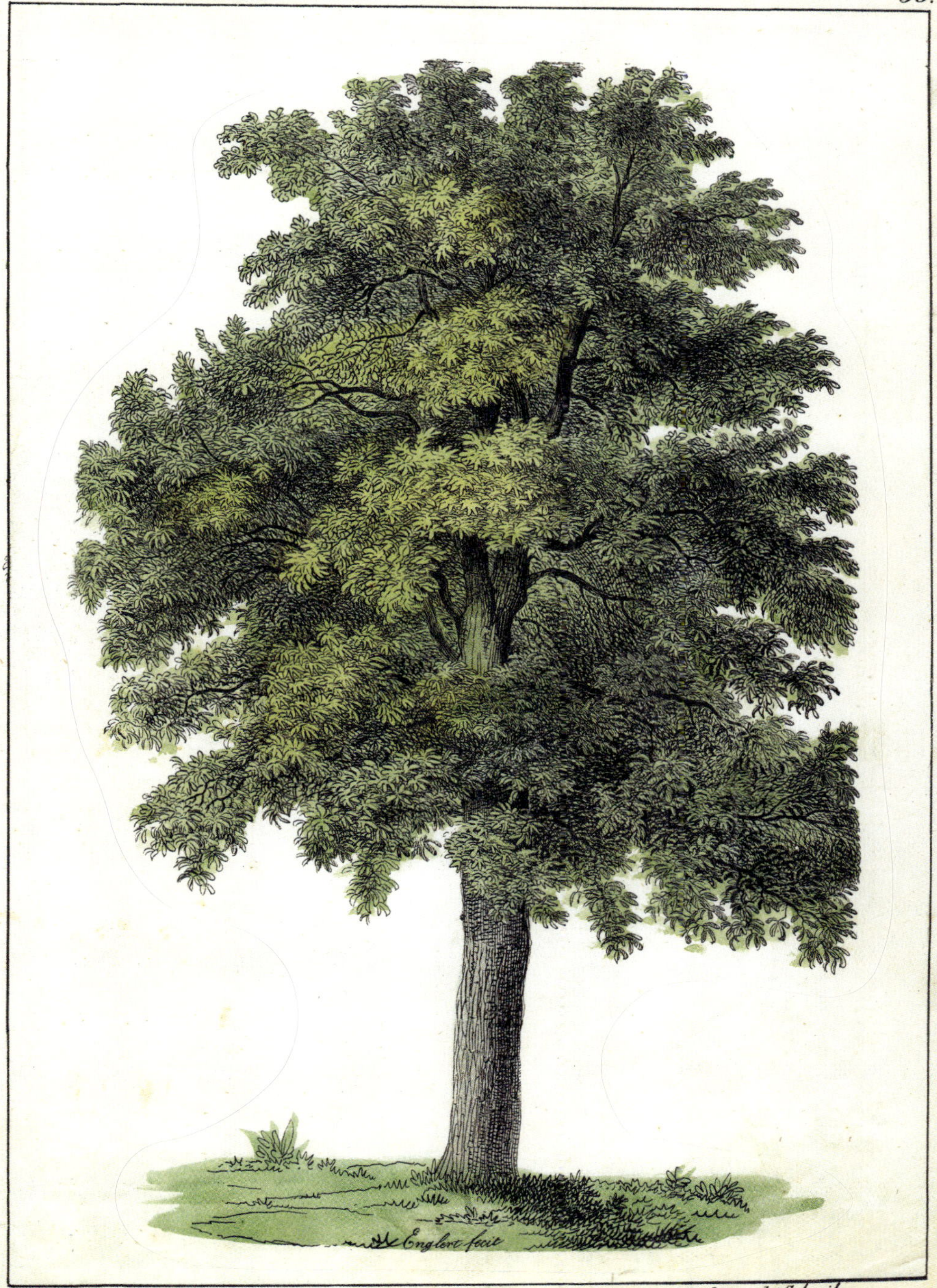

Esslingen bei Schreiber.

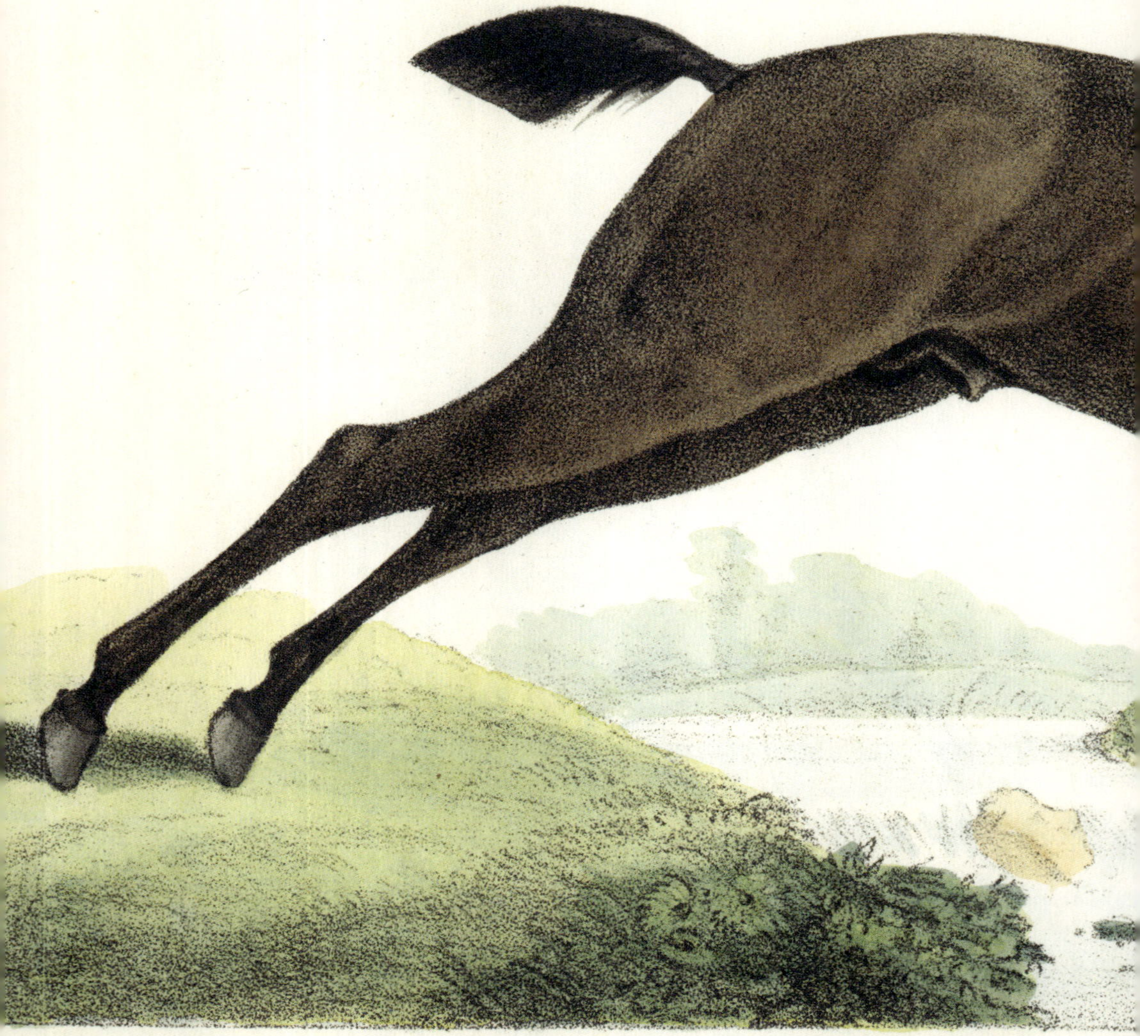

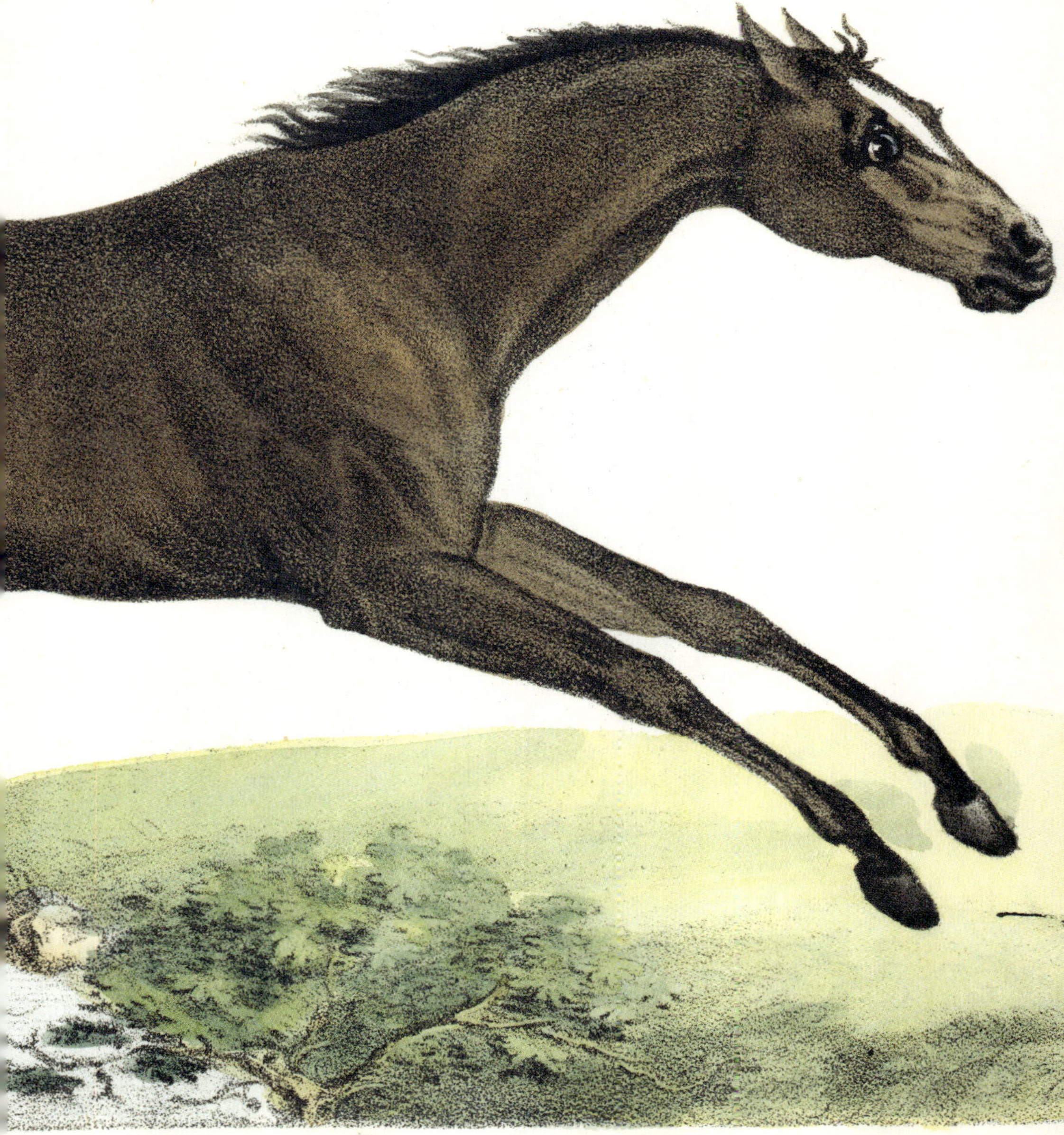

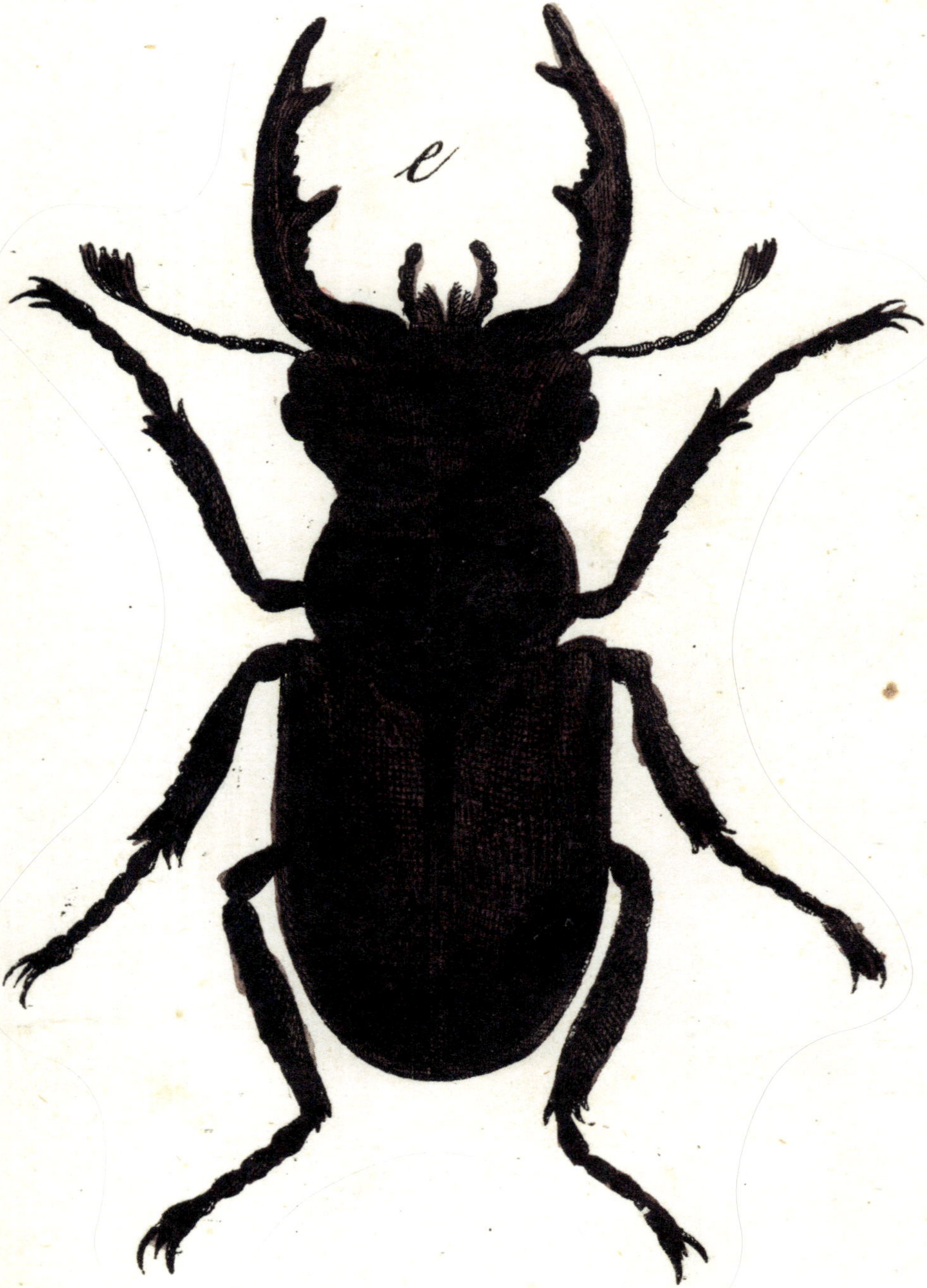
e

T. III.

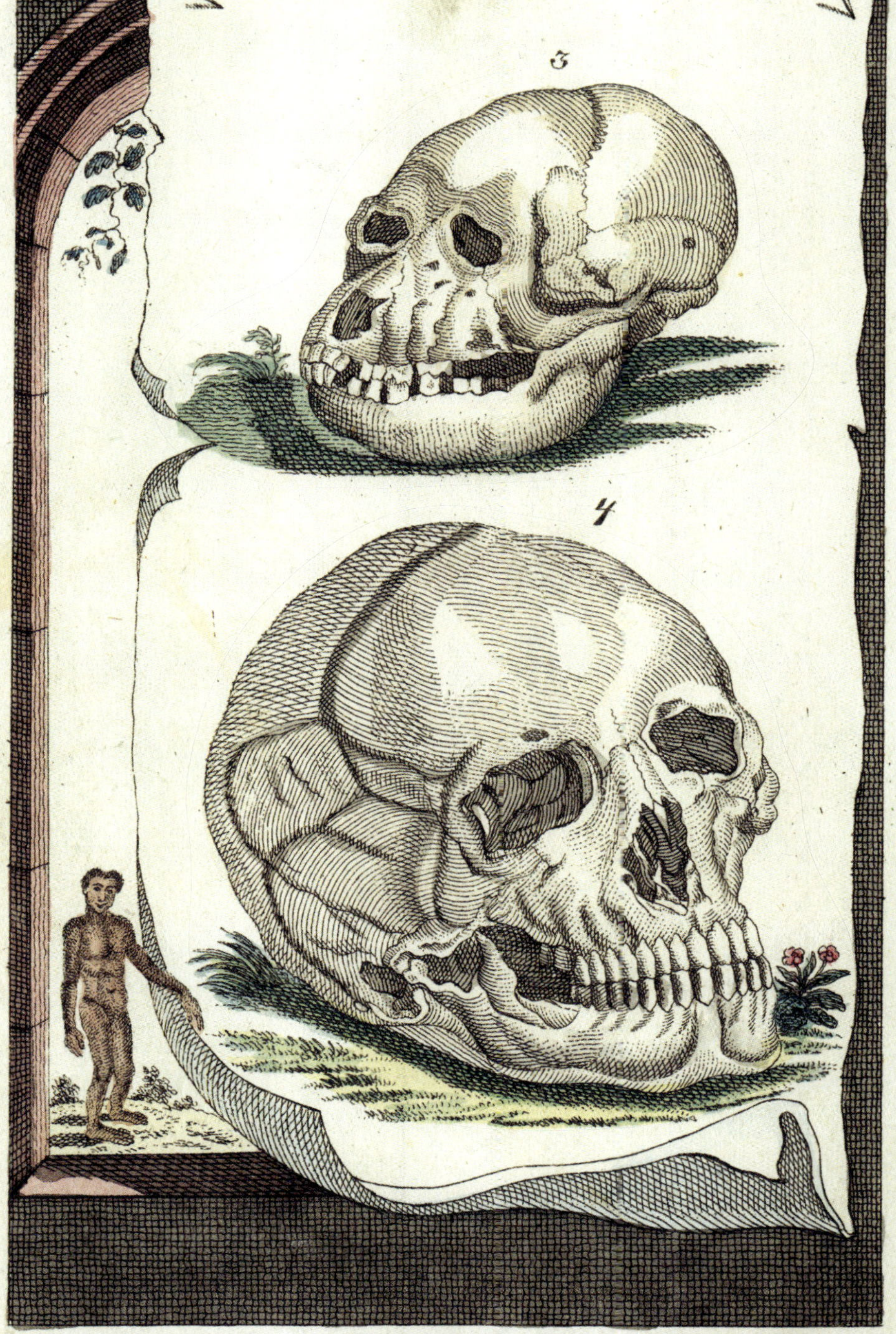

COLBURN'S PHILA. MUSTARD

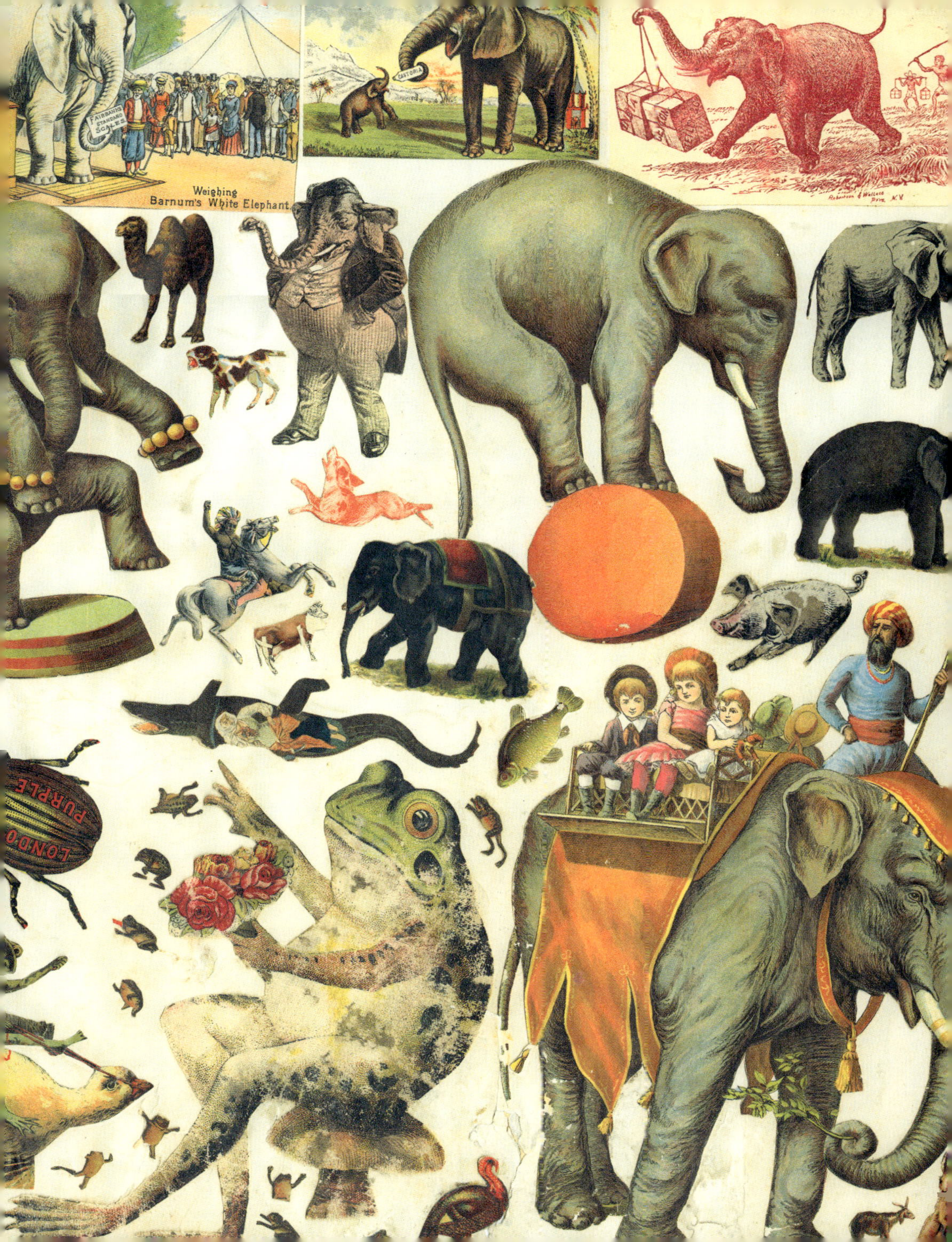
Weighing
Barnum's White Elephant.
CASTORIA
PURPLE

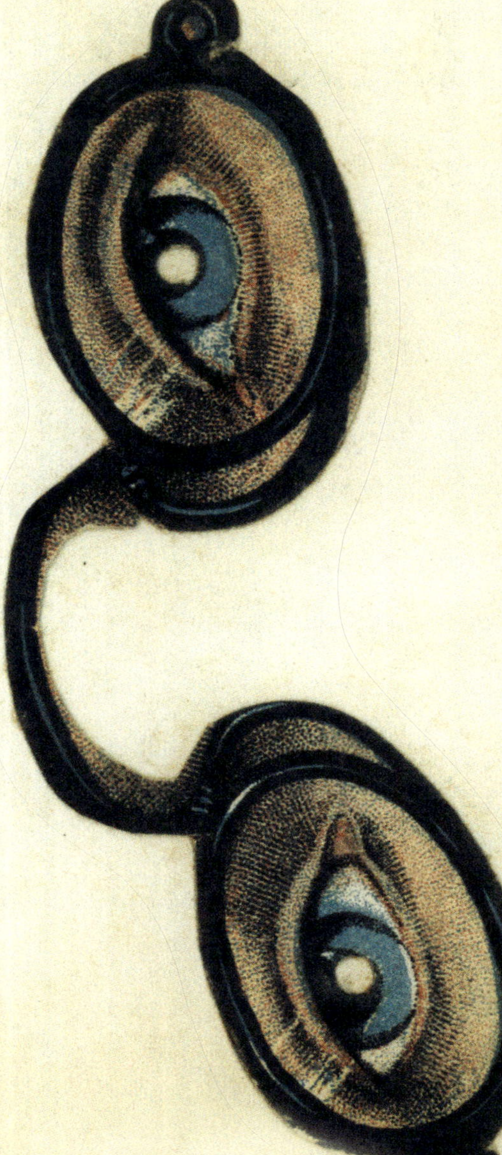

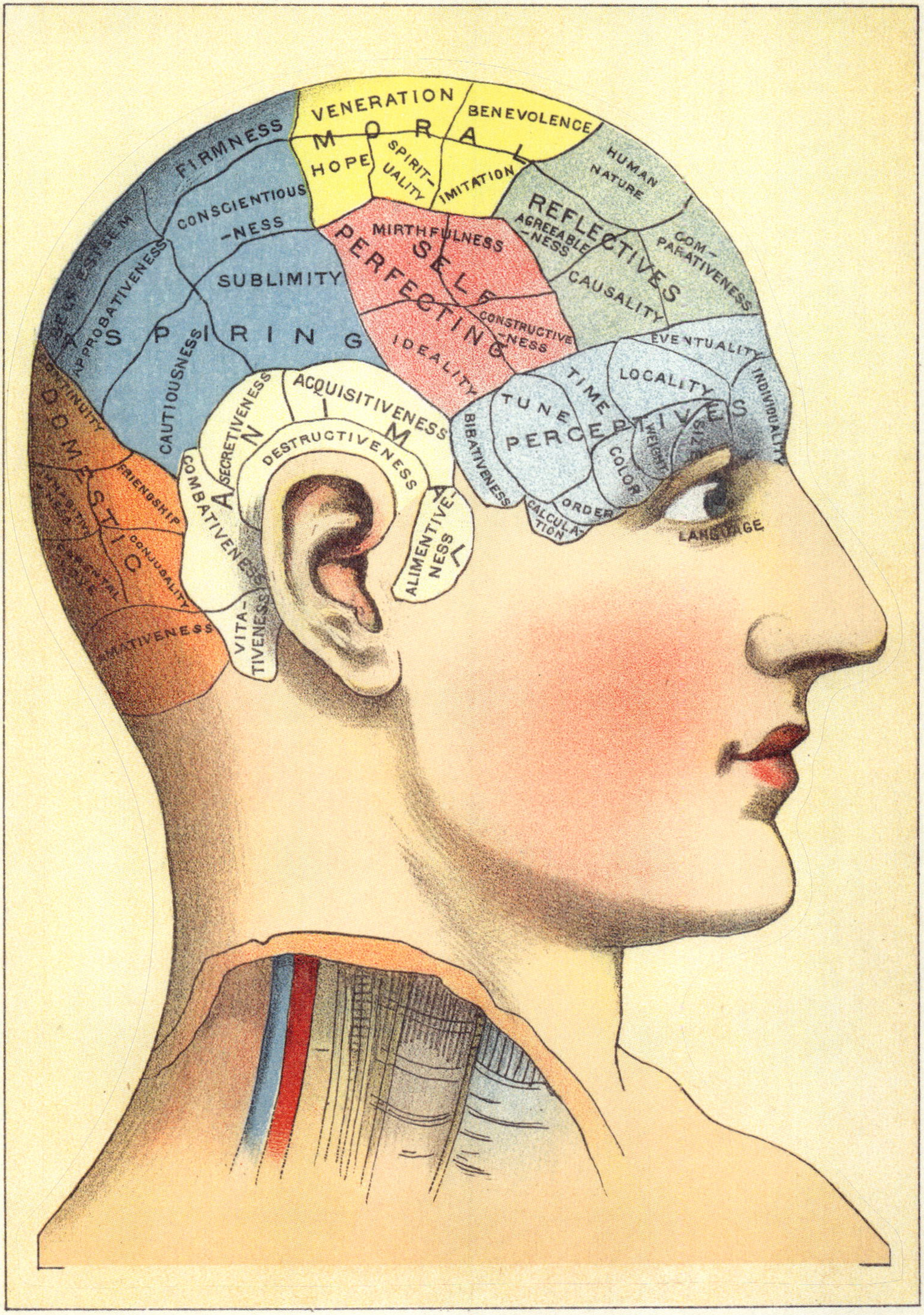

VENERATION
BENEVOLENCE
MORAL
FIRMNESS
HOPE
SPIRIT-UALITY
IMITATION
HUMAN NATURE
CONSCIENTIOUS-NESS
REFLECTIVES
AGREEABLE-NESS
COM-PARATIVENESS
MIRTHFULNESS
SELF PERFECTING
CAUSALITY
SUBLIMITY
APPROBATIVENESS
ASPIRING
CONSTRUCTIVE-NESS
IDEALITY
EVENTUALITY
CONTINUITY
DOMESTIC
CAUTIOUSNESS
SECRETIVENESS
ACQUISITIVENESS
ANIMAL
DESTRUCTIVENESS
TIME
LOCALITY
INDIVIDUALITY
TUNE
PERCEPTIVES
BIBATIVENESS
COLOR
FRIENDSHIP
COMBATIVENESS
ORDER
CALCULATION
LANGUAGE
ALIMENTIVE-NESS
CONJUGALITY
VITA-TIVENESS
AMATIVENESS

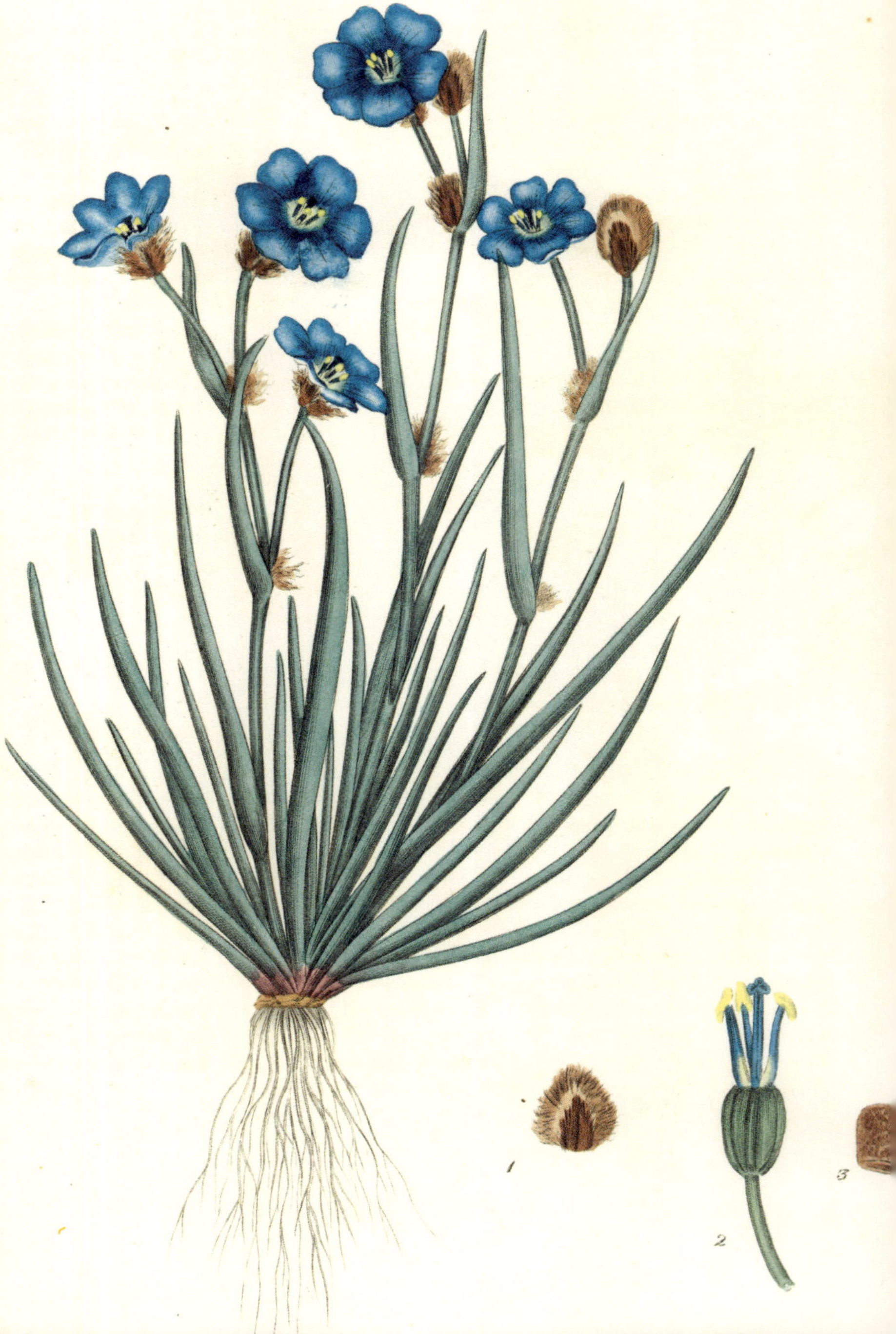
1
2
3

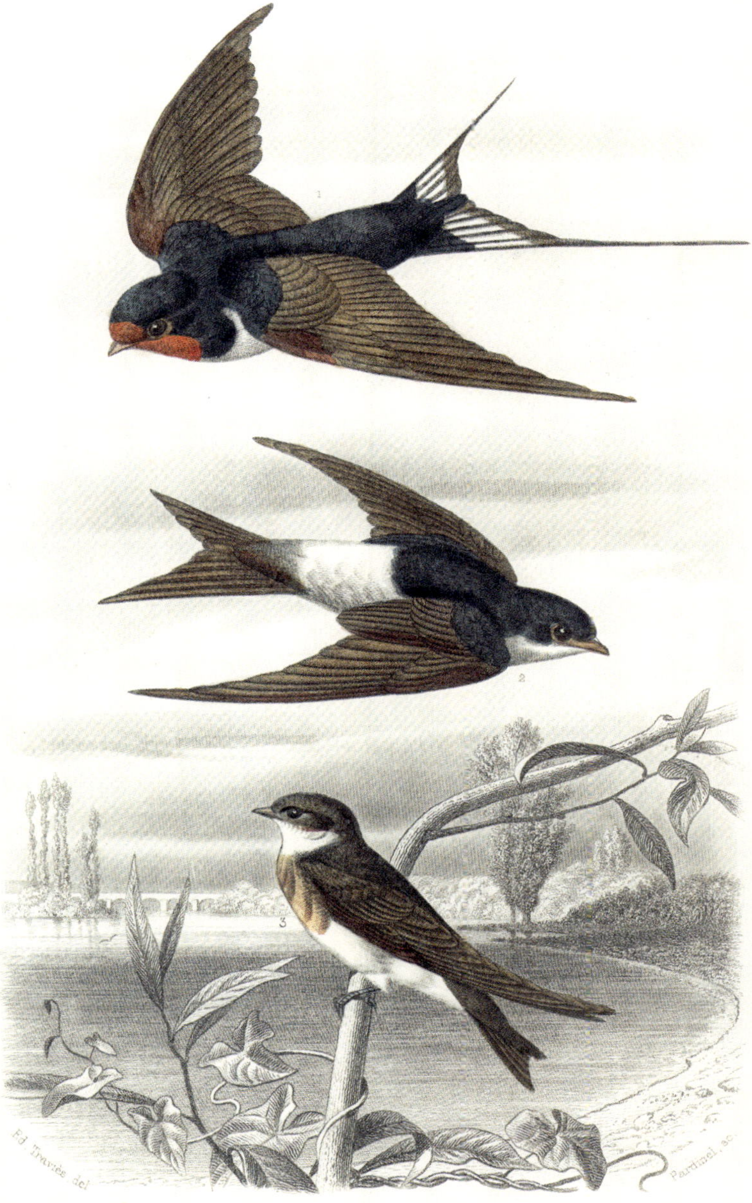

1. L'HIRONDELLE DE CHEMINÉE ——— 2. Id. À CROUPION BLANC

3. L'HIRONDELLE DE RIVAGE.

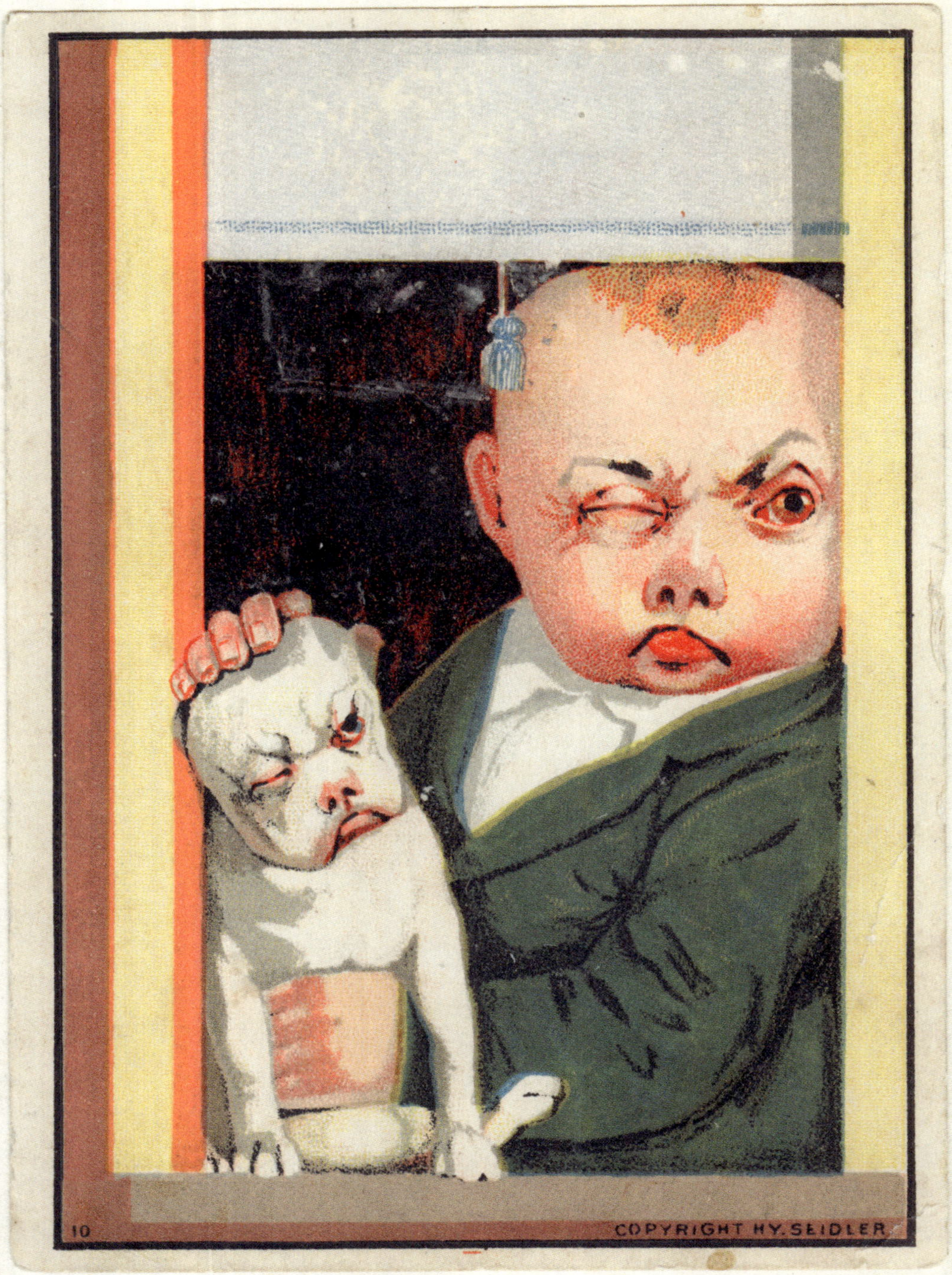
10
COPYRIGHT HY. SEIDLER

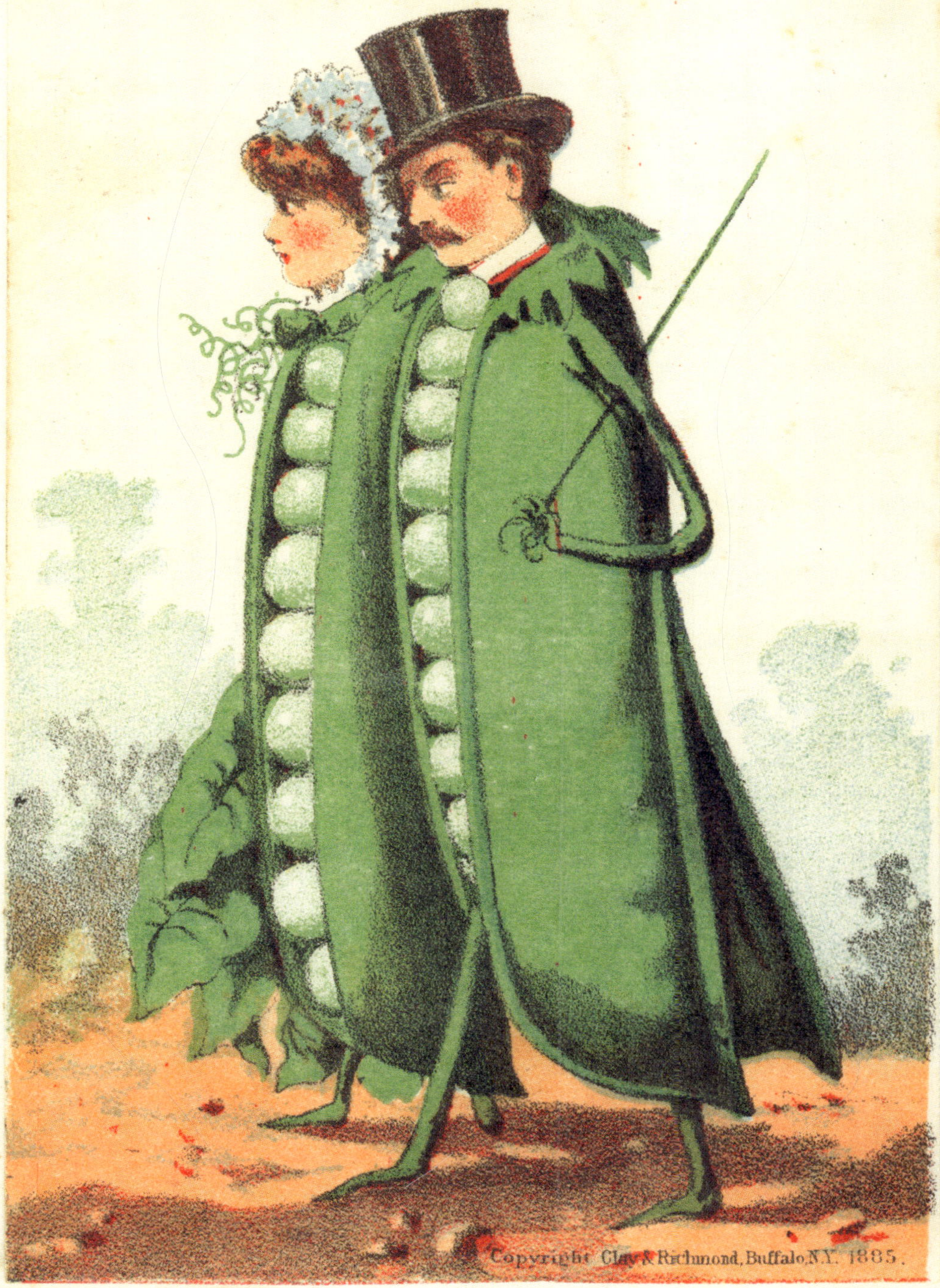
Copyright Clay & Richmond, Buffalo, N.Y. 1885.

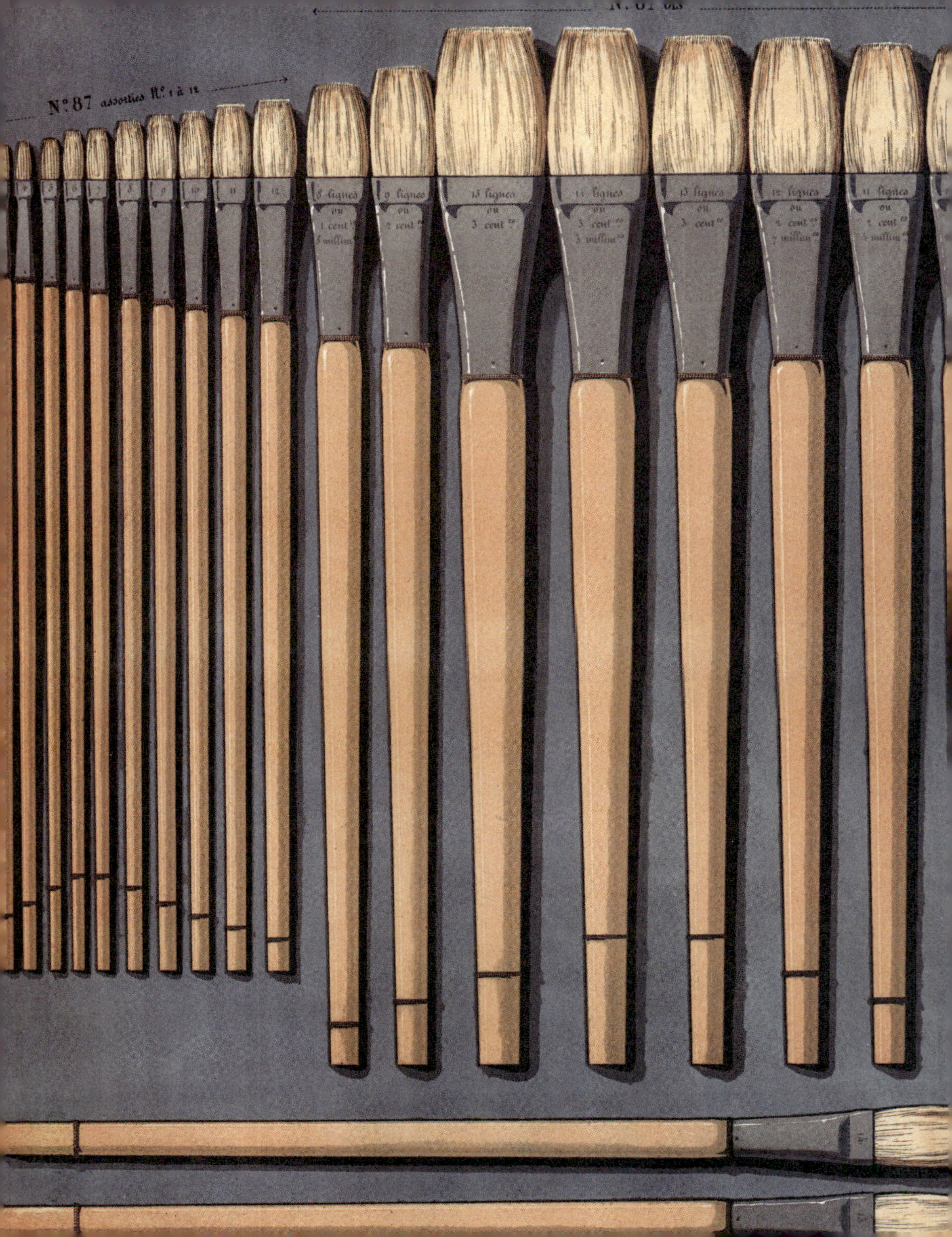

N° 87 assorties N°s 1 à 12
8 lignes ou 1 cent.es 8 millim.es
9 lignes ou 2 cent.es
15 lignes ou 3 cent.es
14 lignes ou 3 cent.es 3 millim.es
13 lignes ou 3 cent.es
12 lignes ou 2 cent.es 7 millim.es
11 lignes ou 2 cent.es

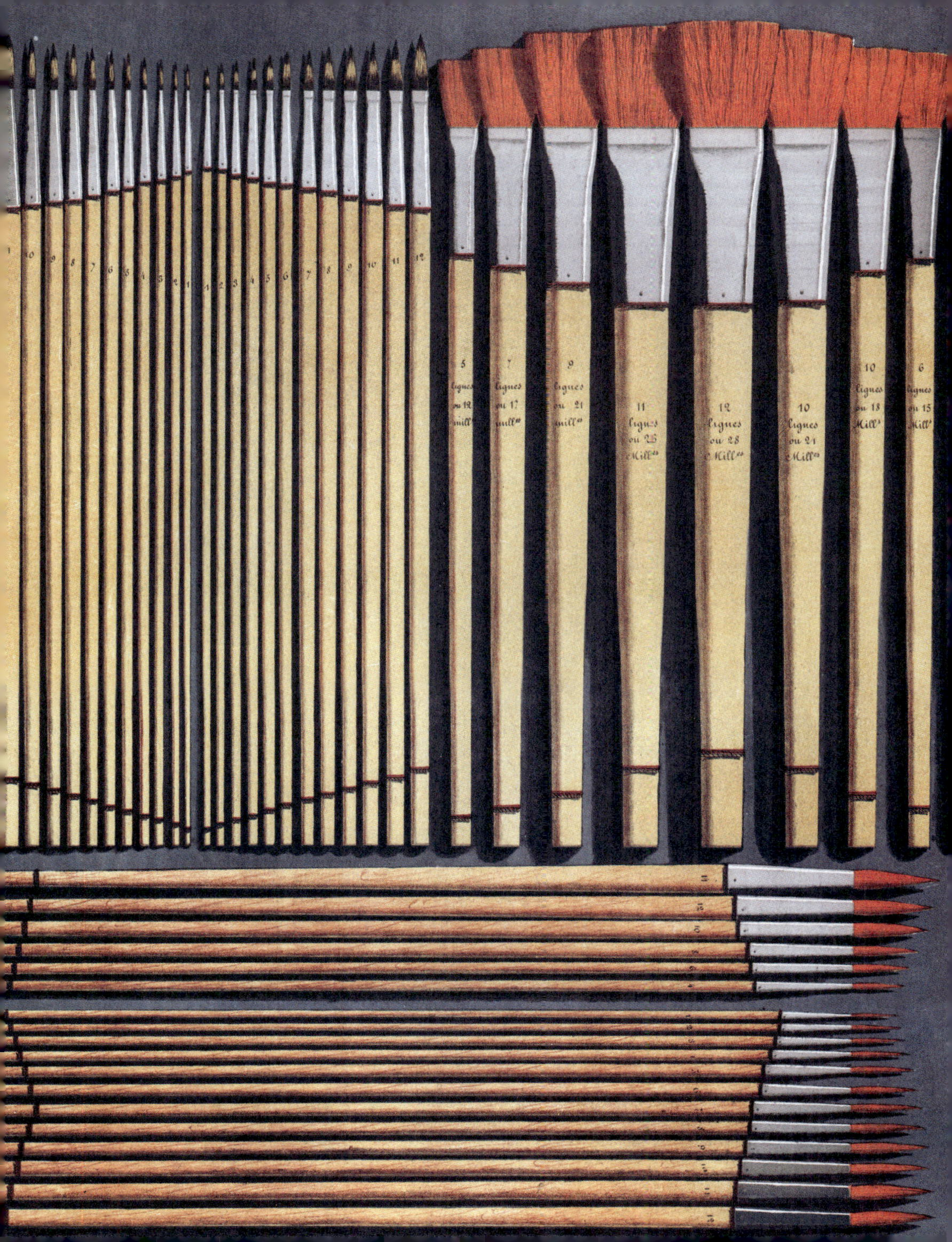
5 lignes ou 12 mills
7 lignes ou 17 mills
9 lignes ou 21 mills
11 lignes ou 25 Mills
12 lignes ou 28 Mills
10 lignes ou 21 Mills
10 lignes ou 18 Mills
6 lignes ou 15 Mills

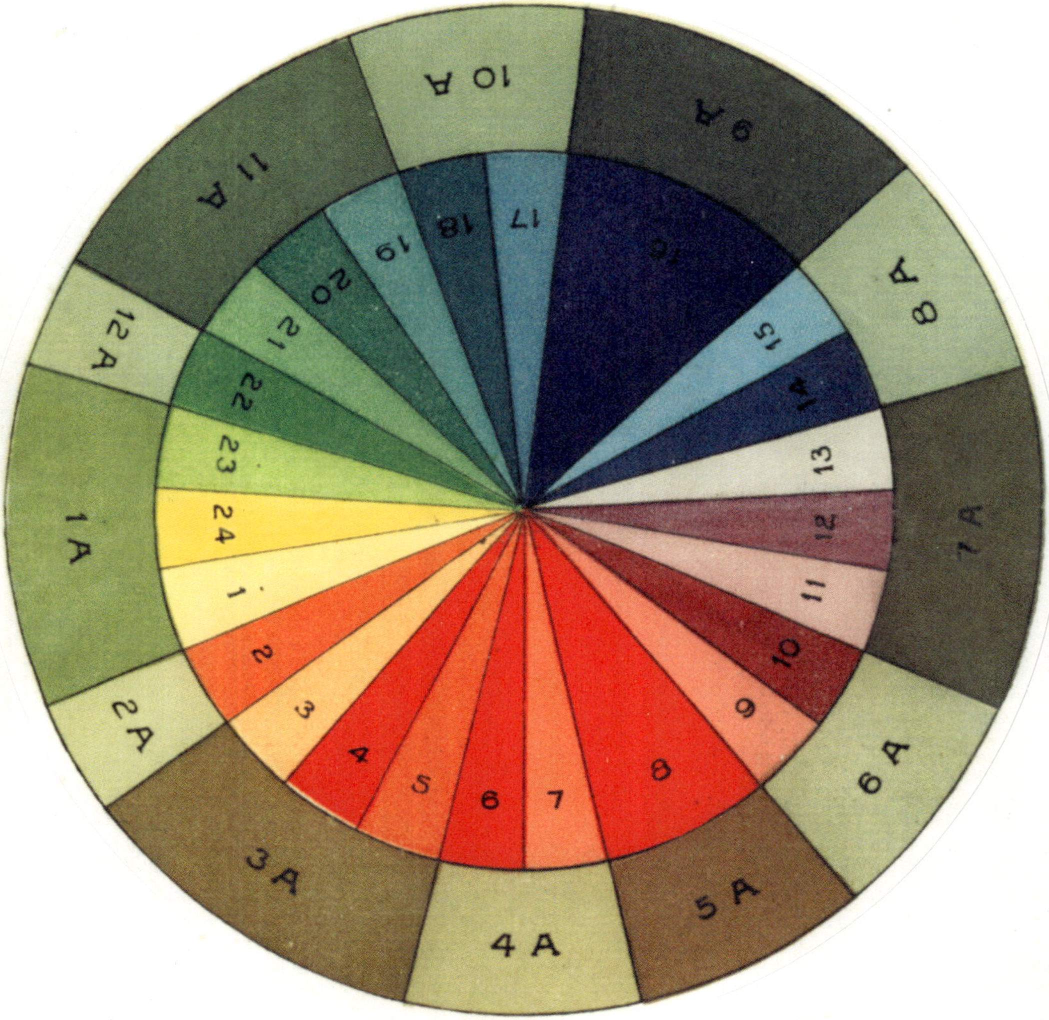

1
2
3
4
5
6
7
8
9
10
11
12
13
14
15
16
17
18
19
20
21
22
23
24
1A
2A
3A
4A
5A
6A
7A
8A
9A
10A
11A
12A

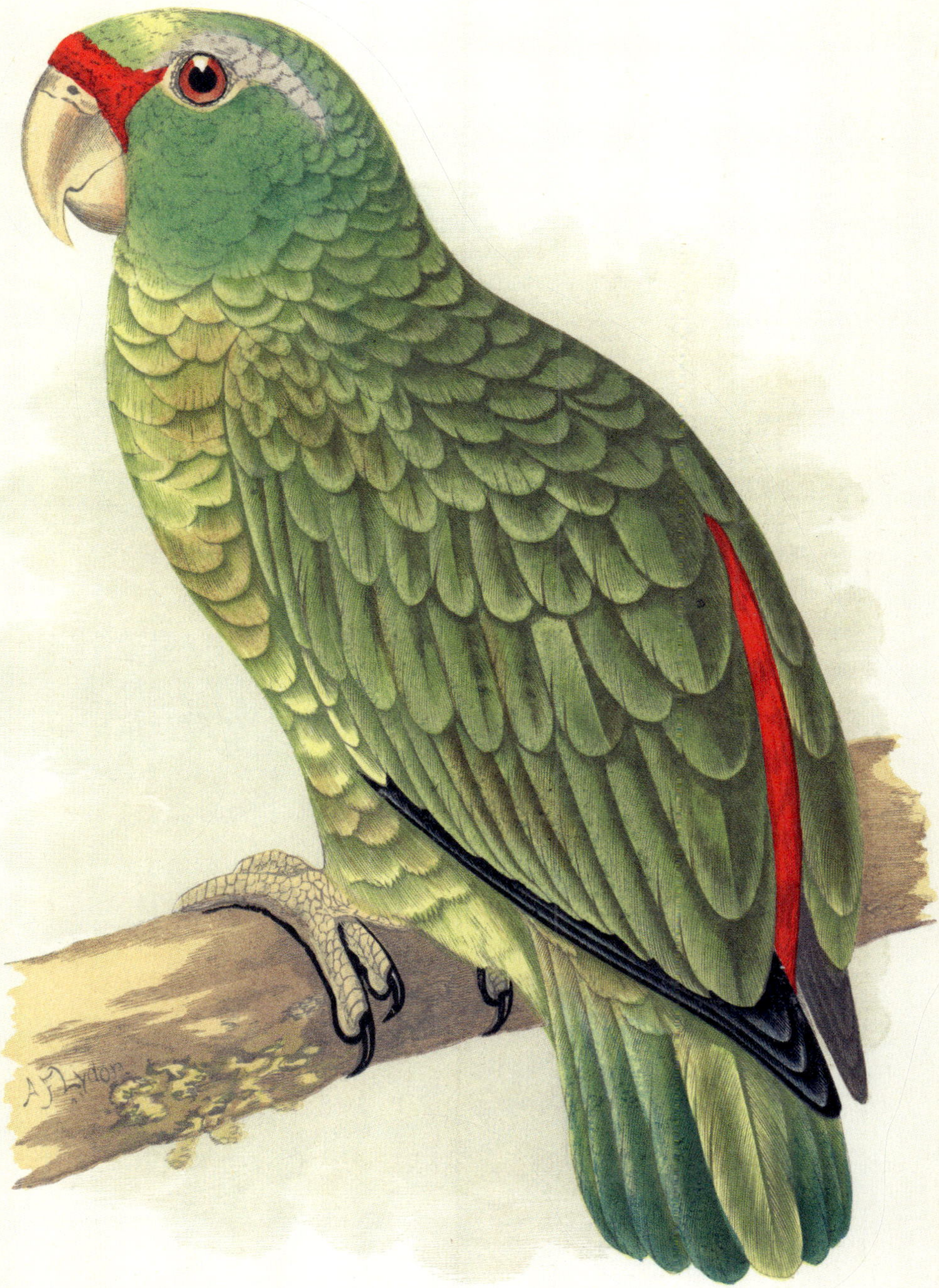
A F Lydon

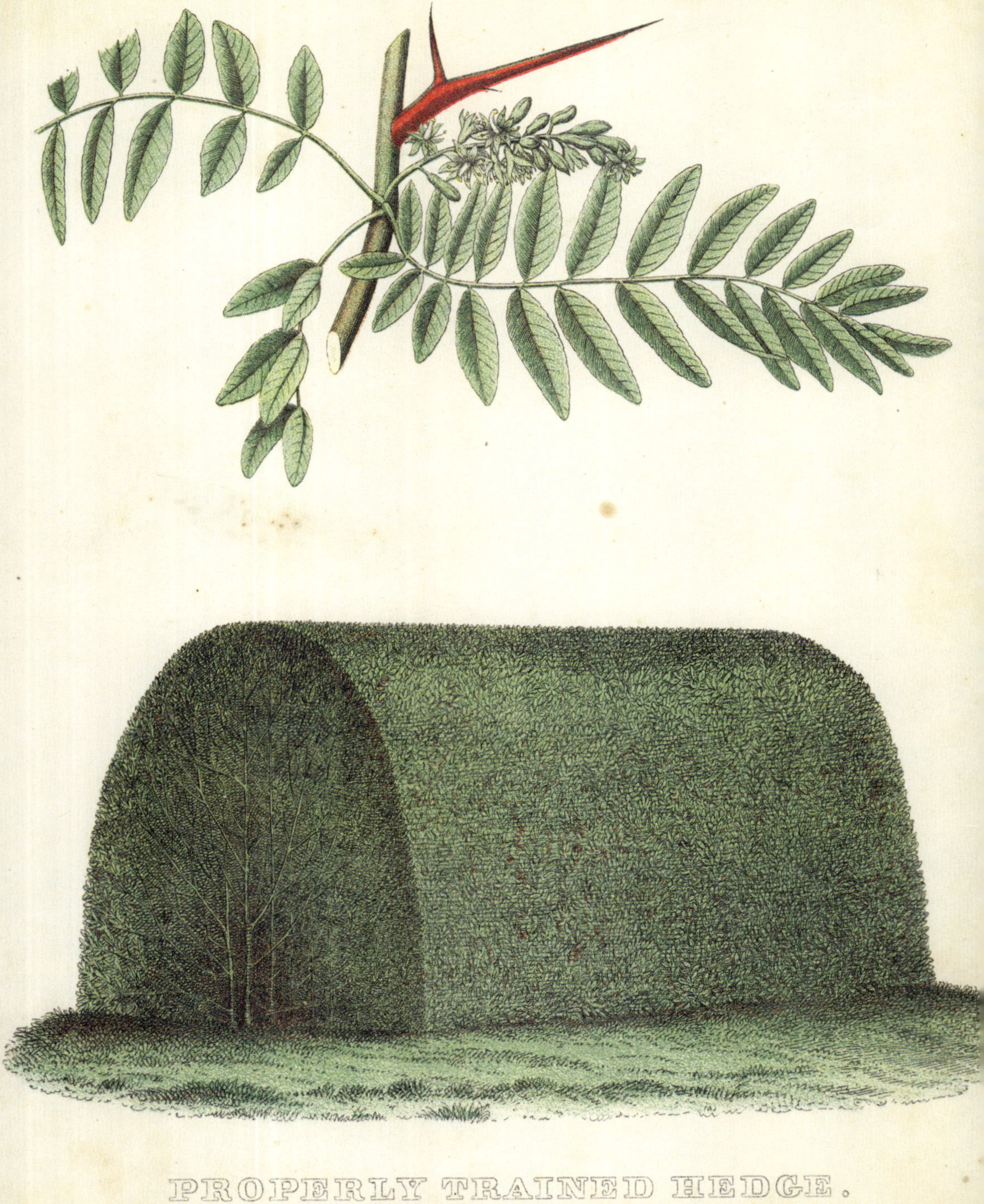

PROPERLY TRAINED HEDGE.

HONEY LOCUST, THORN, LEAF AND FLOWER.

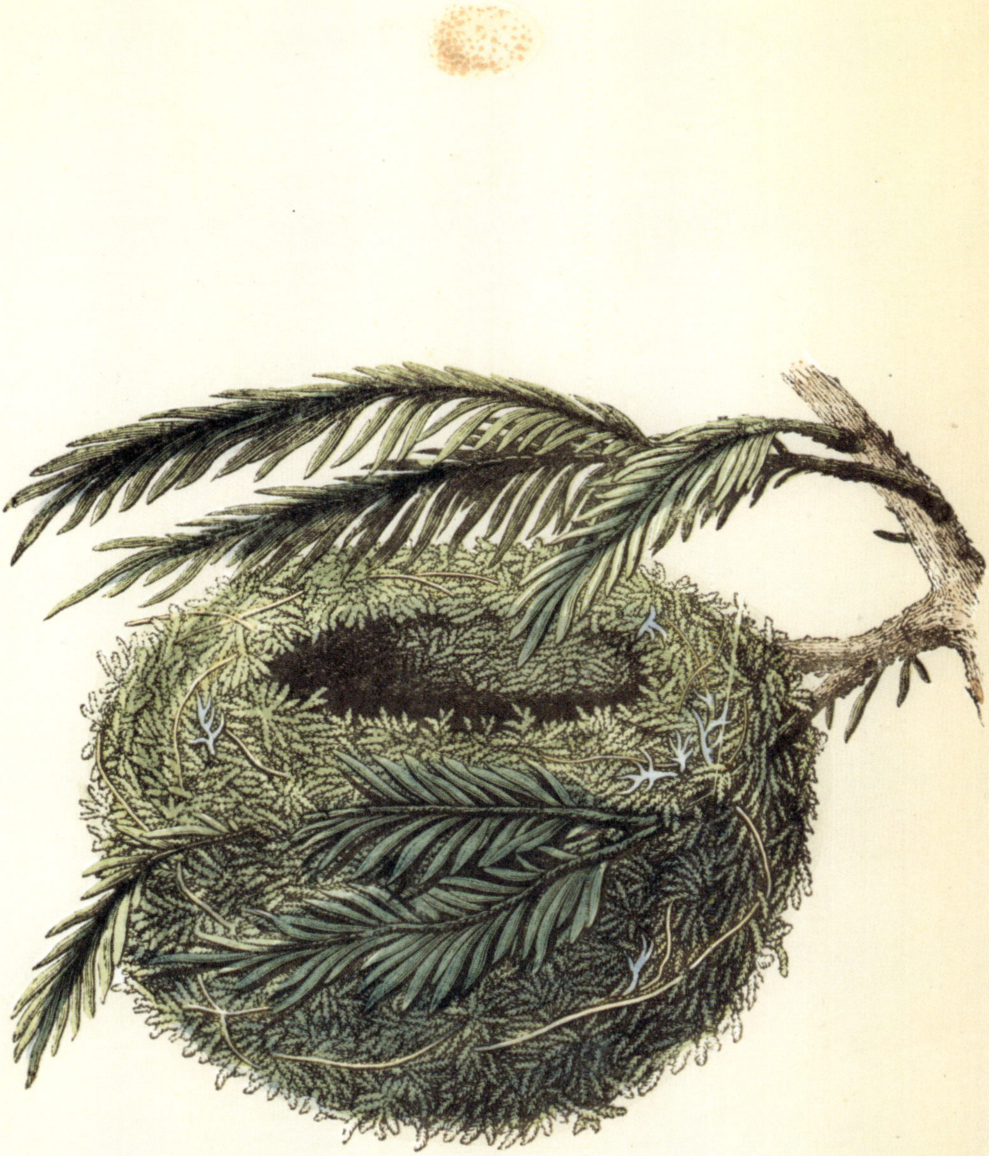

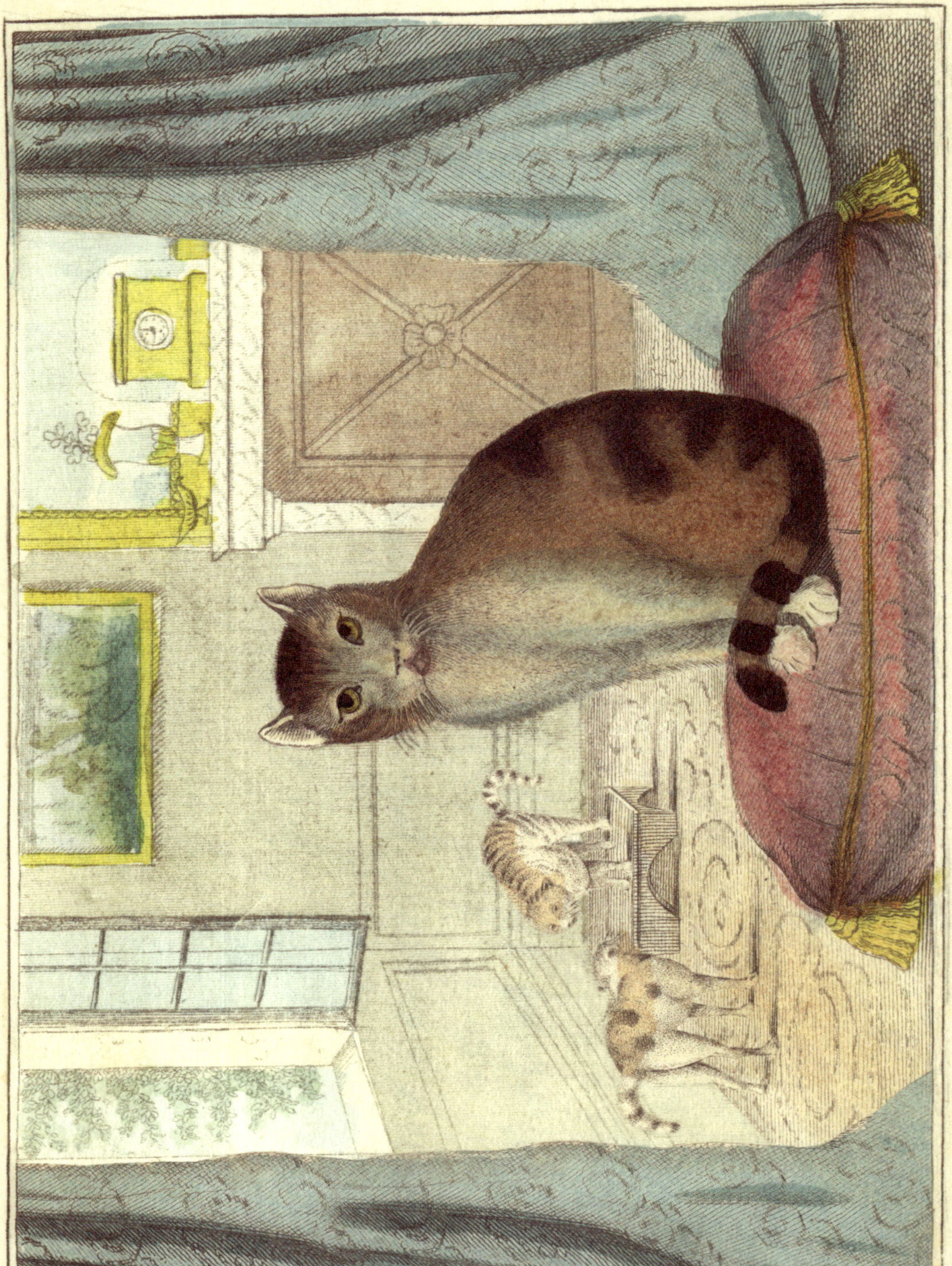

N.790.

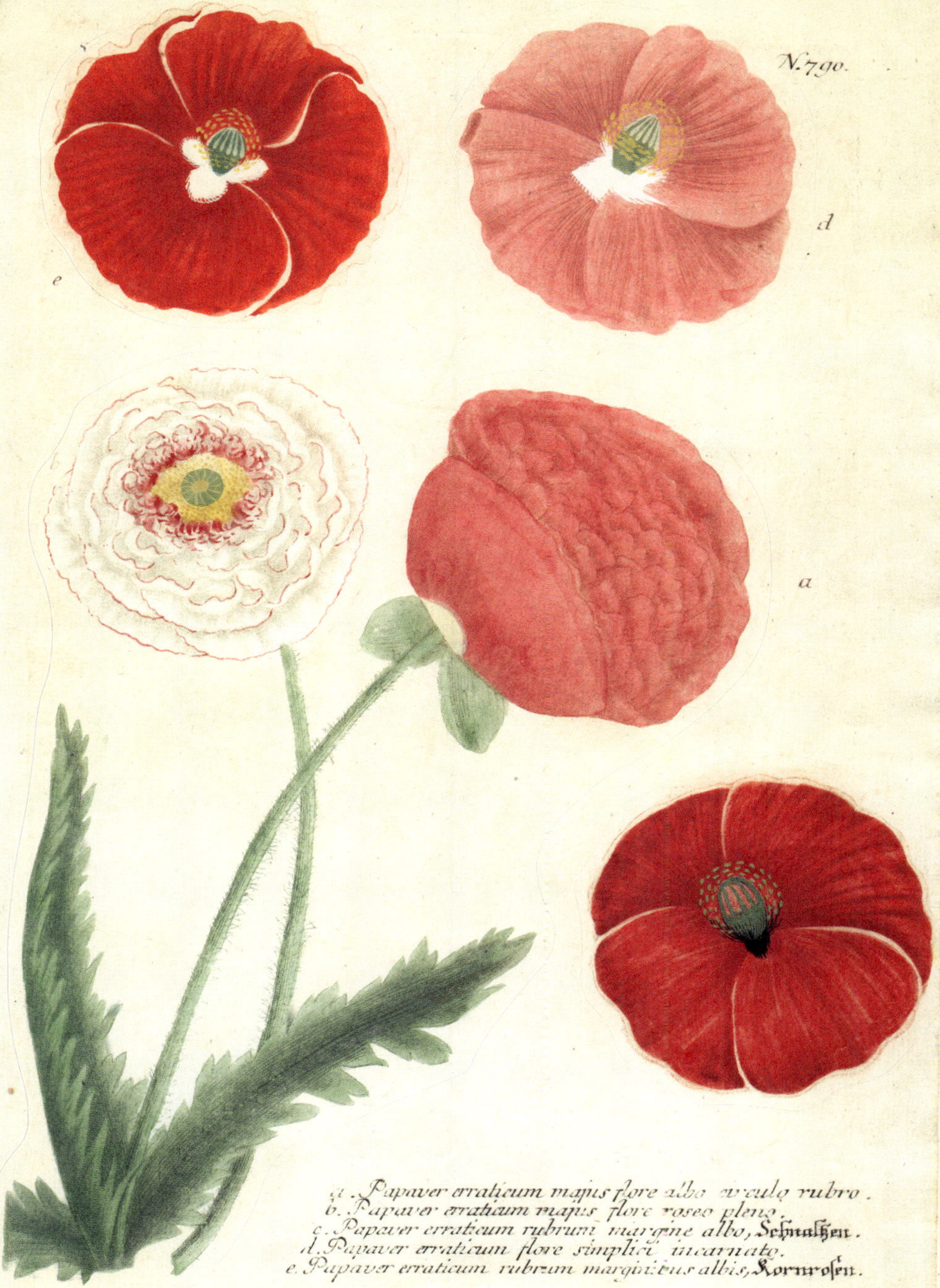

a. Papaver erraticum majus flore albo circulo rubro.
b. Papaver erraticum majus flore roseo pleno.
c. Papaver erraticum rubrum margine albo, Schnalchen.
d. Papaver erraticum flore simplici incarnato.
e. Papaver erraticum rubrum marginibus albis, Kornrosen.

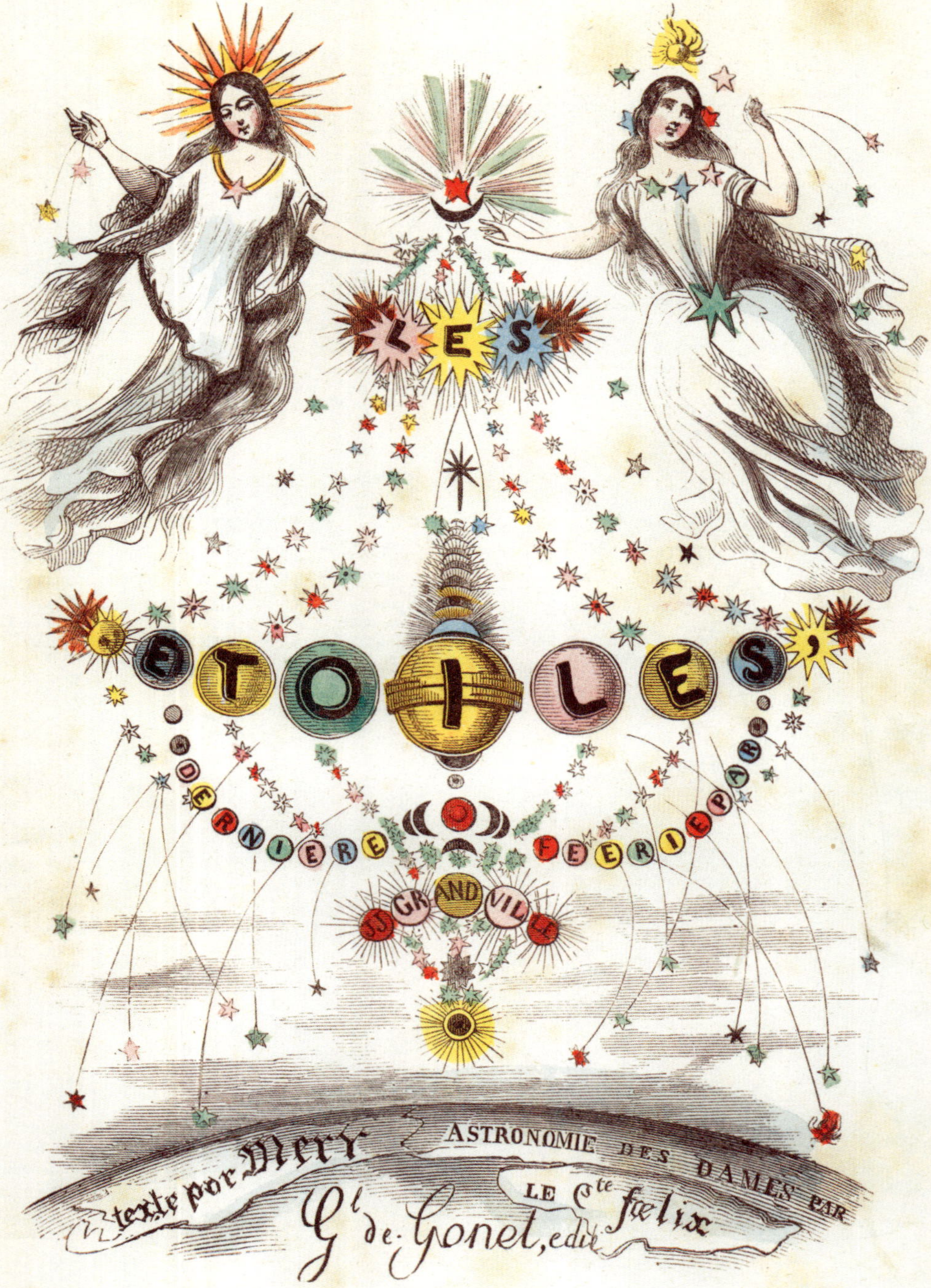
LES
ETOILES,
DERNIERE FEERIE PAR
JJ GRANDVILLE
texte par Mery
ASTRONOMIE DES DAMES PAR
LE Cte Fœlix
Gl de Gonet, edit

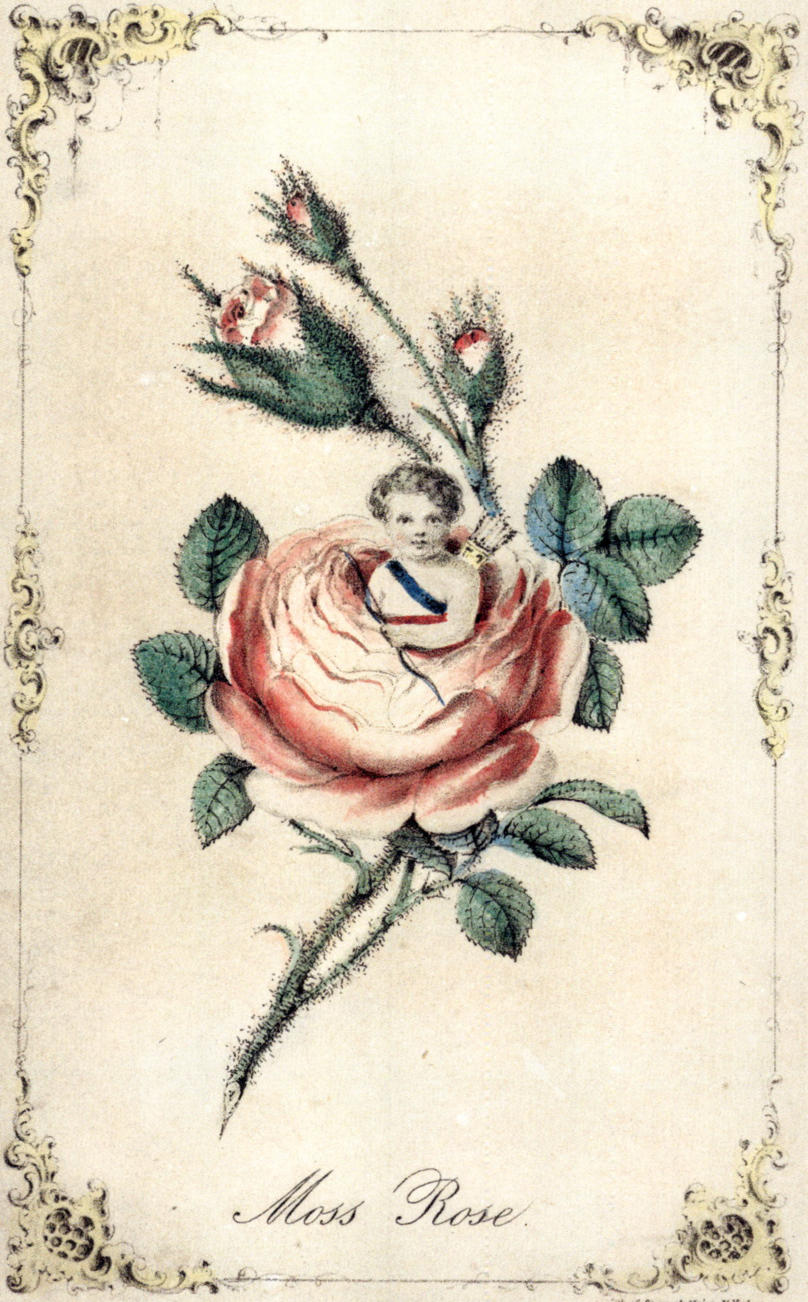

Moss Rose

NEW YORK.
Nafis & Cornish.

Lith. of Sarony & Major N. York.

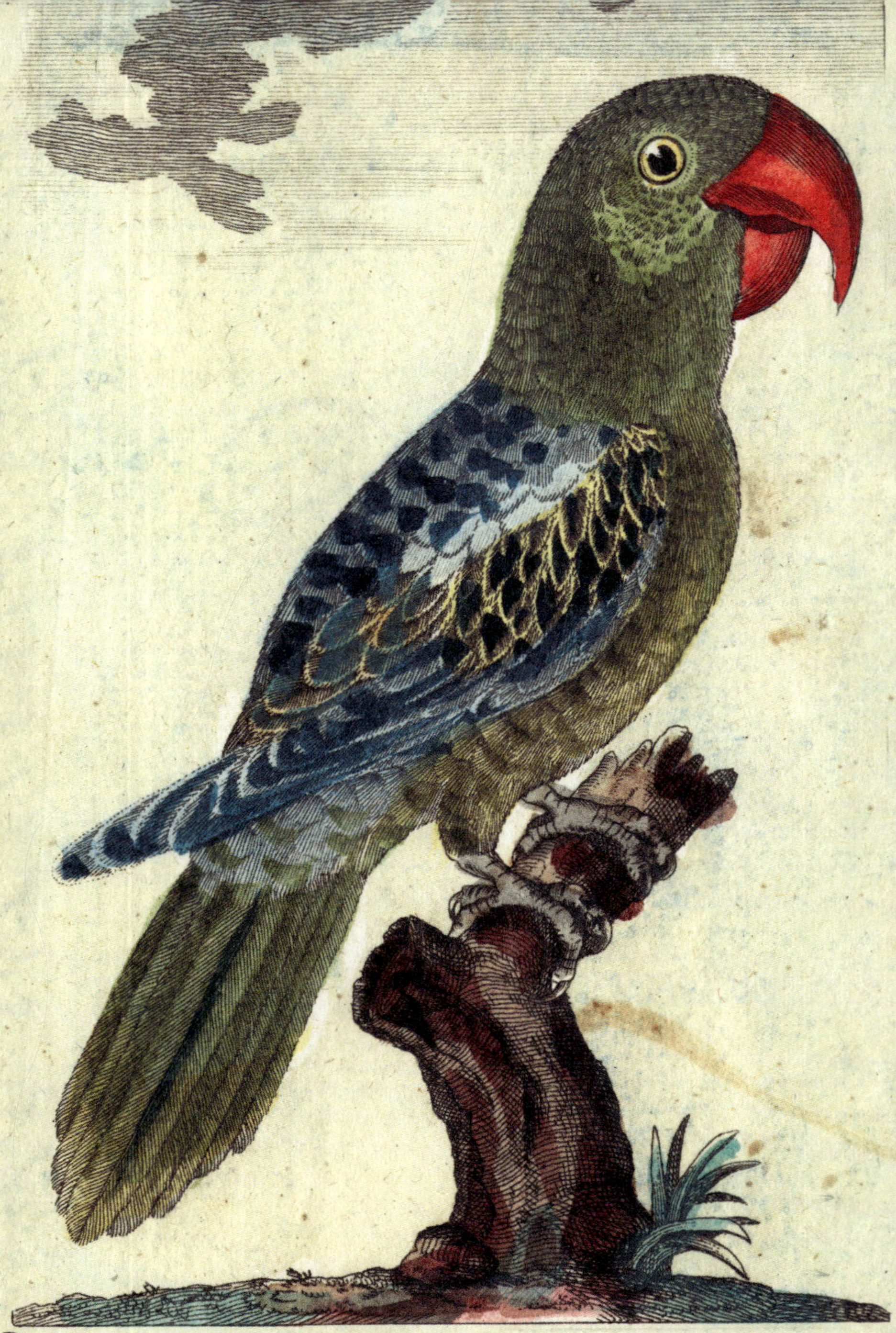

Büff. N. d. Vögel XIX. T.

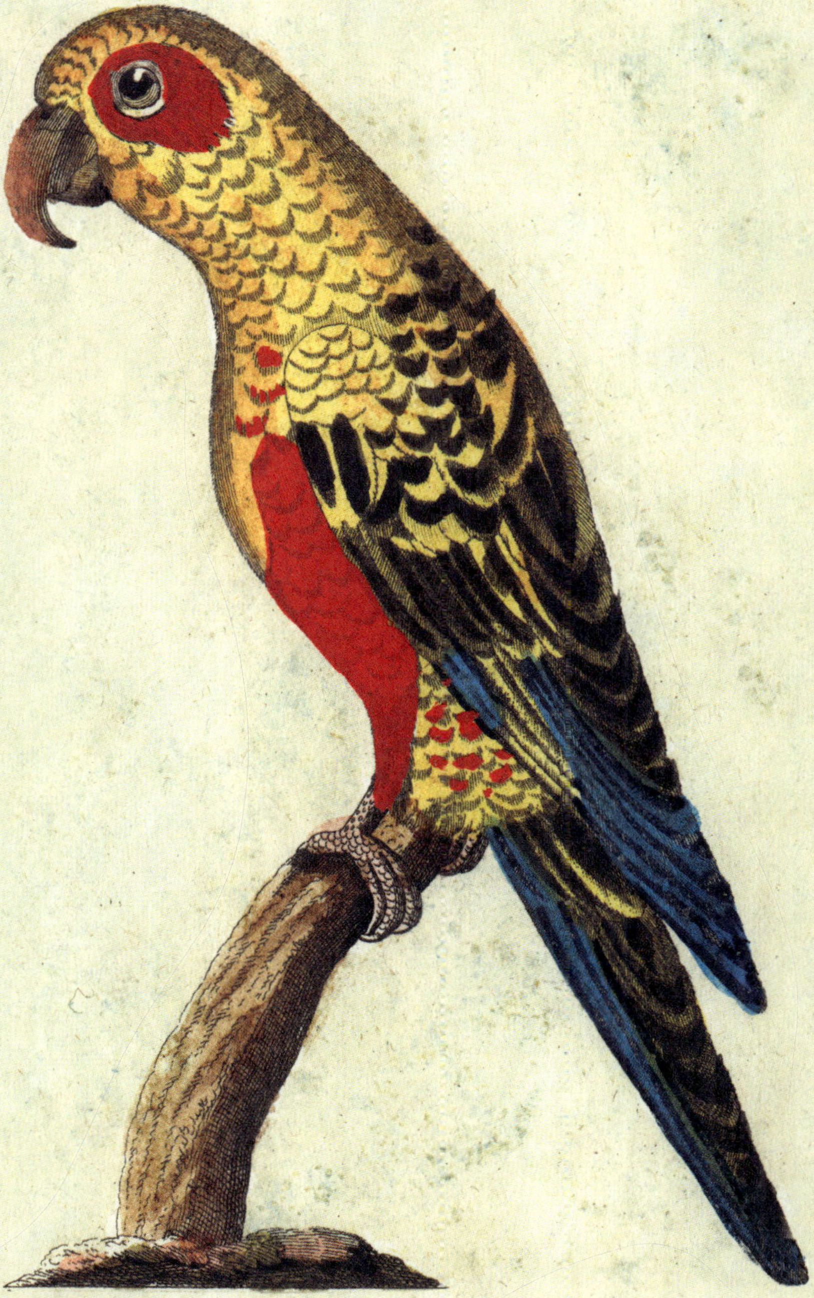

Büff N d Vogel XIX Th

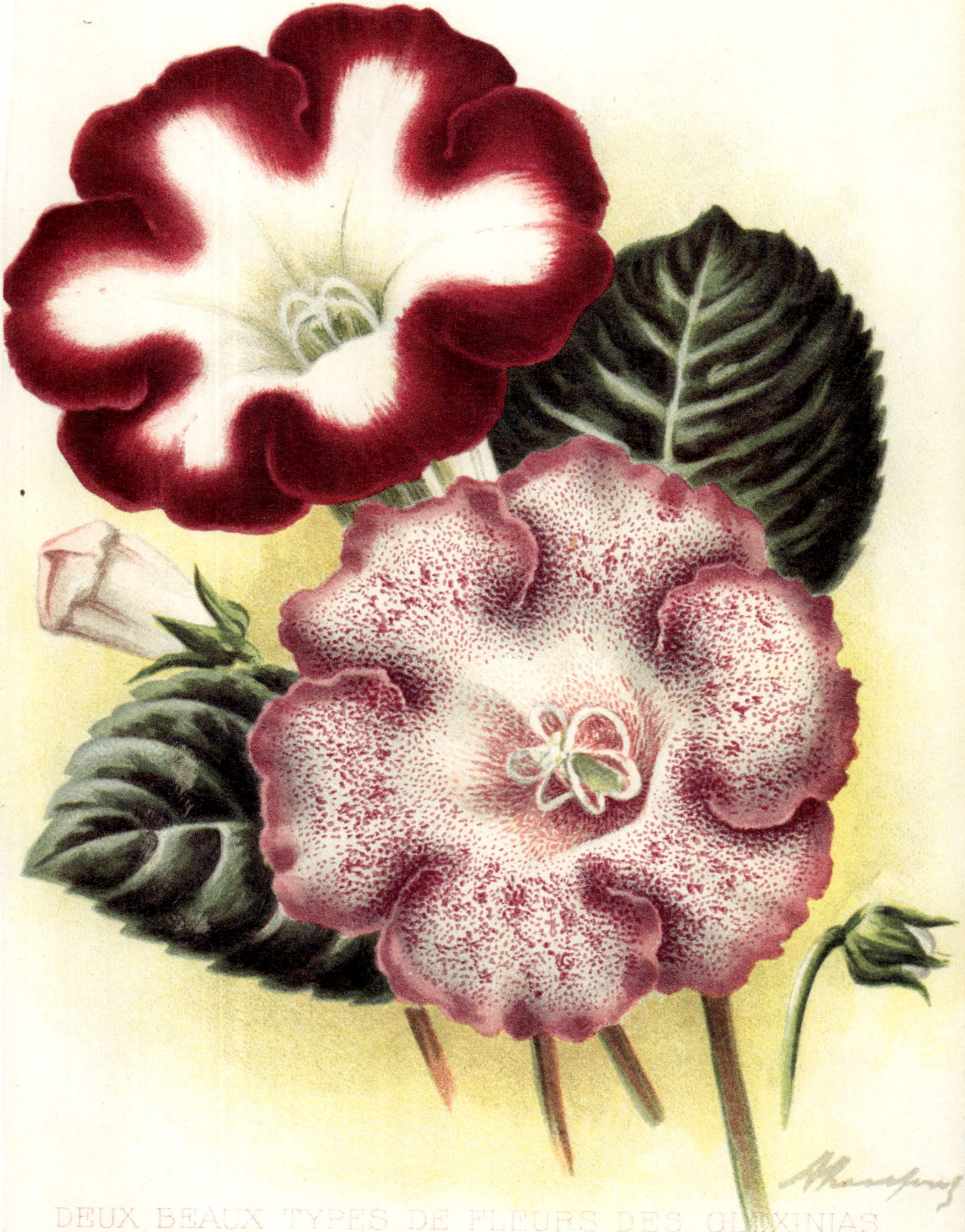

DEUX BEAUX TYPES DE FLEURS DES GLOXINIAS
DE LA RACE KEGELJAN DE NAMUR

2.

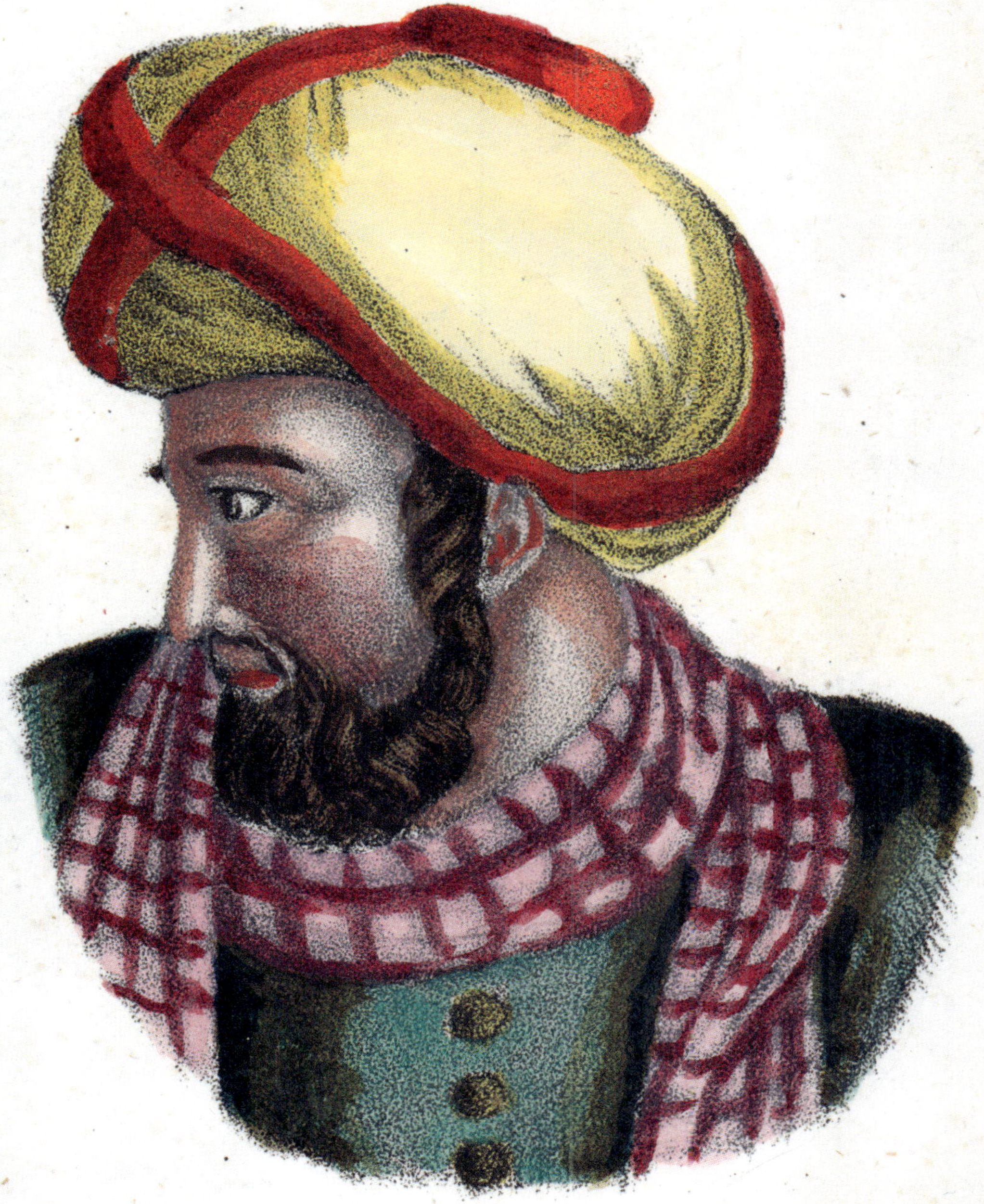

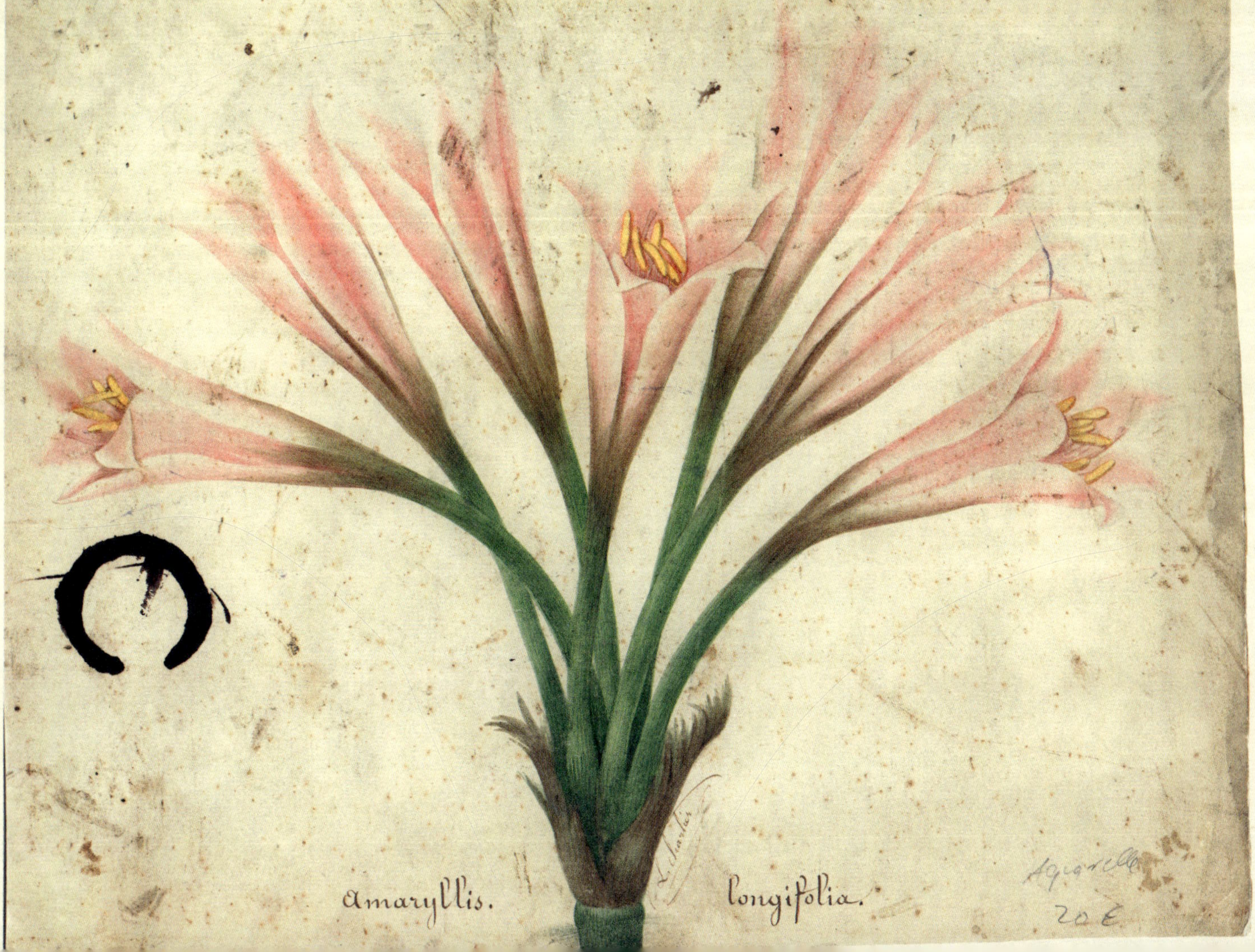

amaryllis. longifolia.

Aquarelle 20 E

ELEPHAS.

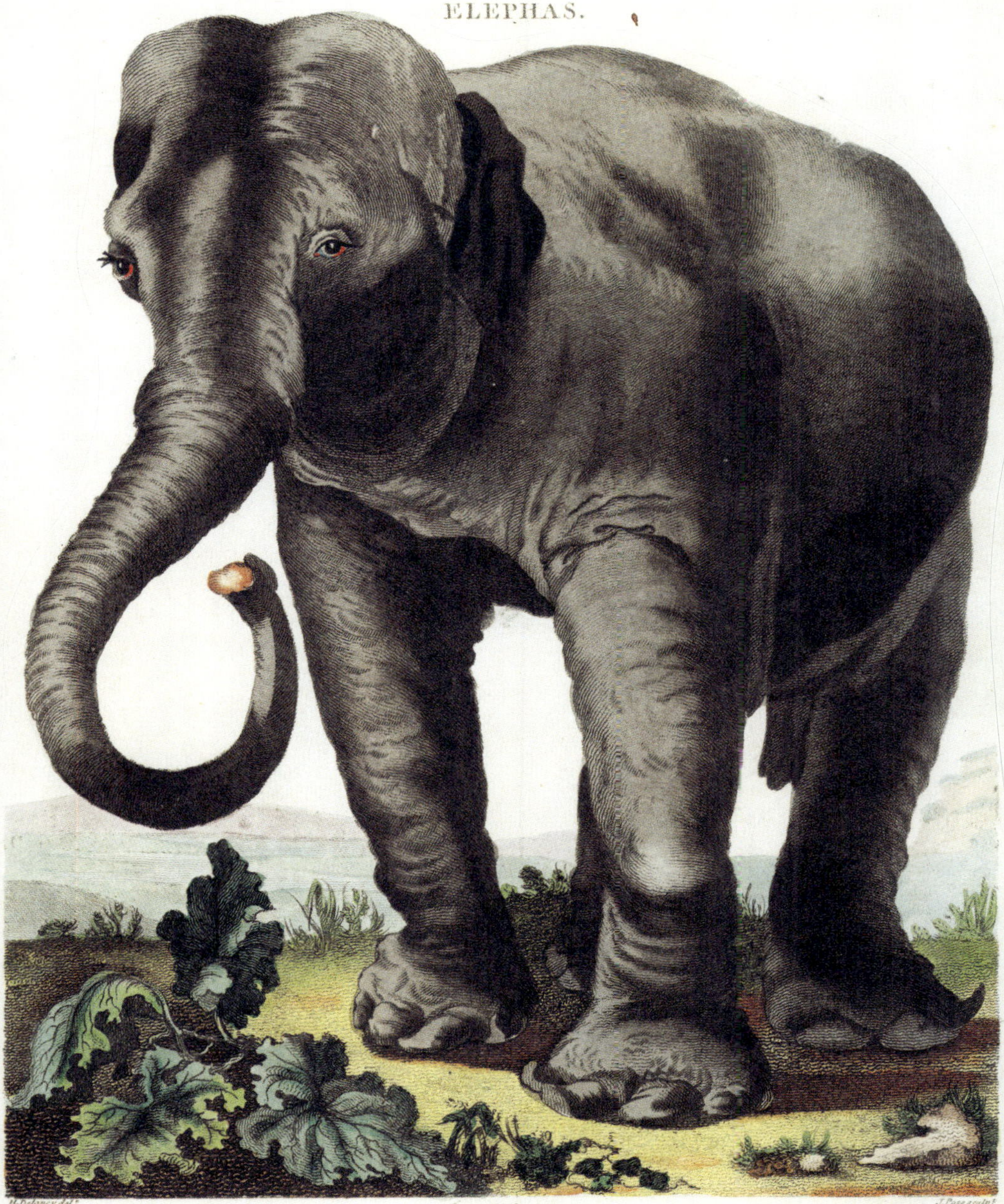

H. Delaney del.t J. Pass sculp.t

The Elephant.

London, Published as the Act directs, September [illegible] by J. Wilkes.

Joseph Campbell
To
Moleson Fitz Randolph

— Deed —
Dated 27th March, 1764.

... February 8th A.D. 1821

To reduce an improper fraction to ... whole or mixed Number

Rule

Divide the upper ... by the lower

... proper terms Result 16 13/19

$19 \,)\, 317 \,(16 \tfrac{13}{19}$

Reduce $\frac{141}{17}$ to its proper terms Result $8 \frac{5}{17}$

$17 \,)\, 141 \,(8 \tfrac{5}{17}$

Reduce $\frac{126}{48}$ to its proper terms Result $2 \frac{5}{8}$

$48 \,)\, 126 \,(2 \tfrac{5}{8}$

Reduce $\frac{3848}{21}$ to its proper terms Result $183 \frac{5}{21}$

$21 \,)\, 3848 \,(183 \tfrac{5}{21}$

6 Reduce $\frac{1245}{22}$ to its proper terms Result $56 \frac{13}{22}$

$22 \,)\, 1245 \,(56 \tfrac{13}{22}$

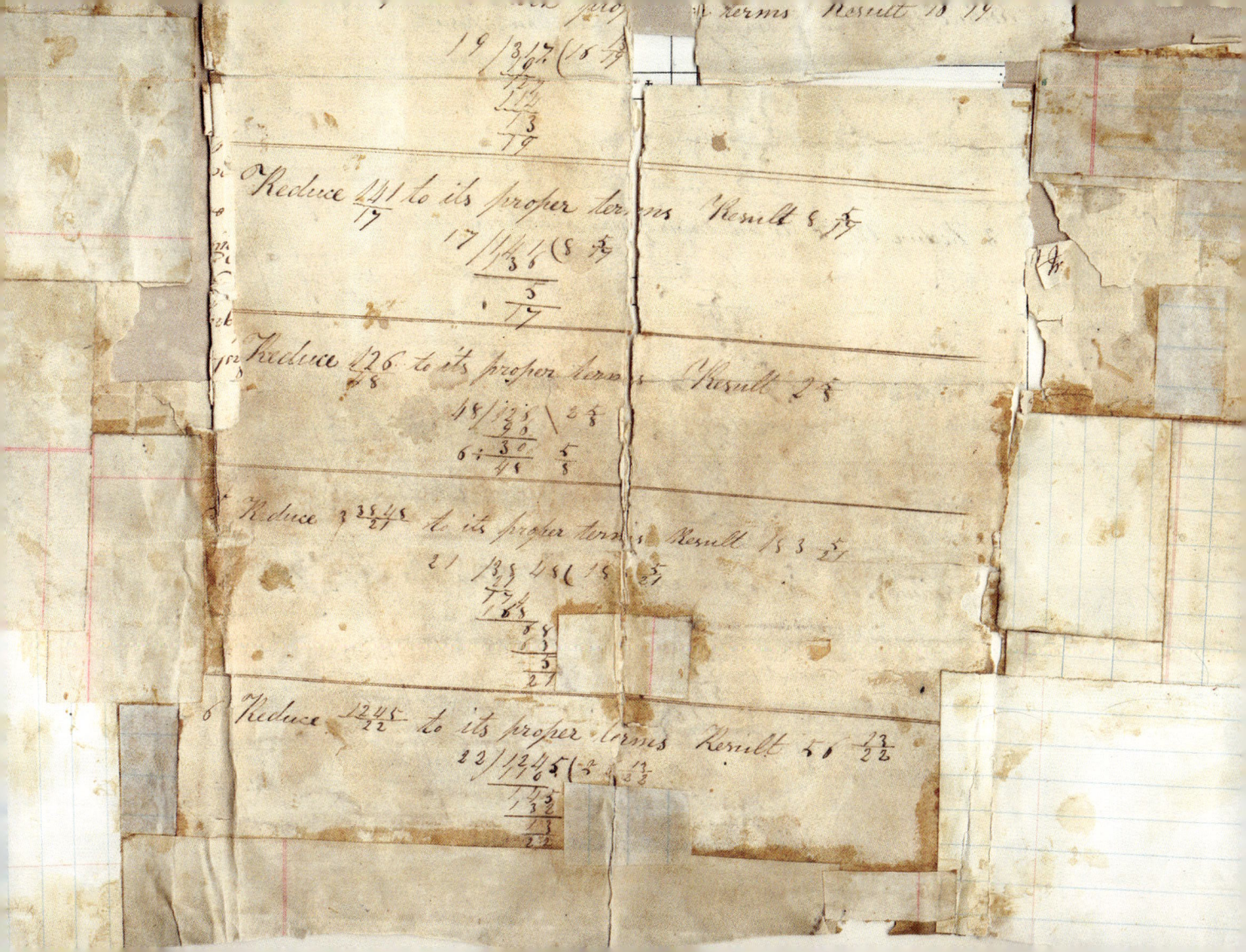

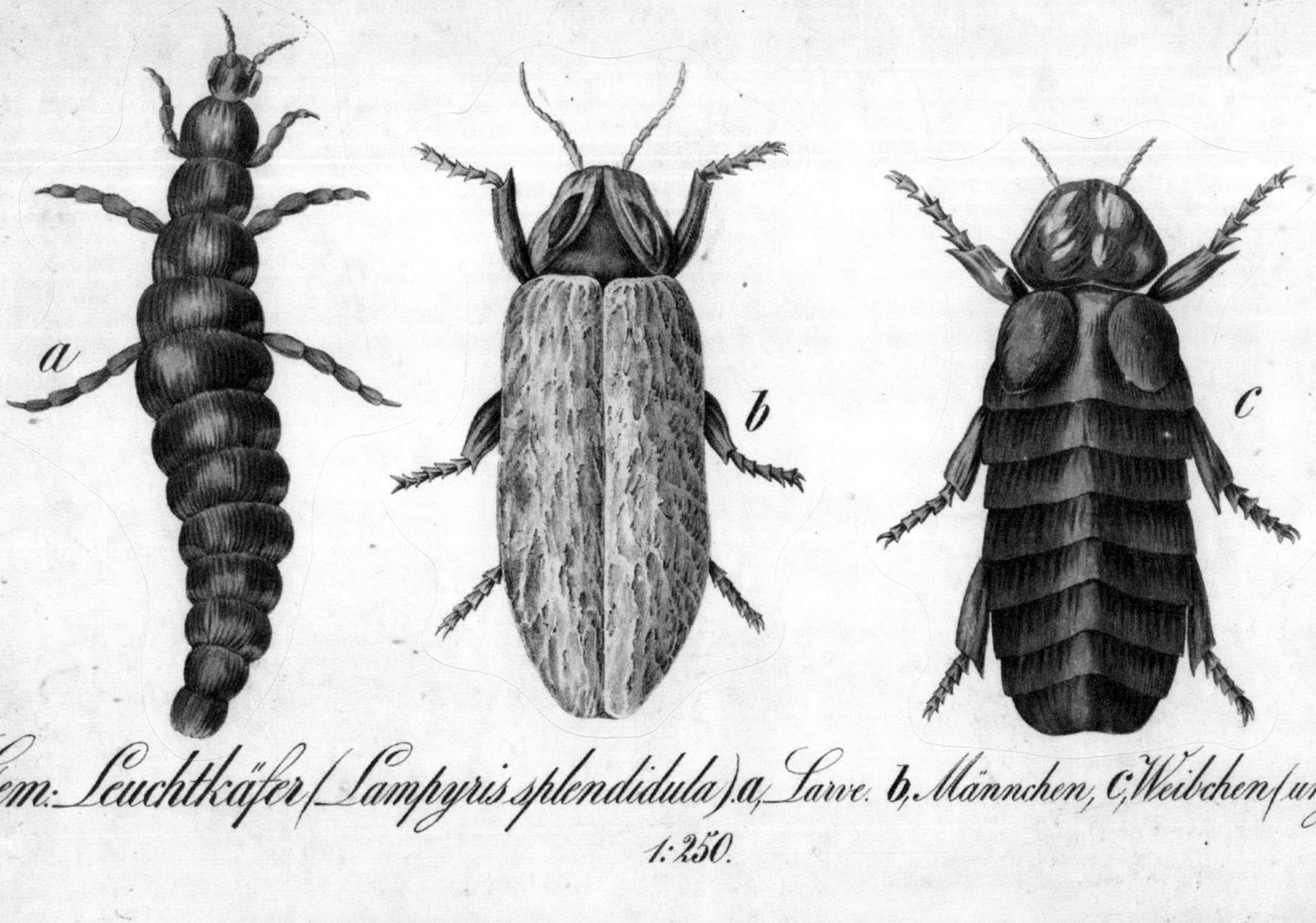

Gem: Leuchtkäfer (Lampyris splendidula). a, Larve. b, Männchen, c, Weibchen (ungef.
1:250.

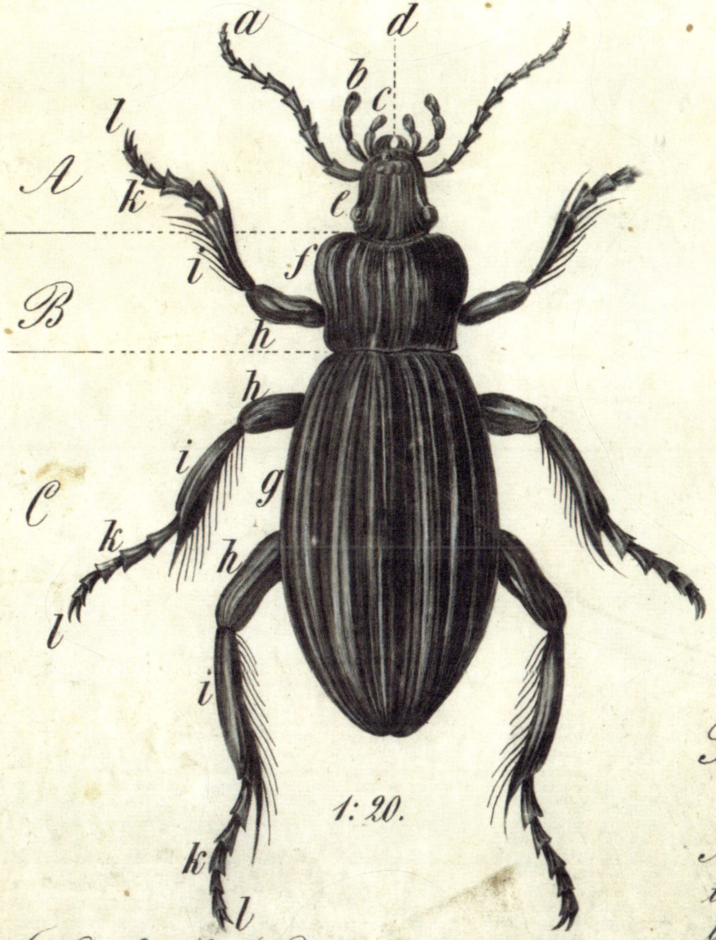

…der Laufkäfer (Carabus coreaceus.)

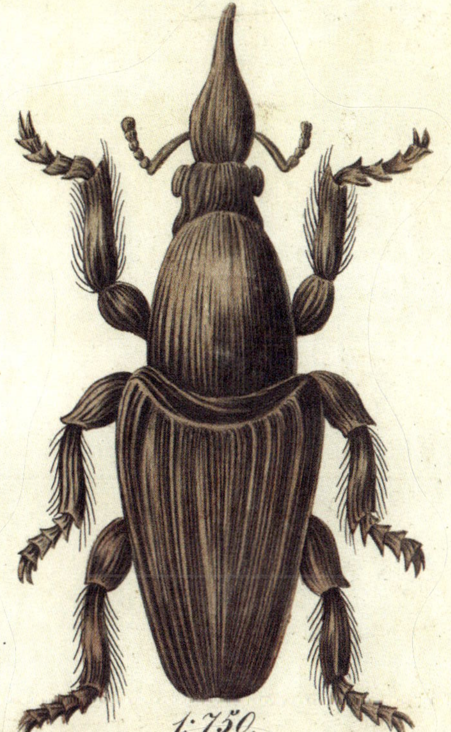

Brauner Kornwurm (Calandra granar…

A. Kopf, a, Fühler (gegliedert), b, Kinnladentaster, c, L… taster, d, Fressverkzeuge (zangenförmig), e, Kopfschild (seit… liegende Augen). B. Brustschild mit dem ersten Fusspaar… derbeine), woran: h, Oberschenkel, i, Unterschenkel, k, Fuss… ke oder Tarsen, l, Klauenglied. C. Hinterleib (Abdomen…

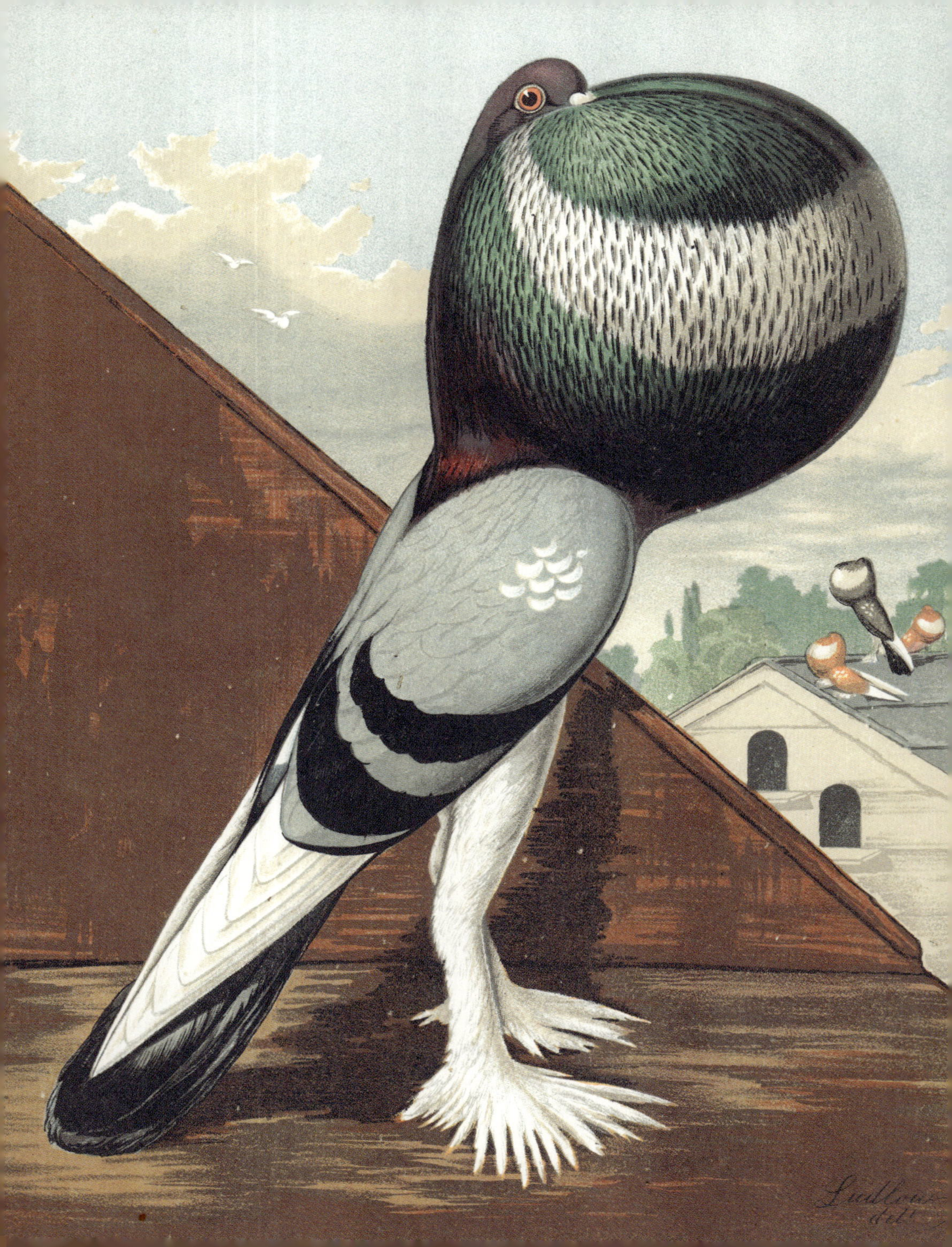
Ludlow
del.

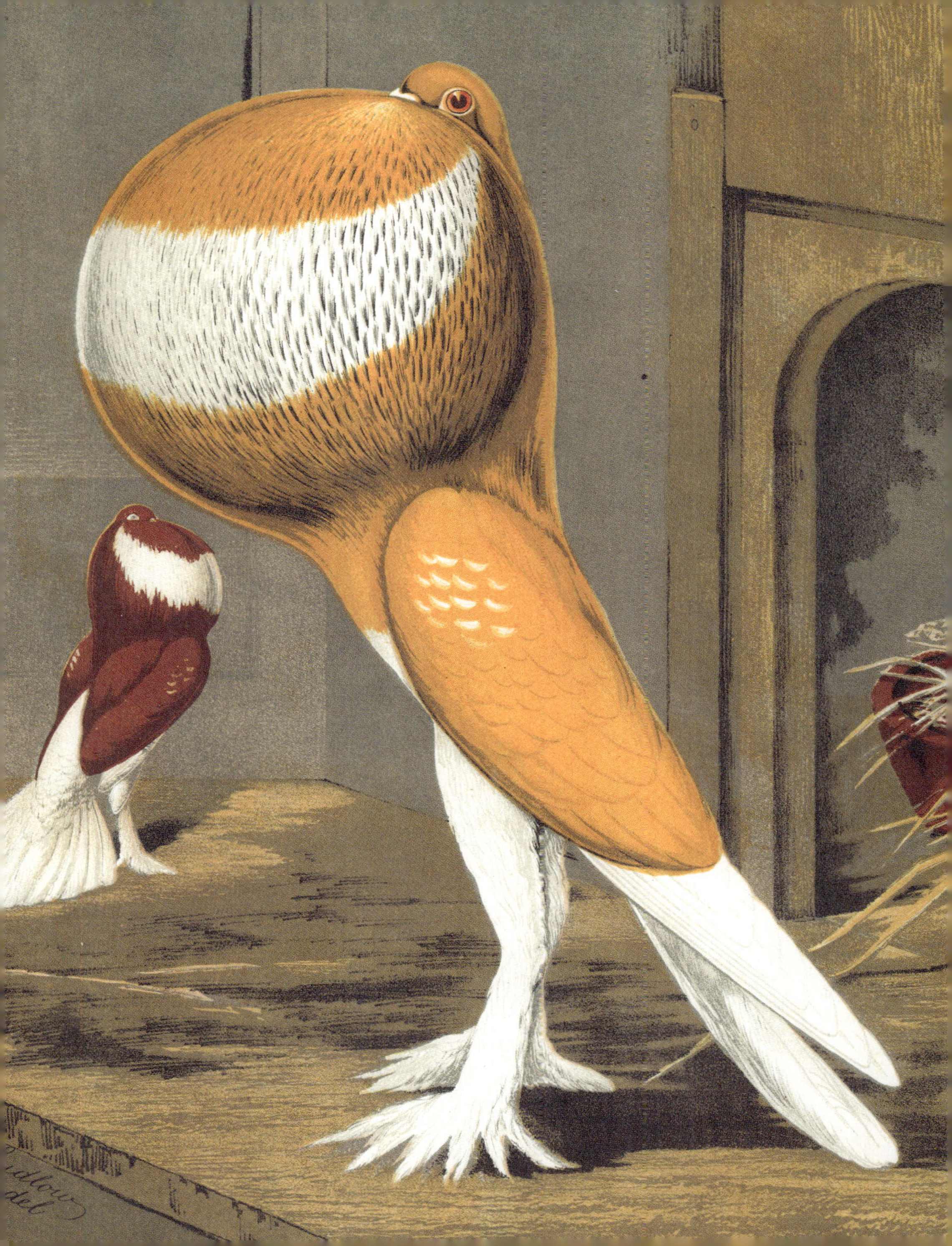

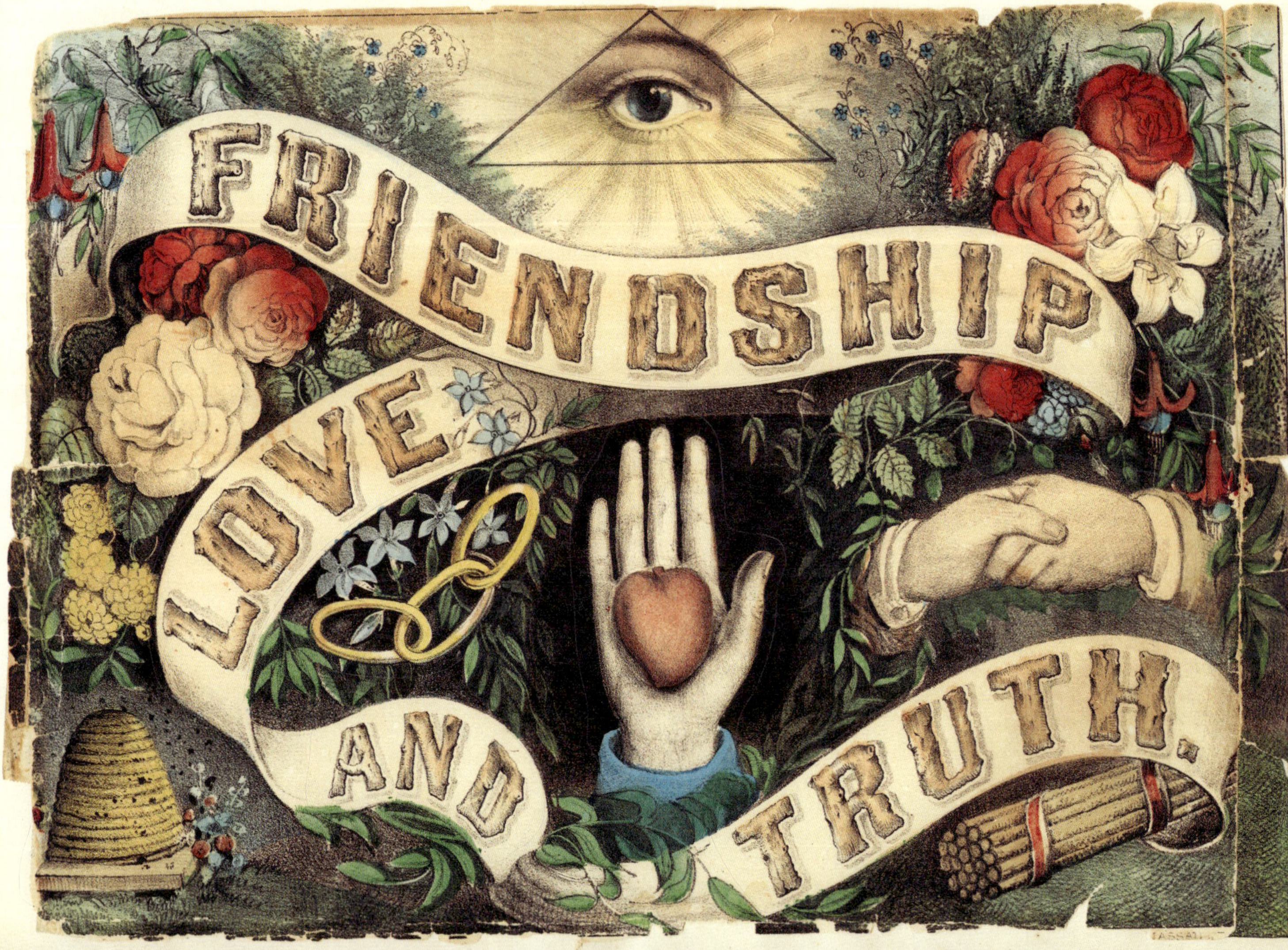
FRIENDSHIP
LOVE
AND
TRUTH.

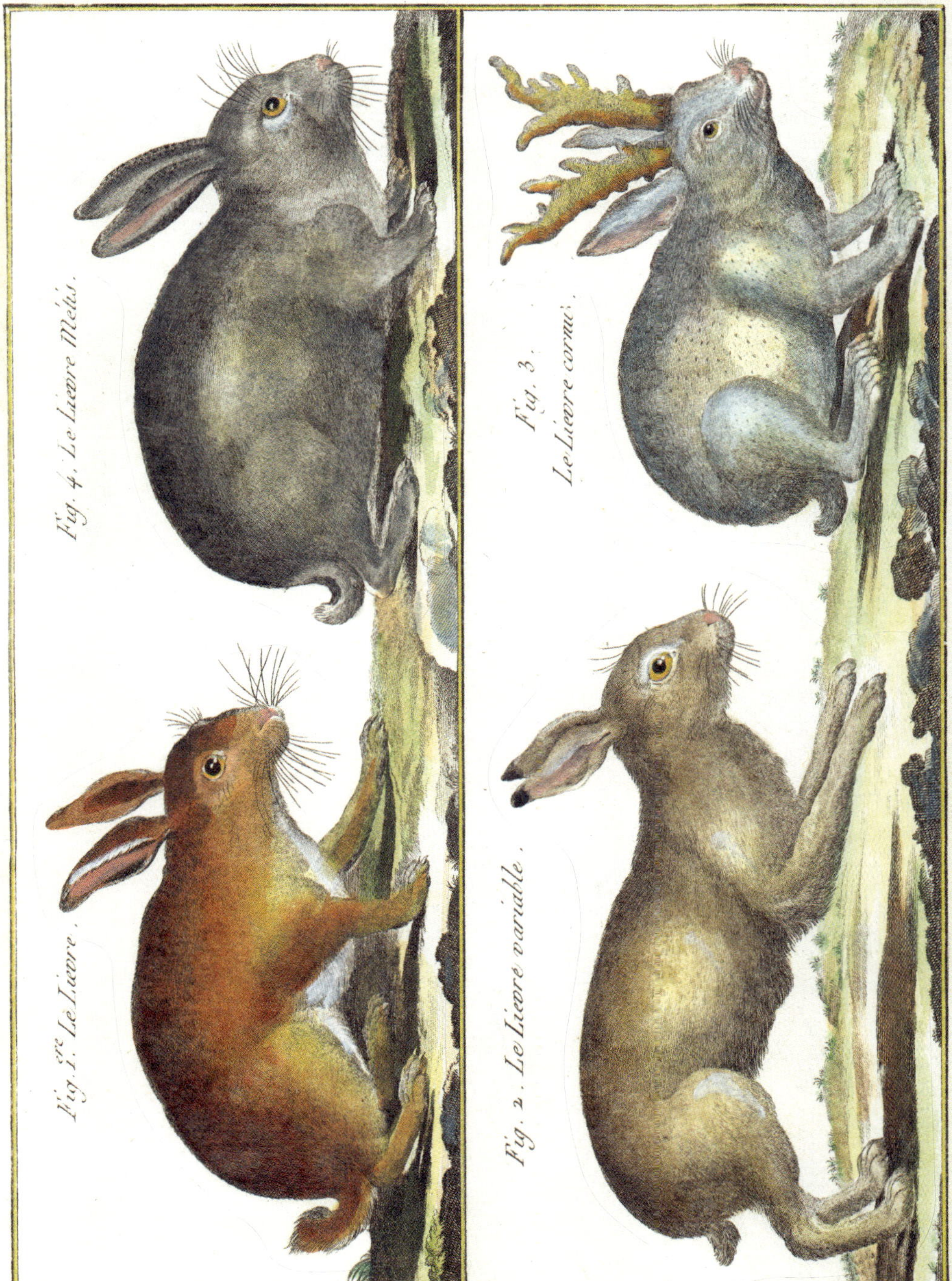

Fig. 1.re Le Lievre.

Fig. 2. Le Lievre variable.

Fig. 3. Le Lievre cornu.

Fig. 4. Le Lievre Métis.

Benard Direxit

Histoire Naturelle, Quadrupèdes.

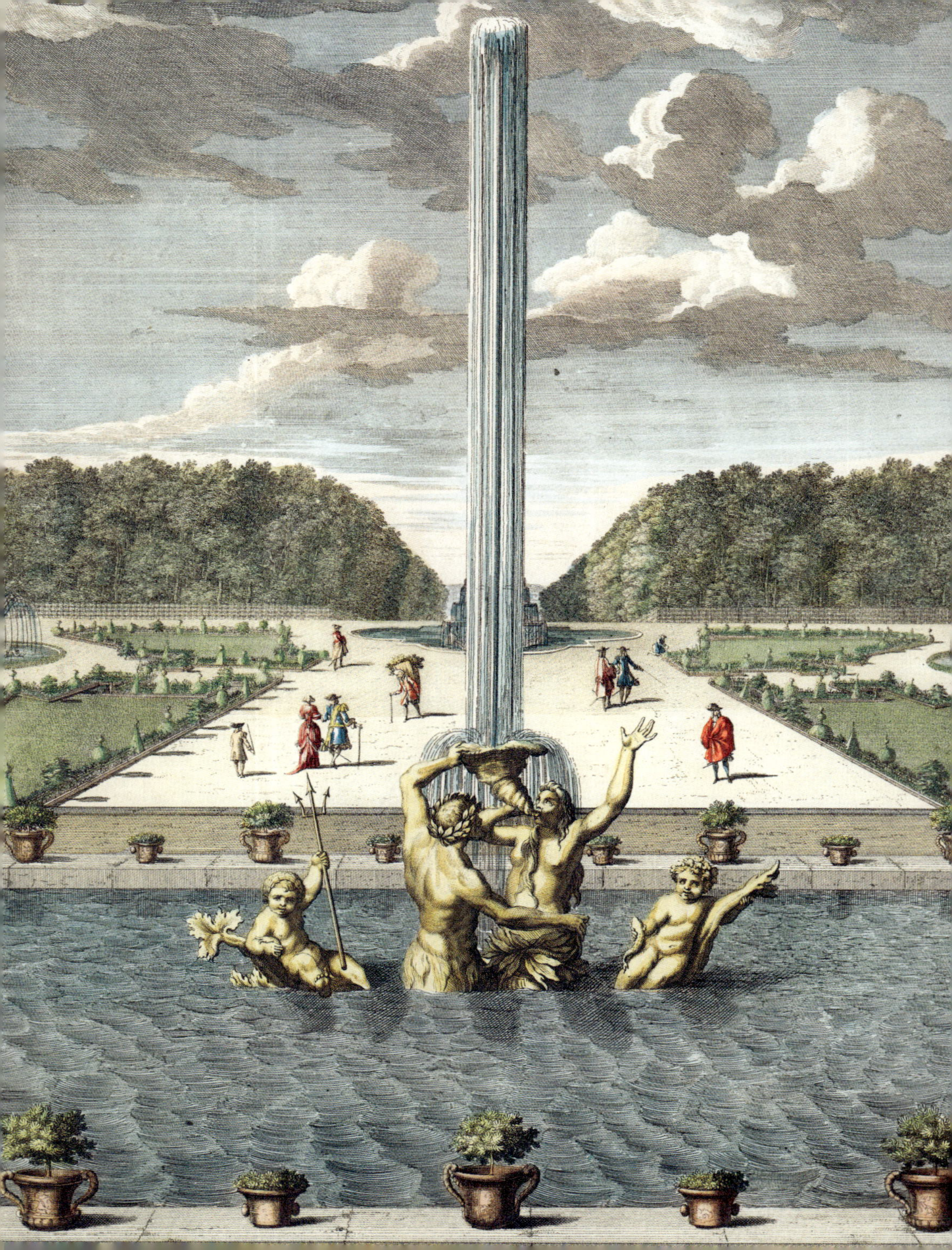

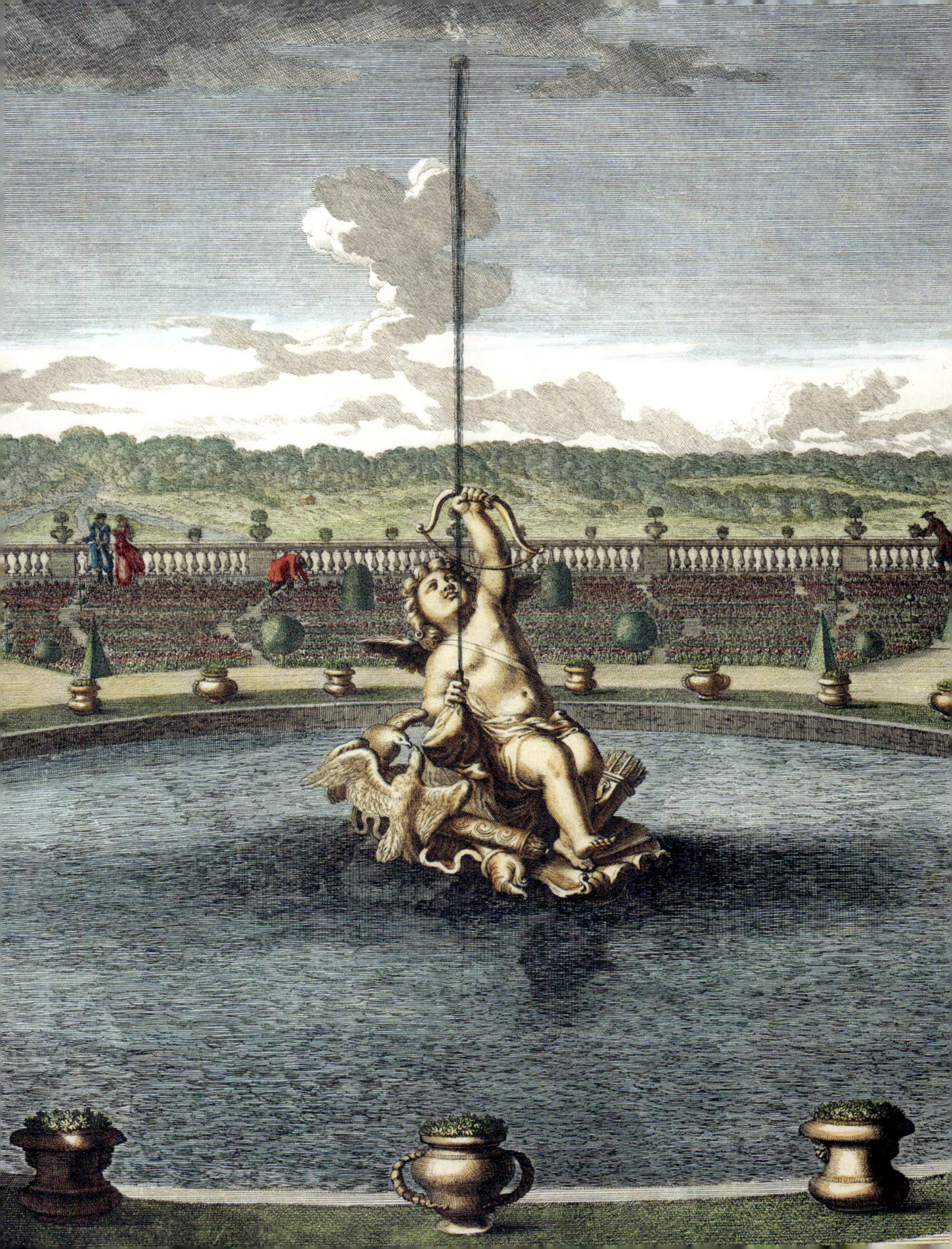

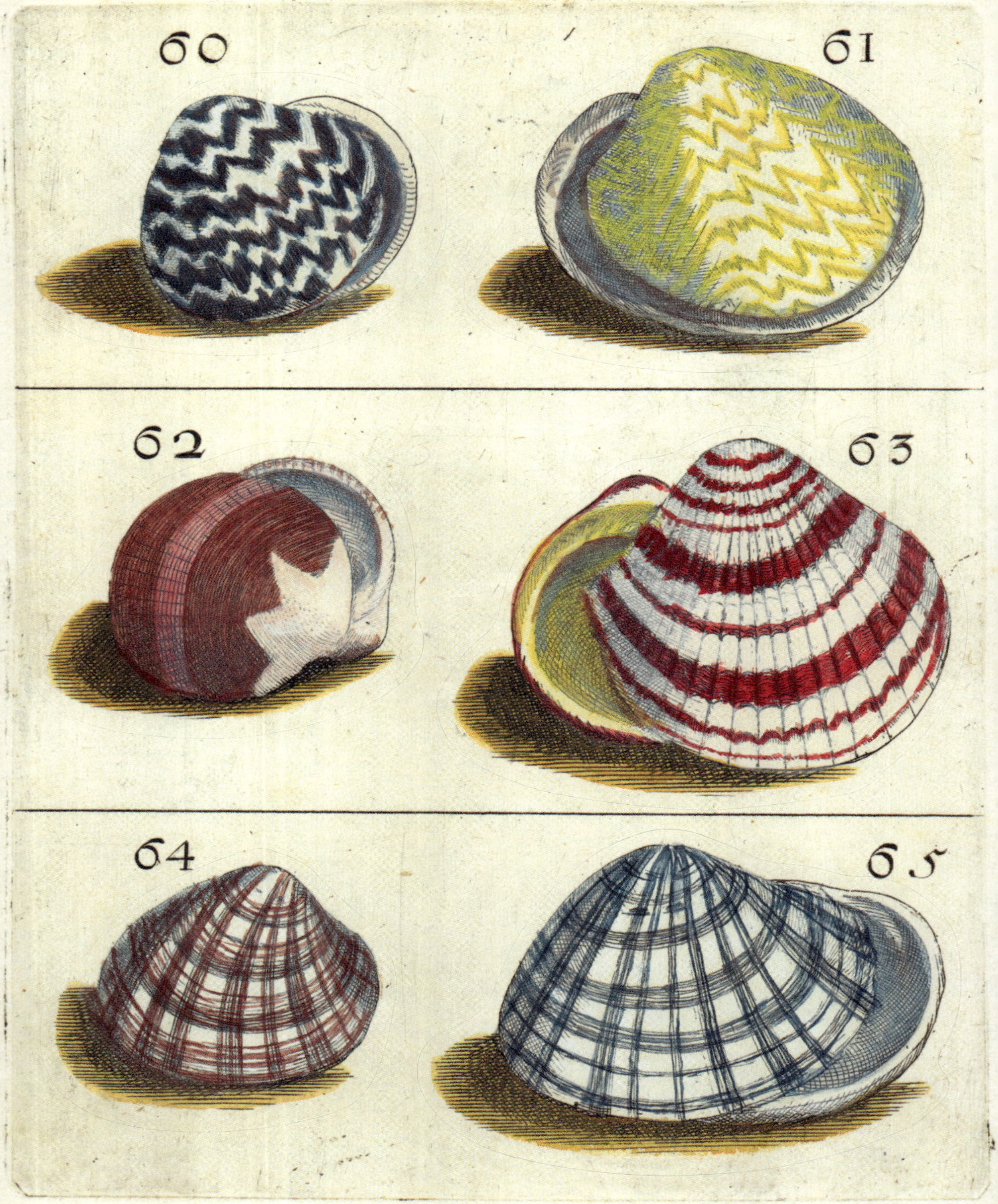
60
61
62
63
64
65

1

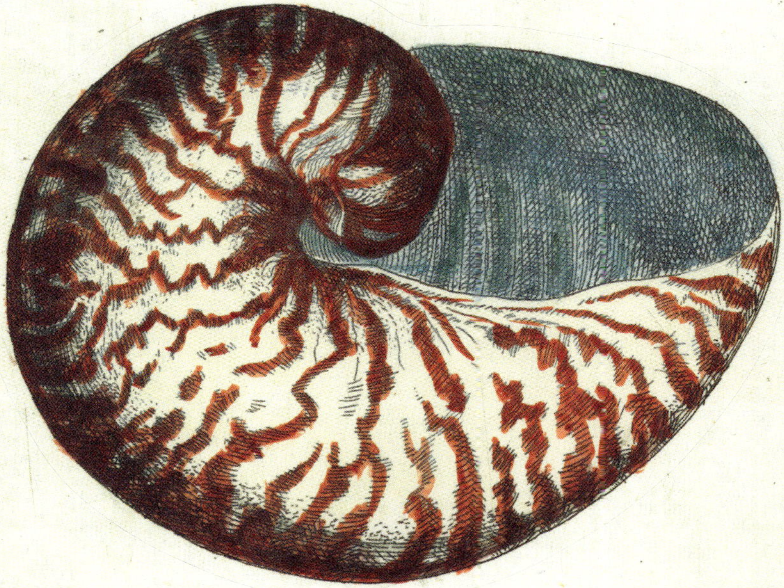

2

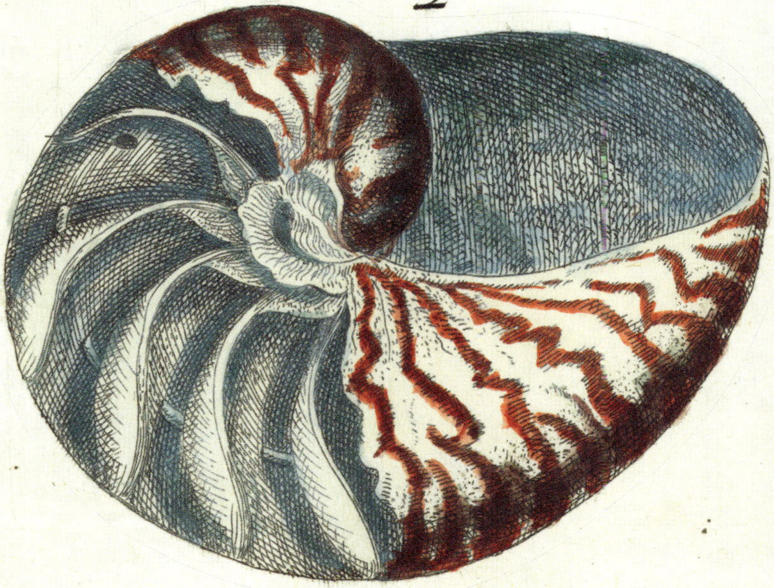

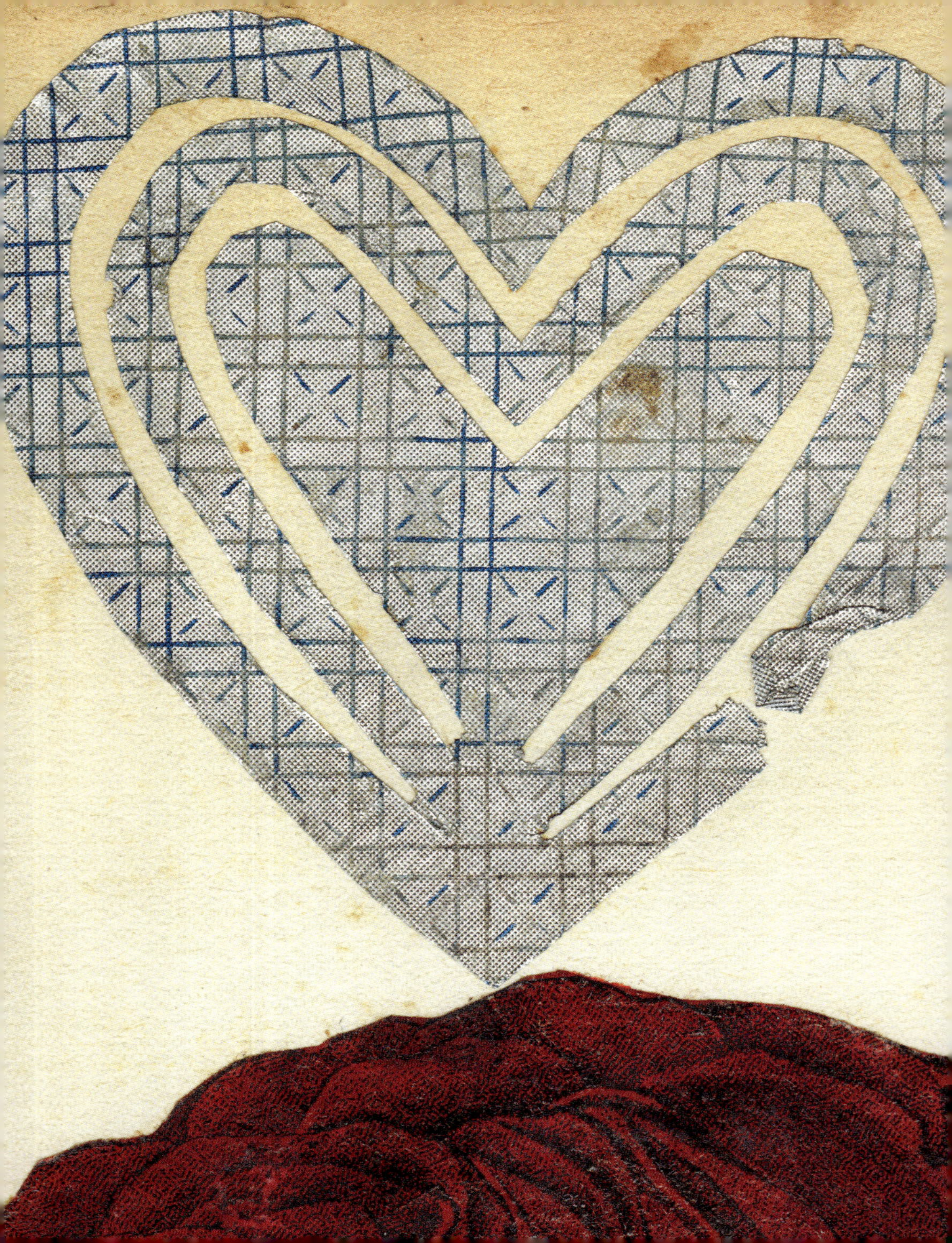

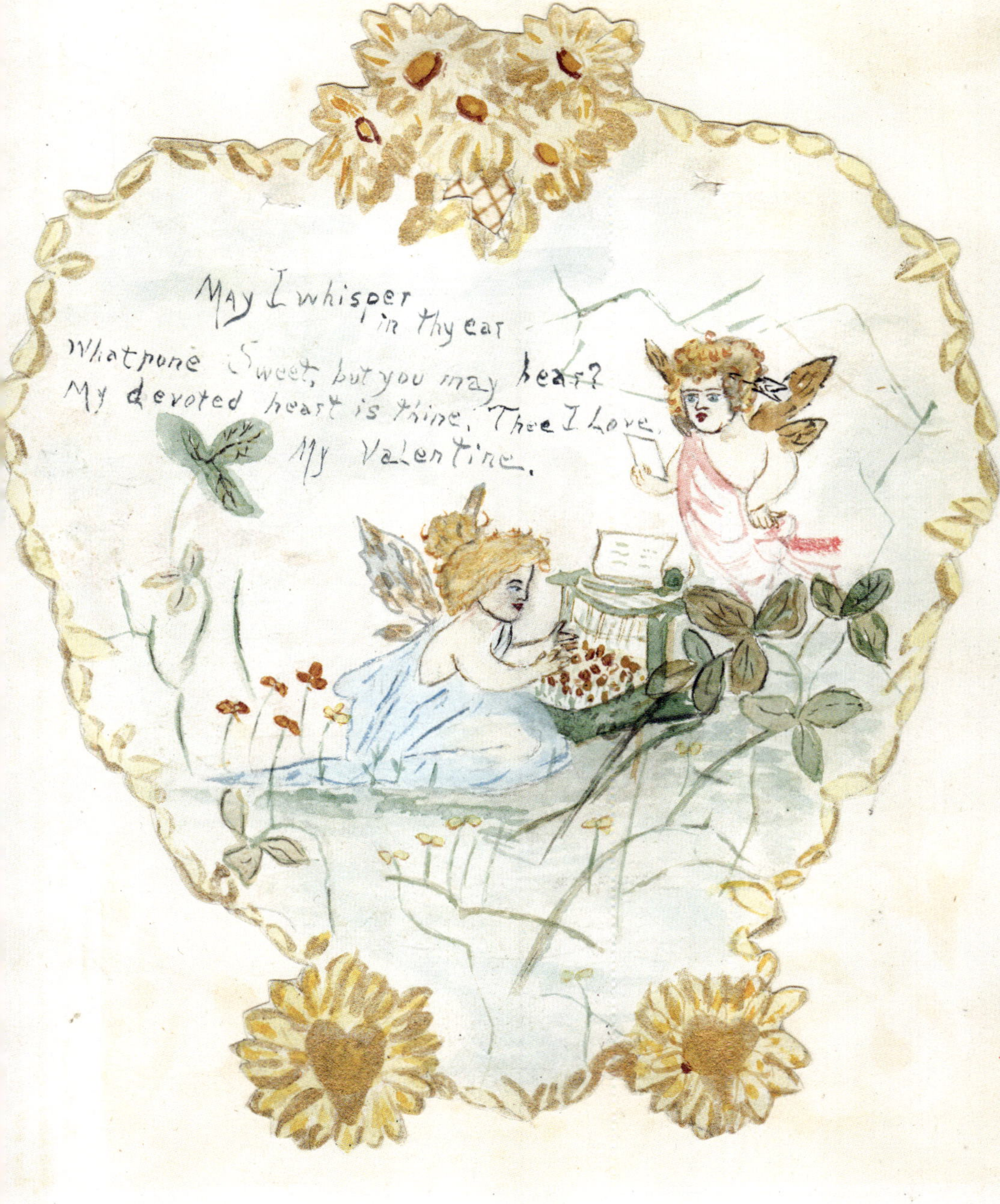
May I whisper in thy ear
What none Sweet, but you may hear?
My devoted heart is thine, Thee I Love,
My Valentine.

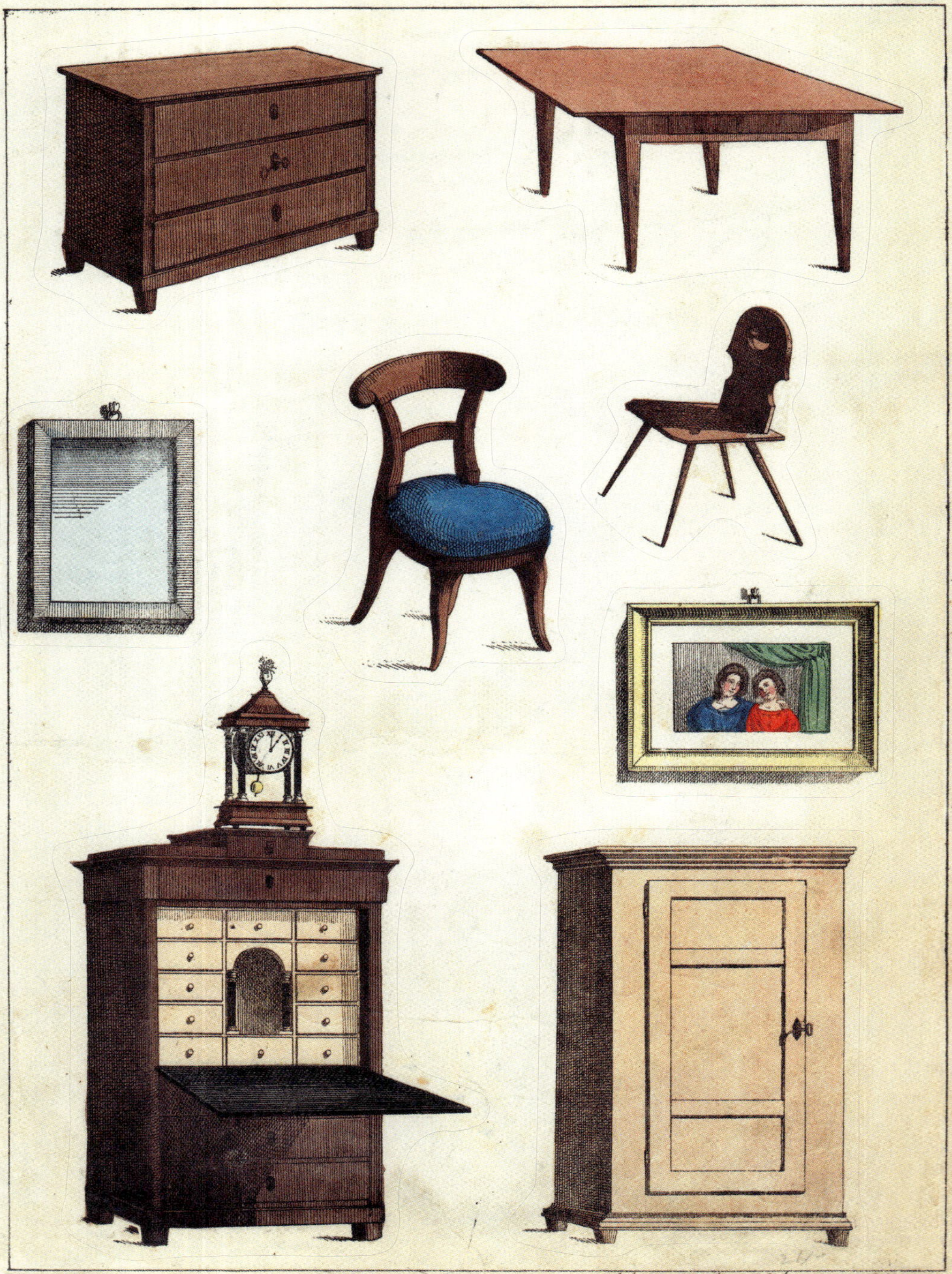

lithographirt bei I. F. Schreiber in Esslingen

T. III.

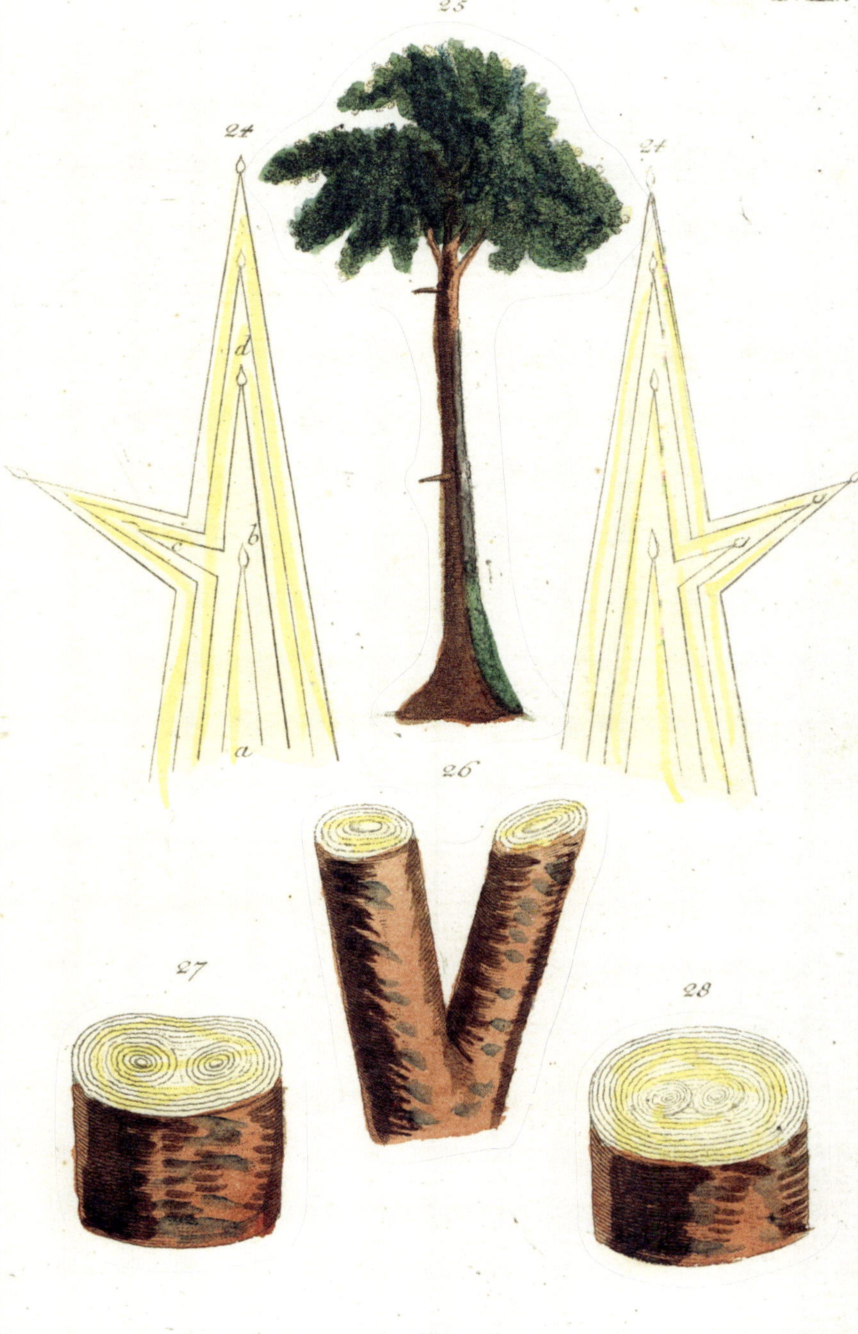

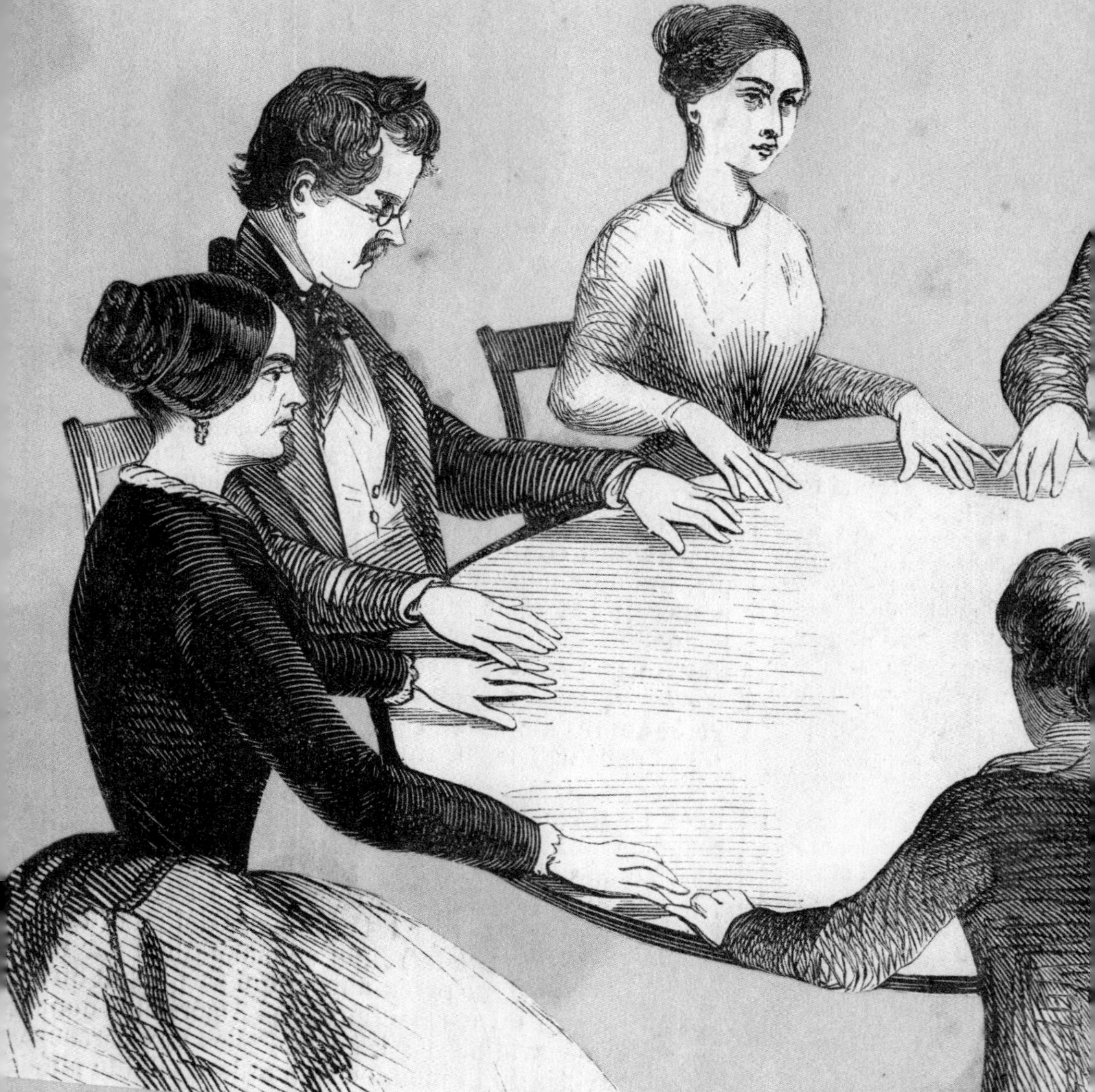

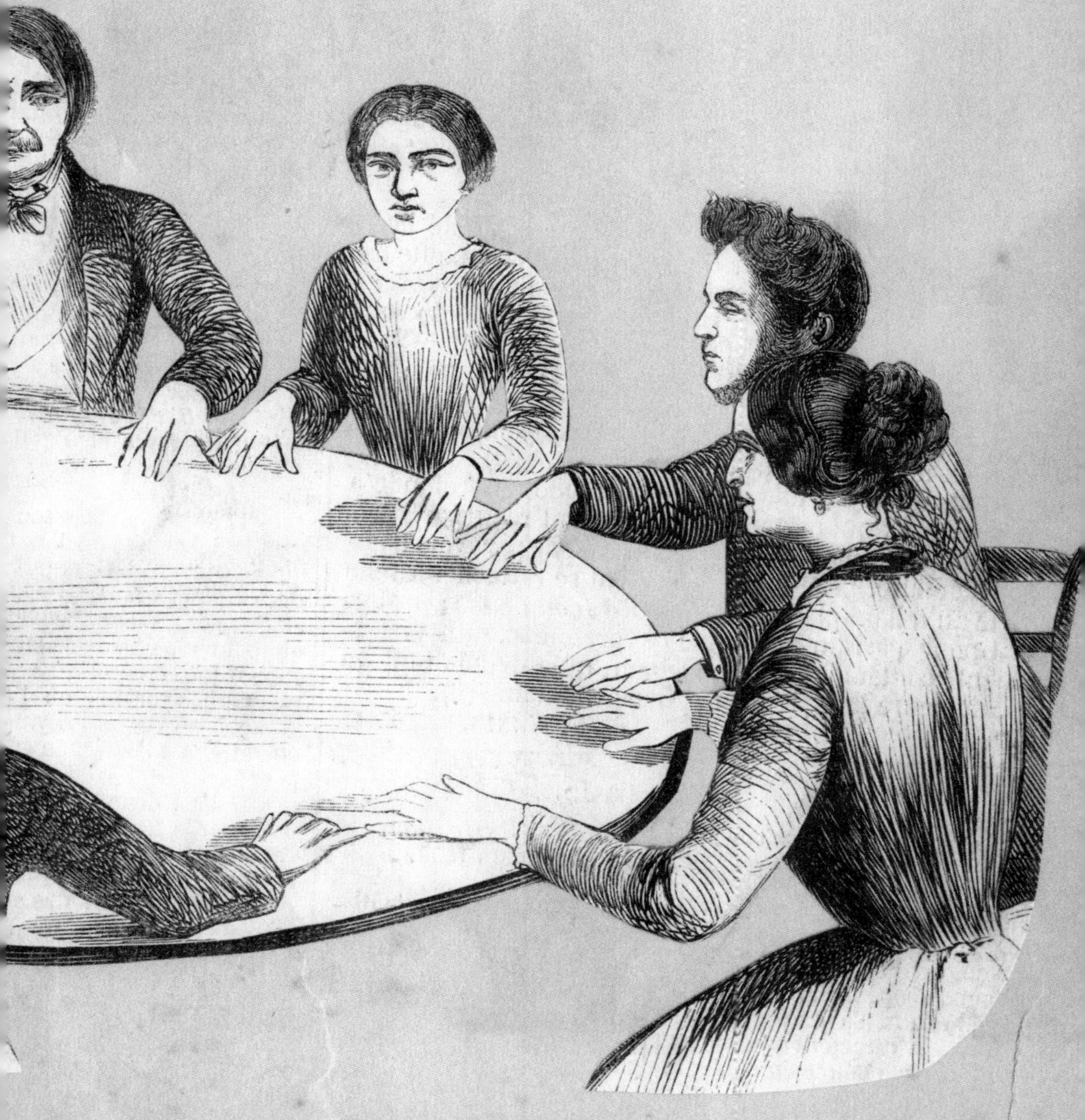

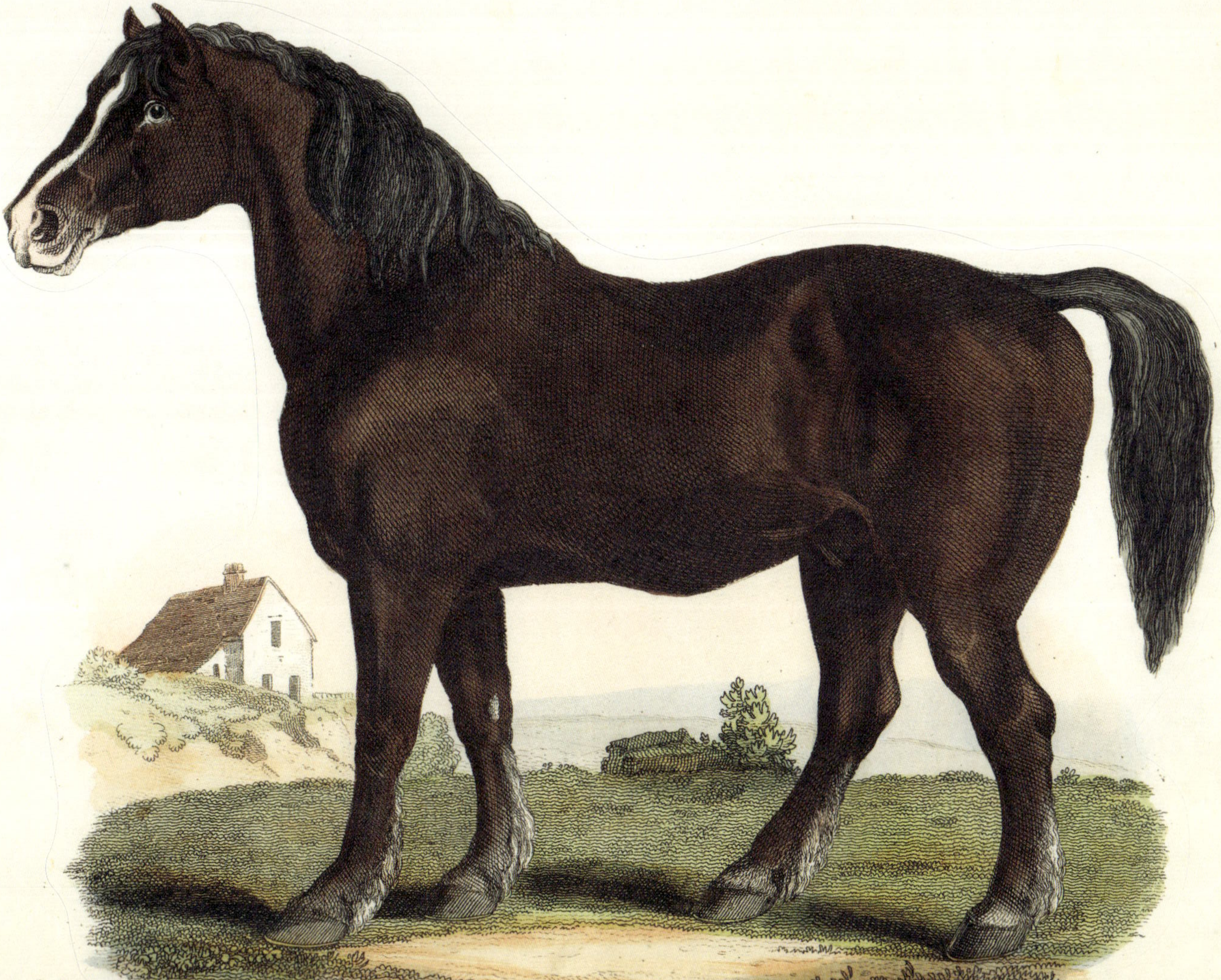

The Dray Horse

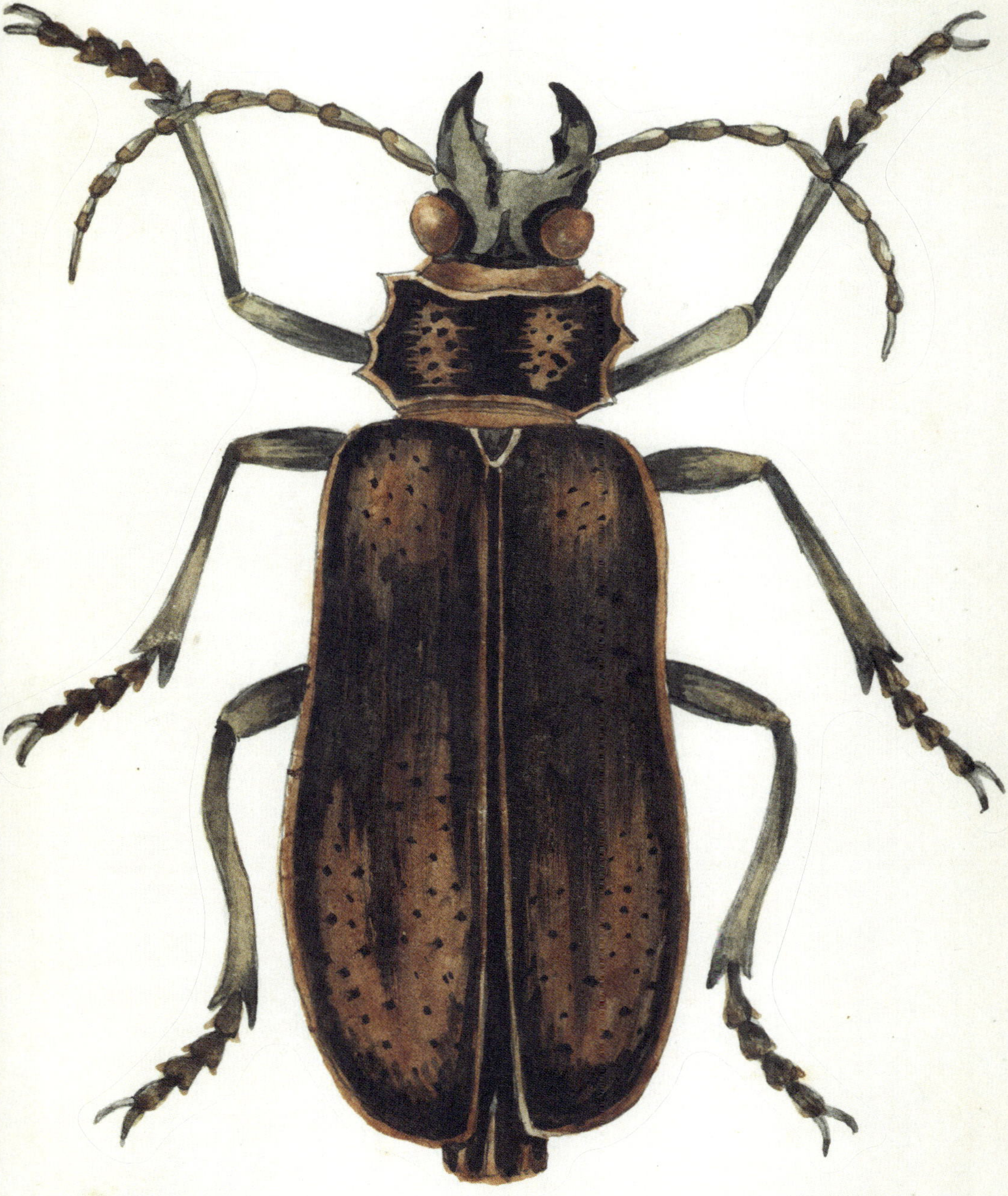

Cerambyx Giganteus (Shaw.)
natural size Inhabits. S. America.

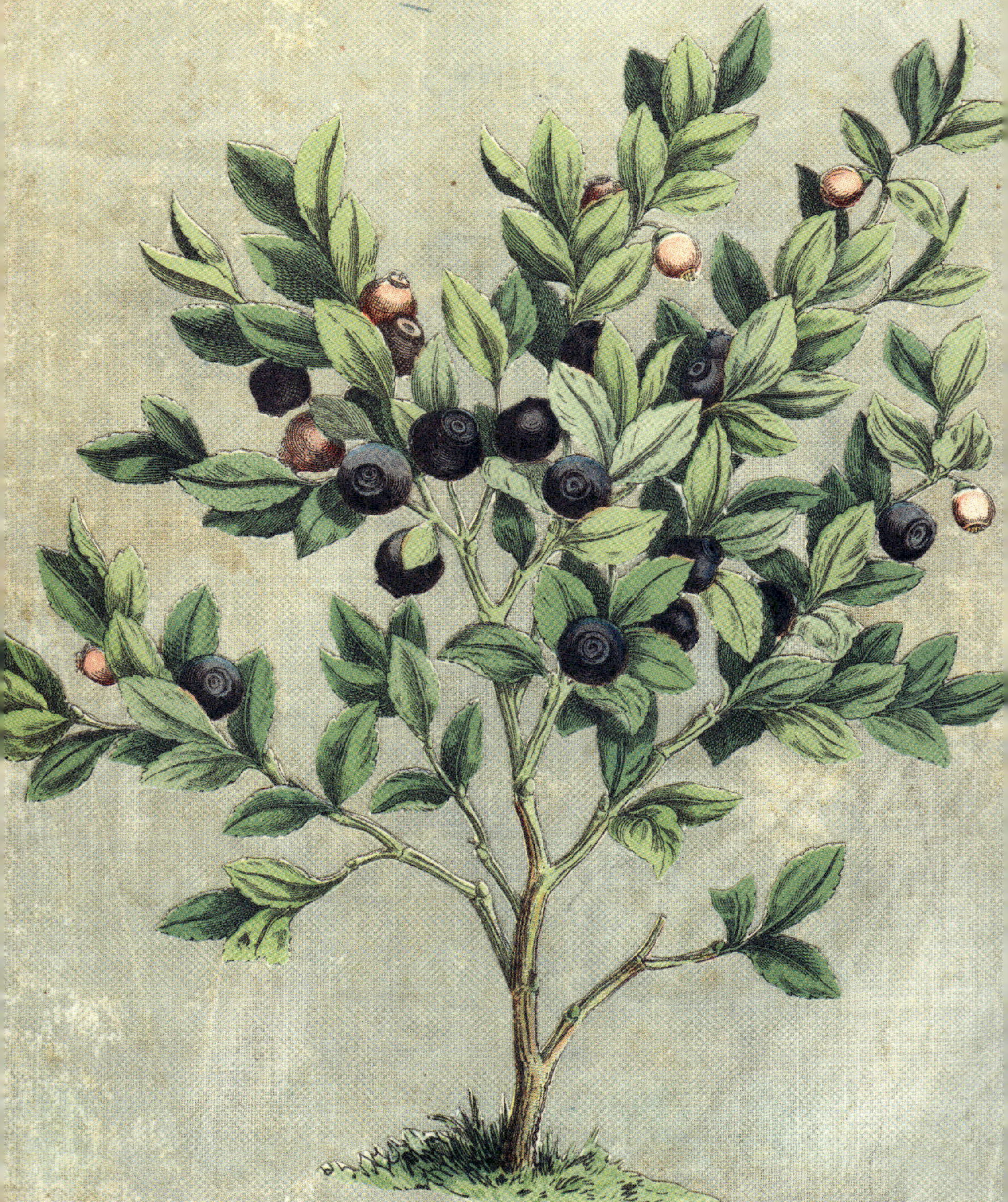

Einfache Fraktur.

2. VII.

A B C D E F G

H I K L M N O

P Q R S T U V

W X Y Z.

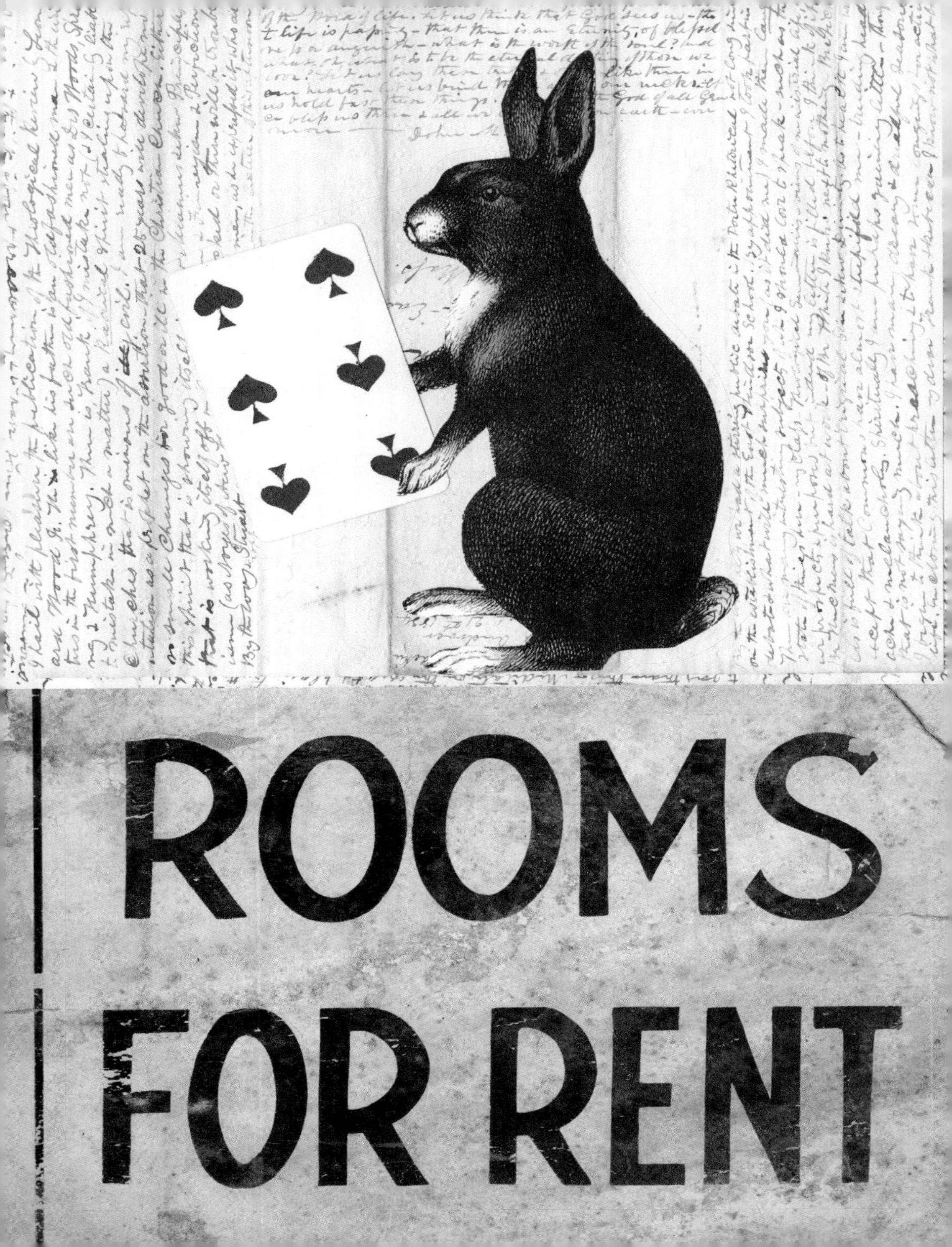
ROOMS
FOR RENT

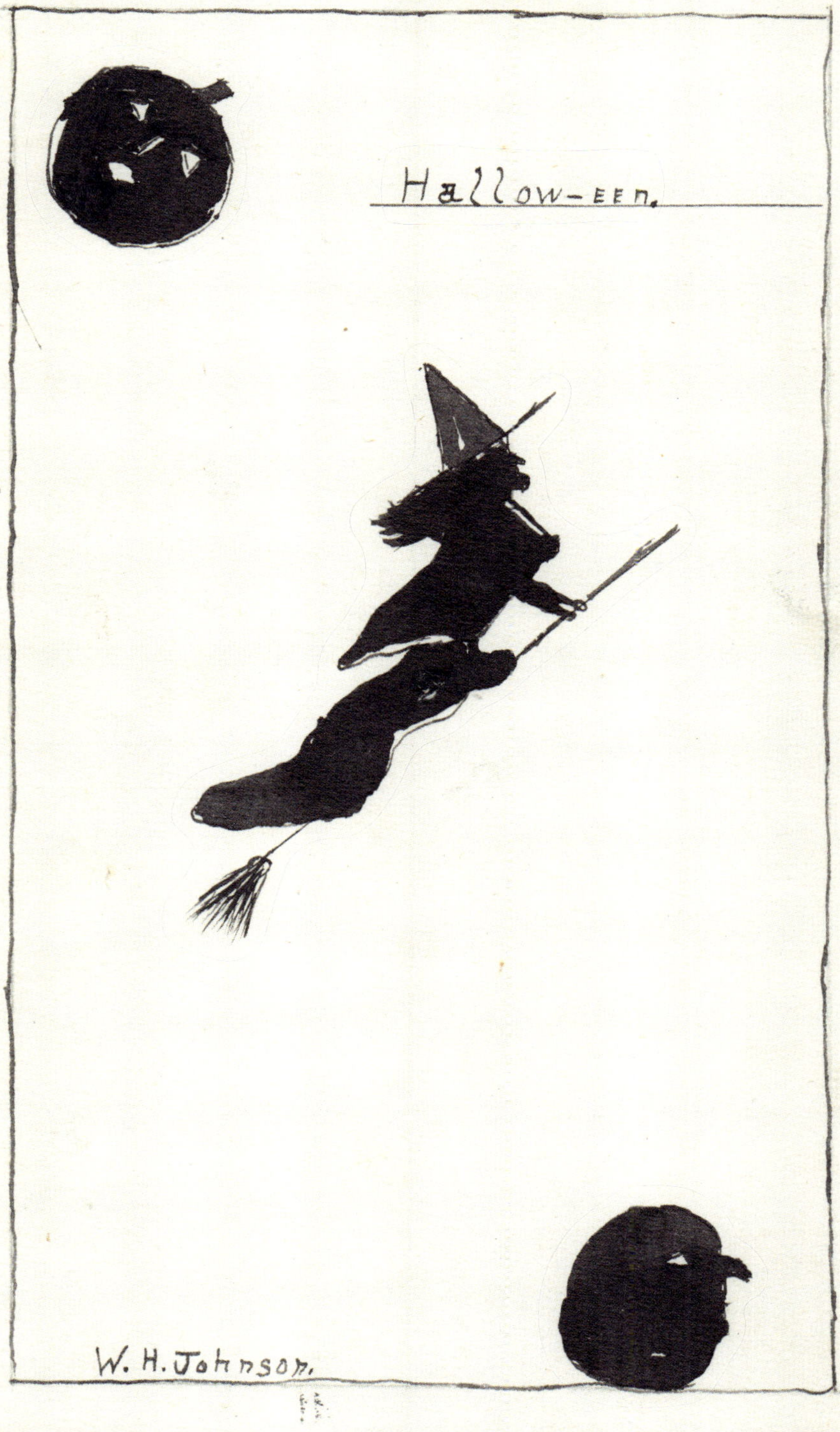
Hallow-een.
W. H. Johnson.

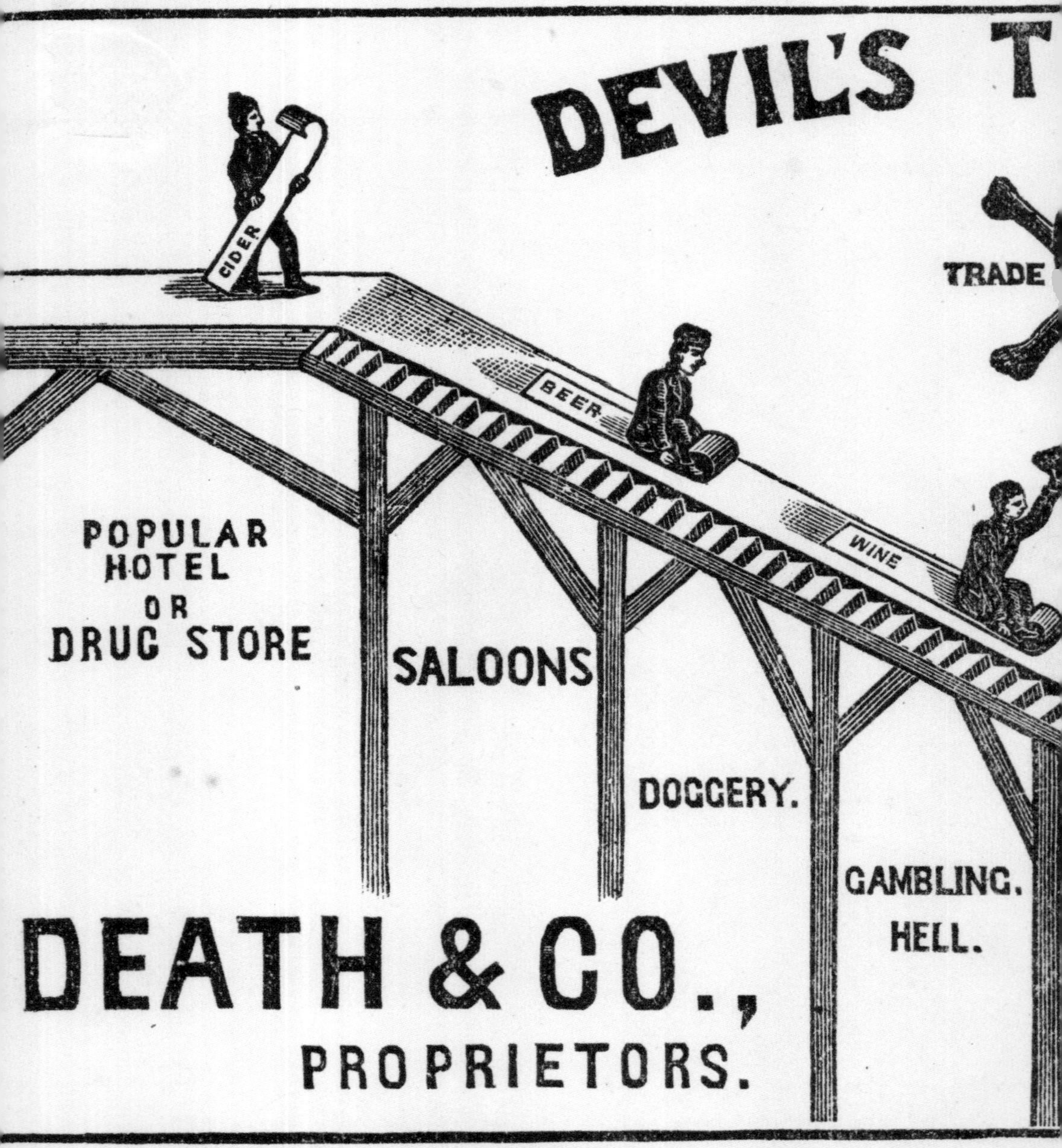

TAXPAYER: I awfully hate to have the boys slide
there's SUCH a REVENUE from it; and——and

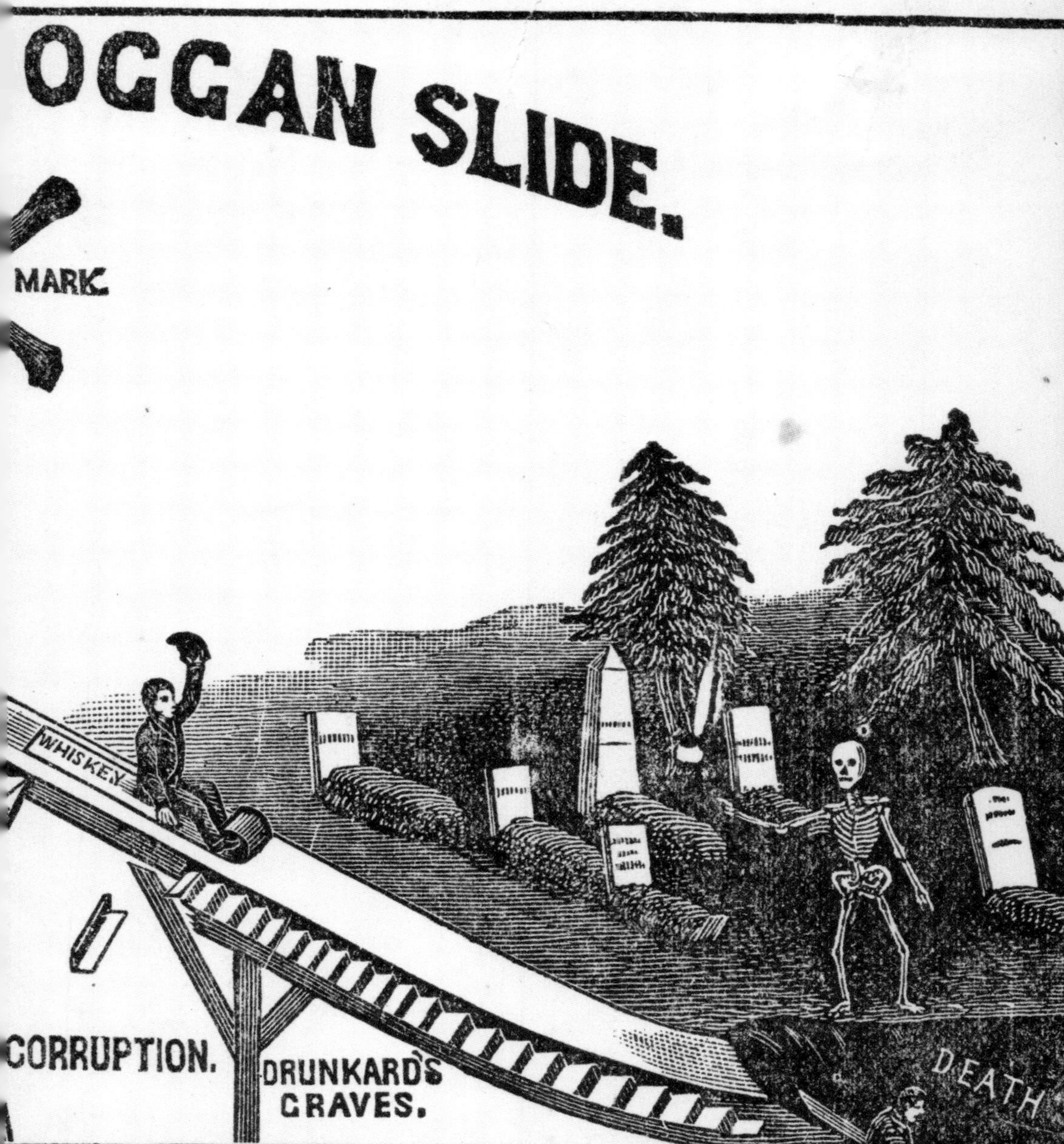

, but I believe in **PERSONAL LIBERTY**—and then
raid I'll be **BOYCOTTED** if I don't let 'em slide.

I.

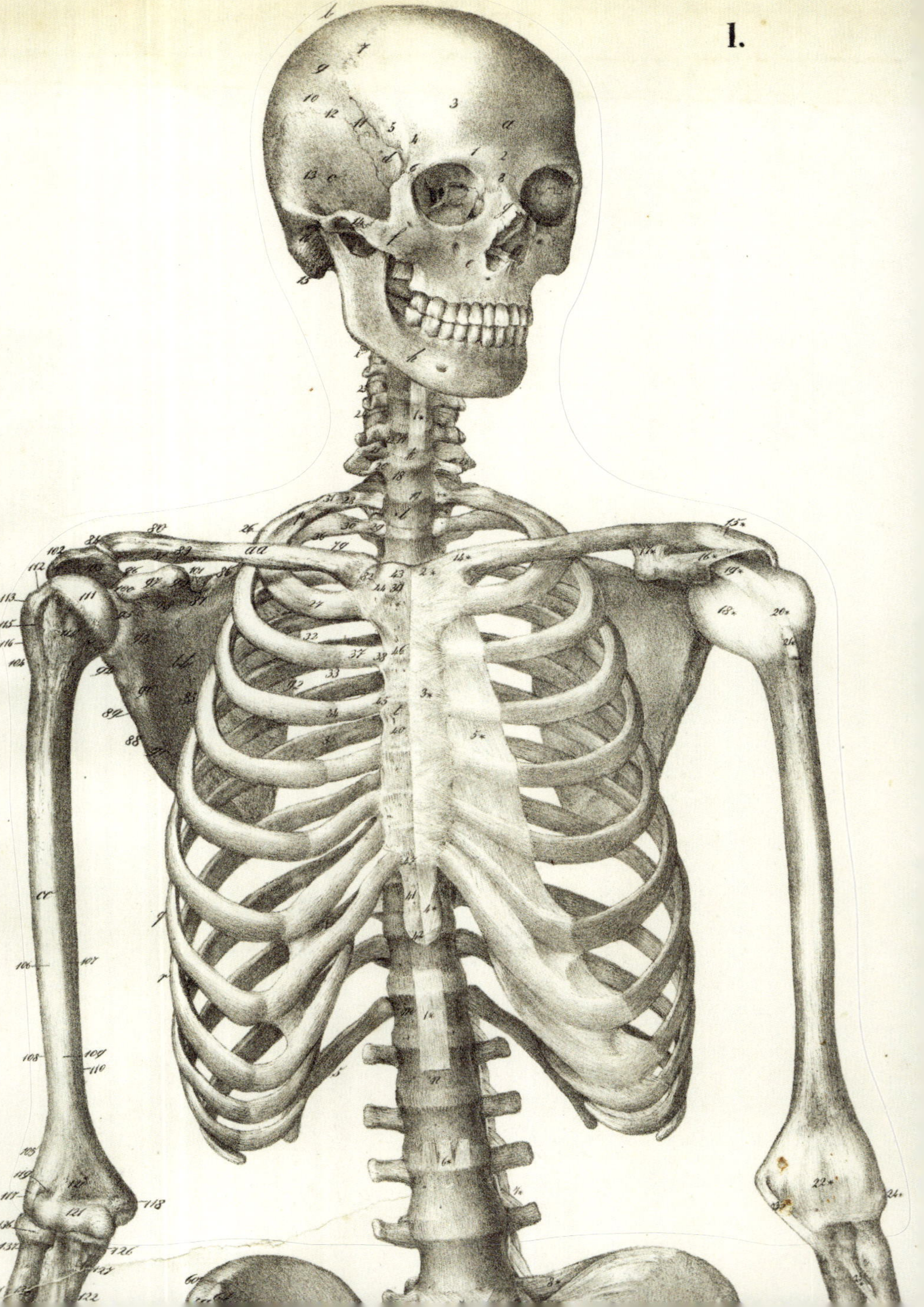

II.

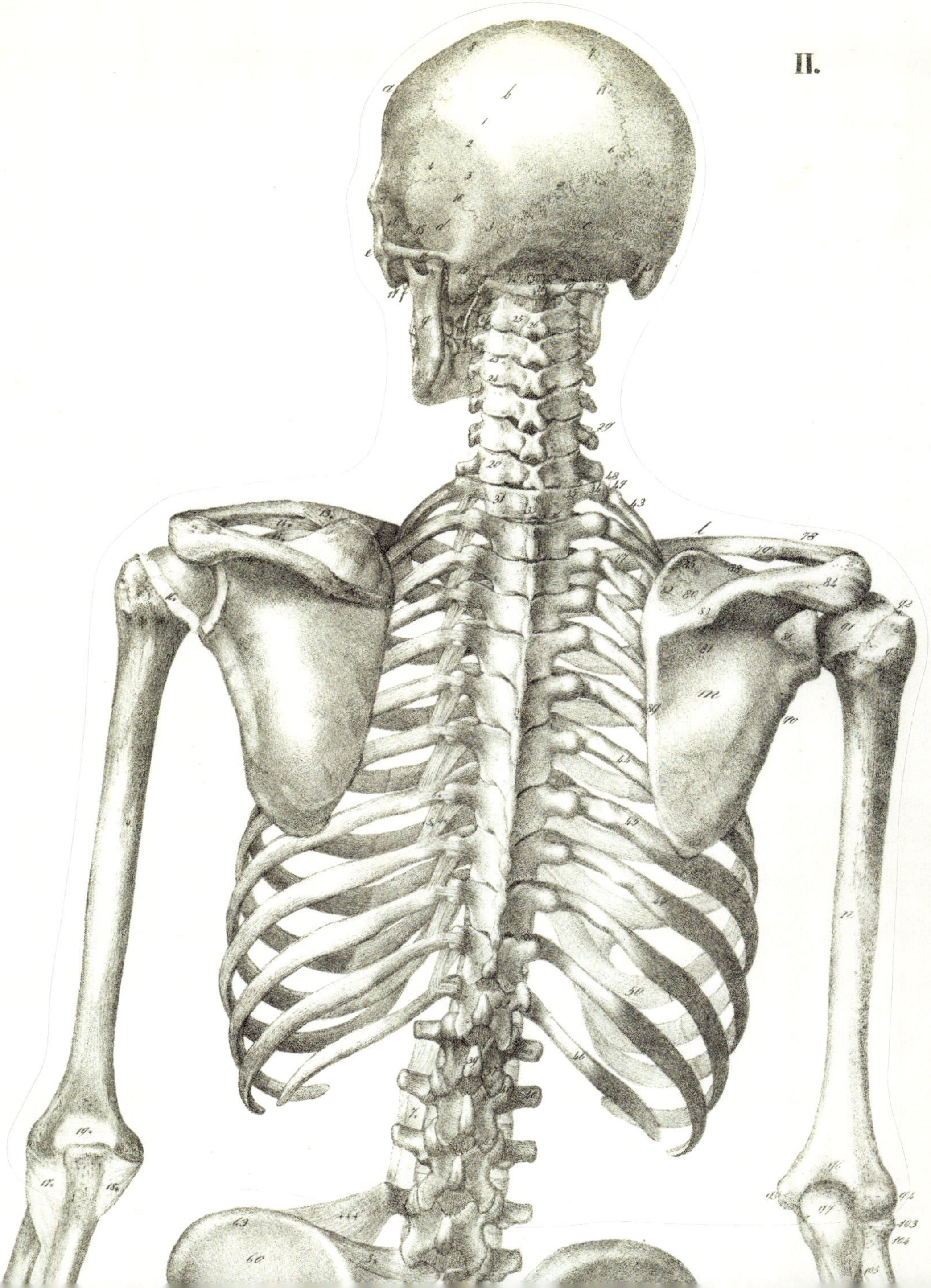

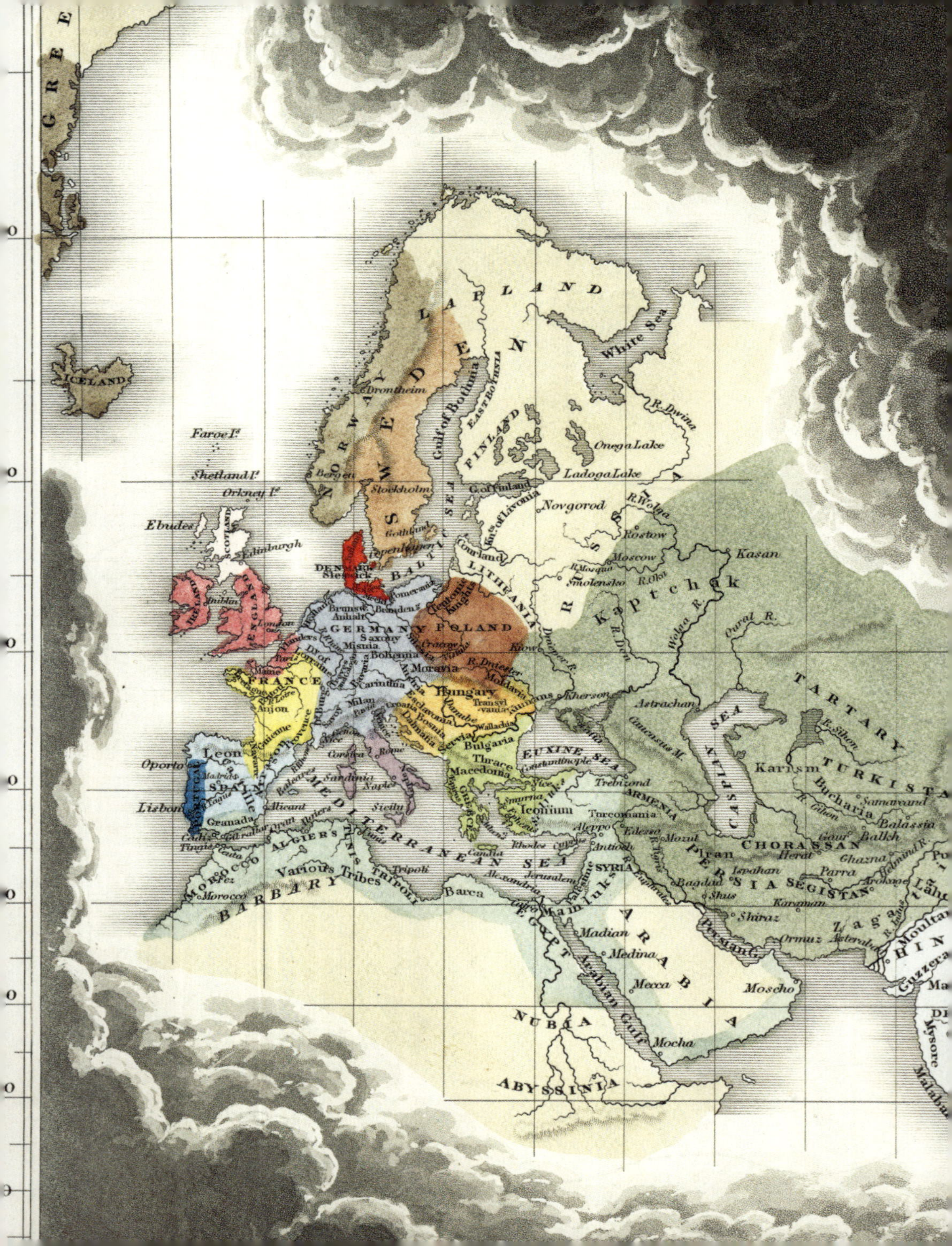

GREE
ICELAND
Faroe I.
Shetland I.
Orkney I.
Ebudes
Edinburgh
Dublin
IRELAND
ENGLAND
London
LAPLAND
SWEDEN
NORWAY
Drontheim
Bergen
Stockholm
Gothland
Copenhagen
DENMARK
Gulf of Bothnia
EAST BOTHNIA
FINLAND
G. of Finland
White Sea
R. Dwina
Onega Lake
Ladoga Lake
Novgorod
R. Wolga
Rostow
Moscow
Smolensko
R. Oka
Kasan
Kaptchak
RUSSIA
BALTIC SEA
Courland
Livonia
LITHUANIA
Teutonic Knights
POLAND
Cracow
R. Dniester
Moldavia
Kiow
Dnieper R.
R. Don
Wolga R.
Oural R.
Brunsw.
Anhalt
GERMANY
Saxony
Misnia
Bohemia
Moravia
Flanders
Paris
Maine
FRANCE
Anjou
Guienne
Provence
Milan
Hungary
Transylvania
Sclavonia
Croatia
Bosnia
Dalmatia
Servia
Wallachia
Bulgaria
Thrace
Macedonia
Constantinople
Kherson
EUXINE SEA
Astrachan
CASPIAN SEA
Caucasus M.
TARTARY
R. Sihon
TURKISTAN
Karism
Bucharia
Samarcand
Balkh
Balassia
Corsica
Sardinia
Rome
Naples
Sicily
Leon
Oporto
Madrid
SPAIN
PORTUGAL
Lisbon
Granada
Alicant
Balearic
MEDITERRANEAN SEA
ALGIERS
TUNIS
TRIPOLI
Tripoli
Barca
MOROCCO
Morocco
Fez
BARBARY
Various Tribes
Candia
Rhodes
Cyprus
Smyrna
Iconium
Trebizond
ARMENIA
Turcomania
Aleppo
Antioch
Edessa
SYRIA
Jerusalem
Alexandria
Cairo
EGYPT
Mamluks
Mozul
Bagdad
PERSIA
Ispahan
Shus
Shiraz
Karaman
Herat
CHORASSAN
Gaur
Ghazna
Parra
SEGISTAN
Persian G.
Ormuz
Zagatai
Moultan
Guzzerat
Mysore
Madian
Medina
Mecca
ARABIA
Arabian Gulf
Moscho
Mocha
NUBIA
ABYSSINIA

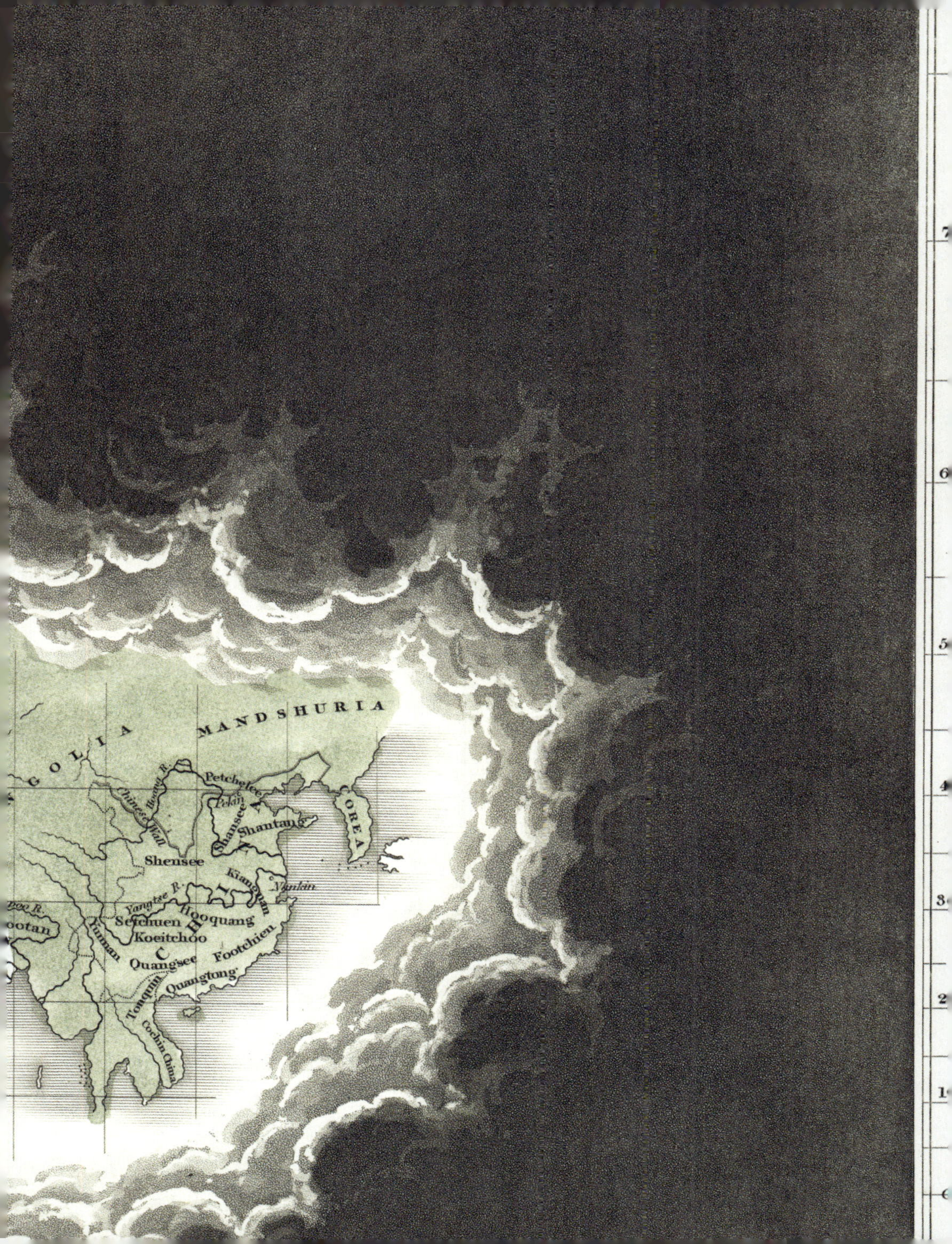

MANDSHURIA
GOLIA
Petchelee
Pekin
Chinese Wall
Shansee
Shantang
COREA
Shensee
Kiangnan
Nankin
Yangtse R.
Hooquang
Setchuen
Koeitchoo
Yunnan
Quangsee
Footchien
Quangtong
Tonquin
Cochin China
ootan

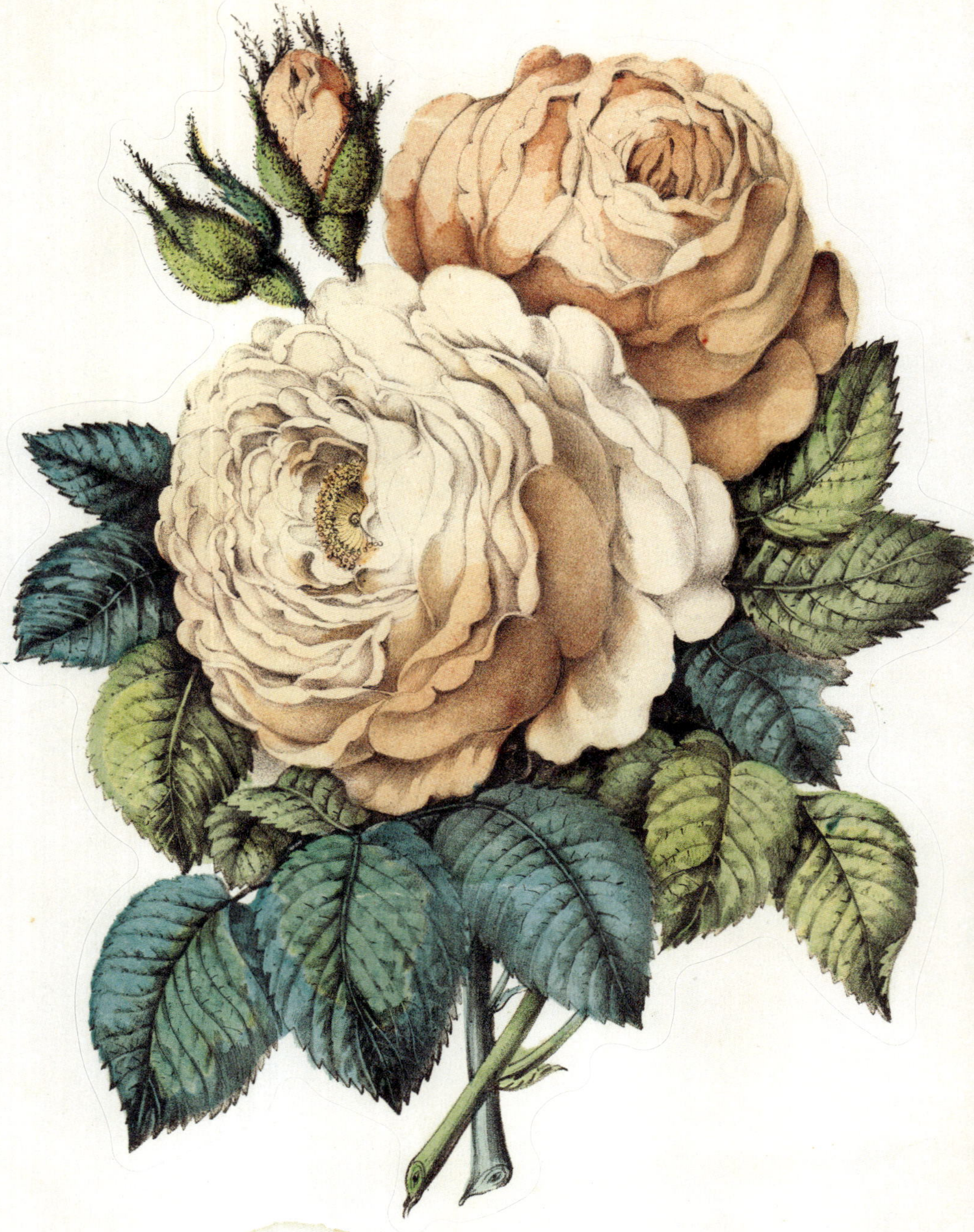

THE ROSE.

NEW YORK, PUBLISHED BY CURRIER & IVES, 125 NASSAU ST.

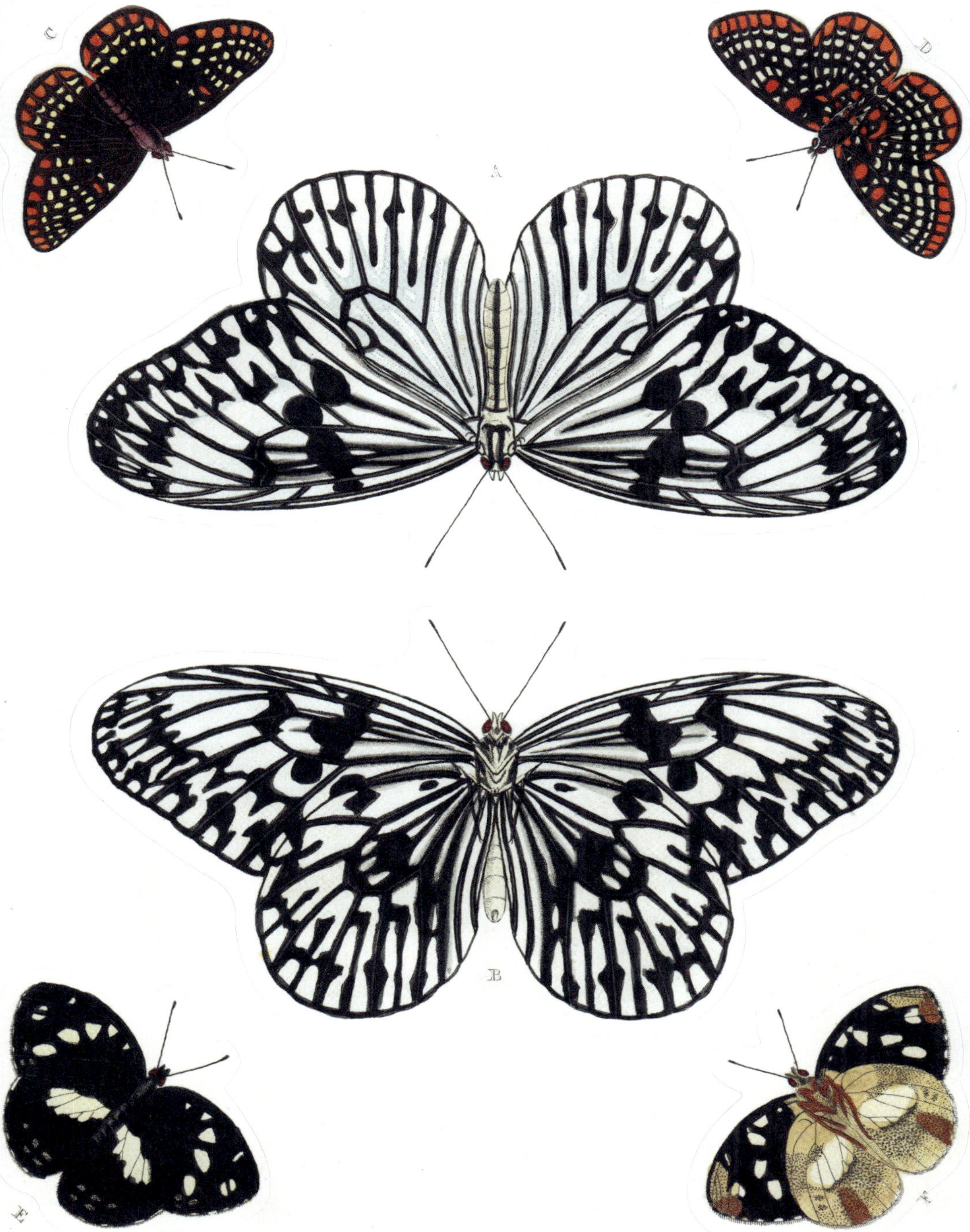
A
B
C
D
E
F

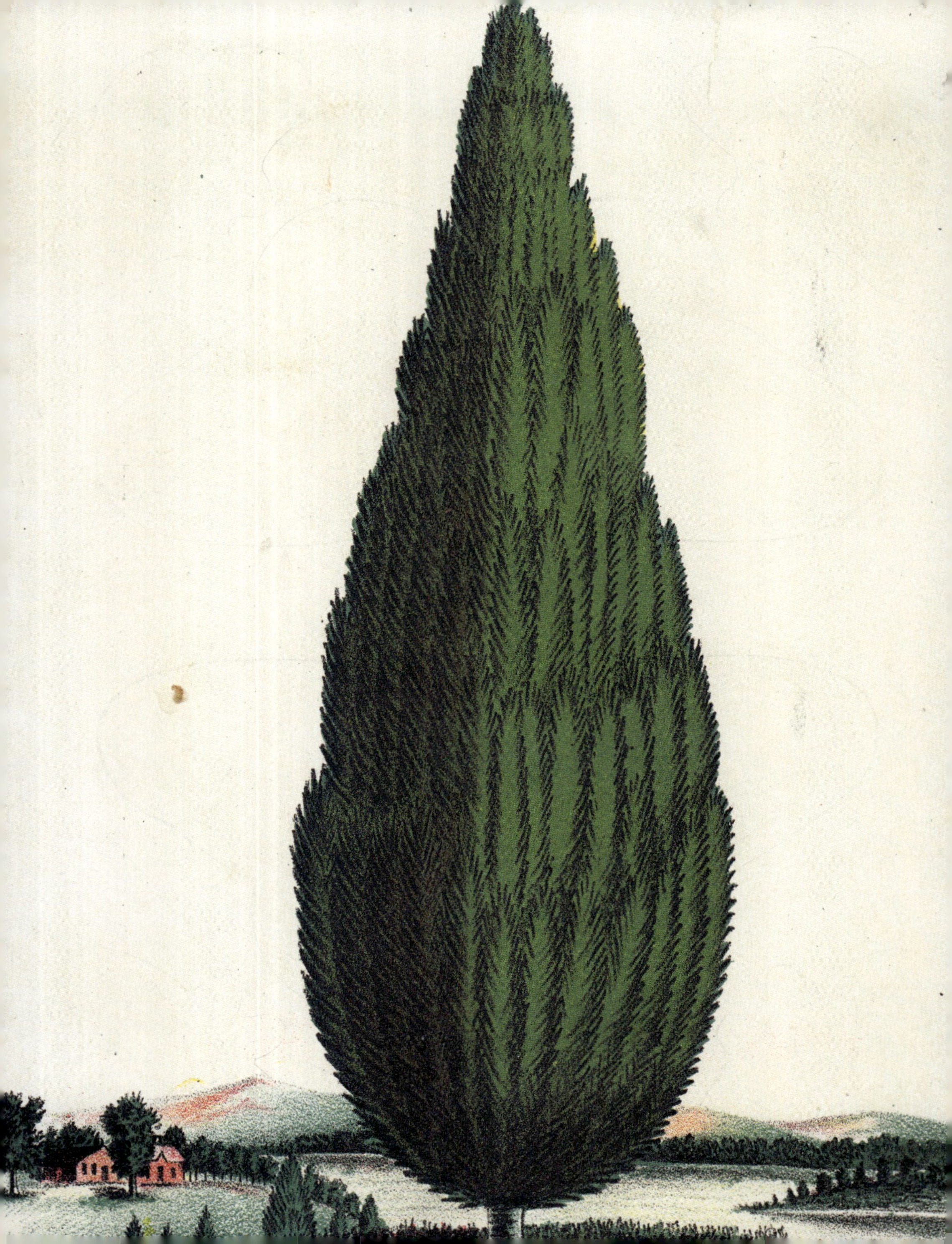

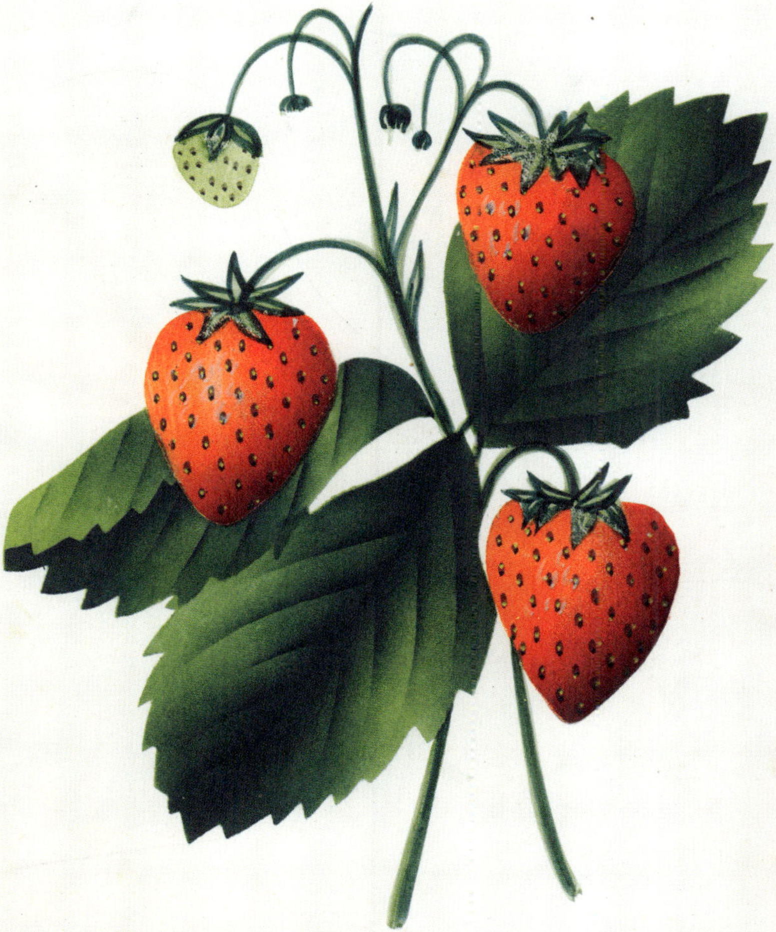

BROOKLYN SCARLET.

20

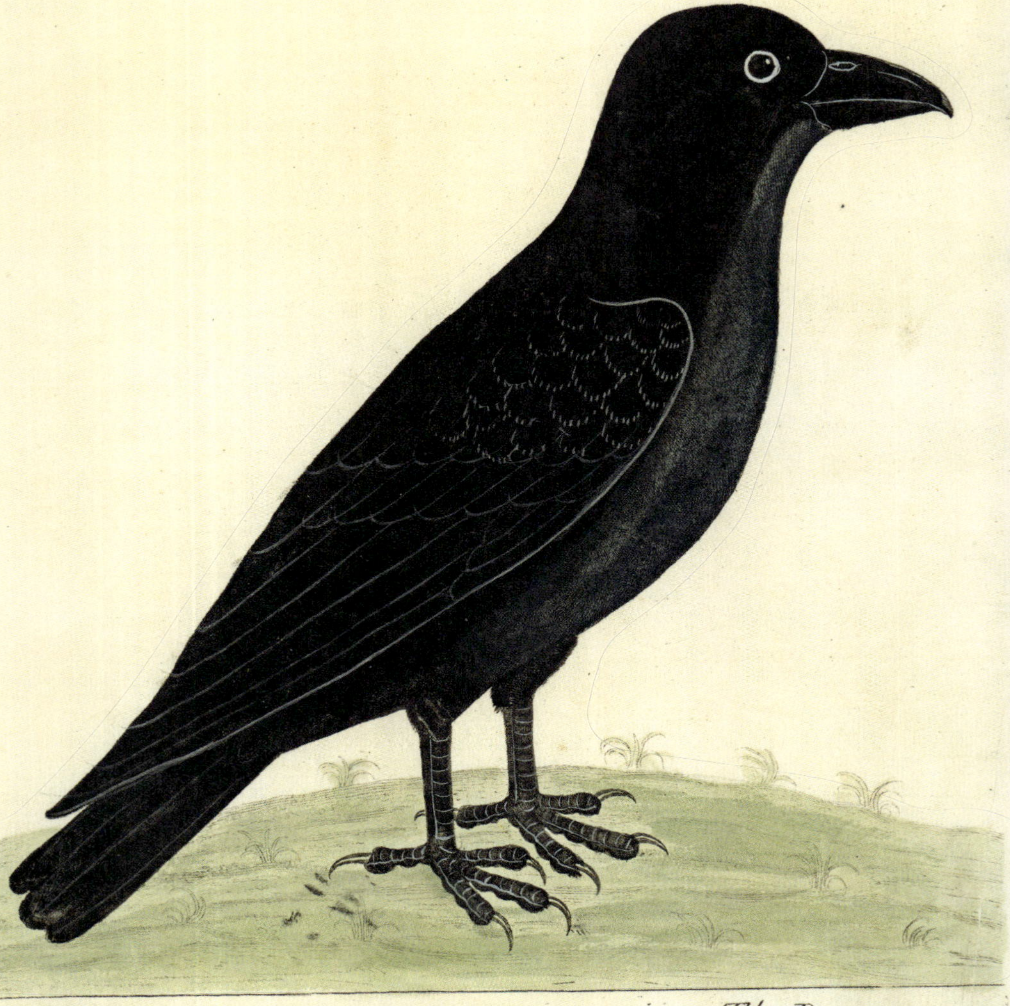

Corvus The Raven

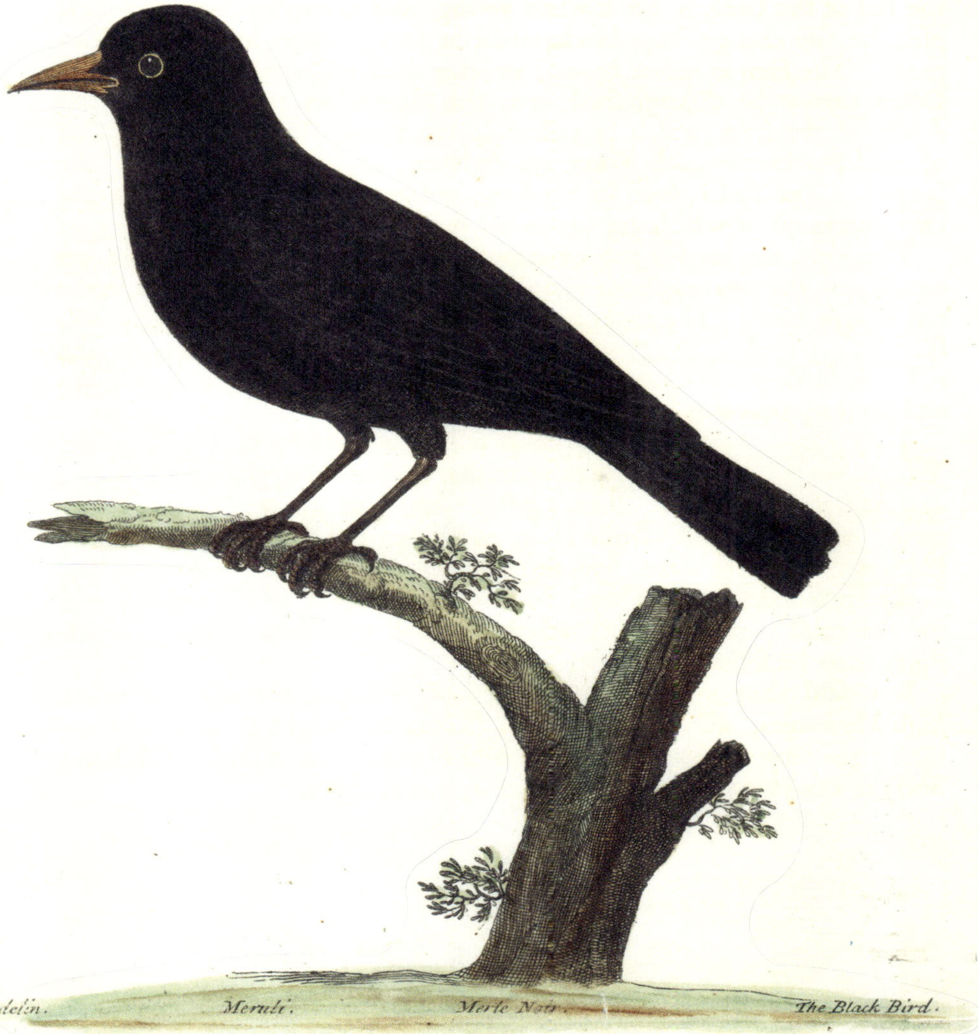

Albin delin. *Meruli.* *Merle Noir.* *The Black Bird.*

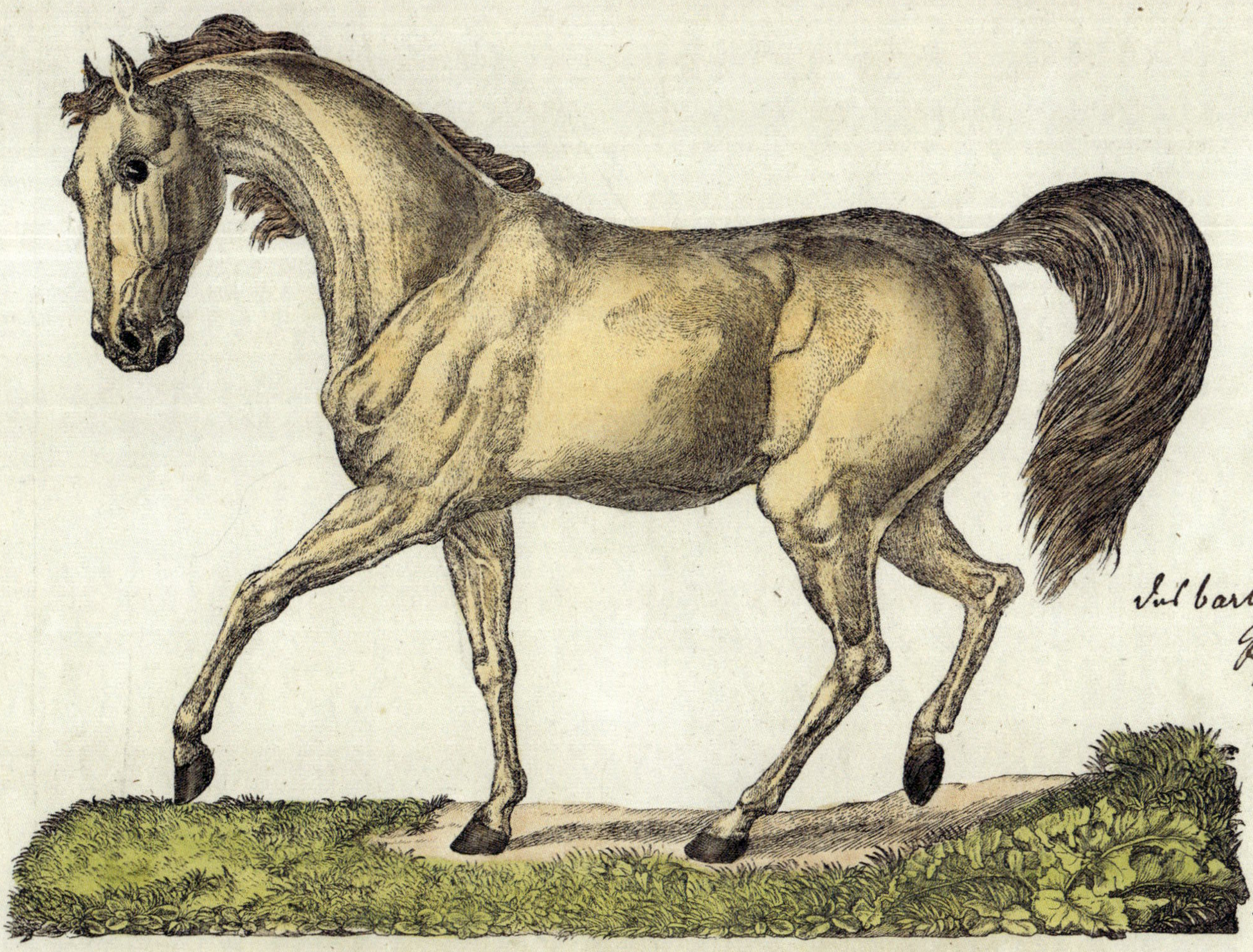

Das barbarische Pferd.

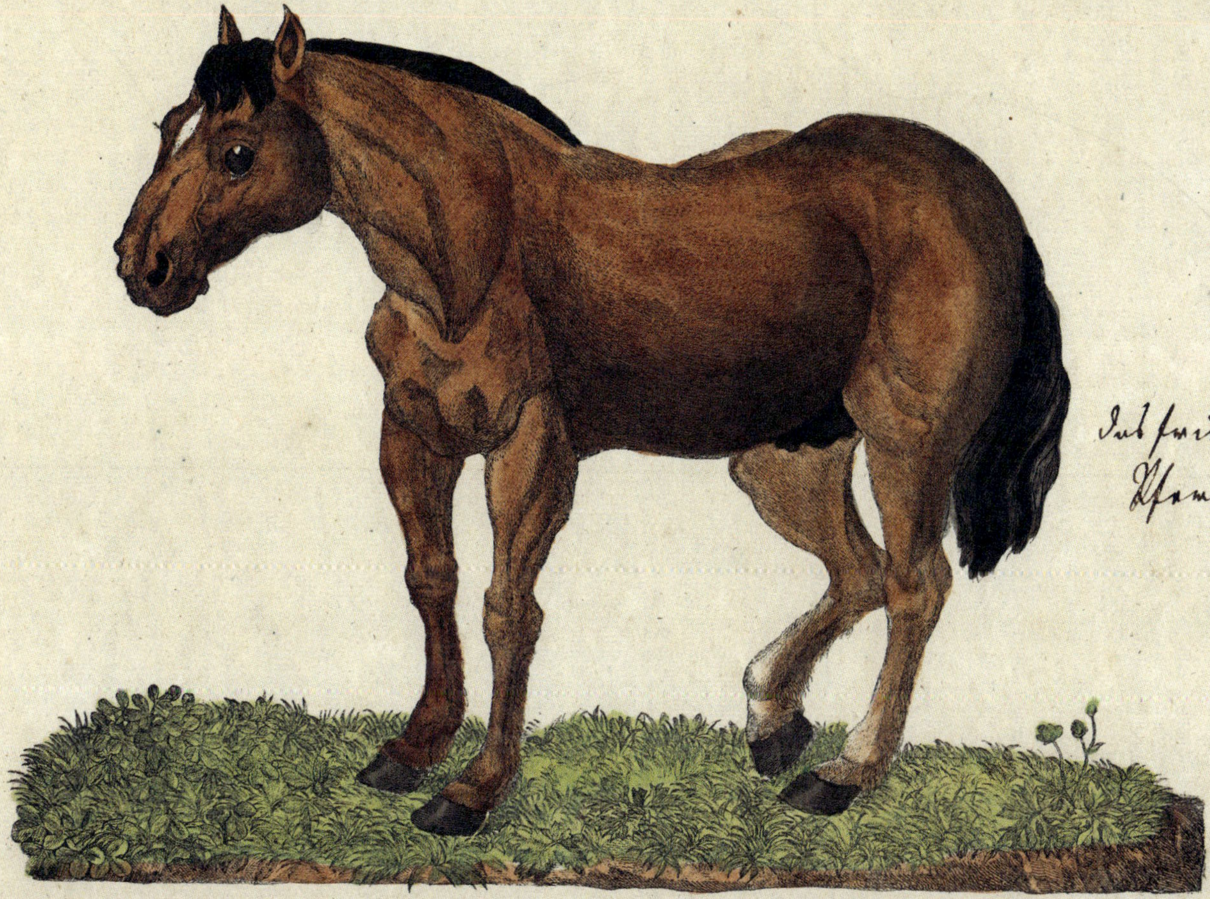

Das friesländische Pferd.

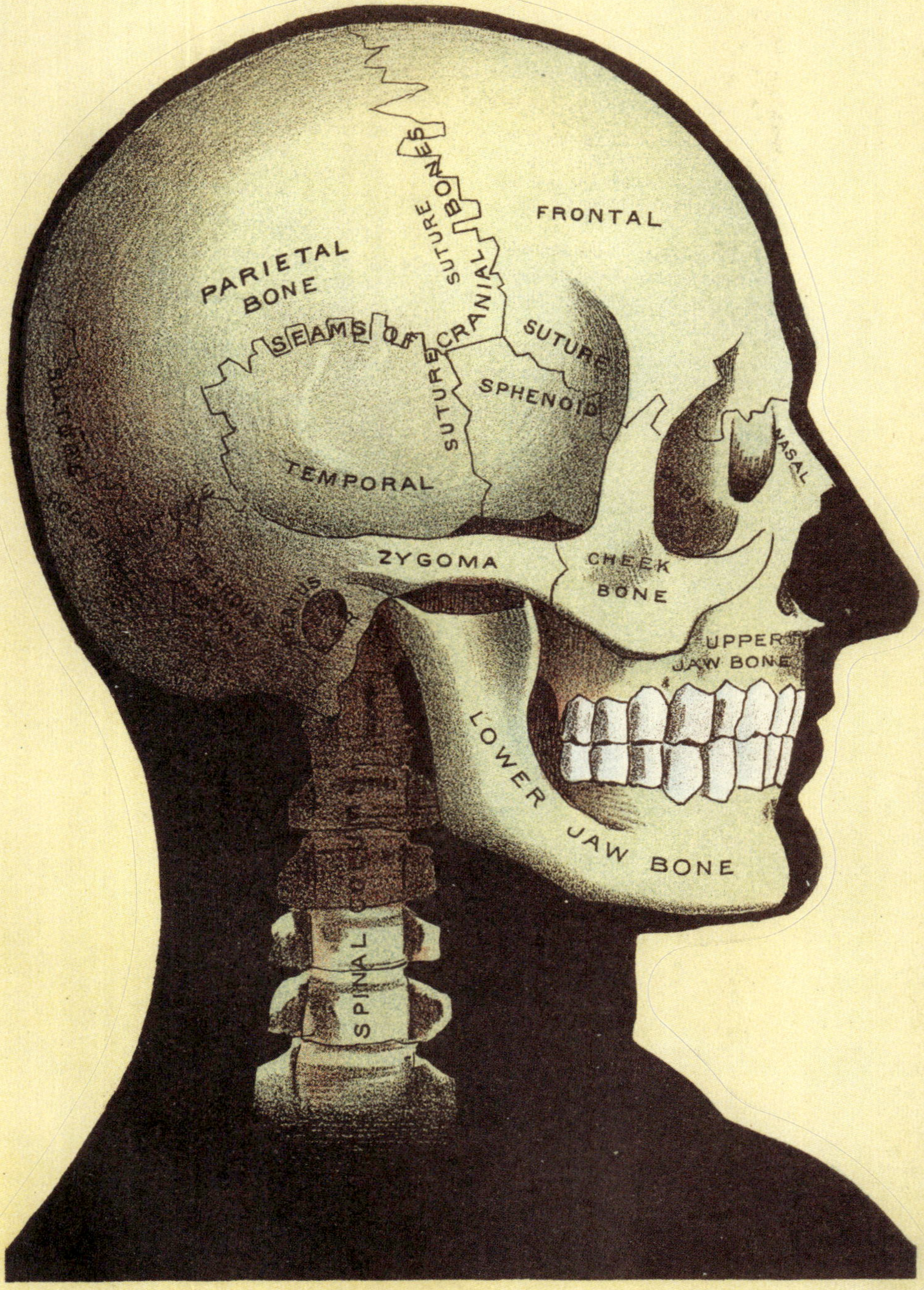
PARIETAL BONE
FRONTAL
SEAMS OF CRANIAL BONES
SUTURE
SUTURE
SUTURE
SPHENOID
TEMPORAL
NASAL
ZYGOMA
CHEEK BONE
UPPER JAW BONE
LOWER JAW BONE
SPINAL

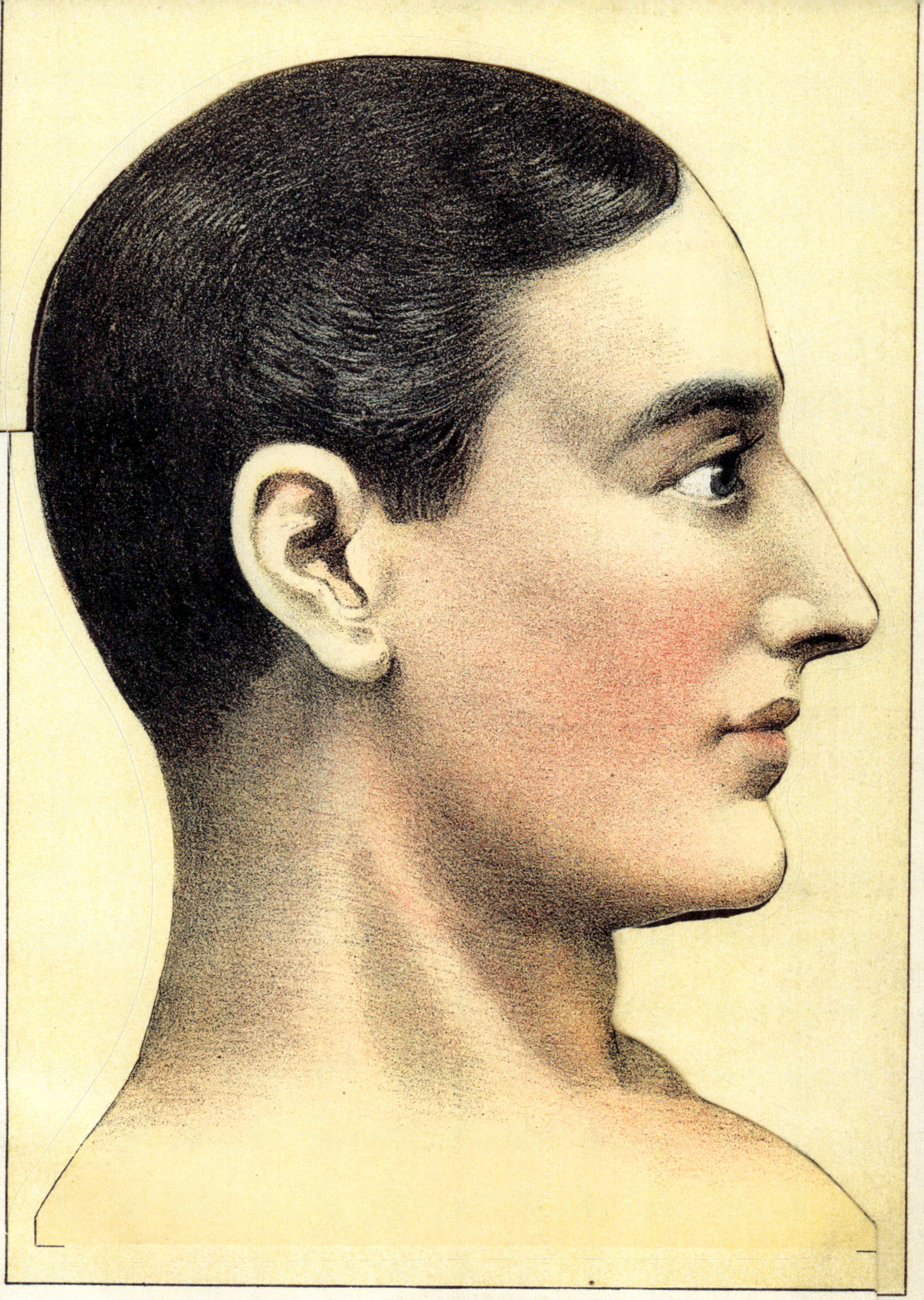

A PICTURE OF PERFECT HEALTH.

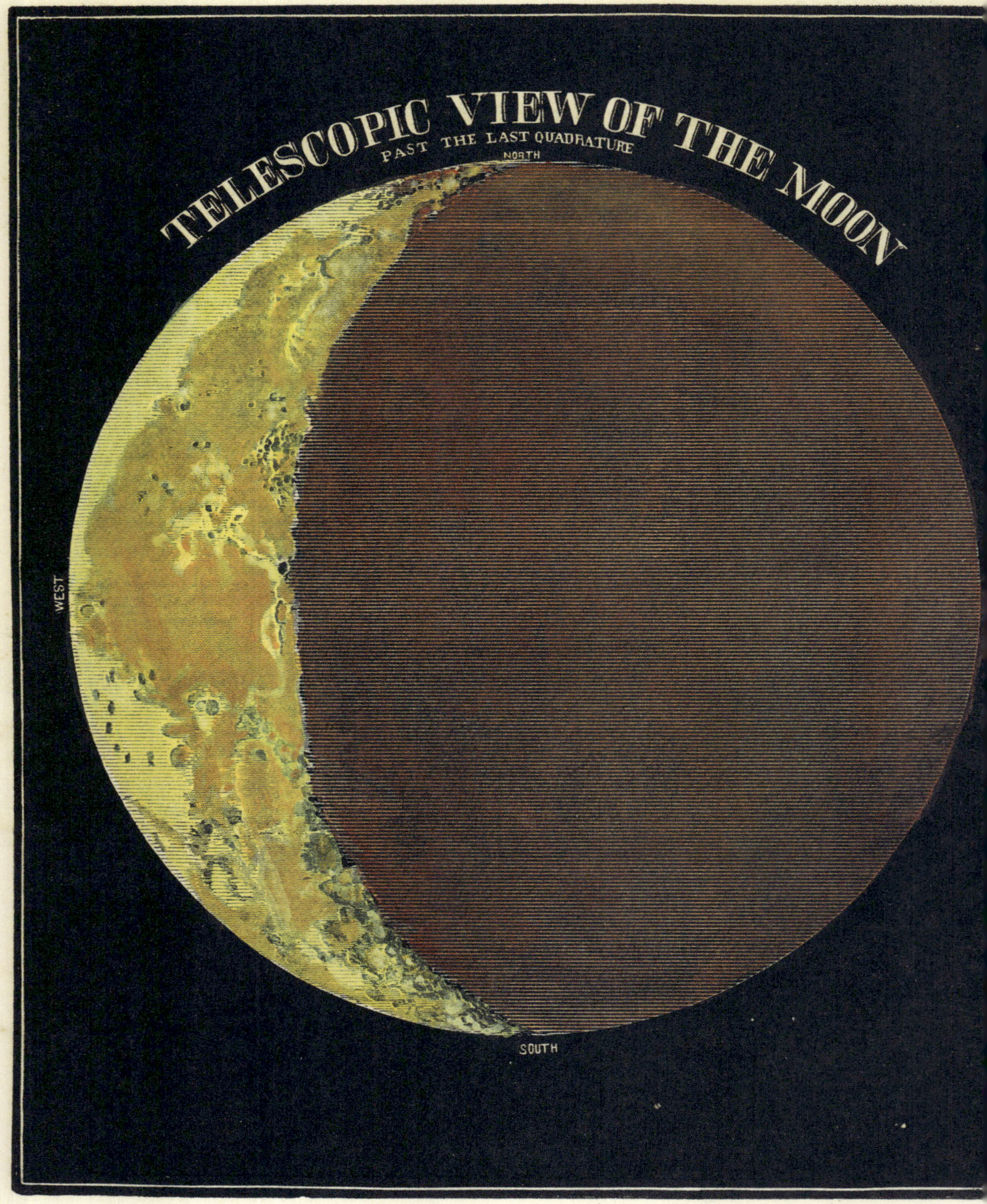
TELESCOPIC VIEW OF THE MOON
PAST THE LAST QUADRATURE
NORTH
WEST
SOUTH

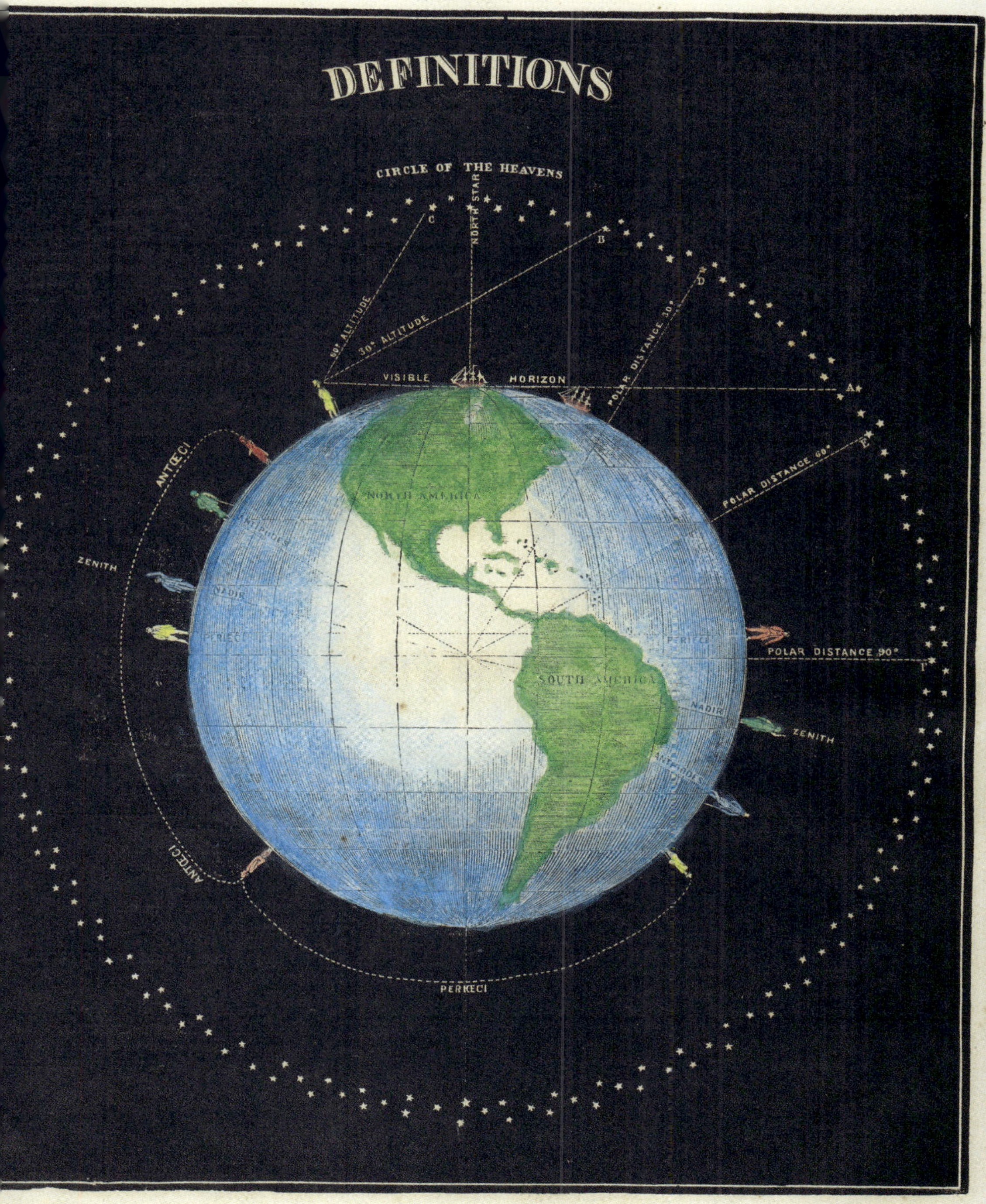
DEFINITIONS
CIRCLE OF THE HEAVENS
NORTH STAR
C
B
D
60° ALTITUDE
30° ALTITUDE
VISIBLE HORIZON
A
POLAR DISTANCE 30°
E
POLAR DISTANCE 60°
NORTH AMERICA
ANTŒCI
ANTIPODES
ZENITH
NADIR
PERIŒCI
SOUTH AMERICA
PERIŒCI
POLAR DISTANCE 90°
F
NADIR
ZENITH
ANTIPODES
ANTŒCI
PERIŒCI

(

Egyptia

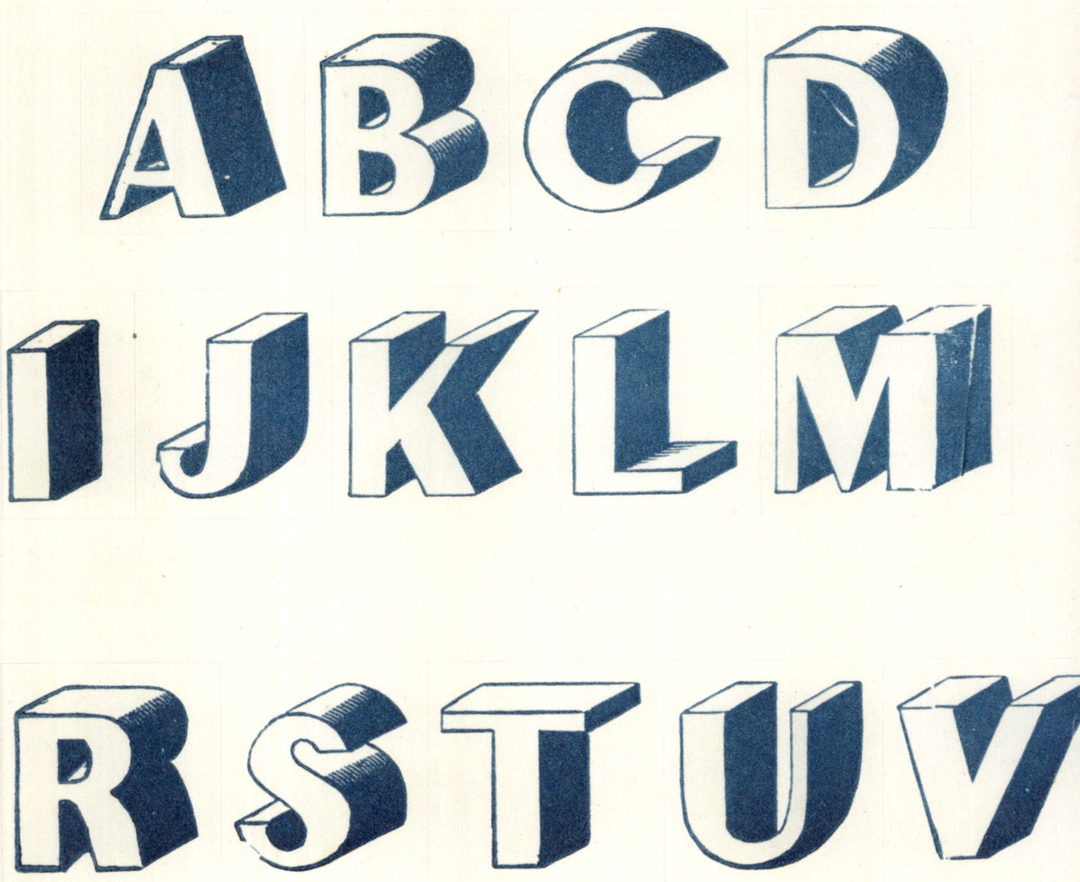

Carving.

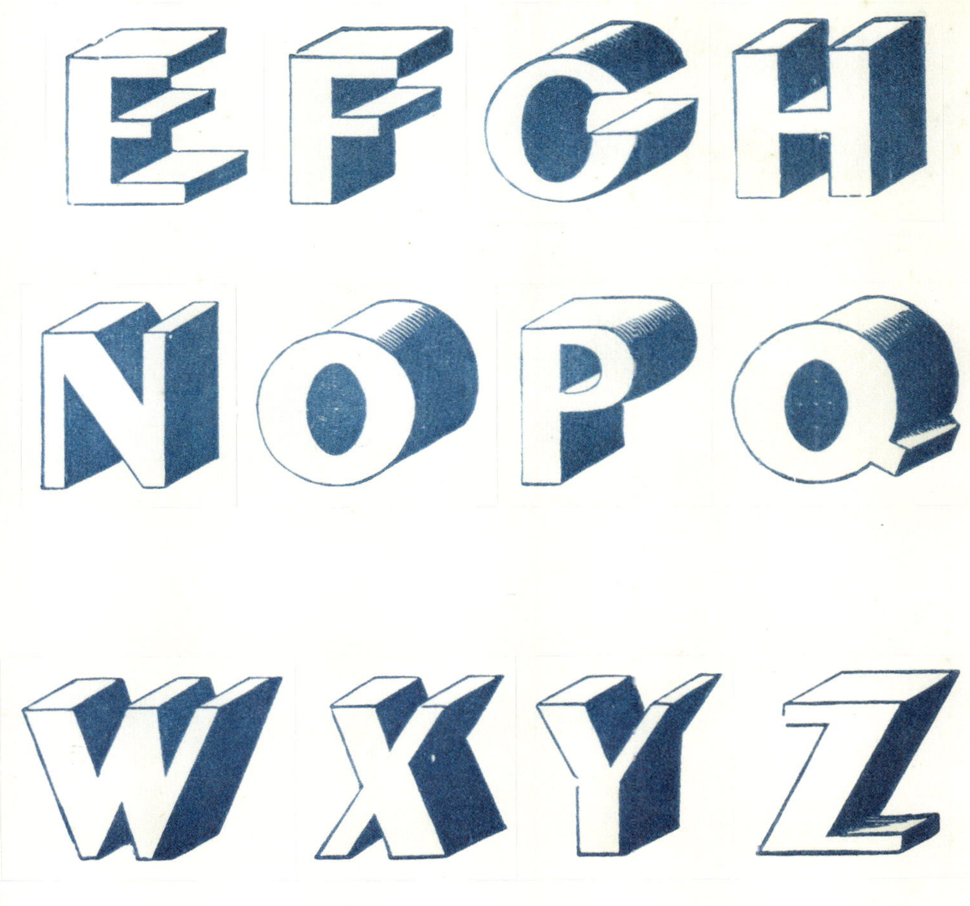

~~Gli ingl~~ Greco, rimettendo ~~[illegible]~~ lo scritto. Non attarimi ~~[illegible]~~

Quanto ci costa poco ~~[illegible]~~ & dover copiare da qualche ~~traduttore~~ cinquantina e settantina versi per ~~volta~~ lezione d'una tragedia di Sofocle, roba da vetrioli, che ~~[illegible]~~ fa ~~[illegible]~~ stancarsi ~~quanto~~ il ~~[illegible]~~ ~~quanto~~ quanto non so che dire... ~~e non basta~~ ~~[illegible]~~ poi prepararsi ~~alla~~ ~~alla~~ ed esser poi costretto prepararcisi per ~~rife~~ poterla ripetere in classe

~~Ma [illegible] questo [illegible]~~

1° Maledetta la ~~quadratura~~ del c[illegible] e quella detta ~~matta~~ di chi ~~l'ha~~ l'ha inventata ~~[illegible] potessi mandare a agli gli accidenti a [illegible]~~

~~Se io potessi avere a mia disp[illegible] qualche accidente da mandare, risparmierei certo di spedirne uno almeno una a~~ quella ~~irrequieta~~ del M.o Ondaro, che non fa ~~[illegible]~~ ~~senza~~ dei poveri studenti di Liceo 1° e 2°

~~[illegible] Professore [illegible]~~ esser costretto a studiar ~~a~~ quella ~~[illegible]~~ me, ~~[illegible]~~ dai miei primi anni ~~[illegible]~~ ho sempre ~~[illegible]~~ odiato la matematica ~~[illegible]~~

~~[illegible]~~ e ~~che~~

a me non potto ~~che~~ avrei piuttosto ~~[illegible]~~ imparare queste costruzioni fantastiche

Se non m'importa — mi fa

conoscere ...

Quella di mi ...

Din don din don, —

Oh! che doppio insolito ...

È inutile che mi confondo tanto

non mi vuol entrare nella testa questa

tura del circolo; mi fece che ... legger

roba, ... quadri la mia testa

legger questa roba! Uff! che

Uhfff! credo quasi quasi

... di più a dormire e mandar

al diavolo la questa ... la geometria! —

Oh! che doppio insolito!

son le campane di

Ah! ora mi rivenga, oggi

Ah! ora ricordo

l'anniversario di Curtatone.

3°

Oggi è l'anniversario di Curtatone

noi abbiamo festa! e le campane

Ah le suonano di santa Croce

Sole le campane suonano

... suonano doppio

e noi abbiamo vacanze; è un giorno

a sante memorie per noi Italiani

per chi sente un po' d'amor di patria

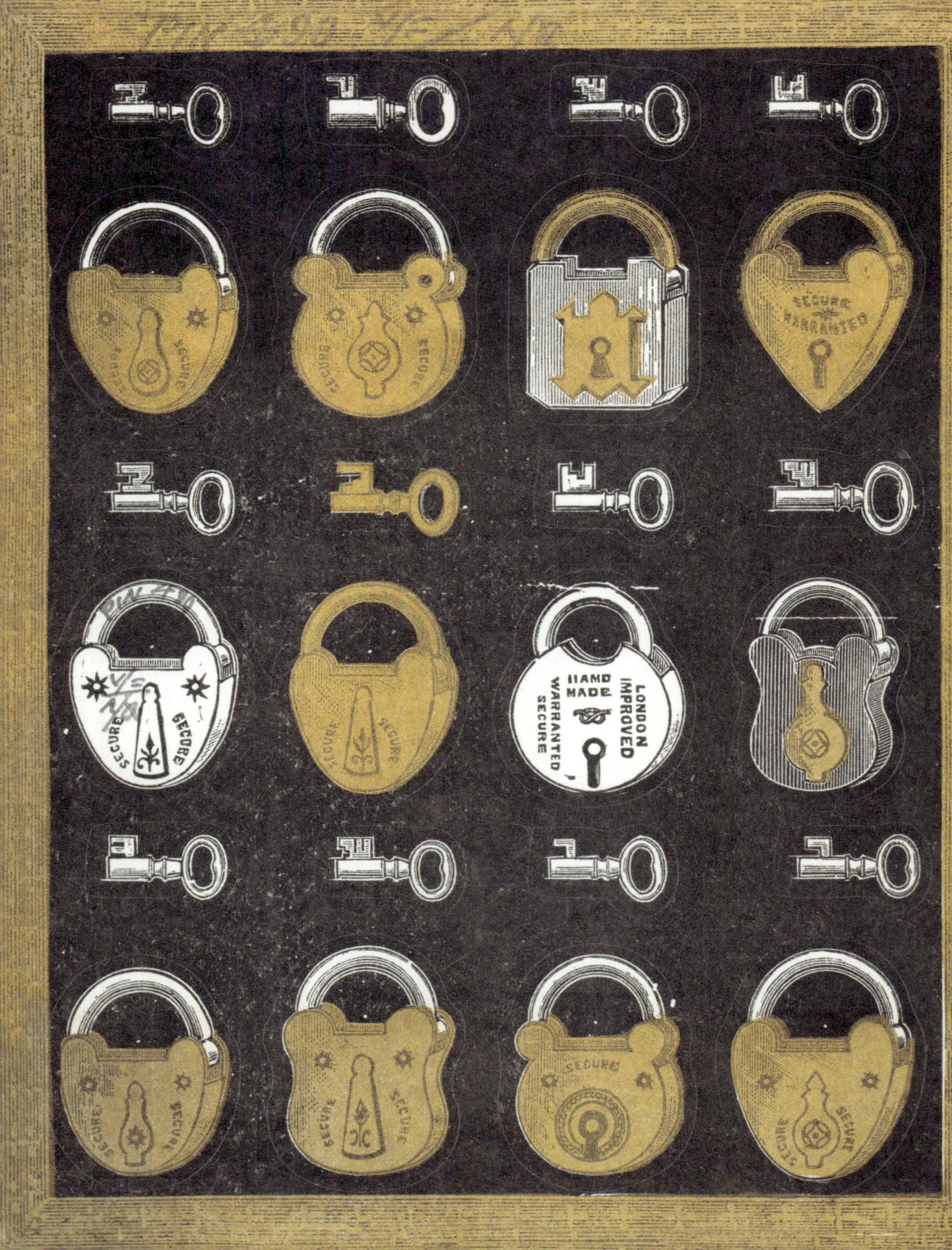
SECURE
SECURE
SECURE
SECURE
SECURE
WARRANTED
SECURE
SECURE
SECURE
SECURE
HAND
MADE
LONDON
IMPROVED
WARRANTED
SECURE
SECURE
SECURE
SECURE
SECURE
SECURE
SECURE
SECURE

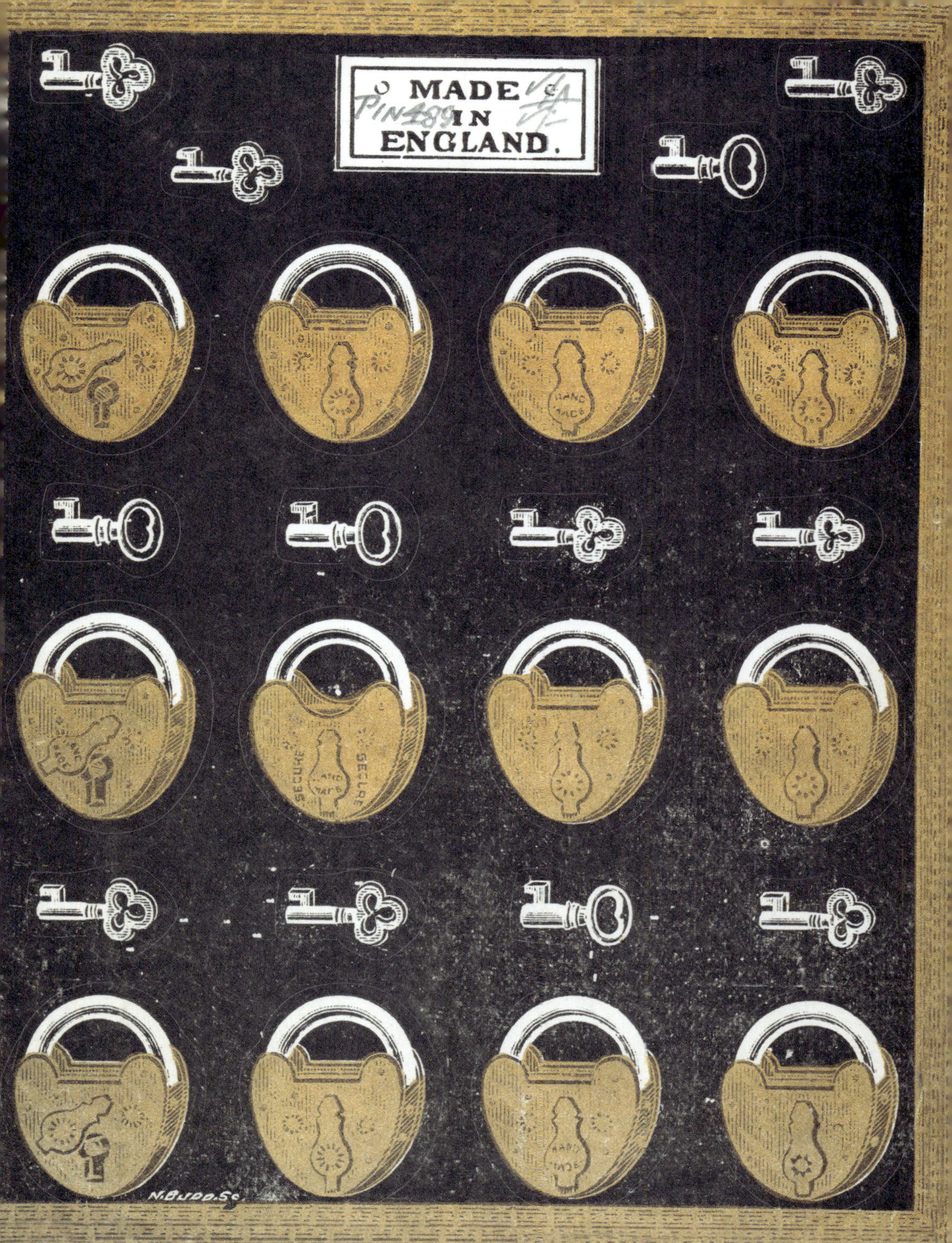
MADE
IN
ENGLAND.
HAND MADE
SECURE
SECURE
N.BUDD.Sc

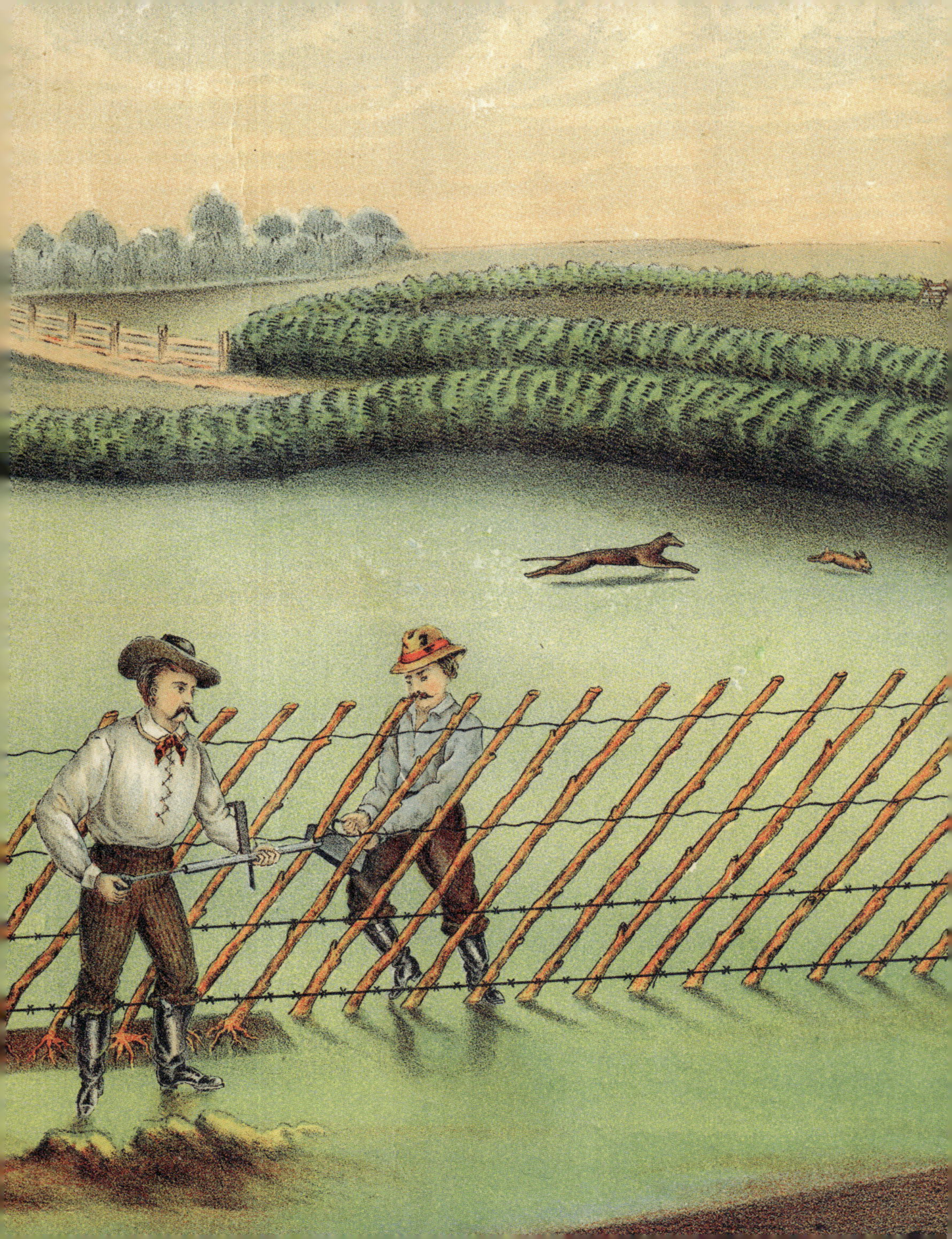

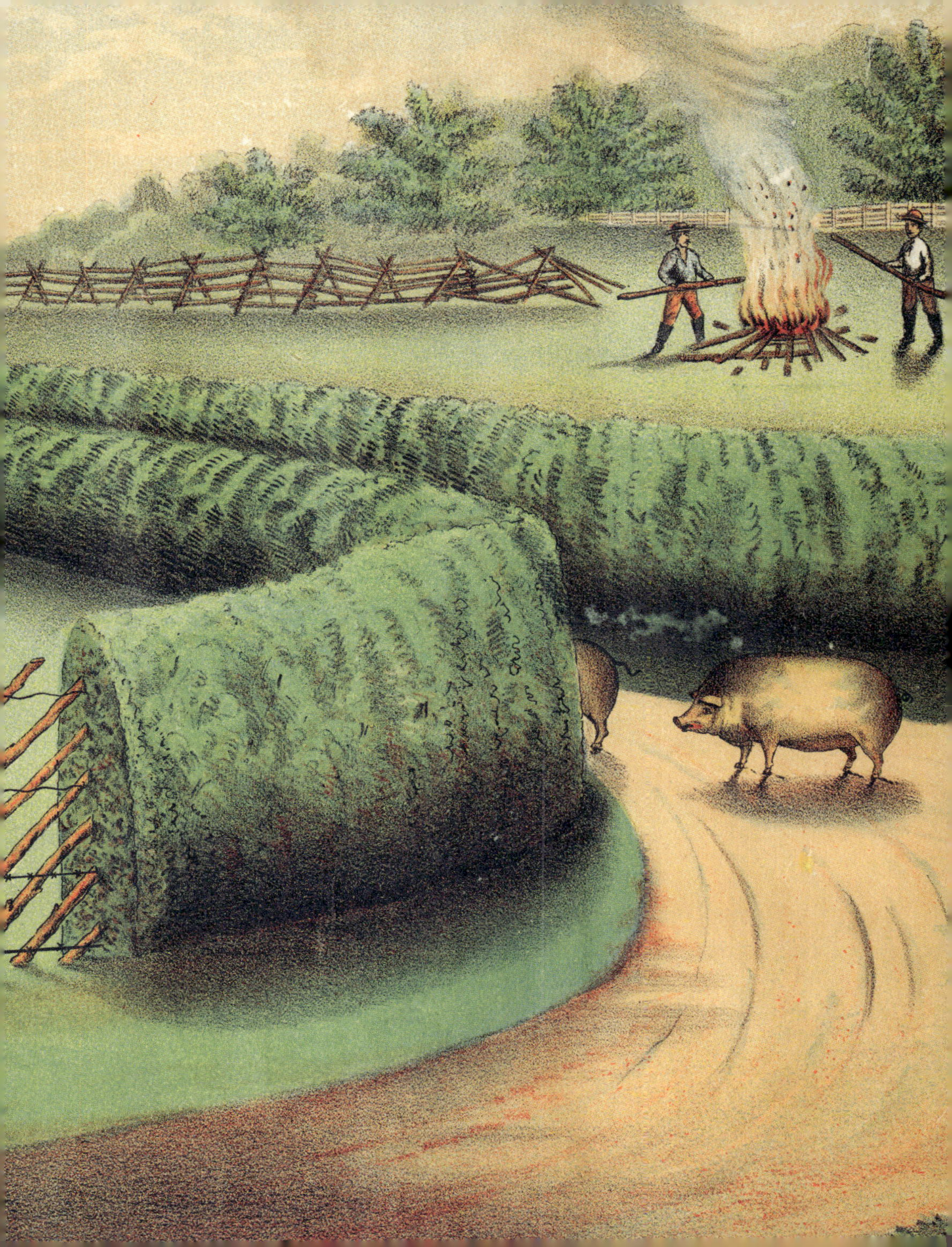

Porcus pumilo Taxus porcinꝰ

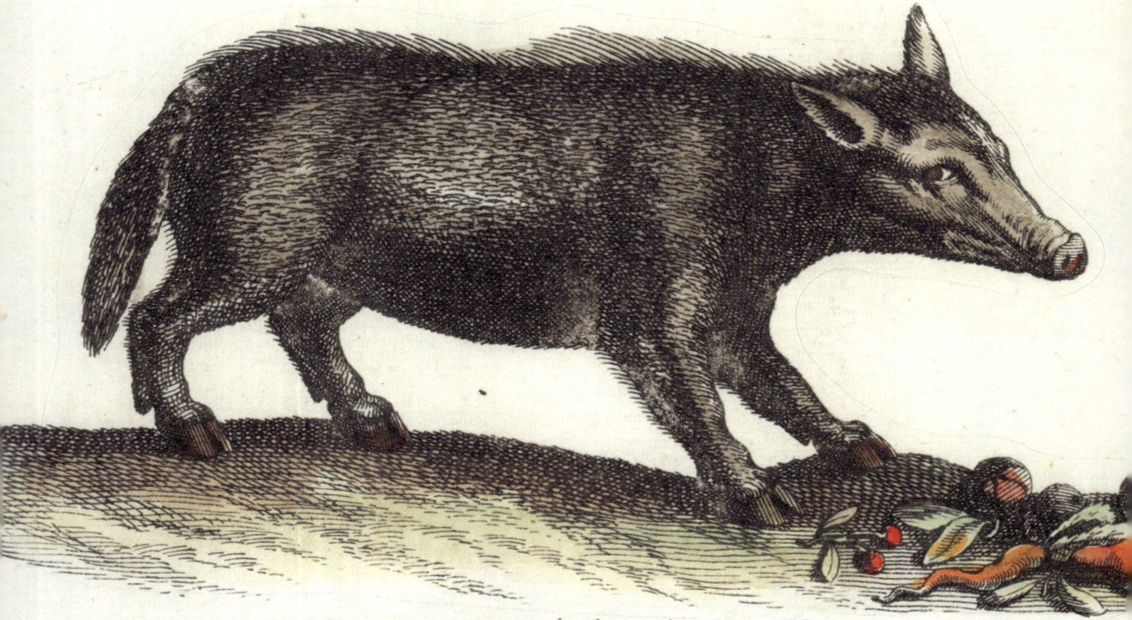

Aper . Wildschwein

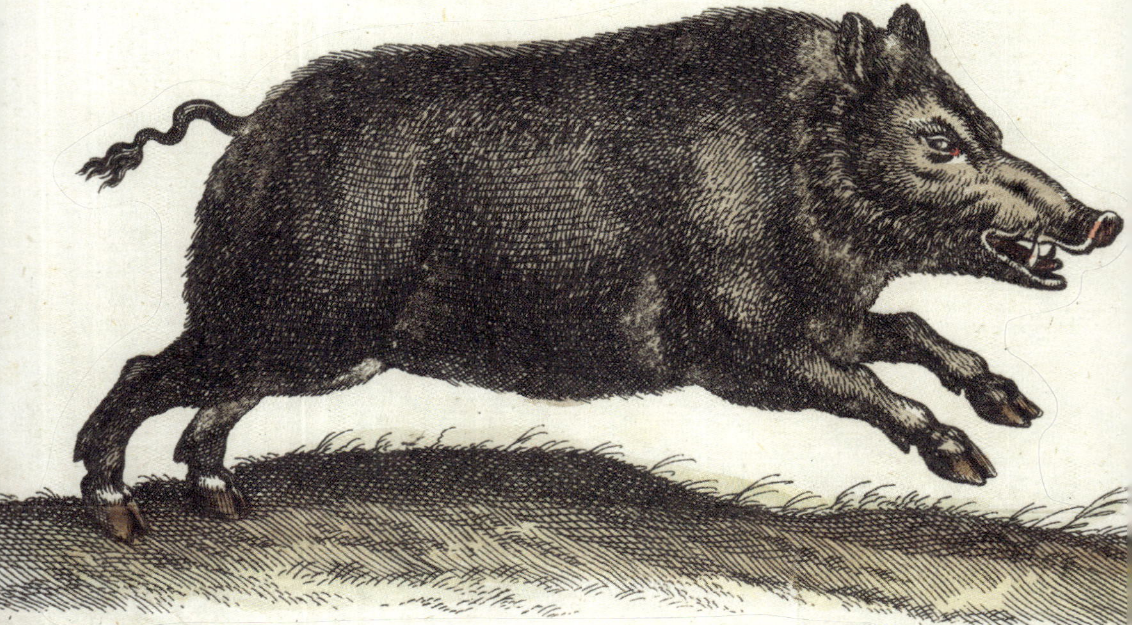

Verres . Eber

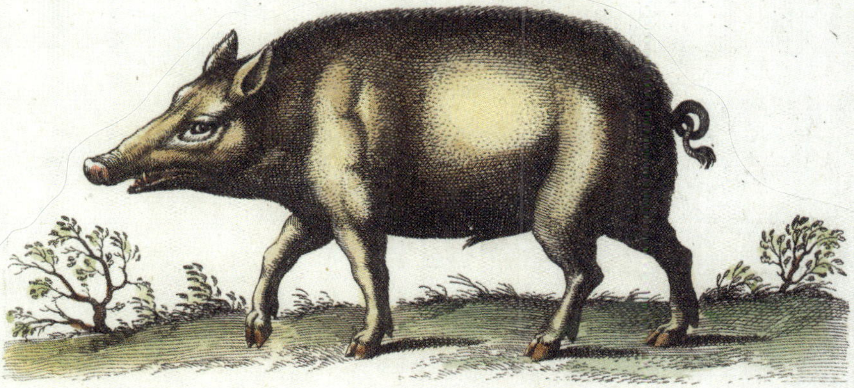

Aper . Wildschwein .

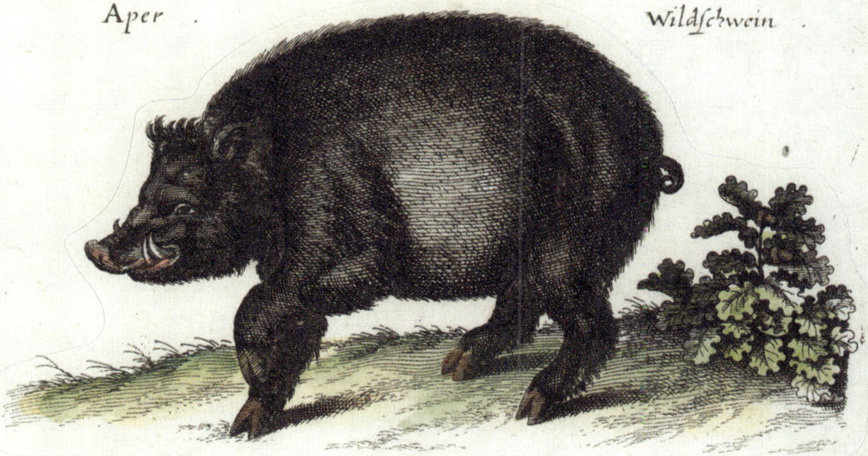

Scrofa Mock

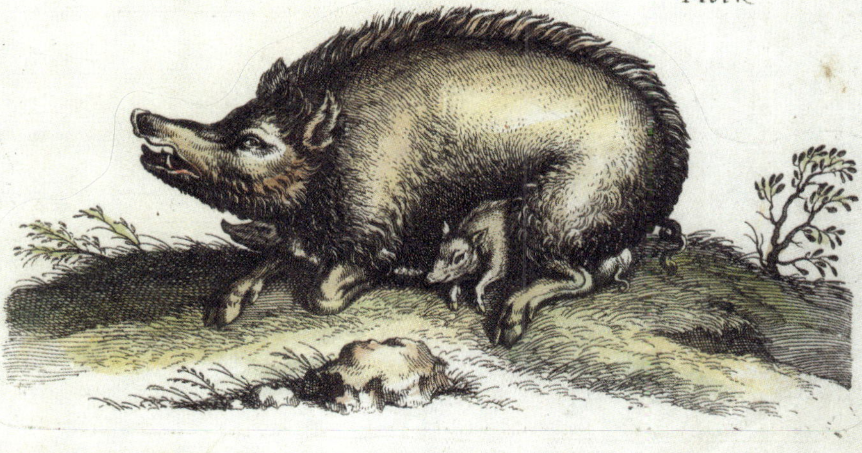

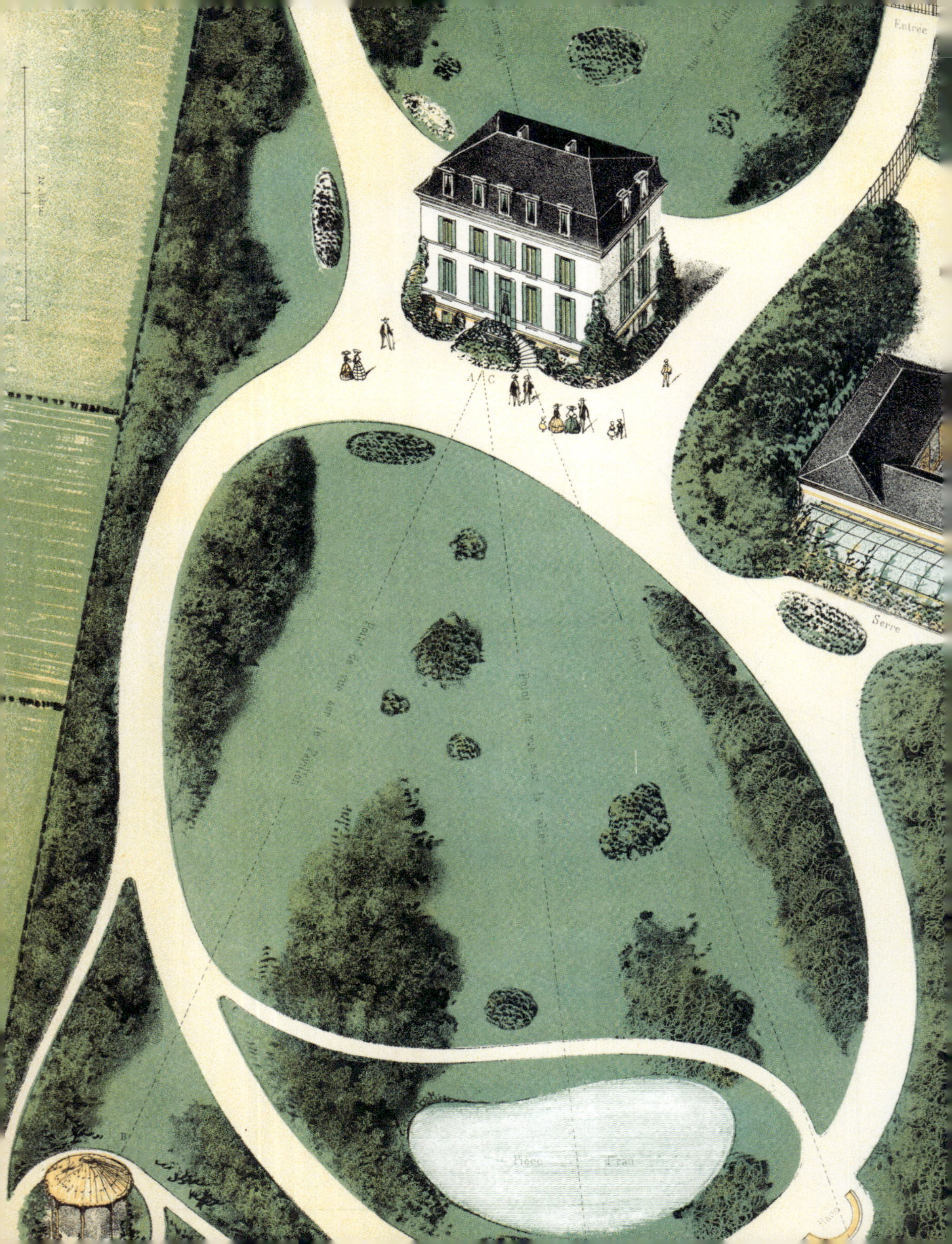

Entrée
Serre
A
C
B
Point de vue sur le Pavillon
Point de vue sur la vallée
Point de vue sur le banc
Pièce d'Eau
Banc

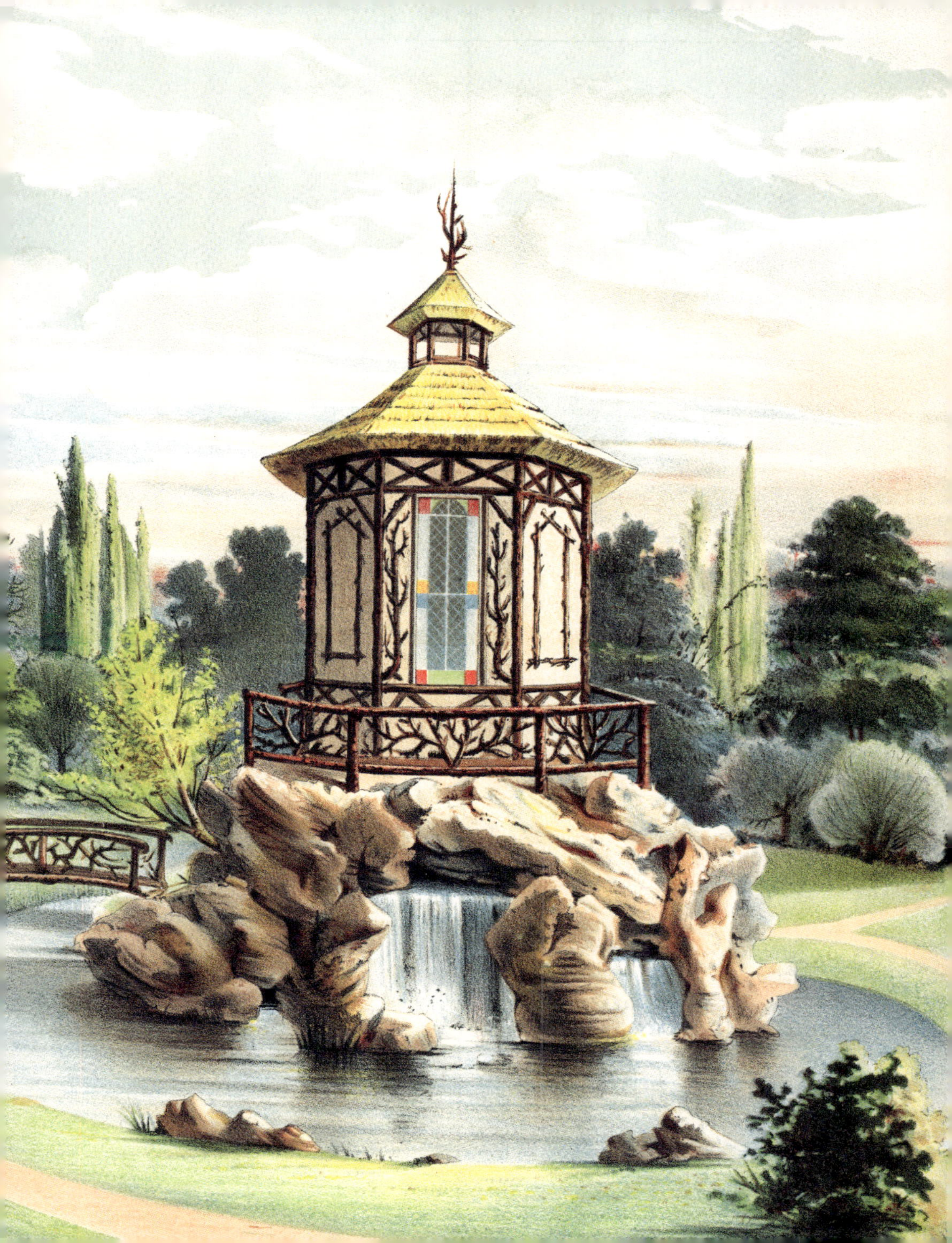

Keep good company
Keep good company
Keep good company
Keep good company
Keep good company
Keep good company

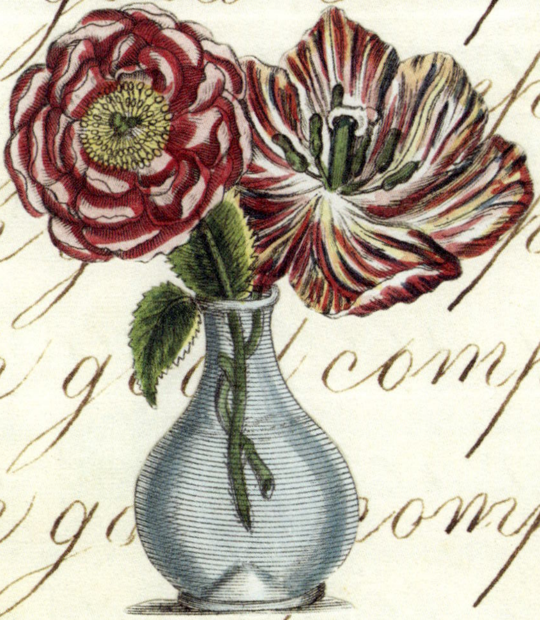

Taf. 227.

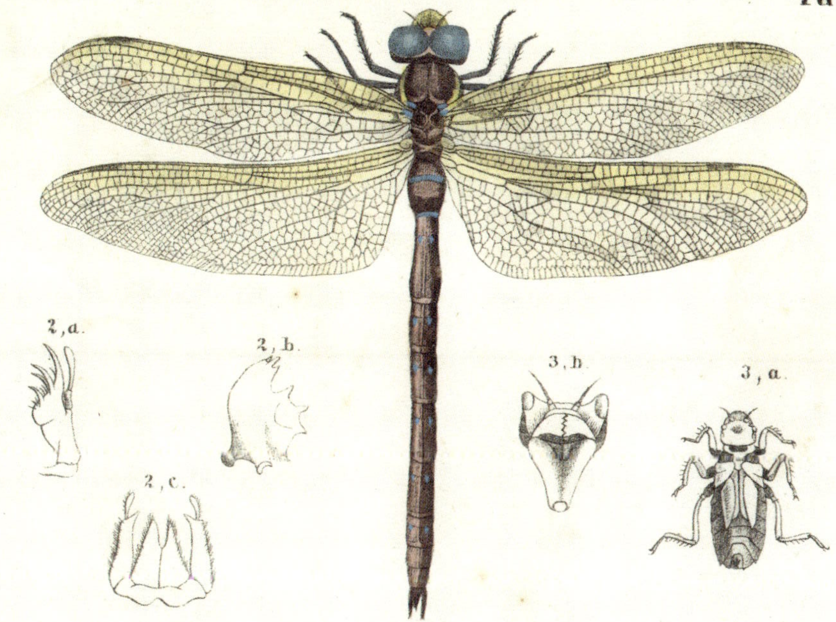

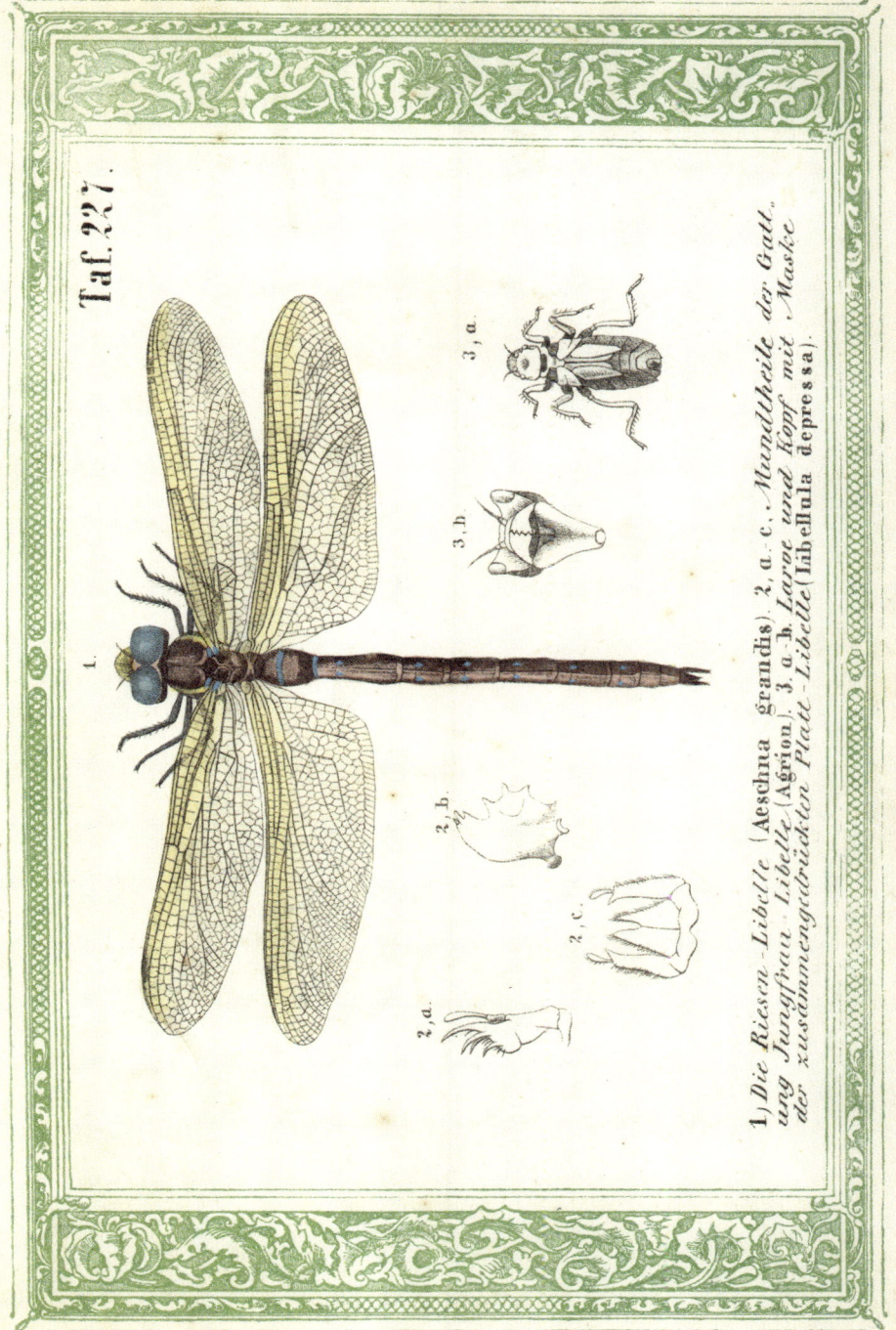

1) *Die Riesen-Libelle* (Aeschna grandis). 2, a.-c. *Mundtheile der Gattung Jungfrau-Libelle* (Agrion). 3. a-b. *Larve und Kopf mit Maske der zusammengedrückten Platt-Libelle* (Libellula depressa).

N. 536.

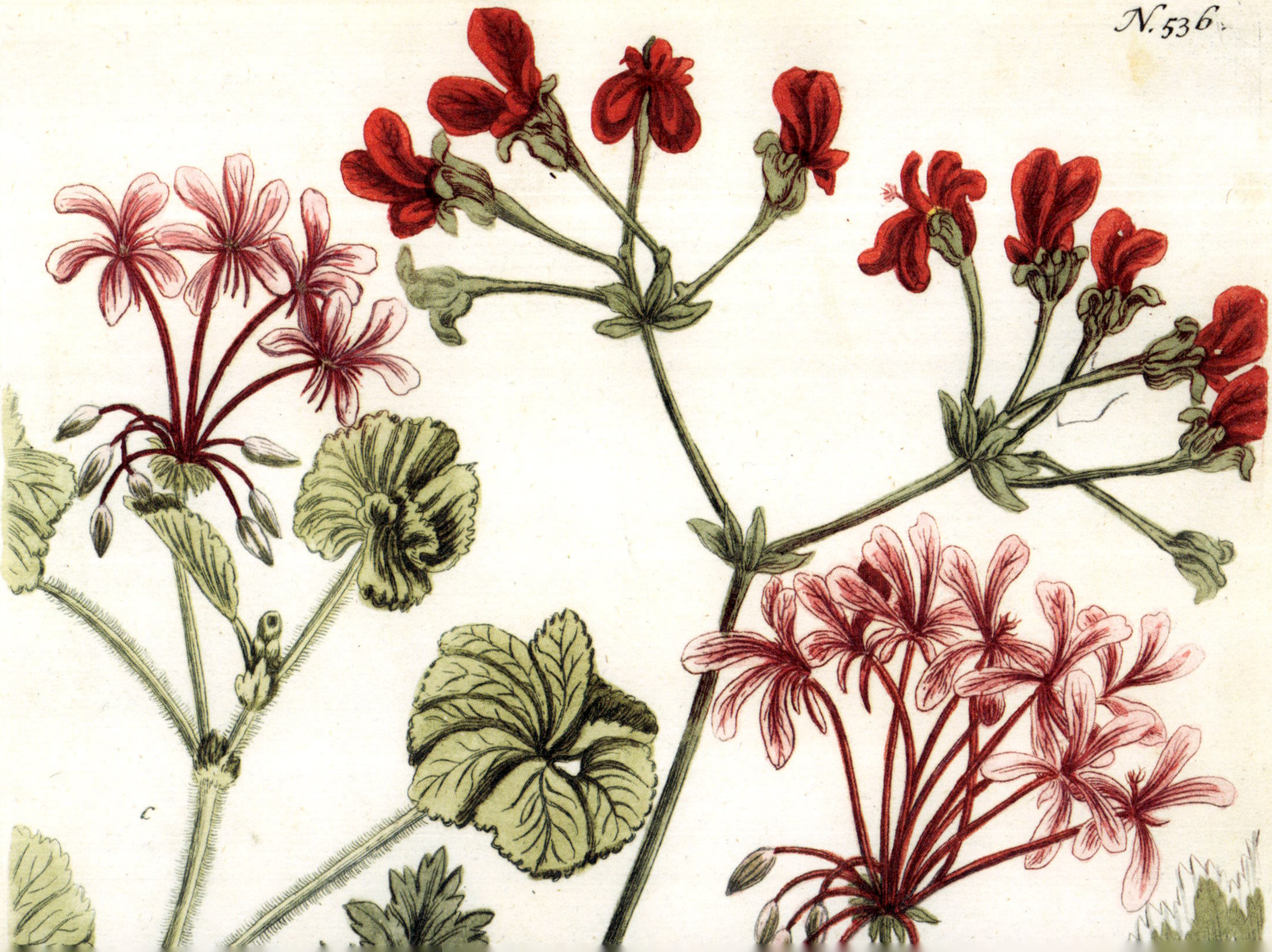

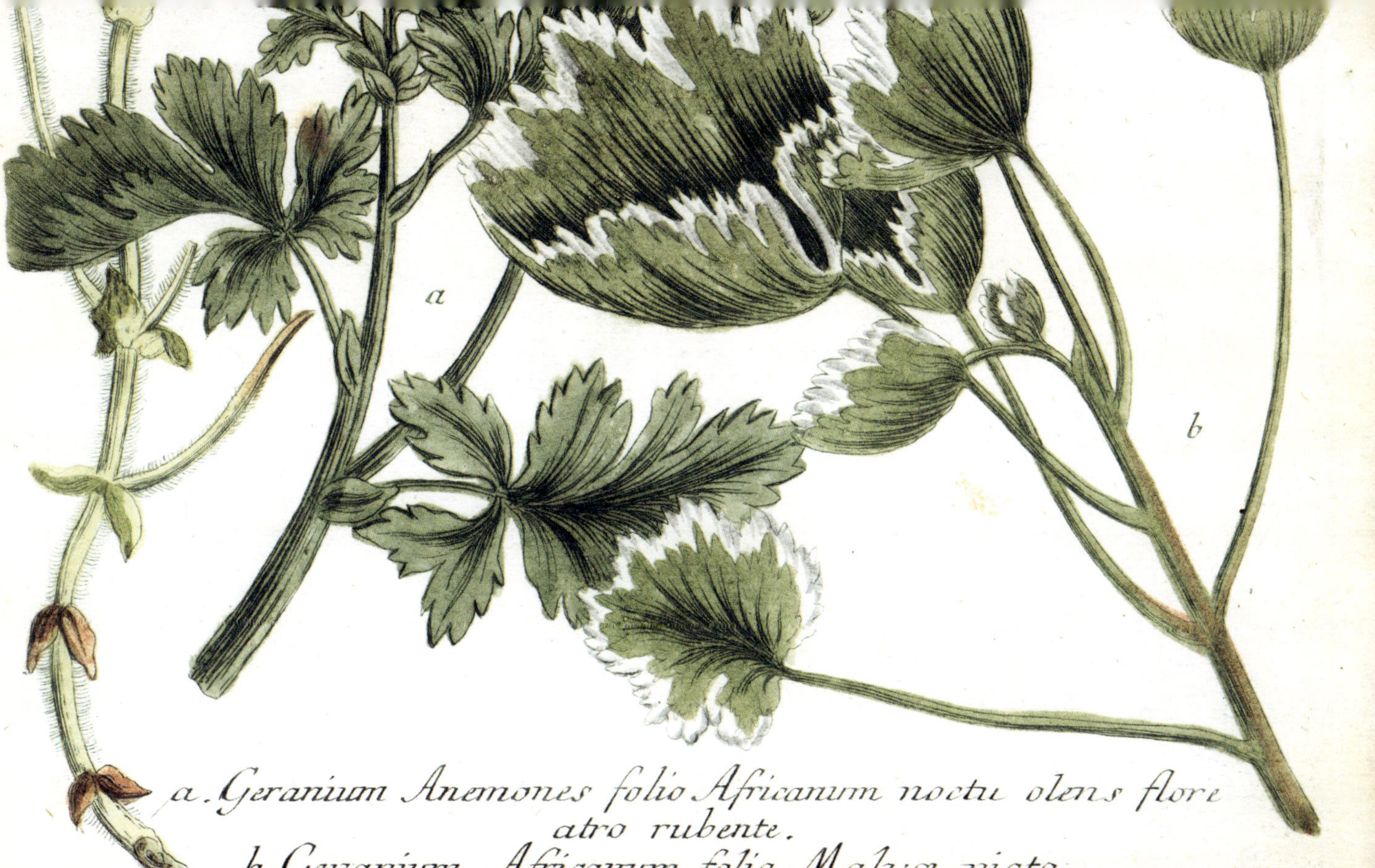

a. Geranium Anemones folio Africanum noctu olens flore atro rubente.
b. Geranium Africanum folio Malvæ picto.
c. Geranium Africanum frutescens Malvæ folio.

s.

Weinman

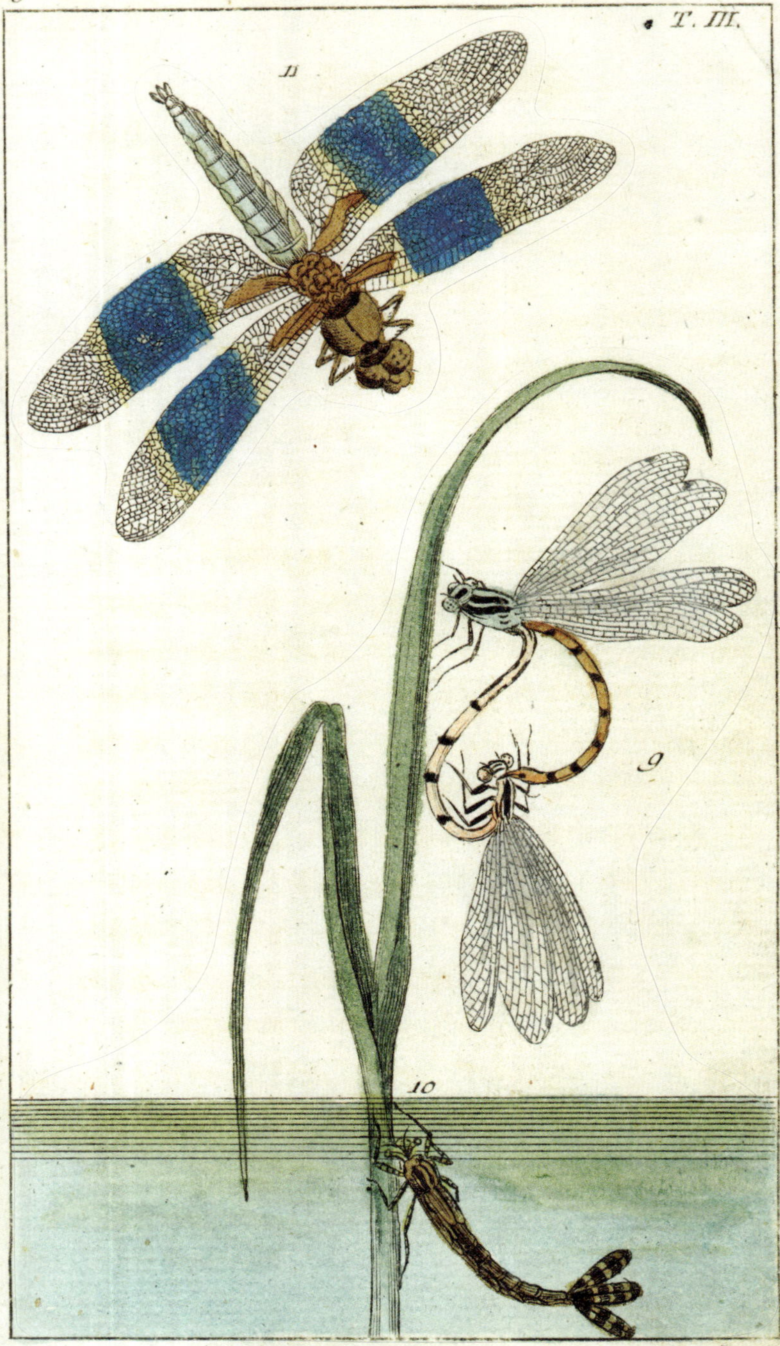
T. III.
11
9
10

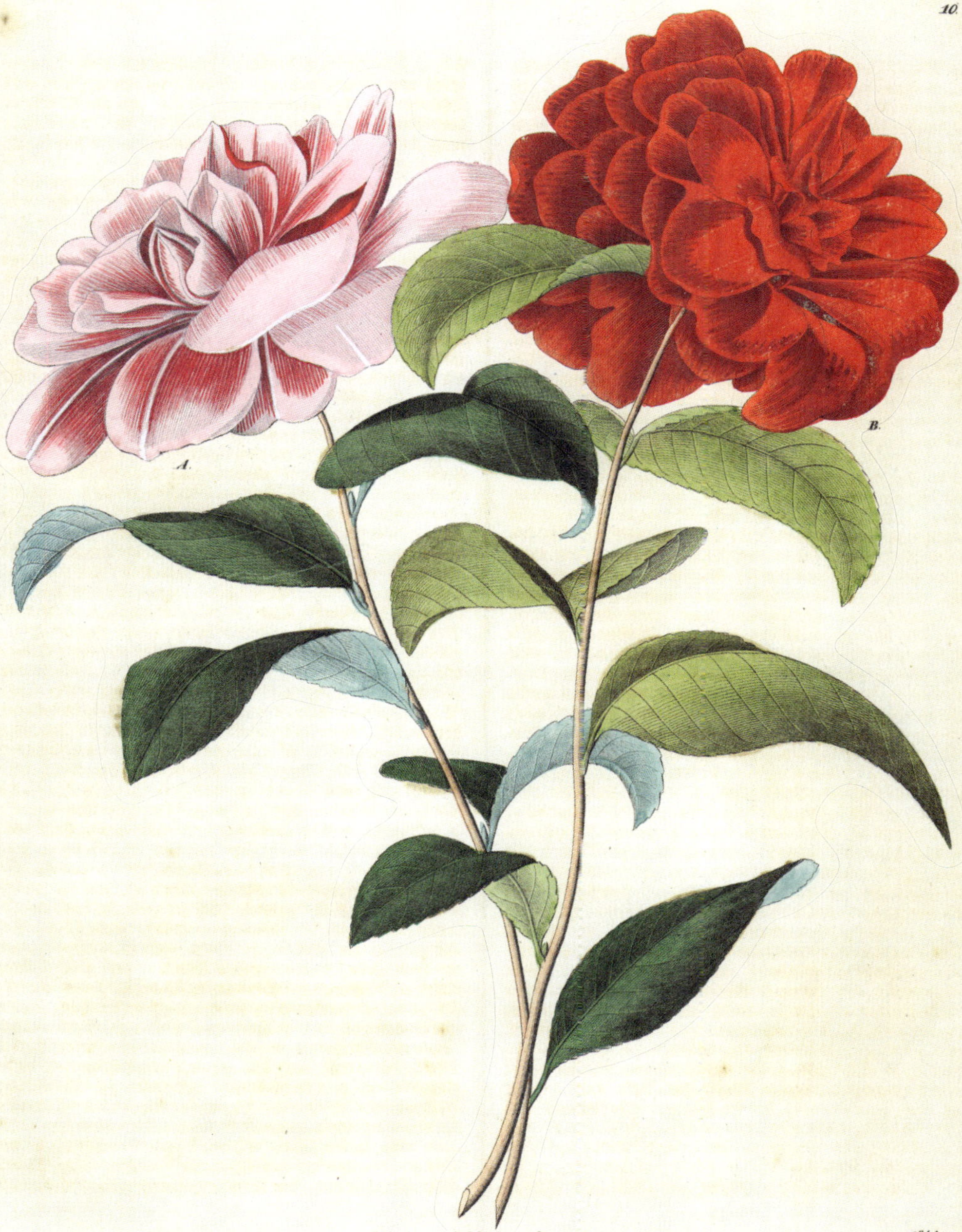

Lith. Anst. v. C. Schach in Stuttgart.

1843.

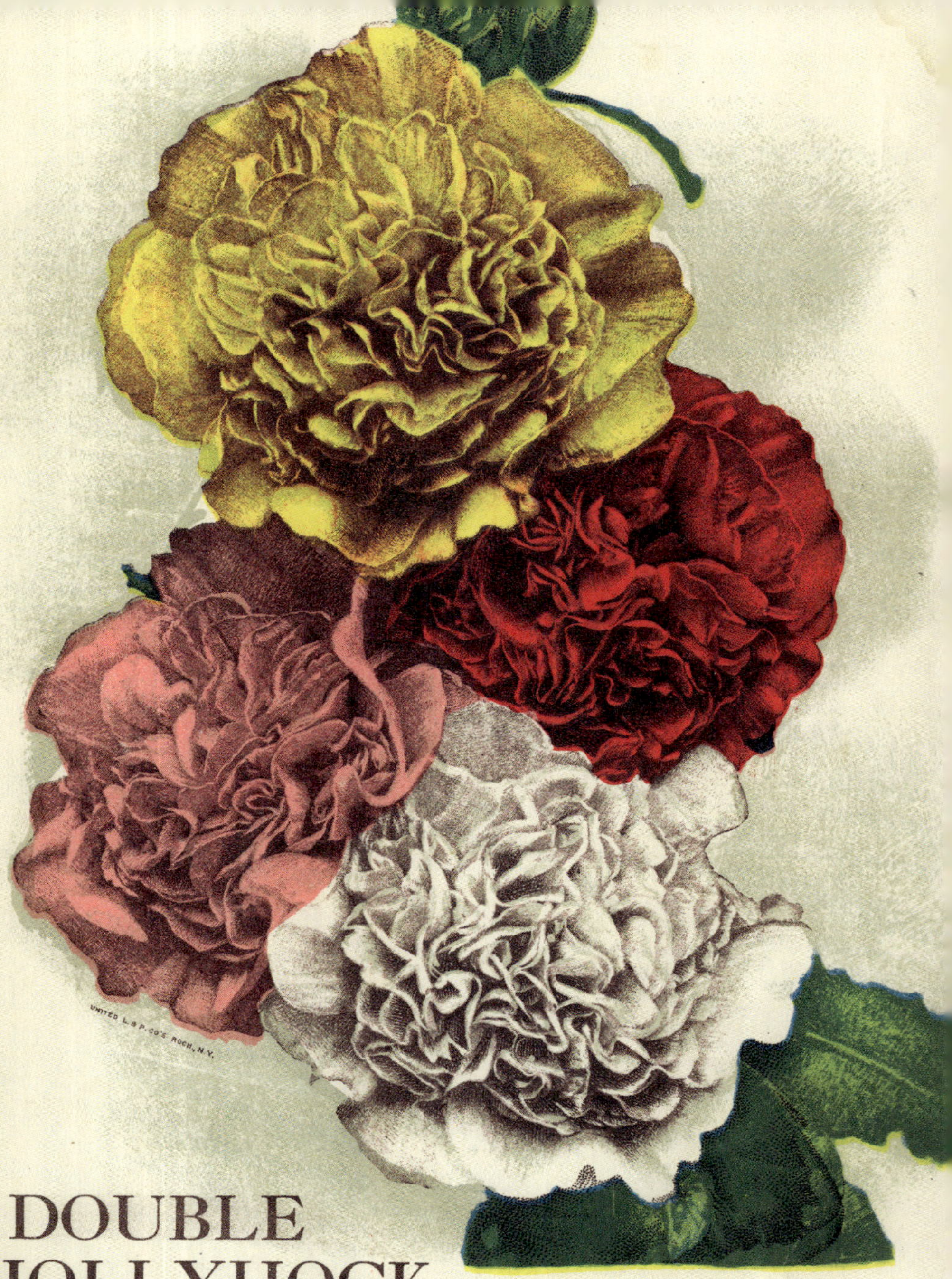

DOUBLE HOLLYHOCK

A Rival of the Rose in Size, Form and Beautiful Colors

OMNIBUS

AND

Other Stories.

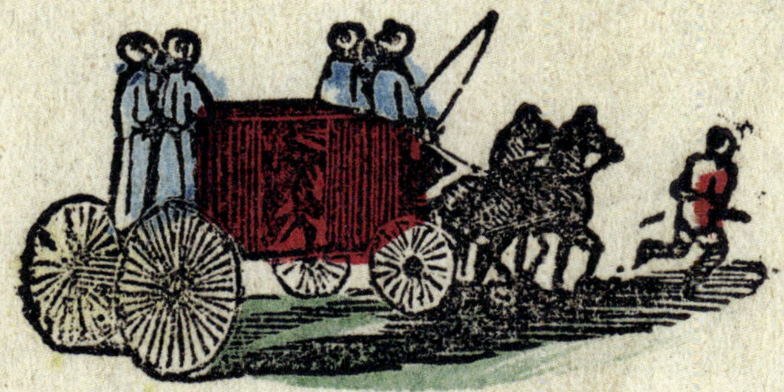

NEW YORK:
LEAVITT & ALLEN.

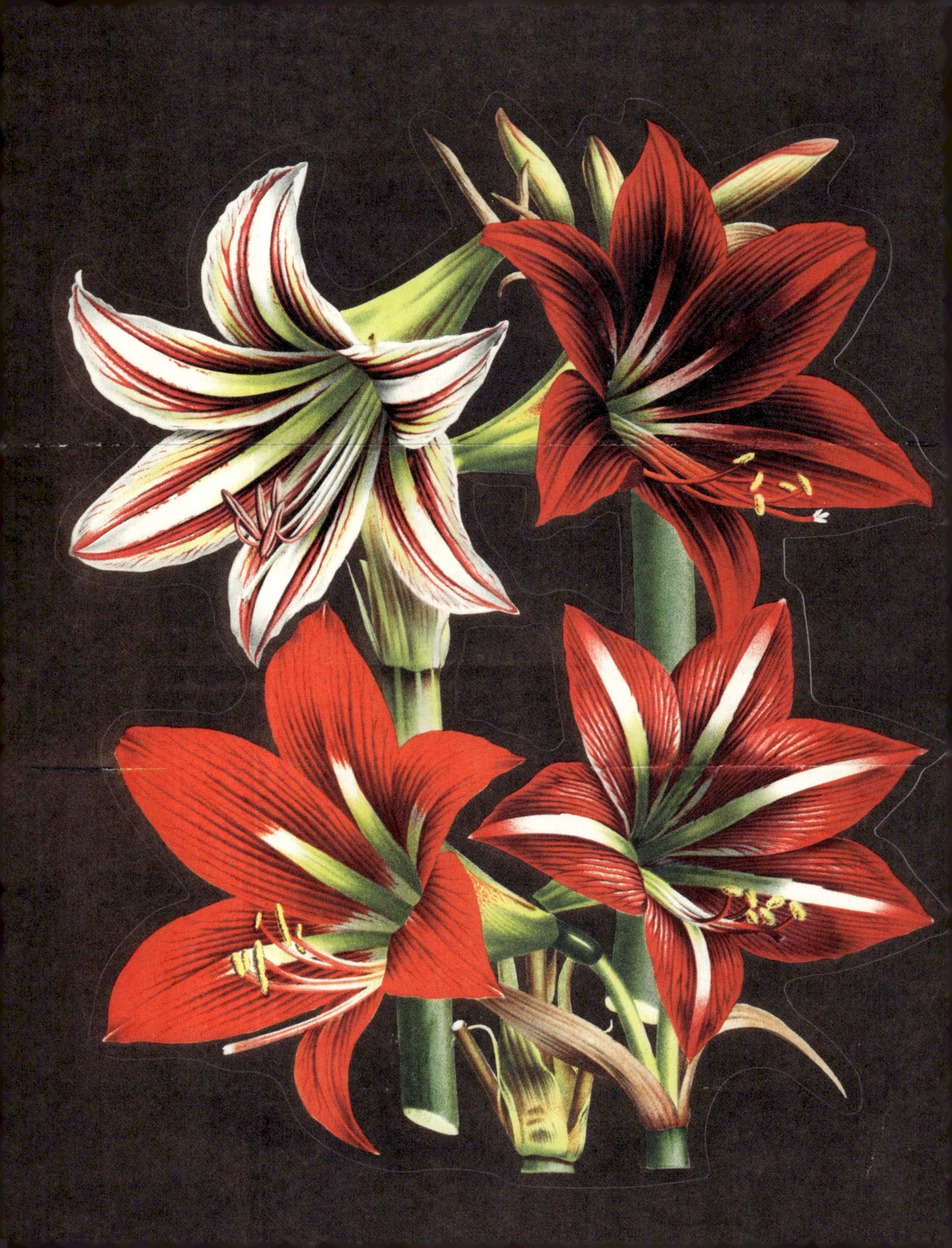

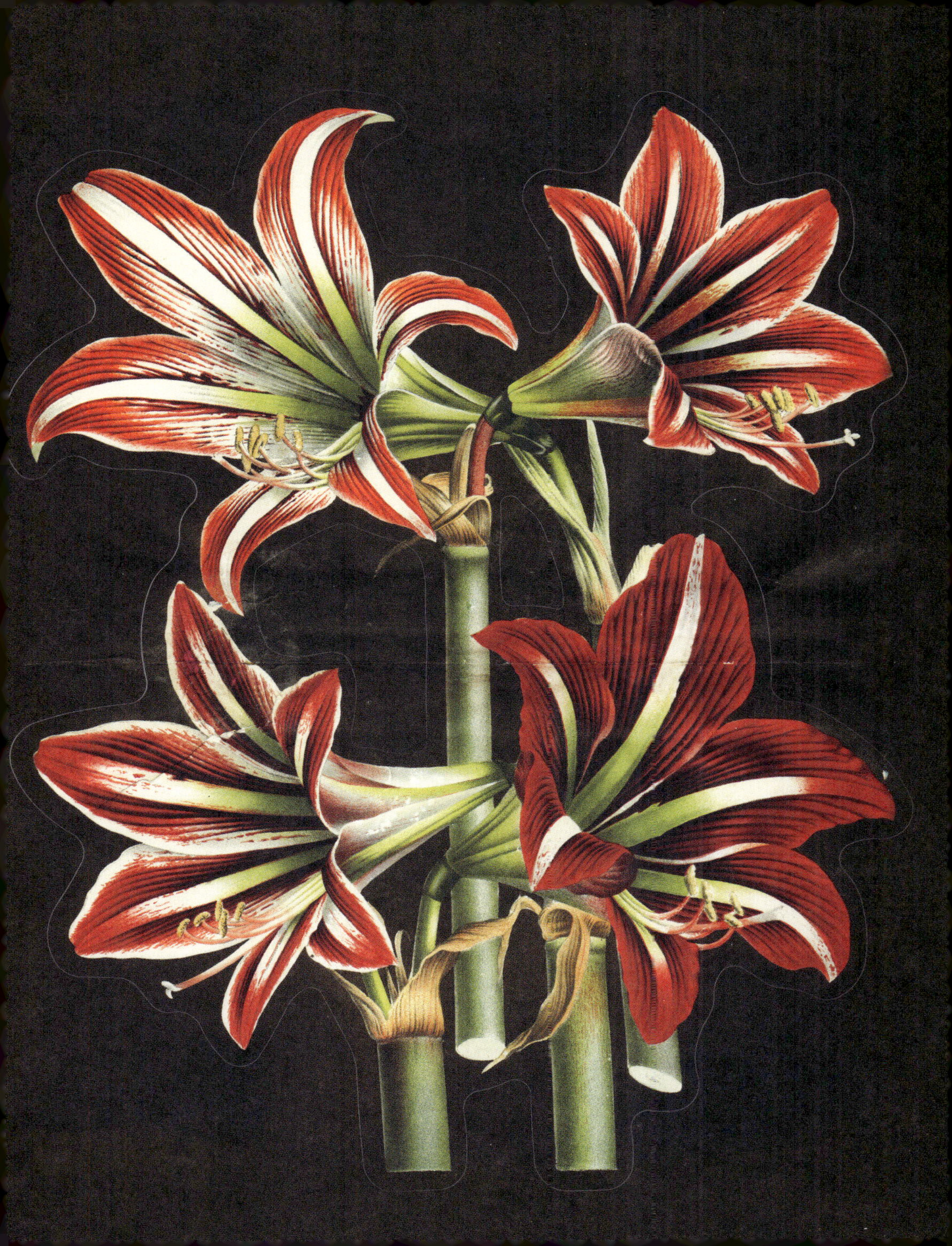

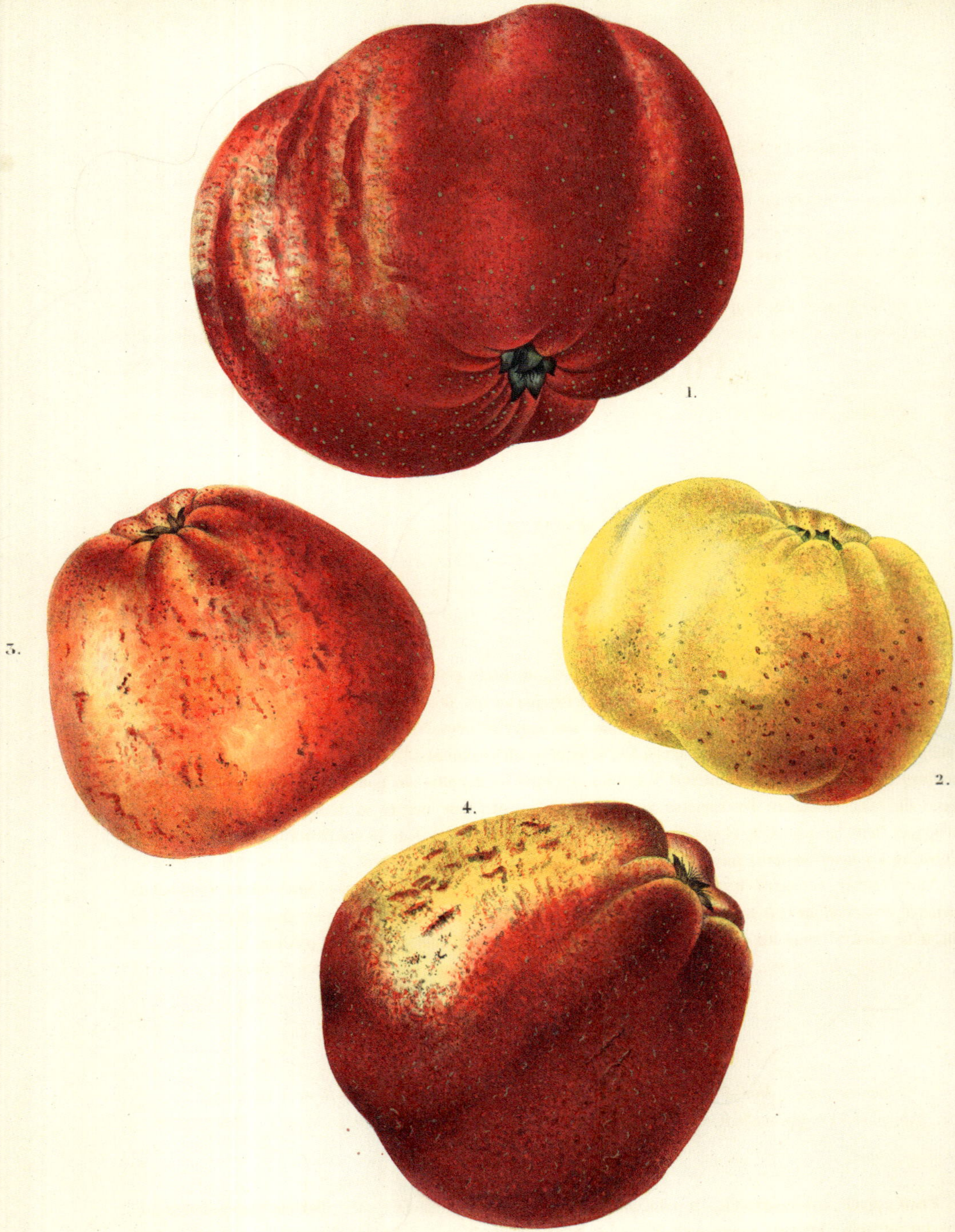
1.
3.
2.
4.

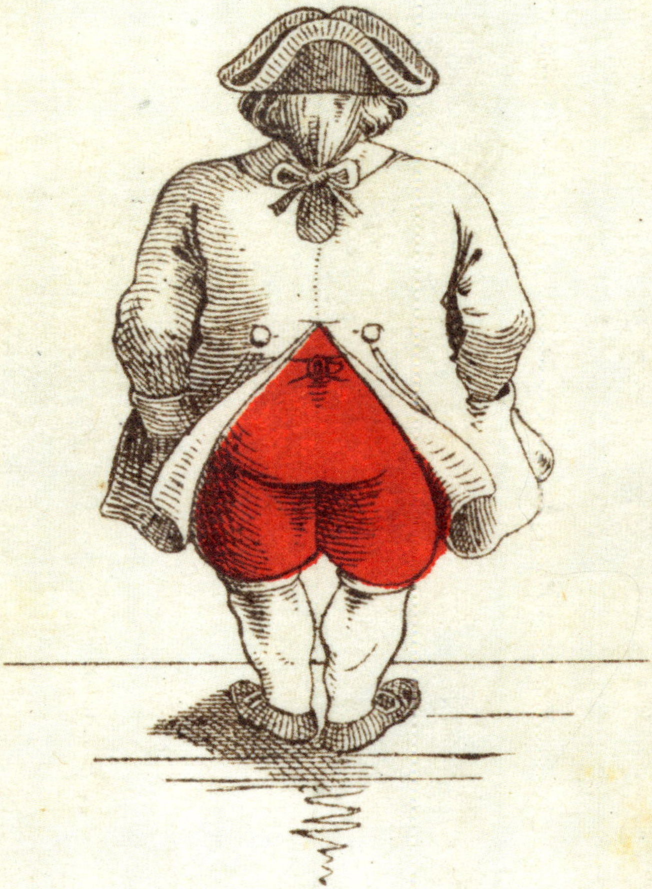

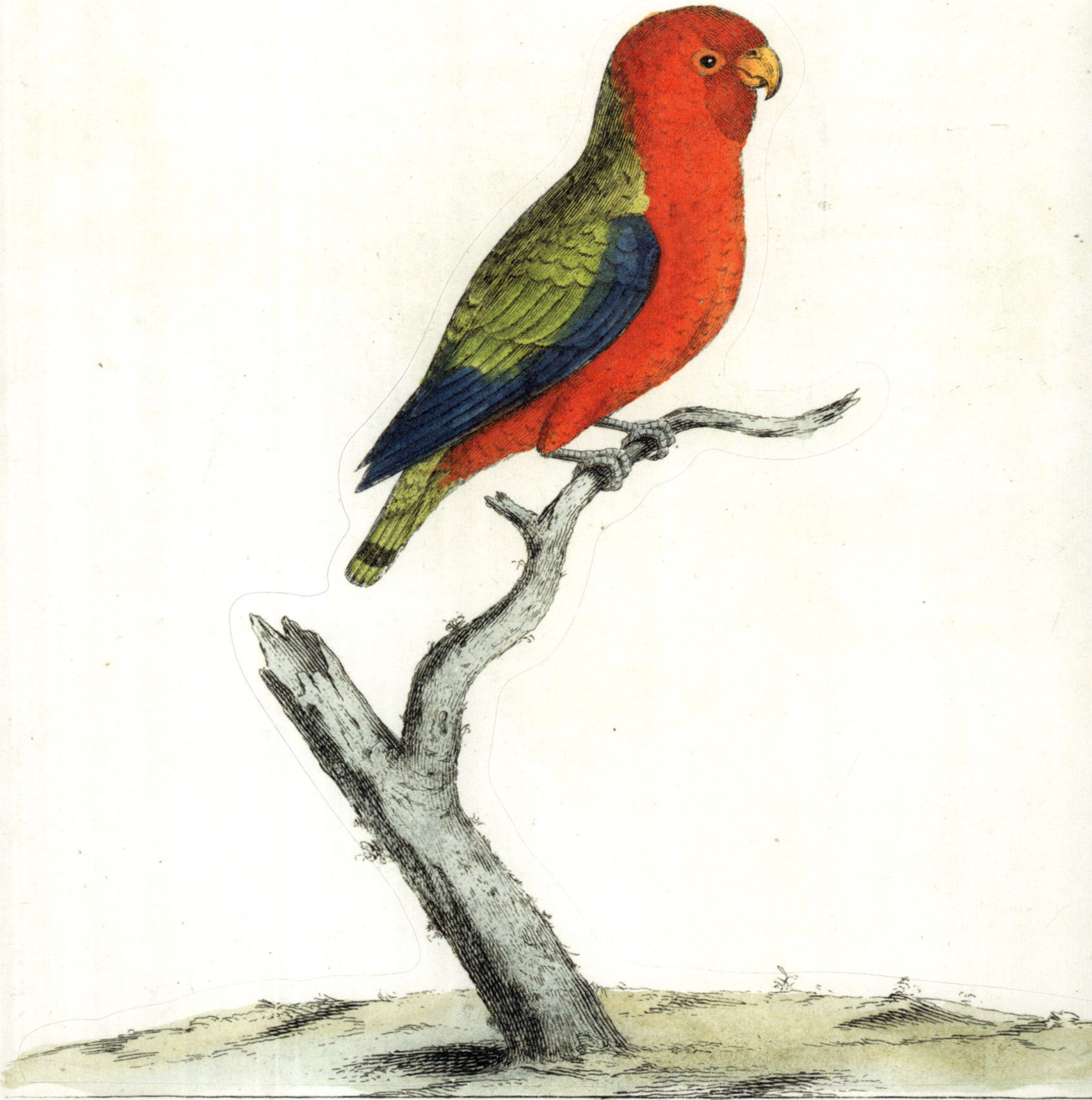

Paroquet from the East Indies

E. Albin del. June 21. 173

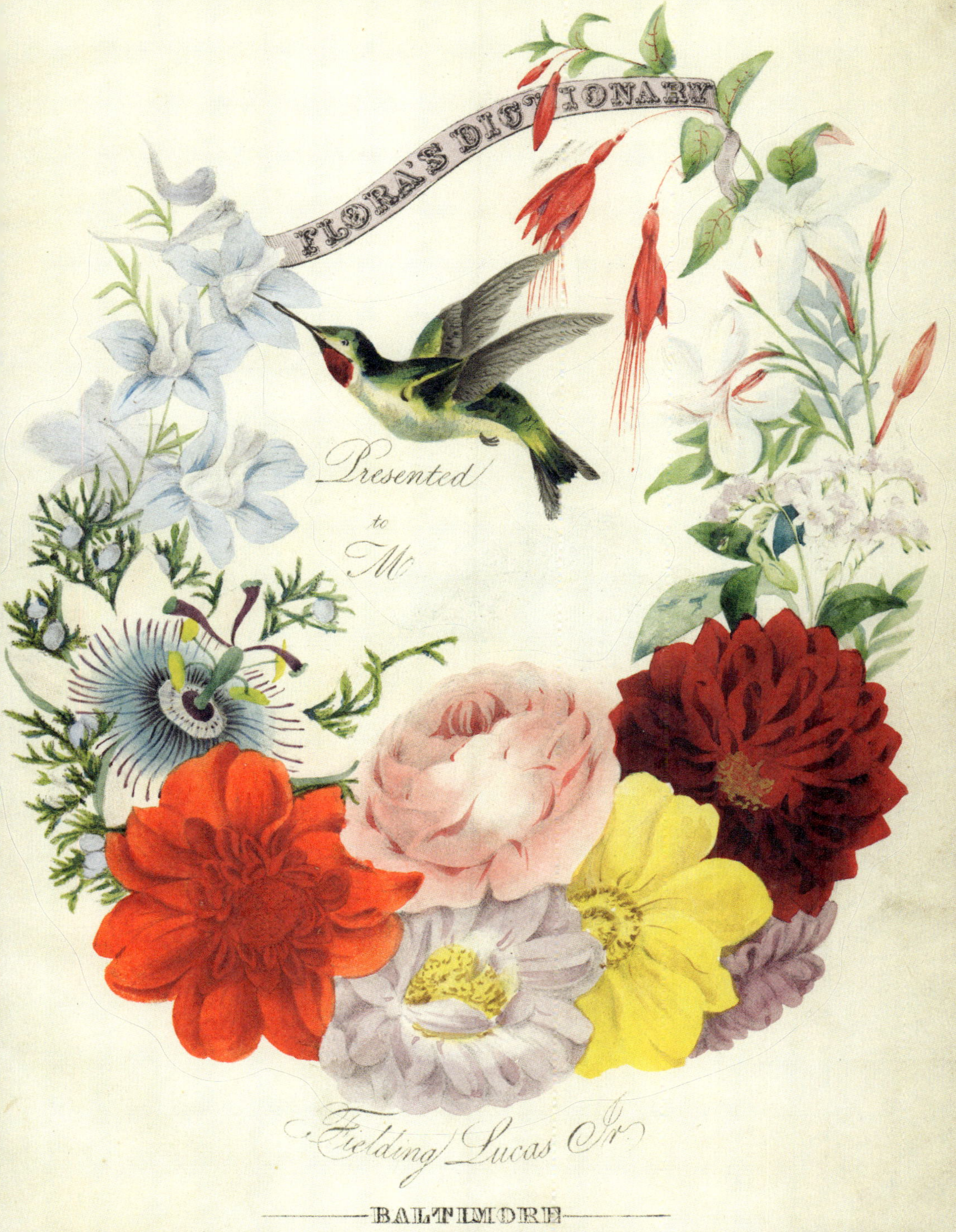
FLORA'S DICTIONARY
Presented
to
Mr
Fielding Lucas Jr
BALTIMORE

BUCEPHALUS. N.° 20.

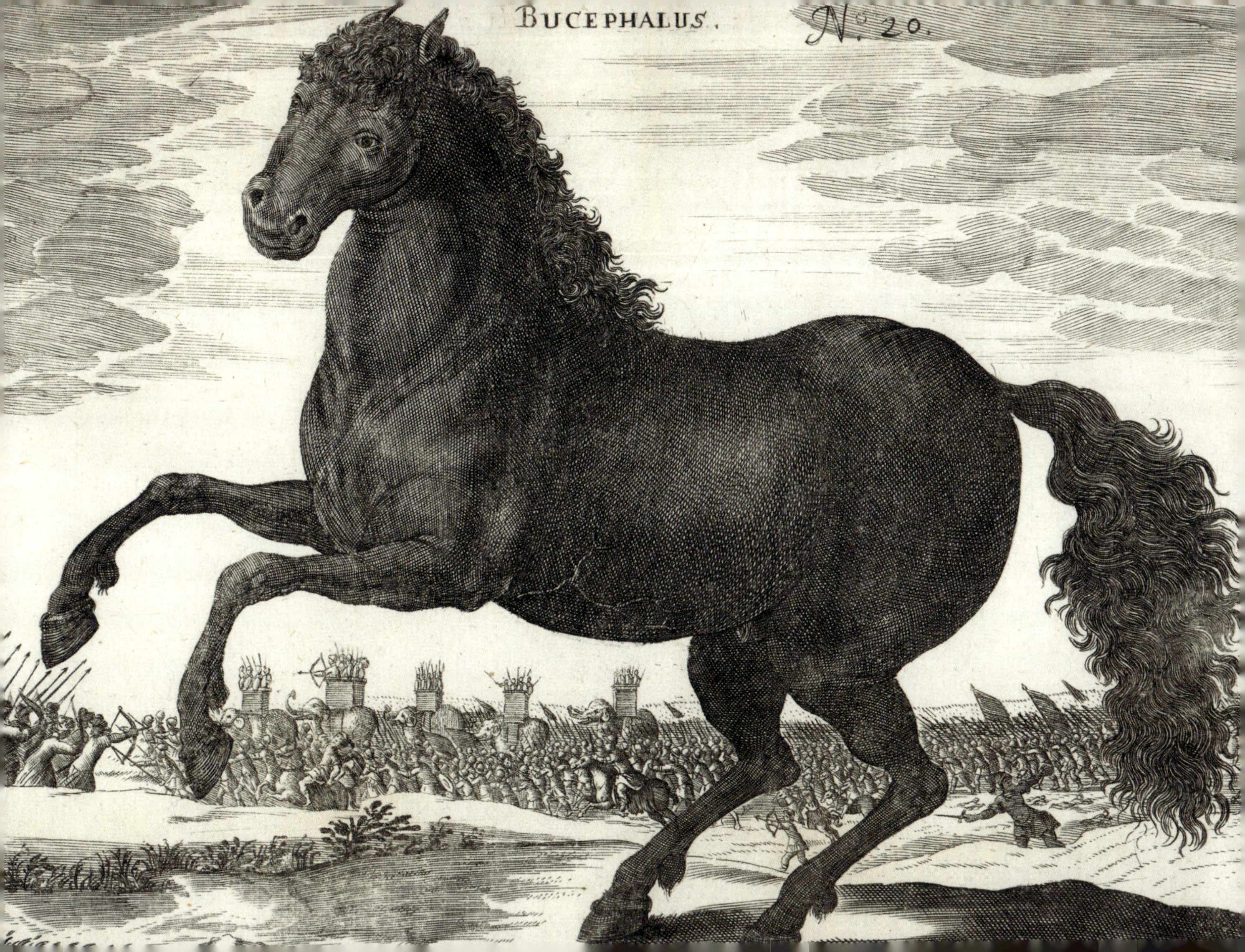

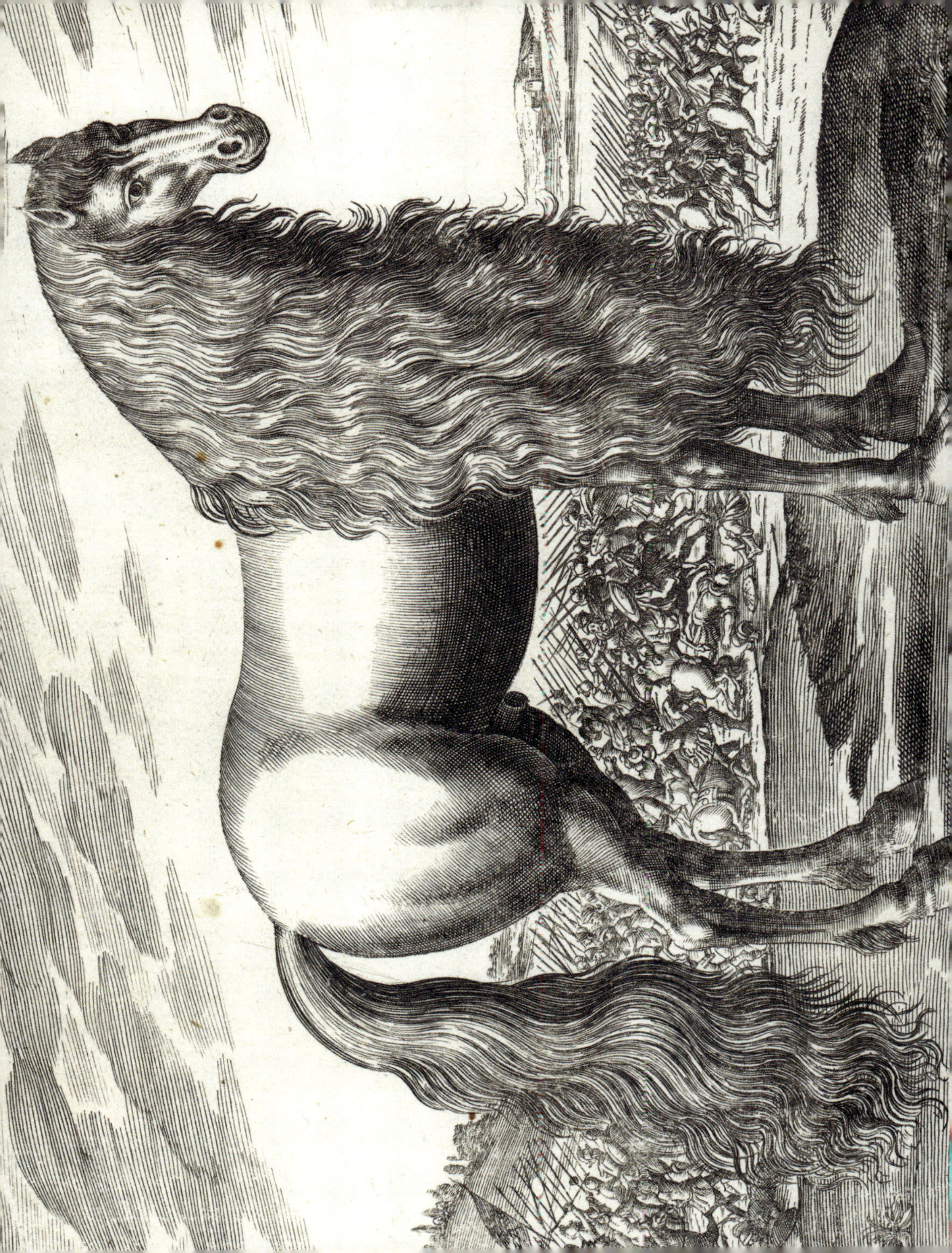

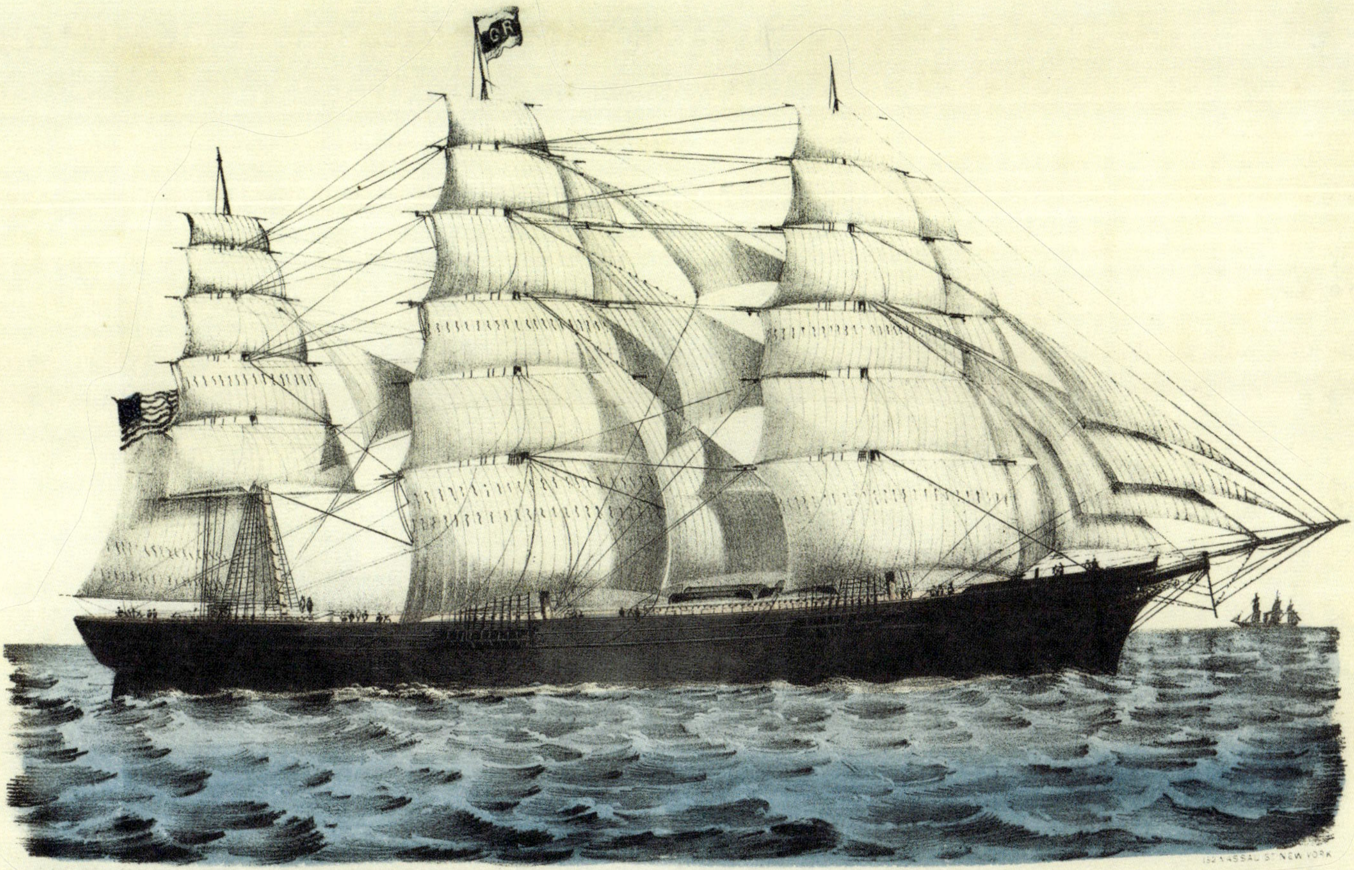

CLIPPER SHIP "GREAT REPUBLIC".

Length on Deck 325 feet. Breadth of Beam 53 ft. Depth of Hold 39 feet. Tonnage per Register 4500.

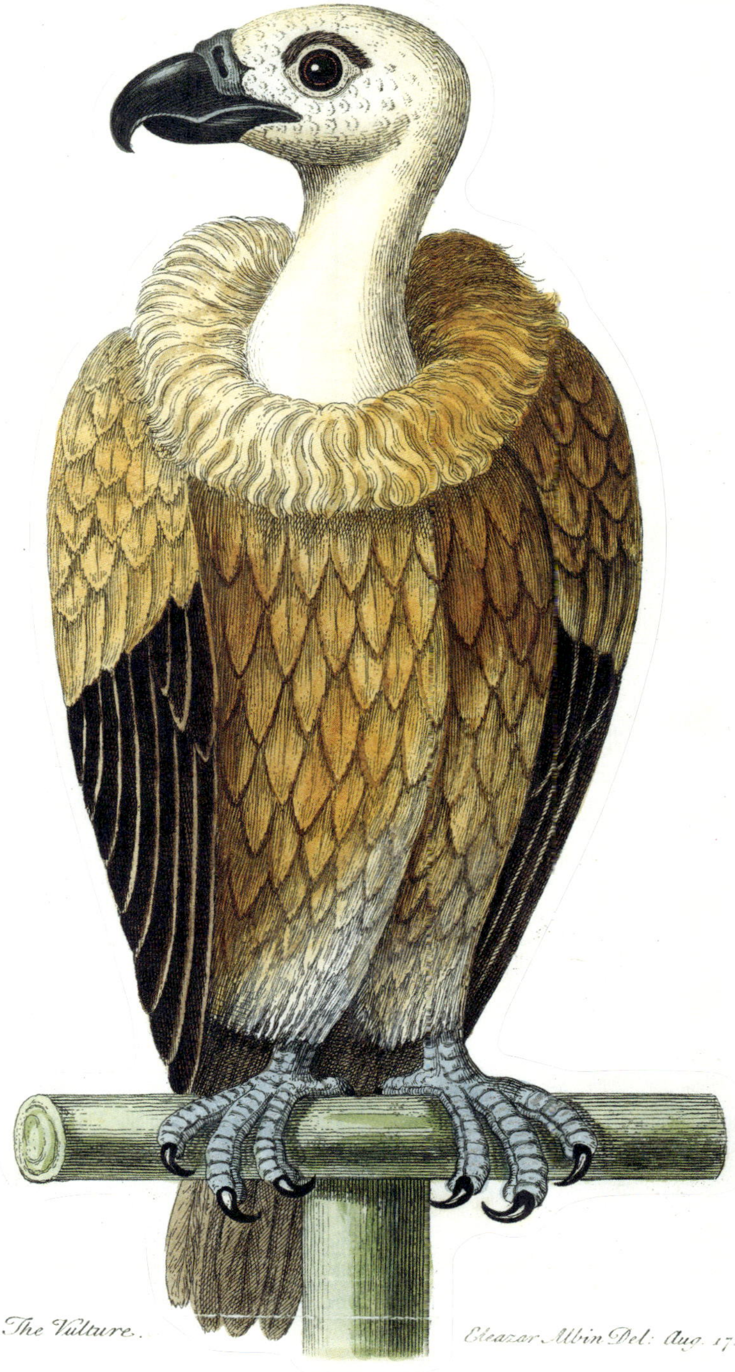

tueris: Vaultour: The Vulture. Eleazar Albin Del: Aug. 17. 1736

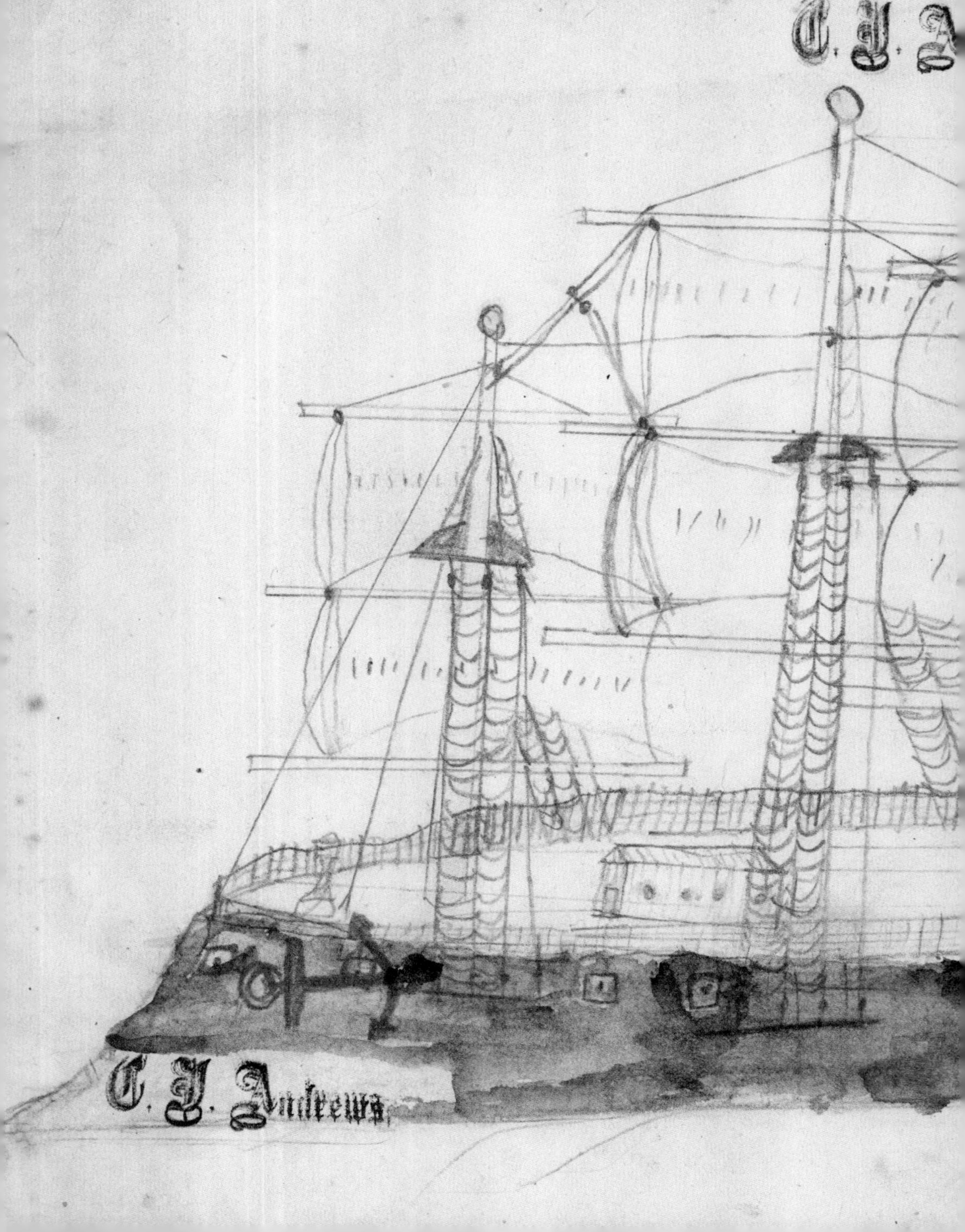
C. J. A
C. J. Andrews

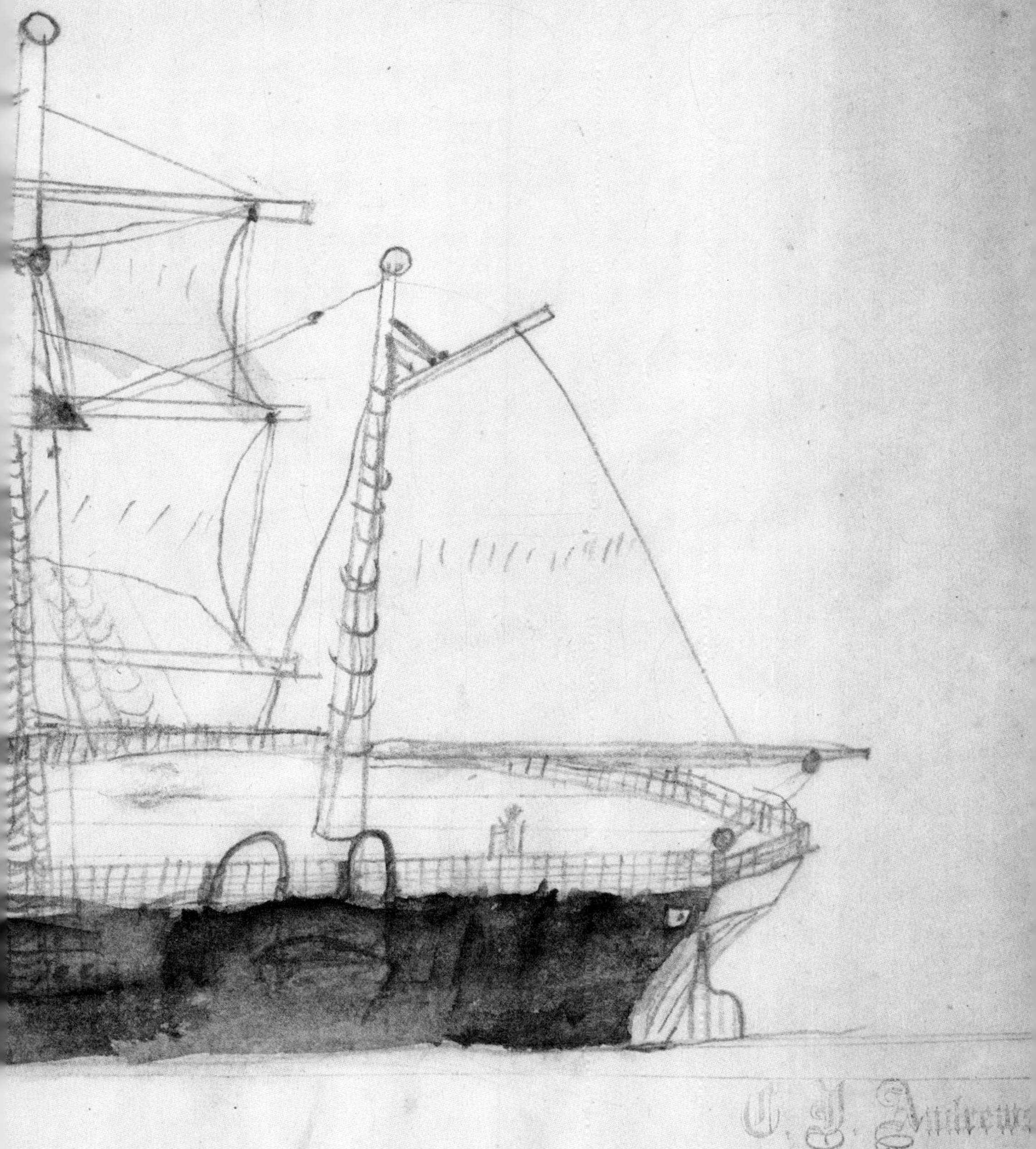
C. J. Andrew

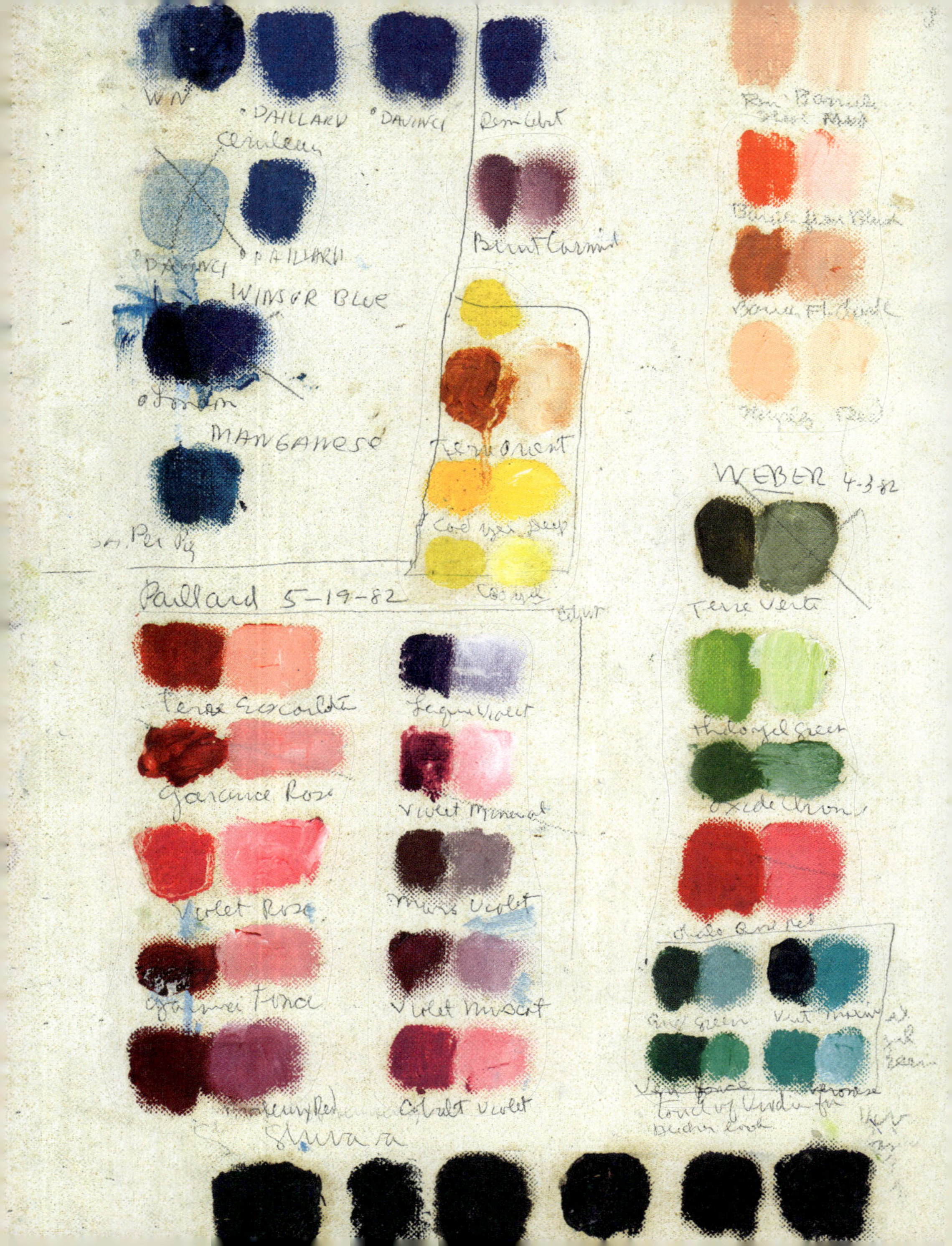
WN
PAILLARD
DAVINCI
PAILLARD
MANGANESE
Burnt Carmine
Paillard 5-19-82
WEBER 4-3-82
Terre Verte
Garance Rose
Violet Rose
Violet Mineral
Mars Violet
Violet Muscat
Cobalt Violet

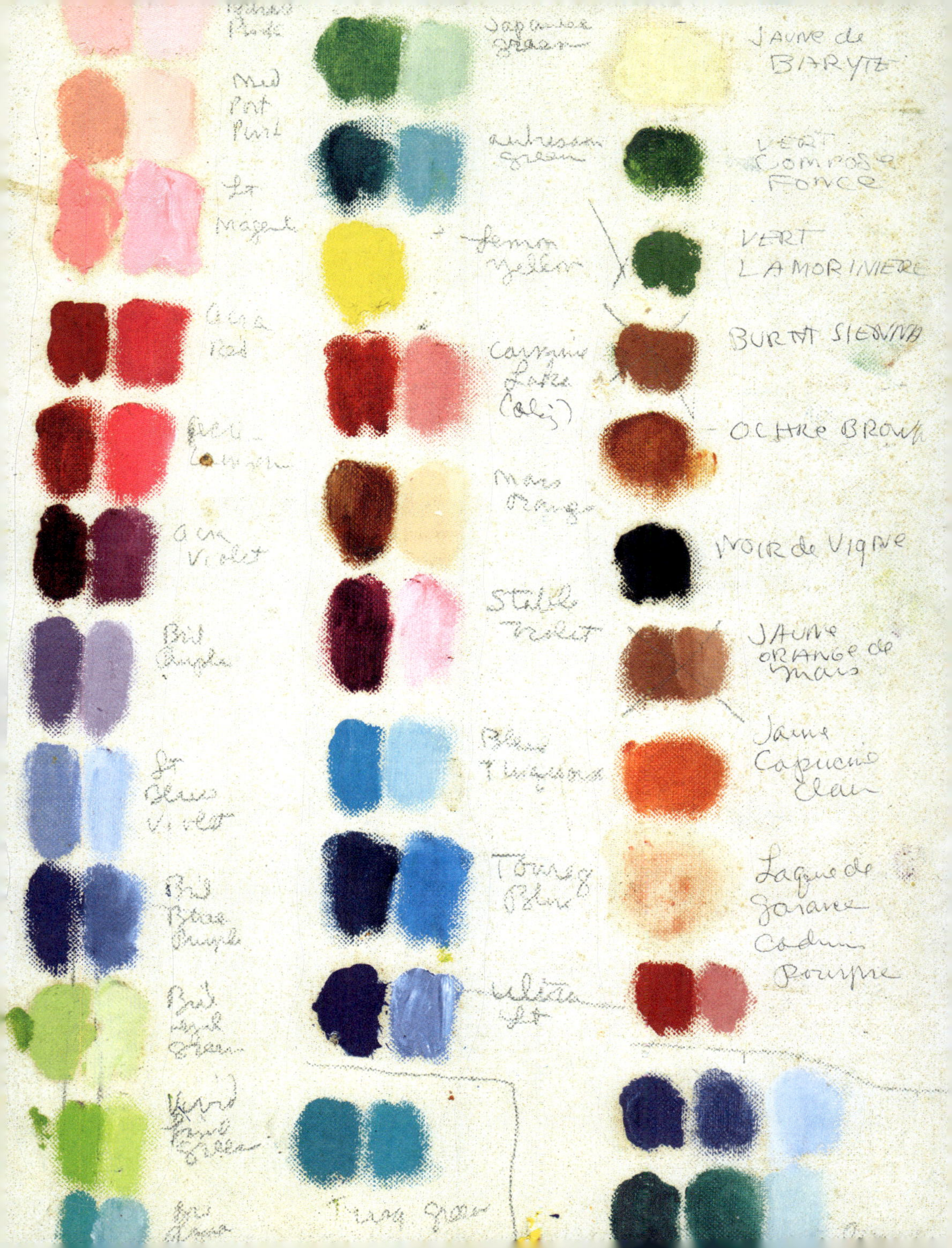

Japanese green
JAUNE de BARYTE
Lt Magenta
VERT COMPOSE FONCE
Lemon Yellow
VERT LAMORINIERE
Acra Red
BURNT SIENNA
Carmine Lake
OCHRE BROWN
Mars Orange
Acra Violet
NOIR de VIGNE
JAUNE ORANGE de Mars
Jaune Capucine Clair
Laque de Garance

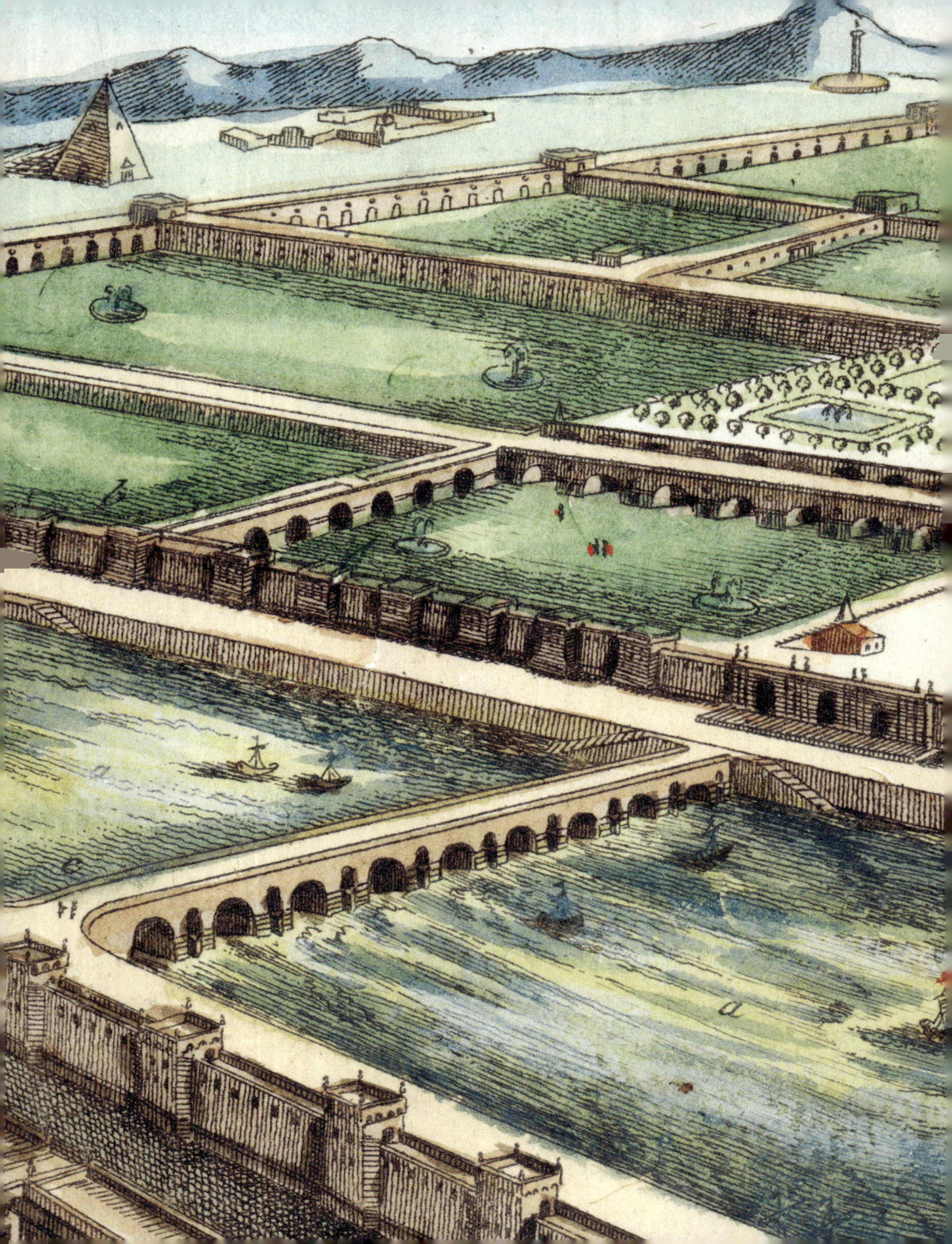

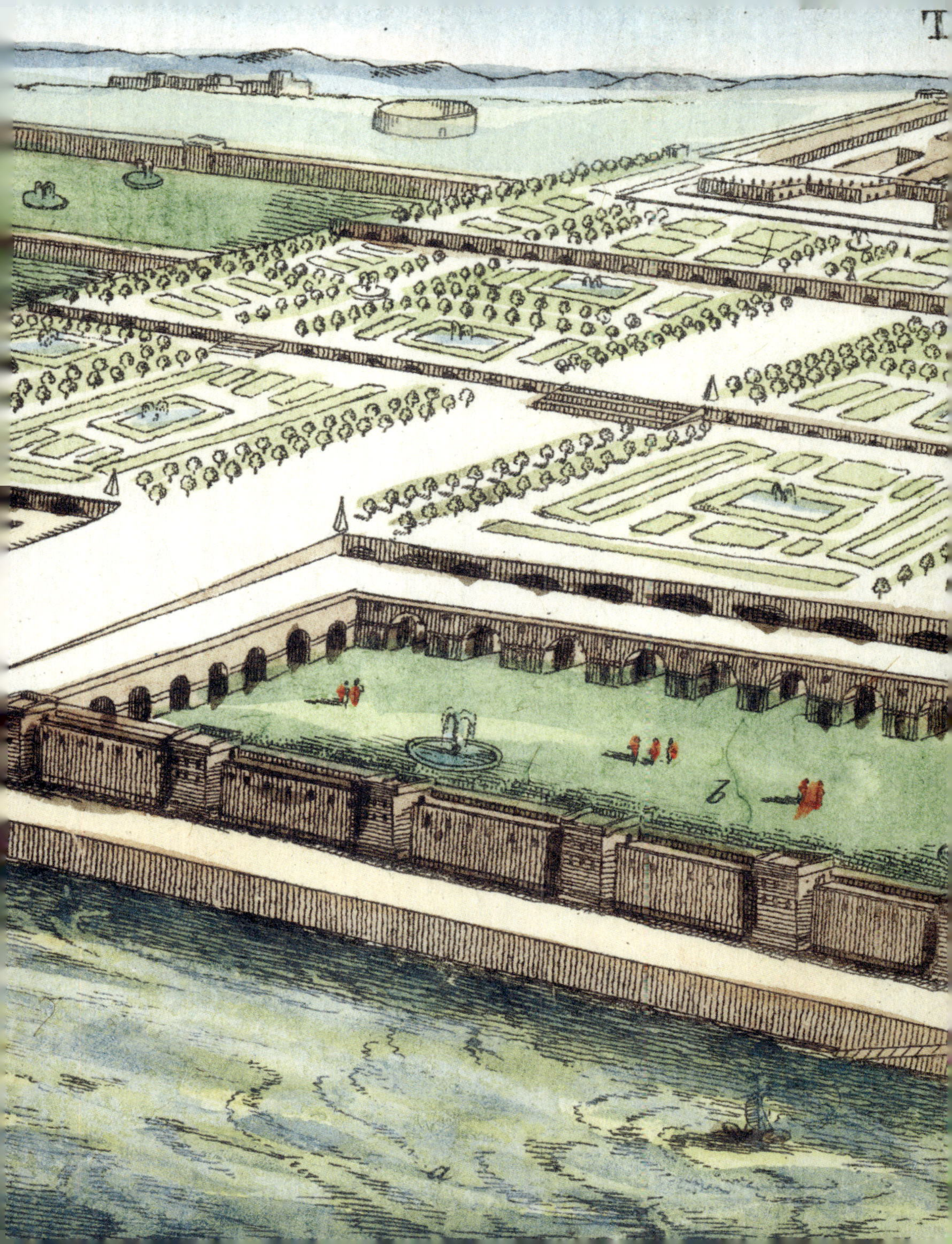
b

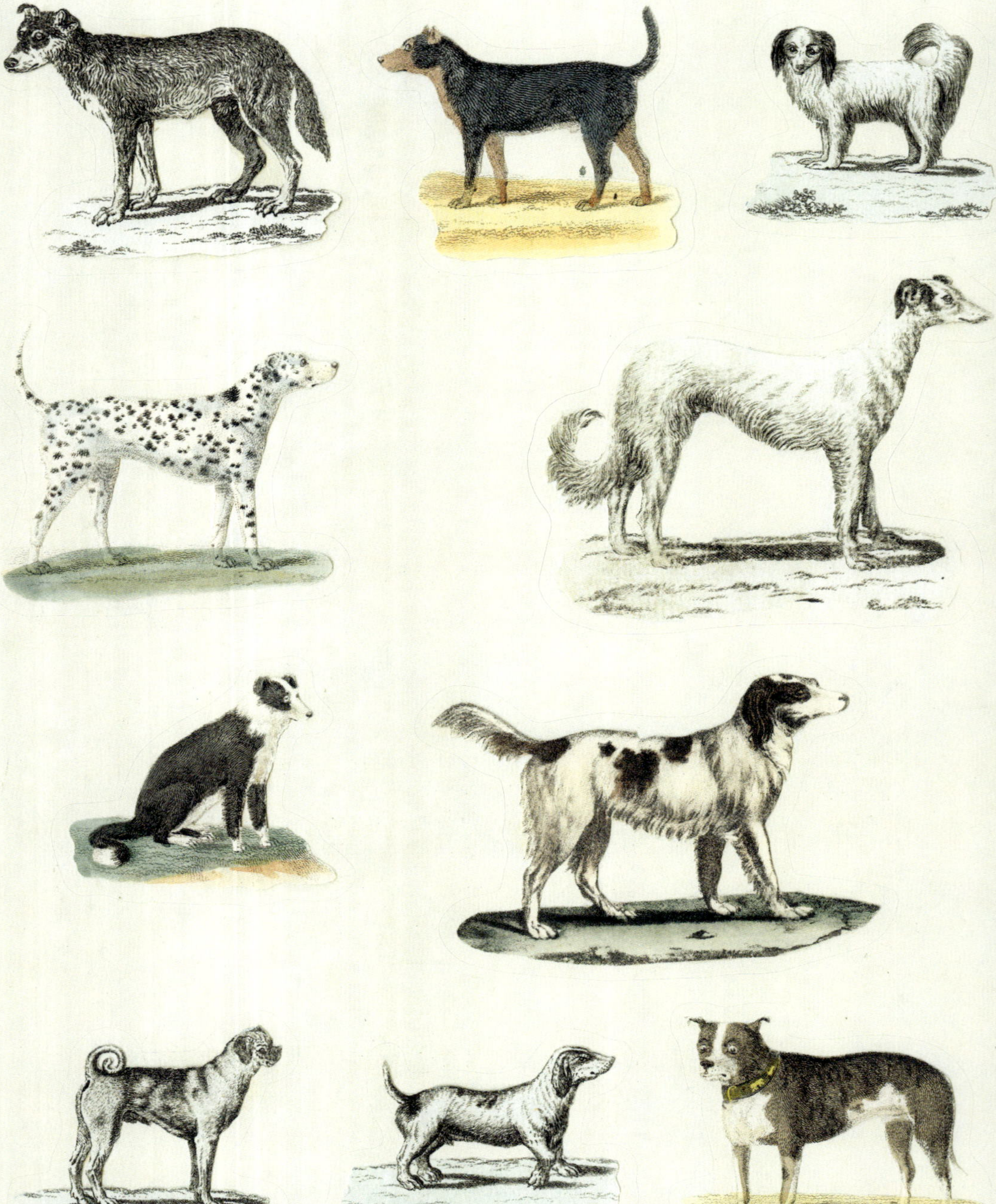

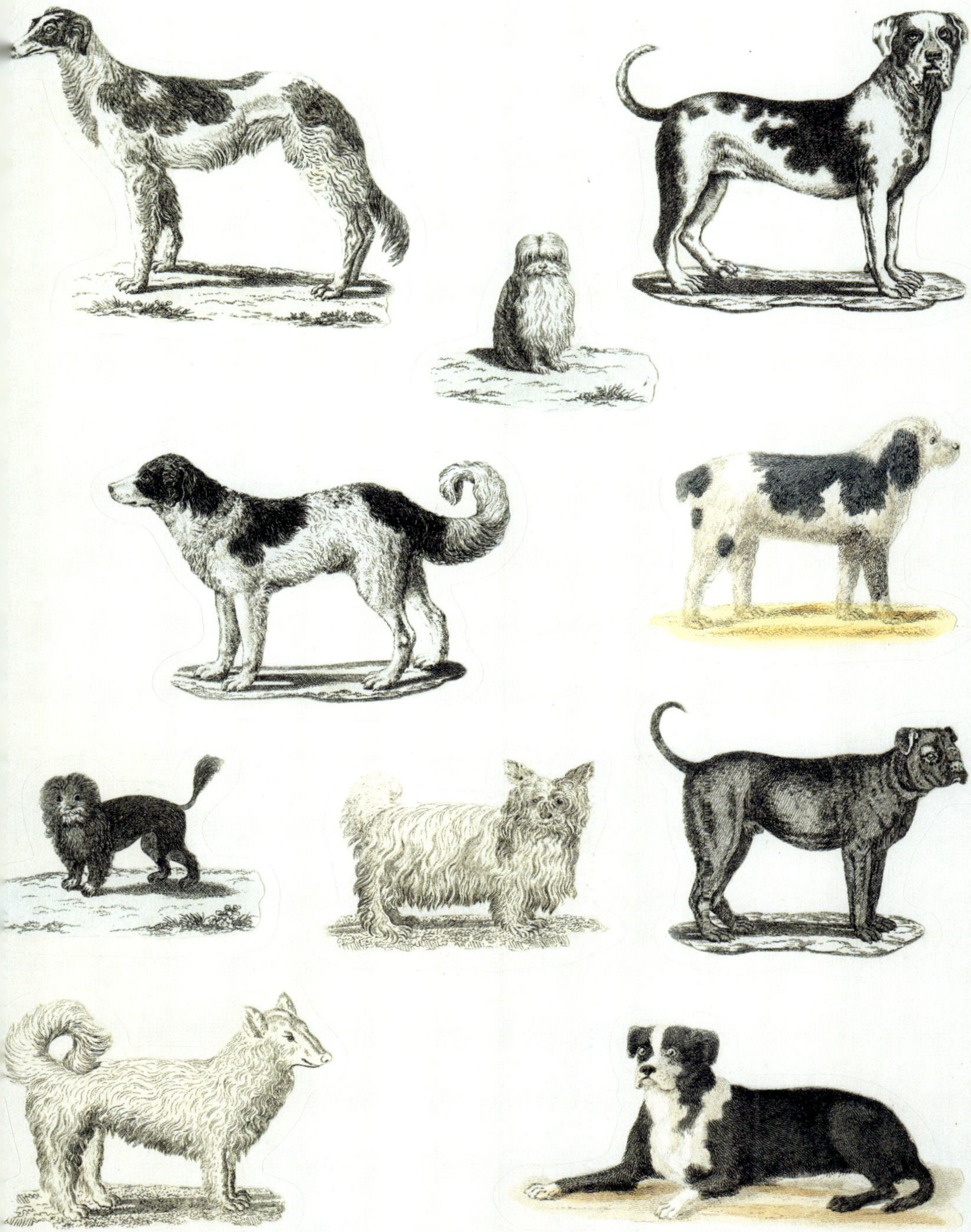

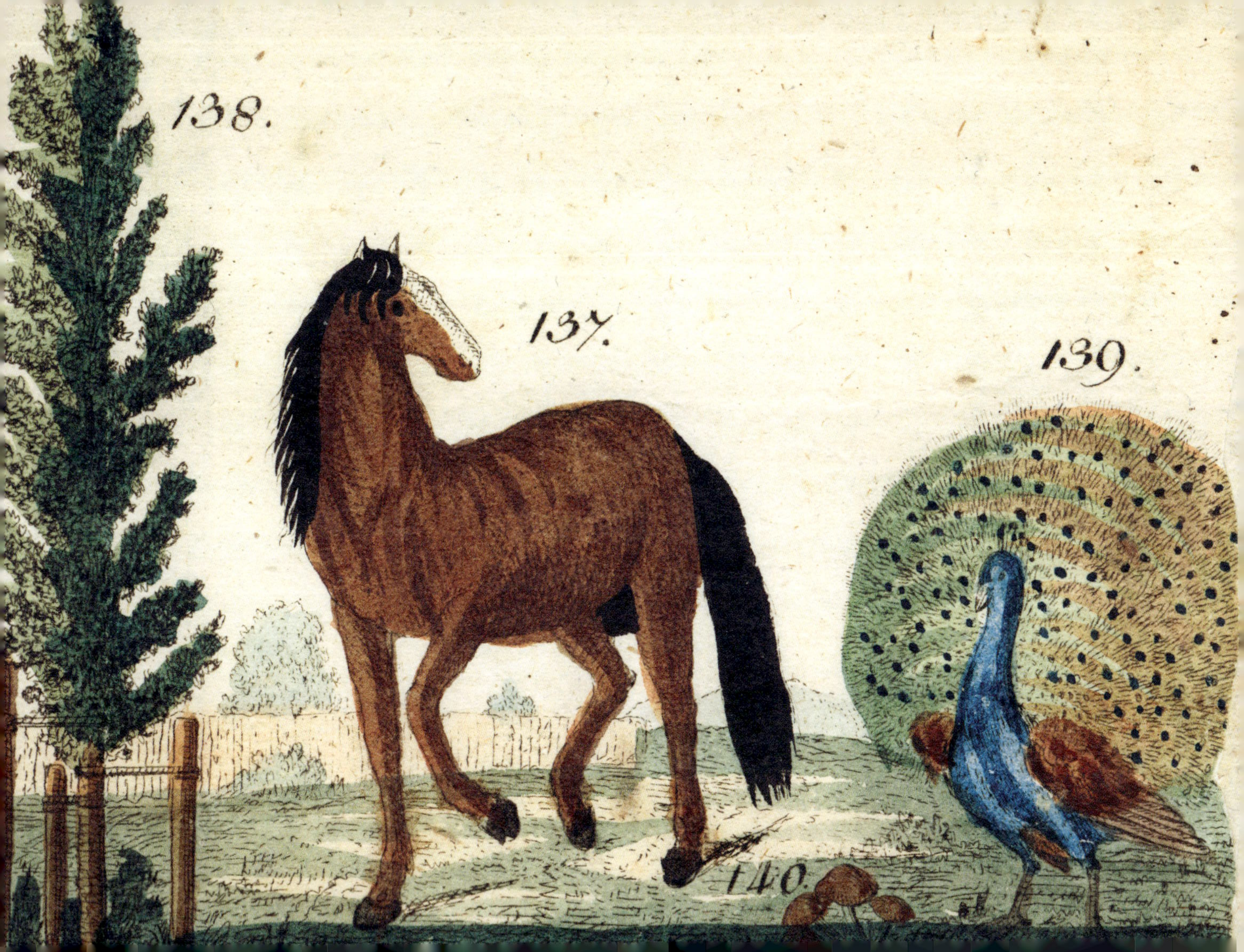
138.
137.
139.
140.

Winter's Cinnamon

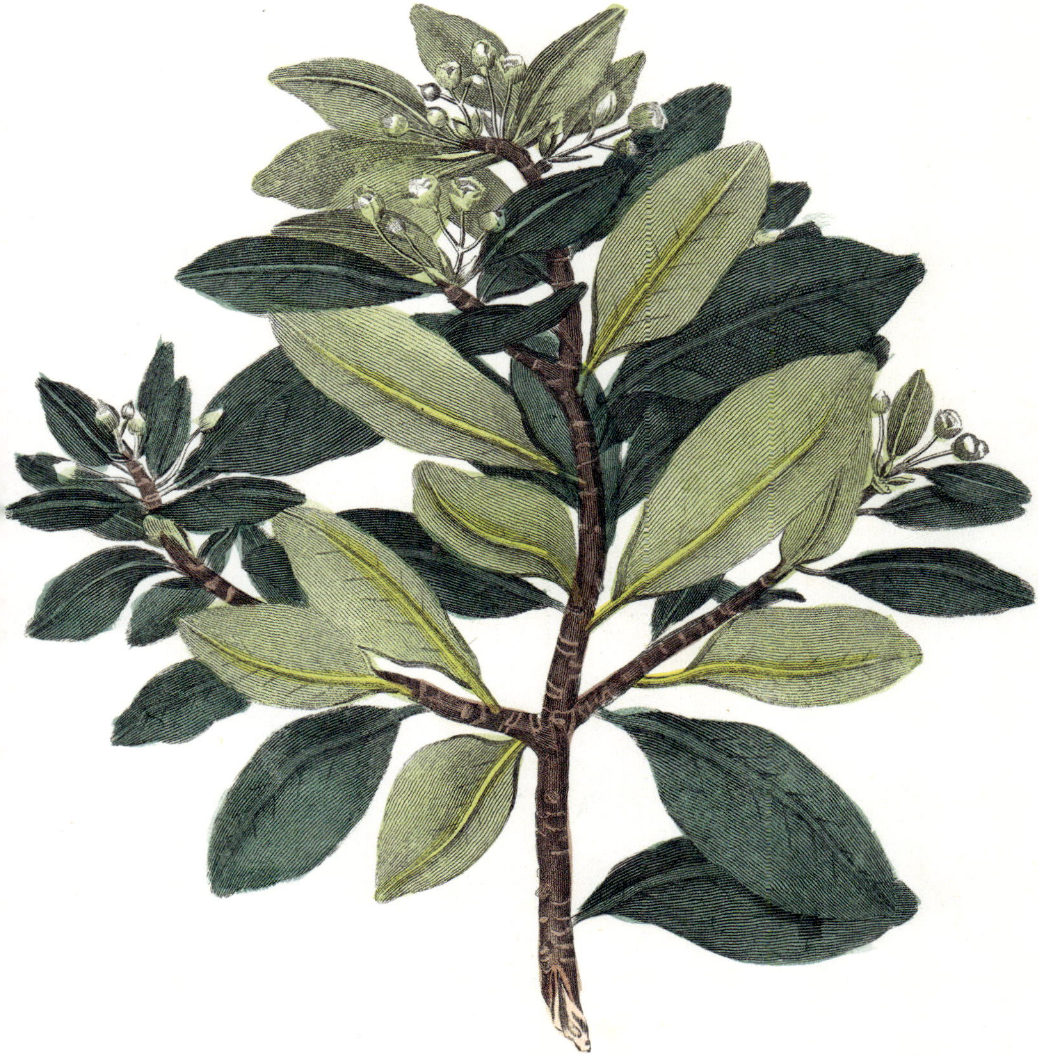

Electric Eel

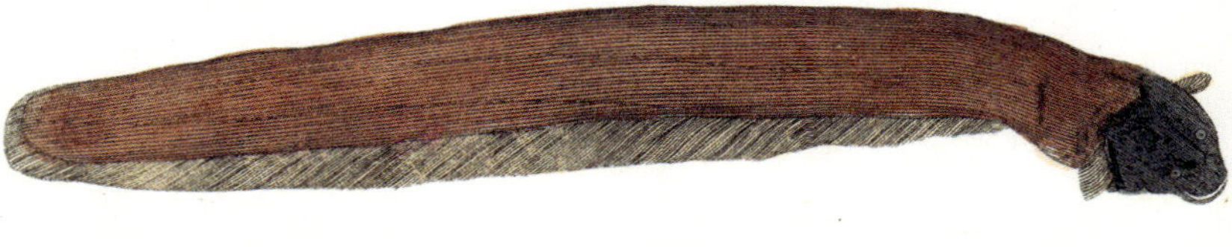

London Published by E. Edwards Crane Court Fleet Street 1816.

20.

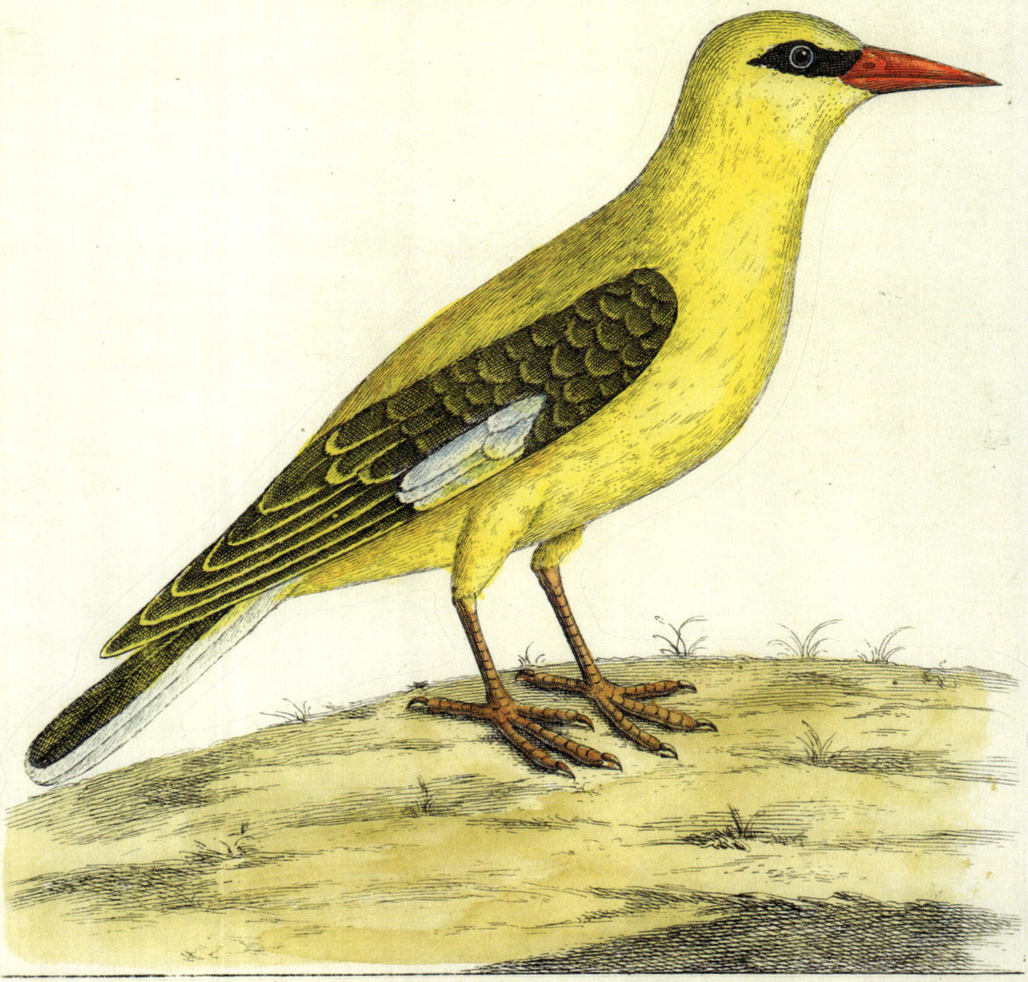

The Yellow Bird from Bengall. *Eleazar Albin Del. Sep. 16 1736.*

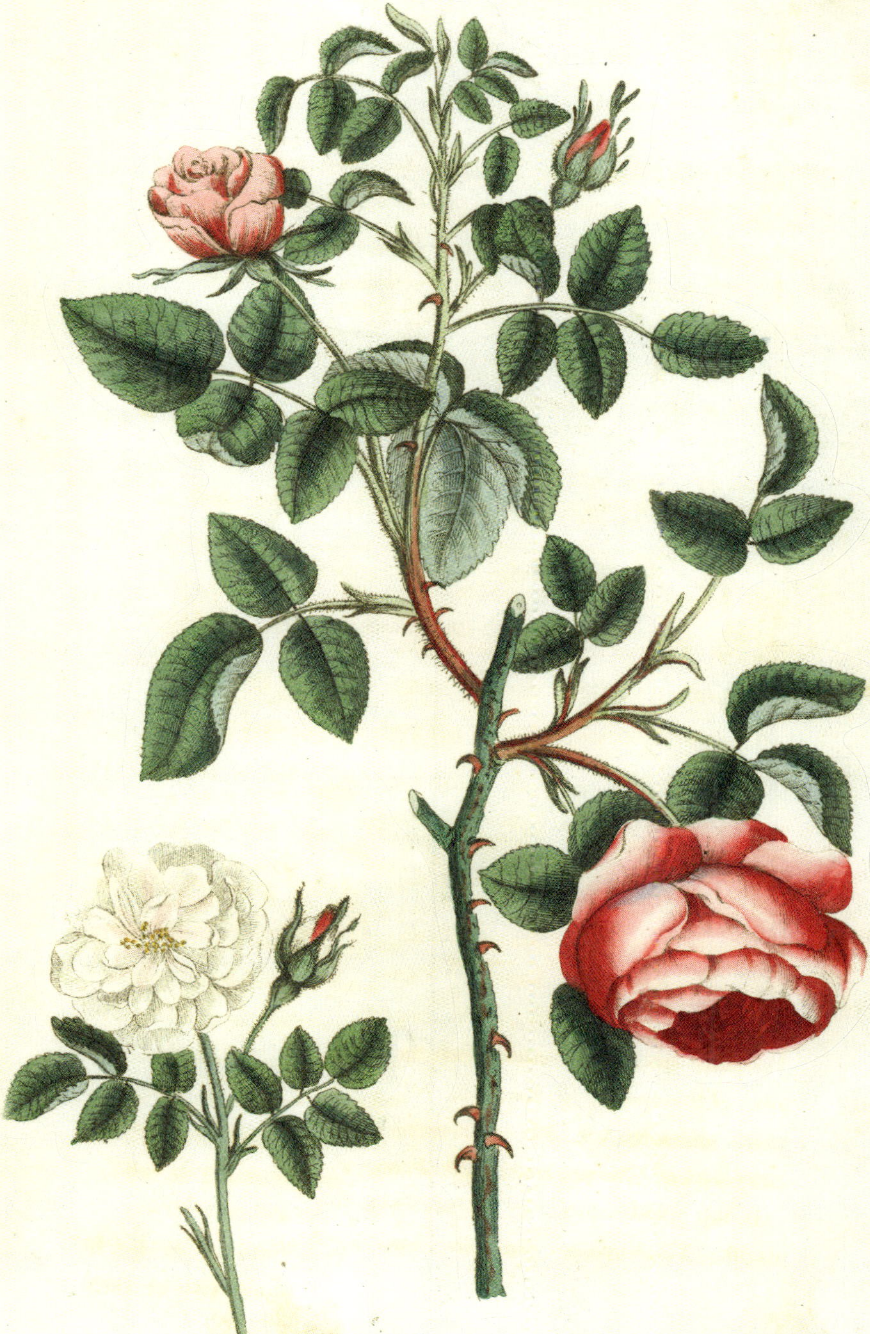

Rosa Centifolia

T. 2.

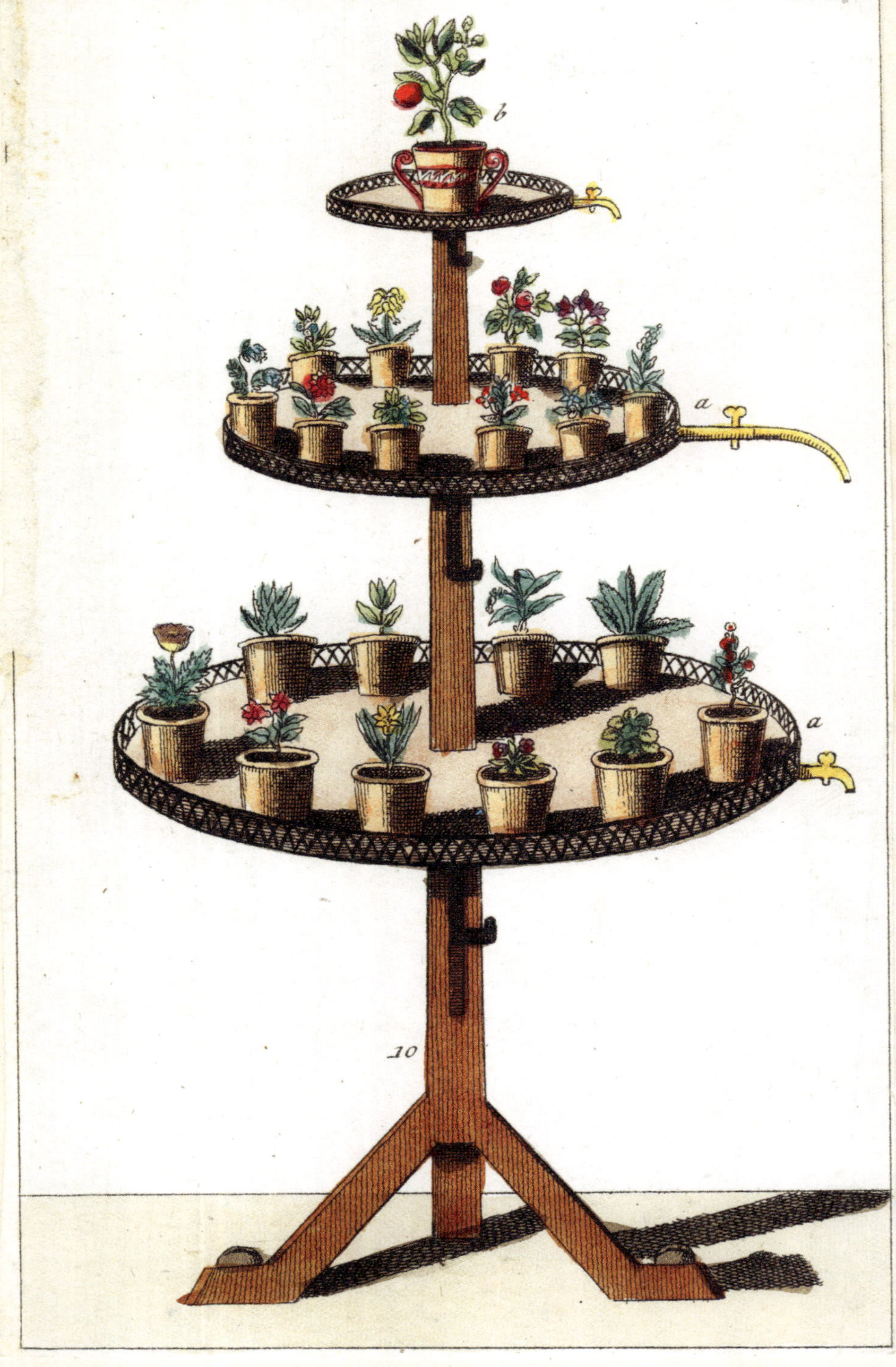

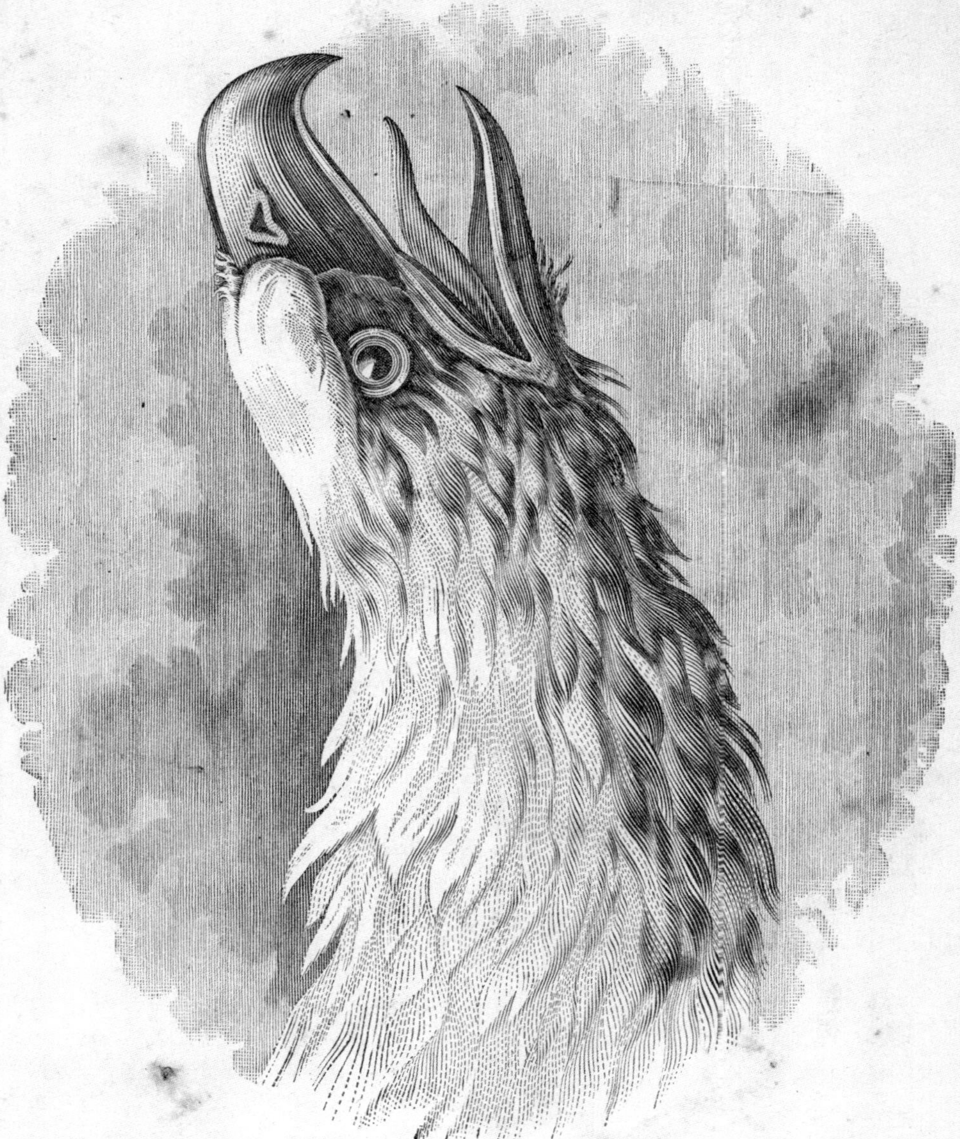

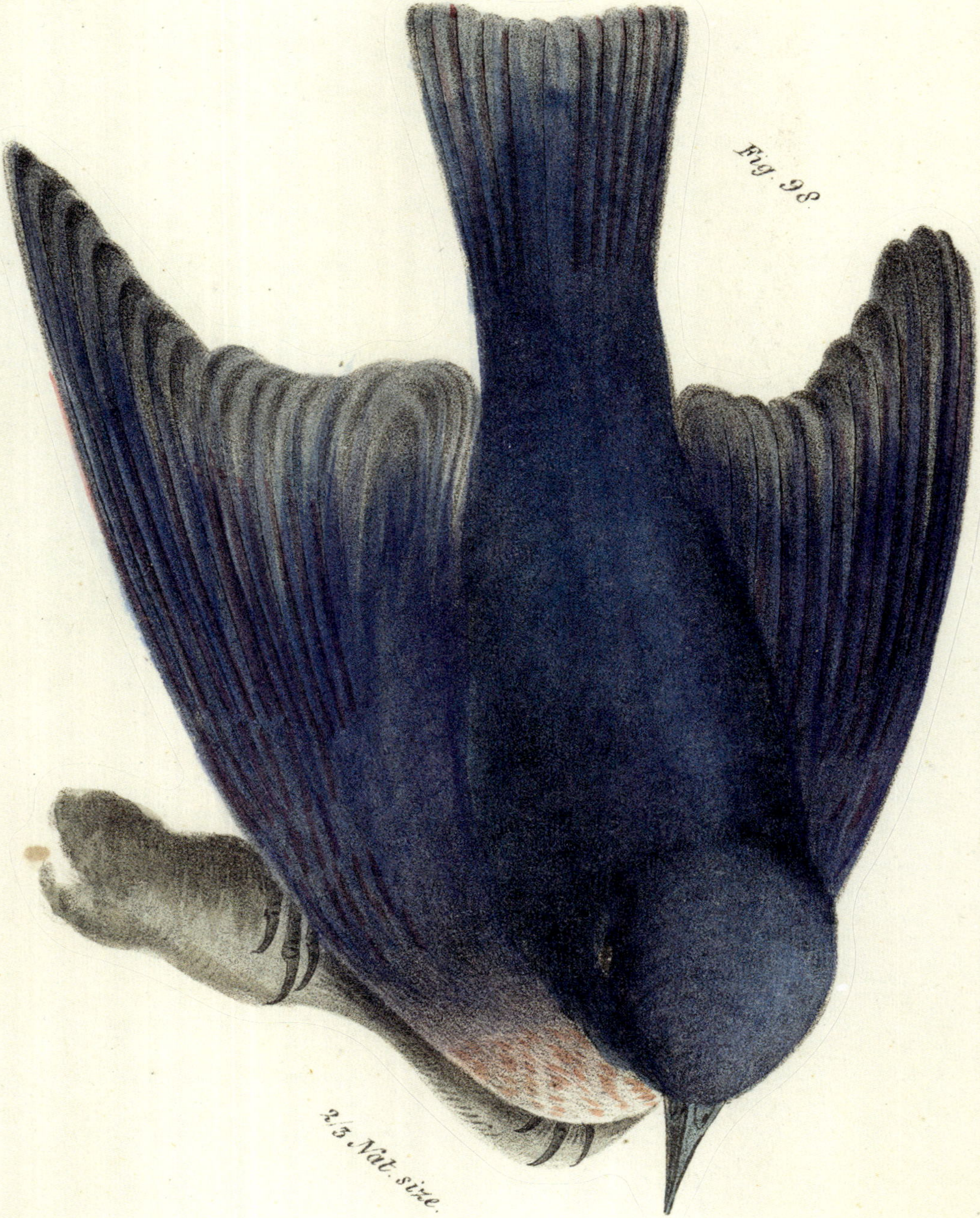

Fig. 99

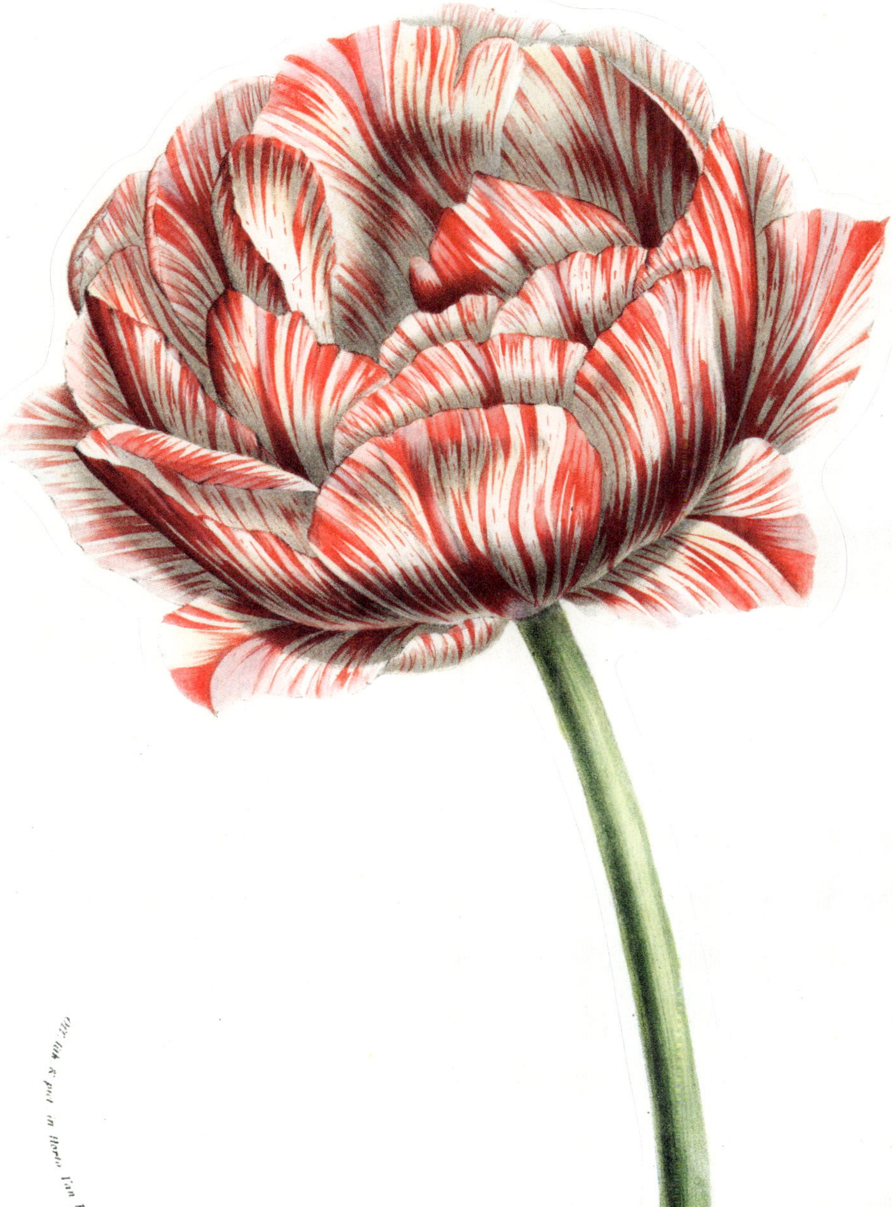

TULIPE DOUBLE HÀTIVE, *MARIAGE DE MA FILLE.*

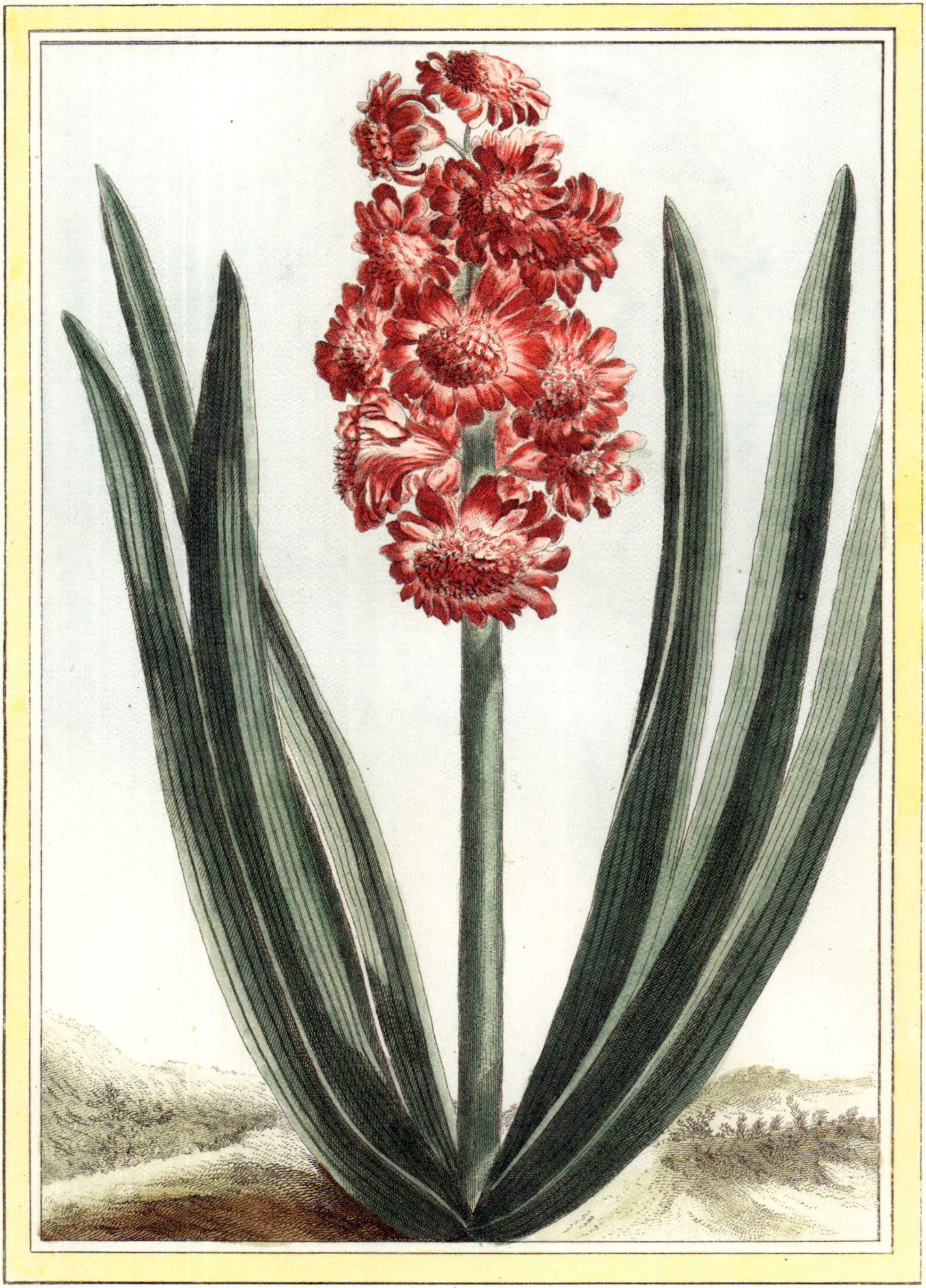

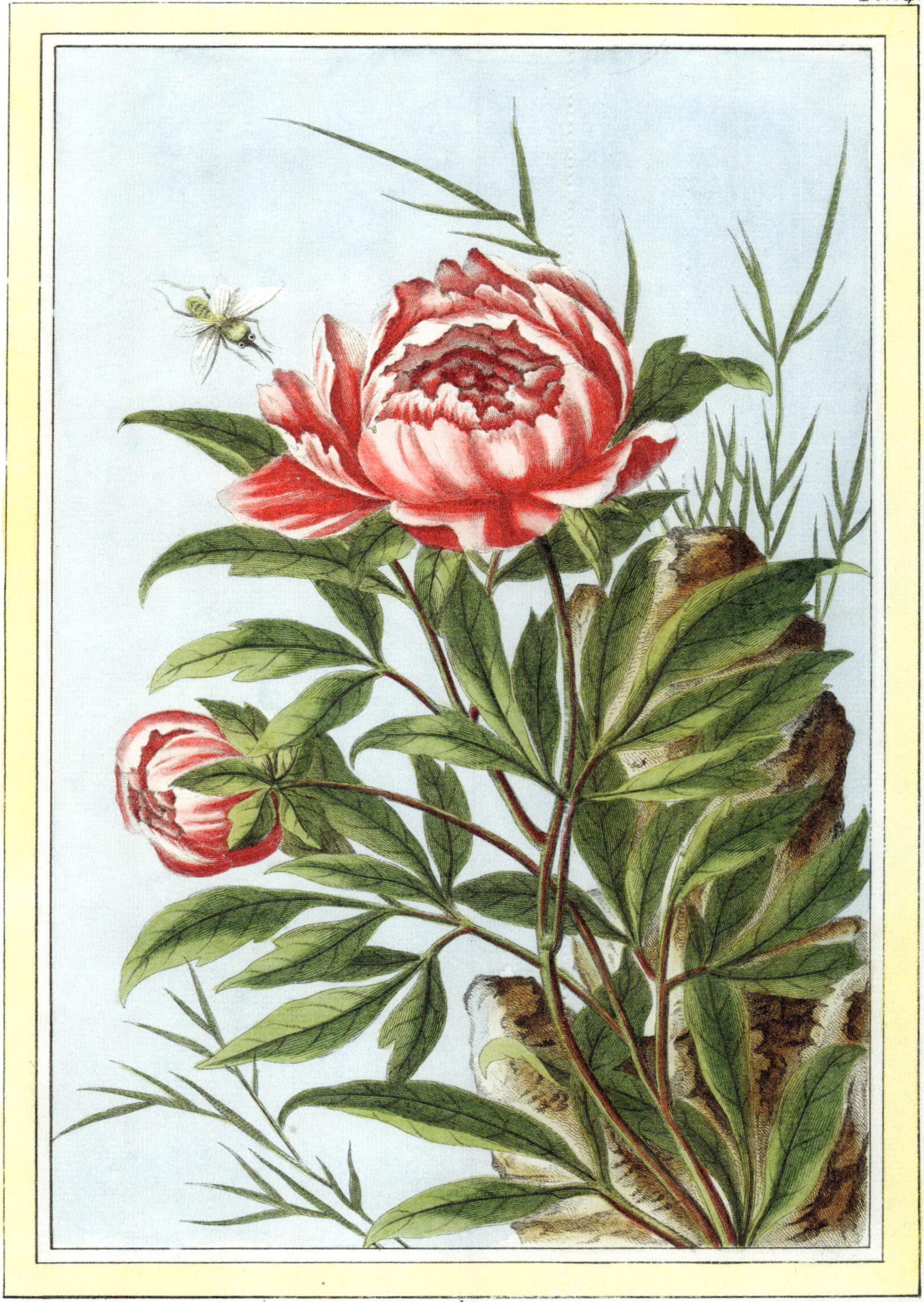

芍

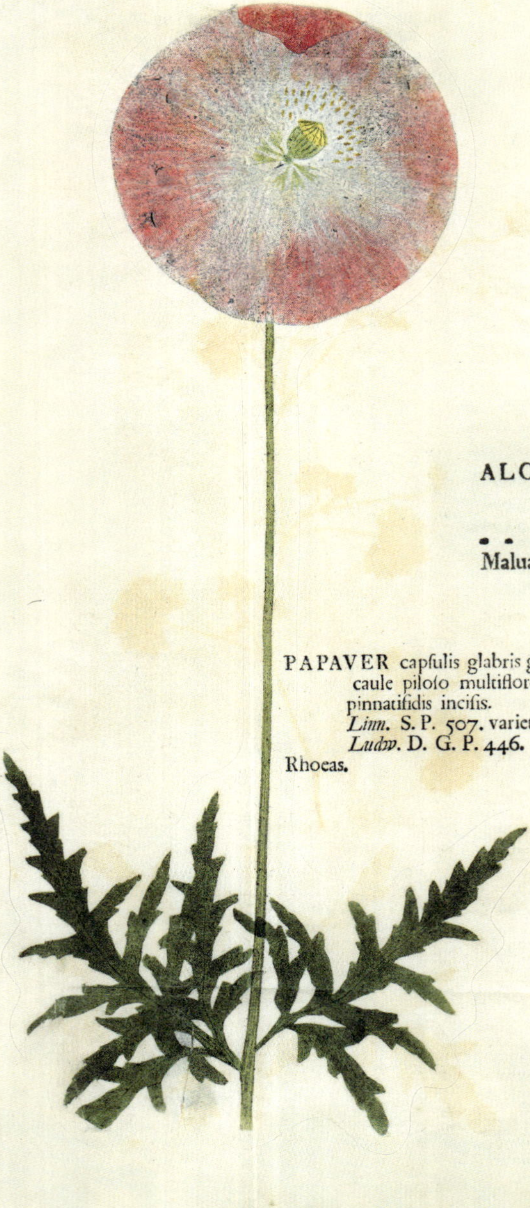

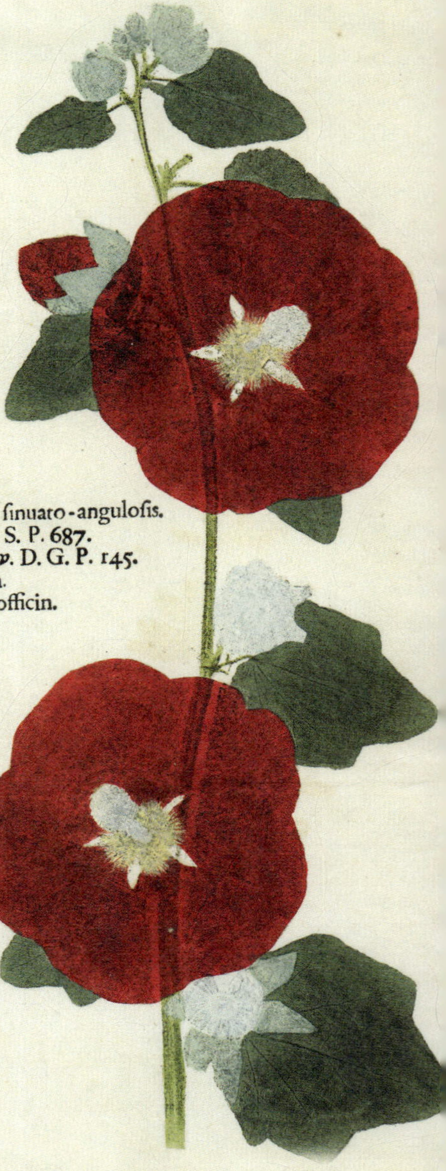

ALCEA foliis ſinuato-anguloſis.
Linn. S. P. 687.
Ludw. D. G. P. 145.
. . . . . roſea.
Malua arborea. officin.

PAPAVER capſulis glabris globoſis, caule piloſo multifloro, foliis pinnatifidis inciſis.
Linn. S. P. 507. variet. α.
Ludw. D. G. P. 446.
Rhoeas.

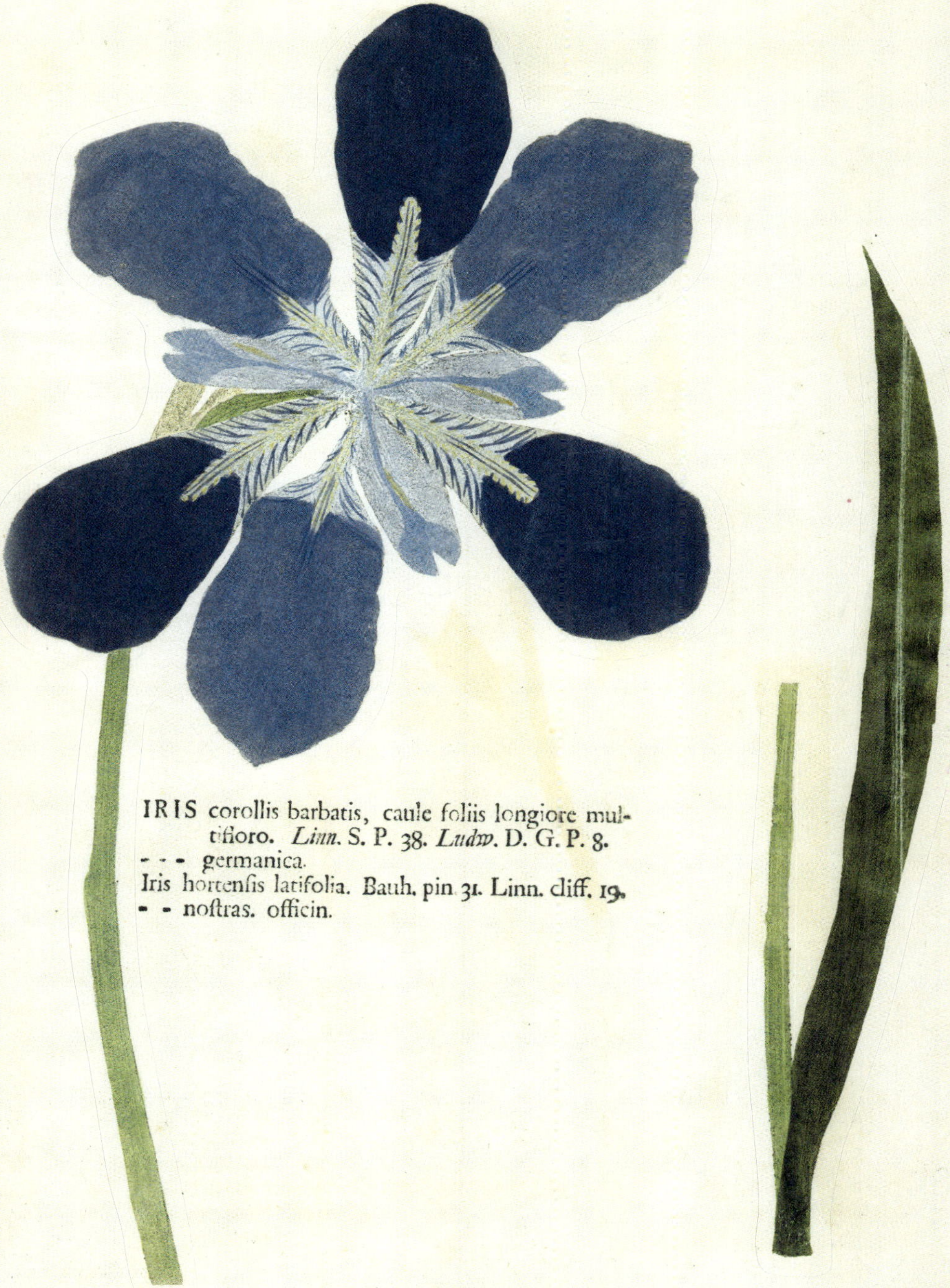

IRIS corollis barbatis, caule foliis longiore multifloro. *Linn.* S. P. 38. *Ludw.* D. G. P. 8.
- - - germanica.
Iris hortenſis latifolia. Bauh. pin. 31. Linn. cliff. 19.
- - noſtras. officin.

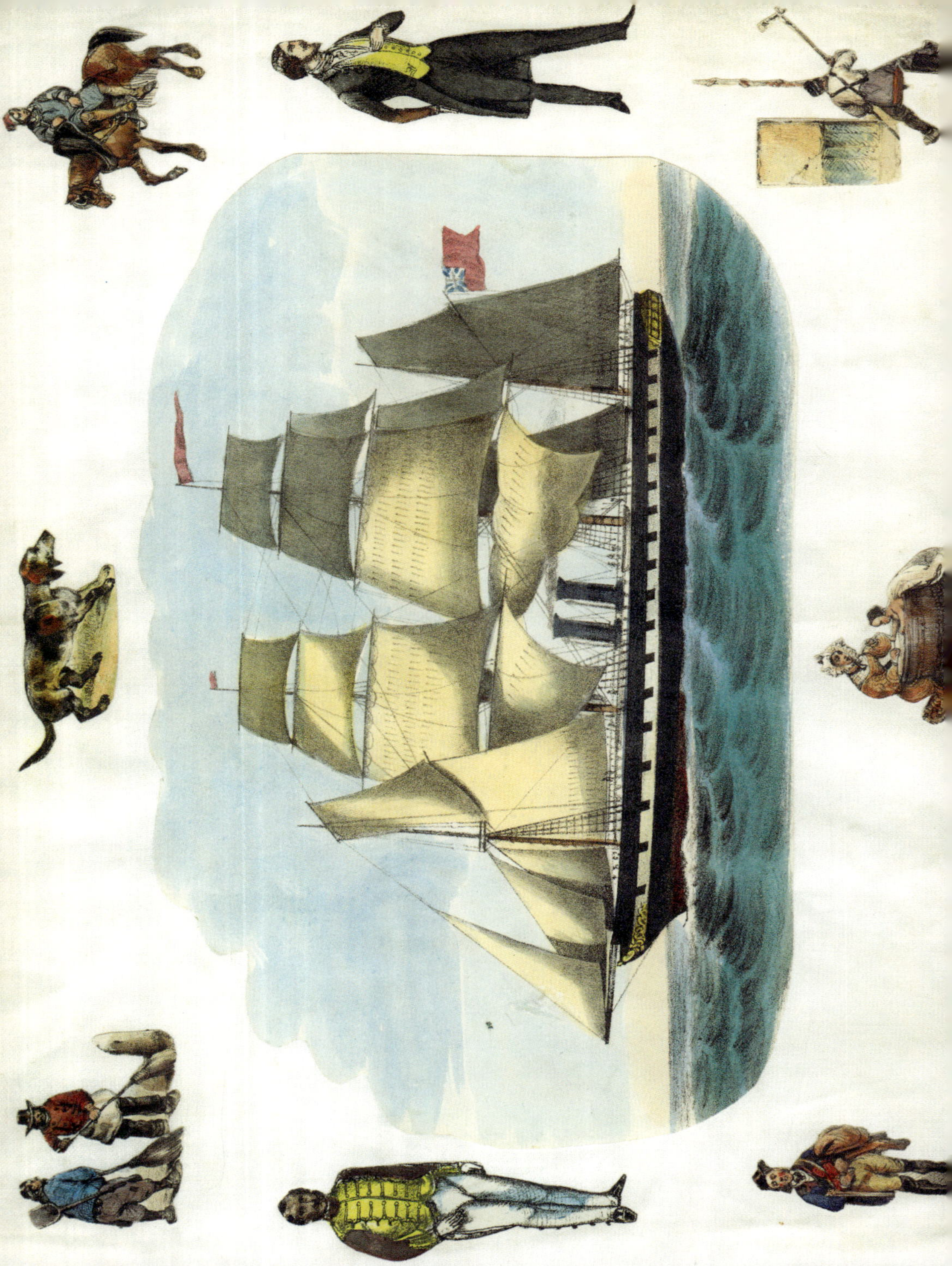

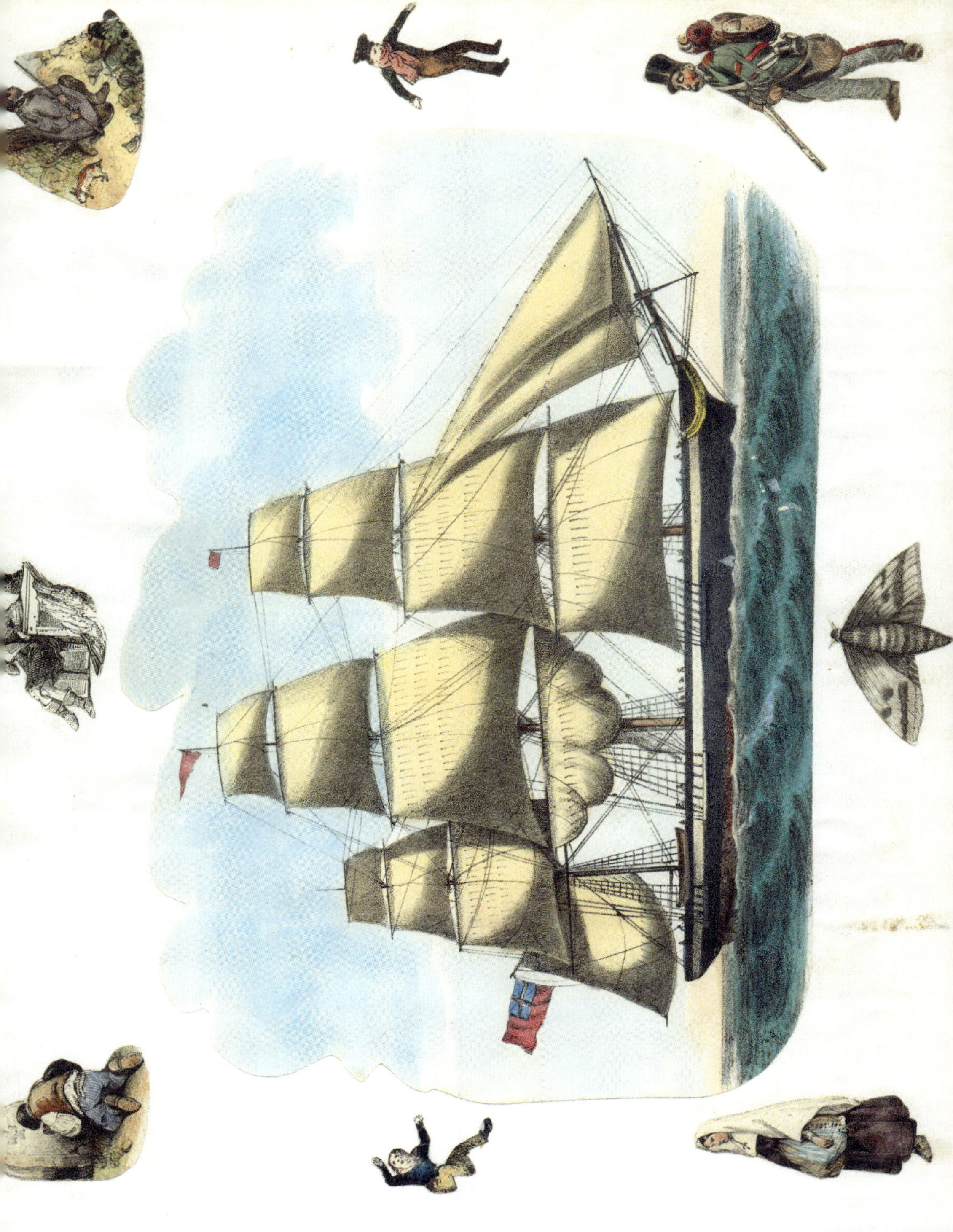

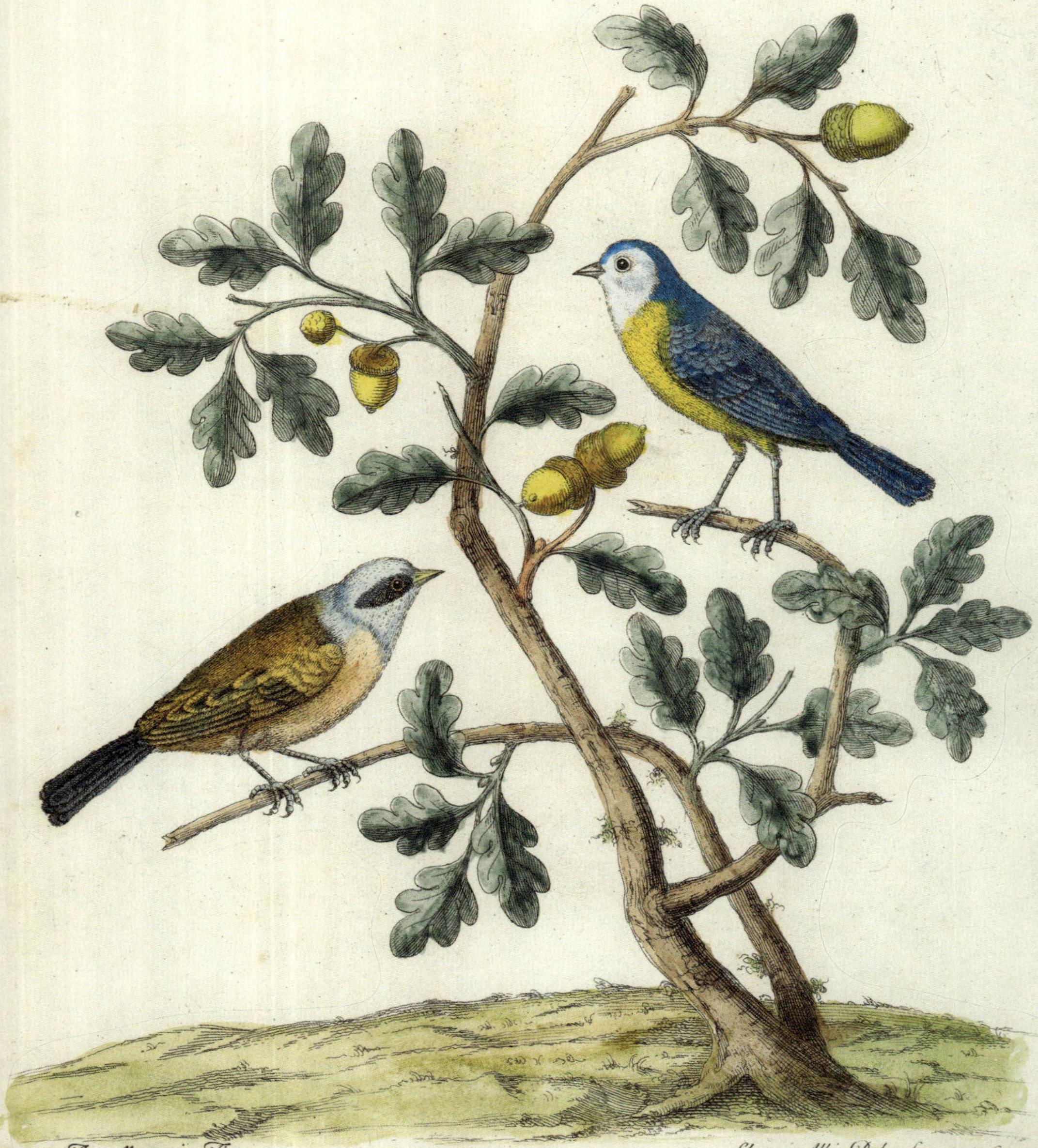

The Mountain Titmouse. *Eleazar Albin Del. Sep. 15 1736*

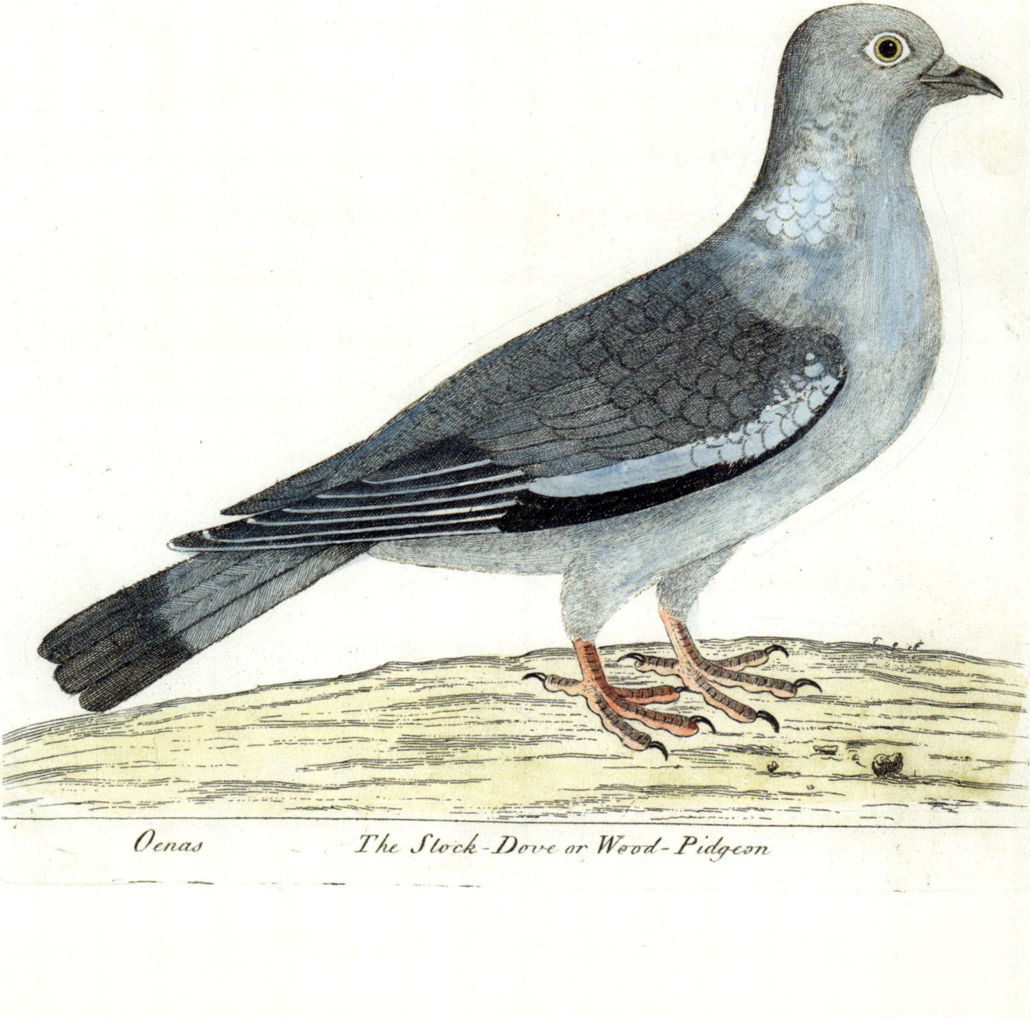

Oenas *The Stock-Dove or Wood-Pidgeon*

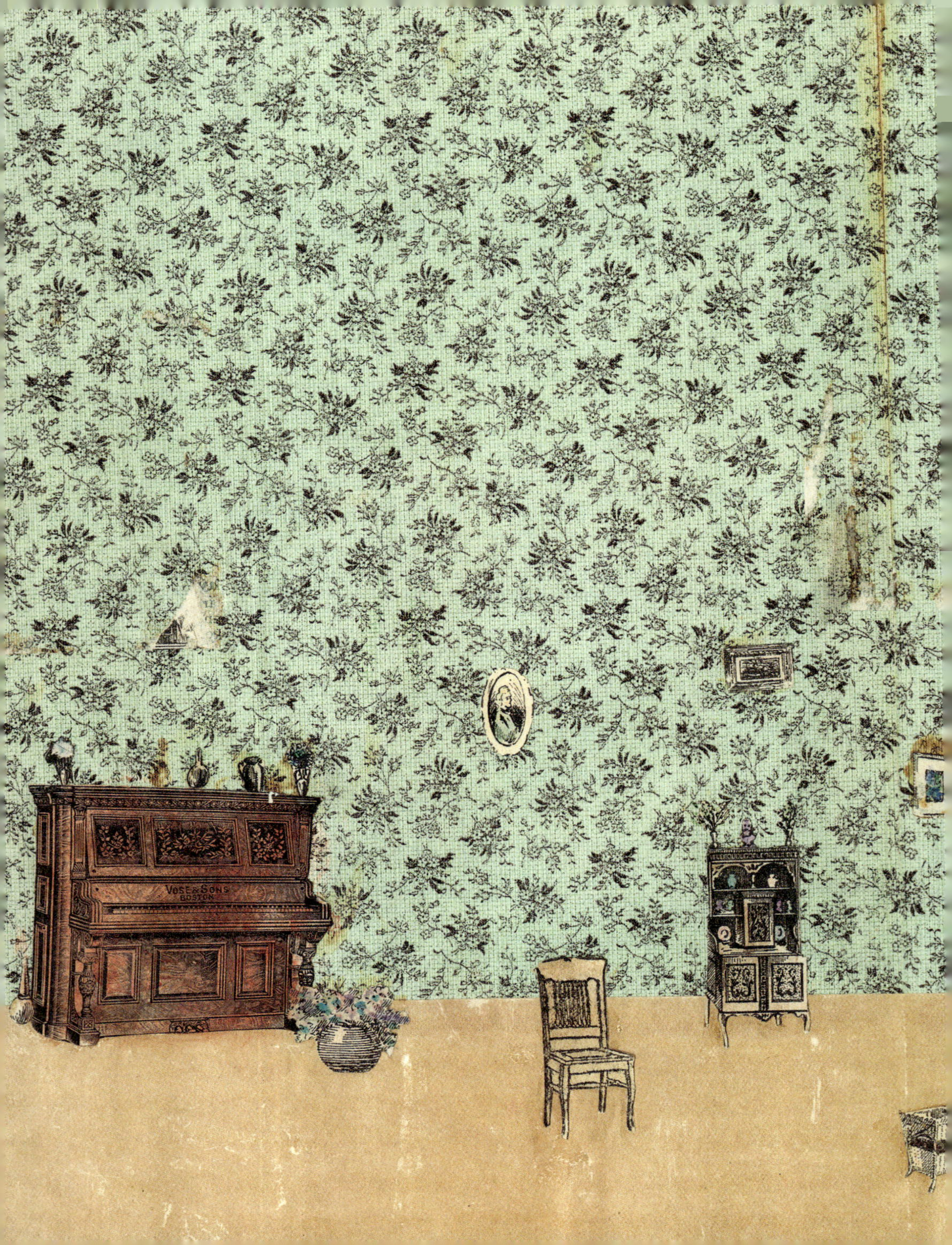
VOSE & SONS
BOSTON

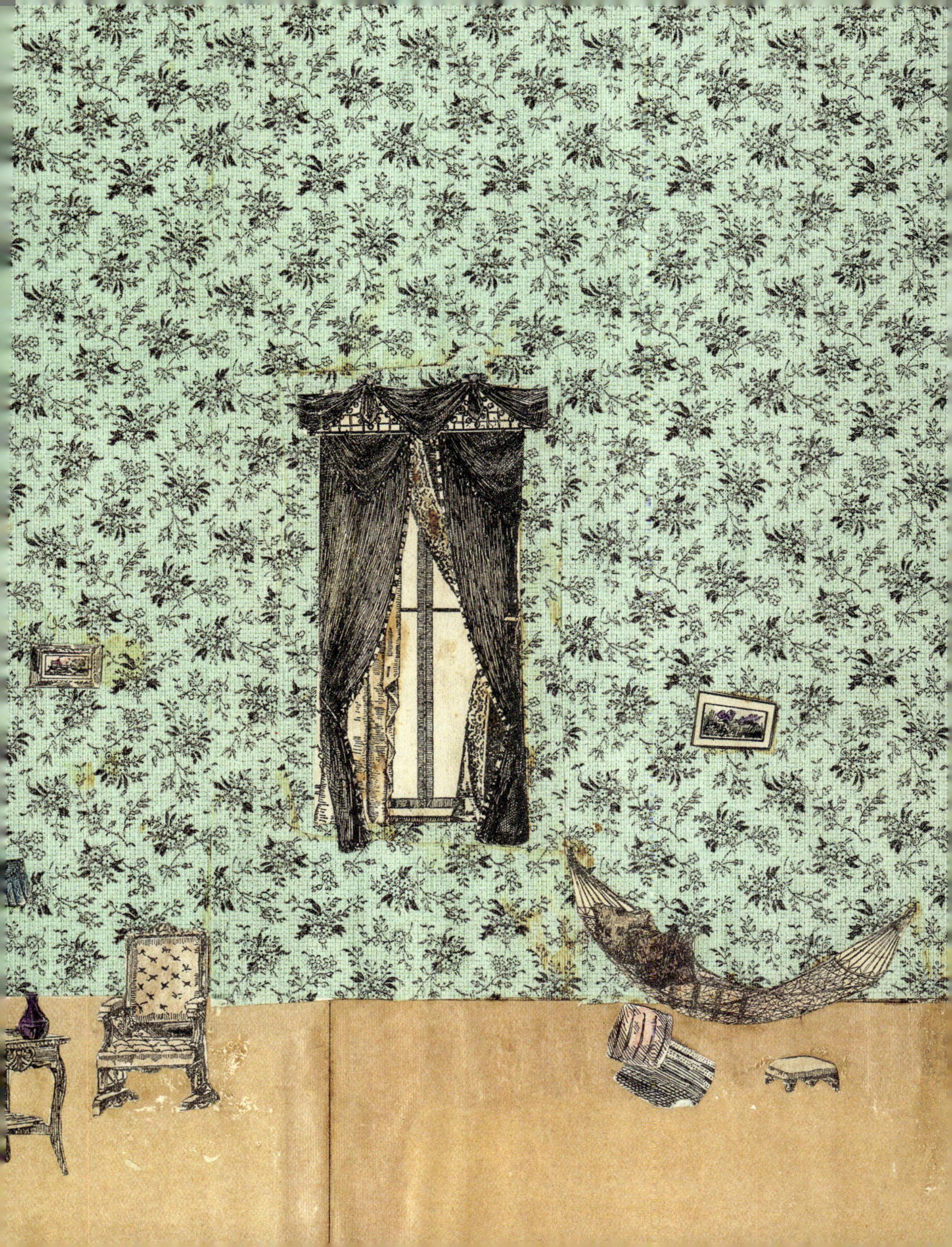

T. XII.

33

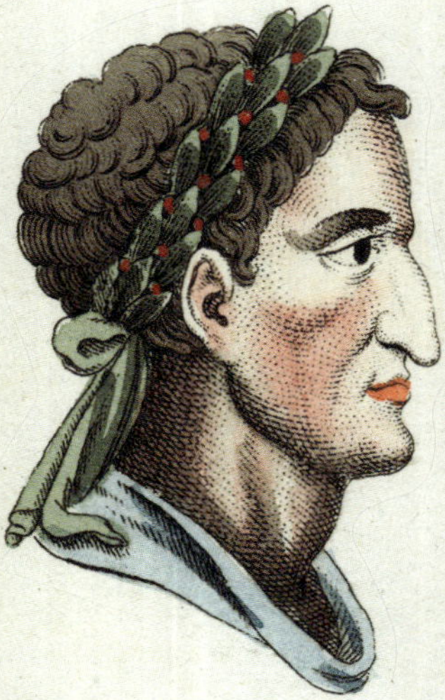

34

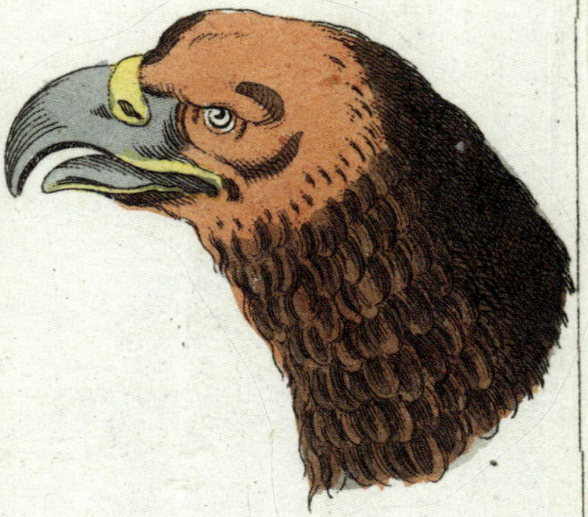

35

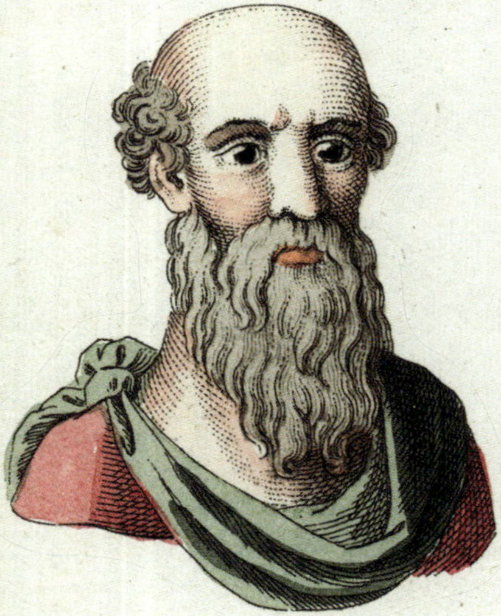

36

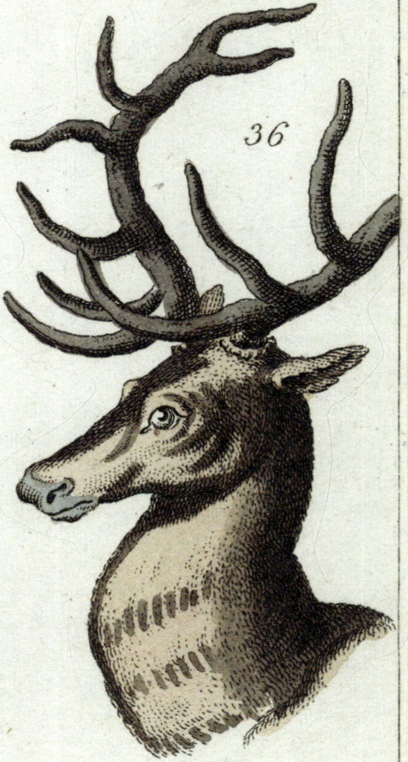

29

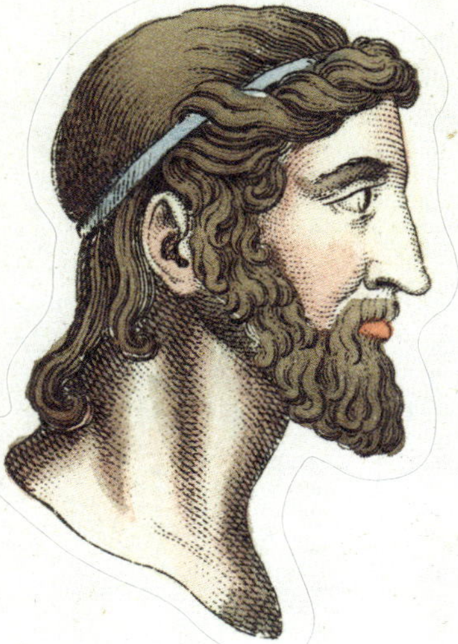

30

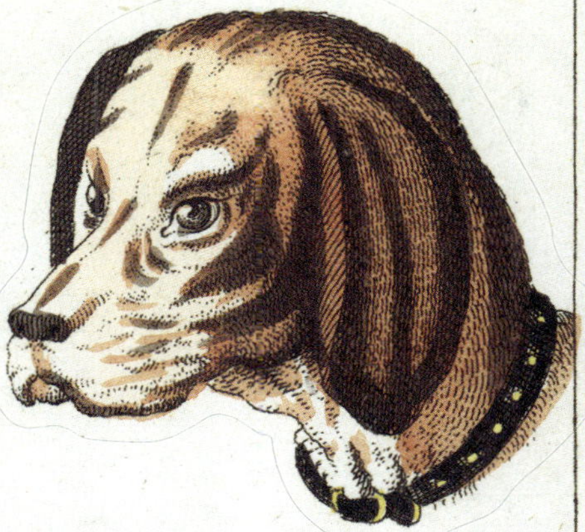

31

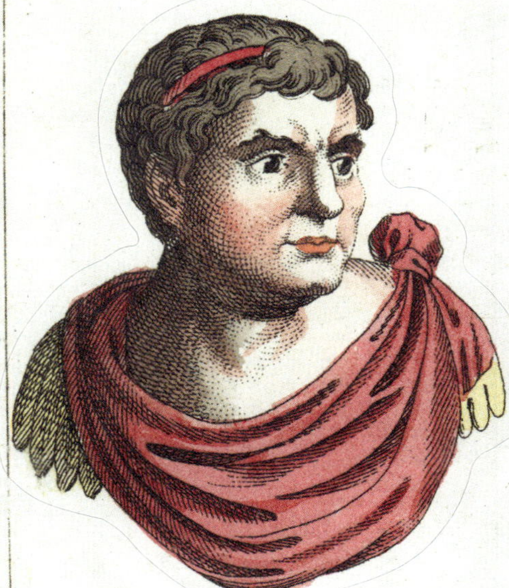

32

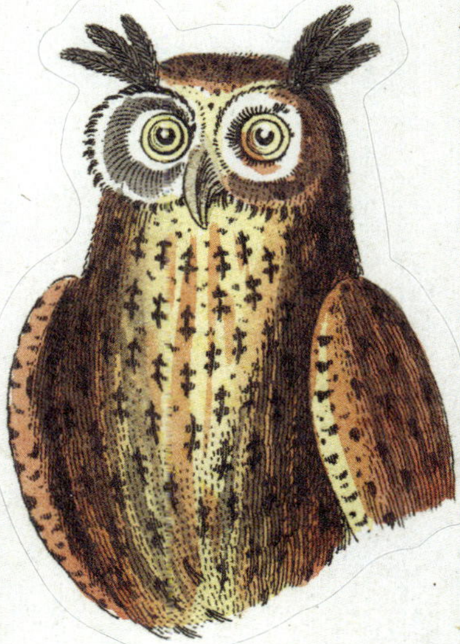

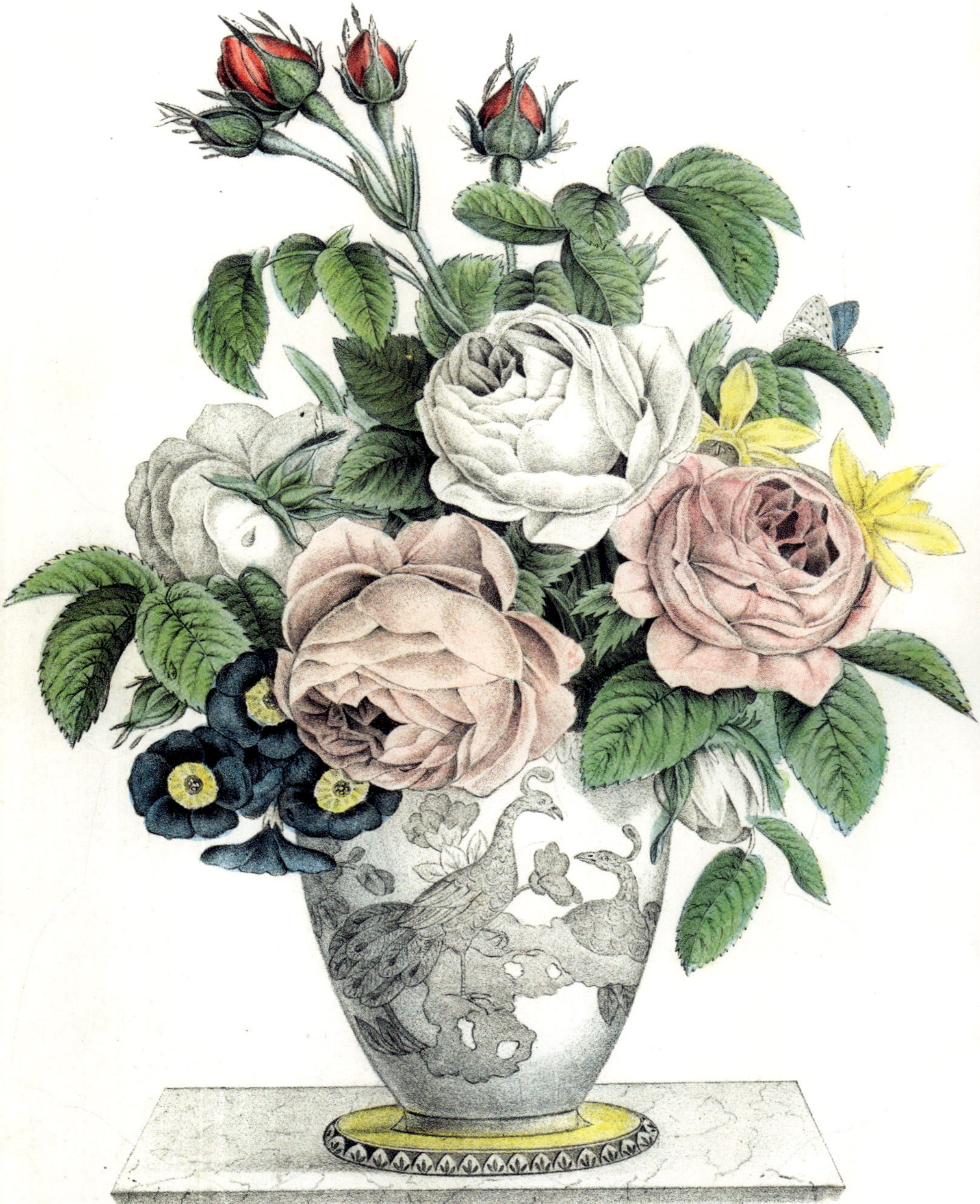

Entered according to Act of Congress in the year 1845 by N. Currier, in the Clerk's office of the District Court of the Southern District of N. Y.

THE BOQUET.

Lith & Pub. by N. Currier, 2 Spruce St. N. Y.

383.

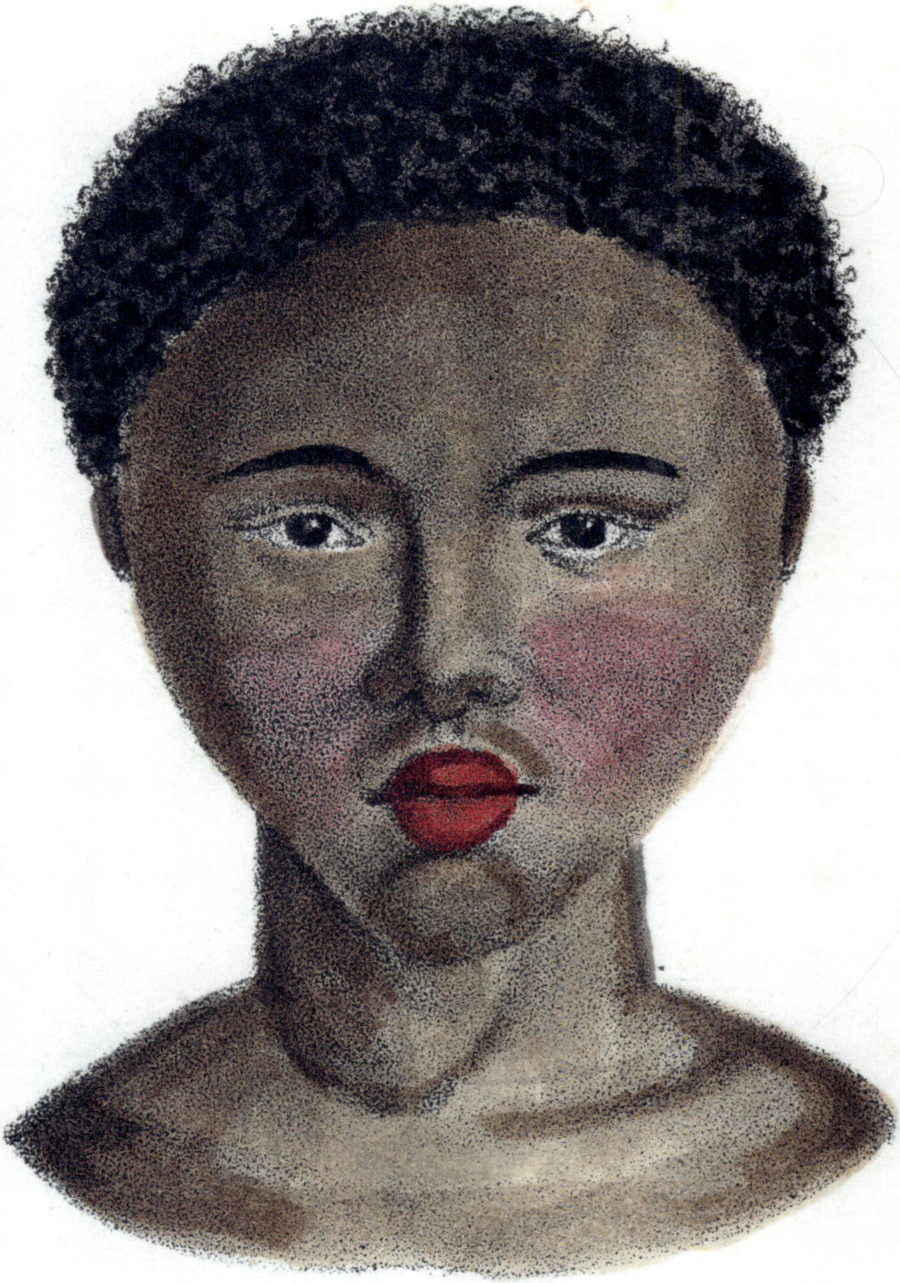

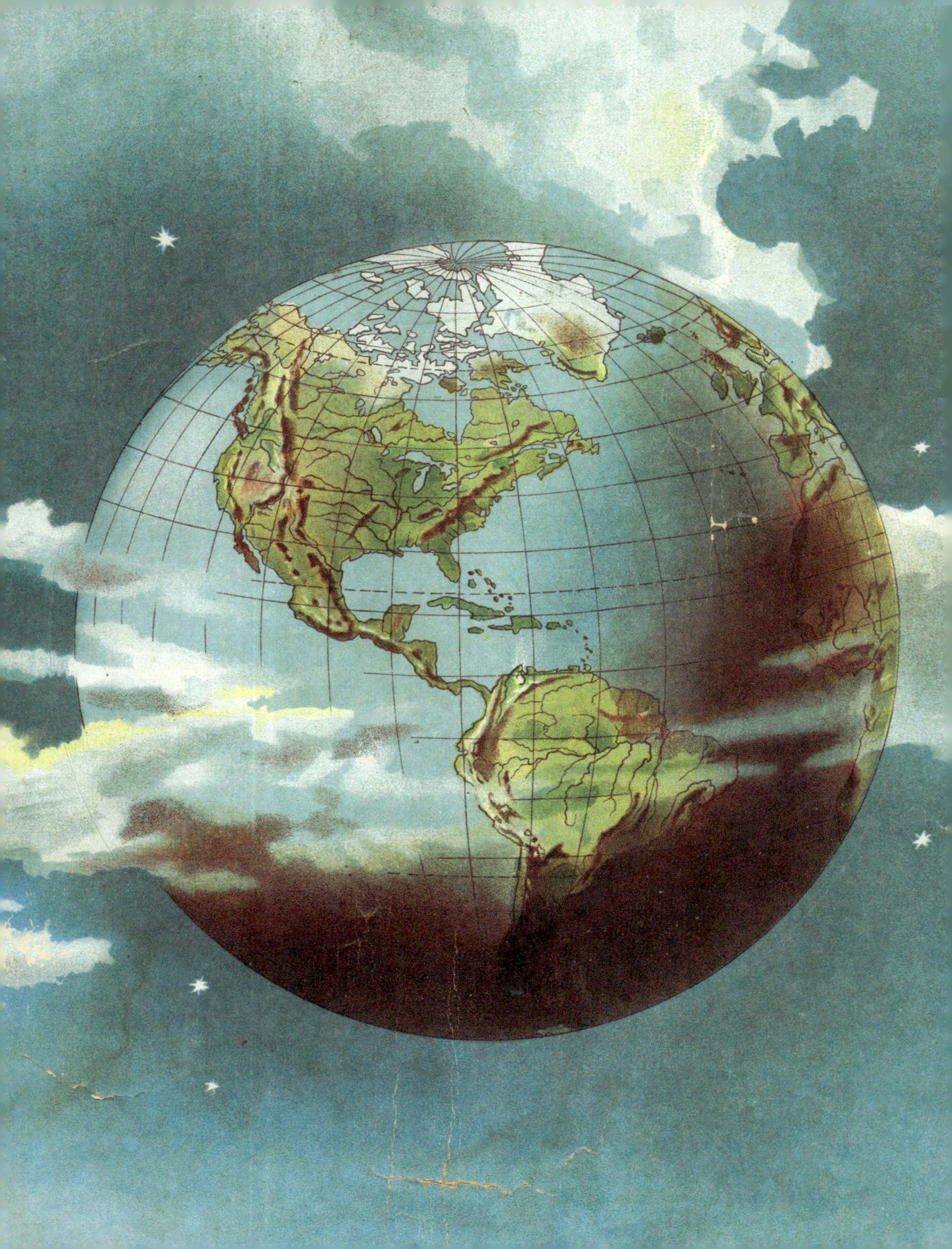

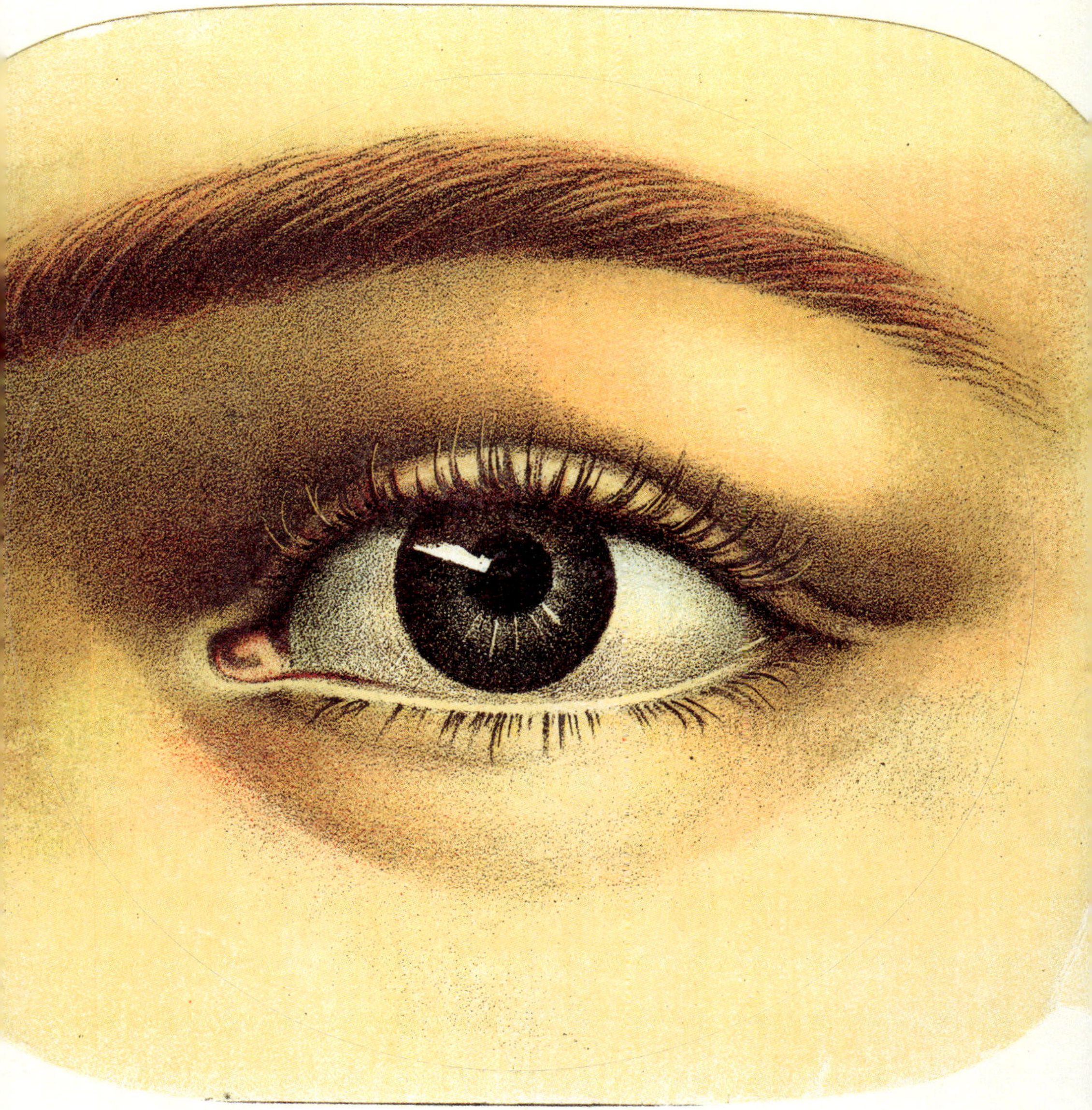

1.

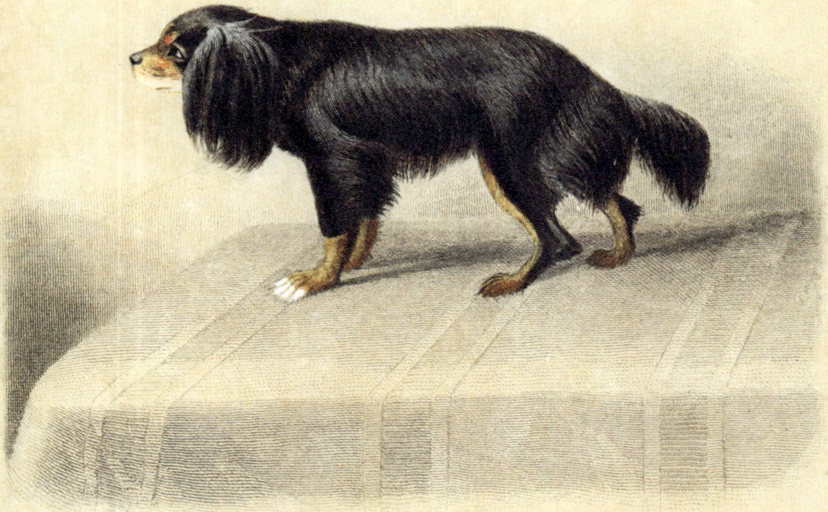

2.

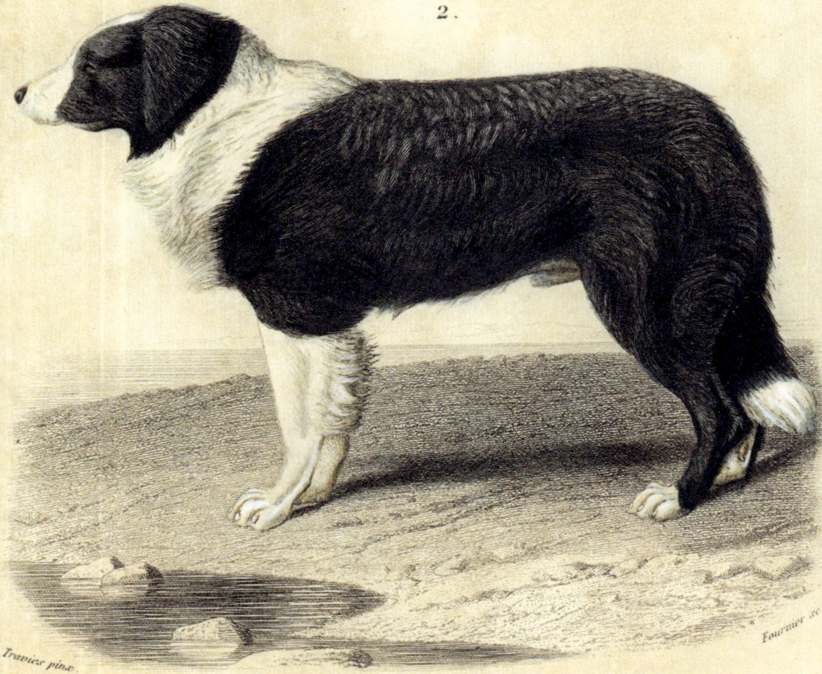

Traviès pinx. *Fournier sc.*

I.re *SÉRIE:* QUADRUPÈDES *SANS OS MARSUPIAUX* (I. G. S.t HIL.)

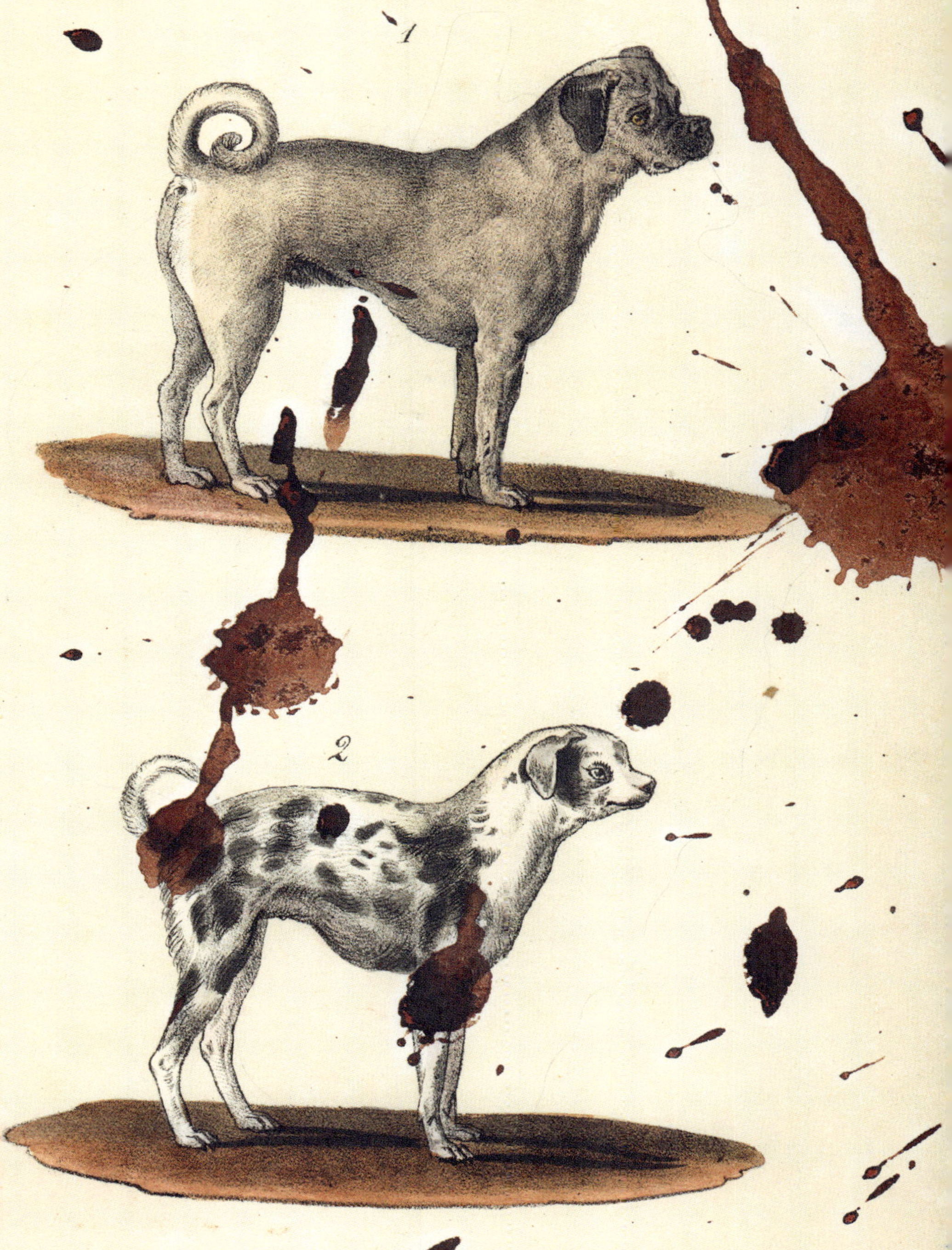

1. *Doguin.* 2. *Roquet.*

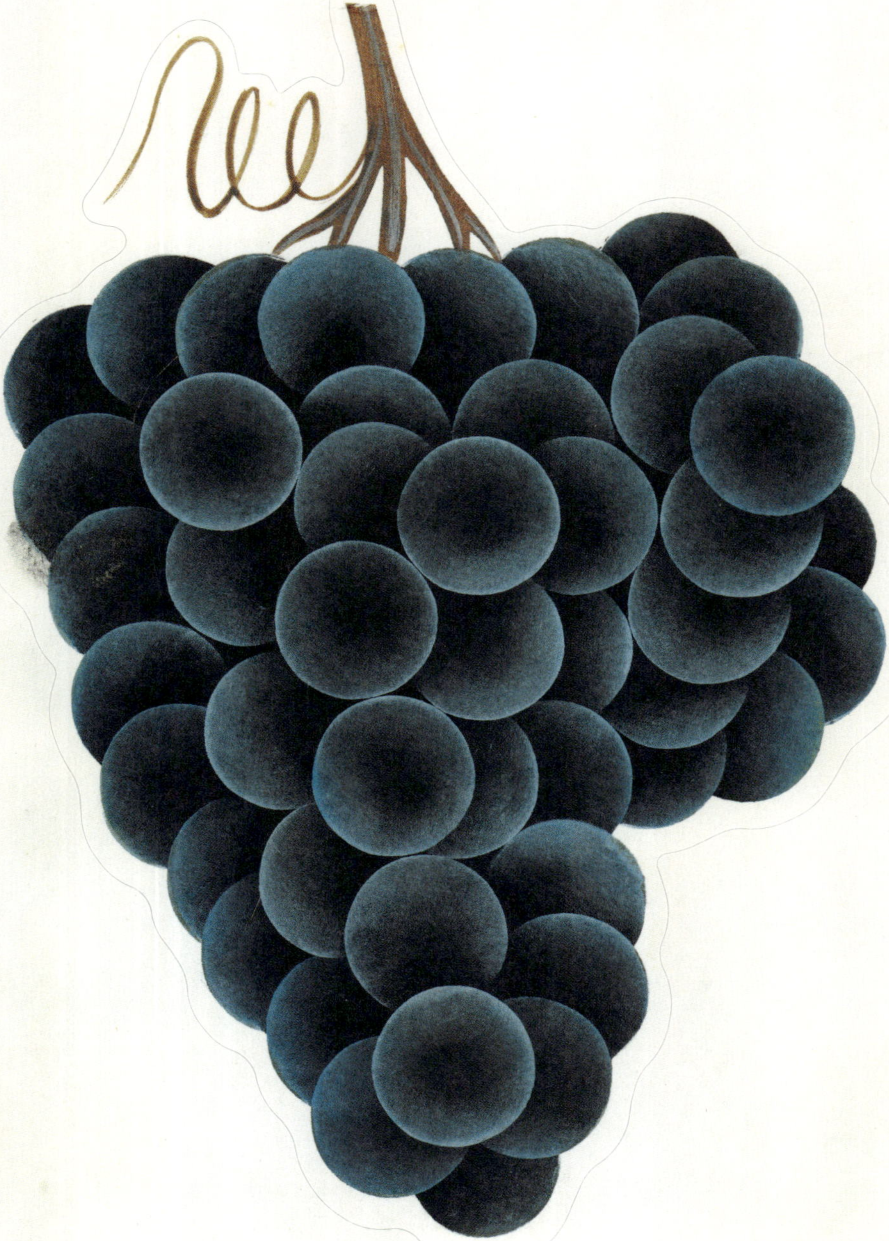

CHAMPION.

Remarkably hardy and very productive. Fruit of fine size and fair quality. Much prized because of its very early ripening and certainty of succeeding where most other sorts fail.

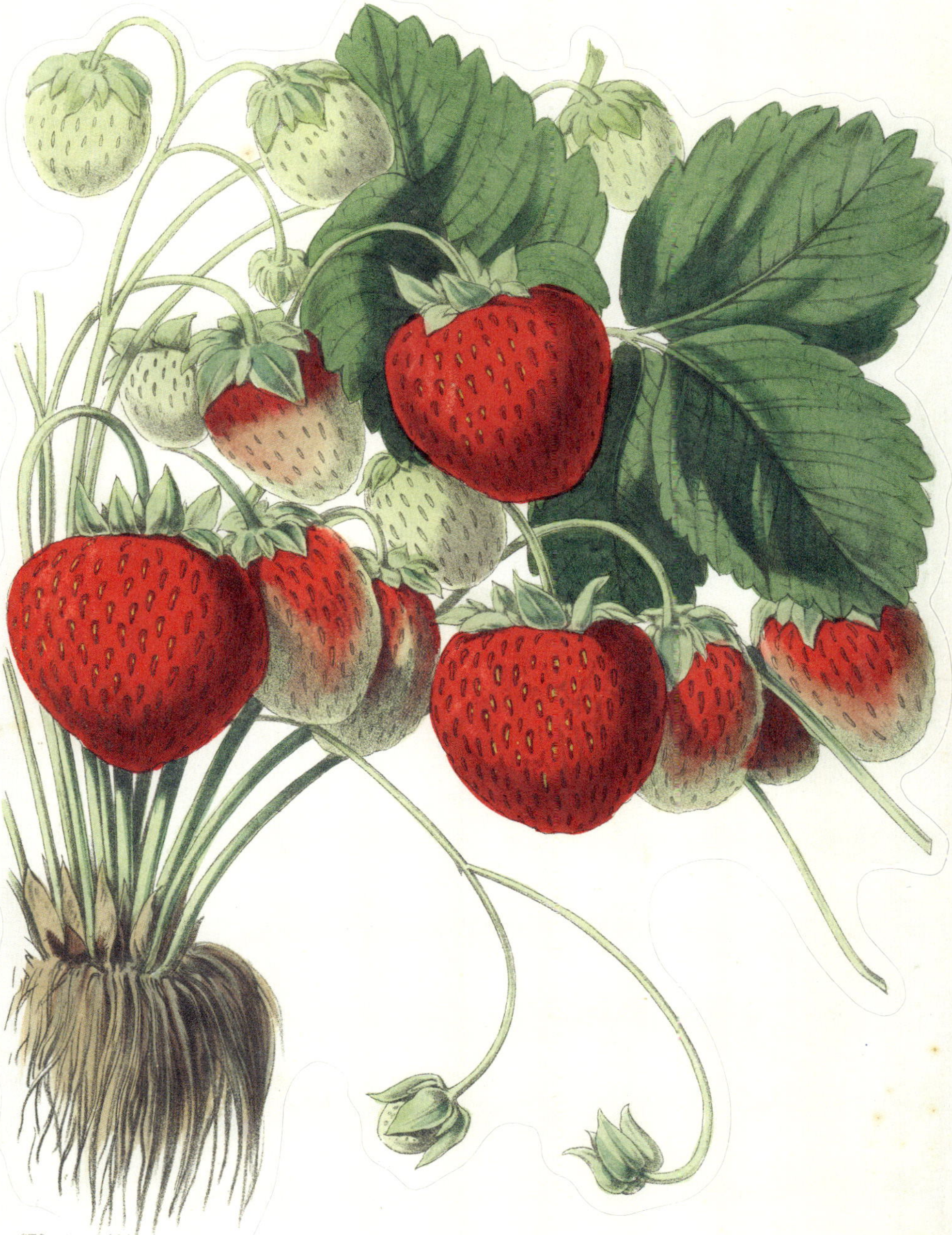

C. T. Rowning del & lith.

Printed by C. F. Cheffins, London.

Strawberry. Prince Arthur

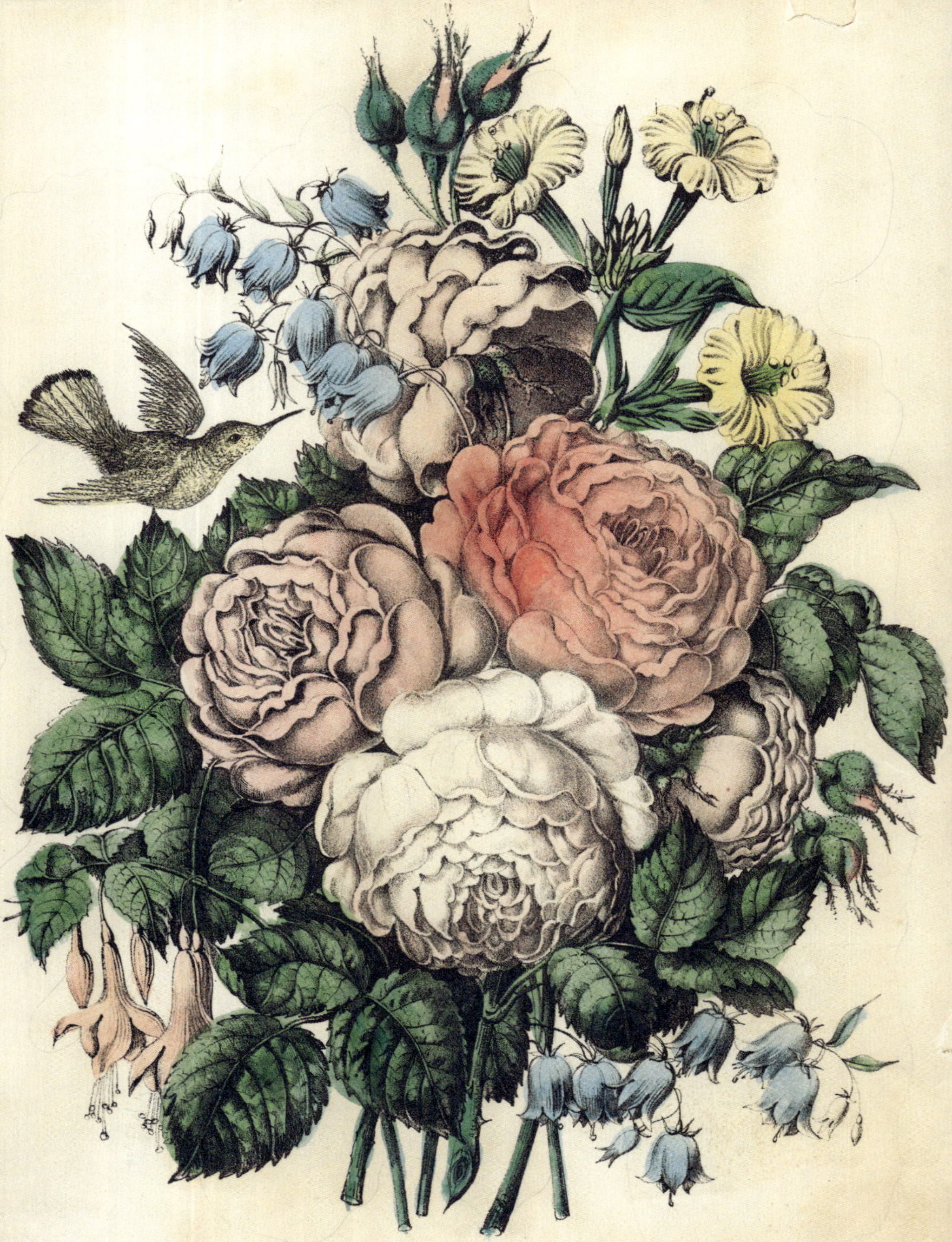

FLOWERS.

ROSES AND BLUEBELLS

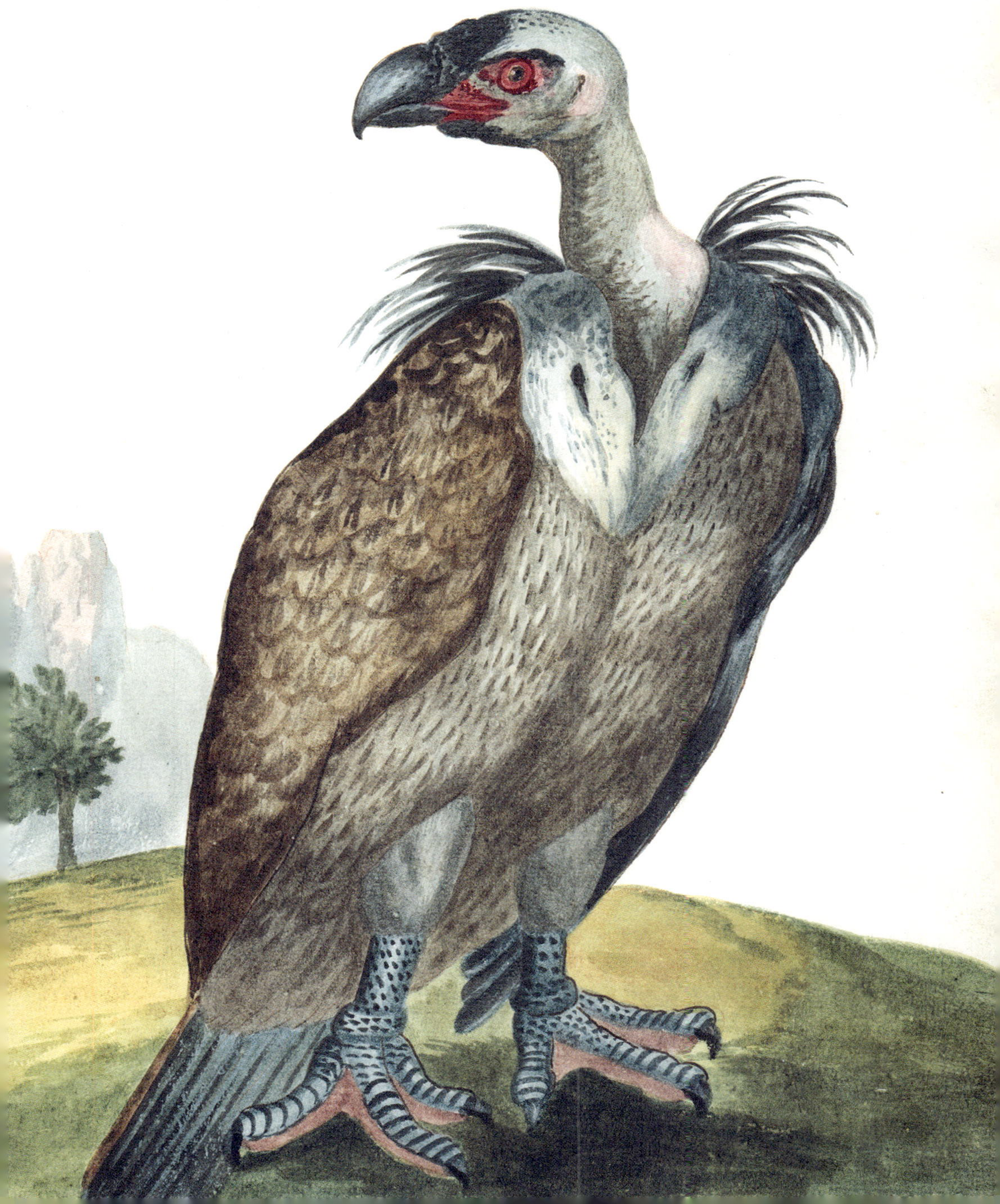

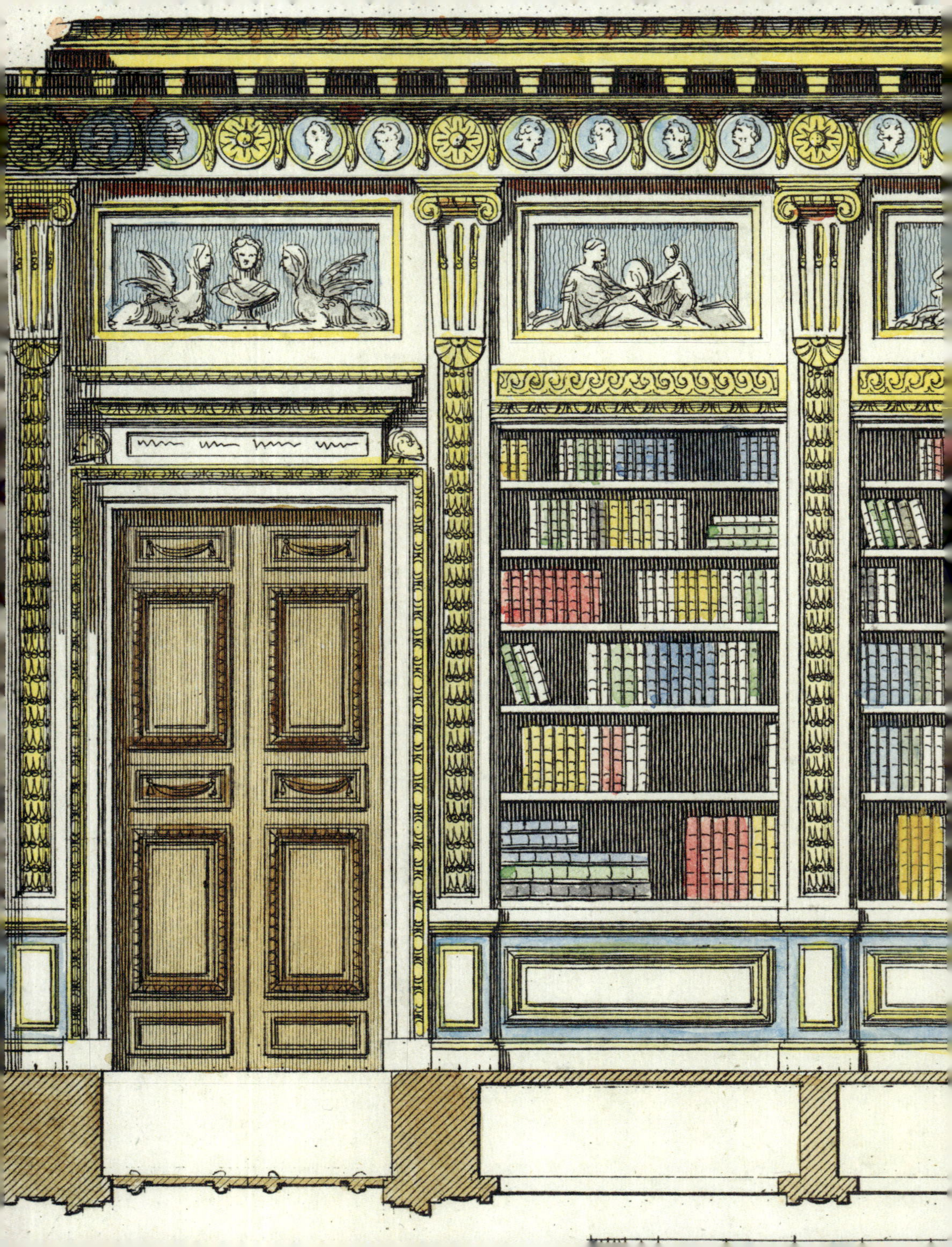

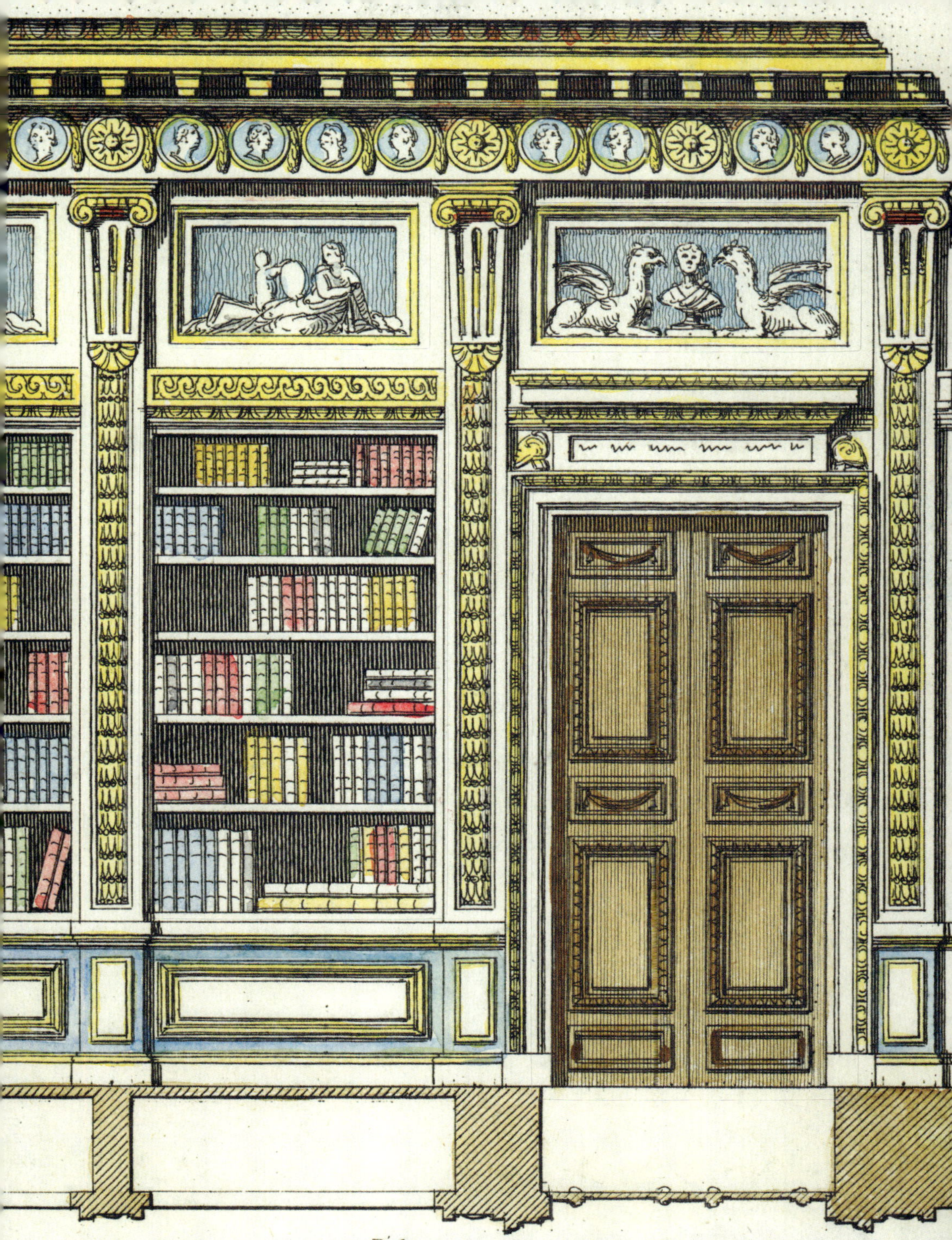

12 Pieds

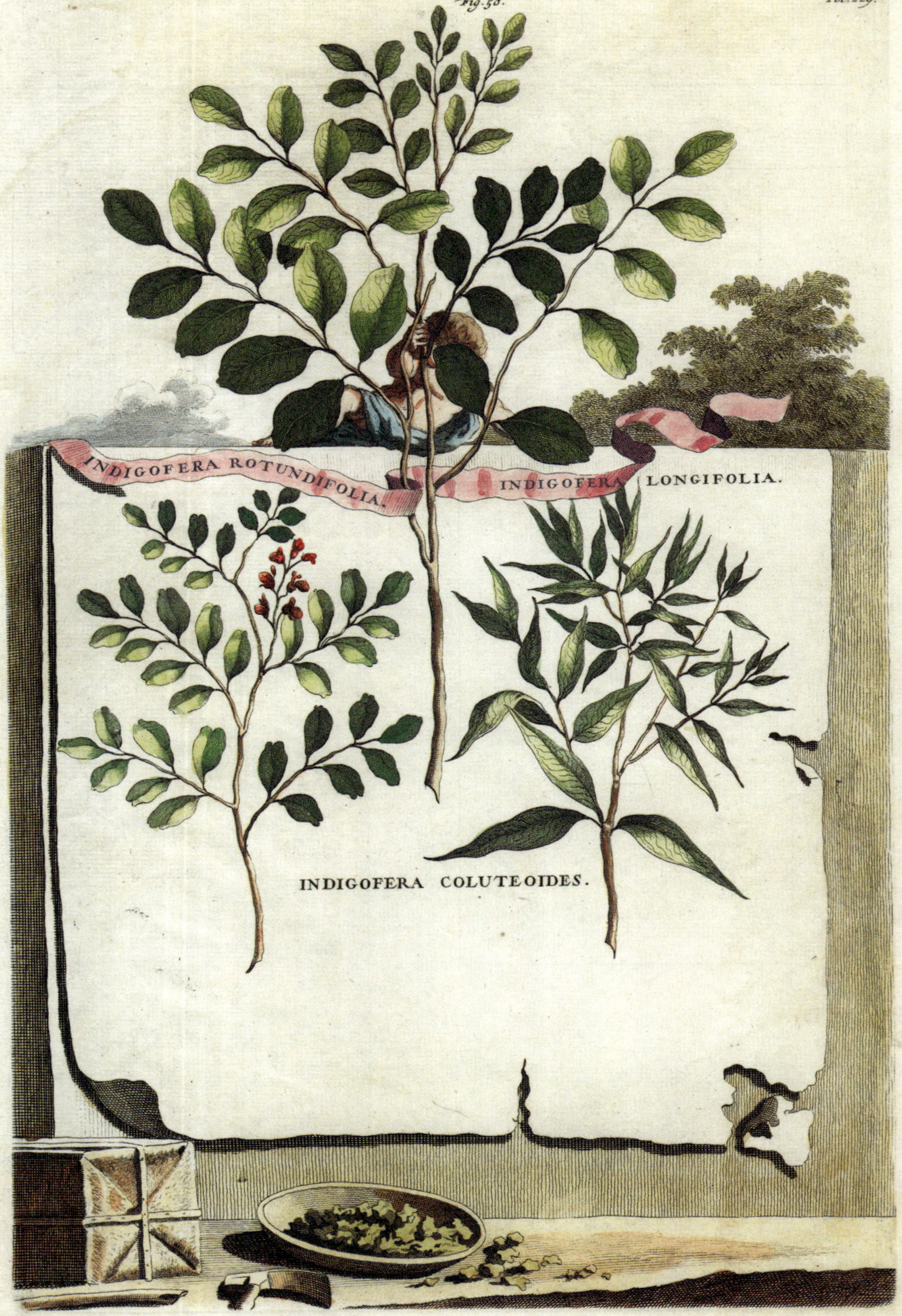
INDIGOFERA ROTUNDIFOLIA.
INDIGOFERA LONGIFOLIA.
INDIGOFERA COLUTEOIDES.

Fig. 111.

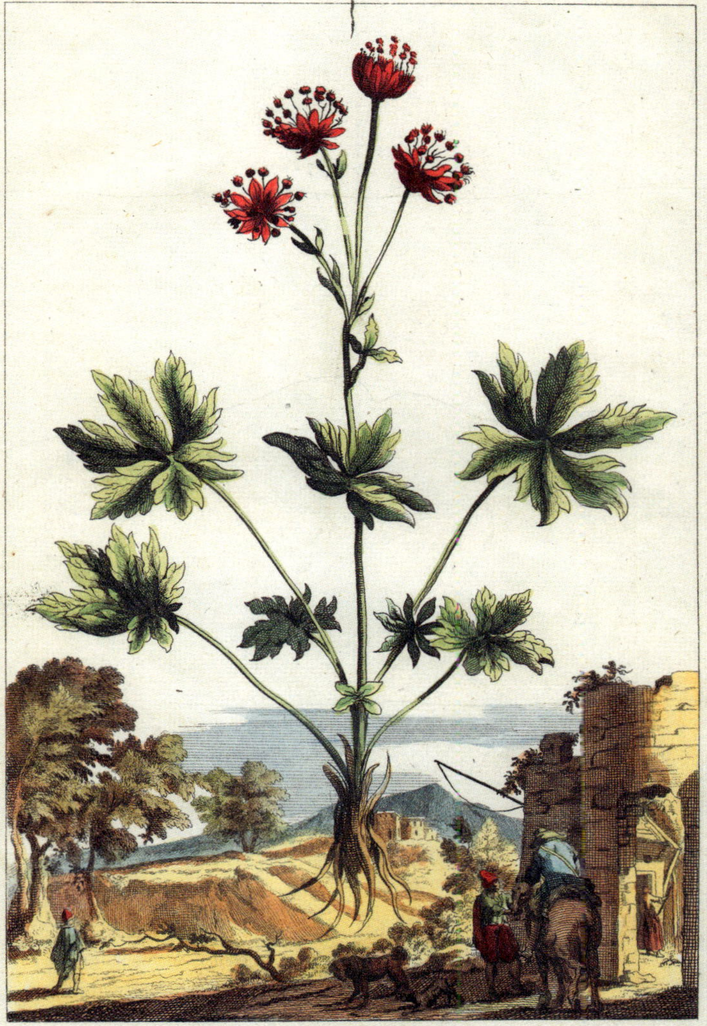

Astrantia Alpina.

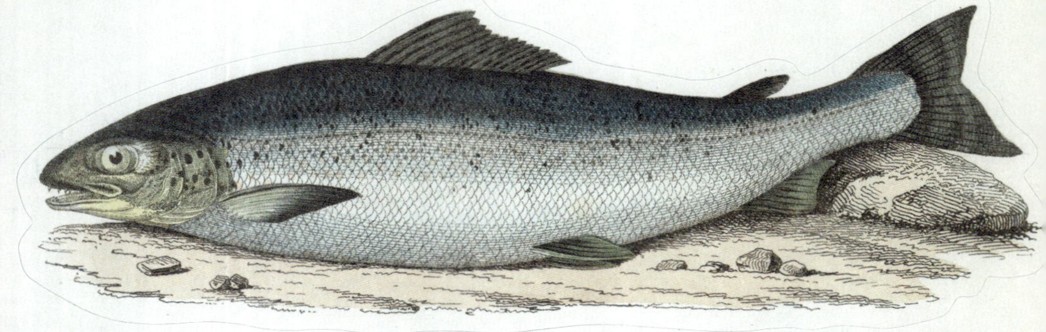

Salmon.

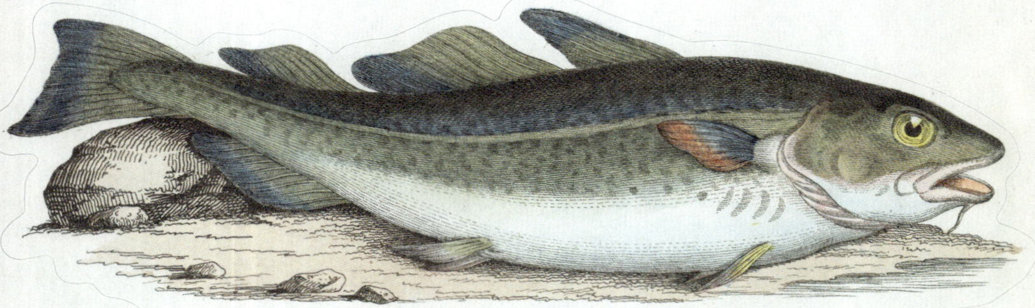

Common Cod.

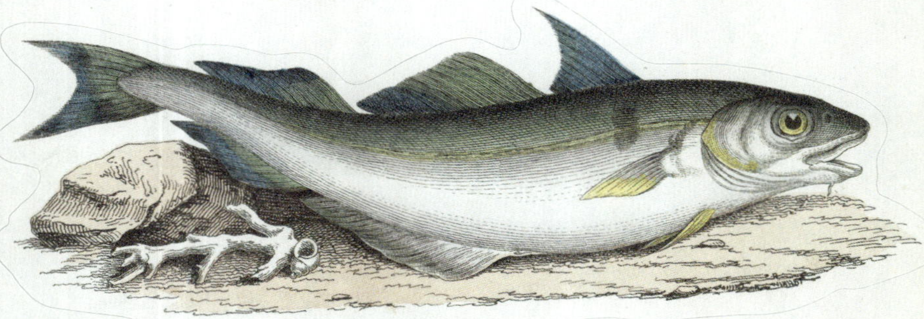

Haddock.

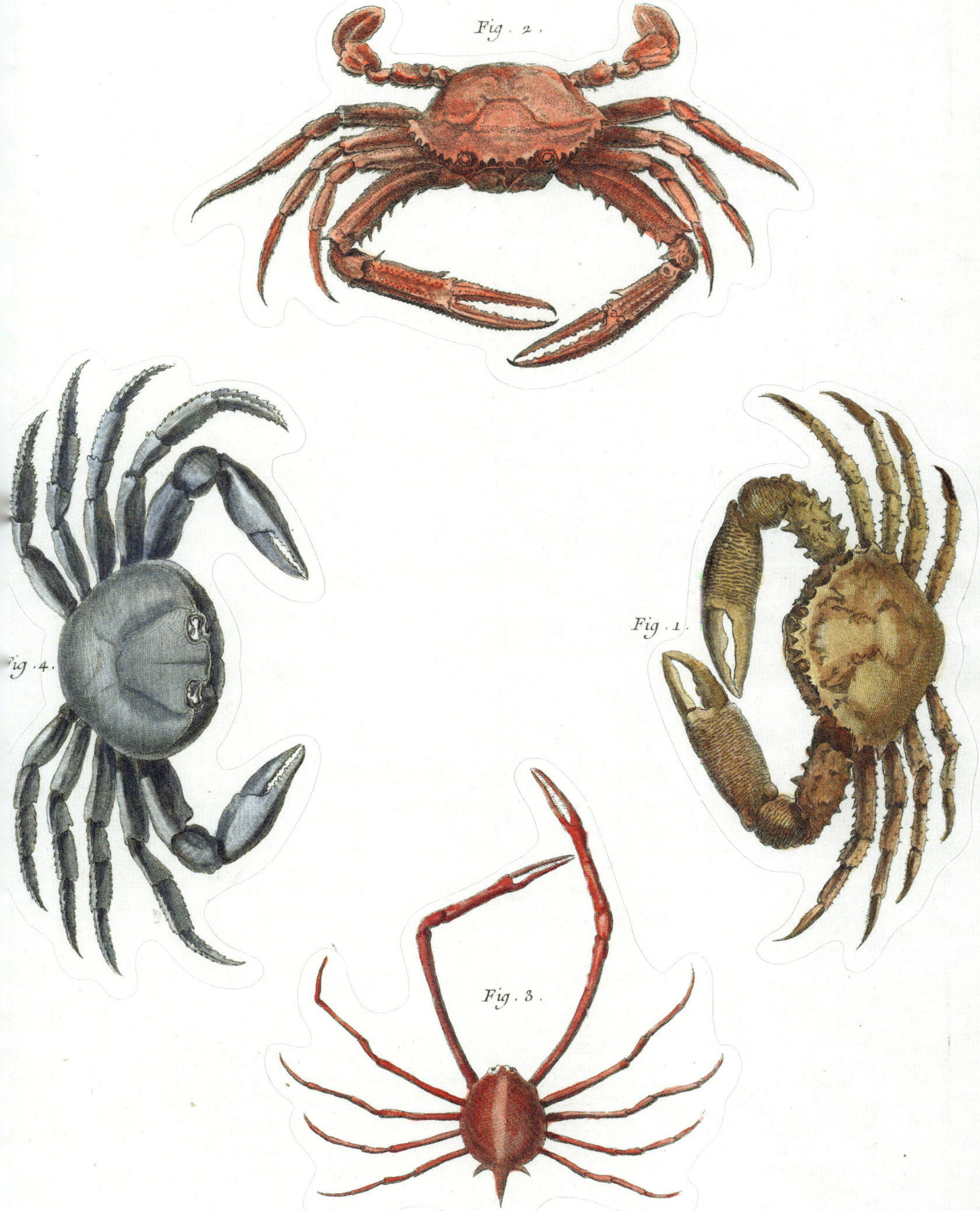

Martinet . Del.

Benard Fecit.

Histoire Naturelle,

Fig. 1. CRABE DE S.T DOMINGUE. Fig. 2. LA SIRIQUE. Fig. 3. CRABE A LONGUES JAMBES. Fig. 4. CRABE VIOLET.

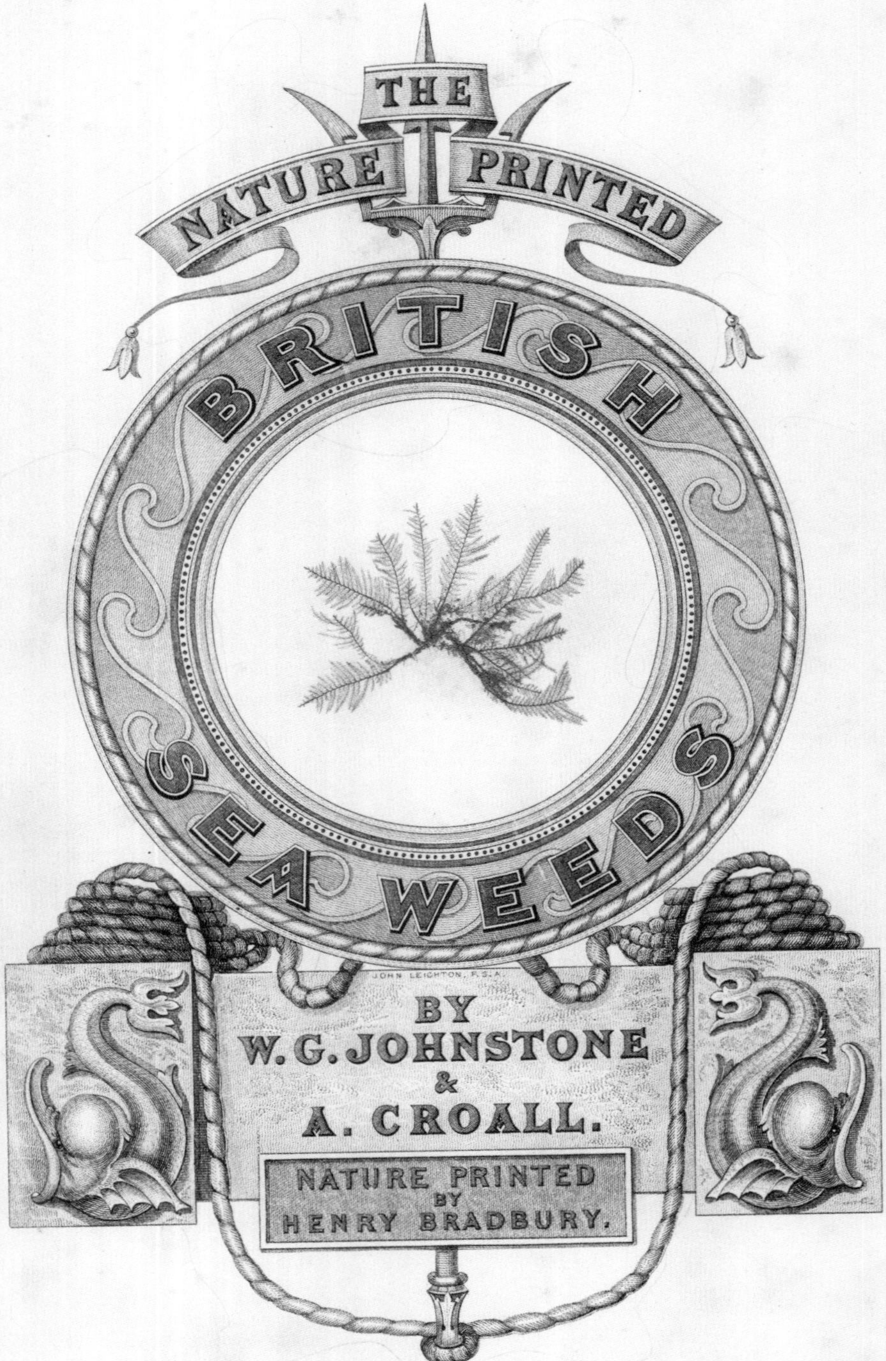
THE
NATURE PRINTED
BRITISH
SEA WEEDS
JOHN LEIGHTON, F.S.A.
BY
W. G. JOHNSTONE
&
A. CROALL.
NATURE PRINTED
BY
HENRY BRADBURY.

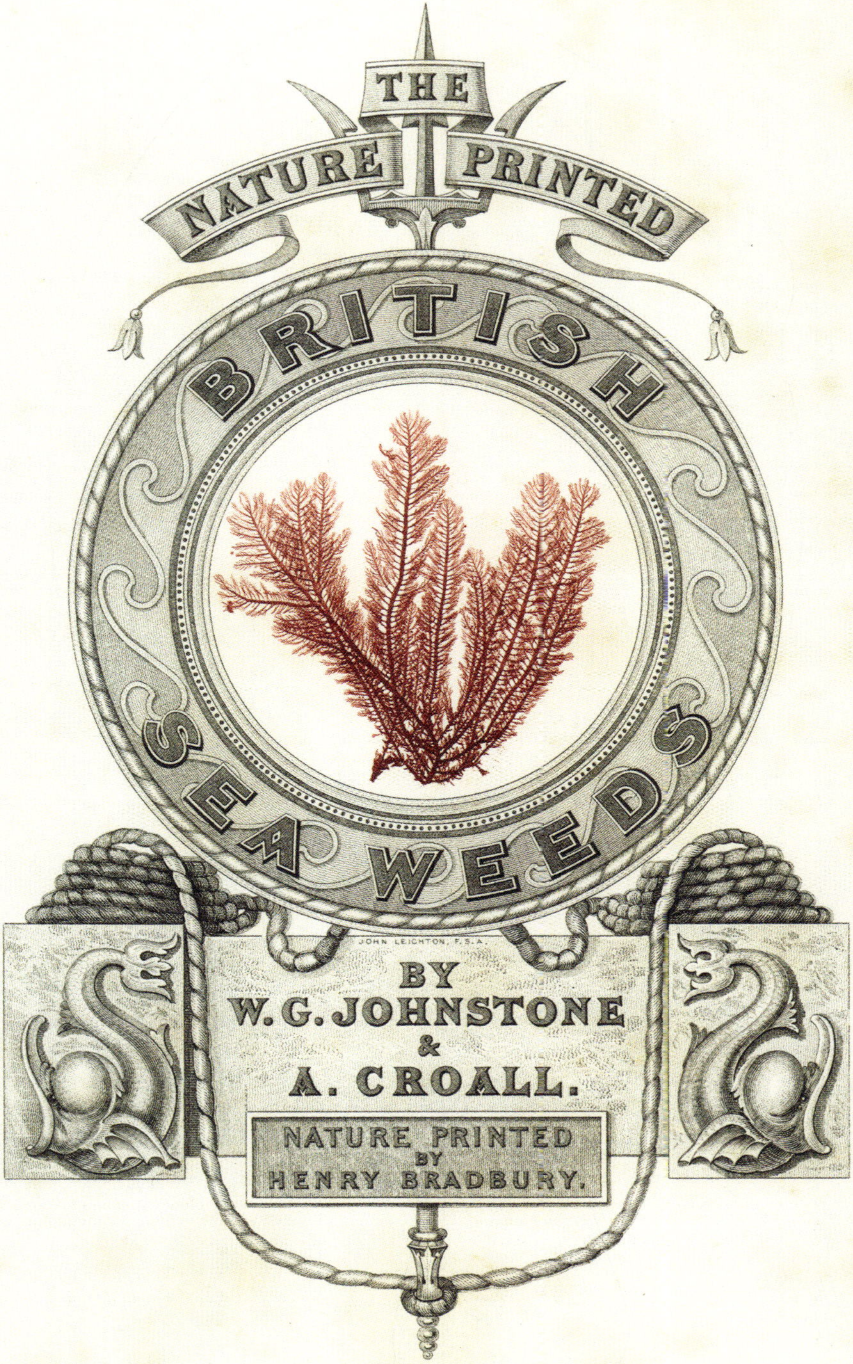
THE
NATURE PRINTED
BRITISH
SEA WEEDS
JOHN LEIGHTON, F.S.A.
BY
W. G. JOHNSTONE
&
A. CROALL.
NATURE PRINTED
BY
HENRY BRADBURY.

LONDON.

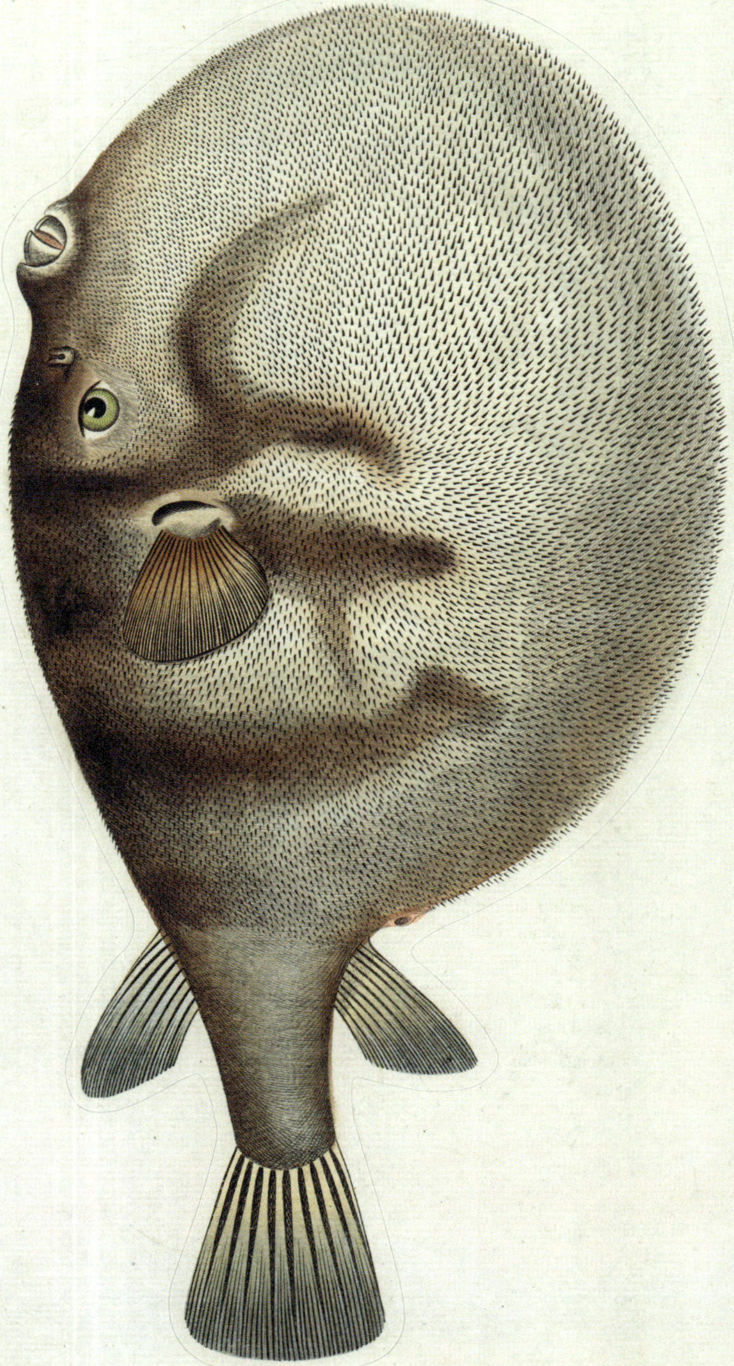

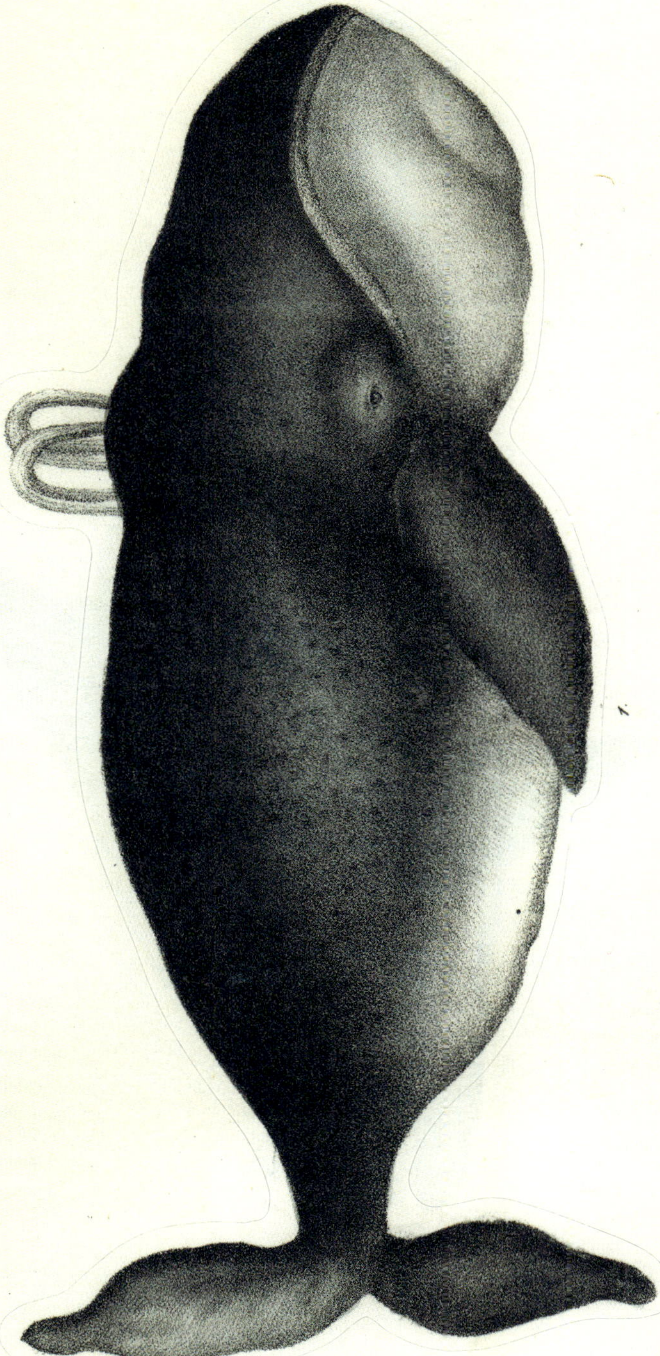

Yours Truly
John Jacob Astor Sen—

... 1.7.1906.

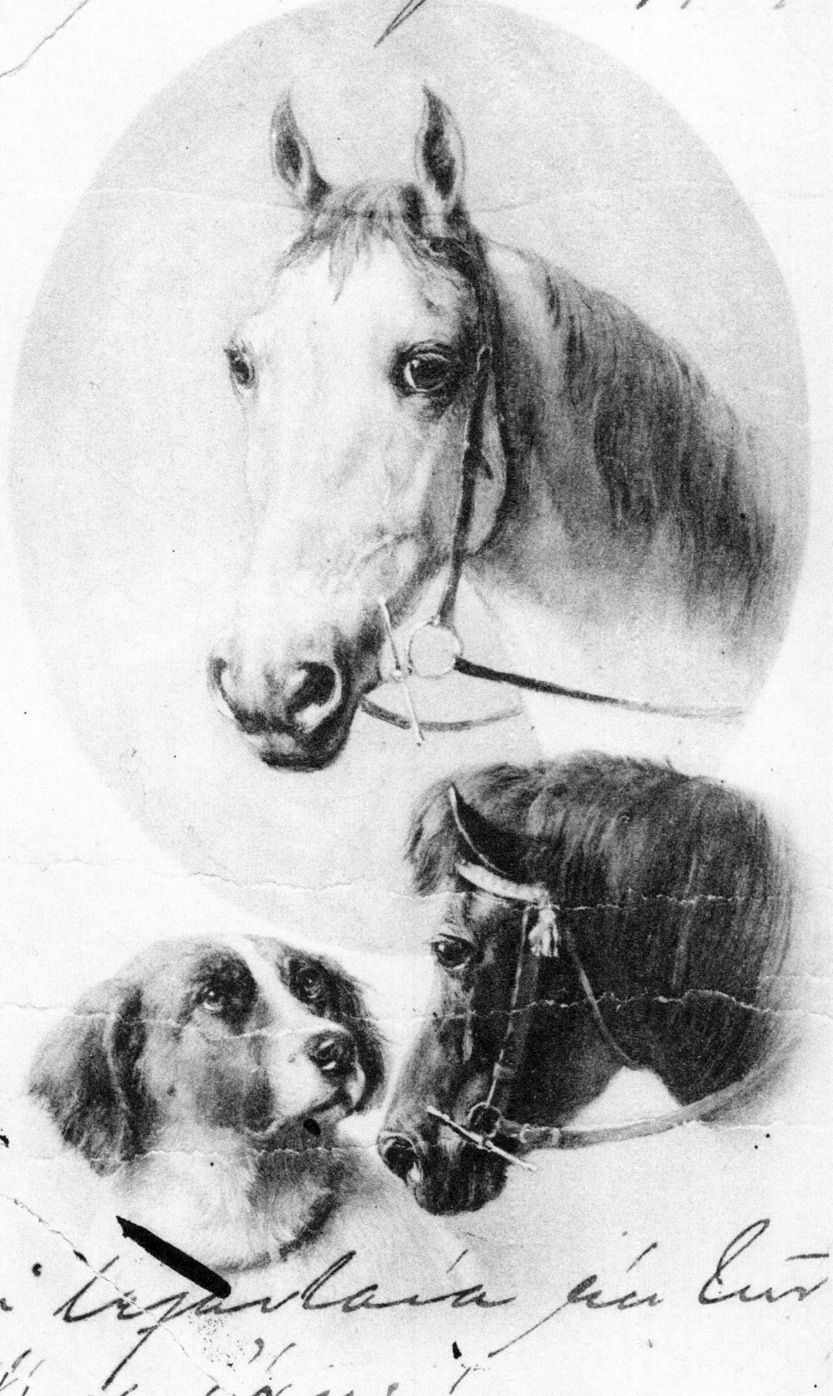

[illegible]

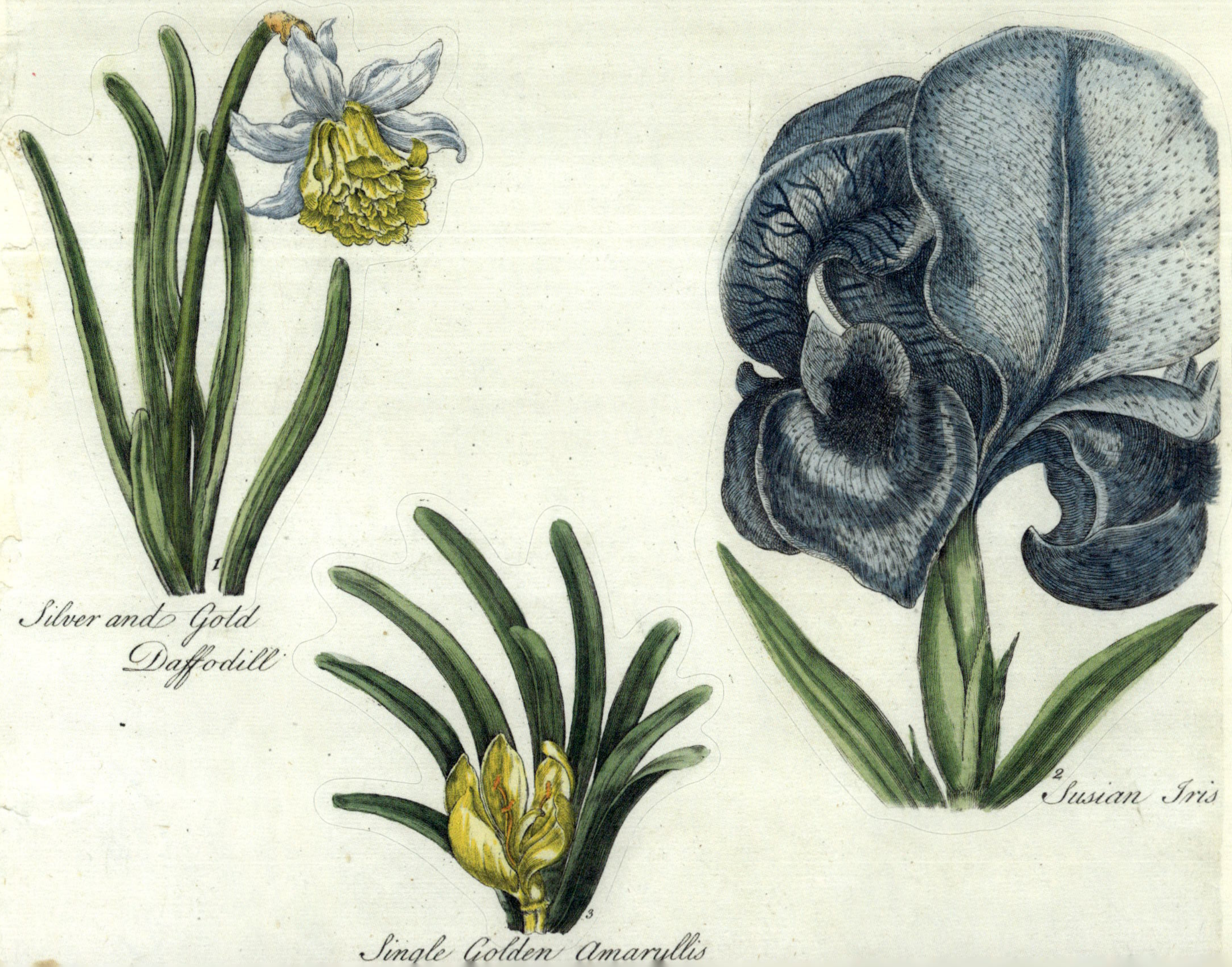
1
Silver and Gold Daffodill
2
Susian Iris
3
Single Golden Amarullis

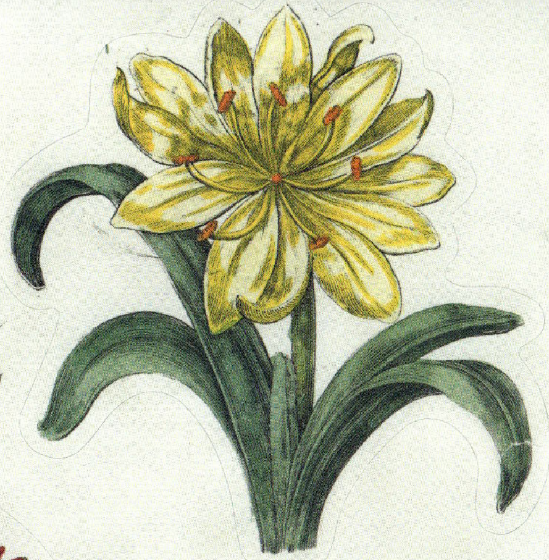

Double Golden 4 Amaryllis

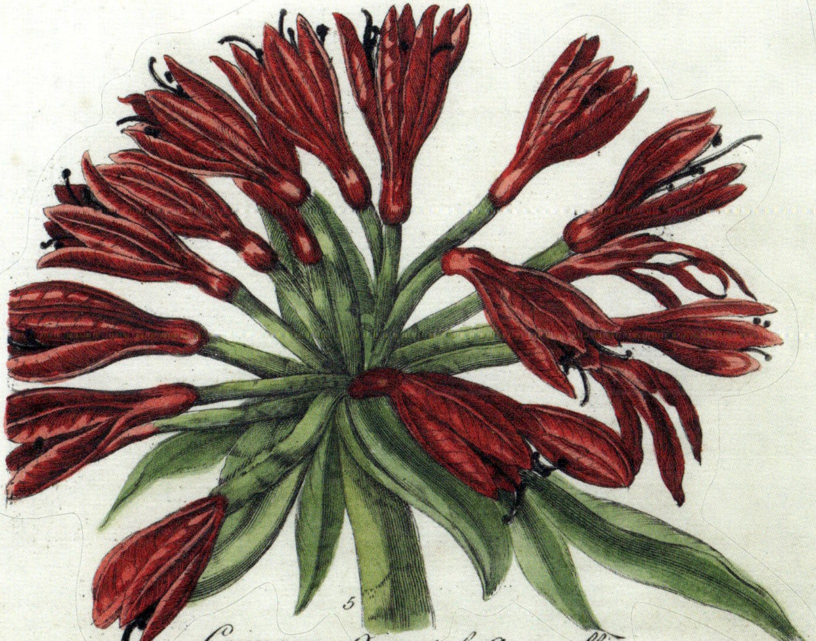

5 Crimson Oriental Amaryllis

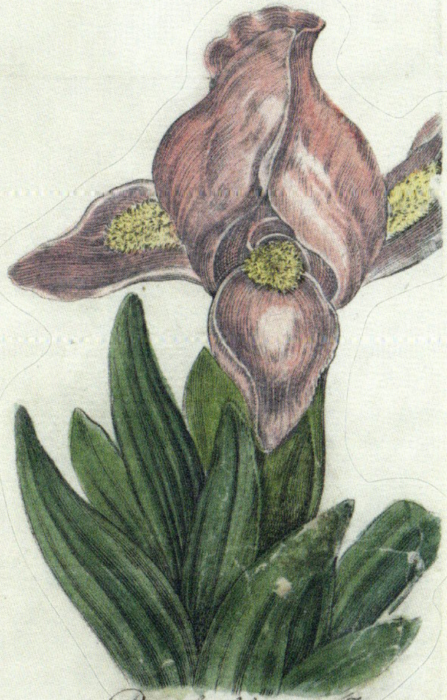

Peach bloom Iris

Fig. 1.

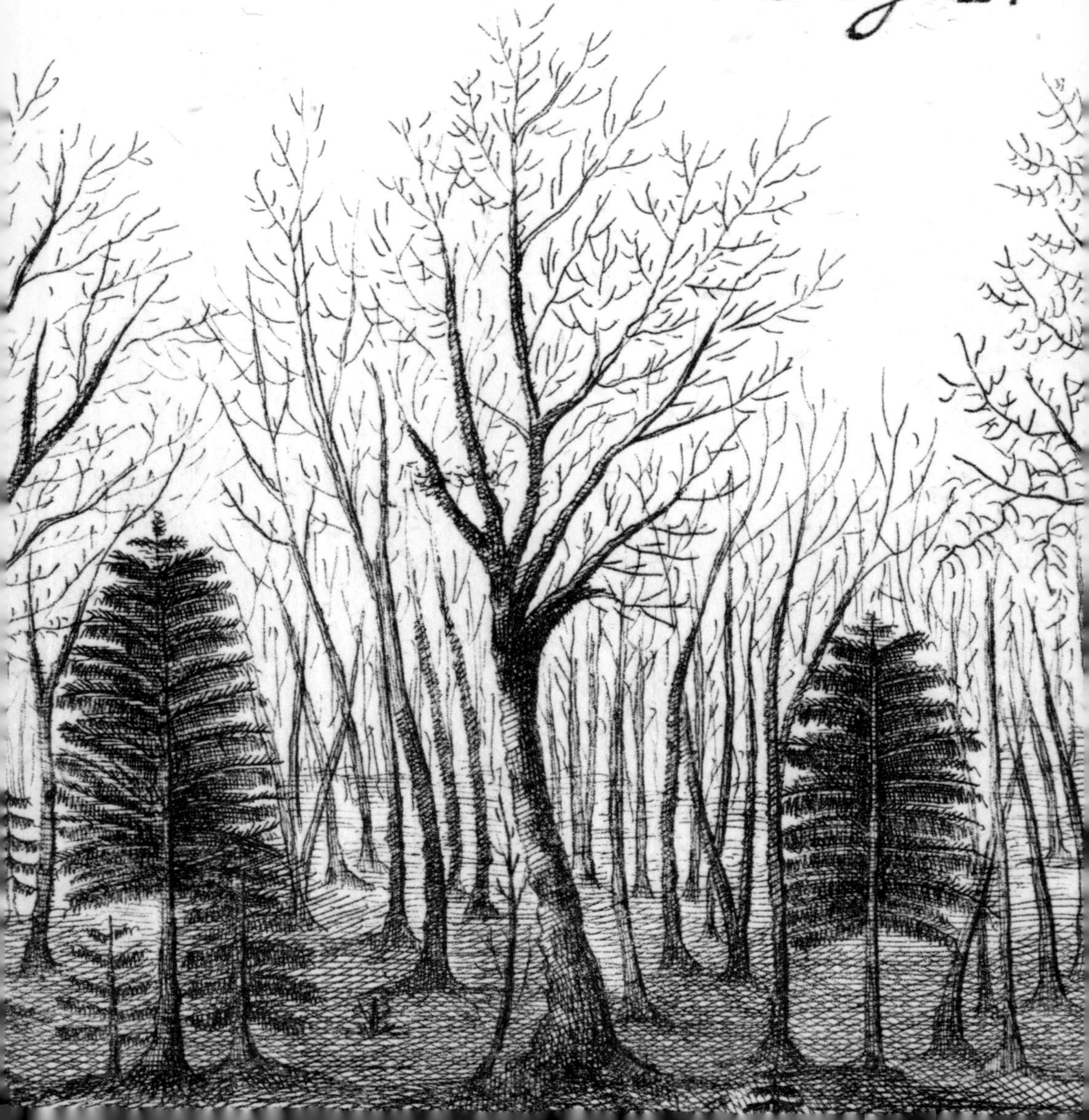

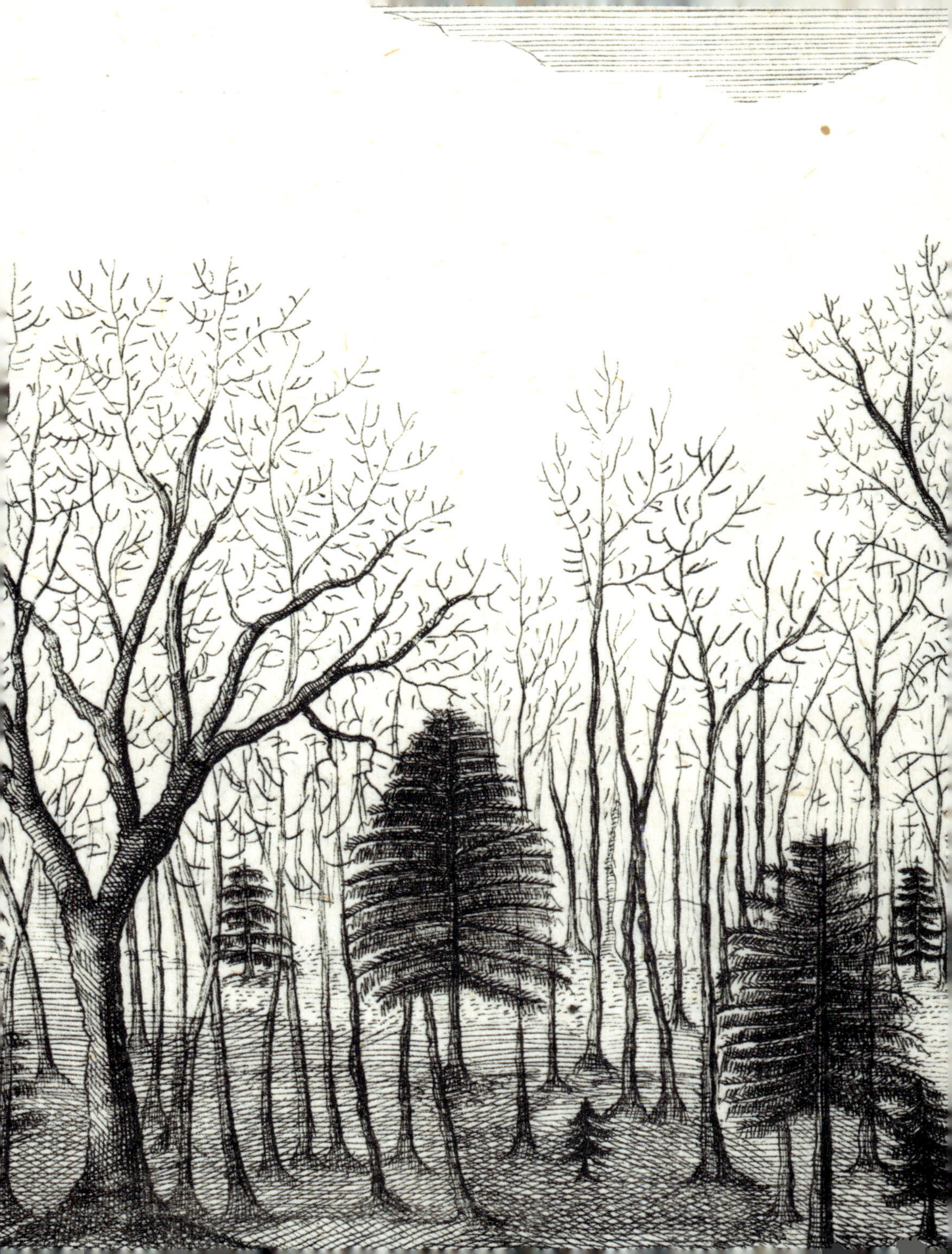

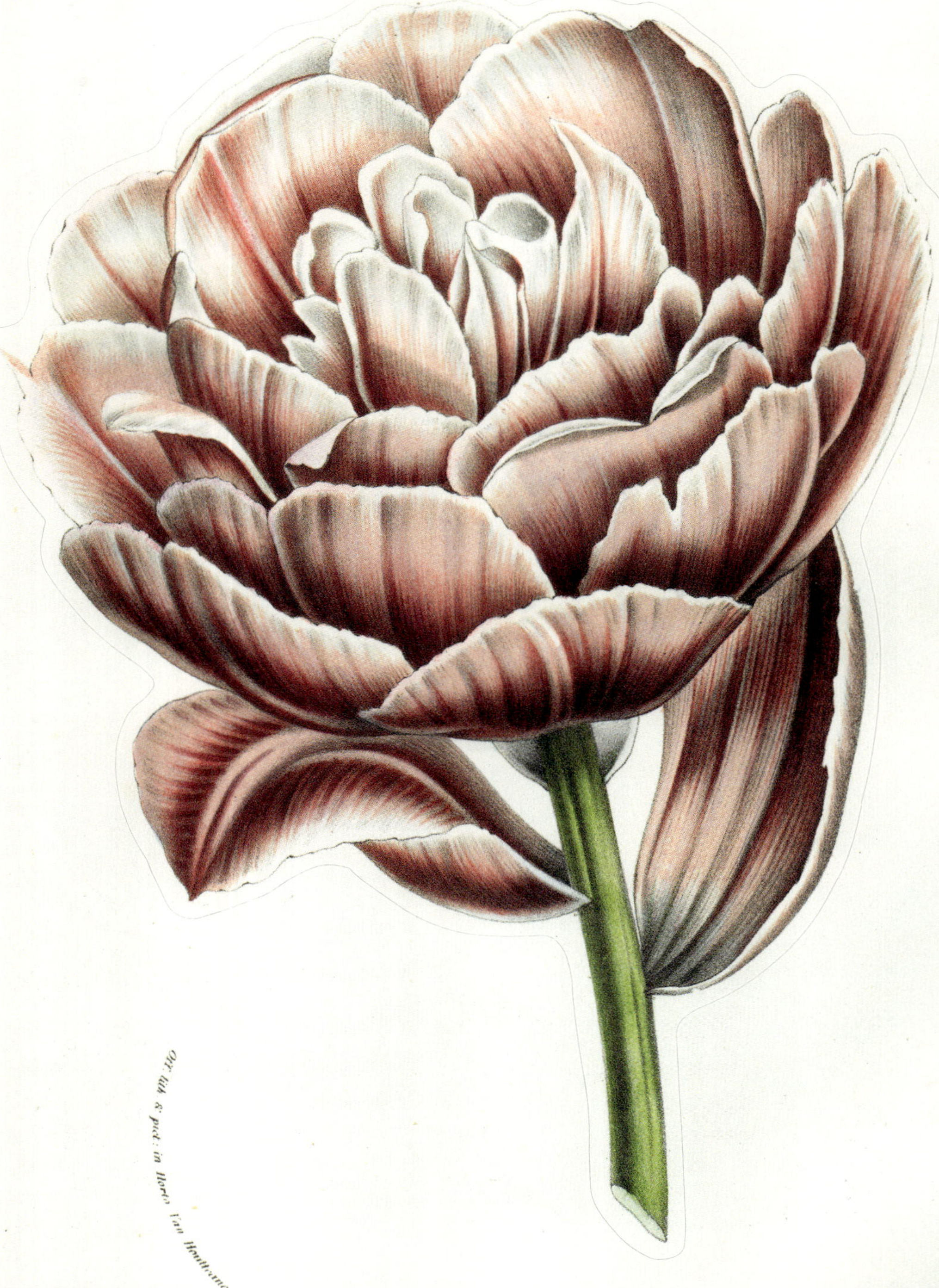

Ort. lith & pict: in Horto Van Houtteano.

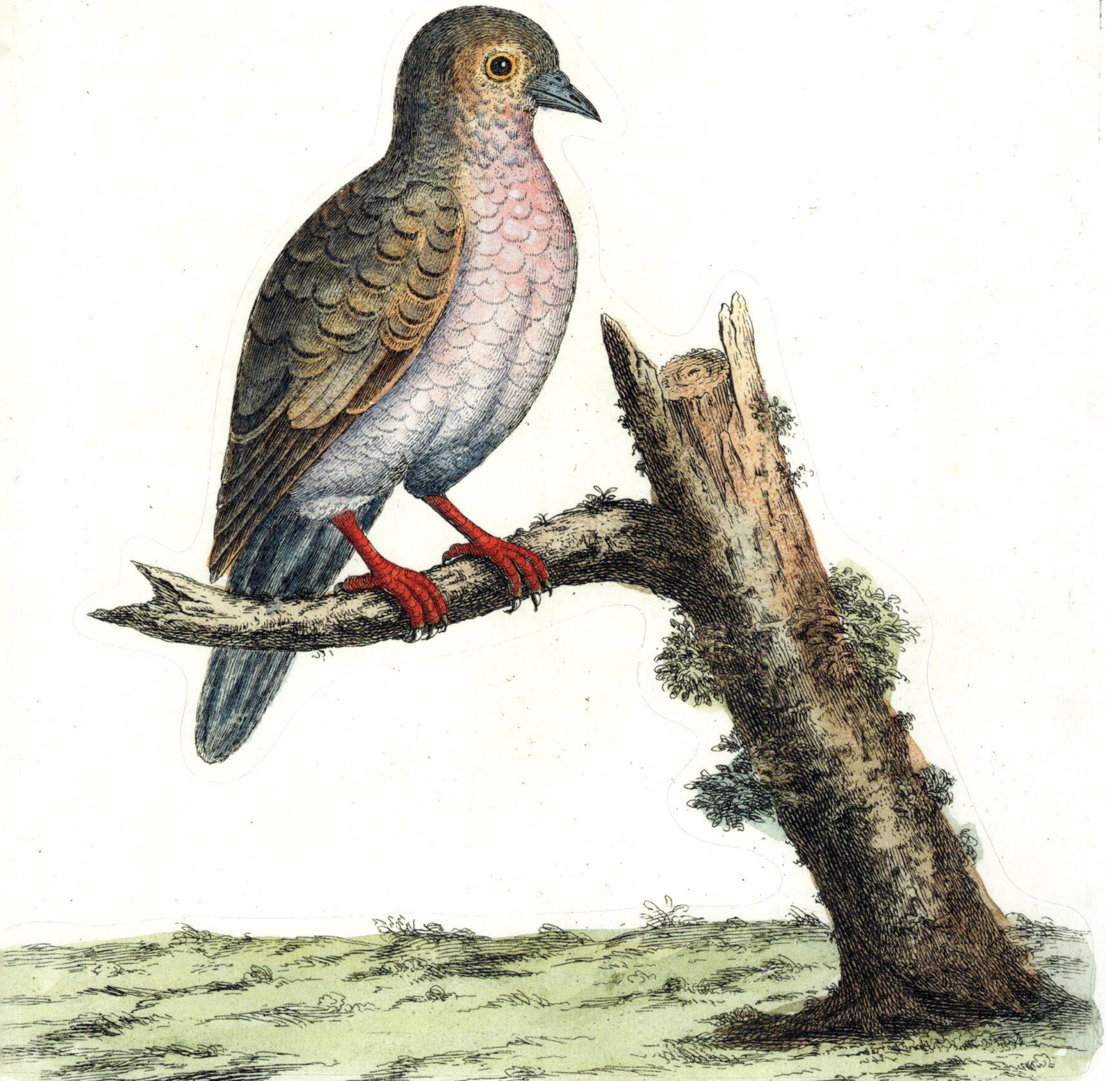

A Dove from China. *Eleazar Albin Del. July 21. 1735.*

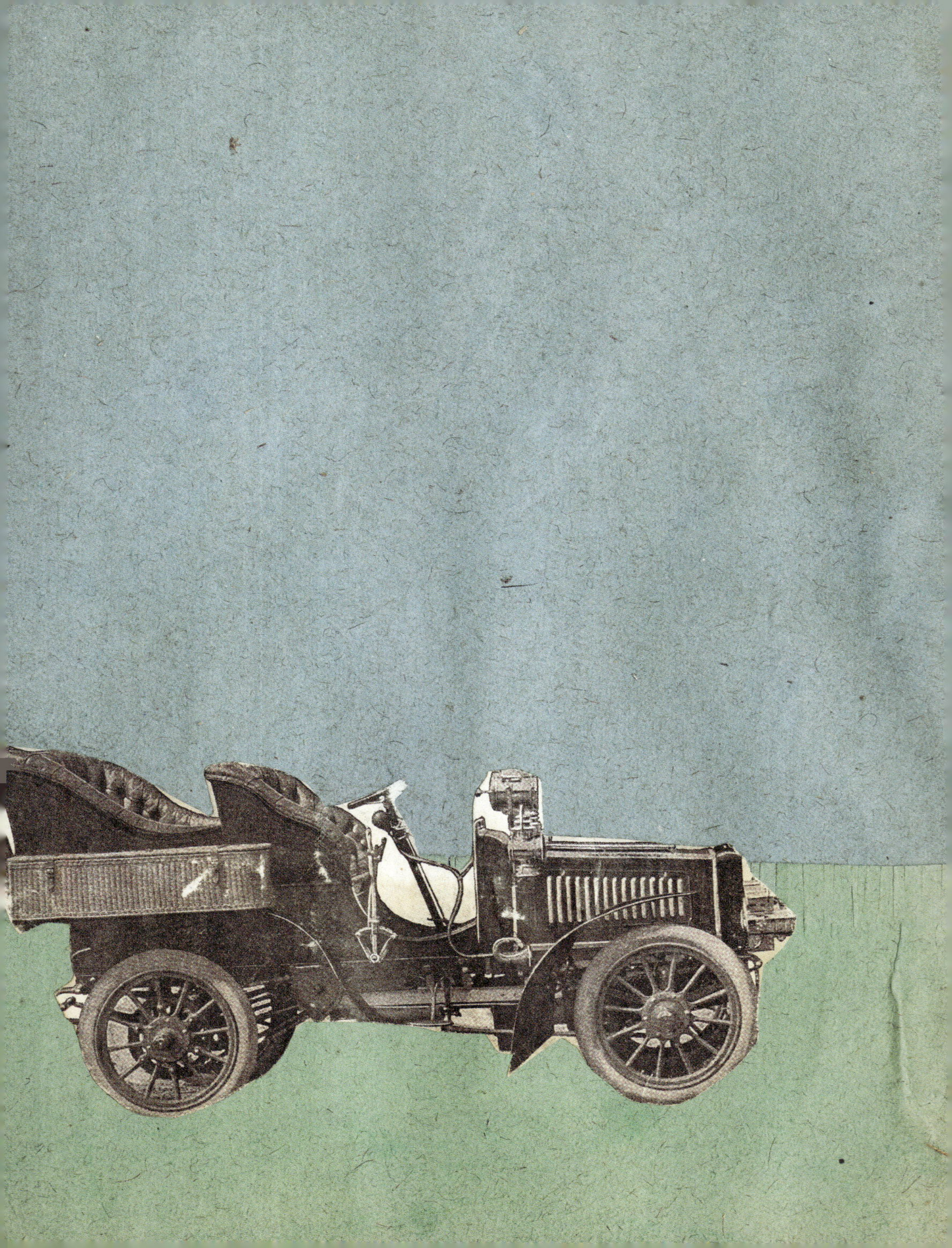

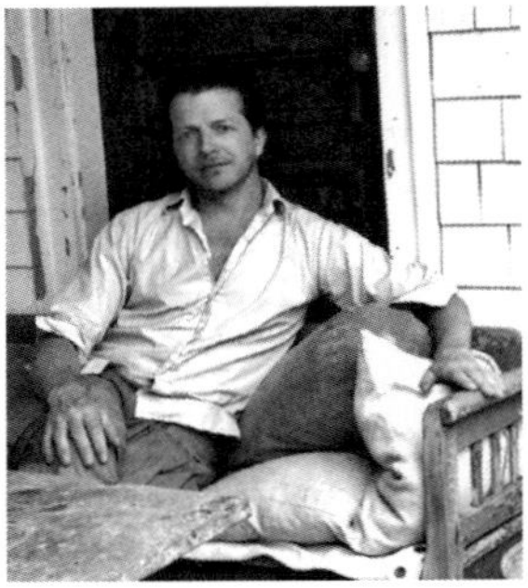

JOHN DERIAN founded the John Derian Company in 1989, and today employs a staff of artisans in his studio in New York City to create his signature decoupage plates, platters, paperweights, coasters, bowls, trays, and more. His designs are available in his own retail shops in New York's East Village—where he also carries vintage and antique imports, bed and table linens, stationery, vintage and new lighting, and an ever-changing assortment of one-of-a-kind curios—as well as in upscale home stores, catalogs, and gift shops around the globe. His work, along with his retail shops, studio, and homes, has been featured in *Vogue*, *T: The New York Times Style Magazine*, *Elle Decor*, *Vanity Fair*, *World of Interiors*, *WSJ Magazine*, *Architectural Digest*, *House & Garden*, *Gourmet*, *Bon Appétit*, *Garden Design*, *New York* magazine, *GQ*, and *W*.